# The Politics of the Environment
Ideas, Activism, Policy

2nd Edition

The continuous rise in the profile of the environment in politics reflects growing concern that we may be facing a large-scale ecological crisis. The new edition of this highly acclaimed textbook surveys the politics of the environment, providing a comprehensive and comparative introduction to its three components: ideas, activism and policy. Part I explores environmental philosophy and green political thought; Part II considers parties and environmental movements; and Part III analyses policy-making and environmental issues at international, national and local levels. This second edition has been thoroughly updated with new and revised discussions of many topics including the ecological state, ecological citizenship, ecological modernisation and the Greens in government and also includes an additional chapter on 'Globalisation, trade and the environment'. As well as considering a wide variety of examples from around the world, this textbook features a glossary, guides to further study, chapter summaries and critical questions throughout.

NEIL CARTER is Senior Lecturer in the Department of Politics at the University of York. He is co-author of *How Organisations Measure Success: The Use of Performance Indicators in Government* (with Rudolf Klein and Patricia Day, 1992) and joint editor of the journal *Environmental Politics*.

# The Politics of the
# Environment

## Ideas, Activism, Policy

## 2nd Edition

## NEIL CARTER

*Department of Politics, University of York*

CAMBRIDGE
UNIVERSITY PRESS

CAMBRIDGE UNIVERSITY PRESS
Cambridge, New York, Melbourne, Madrid, Cape Town, Singapore, São Paulo,
Delhi, Dubai, Tokyo, Mexico City

Cambridge University Press
The Edinburgh Building, Cambridge CB2 8RU, UK

Published in the United States of America by Cambridge University Press, New York

www.cambridge.org
Information on this title: www.cambridge.org/9780521687454

First edition © Cambridge University Press 2001
Second edition © Neil Carter 2007

First published 2001
Second edition 2007
5th printing 2010

Printed in the United Kingdom at the University Press, Cambridge

*A catalogue record for this publication is available from the British Library*

ISBN 978-0-521-86802-0 Hardback
ISBN 978-0-521-68745-4 Paperback

*To Tom and Rosa*

# Contents

# Figures

# Tables

# Boxes

# Preface to the second edition

The writing of the first edition of this book took several years, so it was with some relief when I began to prepare this second edition that I found the basic structure of the book still seemed to work. I have added one chapter – effectively a second on international environmental politics – in which I analyse the relationship between globalisation, trade and the environment, with a specific focus on the World Trade Organisation, the North American Free Trade Agreement and the European Union (EU). The discussion of the EU also serves as an introduction to a supranational organisation that frequently reappears in the two following chapters. Otherwise, all the chapters have been thoroughly updated, with substantially new or revised discussions of many topics, including Bjørn Lomborg, the ecological state, ecological citizenship, the experience of green parties in government, party politicisation, environmental policy integration and the use of market-based instruments.

I would like to thank Elizabeth Bomberg, Meg Huby and Chris Rootes for reading various chapters. I also received excellent advice on various revisions from Andy Dobson, Katarina Eckerberg, Arthur Mol, John Parkinson and Wolfgang Rüdig. Thanks are owed again to my students for sharpening my thoughts and to John Haslam for encouraging me to write this second edition. I would like to thank Susan Baker, and Taylor and Francis, for permission to reproduce her 'Ladder of Sustainable Development' in Table 8.1.

Finally, thanks to Charlie, again, for her love and support, and to Tom, just for being my wee man.

# Acknowledgements

In writing a book that has been as long in gestation as this one, I have inevitably accrued many debts. Andy Dobson, Meg Huby, Andy Jordan, Sue Mendus and Chris Rootes have each read several chapters, and I know that the book is much better for their wise and helpful comments. Brian Doherty, Mat Paterson and Andrew Williams have each commented on a chapter. A wide range of people have helped in small but important ways, including Keith Alderman, Riley Dunlap, Katarina Eckerberg, Dave Humphreys, Janet Jenkins, Arthur Mol and Ben Seel. Many others, too numerous to mention, have contributed in a less formal manner. I should, however, like to make a special fond mention for Dick Richardson, with whom I shared many discussions about green politics and whose enthusiasm and good humour are greatly missed by his many friends. My colleagues at the University of York have provided a friendly, supportive and stimulating working environment. Several cohorts of students who have taken my courses in 'Green Politics' and 'Environmental Policy' have also helped me to develop my ideas. I am also grateful to Nuffield College, Oxford, where I spent Autumn 1997 as a Visitor. John Haslam has been a remarkably patient, supportive and encouraging editor throughout.

Finally, Charlie Burns has been an unfailing source of emotional and intellectual support throughout the often painful process of writing this book. She has read every chapter, usually several times, and offered excellent, constructive advice. I cannot thank her enough.

# Abbreviations

| | | | |
|---|---|---|---|
| ACF | Advocacy Coalition Framework | GJM | Global Justice Movement |
| APP | anti-party party | GMO | genetically modified organism |
| BSE | bovine spongiform encephalopathy | HCFC | hydrochlorofluorocarbons |
| CBA | cost–benefit analysis | HEP | hydroelectric power |
| CDU | Christian Democratic Union (Germany) | HFC | hydrofluorocarbons |
| | | IMF | International Monetary Fund |
| CFC | chlorofluorocarbons | IPCC | Intergovernmental Panel on Climate Change |
| CITES | Convention on International Trade in Endangered Species | IWC | International Whaling Commission |
| COP | Conference of the Parties | LA21 | Local Agenda 21 |
| DDT | dichlorodiphenyltrichloroethane (insecticide) | LCV | League of Conservation Voters (USA) |
| DEFRA | Department for Environment, Food and Rural Affairs | LETS | local exchange trading system |
| | | LRTAP | long-range transboundary air pollution |
| EAP | Environmental Action Plan | | |
| EEA | European Environment Agency | LULU | locally unwanted land use |
| EIA | environmental impact assessment | MBI | market-based instrument |
| EMAS | Eco-Management and Audit Scheme | ME | ministry of environment |
| EPA | Environmental Protection Agency (USA) | MEA | multilateral environmental agreement |
| EPI | environmental policy integration | MEP | Member of the European Parliament |
| EU | European Union | | |
| EU-15 | The 15 EU member states pre-2004 | MP | Member of Parliament |
| EU-25 | The 25 EU member states post-2004 | NAAEC | North American Agreement on Environmental Cooperation |
| FDP | Free Democratic Party (Germany) | | |
| FoE | Friends of the Earth | NAFTA | North American Free Trade Agreement |
| GEF | Global Environment Facility | | |
| GHG | greenhouse gas | NATO | North Atlantic Treaty Organisation |

| | | | |
|---|---|---|---|
| NFU | National Farmers' Union | UNCED | United Nations Conference on Environment and Development |
| NGO | non-governmental organisation | | |
| NIMBY | not in my back yard | UNDP | United Nations Development Programme |
| NSM | new social movement | | |
| OECD | Organisation for Economic Co-operation and Development | UNEP | United Nations Environment Programme |
| POS | political opportunity structure | WCED | World Commission on Environment and Development |
| PPP | polluter pays principle | | |
| PR | proportional representation | WSSD | World Summit on Sustainable Development |
| RSPB | Royal Society for the Protection of Birds (UK) | | |
| | | WTO | World Trade Organisation |
| SPD | Social Democratic Party (Germany) | WWF | World Wide Fund for Nature |

# Glossary

**Anthropocentrism** A way of thinking that regards humans as the source of all value and is predominantly concerned with human interests.

**Biodiversity** The number, variety and variability of living organisms; sometimes refers to the total variety of life on Earth.

**Bioregionalism** An approach that believes that the 'natural' world (specifically, the local bioregion) should determine the political, economic and social life of communities.

**Climate change** Any change in climate over time, whether due to natural variability or to human activity.

**Conservationism** An approach to land management that emphasises the efficient conservation of natural resources so that they can later be developed for the benefit of society.

**Corporatism** A system in which major organised interests (traditionally, capital and labour) work closely together within the formal structures of government to formulate and implement public policies.

**Cost–benefit analysis** A study that compares the costs and benefits to society of providing a public good.

**Decentralisation** The expansion of local autonomy through the transfer of powers and responsibilities away from a national political and administrative body.

**Deep ecology** The pre-eminent radical ecocentric moral theory which has the primary aim of preserving nature from human interference.

**Ecocentrism** A mode of thought that regards humans as subject to ecological and systems laws and whose ethical, political and social prescriptions are concerned with both humans and non-humans.

**Ecological footprint** A measure of the amount of nature it takes to sustain a given population over the course of a year.

**Ecological modernisation** A policy strategy which aims to restructure capitalist political economy along more environmentally benign lines based on the assumption that economic growth and environmental protection can be reconciled.

**Ecologism** A distinctive green political ideology encompassing those perspectives that hold that a sustainable society requires radical changes in our relationship with the non-human natural world and our mode of economic, social and political life.

**Eco-tax** A tax levied on pollution or on the goods whose production generates pollution.

**Environmental impact assessment** A systematic non-technical evaluation, based on extensive consultation with affected interests, of the anticipated environmental impact of a proposed development such as a dam or road.

**Genetically modified organism** New organisms created by human manipulation of genetic information and material.

**Green consumerism** The use of environmental and ethical criteria in choosing whether or not to purchase a product or service.

**Holism** The view that wholes are more than just the sum of their parts, and that wholes cannot be defined merely as a collection of their basic constituents.

**Intrinsic value** The value which something has, independently of anyone finding it valuable.

**Issue attention cycle** The idea that there is a cycle in which issues attract public attention and move up and down the political agenda.

**Limits to growth** The belief that the planet imposes natural limits on economic and population growth.

**Market-based instrument** A policy instrument that internalises into the price of a good or product the external costs to the environment of producing and using it.

**Modern environmentalism** The emergence, from the late 1960s, of growing public concern about the state of the planet, new political ideas about the environment and a mass political movement.

**Moral extensionism** Ethical approaches which broaden the 'moral community' to include non-human entities such as animals, based on the possession of some critical property such as sentience.

**New politics** The view that since the late 1960s the rise of postmaterial values, a new middle class and new social movements has changed the political agenda and led to a realignment of established party systems.

**New social movement** A loose-knit organisation which seeks to influence public policy on an issue such as the environment, nuclear energy or peace, and which may use unconventional forms of political participation, including direct action, to achieve its aims.

**Ozone depletion** Depletion of ozone in the Earth's upper atmosphere which leaves the surface of the Earth vulnerable to harmful ultraviolet radiation.

**Party politicisation** A process whereby the environment ascends the political agenda to become electorally salient and the subject of party competition.

**Pioneer states** Those countries, mostly in Northern Europe, that have taken the lead in developing progressive environmental policies and setting high standards of environmental protection.

**Policy paradigm** A framework of ideas and standards that specifies the nature of a problem and the policy goals and instruments needed to address it.

**Political opportunity structure** The dimensions of the political environment that either encourage people to use collective action or discourage them from doing so, and which shape the development of movements and parties.

**Postmaterialism** The theory that, as material affluence spreads, 'quality of life' issues and concerns tend to replace material ones, fundamentally changing the political culture and values of industrialised countries.

**Precautionary principle** The principle states that the lack of scientific certainty shall not be used as a reason for postponing measures to prevent environmental degradation.

**Preservationism** An approach based on an attitude of reverence towards nature, especially wilderness, that advocates the protection of a resource from any form of development.

**Regime** The principles, norms, rules and decision-making procedures which form the basis of co-operation on a particular issue in international relations.

**Regulation** Any direct ('command-and-control') attempt by the government to influence the behaviour of businesses or citizens by setting environmental standards (e.g. for air quality) enforced via legislation.

**Renewable energy** Energy sources, such as wind, geothermal and hydroelectric, that never run out.

**Resource mobilisation** An approach to collective action which focuses on the way groups mobilise their resources – members, finances, symbols – in turning grievances into political issues.

**Risk assessment** An evaluation of the potential harm to human health and the environment from exposure to a particular hazard such as nitrates in drinking water.

**Sentience** The capacity to suffer or to experience enjoyment or happiness.

**Social justice** The principles that should govern the basic structure of a society, focusing on the distribution of rights, opportunities and resources among human beings.

**Survivalism** Approaches characterised by an overriding preoccupation with human survival, a sense of urgency about an impending ecological crisis and drastic, often authoritarian, solutions.

**Sustainable development** The ability of the present generation to meet its needs without undermining the ability of future generations to meet their needs.

**Technocentric** A mode of thought which optimistically believes that society can solve all environmental problems, using technology and science, and achieve unlimited material growth.

**Traditional policy paradigm** An approach to the environment that treats each problem discretely, gives priority to economic growth and results in reactive, piecemeal and tactical policies and end-of-pipe solutions.

# Introduction

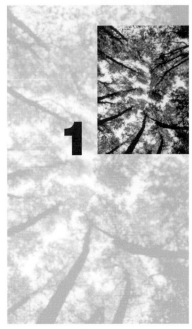

The environment has been on the political agenda since the late 1960s. Much has happened in that time, but is the planet better off? According to one popular heuristic measure of the state of the environment – the **ecological footprint** – things are bad and getting steadily worse.[1] The global ecological footprint of humanity is a measure of the amount of nature it takes to sustain a given population over the course of a year. This global footprint first exceeded the Earth's biological capacity in the late 1970s, since when it has risen steadily, overshooting by almost 40 per cent in 2005 (Venetoulis and Talberth 2006: 12). Moreover, this alarming figure disguises huge disparities among the nations; for example, the per capita footprint (in global hectares) of the USA (108.95) is about seventy times that of Ethiopia (1.56) (Table 1.1). It would be wrong, however, to draw the conclusion that nothing has changed over the last forty years; in practice, the picture is much more complicated, as is illustrated by the following examples.

> **Ecological footprint:** A measure of the amount of nature it takes to sustain a given population over the course of a year.

In April 1986 the Chernobyl nuclear reactor exploded, with catastrophic human and environmental consequences stretching from the Ukraine across much of the Northern Hemisphere. Chernobyl appeared to be the death-knell for the nuclear industry, as most governments stopped commissioning any new nuclear power-stations. Remarkably, twenty years later the nuclear industry is back in favour, with the first new nuclear reactor in the EU for over a decade being built in Finland, the French and British governments planning a new generation of nuclear reactors, and President Bush offering financial incentives to anyone willing to build the first nuclear power stations in the USA in a generation. Ironically, the contemporary justification

**Table 1.1 Ecological footprint estimates, 1961–2001 (global hectares per capita, rounded)**

|  | Ecological footprint | Biological capacity | Ecological balance |
|---|---|---|---|
| USA | 109 | 20 | −89 |
| France | 66 | 11 | −55 |
| Germany | 52 | 8 | −44 |
| Italy | 41 | 8 | −33 |
| Sweden | 66 | 26 | −40 |
| UK | 62 | 10 | −52 |
| Kuwait | 155 | 8 | −147 |
| China | 12 | 8 | −4 |
| India | 4 | 6 | 2 |
| Ethiopia | 2 | 9 | 7 |
| Nepal | 2 | 8 | 6 |

*Source*: Venetoulis and Talberth (2006: 11–13).

for nuclear power is the 'green' claim that it is a carbon-free solution to climate change.

The lifestyle choices of many people are increasingly shaped by environmental considerations: they purchase organic products, recycle drink containers, cycle to work and invest their savings 'ethically' and take 'ecotourist' holidays. Yet global capitalism and consumerist lifestyles grow ever more demanding on the environment. Most people in the industrialised world seem to want more goods, to take cheap flights, to drive their cars and they are wedded to a 'throwaway' culture that results in landfill sites piled high with plastic bottles and obsolete computers.

Citizens have joined environmental groups in their millions, signed petitions and marched on demonstrations. The environmental lobby has become an important actor in national and international politics, while the dramatic stunts of eco-warriors have become a familiar part of the political repertoire. But entrenched business interests and technocratic elites continue to exercise far greater influence over most key policy decisions. Green parties are now an established feature of party politics in many European countries, and have even joined coalition governments in several countries, whilst established parties of all persuasions have adopted a greener rhetoric. However, electoral politics remain dominated by traditional materialist issues, such as the state of the economy, taxation, public order and welfare policy. Governments everywhere have introduced a wide range of environmental protection policies and regulations, and most countries are formally committed to the principles of **sustainable development**, but priority is still almost always given to economic growth over environmental protection. Efforts to build

**Sustainable development:** The ability of the present generation to meet its needs without undermining the ability of future generations to meet their needs.

international co-operation to address global environmental problems such as **climate change** have become a central concern of international diplomacy, yet the USA has refused to agree to make

> **Climate change:** Any change in climate over time, whether due to natural variability or to human activity.

even the limited and inadequate emissions reductions contained in the Kyoto Protocol, and rapidly industrialising major powers such as China and India have not been required to make any commitments.

Whilst there is no doubt that environmental issues have had a big impact on contemporary politics, the frequency with which governments adopt a business-as-usual response to environmental problems raises the cynical thought that perhaps nothing much has really changed. This puzzle is one of many challenges confronting environmental politics, which has rapidly become an established subject of political enquiry.

The rationale behind this book is that environmental politics is a distinctive subject that is worthy of study both in its own right and also for the challenges it poses for the wider discipline of politics. Environmental politics is a wide-ranging subject with three core components:

1. the study of political theories and ideas relating to the environment;
2. the examination of political parties and environmental movements;
3. the analysis of public policymaking and implementation affecting the environment at international, national and local levels.

The broad aim of this book is to provide an introduction to environmental politics that covers all three aspects of this rapidly expanding subject. The primary focus of the book is on environmental politics in the industrialised world. It is the affluent industrialised countries of Europe and North America that are largely responsible for causing contemporary environmental problems and it is essential that they take the lead in solving them. Much of the substance of environmental politics – ideas and theories, parties and movements, policy initiatives – is rooted in the industrialised world too. Although North–South issues and development themes regularly surface in the book, for reasons of substance, practicality and space, the book has a primary focus on advanced industrialised countries. The rest of this introduction identifies the distinctive features of environmental politics and explains the structure of the book.

So, in what ways is environmental politics distinctive? One distinguishing characteristic is that it has a primary concern with the relationship between human society and the natural world. This human–nature relationship connects the extraordinarily diverse set of issues encompassed by environmental politics, which include wilder-

> **Biodiversity:** The number, variety and variability of living organisms; sometimes refers to the total variety of life on Earth.

ness preservation and nature conservation, air, water and land pollution, the depletion of scarce resources such as fish stocks, rainforests and endangered species, the use of nuclear power and biotechnology, and 'global' problems such as **biodiversity** loss, climate change and **ozone depletion**. Traditionally,

**Ozone depletion:** Depletion of ozone in the Earth's upper atmosphere which leaves the surface of the Earth vulnerable to harmful ultraviolet radiation.
**Holism:** The view that wholes are more than just the sum of their parts, and that wholes cannot be defined merely as a collection of their basic constituents.

many of them were (and often still are) treated discretely as separate policy problems. The increasing tendency to conceptualise these problems as 'environmental' reflects the emergence of an environmental discourse, or way of thinking about the world, which has given coherence and political significance to the notion of 'the environment' (Dryzek 2005). Underpinning this discourse is a **holistic** perspective which, rather than examining individual issues in isolation, focuses on the interdependence of environmental, political, social and economic issues and the way in which they interact with each other.

At this point it is important to provide some historical context because the emergence of this wider environmental discourse is a relatively recent development. Of course, many of the problems that we now regard as environmental, such as pollution, deforestation and land degradation, are not new. In the classical world, Plato, Lucretius and Caesar all commented on the problem of soil erosion (Wall 1994a: 2–3). The collapse of the Mayan civilisation hundreds of years ago can probably be attributed to deforestation and soil erosion (Ponting 1992). Much later, however, it was the industrial and scientific revolutions of the eighteenth and nineteenth centuries that really created the conditions for contemporary concern about the environment. In particular, the process of industrialisation contributed to environmental degradation by accelerating resource consumption, urban development and pollution. One of the earliest examples of what we would now call environmental legislation was the 1863 Alkali Act in Britain, whilst in the USA the first legal action against air pollution occurred in 1876 in St Louis (Paehlke 1989: 23). The first wave of concern about environmental issues can be traced to the emergence of conservation and nature protection groups in the latter part of the nineteenth and the early twentieth centuries, reflecting a growing middle-class interest in the protection of wildlife, wilderness and natural resources (Lowe and Goyder 1983). Several leading pressure groups, including the Sierra Club in the USA, the Royal Society for the Protection of Birds in the UK, and the Naturschutzbund Deutschland in Germany, date from this period. The **conservationist** movement established a firm base through the twentieth century as most countries saw a gradual accumulation of policies affecting various 'environmental' issues, ranging from the regulation of industrial pollution to the creation of

**Conservationism:** An approach to land management that emphasises the efficient conservation of natural resources so that they can later be developed for the benefit of society.
**Modern environmentalism:** The emergence, from the late 1960s, of growing public concern about the state of the planet, new political ideas about the environment and a mass political movement.

national parks. Nevertheless, it was not until the emergence of '**modern environmentalism**' – the wave of popular concern about environmental issues that swept across the developed world during the 1960s – that the environmental discourse became widespread (Pepper 1996) (see Box 1.1).

---

**1.1 Evolution of environmental issues**

*First generation: preservation and conservation* (pre-1960s)
Protection of wildlife and habitats
Soil erosion
Local pollution

*Second generation: 'modern environmentalism'* (from 1960s)
Population growth
Technology
Desertification
Pesticides

Resource depletion
Pollution abatement

*Third generation: global issues* (late 1970s onwards)
Acid rain
Ozone depletion
Rainforest destruction
Climate change
Loss of biodiversity
Genetically modified organisms

---

The rise of modern environmentalism highlights a second distinctive feature of the environment as a political subject: unlike most other single issues, it comes replete with its own ideology and political movement (Jacobs 1997: 1). An awareness of historical context is again important, for nei-

**Preservationism:** An approach based on an attitude of reverence towards nature, especially wilderness, that advocates the protection of a resource from any form of development.

ther a green ideology nor an environmental movement existed before the late 1960s. Modern environmentalism differed from the earlier **preservationist** and conservationist movements in two important ways (McCormick 1989: ch. 3). First, it was driven by the idea of a global ecological crisis that threatened the very existence of humanity. The atomic age had brought home the fragility of planet Earth. This perception was nurtured by a series of well-publicised eco-disasters, notably the massive oil spillages from the wrecked *Torrey Canyon* tanker off the Cornish coast in 1967, the blow-out of an oil platform at Santa Barbara, California, two years later, and the mercury poisoning of Minamata Bay in Japan. Following Rachel Carson's 1962 best-seller, *Silent Spring*, which alerted the world to the dangers posed by the synthetic chemicals used in pesticides such as DDT, advances in scientific knowledge were increasingly catapulted out of the laboratory into the public arena. Fierce public debates about the consequences of population growth, technology and resource depletion encouraged people to think increasingly in global terms about the environment (Ehrlich 1968; Commoner 1971; Meadows et al. 1972).

Secondly, modern environmentalism was a political and activist mass movement which demanded a radical transformation in the values and structures of society. It was influenced by the broader 'politics of affluence' and the general upsurge in social movement protest at that time. Modern environmentalism came of age on 22 April 1970 when millions of Americans celebrated and protested on Earth Day; still the largest environmental demonstration in history. The burgeoning environmental movement certainly helped to popularise the environmental discourse. Governments set up environmental ministries and agencies and introduced swaths of new legislation to protect the environment. The watershed 1972 UN Stockholm conference, which examined how a range of global environmental problems affected human life, marked the entry of the environment onto the international agenda. Thus, by the early 1970s, the component parts of environmental politics had started to take shape: the appearance of new political ideas and ways of thinking about the environment; the rise of a mass environmental movement; and the creation of a new policy agenda.

These three core components of environmental politics provide the framework for this book, which is divided into three parts to reflect the distinctive contribution made by each area of study: ideas; parties and movements; and policy.

Part I explores different ways of thinking about the environment. A major theme of the book is to explore whether there is now a sufficiently comprehensive and distinctive view of environmental issues to talk in terms of a green political ideology, or '**ecologism**' (Dobson 2000). In particular, green political thought offers two important insights. One is the belief that we need to reconceptualise the relationship between humans and nature, which prompts many important questions about which parts of nature, if any, have value, on what basis that value may be attributed and whether such value is equal to that of humans. A further critical insight is the conviction that the Earth's resources are finite and that there are ecological

> **Ecologism:** A distinctive green political ideology encompassing those perspectives that hold that a sustainable society requires radical changes in our relationship with the non-human natural world and our mode of economic, social and political life.
> **Limits to growth:** The belief that the planet imposes natural limits on economic and population growth.

**limits to growth** which, unless we change our ways, will be exceeded sooner rather than later. Radical greens draw the conclusion that we need a fundamental reassessment of our value systems and a restructuring of existing political, social and economic systems in order to achieve an ecologically sustainable society. Part I assesses this claim that ecologism is a distinctive ideology. Chapter 2 provides an introduction to environmental philosophy by exploring ethical questions about how humans ought to think about and act towards nature. Chapter 3 outlines and analyses the green political programme and assesses the relationship between green ideas and other political ideologies.

Part II turns to the question of how we get to a sustainable society, with a focus on collective action. Environmental activism is now a very broad church. Green parties have become established in several countries and there are many 'environmentalists' operating within established political parties. Beyond parties, the contemporary environmental movement now encompasses mass-membership pressure groups such as the Sierra Club, international non-governmental organisations (NGOs), including Greenpeace and Friends of the Earth, thousands of local grassroots groups and radical protest groups such as Earth First!. Whether by directly influencing the policy process or indirectly raising public

> **New politics:** The view that since the late 1960s the rise of postmaterial values, a new middle class and new social movements has changed the political agenda and led to a realignment of established party systems.

consciousness about environmental issues through media campaigns and protest activities, the environmental movement has become a significant political actor and agent of change. In Chapter 4 the rise of green parties is examined in the context of the claim that they represent a '**new politics**'. A range of structural and institutional factors is explored to explain why green parties have achieved electoral success in some countries, but failed elsewhere, with a particular focus on Germany, France and Britain. Chapter 5 investigates the impact of environmental issues on party politics. It looks first at the way green parties, notably the German Greens, have dealt with the transition from pressure politics to parliamentary respectability and then into government; secondly, it assesses the impact of environmentalism on established parties, through case studies of Germany, Britain and the USA. Chapter 6 explores the development and achievements of environmental groups, particularly in the USA and Britain, using the dynamic tension between the large, mainstream environmental lobby and grassroots action as a means of exploring some central questions of green agency, or how to achieve political change.

Finally, Part III is concerned with environmental policy; specifically, it examines progress towards the implementation of sustainable development. Whilst governments may be deaf to the radical message of ecologism, many have been influenced by the alternative **policy paradigms** of sustainable development and **ecological modernisation**, which offer the promise of protecting the environment by reforming capitalism. As a result, radical ideas like the '**precautionary principle**', and innovative policy instruments such as **eco-taxes**, have begun to appear on the policy agenda. At an international level, the search for solutions to global environmental problems has engendered unprecedented efforts to secure widescale international co-operation between independent sovereign states to solve problems such as ozone deple-

> **Policy paradigm:** A framework of ideas and standards that specifies the nature of a problem and the policy goals and instruments needed to address it.
> **Ecological modernisation:** A policy strategy which aims to restructure capitalist political economy along more environmentally benign lines based on the assumption that economic growth and environmental protection can be reconciled.
> **Precautionary principle:** The principle that the lack of scientific certainty shall not be used as a reason for postponing measures to prevent environmental degradation.
> **Eco-tax:** A tax levied on pollution or on the goods whose production generates pollution.

tion. However, policymakers have discovered that environmental issues pose distinctive and pressing problems. Chapter 7 explores the environment as a policy problem, identifying its distinguishing characteristics and outlining

**Traditional policy paradigm:** An approach to the environment that treats each problem discretely, gives priority to economic growth and results in reactive, piecemeal and tactical policies and end-of-pipe solutions.

the **traditional policy paradigm**, which has proved unable to cope with the range and intensity of contemporary environmental problems. The resilience of this traditional paradigm is explained by the structural power that capitalism gives to producer interests and by the segmentation of the policy process, but the chapter also explores a range of policy models and frameworks that can help make sense of environmental policymaking and show how change is possible. Chapter 8 analyses the strengths and weaknesses of the alternative policy paradigms of sustainable development and ecological modernisation, and the remaining chapters evaluate how far they have been implemented. Chapter 9 looks at the emergence of international cooperation between nation states intended to address problems of the global commons, with detailed studies of climate change and ozone depletion.

**Regulation:** Any direct ('command and control') attempt by the government to influence the behaviour of businesses or citizens by setting environmental standards (e.g. for air quality) enforced via legislation.
**Market-based instrument:** A policy instrument that internalises into the price of a good or product the external costs to the environment of producing and using it.

Chapter 10 examines the relationship between globalisation, trade and the environment, and assesses the impact of three key institutions: the World Trade Organisation, the North American Free Trade Agreement and the European Union. Chapter 11 investigates progress towards greener government by examining how far environmental policy considerations have been integrated into routine policymaking processes. Chapter 12 analyses the strengths and weaknesses of different policy instruments, concentrating on the key debate between the competing claims of **regulatory** and **market-based instruments**, with particular studies of climate change policies in the energy and transport sectors.

Throughout Parts II and III an informal comparative approach is employed. It is informal in the sense that it makes no attempt to follow a rigorous comparative methodology; but it is comparative in that it uses examples and case studies from several different countries, mostly from Europe, the USA and Australasia, to illustrate the arguments.

Another key theme of the book is that environmental politics, in addition to being a distinctive and fascinating subject worthy of study in its own terms, is important because it challenges established political discourses, political behaviour and policy agendas. Thus the growing significance of environmental politics has seen political philosophers extend mainstream theories of justice to consider whether non-human nature or future generations of humans have interests or rights or are owed obligations. Political ideologies, including conservatism, liberalism, socialism and feminism, have had to respond to the environmental challenge, giving rise to several new hybrid concepts, such as ecosocialism and ecofeminism. Where green parties have achieved electoral success, they have destabilised long-standing party alliances and voting patterns. The growing legitimacy and influence of environmental groups has frequently disrupted established policy networks and challenged the influence of producer interests over the policy process. The sustainable development paradigm forces governments to rethink the way they make policy. Traditional Realist accounts of international relations struggle to account for the growth of co-operation and collective action to prevent environmental degradation. The book will show how the rise of environmental politics has therefore been responsible for a widespread re-examination of established assumptions, interpretations and beliefs about contemporary political ideas and behaviour.

Conversely, core political ideas inform our understanding of environmental politics. Concepts such as justice, democracy and equity are central to green political theory. For example, an analysis of the green commitment to participatory democracy can draw on a rich literature on democratic theory and practice. The political science literature on new politics and **postmaterialism** offers important insights about the development of the environmental movement. The study of environmental policymaking is incomplete without concepts and frameworks drawn from the public policy literature, such as agenda-setting theory or policy network analysis.

> **Postmaterialism:** The theory that, as material affluence spreads, 'quality of life' issues and concerns tend to replace material ones, fundamentally changing the political culture and values of industrialised countries.

Some familiar political dichotomies also resurface. Is the state or the market more effective for achieving environmental policy outcomes? Are centralised or decentralised political structures better at dealing with environmental problems? Most importantly, in debating how to achieve a sustainable society, greens confront the familiar dilemma of reformism versus radicalism. Should environmental activists pursue an evolutionary reform of the capitalist system by getting elected to parliament, or should they seek nothing less than a radical transformation of the system? Should groups adopt conventional or unconventional forms of protest? Is collective action (through green parties and pressure groups) or individual action (by changing lifestyles and **green consumerism**) more effective? In returning to some of these themes in the concluding chapter, I argue that, as the environment has become an increasingly mainstream issue, so the centre of gravity in environmental politics has shifted from a *radical* rejection of contemporary society and a relatively *narrow* concern with ecological issues, to a *reformist* acceptance of capitalist liberal democracy accompanied by a *broader* **social justice** agenda.

> **Green consumerism:** The use of environmental and ethical criteria in choosing whether or not to purchase a product or service.
> **Social justice:** The principles that should govern the basic structure of a society, focusing on the distribution of rights, opportunities and resources among human beings.

### ▶ *Further reading and websites*

Ponting (1992) is a very readable environmental history of the world. Grove (1995) offers a fascinating account of the early history of environmentalism as part of colonial expansion. Wall (1994b) provides an interesting anthology of early green writings. For a history of the rise of environmentalism, see McCormick (1989). Good assessments of the state of the environment can be found in the annual publications by the World Resources Institute (http://www.wri.org/), the numerous United Nations Environment Programme reports (http://www.unep.org/), the Millennium Ecosystem Assessments (http://www.millenniumassessment.org/en/index.aspx) and, for Europe, the excellent European Environment Agency reports (see http://www.eea.eu.int). There are countless books outlining and seeking to explain the environmental crisis, including McMichael (1995), Pickering and Owen (1997) and Lester Brown's annual State of World reports (e.g. Worldwatch Institute 2006) for new developments.

NOTE

1 The ecological footprint is just one of many measures of the environmental impact of human activities. By comparing the ecological footprint of human activities with the biological capacity of the Earth, the footprint metric indicates whether our use of crop lands, forest lands, pasture lands, built space, fisheries and energy is sustainable. Whilst the methodology of measurement is open to criticism and is being continuously refined (Venetoulis and Talberth 2006), it does provide a useful heuristic device for assessing the sustainability of human use of natural resources. See Wackernagel and Rees (1996) and Chambers et al. (2000).

# PART 1

# Theory: thinking about the environment

Part I examines how political theorists think about environmental issues. Specifically, it asks the question: is there a sufficiently comprehensive, coherent and distinctive view of environmental issues to justify talking about a green political ideology which, following Dobson (2000), can be called ecologism?

There has been a phenomenal growth in the literature on environmental philosophy and political thought in recent years. The distinction between *reformist* and *radical* approaches provides a useful shorthand means of categorising two quite different ways of thinking about environmental problems. Broadly speaking, reformist approaches adopt 'a managerial approach to environmental problems, secure in the belief that they can be solved without fundamental changes in present values or patterns of production and consumption' whereas radical positions (i.e. ecologism) argue that 'a sustainable and fulfilling existence pre-supposes radical changes in our relationship with the non-human natural world, and in our mode of social and political life' (Dobson 2000: 2).[1] In short, reformist and radical approaches represent qualitatively different interpretations of environmental problems.

Dobson also makes the bigger and bolder claim that ecologism should be regarded as a distinct political ideology. To cohere as an ideology, ecologism must have three basic features: (1) a common set of concepts and values providing a critique of the existing social and political systems; (2) a political prescription based on an alternative outline of how a society ought to look; (3) a programme for political action with strategies for getting from the existing society to the alternative outline. Ecologism, according to Dobson, passes the test on all three counts. First, it is characterised by two core ideas: a rethinking of the ethical relationship between humans and the natural world, and the belief that there are natural limits to growth. Secondly, it offers an alternative political prescription for a sustainable society. Thirdly, it identifies various strategies for reaching the sustainable society. By contrast, reformist approaches do not add up to an ideology. They offer no distinctive view of the human condition or the structure of society. They are embedded in and 'easily accommodated by other ideologies' (p. 7) such as conservatism, liberalism or socialism.

It is because ecologism encapsulates the most interesting, challenging and distinctive contributions made by environmental political theorists that Part I focuses on its arguments and examines the veracity of the claim that it represents a distinct ideology. Chapter 2 identifies some of the key issues in environmental philosophy by exploring ethical questions about the relationship between humans and the natural world. Chapter 3 outlines the core features of green political thought and examines the relationship between green ideas and traditional political ideologies. There is often a close, and sometimes confusing, relationship between theory and practice in any discussion of political ideology. One further question underlying the discussion in Part I concerns the implications of ecologism for practical political arrangements: what impact has it had on the development of green parties and the wider environmental movement, and what lessons does it have for policymakers?

*Note*

1 Dobson uses the term 'environmentalism' rather than 'reformism', but his is a very particular use of the term which can give rise to confusion, for example, when discussing 'modern environmentalism' or the 'environmental movement'.

# Environmental philosophy

**2**

## Contents

## Key issues

▶ What are the main theories and debates in environmental philosophy?
▶ Does nature have value independent of human needs?
▶ Are some parts of nature more valuable than others?
▶ On what grounds might humans have duties towards the natural world?
▶ Can environmental philosophy provide the ethical basis for a green ideology?

> The central and most recalcitrant problem for environmental ethics is the problem of constructing an adequate theory of intrinsic value for nonhuman natural entities and for nature as a whole.  (Callicott 1985: 257)

Environmental politics is suffused with ethical dilemmas. Should we reduce the employment prospects of poor people in order to save an endangered species? Are draconian controls on population growth justified if we are

13

to reduce the pressure on the natural environment? Is it wrong to eat meat? Environmental ethics, by examining questions about how humans ought to think about and act towards nature, provides a link between theory and practice. It is primarily concerned with values. Does nature have value separate from its role in meeting human needs? If so, why? Which parts of nature possess value and are some parts more valuable than others?

**Deep ecology:** The pre-eminent radical ecocentric moral theory, which has the primary aim of preserving nature from human interference.

There is a strong normative element to environmental philosophy. Many leading contributors are also committed activists whose main objective is to develop a robust environmental ethical theory to underpin green activism. Radical perspectives such as **deep ecology** question the existence of a clear divide between humans and nature and may even push humans off their pedestal at the top of the ethical hierarchy. If ecologism is a separate ideology, then the way the human–nature relationship is conceptualised arguably provides its most distinctive and radical feature.

This chapter provides an introduction to the key debates in environmental philosophy. It considers whether an environmental ethic that attributes value and moral significance to nature is defensible, and whether it is a necessary component of a green political theory. The opening sections stake out the territory covered by environmental philosophy by distinguishing three different types of value, explaining the **anthropocentric–ecocentric** dichotomy and setting out a simple typology categorising the main approaches within environmental philosophy. The core of the chapter consists of a critical analysis of environmental theories of value under the two broad categories of holism and **moral extensionism**. The final section suggests that the search for a pure non-anthropocentric perspective may be fruitless. Ecologism is, and perhaps *should be*, informed by a wide range of value theories – a form of value eclecticism – each of which can contribute constructively to the development of an ethical framework to guide human behaviour towards the environment.

**Anthropocentrism:** A way of thinking that regards humans as the source of all value and is predominantly concerned with human interests.
**Ecocentrism:** A mode of thought that regards humans as subject to ecological and systems laws and whose ethical, political and social prescriptions are concerned with both humans and non-humans.
**Moral extensionism:** Ethical approaches which broaden the 'moral community' to include non-human entities such as animals, based on the possession of some critical property such as sentience.

## ◗ Staking out the territory

### ◗ *Types of value*

A key concept in environmental philosophy is *value*. Unfortunately, not only are there several different *kinds* of value, but there is also little consistency

## 2.1 Defining value

1. *Instrumental value* is the value which something has *for someone* as a *means to an end* which they desire. So, a word processor is valuable to me in so far as it enables me to write, when writing is something I want to do.

2. *Inherent value* is the value something has *for someone*, but not as a means to a further end. A beautiful landscape has value for me,

but not because it enables me to do something further. It is something which I find valuable in itself.

3. *Intrinsic value* is simply the value which something has. No appeal need be made to those for whom it has value. It simply is valuable and is so independently of anyone finding it valuable.

in the way key terms, such as instrumental, inherent and **intrinsic value**, are used. The distinctions between these terms are contested and key writers use them differently.[1] Rather than becoming

**Intrinsic value:** The value which something has, independently of anyone finding it valuable.

embroiled in arcane debates about these distinctions, the three definitions used in this chapter are simply set out in Box 2.1. These terms are not mutually exclusive; being valuable in one way does not preclude something also being valuable in another way.

### ◗ *The anthropocentric–ecocentric divide*

Why is value a key concept in environmental philosophy? A central tenet of green thinking is the belief that the current ecological crisis is caused by human arrogance towards the natural world, which legitimates its exploitation in order to satisfy human interests. Human arrogance towards nature is rooted in *anthropocentrism*: the belief that ethical principles apply only to humans and that human needs and interests are of highest, perhaps exclusive, significance – humans are placed at the centre of the universe, separated from nature, and endowed with unique values (see Box 2.2). Anthropocentrism regards only humans as having intrinsic value, a claim usually based on their capacity either to experience pleasure and pain or to reason, and, furthermore, that only humans have interests. The rest of nature is of instrumental value; it has value and deserves moral consideration only in so far as it enhances human well-being. Non-human nature – the koala bear or brown rat, the field of tulips or tract of wilderness – is simply a 'storehouse of resources' for the satisfaction of human ends (Eckersley 1992: 26). An anthropocentric case for environmental protection will therefore be justified instrumentally in terms of the consequences that pollution or resource depletion might have for human interests. Lead is removed from petrol because it harms human health and fishing grounds are protected because of the threat to a vital economic and food resource. Although there are many powerful instrumental arguments for defending the environment, many greens believe that they are insufficiently

## 2.2 The roots of anthropocentrism

1. *The Bible?*

   The 'historical roots of our ecological crisis' can be located in the despotic Judaeo-Christian world-view, which interpreted Genesis as regarding nature as existing solely to serve mankind and therefore ripe for exploitation (White 1962).

   A different reading of the Bible identifies a strong tradition of stewardship, conservation and concern for non-humans that is 'at least as representative of Christian history as any despotic view' (Attfield 1983: 45). Nor can the Judaeo-Christian thesis explain why a non-Christian country, such as Japan, has an equally strong technocratic-industrial culture and similar levels of environmental damage as Europe and North America.

2. *The Enlightenment?*

   The dominance of anthropocentrism in Western culture is often blamed on the Enlightenment ideas and the scientific revolution of the sixteenth and seventeenth centuries. Francis Bacon, for example, argued that by analysing nature atomistically – breaking it into parts and reducing it to basic components – scientific knowledge could give us mastery over nature, which could then be manipulated for our own ends. Greens are critical of the Enlightenment legacy for encouraging the misconceived belief that humans can master nature and for the apparent lack of concern towards nature that it has engendered – attitudes that, for example, inform scientific enthusiasm for genetically modified products.

   A contrary view points to the great achievements of the Enlightenment: the triumph of reason over traditional authority and the ascendancy of liberal values such as rights, freedom and justice. There is nothing wrong with a disinterested scientific attempt to master nature in order to understand how it works. Without science, how would we even know about global environmental problems such as climate change and ozone depletion? The problem arises when scientific achievements and technologies are misused through ignorance or for immoral reasons.

   See Hayward (1995: ch. 1) for a discussion of ecology and the Enlightenment tradition.

robust to support a strong environmental ethic. For example, anthropocentric arguments generally place the onus on those wishing to protect the environment to make their case, rather than on those wishing to intervene in nature to justify their actions.

One of the key themes in environmental ethics has been the attempt to develop a non-anthropocentric, or *ecocentric* ethic (Eckersley 1992). Ecocentrism rejects the 'human chauvinism' of anthropocentrism and argues that non-human entities also have intrinsic value. Precisely which entities or categories in the non-human world have value varies according to the

**Sentience:** The capacity to suffer or to experience enjoyment or happiness.

writer, ranging through animals, trees, plants and other non-**sentient** living things (both individuals and species), and even inanimate objects such as rivers or mountains. A common thread linking all ecocentric arguments is the belief that to show that some or all of nature has intrinsic value may prove a powerful instrument for defending the environment.

## 2.3 A typology of environmental philosophy

1. *Shallow* perspectives such as 'resource conservationism' and 'preservationism' (see Box 2.5) are concerned about environmental protection, but it remains subordinate to other human interests. Shallow perspectives accept the Sole Value Assumption: that humans are the sole items of value.

2. *Intermediate* perspectives argue that moral consideration should be extended to include certain non-human entities, although the categories included (animals? plants?) and the reasons for extension (sentience? capacity to flourish? protection of diversity?) differ. A large part of environmental philosophy falls within this category, notably 'moral extensionist' positions based on sentience (Singer 1976) and rights (Regan 1983), and the 'ethical holists' (Callicott 1985, 1986; Rolston 1988, 1991). Intermediate positions remain wedded to some version of the Greater Value Assumption: that human interests always

outvalue other considerations and the value of non-humans (Sylvan and Bennett 1994), or, slightly differently, that the value of normal members of a species will never exceed that of humans (Attfield 1993: 22).

3. *Ecocentric* perspectives reconceptualise ethical positions around a non-human-centred attitude to the environment, which involves the rejection of both the Sole and Greater Value Assumptions. Ecocentrics see value residing in the ecosphere as a whole rather than in humans or in individual entities, and that value exists independently of humans. Deep ecology is the most prominent ecocentric position (Naess 1973, 1989; Devall and Sessions 1985), although other 'deep' positions exist, such as 'transpersonal ecology' (Fox 1990).

Adapted, with amendments, from Vincent (1993: 256).

The anthropocentric–ecocentric dualism is a key conceptual distinction in environmental philosophy.[2] For many observers and activists, an acceptance of a non-anthropocentric perspective is the litmus test for being green; it is what distinguishes ecologism from other political ideologies (Eckersley 1992). It will be argued below, however, that the attempt to draw a sharp conceptual distinction between anthropocentrism and ecocentrism is at best misguided, at worst, untenable. For now, it is sufficient to note that this simple twofold typology fails to capture the rich complexity and variation within environmental philosophy. Several commentators have found it helpful to distinguish an intermediate area of environmental concern located between the two poles of shallow (anthropocentric) and deep (ecocentric) environmental ethics (Vincent 1993; Sylvan and Bennett 1994). The three-fold typology outlined in Box 2.3 categorises the different approaches within environmental ethics.

### ▶ *A green theory of value?*

A major concern in environmental ethics has been to construct a green, or environmental, theory of value, based on a concern for the whole environment, not just individual parts of it. A 'theory of value', as Goodin (1992) puts it, is 'a theory of the Good . . . [which] should tell us both *what* is to be valued and *why*' (p. 19). It should provide a set of principles, or a code of conduct, to guide the way we behave towards the environment. However, this ethical enterprise draws on a range of concepts from moral philosophy, which raise various issues that should be flagged up here, as they will keep surfacing in the subsequent discussion.

First, what are the implications of showing that nature, or parts of nature (e.g. animals or plants), possesses intrinsic or inherent value? Greens hope it will encourage us to change our behaviour towards nature, but others might say that it means nothing: just because nature has value does not imply that someone has a moral duty to behave towards it in certain ways. These different interpretations point to two distinct questions which are often run together in the literature: one is a philosophical question about the kind of value that inheres in nature; the other is a more political question about how to motivate people to act on the recognition of that value. It is often difficult to maintain the distinction between the two questions, but this chapter focuses on the former, although the latter issue will also be discussed, especially in the conclusion.

Secondly, some writers argue that if, say, animals do have intrinsic or inherent value, then they also have *interests* (perhaps in living a full life?) or, stronger still, that they possess certain *rights* (a right to life?). They then try to show that the possession of interests or rights creates obligations or *duties* concerning the way we should behave towards animals. However, there is a tendency to make some big jumps here. Consequently, in assessing such claims, it is important to distinguish between the possession of interests or rights and the existence of duties. Just because a chimpanzee might have an interest in living a full life does not necessarily mean that I have a duty to ensure that it can flourish. Similarly, I might concede that a chimpanzee has a right to life but deny that this right gives me an obligation to do all in my power to protect it. Conversely, I might deny that the chimpanzee has a right to life yet still acknowledge that I have duties to it (not to treat it cruelly?). In short, there is no necessary symmetry between rights and duties.

More broadly, without assessing the validity of claims about the interests or rights of animals, it is important to be aware that terms such as interests, rights and duties carry considerable conceptual baggage from moral philosophy. For example, one common approach in political philosophy would argue that only those creatures which are capable of making a contract can be moral agents with corresponding rights and duties. As animals clearly cannot carry out responsibilities or duties, according to this contractarian view, they cannot have rights (Rawls 1973). Of course, there are objections to this interpretation: for example, on what grounds do we ascribe rights to babies or the senile who cannot carry out such duties or responsibilities? The simple point being made here is that debates about the appropriateness and accuracy of applying this kind of human moral discourse to the non-human world lie at the heart of environmental ethics.

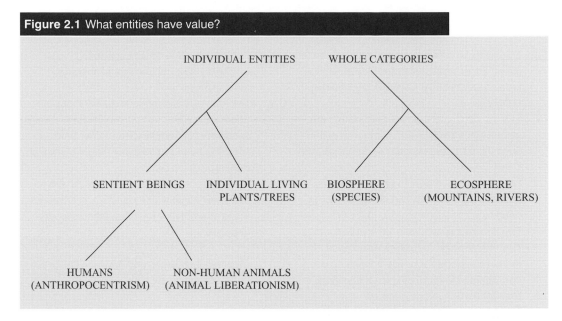

**Figure 2.1** What entities have value?

INDIVIDUAL ENTITIES          WHOLE CATEGORIES

SENTIENT BEINGS    INDIVIDUAL LIVING    BIOSPHERE          ECOSPHERE
                   PLANTS/TREES         (SPECIES)          (MOUNTAINS, RIVERS)

HUMANS              NON-HUMAN ANIMALS
(ANTHROPOCENTRISM)  (ANIMAL LIBERATIONISM)

To summarise, this section has shown that greens object to the anthropocentric basis of most traditional ethical and political theory. They argue
that value should be accorded not simply to humans but also to nature. We
now need to know what *kind* of value (instrumental, inherent or intrinsic)
can be ascribed to nature, what *parts* of nature have value and on *what
grounds* that value is accorded (see Figure 2.1). There are two dominant
ways of approaching these questions in environmental ethics – 'holism'
and 'moral extensionism' – which are critically analysed in the following
sections.

---

### Critical question 1
Is it important to show that nature has value independent of human needs?

---

## ▶ Holistic perspectives

The most radical approaches adopt a holistic analysis of the human–nature
relationship: they include all ecocentric perspectives, notably deep ecology,
and the group of intermediate approaches known as 'ethical holism' (see
Box 2.3). Holism is concerned with the way the different parts of nature
interact with each other in ecosystems and the biosphere – the interdependence and reciprocity that make up the 'whole' – rather than atomistic accounts of nature that focus on individual parts in isolation. A holistic
view of nature holds that everything is connected to everything else, that
the whole is greater than the sum of the parts, that process takes primacy
over the parts and that there is unity of humans and non-human nature

## 2.4 The eight-point platform of deep ecology

1. The flourishing of human and non-human life on Earth has value in itself. This value is independent of their usefulness for human purposes.
2. The richness and diversity of life forms are values in themselves and contribute to the flourishing of human and non-human life on Earth.
3. Humans have no right to reduce this richness and diversity except to satisfy vital needs.
4. The flourishing of human life and cultures is compatible with a substantial decrease in the human population. The flourishing of non-human life requires such a decrease.
5. Present human interference with the non-human world is excessive, and the situation is rapidly worsening.

6. Policies affecting basic economic, technological and ideological structures must change.
7. The ideological change is mainly that of appreciating life quality (dwelling in situations of inherent value) rather than adhering to an increasingly higher standard of living.
8. Those who subscribe to the above have an obligation directly or indirectly to participate in the attempt to implement the necessary changes.

Adapted from Devall and Sessions (1985: 70); Naess (1989: 29); Devall (1990: 14–15).

(Merchant 2005: 77–8). Broadly speaking, holistic theories are prepared to extend the boundaries of moral consideration well beyond individual humans by according intrinsic value to a range of non-human entities (to include animals, plants and even rocks) and to 'whole' categories, such as species and ecosystems. Holists are engaged in two kinds of exercise: a quest for an ethical code of conduct based on the existence of intrinsic value in nature and the development of an ethics based on a changed ecological consciousness or 'state of being' (Dobson 2000: ch. 2). Both approaches can be found in the work of Arne Naess, one of the founders of deep ecology, whose ideas have shaped the development of ecocentrism.

The claim that nature possesses intrinsic value is clearly stated in the eight-point platform for deep ecology drawn up by Naess and Sessions (see Box 2.4): 'The flourishing of human and non-human life on Earth has intrinsic value. The value of non-human life forms is independent of the usefulness these may have for narrow human purposes' (Naess 1989: 29). Naess is informed by the idea of symbiosis: that every entity has value because it is needed by at least one other entity. Nothing and no one is entirely independent, so everything has value. He also extracts a principle of equality from the holistic thesis that everything is interdependent. This principle – Naess calls it 'biocentric egalitarianism' – states that all forms of life have 'the equal right to live and blossom'.[3] Naess does not attempt to produce a scientific case for intrinsic value; instead, biocentric egalitarianism is justified as simply an 'intuitively clear and obvious value axiom'. Thus, with this first theme, Naess seems to be offering the basis for a green theory of value.

The second theme in Naess's work, underpinning the first claim that nature has intrinsic value, is a metaphysical argument about how the closer identification of the human self with nature could provide a rationale for nurturing a higher ecological consciousness. Naess rejects the Enlightenment view that humans are separate from nature and that Man is controller of nature; instead, he adopts a position that is rather similar to the ancient Greek view of Man as part of nature (Nussbaum 1986). Naess favours '*the relational, total-field image*' (1989: 28), which regards the 'relational self' as having a wider understanding of identity based on the perceived continuity between self and nature. He argues that by seeing ourselves as part of nature and by identifying more closely with it, to the extent that the other (nature) becomes part of our self, a self-realisation emerges upon which we can develop obligations to non-human nature. Thus the second theme emphasises the importance of developing an 'ecological consciousness'; by changing the way we perceive and think about nature we can overcome the ecological crisis.

Although both themes were of central importance in early ecocentric writing in the 1970s and 1980s, subsequently the focus has shifted from the quest for an ethical code of conduct towards the second, 'state of being' approach. This shift represents an implicit acknowledgement that the pursuit of intrinsic value theory may be misplaced (Dobson 2000: 46).

Efforts to construct a holistic theory of value have encountered three notable obstacles. First, many writers express their unease about the explicitly intuitive basis upon which Naess accords intrinsic value right across the ecosphere, to include mountains, rivers and cultures. Other holistic theorists have sought to construct a more robust case based on scientific arguments (Callicott 1986; Rolston 1991).[4] Callicott, for example, draws on Hume and Darwin to elaborate a 'bio-empathetic' theory based on the claim that moral sentiments are a product of the evolutionary process. A holistic interpretation of sociobiology and quantum physics holds that there is no significant distinction between the individual self and the environment. If humans could identify more closely with other organisms in the biosphere, they would recognise that they have common interests with non-humans and might then develop moral sentiments towards them. The continuity of self and nature means that, if the individual self is intrinsically valuable, then nature must also be intrinsically valuable.

However, these less intuitive holistic arguments tend to draw rather selective – and contestable – lessons from modern scientific discoveries. For example, contrary to the claims of the holists, the science of ecology does not deny the existence of differences between the self and nature. Its study of individual organisms 'entails no radically holistic ontology' in which 'I and nature are one' (O'Neill 1993: 150). Brennan (1988) offers the more fundamental objection that ecosystems do not operate according to the principles of holism and interdependence.

Yet the idea that someone might have reason to act because they are part of a wider entity, which can itself flourish or perish, is not so strange. Many people think that their well-being may depend partly upon the success of a group to which they belong, such as their nation, local community or fellow workers. The crucial *political* question is membership. Even if holistic arguments are admissible in principle, they will not serve green purposes unless their proponents can show clearly that someone's interests are related to a wide array of living entities.

Secondly, a key feature of holism is that moral consideration is given to whole categories (species, ecosystems) or ecological concepts (diversity, complexity), rather than (or in addition to) individual entities, such as a human being. Holistic accounts perceive the whole to be greater than the sum of its parts: 'Intrinsic value is a part in a whole and is not to be fragmented by valuing it in isolation' (Rolston 1991: 95). Here, Naess and the ethical holists draw on Aldo Leopold's (1949) 'land ethic' thesis which holds that 'a thing is right when it tends to preserve the integrity, stability and beauty of the biotic community' (pp. 224–5).[5] Large 'wholes', such as the biotic community or ecosphere, are sufficiently organised and integrated to have a good of their own and to possess intrinsic value. Thus, in holistic accounts, intrinsic value resides in the general process, rather than the individual expressions, of life (Taylor 1992: 114).

One objection to these arguments holds that a collective entity, such as a species, cannot have intrinsic value because it does not have interests, at least none over and above the sum of those of its individual members (Attfield 1983: 150). Brennan (1986) argues that these wholes are not even wholes in their own right but mere aggregations of individuals. However, even if we accept that a species cannot have interests, the view that the possession of interests is not necessarily a condition for the possession of intrinsic value – even if it is necessary for the attribution of rights – is quite respectable in mainstream moral philosophy (Dworkin 1993).

Perhaps a more powerful criticism is Regan's (1983: 361–2) charge that the holistic focus on the whole species or biosphere is essentially 'environmental fascism' because it ignores or suppresses the rights of individual entities. Eckersley (1992: 60–1) suggests that this problem can be overcome through the concept of 'autopoiesis', or self-renewal – the idea that all entities continuously strive to reproduce their own organisational activity and structure – which attributes value both to the collective whole (species, ecosystem) and to the individual organisms that make it up. Yet the task of producing an ethical code of conduct based on autopoiesis would hardly be straightforward, not least because the idea that 'wholes' have value would have serious implications in any conflict between the interests of the ecosystem and individuals within it. Suppose, for example, it was generally agreed that the good of the biotic community (which would include humanity as a whole) required an immediate reduction in human population to lessen pressure on scarce resources. Would infanticide therefore be justified, or would the rights of individual babies be upheld against the good of the larger biotic community? Some system for reconciling the competing claims of wholes and individual parts would be essential. The absence of any satisfactory method for resolving these trade-offs is a major obstacle to the development of any code of conduct based on holistic assumptions.

Thirdly, perhaps the most controversial feature of all these ethical claims concerns the distribution of value among morally considerable entities. In short, do holders of intrinsic value possess equal amounts of it? Naess's radical concept of 'biospherical egalitarianism – in principle' rejects the 'differential imperative' (Rodman 1980), whereby human attributes are valued as higher than, rather than simply different from, those of other species. The inference is that humans possess no greater moral significance than koalas, rats or mosquitoes. To avoid one obvious objection, Naess (1989) appended the clause 'in principle' because 'any realistic praxis necessitates some killing, exploitation and suppression' (p. 28). Nevertheless, the doctrine has still, not surprisingly, provoked enormous controversy. How much killing, exploitation and suppression is acceptable? Of whom? By whom? On what grounds?[6] In response to an array of withering attacks on the unworkability of the principle, Naess tried to clarify his position:

> The principle of biospherical egalitarianism defined in terms of equal right, has sometimes been misunderstood as meaning that human needs should never have priority over non-human needs. But this is never intended. In practice, we have for instance greater obligation to that which is nearer to us. This implies duties which sometimes involve killing or injuring non-humans.
> (Naess 1989: 170)

However, this qualification denudes the principle of its radicalism; it now merely provides a guideline to help adjudicate when the needs of different species conflict. For example, 'You shall not inflict unnecessary suffering upon other living beings' (ibid.: 171); but what is unnecessary? In his defence, Fox (1990: 223–4) makes clear that Naess is not in the business of producing moral 'oughts'; rather, he is simply making 'a statement of non-anthropocentrism'. Yet there are further problems with Naess's reformulation.

It seems that Naess believes we owe a greater duty to those closest to us (family? friends? pets?) than to someone (a starving Ethiopian?) or something (a Brazilian rainforest?) far away. If so, it seems rather strange that a holistic thinker should focus on one 'local' ecosphere, as opposed to the entire planet. There is also a broader issue here concerning the way that the 'community' is privileged by those holistic theories influenced by the 'land ethic'. The claim seems to be that the community possesses intrinsic value because we are all parts of the same 'whole' (the biosphere or ecosphere). It was argued above that, even if we recognise our interdependence with the natural world, it does not also imply acceptance of a moral relationship. Conversely, we often recognise obligations to those with whom we share no sense of interdependence or community, such as Sudanese famine victims. In this sense, the community argument may erect barriers that prevent us from fulfilling obligations to the needy in poorer countries because of the primary obligations we might owe to those in our own community. Consequently, community may be both too exclusive (of those suffering elsewhere) and too inclusive (of those in the community with a lesser claim on grounds of need or well-being) to provide the basis of an ethical code.

Another implication of the reformulated principle is that Naess clearly regards humans as having priority over non-humans, which seems to place him in the anthropocentric camp. Most other holists adopt a similar position.[7] Typically, they construct hierarchies of value-holders – humans, higher mammals, animals, plants and so on – in which humans always seem to come out on top. Mathews (1991), for example, defines 'the degree of power of self-maintenance' (i.e. complexity) as the criterion for determining priority in conflicting moral claims, a characteristic that (coincidentally?) humans possess in abundance. Put differently, in adjudicating conflicts between values, it seems that ecocentric writers ultimately fall back on arguments that privilege humans. Alternatively, they avoid the challenge of providing moral codes of conduct altogether.

Thus, to summarise, Naess does little more than stipulate that nature possesses intrinsic value; many writers would simply deny this claim. The 'scientific' grounds on which nature is accorded intrinsic value are also strongly contested. Even if we accept that nature does have intrinsic value, it is not clear what that implies. Holistic arguments provide little guidance on how to resolve dilemmas when different parts of nature conflict with one another. So, in practice, the claim that nature has intrinsic value simply sits there; it does not tell us how we should behave towards nature.

Consequently, it is not surprising that deep ecologists have focused increasingly on developing the second key theme in Naess's work – the concept of the 'relational self'. Warwick Fox (1990), with his concept of 'transpersonal ecology', is one of the more sophisticated exponents of this approach,[8] which explicitly rejects intrinsic value theory. Fox, whose work bears the imprint of psychology (notably Maslow 1954), argues that the 'self' should be extended beyond the egoistic, biographical or personal sense of self to produce 'as expansive a sense of self as possible' (Fox 1990: 224). Instead of regarding ourselves atomistically – as separate and isolated from everyone and everything else – we should seek to empathise with others, particularly with animals, plants and wider nature. Humans should try to experience a lived sense of identification with other beings; for if someone's sense of self can embrace other beings, then there is little need for moral exhortation to behave in a caring way towards those beings (Eckersley 1992: 62). This 'state of being' approach therefore focuses on the normative question of how people might be motivated to develop a higher ecological consciousness.

Rather than issue moral injunctions, Fox prefers an 'experiential invitation' to individuals to experience our oneness with the world, to engage in wider identification and move towards a more expansive sense of self (pp. 244–5).[9] He believes that the exercise of providing moral 'oughts' simply reinforces the traditional idea of an atomistic volitional self (and reinforces the belief that 'man' is the controller of nature, rather than a part of it). Yet this dismissal of ethical codes may be a little disingenuous; in reality, as Fox concedes, it partly reflects the failure of deep ecologists to make a robust case for intrinsic value, without which moral injunctions may lack normative force. Consequently, Fox (and other exponents of the 'state of being' school) choose to avoid the issue: 'Rather than convince us through logic and morals, they try to convert us through their example and experience' (Lucardie 1993: 31). In practice, humans may need a code of conduct to help them make choices between different courses of action. Human actions unavoidably involve intervention in the natural world, but a greater capacity to identify with that world will not itself resolve tricky conflicts of interest. On the contrary, a higher ecological consciousness would be more likely to sharpen and intensify the range and complexity of conflicts, which would increase the need for some form of ethical code of conduct.

There may also be a paradox at the heart of transpersonal ecology because it allocates a central role to the 'individual', who can only reach complete self-fulfilment by choosing to live a life at one with nature; yet the essence of holism is the importance of whole systems and species, which surely implies a downgrading, or even a denial, of the autonomous individual. There seems to be a strong anthropocentric flavour to this quest for 'self-realisation'. Although Fox is genuinely searching for a different ecological conception of the self – a means of raising ecological consciousness – the psychological language and the emphasis on the experiential convey the impression that personal (human) transformation is the ultimate goal (Taylor 1991; Sylvan and Bennett 1994: 110). Put differently, transpersonal ecology looks more like a form of enlightened self-interest – a criticism Fox himself directs at the ethical holists – driven by the belief that individuals have an interest in and a duty to protect nature because they are at one with it.

A sympathetic interpretation of the two themes running through holistic approaches, although perhaps not one that Fox would accept, is that they separate justificatory questions about why it is right to do something from motivational questions about how to persuade people to do what is right. Thus it might be argued that holists are claiming that: (1) it is right to respect nature because it has intrinsic value; and (2) what will motivate us to respect nature is a recognition of our own relational status, or interdependence, with nature. So the appeal to self-interest comes in only at the level of motivation, not at the level of justification.

Although this approach might be philosophically legitimate, it still encounters some of the difficulties outlined above. For example, this synthesis still has to convince us of the intuitive stipulation that nature has intrinsic value. In practical terms, it is questionable whether the individualistic focus on the self can provide a basis for the broader political transformation of society that greens seek. If the aim is to reach out to a wider human audience – to educate and persuade people of the need to raise their ecological consciousness – then holistic perspectives need to do a better job. One characteristic of deep ecology writing is that it is often couched in mystical or spiritual language. Indeed, Devall (1990) explicitly describes the experiential approach as evocative of what he admits is 'primarily a spiritual-religious movement' (p. 160); we are encouraged 'to think like mountains'. This mysticism may appeal to some people, but many will find it alienating.

Overall, holistic arguments have potentially far-reaching implications: removing narrow human interests from centre-stage, attributing value to non-human entities and nurturing a new ecological consciousness. They represent a radical enterprise that seeks to push back the boundaries of conventional political philosophy by replacing anthropocentric moral reasoning with an ecocentric moral sensibility. Whether or not we judge them successful in this task, they draw our attention to the importance of developing an ecological consciousness that will encourage us to alter our relationship with nature. Holism also shows that concepts developed in traditional liberal moral philosophy do not always serve us well when we are considering non-human nature. Each attempt to develop an ethical code of conduct has foundered badly. Yet green political theory might benefit from identifying a clear set of ethical principles to provide a framework for laws and policies which, in turn, could act as a powerful legitimating force to change attitudes and behaviour towards nature. 'Moral extensionism' is a different approach to producing such a code.

### Critical question 2

Is the quest for an ethical code of conduct based on the interdependence of nature doomed?

## ▶ Moral extensionism

'Moral extensionism' broadens the 'moral community' to include non-human entities, notably animals, based on the possession of some critical property such as sentience or the capacity to reason. The 'expanding circle' of moral concern is usually justified on the grounds that the morally relevant property – sentience, consciousness, rationality – is a capacity that humans share with non-humans.[10]

### ▶ Animal liberationism

Animal liberationism is the best-known example of moral extensionism. It might appear surprising that the animal liberation literature is at the margins of green political thought.[11] After all, an advocate of animal rights

## 2.5 Conservationism and preservationism

Conservationism and preservationism were two early currents of environmental thinking that gave birth to the first wave of 'environmental' pressure groups in the nineteenth and early twentieth centuries.

'Resource conservationism' refers to the ideas of modern land management popularised by Gifford Pinchot early in the twentieth century. His doctrine of conservation abhorred the wasteful exploitation of nature. Pinchot commended the use of scientific management techniques in developing land for the wider benefit of society rather than for a privileged few.

'Preservationism' represents an attitude of reverence towards nature, especially for the wilderness of the USA and Australia. Its leading exponent was John Muir of the Sierra Club, whose writings had a greater emphasis on the interrelation of humanity and nature.

Both approaches were clearly anthropocentric, although in preservationism humans were not the sole source of value. Conservation involves managing a resource for later consumption whereas preservation will protect a resource from any interference. Or, as Eckersley (1992) puts it, 'whereas Pinchot was concerned to *conserve* nature *for* development, Muir's concern was to *preserve* nature *from* development' (p. 39).

See Eckersley (1992: ch. 2) and Oelschlaeger (1991).

explicitly traverses the anthropocentric–ecocentric divide by granting moral consideration to non-humans. Yet animal liberationists employ ethical arguments that have set them apart from ecocentric theory. In part this divergence can be explained by the origins of the animal rights movement. Whereas contemporary environmentalism is rooted in early conservationist and preservationist movements (see Box 2.5), animal liberationism emerged from the separate animal protection tradition. Animal liberationists have mobilised their arguments in support of vegetarianism, and in opposition to hunting, the fur trade, modern farming practices and vivisection. The animal liberation literature has focused on protecting individual creatures (rather than whole species) by employing prevailing moral discourses to argue that the moral consideration shown to humans should be extended to a range of non-human creatures. The two main approaches within animal liberationism – utilitarianism and animal rights – are represented by the leading theorists, Peter Singer and Tom Regan.

Singer (1976, 1979) proposes a utilitarian argument in which actions should be judged by their consequences, i.e. the pleasure or pain, happiness or well-being they produce. He develops Jeremy Bentham's observation that to determine which creatures should receive moral consideration, the question we should ask is 'not, Can they *reason*? nor Can they *talk* but, *Can they suffer*?' (Singer 1979: 50). Singer argues that *sentience* – 'the capacity to suffer or experience enjoyment or happiness' (ibid.: 50) – is 'a prerequisite for having interests at all'. What he broadly means by 'interests' here is the opportunity for creatures to live their lives to the full. Without sentience, Singer argues, we can have no interests. A stone has no feelings and cannot suffer, so a boy kicking it along the street is not harming its interests.

Conversely, a mouse does have an interest in not being treated in this way because it will suffer. Singer argues that the principle of equal consideration of interests should consequently be applied to all creatures that can suffer: sentience 'is the only defensible boundary of concern for the interests of others' (ibid.: 50). Singer's definition of sentience includes a range of life-forms such as birds, reptiles, fish and some crustaceans, drawing the line 'somewhere between a shrimp and an oyster' (Singer 1976: 188).

Regan (1983) develops a rights-based approach to animal protection. All 'subjects-of-a-life' – individuals who have beliefs, desires, perception, memory and a sense of the future, an emotional life and a psychophysical identity over time (p. 243) – are either 'moral agents' or 'moral patients' possessing equal intrinsic value.[12] Thus he extends the moral community from humans to include many animals. Everyone within that moral community is entitled to respectful treatment. Just as human moral agents should respect the rights of, and have a prima-facie duty not to harm, individual human moral patients (the handicapped, senile and infants), so individual non-human moral patients (mentally normal mammals over the age of one year) have an inviolable right to be treated with respect and allowed to 'live well'.

Thus animal liberationists differ from holists in two important respects. First, they extend the moral community to include a range of sentient creatures, but they do not venture as far into nature as the holists. Secondly, both Singer and Regan focus on the intrinsic value that resides in the capacities and interests of *individual* creatures rather than in wholes (ecosystems, species). The key difference between the two writers is that Singer employs utilitarianism whereas Regan uses a rights-based argument. The work of both writers has been subjected to extensive review and, for reasons of space, the following critical discussion focuses on the writings of Singer as probably the best-known exponent of animal liberationism.[13]

Singer's argument is vulnerable to some of the familiar criticisms of utilitarianism. Although animal liberation is concerned with the welfare of individual animals, ironically one weakness of utilitarianism is that it is not always very good at defending the individual (Williams 1973). A consequentialist argument such as utilitarianism places intrinsic value only in 'states of affairs' – suffering or enjoyment – rather than in the individuals who are experiencing that suffering or enjoyment. So the principle of maximising aggregate pleasures over pains in a given population of individuals might result in significant harm being inflicted on one or two individuals in order to improve the net welfare of a larger group of individuals. Hence utilitarian calculations may provide the individual creature with only a limited, rather than an absolute, obligation that its interests be respected by humans.

A different response is to reject sentience as a sufficient criterion to be a rights-holder, or to receive equal consideration, and instead to argue that other attributes, notably the ability to reason or to talk, set humans apart from other species. Many political philosophers argue that the inability to reason means that animals cannot enter into reciprocal agreements or discharge moral obligations, so they cannot be the subject of moral rights or obligations. Singer acknowledges that animals are unable to comprehend the requirements of acting as moral agents, but points out that the same is true of various groups of human moral patients, such as those with learning difficulties, the senile or infants, who can neither reason nor talk – yet their interests are still protected. Singer argues that the implicit grounds on which such moral patients receive moral consideration is due to their capacity to suffer (i.e. sentience). Logically we should therefore extend equal consideration to the suffering of other sentient creatures, such as factory-farmed livestock. Indeed, Singer (1979: ch. 3) condemns as 'speciesists' those who would treat the suffering of humans as more important than the suffering of other species.

Other criticisms focus on the internal consistency of the arguments. In particular, should all sentient creatures receive *equal treatment*? Equality across species might suggest that rats, cats and humans should all be accorded equal treatment, but few humans would be happy with the idea that a drowning cat, let alone a rat, might be pulled from a pond before a human. In practice, Singer says that all sentient creatures should receive equal consideration, but that does not imply that they should receive equal treatment. As a utilitarian, Singer is concerned with the total or aggregate consequences in each particular situation. He argues, perhaps a little conveniently, that the capacity for human suffering is generally of a higher order than for other creatures (Singer 1979: 52–3). For example, the human capacity to anticipate oncoming death, perhaps through a terminal illness, often makes our suffering much greater. In particular, human capacities such as self-awareness, intelligence and planning for the future make human life more valuable than that of creatures not possessing those capacities.[14] Singer anticipates that human suffering will therefore receive greater weight in the utilitarian calculus. On a straight choice, a human life will, almost always, outweigh that of an animal. Indeed, it may be legitimate to use mice in medical experiments if the outcome is to relieve suffering for even a small group of humans.

This line of argument suggests a weakness in Singer's claim that all sentient creatures have an interest. By attributing greater weight to capacities such as self-awareness and planning, one inference is that Singer shows that humans have interests whilst other sentient creatures simply feel pain. It suggests that a stronger definition, by which 'having an interest' involves plans, projects and purposes, is more valid. Creatures lacking those capacities are, arguably, creatures without interests. Applying this definition would rein back attempts to extend value to a wide range of species, but it would not necessarily confine it solely to humans. Certainly apes have some of these superior capacities,[15] whilst other sentient creatures, such as mice, may not possess such capacities – and therefore do not have interests (see Box 2.6). Of course, it does not necessarily follow that humans can treat

Based on a book by Cavalieri and Singer (1993), the Great Ape Project seeks: 'the extension of the community of equals to include all great apes: human beings, chimpanzees, bonobos, gorillas and orang-utans. The community of equals is the moral community within which we accept certain basic moral principles or rights as governing our relations with each other and enforceable in law'. Its key principles are:

*The Right to Life*. Killing is justified only in very strictly defined circumstances, e.g. self-defence.

*The Protection of Individual Liberty*. No one must be imprisoned without due legal process. Unless a crime has been committed, a creature is entitled to immediate release.
*The Prohibition of Torture*. No deliberate pain may be inflicted on anyone.

In June 2006 the Spanish Parliament considered a proposal to give legal rights to non-human great apes.

See http://www.greatapeproject.org.

mice however they please. Whilst mice might not have interests or rights, humans might still have a duty to treat them in certain ways.

Putting aside the above objection, if human suffering or well-being is always given more weight, what practical benefits for animals flow from the sentience thesis? According to Singer, quite a lot, as the requirement to stop inflicting 'unnecessary' suffering on animals would result in radical changes to human diets, farming methods, scientific experimental procedures, hunting, trapping and wearing of furs, and areas of entertainment like circuses, rodeos and zoos (Singer 1979: 53). The outcome of this dramatic change in attitudes and behaviour would be a massive reduction in the quantity of suffering.

Rights-based arguments have received particularly stern treatment from traditional ethical theorists, notably because they seek to ascribe a liberal principle, which was developed to fit uniquely human attributes, to animals. Nash (1989), for example, suggests that extending rights to animals is simply a logical progression of liberal ethical theory, which historically has gradually extended its reach to slaves, women, blacks and other excluded groups. Critics counter that this argument founders on a faulty analogy between humans and animals: to extend equal consideration to non-white humans on the grounds of their common humanity (i.e. denying the relevance of skin colour as an indicator of moral standing in society) is qualitatively different from arguments about our relationship with animals (Taylor 1992: 60–1). Indeed, it might be regarded as offensive to compare the struggle for animal rights with the women's emancipation, civil rights and anti-slavery movements. Clearly, an acceptance of Regan's argument depends on the persuasiveness of his 'subject-in-a-life' criterion as the basis for attributing intrinsic value to some animals.

From a holistic perspective, animal liberationism does not go nearly far enough and cannot alone provide the framework for a broad environmental, or ecological, ethic (not that it claims to do so). The focus on the individual creature ignores the holistic message that solutions to environmental problems should be sensitive to the interdependence of the natural world. Certainly, animal liberationism offers no prima-facie case for extending moral consideration beyond individual animals. Utilitarian and rights-based arguments attribute no moral standing to non-sentient entities such as insects, plants and rocks. By focusing on the well-being of individual creatures, animal liberationists deny that any value can reside in collectives, such as a species. Thus, the loss of the last two members of a species – perhaps the last two giant pandas – would be no more morally significant than the loss of two stray mongrel dogs. Ecocentrics also point out that animal liberationist arguments may encounter the 'problem of predation' – the logical, if absurd, argument that humans should intervene in the food chain to turn non-human carnivores, such as cats, into vegetarians, or at least to minimise the suffering of their prey (Eckersley 1992: 45).

It is certainly hard to see how either the sentience or the 'subject-in-a-life' argument could be used to justify the existence of *intrinsic* value in species or ecosystems, let alone the wider biotic community or ecosphere. Attfield argues that sentience is a sufficient but not a necessary condition for moral consideration. He claims that trees and plants also have a good of their own, defined as their flourishing, or capacity to flourish, which gives them moral standing (Attfield 1983: 154). Yet biological science suggests that a tree is incapable of having any experience. Moreover, Attfield tempers the potentially 'devastating' ethical implications of this view by pointing out that moral *standing* should not be confused with moral *significance*, as they involve quite separate judgements (Attfield 1983: 154). An organism may have intrinsic value (standing), but that value may be extremely low (significance). Thus Attfield constructs a hierarchy of supremacy based on attributes, such as sentience, consciousness and cognition, that privilege human interests over all others, with plants sitting at the bottom of the pile. In practice, like animal liberationism, this weak anthropocentric ethic might do little more than hasten the demise of factory farming and similar 'unnecessary' practices.

An *instrumental* case in support of environmental protection might be built on the argument that the interests of a sentient creature demand that its natural habitat – nesting sites, breeding grounds, food sources – should be protected (Eckersley 1992: 43–4). In a similar vein, Benton (1993) draws on both socialist and ecocentric theory to develop the rights-based approach. Although he retains an analytical focus on the individual as the bearer of rights, Benton rejects the disembodied, atomistic individual of liberal thought for a wider view of the individual in relationship with other persons (the socialist focus on the individual in society) and with ecological conditions (the ecocentric view). He argues that if priority is attributed to individual (human and non-human) autonomy, then the same moral priority must be given to the material conditions – notably protection of the environment – that enable that individual autonomy to be exercised (see Chapter 3).

However, at root, this argument appears to be qualitatively similar to other instrumental anthropocentric arguments that support environmental protection (see below, pp. 34–5).

Nevertheless, animal liberation arguments are often dismissed too easily by ecocentrics. Utilitarian and rights-based arguments for animal liberation have undoubtedly made an important contribution to environmental ethics. A major strength of both approaches is the way they build a case for animal protection by extending a familiar moral discourse beyond humans. The language and the form of argument employed in this liberal discourse are less likely to alienate the reader, although their radical conclusions might. Singer's claim that the moral community should be based on the capacity for sentience rather than the capacity to reason or talk is powerfully made and conforms with the intuitions of many people – especially the pet-owner or lover of wildlife (see Box 2.6). Regan's strategy of employing rights as a means of protecting and furthering the interests of animals also sits comfortably within the traditions of liberal thought. Both approaches have tapped the widespread contemporary unease about the treatment of animals, as in factory farming or vivisection, and the way it offends our 'humanitarian' sensibilities. They also suggest many practical policies – bans on hunting for sport, the regulation of factory farming, the abolition of veal crates – that have widespread appeal. Admittedly, these same strengths, couched as they are in a conventional anthropocentric individualist moral discourse, limit the potential of animal liberationism to underpin a broader environmental ethic. Nevertheless, one knock-on effect might be that once people accept that some animals are worthy of moral consideration, the more radical claim that further parts of the natural world also have value may become more acceptable.

---

### Critical question 3
Are animal liberationists environmentalists?

---

▶ *Moral extensionism as an environmental ethic*

The flourishing of environmental ethics in recent years has produced a wide range of moral extensionist theories (Brennan 1988; Norton 1991; Goodin 1992; Benton 1993; O'Neill 1993; Hayward 1995; Dobson 1998; Wissenburg 1998; Barry 1999a, *inter alia*). These are generally intermediate perspectives, which accept the Greater Value Assumption that humans are the only creatures able to value, but that humans are not the only bearers of value (see Box 2.3).

One interesting approach involves the use of intuitive arguments about 'naturalness' and the special significance of nature to humans, as grounds for ascribing inherent value to nature. Goodin (1992) outlines a green theory of value based on the idea of 'naturalness'. He argues that natural objects have value because they are the product of a natural process rather than an artificial, human process.[16] Naturalness has value because (1) humans want 'some sense and pattern to their lives'; (2) people want their own lives set in some larger context (to which they are connected); (3) it is the products of natural processes, untouched (or lightly touched) by human hands which provides that larger context (p. 37).[17] Similarly, Dworkin (1993) talks of the 'sacredness' of nature and the importance of respecting 'nature's investment' to support his claim that nature has intrinsic value. He argues that people wish animal species to be preserved because of 'respect for the way they came into being rather than for the animals considered independently of that history . . . we consider it wrong, a desecration of the inviolable, that a species that evolution did produce should perish through our acts' (ibid.: 78). Consequently, the extinction of a species is 'an intrinsically bad thing to do . . . a waste of nature's investment' (ibid.: 78).

There are weaknesses in this approach. Dworkin (1993) concedes that there is inconsistency in what we regard as sacred and inviolable. We might regard a rare species of exotic bird or the Siberian tiger as sacred, whilst not overly regretting the extinction of pit vipers or rats. Nor do we treat everything produced by nature as inviolable; we are prepared to mine coal or chop down trees to build a house. In short, this kind of intuitive argument is necessarily selective. Similarly, Goodin's (1992) theory of value rests heavily on the intuitive claim that humans have a psychological need for something larger than themselves; yet that intuition is open to dispute. Even if we have such a need, is 'nature' the only means of satisfying it? For many people religion provides this larger context. Others would say that phenomena which touch nature neither lightly nor lovingly – feats of technological wizardry such as huge skyscrapers in Los Angeles, or atomic bombs – may also inspire us to contemplate something larger than ourselves. What makes the village preferable to the city is not that it is in better balance with nature but that it required less human intervention in nature. Put differently, for Goodin, value resides not in protecting nature from harm for its own sake, but in humans deriving 'satisfaction from reflection upon its larger setting' (ibid.: 52). In this sense, it appears that nature has inherent value (see Box 2.1).

Another theme in several intermediate approaches involves drawing an important distinction between constitutive and instrumental value in a flourishing human life. O'Neill (1993) constructs an environmental ethic around Aristotle's idea of objective human good. The Aristotelian objective is the flourishing of human life. The constitutive parts of this 'good life' include a range of liberal values, notably autonomy, and a range of positive relationships with contemporaries, across generations and, crucially, with nature. The flourishing of non-human creatures, therefore, 'ought to be promoted because they are constitutive of our own flourishing' (ibid.: 24).

Despite the prima-facie anthropocentrism, O'Neill claims that this involves no reversion to narrow instrumentalism. Rather, just as Aristotle taught us to care for our friends for their own sake, and not for the benefits it may bring to us (such as self-satisfaction or anticipated reciprocity), so we should promote the flourishing of non-human living things as an end in itself. Thus, 'care for the natural world is constitutive of a flourishing human life' (ibid.: 24). Similarly, Raz (1986) offers the example of a close relationship between a man and a dog. The man's life is richer and better because of that relationship. So the dog has value not just because it causes feelings of security and comfort in the man (instrumental value) but because of the constitutive role it plays in enhancing the quality of his life (inherent value)[18] (see Box 2.1). Raz suggests that this kind of inherent value is insufficient to justify according rights to dogs, although it may still be sufficient to create duties to protect or promote their well-being (Raz 1986: 178).

The approaches above are just two examples from a range of moral extensionist frameworks. Neither is complete, but both have something interesting to offer. The existence of these intermediate theories of value suggests that the search for a single definitive value system to underpin an environmental ethic may be doomed. Instead, green political theorists might be better advised to accept familiar intuitive arguments, like Dworkin's, that a plurality of value theories exist and that there is no hierarchy among them. This notion of a plurality in value theories is not controversial in itself. However, while many writers argue that we need to determine which is the 'right' or 'best' theory, the suggestion here is that there may be some advantage in accepting an eclectic spread of theories.[19]

First, it allows for different considerations to apply in different cases. A single value theory may be good at dealing with one type of ethical problem but less helpful for another. An eclectic approach recognises the virtue of drawing on a range of value theories – utilitarian, rights-based, ecocentric and so on – to help deal with different types of problem. Thus Brennan (1992: 28) argues that the value systems we use to justify (1) killing a badly injured animal to put it out of its suffering; (2) preserving the life of a human in severe pain; (3) protecting a (non-sentient) tree by forcibly restraining a vandal from damaging it, might involve different moral considerations. Secondly, the sheer complexity of many environmental issues suggests that there may be more than one way of viewing the same problem, as is often the case in public policy. Perhaps no single value system provides an exhaustive framework for dealing with a problem. Indeed, an environmental ethic might also draw on a range of *anthropocentric* arguments about how humans should treat other humans, such as the need for intragenerational justice and the obligations we owe to future generations (see Chapter 3). Such explicitly anthropocentric debates are often excluded from green political theory, but with the increasing dominance of the sustainable development discourse in public policy they have gained in significance (Dobson 1998).

This observation resonates with the 'convergence thesis' outlined by Norton (1991).[20] He argues that the differences between opposing wings of the environment movement are more apparent than real; in particular, although ecocentric and anthropocentric defences of the non-human world may come from different starting points and apply different value systems, they can end up producing more or less similar solutions. Norton emphasises the importance of anthropocentric arguments that act in the interests of future generations (see Box 3.4):

> introducing the idea that other species have intrinsic value, that humans should be 'fair' to all other species, provides no operationally recognizable constraints on human behaviour that are not already implicit in the generalized, cross-temporal obligations to protect a healthy, complex, and autonomously functioning system for the benefit of future generations of human beings. Deep ecologists, who cluster around the principle that nature has independent value, should therefore not differ from longsighted anthropocentrists in their policy goals for the protection of biological diversity.
>
> (Norton 1991: 226–7)

The policy convergence that Norton perceives between ecocentrics and future-generation anthropocentric perspectives provides a good illustration of value eclecticism in practice. From this perspective, rather than regarding ecocentrism as an attempt to replace conventional human-centred moral principles with a new framework that encompasses the natural world, it might be regarded as a new *supplementary* dimension that can contribute to a richer, more informed moral synthesis.

---

### Critical question 4

Is 'value eclecticism' a firm basis for a green political theory?

---

## ▶ Conclusion: Breaking down the anthropocentric–ecocentric divide

One of the distinguishing features of ecologism is the view that humans are not necessarily seated at the top of the ethical hierarchy. Holistic arguments that draw attention to the interdependence of ecosystems have forced political philosophers to reappraise the human–nature relationship and to think seriously about the duties we owe to the natural world.

Yet it has been argued here that all ecocentric accounts ultimately employ some form of anthropocentric argument – the idea that human needs and interests are of highest, and even exclusive, value and importance. Attempts to develop an ethical code of conduct based on the existence of intrinsic value in nature have struggled to apply traditional ethical concepts to unfamiliar entities and categories, such as species and ecospheres, and they have fallen back onto hierarchies of value which always concede priority to human interests in all critical inter-species conflicts.[21] Although 'state of being' ecocentrics have resisted the path of issuing ethical injunctions, the centrality in their work of the individual self also fails to avoid the trap of anthropocentrism, and they too concede priority to humans in conflicts of interest. Indeed, an ecocentric position that denied the existence of a clear and morally relevant dividing line between humankind and the rest of nature is, arguably, untenable. Certainly, any principle along the lines of biocentric egalitarianism would be impossible to implement. Taking it to the extreme, how could a human justify killing any animal or fish, or consuming a vegetable, bean or berry? All involve some restraint on another entity's capacity to live and to flourish. Humans must place themselves above other species and entities 'simply to live' (Luke 1988: 521). No ecocentric denies that humans have the right to live and to flourish, but to do so inevitably involves the denial of other entities that same right. If it is accepted that a pure non-anthropocentric position is impossible or, at least that every deep ecologist employs some form of anthropocentric argument, then it is a nonsense to talk about an ecocentric–anthropocentric dichotomy in such stark terms.

A more fruitful approach regards these philosophical debates as 'between relative positions concerning the moral weight we should give to the natural environment in relation to human interests' (Taylor 1991: 580). It is helpful also to distinguish between 'strong anthropocentrism', which retains the Sole Value Assumption, and 'weak anthropocentrism', which concedes that nature may have some non-instrumental value.[22] Thus weak anthropocentrism means that the human–nature relationship need not always be reduced to purely human interests (Barry 1999a). Rather than define different perspectives according to which side of the ecocentric/anthropocentric divide they lie, they can be located along a *continuum*, which moves from ecocentrism through various gradations of anthropocentrism to 'strong anthropocentrism'.

If the ecocentric/anthropocentric divide is redundant, where should the boundary of ecologism lie? Which perspectives fall within ecologism, and which fall outside? One obvious division would include within ecologism all weak anthropocentric or intermediate perspectives that reject the Sole Value Assumption. This delineation encompasses all those perspectives that make the qualitatively significant step of conceding some intrinsic or inherent value to the non-human world. Thus a crucial defining feature of ecologism might be that it includes all perspectives which concede *humans will always be the distributors of value, but they are not necessarily the only bearers of value.*

It is not always clear what practical implications might flow from the attribution of value to non-human entities. Do animals or (parts of) nature have interests and/or rights? If so, what does that mean in practical terms? What duties do we owe towards nature? This chapter has shown the difficulties encountered in trying to develop environmental codes of conduct. None is entirely convincing, but many have something interesting to offer. If any conclusion can be drawn from these debates, it is that perhaps too much emphasis has been placed on the need for a robust case for intrinsic value or for rights. There may be most mileage in those intermediate approaches that recognise the existence of inherent value in non-human forms – from which it can then be argued that, whilst non-human entities may not have rights, humans do have duties not to do certain things to them. Whatever position is adopted, the advantage of a broad definition of ecologism is that it includes a wide range of perspectives, all of which seek to generate a higher ecological consciousness that 'will turn the tables in favour of the environment, such that the onus of persuasion is on those who want to destroy, rather than those who want to preserve' (Dobson 2000: 59).

There are also *political* advantages in adopting this broad definition if it helps open up environmental philosophy to a wider audience. One inference frequently drawn from the conventional dichotomy is that ecocentrism represents the boundary of ecologism. Much ink has been spilt discussing this point, often in the form of a polarised debate about doctrinal purity – about being 'greener than thou' – reminiscent of the fratricidal conflicts associated with other 'isms' such as socialism and feminism. Ecocentrics tend to dismiss other positions for being insufficiently 'deep' and, in so doing, have claimed the moral high ground: 'After all, who would embrace a shallow view of any subject which one genuinely cares about, when a deeper view is available?' (Goodin 1992: 43). Such exclusive attitudes are harder to sustain if it is accepted that a pure ecocentric position is untenable and that a wider range of ideas can be incorporated within the ambit of ecologism. The inclusion of intermediate perspectives does not denude ecologism of its radicalism; rather, deep ecology would colonise the most extreme ecocentric wing of a broad church encompassing a wide range of philosophical and political positions. After all, the boundaries of all ideologies display a Plasticine-like quality, being both malleable and movable, as illustrated by the breadth of different positions within socialism (from Marxism to social democracy).

However, an ideology also needs a coherent political dimension. Ecocentrics are criticised for being more concerned with getting the philosophy right – by, for example, elevating the anthropocentric–ecocentric debate into a litmus test for greenness – rather than developing a practical political programme for change (Taylor 1991; Barry 1999a; Dobson 2000). In so far as ecocentrics do think 'politically', they emphasise the need to change individual consciousness, with a heightened awareness of our proper place in nature as the preferred path to ecological salvation (e.g. Devall 1990). This interest in personal transformation is reflected in an apparent lack of interest in wider issues of political change in society. The message seems to be: 'if you cannot change the world, change yourself' (Barry 1994: 390). The next chapter examines attempts to develop a broader political dimension to ecologism.

## ▶ *Further reading*

The collections edited by Gruen and Jamieson (1994), Elliot (1995), Botzler and Armstrong (1998), Smith (1999), O'Neill et al. (2001) and Light and Rolston (2003), and the accessible textbook by Des Jardins (2002), all provide good introductions to the sheer breadth and variety of environmental philosophical writing. The Sessions (1995) reader is a good introduction to deep ecology; see also Devall and Sessions (1985) and Naess (1989). Fox (1990) is, arguably, the most sophisticated ecocentric analysis. Eckersley (1992) offers the best sympathetic survey of ecocentric writing. Good discussions of environmental philosophy can be found in Hayward (1995), Barry (1999a), Dobson (2000) and Pratt et al. (2000). The journals *Environmental Ethics*, *Environmental Values* and *Environmental Politics* provide a good coverage of contemporary developments and debates.

NOTES

1 Some writers use 'extrinsic value' in preference to 'instrumental value'. Some use either 'inherent value' or 'intrinsic value', but not both; others distinguish 'inherent' and 'intrinsic' value, but with little consistency in meaning. Intrinsic value is a particularly tricky concept, with at least three different uses of the term (O'Neill 1993: 9).
2 Several typologies stake out a similar territory in environmental philosophy, notably the shallow/deep ecology cleavage formulated by Arne Naess (1973).
3 Naess (1989) later acknowledged that 'ecosphere' is a more accurate term than 'biosphere' to indicate that 'life' refers also 'to things biologists may classify as non-living: rivers, landscapes, cultures, ecosystems, "the living earth"' (p. 29).
4 A common criticism of holistic arguments is that they commit the 'naturalistic fallacy' of deriving an 'ought' from an 'is', i.e. they shift from a description of the way nature works (how it 'is') to a prescription for an ethical system (how we 'ought' to behave). Whilst a familiarity with scientific developments might inform a debate about ethics, it cannot in itself justify a philosophical or political theory: 'appealing to the authority of nature . . . is no substitute for ethical argument' (Eckersley 1992: 59). See Taylor (1992), Lucardie (1993) and Hayward (1995). For a defence from deep ecology, see Fox (1990: 188–93).
5 Barry (1999a: 124–5) points out that this sentence is usually taken out of context and that Leopold's land ethic does not support a deep ecology perspective based on the intrinsic value of nature.
6 The populist accusation that ecocentrics are misanthropic does them an injustice. Ecocentrics object to human chauvinism, not to humans; they want humans and human culture to blossom and flourish, alongside other species. Their emphasis on the welfare of the non-human world is an attempt to correct an imbalance in philosophical and social science theory (Eckersley 1992: 56–7).

7 Ethical holists, such as Rolston and Callicott, can be placed in the intermediate category (Box 2.3) anyway, because they explicitly or implicitly concede ultimate moral superiority to humans (Vincent 1993). The question here is whether 'ecocentrics' also fall back on anthropocentric arguments.

8 Other prominent deep ecologists include Drengson (1989), Mathews (1991) and McLaughlin (1993).

9 There is some slippage in Fox's use of the concepts of the 'self' and 'identification'. Plumwood (1993: 176) detects three 'shifting, and not always compatible' types of self – indistinguishability, expansion of self and transcendence of self – a lack of clarity that contributes to confusion.

10 The ethical holists are extensionists in so far as they seek to extend moral consideration based on intrinsic value, but their reliance on holistic arguments distinguishes them from the animal liberationist focus on individual living entities (Vincent 1993).

11 The term 'animal liberation' is preferred to 'animal rights' because the latter may be used in a narrow sense to refer to rights-based approaches (e.g. Regan), whilst the former also includes utilitarian perspectives (e.g. Singer).

12 Regan actually uses the term 'inherent value' where here 'intrinsic value' is preferred (see Box 2.1).

13 The discussion focuses on those issues with most relevance to the development of an environmental ethic. For a broader discussion of animal liberation issues, see Clark (1977), Benson (1978), Midgley (1983), Benton (1993), Gruen (1993) and Garner (2005).

14 Singer (1979: ch. 3) does distinguish between pain and death. Whilst 'pain is pain' and pain of similar intensity will be equally bad for all sentient creatures, the various 'superior' capacities for self-awareness and so on mean that the life of humans is more valuable than that of those creatures which do not possess those capacities.

15 Recent research, for example, has shown a chimpanzee picking up a stick *en route* to rooting out a termite nest, and an orangutan using a piece of cardboard to pick a lock on its cage (Goodall 1986). See also Benton (1993).

16 Goodin (1992) argues that only humans can impart value to nature, but the characteristics of nature that give value 'must necessarily be separate from and independent of humanity' (p. 45).

17 Goodin recognises the obvious conflict between the idea of humans being part of nature and the concept of naturalness. He argues that we cannot expect nature to be 'literally' untouched, rather it should be touched 'lightly' or 'lovingly' (Goodin 1992: 53). He illustrates this idea of the 'modesty of creation' by comparing a small English village with Los Angeles, where humanity has ridden roughshod over nature.

18 Raz talks of 'derivative' intrinsic value, which roughly corresponds to the definition of 'inherent value' used here and he uses 'ultimate value' where 'intrinsic value' is used here.

19 Here value eclecticism bears some similarity to Brennan's (1992) case for 'moral pluralism' – that we should 'think in terms of a plurality of values, and an associated plurality of principles' (p. 27) – and draws on some of his arguments.

20 Value eclecticism diverges from moral pluralism here because the latter assumes that there are many values and that they will not converge, so any choice between values will involve a loss of value. Put differently, an argument for convergence is an argument against pluralism.

21 See discussion of the 'Great Chain of Being' in Barry (1999b: 40–3).

22 Several writers make a similar distinction between weak/strong, soft/hard and human-centred/human-instrumental anthropocentrism (Luke 1988; Norton 1991; Barry 1999a; Dobson 2000).

# Green political thought

**3**

## Contents

## Key issues

▶ Is there a distinct and coherent green ideology?
▶ What would a 'green' society look like?
▶ What are the distinguishing principles of green political theory?
▶ How have traditional political doctrines responded to the green challenge?
▶ Where does green politics lie on the left–right spectrum?

Is ecologism a distinct and coherent ideology? Do the two core ideas underpinning the ecological imperative – the need to reassess human–nature relations (discussed in Chapter 2) and the existence of ecological limits to growth – supplemented by a set of principles drawn from other doctrines, justify talking about ecologism as an ideology in its own right? If so, can it accommodate the broad range of competing perspectives and discourses within contemporary green political thought?

This chapter has two parts. The first part examines the central themes of ecologism. It starts by assessing the significance of the 'limits to growth' thesis as a green principle. As all ideologies need a vision of the 'good society' different from our own, the next section outlines the main features that characterise the dominant model of a green sustainable society. The following sections assess whether the driving idea behind green politics – the ecological imperative that we need to save the planet – requires that a green polity be built on the core political principles that characterise most versions of a green society, namely grassroots democracy, **decentralisation**, social justice and non-violence. The second part of the chapter focuses on the way traditional political doctrines have responded to the environmental challenge. The concluding section draws these themes together by arguing that ecologism does represent a new and distinct ideological tradition that is broad enough to encompass several, often competing, green perspectives.

> **Decentralisation:** The expansion of local autonomy through the transfer of powers and responsibilities away from a national political and administrative body.

## ▶ The central ideas of ecologism

### ▶ *The limits to growth*

The publication of *The Limits to Growth* (Meadows et al. 1972) provoked a massive international debate about the existence of ecological limits to economic and population growth.[1] The authors used systems theory and computer modelling techniques (a new concept in the early 1970s) to analyse the complex interdependencies between five key variables: industrial output, resource depletion, pollution, food production and population growth. The computer simulations charted predicted outcomes up to 2100 if each variable continued growing at existing rates, and then for six permutations based on different assumptions about the growth of each variable. However, the interconnectedness of the variables meant that every attempt to address a single problem (e.g. resource depletion) simply pushed problems elsewhere (technical developments that double resource availability increase output, resulting in higher pollution). The authors concluded that if existing growth trends in each variable continued, 'the limits to growth on this planet will be reached sometime within the next one hundred years' (Meadows et al. 1972: 23).

## 3.1 Survivalism: leviathan or oblivion?

Many environmental theorists in the early 1970s had an overriding preoccupation with human survival. The leading environmental 'doom-sayers' were driven by a sense of urgency about the impending ecological crisis, which prompted them to recommend drastic – often authoritarian – solutions.

Garrett Hardin's (1968) famous essay on the 'Tragedy of the Commons' (see Box 7.1) warned that, in a world of finite resources, freedom in the unregulated commons brings ruin to all. He proposed the illiberal solution of 'mutual coercion, mutually agreed upon by the majority of people affected'. His 'lifeboat ethic' (Hardin 1977) callously recommended that 'developed' countries should abandon 'less developed' countries if their governments refused to control population growth and prevent ecological destruction. Thus rich countries in the North would be the 'lifeboats' loaded with survivors, cutting off aid to the poor nations of the South, who would 'drown' (even though the North consumes most resources and places most pressure on fragile ecosystems).

Robert Heilbroner (1974) and William Ophuls (1977) concluded reluctantly that the management of the commons required a strong central authority to persuade self-interested people to change their ways. For Heilbroner, only a centrally planned, authoritarian state – ruled by a monastic government that combined religious orientation and military discipline – could force the required sacrifices and restructure the economy along ecologically sustainable lines. Ophuls envisaged a strong central authority dominated by 'ecological mandarins' who would govern by the application of ecological principles. If self-restraint was not forthcoming, then mildly coercive methods were needed in the short term to avoid resorting to more draconian methods in the longer term.

The illiberal recommendations of survivalism have been attacked from all sides: by capitalists and socialists, the Catholic church and ecofeminists. Despite the emphasis on practical solutions, the draconian prescriptions of survivalism seem impractical in a modern world dominated economically by global capitalism and politically by liberal democracy.

See Eckersley (1992) and Dryzek (2005: ch.2) for a wider discussion of survivalism.

---

The *Limits to Growth* report was enormously significant in the development of environmental thought.[2] The immediate impact of its apocalyptic message was to catapult environmental issues into the public eye and onto the political agenda. Its pessimism also resonated with the contemporary '**survivalist**' concern (see Box 3.1) about population growth (see Box 3.2).

> **Survivalism:** Approaches characterised by an overriding preoccupation with human survival, a sense of urgency about an impending ecological crisis and drastic, often authoritarian, solutions.

In the longer term, 'the belief that our *finite* Earth places limits on industrial growth' has become a 'foundation-stone of radical green politics' (Dobson 2000: 62; emphasis added). Specifically, greens draw several lessons from the 'limits to growth' thesis (Martell 1994: 27–33; Dobson 2000: 63). First, the concept of finitude underpinning the 'limits to growth' thesis is unique to ecologism; it implies that any future sustainable world will be characterised by material scarcity rather than abundance. Secondly, by plotting the combined impact of the five variables, the report underlined the *interdependent*

## 3.2 Population growth

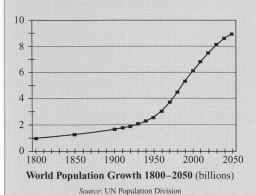

**World Population Growth 1800–2050** (billions)

*Source*: UN Population Division

Paul Ehrlich's best-seller *The Population Bomb* in 1968 with its neo-Malthusian thesis that population growth was exponential. Many greens believe that only by reducing the world's population can global consumption be cut to sustainable levels. Population control is controversial because many suggested solutions are authoritarian and/or discriminate against poorer countries, as illustrated by Hardin's 'lifeboat ethic' (see Box 3.1), and by proposals to cut off food aid to poor countries unless their governments introduce compulsory sterilisation programmes or to impose stronger immigration controls to protect rich countries from refugees from the South. Some environmentalists are also enthusiastic about the Chinese 'one child per family' policy.

The flourishing of human life and cultures is compatible with a substantial decrease of the human population. The flourishing of non-human life requires such a decrease.

(Fourth principle of the deep ecology platform)

World population grew dramatically during the twentieth century, reaching 6 billion in October 1999. The rate of growth has, however, slowed and global population is expected to peak at 9 to 10 billion around 2060, with most growth in less developed countries.

Population control has been a key issue in environmental writing since the publication of

Green parties today, well aware of the sensitivities surrounding population issues, tend to downplay it and pointedly reject coercive methods. Indeed, most evidence suggests that economic and social develop-ment, by reducing poverty, providing for basic needs and improving female literacy and entry to the workforce, is the most effective means of slowing population growth (Harrison 1993; Sen 1994).

relationship between humans and nature, which teaches us that problems cannot be separated and treated in isolation (see Chapter 7). Thirdly, the current pace of economic growth is *exponential*, so that the gradual build-up of environmental problems may produce a sudden catastrophic outcome. This point is often illustrated by the following riddle. On what day will a pond be half covered with lilies, if the coverage doubles every day and will cover the entire pond on the thirtieth day? The answer is the twenty-ninth day (Brown 1978). The message is that policymakers need foresight to act early enough to prevent the catastrophic outcome predicted by *Limits to Growth*. Lastly, short-term technological fixes are insufficient because they do not address the underlying economic, social and political causes of the environmental crisis; they may delay destruction, but they will not prevent it. Overall, *Limits to Growth* suggests that ecological destruction is inextrica-bly linked to prevailing economic, social and political systems. Greens have concluded that only if these arrangements are radically transformed can environmental apocalypse be averted.

Subsequently, the 'limits to growth' thesis has been subjected to widespread criticism (Cole et al. 1973; Martell 1994; Beckerman 1995, *inter alia*). The easiest target has been its empirical claims, particularly about resource depletion, most of which have proven inaccurate because new reserves of oil, gas, coal and other minerals have been discovered (Beckerman 1995, 2002). In short, many indicators suggest that the state of the environment is healthier than predicted in *Limits to Growth*. It is now commonly agreed that the prediction of crisis by 2100 was overly pessimistic. The computer modelling used was very primitive, many of the assumptions were inaccurate and much of the data was flawed. Although updated versions of the *Limits to Growth* report try to meet some of these criticisms (Meadows et al. 1992, 2004), these are serious weaknesses. They show that the sense of urgency that *Limits to Growth* provoked, along with later publications in a similar survivalist vein such as the *Global 2000 Report to the President* published in 1980 and the annual Worldwatch Institute *State of the World* reports, may have been misplaced. These survivalist publications have also been fiercely attacked for underestimating the technological and political capacity of humans to adapt. This Promethean assault, once spearheaded by the economist Julian Simon (1981), has been reinvigorated since his death by Bjørn Lomborg (2001), a Danish statistician and political scientist (Dryzek 2005: 52–6) (see Box 3.3). Overall, their message is that broad trends show that economic growth ultimately improves environmental quality so we must do nothing that might hamper the operation of markets and free trade (see Chapter 10) and we can be confident that humans will find ways to solve any environmental problems that do emerge.

Nevertheless, the basic idea that there are ecological limits to growth remains potent, particularly with the emergence since the 1970s of a new range of global problems such as climate change and ozone depletion. Indeed, in 1995 a group of leading economists joined the fray by declaring that economic growth must sooner or later encounter limits imposed by the Earth's environmental carrying capacity (Arrow et al. 1995). If the great and the good of a discipline known more for its hostility to environmentalism are calling for institutional redesign to deal with pending ecological crisis, then there must be something in the idea (Dryzek 2005: 34). Perhaps greens need not be too defensive about drawing lessons from the 'limits to growth' thesis.

Finally, the 'limits to growth' debate also acted as a catalyst for an important debate in political philosophy about intergenerational justice, for it suggested that our actions now are likely to have a dramatic impact on the kind of world that we pass on to future generations of people not yet born. If so, do we have an obligation to future generations to protect the environment – to conserve resources, prevent pollution, avoid environmental degradation – so that the world they inherit is no worse (or even better) than

## 3.3 Bjørn Lomborg: *The Skeptical Environmentalist*

Lomborg, an ex-Greenpeace member, attacks environmentalists for constantly reciting the 'litany' of environmental fears about disappearing resources, overpopulation, biodiversity loss and pollution. He argues that this litany is inaccurate, and, fuelled by the need for environmental groups to raise funds and the media's search for 'bad news', it creates a climate of fear, which encourages bad policy decisions. In reality, he asserts that 'Mankind's lot has actually improved in terms of practically every measurable indicator' (2001: 4) and he marshals a huge array of statistics about key trends to show that natural resources, energy, food are actually becoming more abundant; people are eating more and living longer; species loss is exaggerated; forests are not disappearing; and pollution improves with economic growth. So, rather than introduce costly and ineffective policies to alleviate environmental problems that either do not exist or which we can do little to prevent, notably climate change, he recommends instead that efforts be concentrated on improving health and diets to alleviate poverty and save lives.

Lomborg has provoked huge criticism from the academic and environmentalist communities. He is criticised for creating a 'straw person', a survivalist environmental litany that few people today really believe. He is widely condemned for 'bad science', including the selective use of evidence, the misinterpretation of key sources, a focus on quantity not quality (e.g. comparing old growth tropical rainforests with timber plantations) and a general insensitivity to the workings of complex ecosystems. A special issue of *Scientific American* (January 2002) had leading scientists lining up to attack him and Lomborg was even taken to the Danish Committee on Scientific Dishonesty, where he was found to have used dishonest methods, although this decision was overruled by the Ministry of Science in December 2003.

The publicity that Lomborg has attracted reflects the high stakes involved: environmentalists are sensitive to the 'cry wolf' charge that they are self-interestedly exaggerating the extent of the eco-crisis; anti-environmentalists (ranging from big business to the right-wing Danish and US governments) are keen to publicise any attempt to undermine the green case.

See Lomborg (2001), Jamison (2004), Dryzek (2005: ch. 3), Dryzek and Schlosberg (2005: chs. 5 & 6); the anti-Lomborg website: www.mylinkspage.com/lomborg.html; and his replies on www.Lomborg.com.

today? Future-generations arguments provide a powerful anthropocentric case for environmental protection that can supplement the ecocentric arguments discussed in Chapter 2 (see Box 3.4).[3]

---

### Critical question 1
Must green politics be based on the idea of limits to growth?

---

## ▶ *A green programme for a sustainable society*

If ecologism is a distinct ideology, then it should be possible to identify a vision of the good society based on ecological principles that is fundamentally different from other ideologies. This section outlines the central

## 3.4 Obligations to future generations

The concept of intergenerational justice provides a powerful *anthropocentric* case for sustainability. Environmental protection is justified because our actions now will clearly have an effect on those still to be born; climate change, resource depletion, nuclear waste and biodiversity loss will all pose problems for future generations. However, there are problems inherent in the attempt to extend moral considerations to future generations.

1.  The problem of *reciprocity*: why should we consider the interests of future people, who cannot offer us anything in return? This difficulty is acute for those who see justice as a matter of mutual advantage (e.g. Gauthier 1986), but such theories also have difficulty explaining obligations to existing people, notably the poor and needy. So, while theories of mutual advantage pose problems for future generations, they are also problematic in other, independent, ways.
2.  The problem of *knowledge*: it may be objected that we cannot know what future generations will want or need (Golding 1972). However, against this, Barry (1991) argues that, whatever their wants, 'they are unlikely to include a desire for skin cancer,

soil erosion, or the inundation of all low-lying areas as a result of the melting of the ice-caps' (p. 248).
3.  The problem of *scope*: it is sometimes argued that people who do not yet exist cannot have rights or interests. This consideration raises very complex issues about the possibility of benefiting or harming those who do not yet exist – and may never exist (see Parfitt 1984).

If we conclude that we do have obligations to future generations, many practical issues arise, including:

1.  How strong is the obligation? Is it the same as that which is owed to people living now? Is it stronger for the immediate next generation than for later generations? Does the obligation diminish as it gets further away (in time) perhaps because we can share it with intervening generations? Does the satisfaction of future *needs* trump current *wants*?
2.  What kind of obligation might we have towards future generations? Are we obliged to ensure they are no worse off than us or should we seek to improve their welfare?

In short, how much sacrifice is needed today?

characteristics of a green sustainable society. Of course, just as any definitive list of the core principles of socialism, liberalism or conservatism would be open to dispute, there is also considerable variation among the contrasting interpretations or discourses (Dryzek 2005) of ecologism. This account builds on the so-called 'four pillars', or core principles, of green politics identified by the German Greens in the 1980s – ecological responsibility, social justice, grassroots democracy and non-violence (see Box 3.5) – supplemented by the writings of green theorists, activists and academics.[4]

*Ecological responsibility*, or sustainability, is the primary aim of green politics and flows directly from the idea of limits to growth. A sustainable society has the capacity to last because the ecological carrying capacities of the planet are not exceeded. If the planet (and human society) is to survive, then development – economic, social, political – must be self-sufficient

---

### 3.5 The 'four pillars' of green politics

The 1983 political programme of Die Grünen, the German green party, set out four core political principles which have subsequently been adopted by most green parties elsewhere:

1. ecological responsibility
2. grassroots democracy
3. social justice
4. non-violence

The concept of ecological responsibility, or sustainability, is informed by the two core ideas of ecologism: (1) the need to recast human–nature relations; (2) the limits to growth. However, it is less clear how the *practical* political commitments to grassroots democracy, social justice and non-violence reflect these two ideas. If the primary aim of ecologism is to achieve a sustainable society, does it really matter how we get there and what the green polity looks like?

---

and geared towards the satisfaction of basic needs. Development must be guided by the principle of futurity so that the impact of economic activities on natural resources today does not prevent future generations of humans from meeting their needs and will allow non-human nature to flourish; thus futurity mixes the anthropocentric aim of protecting future generations of humans with the ecocentric aim of preserving the well-being of non-human nature.

The sustainable economy will require a fundamental transformation in attitudes to economic growth, consumption, production and work.[5] The relentless pursuit of economic growth that characterises the existing capitalist economic system creates a range of environmental problems, notably resource depletion, destructive production and pollution. In contrast, greens advocate 'an economic system oriented to the necessities of human life today and for future generations, to the preservation of nature and a careful management of natural resources' (Die Grünen 1983: sect. 1, p. 7). If we aim to satisfy 'needs not wants', the pressure for continual economic growth would be removed. Many greens advocate a steady-state economy in which the levels of population and wealth are kept constant (Daly 1992), or dramatically scaled back (Georgescu-Roegen 1971).

Greens identify consumption, in particular 'unnecessary' consumption, as a major problem. They argue that the rate of economic growth is maintained by the creation of artificial wants, through advertising, fashion and peer pressure, that generate the unnecessary and wasteful levels of economic activity characteristic of the consumer society. The 'needs not wants' principle poses an explicit challenge to the supremacy of the profit motive. Greens believe that the pursuit of profit stimulates activities that create unnecessary consumer wants and encourages wasteful production strategies such as built-in obsolescence. Instead, a green economy would be based on production primarily for use rather than profit, and would thereby rule out such frivolous consumption. In this *conserver* society, people would be educated to consume less, thereby reducing production, protecting resources

## 3.6 Greens and technology

Greens believe that the *control of technology* is a prerequisite for effective environmental protection. A suspicion of 'high' technology has been a constant theme of modern environmentalism, from Rachel Carson's (1962) warnings about poisonous synthetic chemicals and pesticides, through fears about nuclear power, to contemporary concern about genetically modified organisms. Greens question the widespread assumption that technological solutions will always be found to environmental problems and that the benefits of technology always outweigh its costs.

Greens are not simply Luddite opponents of all forms of technological progress. They recognise that some technologies, such as medical advances, have dramatically improved the quality of life. Some greens see modern information technology playing a key role in a green society characterised by small, high-tech cottage industries, although others point out that the production and use of these technologies massively deplete resources and generate pollution.

What all greens seek is greater democratic control over the development and use of technology. So, consistent with their commitment to economic and political decentralisation, greens would remove the control of technology from central government and big corporations and place it in the hands of the community. Following the ideas of Gandhi and Schumacher, they advocate wider use of intermediate and appropriate technologies, such as wind power and other forms of renewable energy, which are congruent with the needs, skills, culture and environment of local communities.

and cutting pollution. Environmental damage from production can be minimised by using renewable resources, reusing goods, recycling materials and adopting cleaner technologies.

Greens also believe that the rejection of the consumer society will improve the quality of life because a society based on material acquisition is, at best, undesirable, at worst, ethically wrong. As Trainer (1985) puts it: 'Our main problem is that most people hold the disastrously mistaken belief that affluence and growth are possible – and worse still that they are important. Our chief task is to spread the understanding that being able to buy and use up more and more expensive things is hollow and senseless' (p. 249). Furthermore, in a society dominated by the pursuit of economic growth and consumption, there is little time for active citizen participation in the democratic activities of the polity (Barry 1999a: 175). Thus consumerism restricts the opportunity for liberty and self-determination. On either count, greens believe that any quantitative reduction in the overall material standard of life in the sustainable economy will be more than compensated for by the resulting benefits, both material, such as improved craftsmanship, healthier food and safer communities, and 'spiritual' in terms of personal happiness, individual fulfilment and a more co-operative society.

Greens are firmly committed to the 'small is beautiful' philosophy of Fritz Schumacher (1975). The sheer size and complexity of large-scale production and modern technologies damage the environment in many ways (see Box 3.6). For example, pollution is concentrated in one area so that 'hotspots' stretch the carrying capacity of the local ecosystem to the limit. The spatial separation of workplace and home increases traffic volume because employees travel long distances to work and the finished product is then transported nationally or internationally to consumers. Thus the price of economic efficiency arising from economies of scale is massive resource consumption and traffic pollution. Instead, the green economy would be characterised by decentralised, small-scale production within a self-sufficient local community. Production would be for local needs rather than for commercial trade further afield. Agricultural production would use less intensive, organic farming methods and serve the local community. Consequently, traffic volume would fall, as fewer journeys would be made and people would travel shorter distances to work, by foot, bicycle or public transport. Overall, resource consumption would drop dramatically.

The green economy would not dispense with money, but it would be a non-capitalist market economy with less trading activity. It might look like the local exchange trading systems (LETS) that have gained some popularity in recent years. In LETS, goods, skills and services are exchanged or bartered within a closed local network of individuals. No money changes hands. The aim is exchange and trade, not accumulation (see Barry 1999a: ch. 6). There would be less emphasis on paid work in the formal economy. Greater value and social recognition would be attributed to the wide range of tasks that currently do not normally count as paid labour, such as parenting, housework and community voluntary work. Greens support basic income schemes in which everyone would receive a non-means-tested income to ensure economic security for all and to allow people to adopt a more fulfilling lifestyle less dependent on the whims of the market-place (Robertson 1985).

What kind of political institutions would be needed to support the sustainable society? The clarion call of the greens – 'Think global, act local' – underpins the principle of political *decentralisation*. Political power would be located at the lowest 'appropriate' level to encourage what Kirkpatrick Sale (1980) has called 'politics on a human scale'. In its most radical deep ecology and ecoanarchist forms, the green polity would consist of small self-governing communities. Sale proposes that the basic unit of the sustainable society should be the 'bioregion': an area of land defined by the natural, biological and geological features that give an area its identity, such as watersheds or mountain ranges, rather than the human political boundaries represented by towns, states or countries (Sale 1980, 1991; Tokar 1992). Social and economic life within that community should be self-sufficient, requiring no more than the resources available within that bioregion.

Green politics is not, however, confined to the concept of sustainability. As we have seen, greens identify moral as well as environmental reasons for cutting back on consumption and changing our lifestyles. The fact that we over-consume and degrade the environment is not just bad for the environment, but also evidence that we are 'bad people'. Green politics has a view on how a 'good person' should behave in the 'good (green) society', as illustrated by the centrality of the three remaining pillars to green politics. First, green party organisations are typically modelled on participatory democracy. The green state would be a *grassroots democracy*; indeed, participatory democracy would extend beyond political institutions into the economic arena, where the basic form of collective work organisation would be the worker co-operative or commune. Secondly, green politics emphasises *social justice*. A principle of intragenerational equity regards distributional equity, particularly between the rich North and the poor South but also within each country, as a prerequisite of sustainability. A principle of intergenerational justice requires justice towards unborn future generations (see Box 3.4). The need to protect biodiversity leads greens to favour diversity in human relations, specifically opposing all forms of discrimination based on race, gender, sexual orientation or age. Thirdly, greens espouse *non-violence*, opposing international violence (war, armies, nuclear weapons), and are committed to non-violent civil protest.

Thus greens have a broad and radical vision of what a sustainable society might look like. Inevitably, this programme has attracted extensive criticism. Few people would deny that the economic and social prescriptions outlined here would help reduce environmental destruction, but many sympathisers question whether such wholesale reform of economic activity and individual lifestyles is really necessary or desirable, let alone feasible. Unease about the radical prescriptions proposed by many greens has contributed to the popularity of *sustainable development* (see Chapter 8), which outlines an alternative policy paradigm based on the reform of the existing capitalist system, rather than the more fundamental transformation of society outlined above.

However, this chapter is concerned with the content and coherence of ecologism as a radical and distinct green ideology. This section has shown that, although sustainability is the central imperative of ecologism, greens have yoked it to a more general understanding of what a good society and a good person will be like. This begs a fundamental question: does a commitment to sustainability *necessarily* imply a commitment to the principles of participatory democracy, social justice, non-violence and decentralisation – or is the relationship merely contingent?

### Critical question 2
Is the radical green vision of the sustainable society an unattainable utopia?

### ▶ *Does sustainability require specific political arrangements?*

The primacy of the ecological imperative is the driving feature of green ideology. If the objective is to save the planet, does it matter how we do it? Suppose the 'survivalist' prescription of an authoritarian, centralised and inequitable society were the most effective means of achieving sustainability.

Put differently, how can greens be certain that the principles of democracy, decentralisation, social justice and non-violence are the best means of reaching the sustainable society?

Goodin (1992) provides the best formulation of this problem with his distinction between the green *theory of value* and the green *theory of agency*. He argues eloquently that the significance greens attribute to the theory of agency – the means of getting there – is wrongheaded. Instead, the green theory of value, which underpins the case for sustainability, should take priority (Goodin's own theory of value is outlined in Chapter 2). This ecological imperative provides the unified moral vision that binds the green agenda together; without it the green message lacks legitimacy, coherence and direction. Goodin's vision is consequentialist: 'it is more important that the right things be done than that they be done in any particular way or through any particular agency' (ibid.: 120). In any irreconcilable conflict between the two, the theory of agency will always be subordinate to the green theory of value. It may be desirable that Good actions coincide with Right actions – that democratic, non-violent methods achieve the sustainable society – but it is not essential. Put simply (and simplistically), green ends justify the means.[6]

Most radical greens recoil at the consequentialist implications of Goodin's thesis because it might justify using authoritarian or coercive measures to reach a sustainable society. So, are there good grounds for rejecting Goodin's claim that ecological outcomes trump procedures? It is not enough for greens, rooted as many activists are in the emancipatory new social movements and New Left of the 1960s and 1970s (see Chapter 4), simply to express a preference for participatory democracy, non-violence and egalitarianism. They also need to show that without them an ecologically sustainable society is unattainable. If they cannot do so, then perhaps greens must either drop their radical political and moral agenda, or concede that environmental outcomes are less important to them than doing things the 'right' way.

The force of Goodin's argument stems from distinguishing between the theories of value and agency. Eckersley (1996) argues that this sharp delineation is flawed, and that greens are right to say that the means are as important as the ends. She criticises Goodin's own theory of value for being too narrowly based on the non-human world, and therefore providing an insufficient grounding for a green political theory. Instead, the green theory of value should be expanded to incorporate the value of autonomy and self-determination: 'the freedom of human and non human beings to unfold in their own ways and live according to their "species life"' (Eckersley 1996: 223). If moral priority is attributed to autonomy, then it is essential to establish political arrangements that will allow human (and non-human) autonomy to flourish, such as social justice, non-violence and grassroots democracy. This emancipatory interpretation of green politics suggests a blurring of the Right and the Good so that the *way* something is done is part of what makes it the *right* thing to do – a clear rejection of Goodin's consequentialist position. In short, a green theory of agency can be grounded in a green theory of value.

Whether this interpretation enriches ecologism is open to debate. Eckersley's argument, despite the reference to enhancing the autonomy of 'non-humans', seems self-consciously anthropocentric. It is also explicitly individualistic, since autonomy is precisely the value made paramount in liberal individualism. Giving moral priority to individual autonomy seems odd in an environmental theory. But it may be that encouraging individual human autonomy is the best *means* to the sustainable society because it can contribute to changing the way people behave (although it is through exercising our autonomy as consumers that we have caused many of the ecological problems we face today).

Alternatively, greens might argue that change should be justified to further the wider *social* good, rather than to allow *individual* autonomy to flourish. Thus another 'green' riposte to Goodin might hold that ecologism is not only about sustainability, but also about creating the good society in which, for example, self-interested materialism is rejected as morally unacceptable. We return to these two arguments below in examining whether participatory democracy, decentralisation and social justice and, briefly, non-violence (see Box 3.7) are the political arrangements most suitable to bring about sustainability.

---

### Critical question 3
Do green 'ends' justify the 'means'?

---

## ▶ *Must green politics be democratic?*

The uneasy relationship between ecological concerns and democracy is a central issue in green political theory, and a good example of the means/ends debate. Most greens declare that democracy, specifically participatory democracy, is a core principle of ecologism. However, if Goodin is correct, the primacy of the ecological imperative might justify sacrificing democratic principles to protect the planet. This kind of consequentialist thinking underpins the eco-authoritarian argument of the survivalists that ecological imperatives such as population growth and resource depletion demand swift, decisive and drastic government action (see Box 3.1). A strong authoritarian government, unhampered by the need to win elections or protect liberal rights, might coerce self-interested individuals into acting in the collective interest by, say, producing fewer children and living more frugal lifestyles.

Most contemporary greens find these authoritarian solutions repugnant and want to rule them out of court for contravening the ecological principle of democracy. Yet on what grounds is democracy a core green principle? After all, it is obvious that democratic procedures may not always generate environmentally beneficial outcomes. For example, most experts agree that

### 3.7  Is non-violence a green principle?

Green politics is informed by a concern not to harm the natural environment, yet there is no entirely satisfactory distinctive *green* justification for non-violence.

Modern warfare is clearly bad for the environment for it wreaks devastation upon it. Yet war is an extreme case. Within civil society, it is important to distinguish between violence against people and violence against property. Almost all greens reject the former, but many would regard the latter as legitimate and there are certainly numerous examples of environmental activism directed against property, whether it is spiking bulldozers, pulling up GM crops or smashing up McDonald's outlets (see Chapter 6). Thus it is important to be clear about what is meant by 'violence'.

The green commitment to non-violent protest in civil society has a practical explanation arising from the close links between the green movement and the peace, anti-nuclear and women's movements, which all rejected the use of violence against people. The use of well-rehearsed, *anthropocentric* arguments against non-violence that originated in other political struggles – anti-militarism, fear of nuclear accidents, the links with male violence – explains why non-violence has not figured prominently in debates within green political theory.

At the level of green *principle*, where there is a trade-off between non-violence and other green ends, such as achieving a sustainable society, greens need to show that non-violence is a prerequisite for achieving that end. Otherwise it will be trumped by the ecological imperative. However, at the level of *strategy*, a principle of non-violence places the onus on opponents to show why coercive or violent methods might be superior.

See Doherty (1996) for a wider discussion of non-violence and green politics.

climate change prevention requires tough restrictions in car use and high petrol taxes. Yet governments are reluctant to implement such unpopular policies because an angry electorate might vote them out of office. As Goodin (1992) puts it: 'To advocate democracy is to advocate procedures, to advocate environmentalism is to advocate substantive outcomes: what guarantee can we have that the former procedures will yield the latter sort of outcomes?' (p. 168). He is not suggesting that democratic procedures are illegitimate or undesirable; it is just that when it comes to choosing between procedures, the ecological imperative should always trump democracy.

However, Goodin simply asserts that the theory of value takes priority without properly discussing how policies will be derived from it (Hayward 1995). One practical argument for democracy is that infallible green policies will not simply drop like apples from a theory of value, so the means of reaching decisions do matter. Those arguments that defend the use of non-democratic methods often contain an implicit technocratic assumption that a governing elite of politicians, scientists and professionals knows best; Ophuls (1977) even talks of a 'priesthood of technologists' (p. 159). The implication is that certain ecological decisions should be made by those people possessing this 'superior knowledge' (Saward 1996: 80) and not left to the whims of democratic procedures. This argument effectively privileges science over other forms of knowledge and understanding of ecological issues, and gives power to an elite minority. Whilst technical knowledge is, of course, critical in many ecological decisions, it provides only part of the picture. A wide range of alternative perspectives and considerations – non-technical, local, ethical, social, political – should also be included in the decision-making process to ensure a more informed decision that can attract widespread support (Barry 1999a: 199–201). Greens argue that participatory democracy offers the best means of including these factors in the decision process.

The case for participatory democracy starts from a critique of liberal democracy. Greens argue that liberal democracy is unable to produce the best decisions because it is characterised by hierarchy, bureaucracy, individualism and material inequalities. It offers limited opportunities to participate in the public sphere. For example, Porritt (1984) complains that 'The representative element of the system has insidiously undermined the element of participation, in that turning out to vote now and then seems to have become the be-all and end-all of our democracy' (p. 166). Consequently, liberal democracy nurtures an atomised individualistic focus on the private sphere, which makes it a poor breeding ground for the ecological consciousness and responsible citizenship needed to bring about a sustainable society. Greens want to replace representative democracy with participatory democratic procedures based on a discursive or deliberative model (see Dryzek 1990; Smith 2003). These radical forms of democracy presume active citizen participation in governance in institutions such as political parties, local government, neighbourhood assemblies, voluntary associations and the workplace. The green case thus plugs into a much broader tradition of radical democratic theorising in seeking a society where widespread participatory democracy means citizens are fully, freely and actively involved in the decisions that shape their lives (Pateman 1970; Barber 1984). Greens frequently invoke the ancient Greek city state, or more contemporary examples such as the New England town meeting (Tokar 1992: 104), to argue that face-to-face democracy would produce communities that are more in tune with, and therefore considerate towards, their natural environment.

Greens employ two related arguments to support the claim that participatory democracy will result in beneficial environmental outcomes. First, participatory democracy should produce more responsive government. Institutions would be more responsive and accountable because power would be shifted away from the hands of the few: from central government to local communities, from managers to workers, from the central party bureaucracy to the local branch (Goodin 1992: 127–8). Environmental protection would be improved if more people had a say because the decision-making process would draw on a wider range of interests (i.e. beyond the political, business and professional elites who currently dominate). The greater diffusion of information necessary for participatory democracy to operate will provide more ammunition for local communities to protect their environment and, conversely, may enhance the speed with which evidence of environmental damage is communicated to decision-makers. By forcing the institutions of civil society to respond to popular demands, participatory democracy is more likely to produce, if not morally perfect outcomes, then at least morally better ones (ibid.: 128). Of course, a participatory democratic decision may still give greater priority to material well-being than to environmental protection, perhaps by allowing a factory to release high levels of pollutants in order to protect jobs in the local community. Nevertheless, by virtue of the improved responsiveness gained from drawing on a wider circle of interests, knowledge and skills, there is, on balance, a strong, if not overwhelming, instrumental case for saying that participatory democracy makes ecological outcomes more likely.

A second green argument for participatory democracy is that it will create the conditions for the development of greater individual autonomy. In liberal democracy, material inequalities, bureaucratic hierarchies and divisions of labour in work and home deny the majority of citizens the opportunity to shape their own lives; they are unable to become self-determining agents. If democratic structures and opportunities to participate were prevalent in all walks of life – at work, at school, in neighbourhood assemblies – then people should learn to participate simply by participating (Pateman 1970: 42–3). This involvement should nurture a 'democratic personality', which shows greater respect for, and more responsibility towards, fellow citizens (Gould 1988). Discursive democracy, by encouraging citizen involvement and deliberation, enables preferences to be altered and encourages behaviour that conforms to publicly agreed norms. Replacing the self-contained individual of liberal democracy whose identity is only occasionally expressed in the public sphere (notably by voting), the individual in a participatory democracy is more likely to be a public-spirited citizen keen to promote collective activities and community identity. At this point, greens give the arguments for participatory democracy an ecological twist by suggesting that this radical conception of democratic citizenship can also nurture 'an ecological citizenship capable of developing and giving expression to collective ecological concerns' (Plumwood 1996: 158). At the very least, active citizen participation will educate individuals about environmental issues because they will have access to more information and the opportunity to exchange knowledge and views with fellow citizens. Further, once the shift from 'self-regarding' individual to 'other-regarding' citizen has been made, it is a much smaller step to extend that public concern to foreigners, future generations and non-human nature (Eckersley 1996; Barry 1999a). In short, participatory democracy can help nurture an ecological consciousness.

If so, this second argument substantially strengthens the first claim that participatory democracy improves institutional responsiveness: whereas better responsiveness is concerned with the *aggregation* of preferences, greater autonomy should also produce a *transformation* of preferences (Elster, quoted in Barry 1999a: 226). Indeed, it is the aggregation of preferences that (in part) has contributed to ecological problems, such as mass consumerism or public resistance to measures aimed at reducing car use. If participatory democracy takes preferences as given and simply provides a more effective way of aggregating them, then governments may be *less* likely to introduce progressive environmental policies. Instead, greens want to alter human preferences because the radical transformation to a sustainable society will be easier to achieve if people can be persuaded by the force of argument that it is right for them to change their beliefs, attitudes and behaviour, rather than being told to do so (Barry 1999a: 228).

To return to the discussion at the end of the previous section: Eckersley argues that ecological ends justify democratic means because moral priority should be given to nurturing the autonomy of members of the human and non-human community. Participatory democracy is one of the conditions necessary to construct a society in which the conditions for human autonomy prevail. Thus the connection between ecology and democracy is no longer merely contingent. Moreover, authoritarianism is 'ruled out at the level of green principle' because it 'fundamentally infringes the rights of humans to choose their own destiny' (Eckersley 1996: 223).

However, an alternative green riposte to Eckersley might justify participatory democracy on the different grounds that its communicative and deliberative procedures provide the best *means* of changing individual preferences and facilitating the ecological citizenship necessary for the good society. Hence participatory democracy is a core green principle because it contributes to the *common good*, not because moral priority should reside with individual autonomy.

Whichever justification is accepted, how practical is this vision of a participatory democratic polity? It is significant that green theorists and activists have become increasingly reconciled to the continued existence of the (albeit reformed) representative institutions of liberal democracy (see Doherty and deGeus 1996). Even where a powerful case is made for a distinctive 'ecological democracy', it is presented as a model of a 'post-liberal democracy, not an anti-liberal democracy', which would retain many elements of the liberal democratic state (Eckersley 2004a: 138). But many greens now see deliberative democratic procedures as *supplementing*, rather than replacing, reformed liberal democratic institutions. Thus the provision of more opportunities for greater citizen participation could operate alongside attempts to encourage greater 'institutionalised self-criticism' and 'reflexiveness' in existing institutions by making them more open, transparent and accountable (Paehlke 1989; Beck 1992; Barry 1999a). The ascendancy of the sustainable development paradigm has been the catalyst for widespread democratic institutional innovation along these lines during the last decade, including roundtables, citizen juries and extended referenda (see Chapter 11). It is a moot point whether this 'downgrading' of participatory democracy undermines the case for democracy as a core green principle. However, the arguments made here could be used to reformulate a green principle of democracy, which would require an extensive *democratisation* of existing institutions and procedures – even if this falls short of pure participatory democracy.

---

### Critical question 4
Can a liberal democracy be ecologically sustainable?

---

▶ *Must a green polity be decentralised?*

Goodin (1992) observes that 'If there is anything truly distinctive about green politics, most commentators would concur, it must surely be its emphasis on decentralisation' (p. 147). Decentralisation is a constant, oft-repeated theme in party programmes and theoretical tracts. The green case for political decentralisation, as with participatory democracy, draws on a range of intellectual traditions, most notably anarchism, but greens again add a distinctive ecological slant.[7] They follow the anarchist tradition in favouring decentralisation because it creates 'human-scale' political institutions. The underlying assumption is that only in a small community can individuals regain the sense of identity lost in the atomised, consumerist society. This idea informs, for example, the 'small is beautiful' philosophy of Schumacher (1975), the **'bioregionalism'** of Sale (1980, 1991) and the 'libertarian municipalism' of Bookchin (1989: 179–85). As Goldsmith et al. (1972) put it: 'it is probable that only in the small community can a man or woman be an individual. In today's large agglomerations he is merely an isolate' (p. 51). Sale (1991: 64) anticipates that the population of a bioregion will not exceed 10,000 people – small enough for individuals to feel sufficiently attached to their community to participate meaningfully. Citizens need to be able to meet to discuss issues openly, suitably informed about the issues affecting their community, able to understand the implications of their decisions and knowing that their participation may have some influence (Goodin 1992: 149). Thus a decentralised community is a precondition for a flourishing participatory democracy. Greens hope that the combination of decentralisation and participatory democracy will produce fulfilled, other-regarding autonomous citizens prepared to accept the material sacrifices required of a low-consumption sustainable society.

> **Bioregionalism:** An approach that believes that the 'natural' world (specifically, the local bioregion) should determine the political, economic and social life of communities.

Greens make a further distinctive ecological argument for political decentralisation, which holds that policy decisions made by the local community should be more sensitive to the environment. Sale (1980) takes this line furthest by arguing that we should learn from nature by basing the decentralised community on the natural boundaries of the bioregion such as mountain ranges and watersheds. In the bioregion, human communities will become 'dwellers in the land': closer to nature and more respectful of it, more knowledgeable about the capacities and limits of the immediate physical surroundings and, therefore, able to cohabit more harmoniously with natural landscapes.[8]

Decentralisation may be a necessary condition for participatory democracy, but there is no guarantee that a decentralised society will be democratic. Sale (1980) concedes that a society based on a natural bioregion may not always be characterised by democratic or liberal values because another 'natural' principle, diversity, implies that bioregional societies should boast a wide range of political systems, some of which, presumably, might be authoritarian. Even if the political system is democratic, there may be drawbacks about life in a small community. Social control mechanisms may prove oppressive if, as Goldsmith et al. (1972) suggest, offenders are brought to heel by the weight of public opinion. Discrimination against minorities or non-conformist opinion may be rife. Small parochial societies may also be intellectually and culturally impoverished, perhaps reducing innovation in clean technologies (Frankel 1987). So, ironically, the homogeneous decentralised society may lack the diversity that ecologists value.

Another difficulty with decentralisation is that many environmental problems are best dealt with at the national or international level. Global commons problems do not respect the political boundaries between existing nation states, let alone small bioregions. Problems such as climate change and ozone depletion require co-ordinated action across communities and nations, which implies international co-operation between centralised nation states (see Chapter 9). The green slogan 'Think global, act local' may therefore provide an inadequate strategy for dealing with problems of the global commons. Relying on local communities alone to protect the environment assumes that the local community has full knowledge about the causes, impact and solutions to a particular problem; even then, it 'makes sense only when the locals possess an appropriate social and ecological consciousness' (Eckersley 1992: 173).

Greens counter this criticism by stressing that they advocate decentralisation to the lowest 'appropriate' level of government (Schumacher 1975; Porritt 1984). If local communities need to co-ordinate action to deal with transboundary problems, greens insist they must do so 'as independent agents negotiating arrangements that are mutually agreeable to all concerned' (Goodin 1992: 152). Underpinning most 'ecoanarchist' accounts is a deep distrust of the state (Bookchin 1989; see also Barry 1999a: ch. 4), which leads them to reject a central co-ordinating agency that could encroach on the sovereignty of the autonomous decentralised community. Thus Bookchin (1989) talks of a 'humanly scaled, self-governing municipality freely and confederally associated with other humanly scaled, self-governing municipalities' (p. 182).

There are many reasons why this response is flawed. What if the communities are unwilling to act? Co-operation *within* a community may not result in a benevolent attitude towards the outside world. Small parochial communities often define themselves by reference to those outside, so they may be quite averse to considering wider questions, such as the possibility of environmental damage elsewhere. They may even try to free-ride on other communities by producing pollution that damages those living downstream or downwind. Hostility or indifference between communities may be accentuated by the existence of economic inequalities between them; perhaps a poor community might feel less co-operative towards a richer neighbour. It is not difficult to imagine a community being highly sensitive towards its own local environment but unconcerned by damage further afield. It may, therefore, require a central agency (the state?) to persuade localities to change their behaviour. Even if all communities were willing to act collectively to protect the environment, there would still be a role for a central agency to co-ordinate their actions. Yet, resolute in its rejection of such a central agency, the green anarchist model gives no adequate explanation of how the necessary co-ordination might take place (Goodin 1992; Martell 1994).

On balance, the problem lies not with decentralisation *per se*, but with the way the dominant ecoanarchist model, characterised by its distrust of the state, narrowly defines it. Decentralisation does not mean that there should be no central state, let alone no state at all, yet that is what many greens seem to want. Indeed, where international co-ordination is required, green distrust of the state sometimes overrides the ecological imperative. This ecoanarchist model of decentralisation has come under strong attack from writers sympathetic to green politics (Eckersley 1992; Goodin 1992; Martell 1994; Barry 1999a, *inter alia*). Indeed, the emergence of a debate about the nature of the 'green state' has been one of the most significant contemporary developments in green political theory (Eckersley 2004a; Barry and Eckersley 2005; Paterson et al. 2006). Most contributors to this debate are working towards a green theory of the state; in short, they want to transform the state rather than abolish it.

Eckersley (2004a) offers the most developed model of a green state. She identifies three major challenges to the transition to a green world: the anarchic system of sovereign nation states (see Chapter 9), the promotion of capital accumulation and the 'democratic deficit' of liberal democratic state capitalism. She also highlights three countervailing positive trends – environmental multilateralism (see Chapter 9), ecological modernisation (see Chapter 8) and deliberative/discursive democratic practices (see Chapter 11). Together, these trends underline the continuing significance of the nation state. Rather than accept the popular view that globalisation has rendered the sovereign state largely impotent, she argues that the state is still the most important political institution in the struggle against global environmental destruction; it is one of the few institutions with the capacity and legitimacy to implement the radical changes that greens demand (p. 7). It is therefore essential that this powerful state be sympathetic to green objectives; moreover, if it is to fulfil the role of 'public ecological trustee' (p. 12), then it should also be a 'good' state. Sovereignty and democracy are key elements in Eckersley's model. A green state will recognise its responsibilities to those who live beyond its border, because environmental problems do not respect traditional territorial boundaries of the sovereign nation state. Her theory of 'ecological democracy', based on principles of deliberative democracy, holds that 'all those potentially affected by ecological risks ought to have some meaningful opportunity to participate, or be represented, in the determination of policies or decisions that may generate risks' (p. 243). Thus Eckersley recasts the state in a new role, as an ecological steward and facilitator of transboundary democracy, rather than a selfish actor jealously protecting its own territory.

The starting point for Eckersley, in contrast with the ecoanarchist model, is the nation state. Not all these revisionist green theorists embrace the nation state as readily as does Eckersley. Most want to see some degree of decentralisation to 'appropriate' levels, with the onus resting more on the proponent of centralisation to argue that specific powers or responsibilities should reside at a higher level. This kind of reinterpretation would leave decentralisation as a core principle of ecologism, but the kind of state it would produce would look very different from the ecoanarchist model.

To summarise, sustainability may not always be best achieved by political decentralisation. However, greens need not abandon decentralisation, because ecologism is not simply concerned with achieving the right (short-term) outcomes. The case for decentralisation can also be based on its contribution to achieving a good society; although centralisation might sometimes produce better outcomes, if the long-term aim is to create people with the dispositions most likely to be conducive to sustainability, then decentralisation should make this more likely. As with democratisation, decentralisation is not just about getting the right outcomes now; it is also concerned with nurturing a good society inhabited by ecologically concerned citizens.

## ▶ *Must a green society be egalitarian?*

Green theorists generally attribute great importance to 'social justice', but their treatment of the complex relationship between social justice and environmental issues has, until recently, been rather undeveloped (see Box 3.8). Social justice is a highly contested concept. The definition used by greens locates them firmly within the camp of those who link justice with equality. Greens seek a sustainable society characterised by social and economic equality, but why should this be good for the environment? Is there a causal relationship between social justice and sustainability so that, for example, the alleviation of poverty will benefit the environment? Or will inequitable policies sometimes be compatible with sustainability? Is equality a necessary condition for effective participatory democracy and political decentralisation? This section identifies three arguments supporting the claims of social justice to be a core green principle.

## 3.8 Defining social justice

Social justice is concerned with the principles that should govern the basic structure of a society, including the regulation of the legal system, the economy and welfare policy. Theories of social justice generally deal with the distribution of rights, opportunities and resources among human beings.

There are many competing accounts of justice with distribution based variously on principles such as needs, desert, entitlement, utility and equality. A broad division can be identified in modern theories of justice between those which link justice to some notion of equality and those which link it to entitlements, or rights. By defining social justice in terms of social and economic equality, greens adopt a socialist or welfare-state liberal conception of justice. By contrast, Nozick (1974) argues that justice requires that we get the things that we are entitled to – because we have, say, a right to property. If that means some people get more than others, then so be it, because Nozick does not think that inequalities are *in themselves* unjust. However, not all who define

justice by reference to rights are anti-egalitarian (e.g. Benton 1993).

Theories of social justice have, until recently, been largely silent about environmental issues. This is partly explicable by reference to the individualism inherent in liberal theories of justice. The problem here is that environmental goods – the reduction of acid rain or preservation of an endangered species – are not normally distributed to individuals. Yet most policies intended to protect the environment will have distributional implications, perhaps because they will require public expenditure or involve restrictions on the behaviour of individuals (car drivers or hunters), and they will certainly affect some people more than others (Miller 1999).

However, even when modern theories of justice are not individualistic, they are nevertheless anthropocentric in that they explicate value as value for and to human beings (whether individually or collectively). They therefore have difficulty in explaining the intuition that nature might have either inherent or intrinsic value.

First, some greens base their commitment to equality on a lesson from nature (Dobson 2000: 22). The holistic message is that nature consists of a mass of interdependent entities with each part having some value to other parts. Therefore no part is independent of, or superior to, any other part; hence the principle of equality (Dobson 2000: 24). Aside from the weaknesses in the holistic case discussed in Chapter 2, it is hard to see why interdependence necessarily implies equality. After all, there are many interdependent human relationships (employer/employee, landlord/villein, teacher/pupil) where equality would not normally exist. In short, the argument from nature is fundamentally flawed.

Secondly, social injustice contributes to environmental degradation. There is little doubt, for example, that poverty in less developed nations, by encouraging over-intensive farming and the cultivation of marginal land, results in environmental problems such as desertification and deforestation. Economic inequality between North and South is underpinned by an international trading system that encourages less developed countries to produce cash crops for Northern consumption (rather than developing a self-sufficient economy), primarily to pay off debts to those same countries and their financial institutions. Countless social conflicts over 'pollution burdens', environmental entitlements and access to natural resources represent and contribute to a growing 'environmentalism of the poor' in less developed countries that is underpinned by the widespread perception of ecological injustice (Martinez-Alier 2003). It is clear that in many respects the alleviation of poverty will contribute to sustainability. For example, 'development' seems to be the most effective solution to overpopulation. Greater social and economic equality for women, improved female education and literacy, universal access to family planning programmes and the provision of maternal and child health care of good quality are the best means of controlling population growth (see Box 3.2).

Poor and minority communities in affluent nations also bear the brunt of environmental harms because they tend to live near to and work in the most polluting industrial facilities and they are exposed to the highest levels of pollutants. Moreover, they lack the financial resources to afford less environmentally damaging goods or to invest in energy conservation. In the USA in particular, a powerful sense of injustice arising out of these inequities, and fuelled by a plethora of social conflicts over polluting factories, the siting of toxic waste facilities and road construction has contributed to the emergence of the environmental justice movement (Bullard 2000; Roberts and Toffolon-Weiss 2001; Visiglio and Whitelaw 2003). (See Chapter 6.)

Yet the relationship between social justice and sustainability is more complex than is suggested by the simple conclusion that poverty is bad for the environment. In particular, many environmental problems are the result of affluence. Major global problems – climate change, ozone depletion, acid rain – have been caused primarily by development in the advanced industrialised nations of the North. Conspicuous consumption, high levels of car ownership and the extensive use of air conditioning, for example, are key characteristics of rich nations and all massively damaging to the environment. Of course, the redistribution of wealth from the affluent North to the less developed South, and from rich to poor within individual nations, might have an overall positive impact on the environment, simply by cutting out the extremes of wealth and poverty. It is not axiomatic, however, that greater economic equality will reduce damage to the environment; it might just lead to different types of degradation, or a sharing out of the responsibility for causing it as poorer nations are able to increase consumption. Moreover, a key issue in North–South environmental diplomacy is that of 'catch-up': poorer Southern countries want the material benefits of development – refrigerators, washing machines, cars – that the affluent North has experienced. Why should they be denied these opportunities by accepting a steady-state economy? Yet catch-up for the South is certain to have some negative consequences for sustainability because it will inevitably result in higher levels of consumption.

It is also important to consider the impact of sustainability on social justice. Every policy aimed at resolving an environmental problem will have a distributional impact. The closure of a heavily polluting factory will have a negative distributional impact on the employees who will lose their jobs. A policy to reduce petrol consumption through fuel taxes or restrictions on car use will discriminate more heavily against someone who is dependent on a car, because they need it for work or they live in a remote rural area, than someone who has no car or who can easily switch to public transport. In short, there will be many occasions when a choice has to be made between social justice and sustainability.

A third argument suggests that social justice may have a close functional relationship with other components of the green programme, notably the steady-state economy, participatory democracy and decentralisation. A more egalitarian society may be an essential condition of the transition to a steady-state economy. Currently, the gross economic and social inequalities that are integral to capitalist accumulation and wealth creation are legitimated politically by a trickle-down effect that raises the absolute standard of living of low-income groups (even though relative poverty increases) and by a costly welfare state that provides a safety net for the very poorest members of society. This situation is made possible by continued economic growth and an ever-expanding economic pie, but would these inequalities still be acceptable if the economy were static? People may accept inequality when their own material lot is improving, but they are likely to resent it deeply if they are getting poorer in absolute terms. Moreover, the greater transparency of a democratic, decentralised sustainable society would make the persistence of inequality more obvious. Any shift to more frugal consumption patterns and simpler lifestyles is likely to prove more acceptable where everyone is seen to be making similar sacrifices; if not, inequality is likely to be a potential source of social conflict. If this argument holds true at the level of an individual country, it is even more valid on the international stage. Without a major reduction in intragenerational inequality between North and South, by means of debt relief, aid, technology transfer and reform of international trading agreements, there is likely to be only limited progress towards resolving global environmental problems (see Chapters 9 and 10).

The radical forms of participatory democracy and decentralisation desired by greens may also be unworkable without something approximating to equality of wealth and income. It is hard to envisage participatory democracy functioning effectively if the face-to-face interactions that it requires bring individuals of vastly different wealth (and hence power?) together on a regular basis. Indeed, the extension of participatory democracy across society, especially in the workplace, where it should result in narrower income differentials, will in itself contribute to greater equality, partly by making the many sources and forms of inequality more transparent to ordinary people and fuelling demands for their removal (Carter 1996). Similarly, it is more likely that decentralised communities would co-ordinate environmental policies and accept reductions in consumption if the standard of living in each was reasonably similar. The existence of significant disparities in material wealth might encourage poorer communities to seek economic parity with their neighbours.

Overall, there are good reasons for regarding social justice as a core green principle. Admittedly, the relationship between social justice and sustainability is complex and uncertain. Many environmental measures will have a negative impact on social justice; it is therefore incumbent on governments to ensure that disadvantaged groups are compensated in other ways. Nevertheless, on balance, greater equality should benefit sustainability both by alleviating poverty and by facilitating democratisation and decentralisation. Underpinning both arguments is the powerful pragmatic political imperative: 'no justice, no cooperation; no cooperation, no solution' (Connelly and Smith 2003: 31). This mantra of poor Southern nations has catapulted equity issues to the forefront of international environmental diplomacy (see Chapter 9). Similarly, equity considerations are critical in persuading individual citizens to support sustainable policies and become ecological citizens. In short, the pursuit of social justice is a core green principle because it should ease the transition to a sustainable society.

It has been argued in the preceding sections that participatory democracy, decentralisation and social justice (or reformed versions of these concepts) can be regarded as essential components of a sustainable society (and of the means of getting there), although the case for non-violence seems less persuasive. The discussion has also brought out the importance of *ecological citizenship* as a critical ingredient of a green theory of agency. This concept of ecological (or green or environmental) citizenship has attracted growing interest amongst green theorists (Barry 1996, 1999a; Christoff 1996a; Dobson 2003; Dobson and Sáiz 2005; Dobson and Bell 2006). Whichever theoretical approach is adopted (see Box 3.9), there is consensus over the need for active ecological citizenship because of the recognition that the transition to a sustainable society requires more than institutional restructuring: it also needs a transformation in the beliefs, attitudes and behaviour of individuals. Greens recognise that the radical changes necessary for sustainability are only possible if undertaken willingly by individual citizens. As Barry puts it, 'Citizenship . . . emphasizes the duty of citizens to take responsibility for their actions and choices – the obligation to "do one's bit" in the collective enterprise of achieving sustainability' (1999a: 231). Ecological citizenship needs to be nurtured at the level of the (reformed) state, through the deliberative processes engendered by democratisation, decentralisation and egalitarianism, but its effect would spill over from the political sphere into the realms of economic and social activity. This belief that human nature can be changed and preferences transformed – making people less individualistic and materialistic – is an important defining characteristic of ecologism, which, as the following section shows, shapes its relationship with other ideologies. Indeed, the above discussion shows how ecologism has

## 3.9 Ecological citizenship

Andrew Dobson (2003) argues that ecological citizenship is a particular form of post-cosmopolitan, non-territorial citizenship, which stresses responsibilities rather than rights, and regards those responsibilities as non-reciprocal rather than contractual, thereby contrasting with traditional liberal and civic republican notions of citizenship obligations. For him, ecological citizenship has four defining characteristics:

1. It is non-territorial. Conventional notions of citizenship are located within the nation state, but because many environmental problems are international and do not respect national boundaries, ecological citizens have to operate both within and beyond the state.

2. It takes place in both the public and the private realms. Citizenship is traditionally concerned with the way individuals behave in the public sphere, but the private acts associated with day-to-day lifestyles have public implications (by contributing to environmental degradation), so ecological citizenship must encompass the private realm.

3. It is associated with virtues that enable citizens to meet their obligations; in particular, the social justice needed to ensure a just distribution of ecological space, whilst care (and compassion) is required for the effective exercise of justice.

4. It involves a range of non-contractual responsibilities – notably an obligation to ensure that our ecological footprints are sustainable – that are owed to strangers near and far (including future generations), but without any expectation that they will be reciprocated.

Dobson's model of ecological citizenship has attracted a number of criticisms, such as for using the nebulous notion of 'post-cosmopolitan' citizenship and over who is eligible to be an ecological citizen. For greater detail, see the exchange between Dobson (2006) and Hayward (2006a, b) in *Environmental Politics*, vol. 15, no. 3.

been informed by contributions from different ideological traditions. This infusion of ideas raises questions about the distinctiveness of ecologism and its relationship with other political traditions.

## ◗ Traditional political ideologies and the green challenge

Ecologism is an ideology built on two main ideas: a reconceptualisation of the human–nature relationship away from strong anthropocentrism and an acceptance of the idea of limits to growth. It draws its subsidiary principles, such as participatory democracy, decentralisation and social justice, from other political traditions, but the relationship is not all one way. Ideas developed by ecologism have begun to influence established political ideologies. So, whereas the first part of this chapter showed how ecologism has given a green slant to concepts borrowed from other traditions, this second part shows how those other traditions have responded to the challenge posed by ecologism. The discussion starts with those political traditions based on individualism and a belief in social order – conservatism, liberalism, authoritarianism – and continues with those traditions that seek human emancipation through political, economic and social change – socialism, feminism, anarchism. It is argued that this second group of ideologies is closest to ecologism.

## ▶ *Conservatism and neo-liberalism*

There seems little in common between ecologism and the neo-liberal and conservative New Right with its enthusiasm for the market and the defence of the individual. Indeed, the New Right has been particularly hostile towards environmentalism (e.g. Ridley 1995; see also Paehlke 1989: ch. 8; Rowell 1996). Environmentalists are dismissed as 'doomsayers' and environmental regulations attacked for constraining free trade. The emergence of 'free market environmentalism' (Anderson and Leal 1991; Moran et al. 1991) reflected less a concern for the environment *per se* than an extension of a set of economic canons – the hegemony of the market and the sanctity of property rights – to incorporate a new problem. Environmental problems are blamed on the 'Tragedy of the Commons', which, it is argued, arises from the absence of clear, enforceable and tradeable property rights; put differently, the market solution is to privatise public goods, such as endangered species. The libertarian notion of justice based on entitlements contrasts sharply with the green conception of justice based on equity (see Box 3.8). In short, there is nothing that cannot be solved by the market; if there is an environmental problem, then trust the market to sort it out.[9]

Traditional conservative writing, although less overtly hostile, has also been critical of environmentalism: quick to condemn greens as dangerous radicals or socialists in disguise. Typically, green parties are compared to a water melon: 'green on the outside; red on the inside'. Yet there are many similarities between traditional conservatism and green principles (Pilbeam 2003; Scruton 2006). Both share a deep suspicion of Enlightenment ideas of progress and rationality, whilst drawing comfort from Romantic and nostalgic visions of a pre-industrial past. The principle of conservation – common to both doctrines – represents a desire to protect our historical inheritance and maintain the existing order for ourselves and for our descendants. As Scruton (2006) observes, 'Conservatism and conservation are in fact two aspects of a single long term policy, which is that of husbanding resources' (p. 8), by which he means social, material and economic capital. The conservative philosopher Edmund Burke stressed the importance of partnership between past, present and future generations. This idea informs the conservative notion of 'stewardship' – holding land in trust for the next generation and for the wider nation – which has something in common with future-generation arguments. Both doctrines display respect for stability and tradition. Change, where necessary, should involve organic, gradual adaptation, not revolution. The green 'precautionary principle' resonates with the conservative scepticism about radical technical or social experimentation.

Both doctrines reject liberal individualism, believing that individuals flourish best when embedded within strong, supportive communities. Overall, Gray (1993) observes that 'Concern for the integrity of the common environment, human as well as ecological, is most in harmony with the outlook of traditional conservatism' (p. 124).

Despite these affinities between conservatism and ecologism, the attempt by Gray (1993) to appropriate environmentalism for conservatism represents a rare exercise in linking the two doctrines.[10] This omission reflects a fundamental difference between the two traditions that Gray, in his attempt to 'rescue' environmentalism from its radicalism, rather misrepresents. Put simply, conservatism tends to see human nature as fixed and immutable whilst ecologism, as the discussion above showed, believes it is both possible and desirable to transform people. More broadly, whereas conservatism seeks to protect the status quo, ecologism seeks the radical transformation of the economic, political and social system. Core green principles, such as participatory democracy, egalitarianism and non-violence, contrast sharply with the conservative preference for authority, hierarchy and (where necessary) coercion. Conservatism has little to say about limits to growth and dismisses any attempt to extend value beyond humans. Not surprisingly, despite certain common ideas, ecologism and conservatism have drawn few explicit lessons from each other.

## ▶ *Classical liberalism*

The discussion of environmental ethics in the previous chapter showed how many green theorists have employed a liberal rights discourse or, following Bentham, mobilised utilitarian ideas to justify extending obligations to non-humans. It was John Stuart Mill, in his *Principles of Political Economy*, who first developed the idea of the steady-state economy, whilst several key liberal ideas such as toleration, deliberation and the civic society have informed ecologism.

Yet there is much in liberalism that seems incompatible with ecologism. Like conservatism, liberalism is '*incurably* anthropocentric: unable to appreciate nature as anything but resources' (Wissenburg 2006: 23). The centrality of the individual in liberal thought contrasts sharply with holistic arguments about interdependence. Whereas ecologism implies state intervention in pursuit of the common good, the liberal state is neutral, favouring no specific theory of the good and making no judgements about the ethical worth of different lifestyles (de-Shalit 2000: 92; Wissenburg 2006). Liberalism insists on the importance of individual property rights, with the implication that people should be allowed to pursue materialistic lifestyles and be free to use property as they choose. Liberal ideas such as representative government, market freedom and the pursuit of individual private gain sit uneasily alongside the green acceptance of collective solutions to environmental problems, intervention and the need for constraints on individual lifestyles (Martell 1994: 141).

Several political theorists have tried to 'rescue' liberalism for the environment, arguing that many of the apparent differences can be resolved (Wissenburg 1998, 2006; de-Shalit 2000: ch. 3; Stephens 2001; Bell 2002; Hailwood 2004). Typically, however, they still concede that fundamental differences remain. Wissenburg (2006), for example, argues that classical liberalism can be modified to accept limits to its neutrality and to rid itself of its neutral bias by, for example, conceding some institutional representation to non-human interests. Indeed, he claims that the question now is not '*whether*, but . . . *to what degree* can liberalism be green?' (p. 31), although he recognises that only some liberal thinkers have made significant moves in this direction. Moreover, he also acknowledges remaining differences, with liberalism committed to the importance of individual private property and unwilling to recommend any specific good life, specifically the frugal lifestyle of the sustainable society.

# ▶ *Authoritarianism*

The legacy of survivalism suggests that ecologism has more in common with authoritarian thinking, although this is a linkage that is distressing to most greens and seized upon by opponents to berate environmentalism.

It is important, first, to dismiss any suggestion that green politics can be linked to fascism, despite the best efforts of Anna Bramwell, one of whose polemics is entitled *Blood and Soil: Walther Darré and Hitler's 'Green Party'*. The Nazi enthusiasm for biological metaphors and spiritualism was reflected in their view of man as at one with nature, which is embodied in the idea of 'blood and soil', i.e. human attachment to land and place. The Nazis also set up nature reserves and experimented in deciduous reforestation, organic farming and alternative forms of energy. However, the vast bulk of Nazi ideas, principles and policies directly conflict with those of ecologism. The existence of a few 'ecological ideologues' does no more than show that National Socialism was open to ecological ideas; indeed, 'the ecologists were eventually seen as hostile to Germany's national interests' (Bramwell 1989: 205). The few similarities should not be over-exaggerated. As Vincent (1993) observes, just because the Nazis employed 'socialist methods or favoured ancient German traditions does not mean that either socialism or conservatism are eternally besmirched' (p. 266).

There is a stronger case for identifying an authoritarian wing within ecologism dating from the survivalist writings in the 1970s (see Box 3.1). Driven by their overriding preoccupation with human survival and strong sense of urgency, the survivalists were prepared to recommend strict government controls on individuals and organisations, even if it meant suppressing liberal values. Nevertheless, it has been argued above that the centrality of green principles of democracy and social justice effectively places these authoritarian perspectives outside the ambit of ecologism. Ironically, the main impact of survivalism was to provoke a reaction against this authoritarian strand of thinking, which gave green politics its powerful emancipatory character. Contemporary green theorists now go out of their way to distinguish themselves from the authoritarian tradition.

### ▶ *Socialism and Marxism*

Ecologism has an ambivalent relationship with socialism. Many greens emphasise the sharp differences between the two doctrines, in particular the socialist commitment to unconstrained economic growth, and they point to the poor environmental record of countries in the former Soviet bloc as evidence that socialist central planning is no better for the environment than capitalism. Indeed, Porritt (1984) regards both capitalism and socialism as forms of the 'super-ideology' of *industrialism*. Conversely, socialists condemn environmentalists for failing to recognise capitalism as the source of environmental ills and for seeking to protect middle-class privileges such as access to the countryside, whilst ignoring basic social issues such as poverty (Enzensberger 1974). However, several theorists have sought to build links between the opposing camps – often for reasons of practical politics – and the manifestation of this convergence is a body of writing known as *ecosocialism* (Gorz 1980; Frankel 1987; Ryle 1988; Benton 1993; Pepper 1993; Hayward 1995; Sarkar 1999).

There are, of course, several distinct traditions of socialism, which can be broadly divided into revolutionary doctrines, such as Marxism, and reformist approaches, such as social democracy. Most versions are characterised by two related features that seem to set socialism apart from ecologism: its anthropocentrism and its commitment to economic expansion. First, socialism, like capitalism, sits firmly in the Enlightenment tradition in striving for human mastery over nature and assuming that greater freedom will be achieved through material accumulation. Thus Marx believed that alienated humans could attain freedom by mastering, transforming and manipulating nature, none of which was tempered by any great concern for the non-human world. Contemporary Marxists have condemned green ideas such as the steady-state economy as regressive and anti-working class. Yet some socialists point out that mastery does not have to result in environmental destruction; it might imply a more ecologically benevolent notion of stewardship (Pepper 1993: 221). Others have tried to 'rescue' Marxism for ecology by, for example, reinterpreting his early writings on the dialectical theory of human–nature relations (Dickens 1992; Benton 1993).[11] Nevertheless, the socialist tradition, including ecosocialism, bases its concern for the environment firmly on human-centred motives, which suggests that there is little scope for reconciling the contrasting views of human–nature relations.

Secondly, socialism is committed to the pursuit of economic growth. Marxism anticipates human emancipation occurring in a communist utopia characterised by material *abundance* where the economic pie is sufficiently large to satisfy everyone's needs. By contrast, the utopian green sustainable society would experience some degree of material *scarcity*. Whereas socialists have little problem with economic growth and wealth creation *per se*, greens believe that in a finite planet unconstrained economic growth is simply unsustainable. Socialists argue that environmental ills should be blamed specifically on capitalism, not industrialism (and they dismiss the record of the former state socialist countries as irrelevant because they were never truly socialist). It is capitalism, characterised by the dominance of the competitive and dynamic market, the need to accumulate capital, the unbridled pursuit of profit, the use of destructive technologies and the hegemony of economic interests, which has created the contemporary ecological crisis. By creating new goods and wants, capitalism nurtures the consumerist ethos, whilst contributing to wider and deeper poverty, which socialists see as the underlying cause of environmental problems: 'It is the accumulation of wealth and its concentration into fewer and fewer hands which creates the levels of poverty that shape the lives of so many people on our planet, thus making it a major determinant of the environment which people experience' (Weston 1986: 5). Socialists despair that greens, with their 'naive' analysis of society, miss the real target, namely the capitalist system, its institutions and power relations.

It is on this second point that ecosocialism has started to build a bridge between socialism and ecologism. In particular, some writers in the ecosocialist tradition concede that there may be ecological limits to growth, and that unrestrained economic expansion is unsustainable (Ryle 1988; Benton 1993; Hayward 1995). If the central socialist goal of changing the ownership and control of the means of production is insufficient to prevent environmental degradation, then the assumption that material accumulation is the surest path to human emancipation is also brought into doubt. Ecosocialists argue that economic growth must take account of ecological limits and they challenge the 'productivity' ethos of industrial society (Ryle 1988). At a strategic level, the 'industrialism or capitalism' debate has little immediate significance because the global hegemony of capitalism, reinforced by the collapse of the Soviet bloc, clearly makes it the main adversary for both greens and socialists. Thus ecosocialism encourages greens to focus their attention on capitalism as the root cause of ecological problems.

The emergence of ecosocialism has encouraged a process of mutual learning on other issues too. Socialism presses greens to consider how change might be achieved when confronted by the institutions and power relations associated with global capitalism, such as multinational corporations, international financial markets and trade liberalisation. Ecologism is rather hazy about how the change to a sustainable society is to occur, and who will take the lead in bringing it about. Socialists question whether the green emphasis on changing individual values, lifestyles and consumption patterns, combined with a focus on micro-level community politics, is sufficient to overcome the might of global capital. Conversely, socialism has endured many setbacks since the 1980s, which combined with the decline of the industrial proletariat (the key agent for socialist change), have forced socialists to cast around for new allies. Not surprisingly, there seems to be considerable common ground with the ecological movement, as illustrated by the red–green coalitions that have emerged in several countries (see Chapter 5). The consensus between ecologism and socialism across a range of common core principles, notably social justice, equality and democratisation, has led theorists from both camps to explore the potential of new social movements and rainbow coalitions of issue movements – socialists, greens, feminists, anti-racists, gay rights – as agents for change (see Part II). Most socialists might agree with Gorz (1980) that 'the ecological movement is not an end in itself, but a stage in a larger struggle. It can throw up obstacles to capitalist development and force a number of changes' (p. 3). However, for now, socialists and greens share a common foe: capitalism.

Ecosocialists have also contributed to the reassessment of the role of the state within green political theory (Hayward 1995). Whilst greens traditionally distrust the state, socialists see it as playing a central role in bringing about social change. Socialist solutions to environmental problems mirror the approach to other problems: a reformist socialist strategy uses a central interventionist state to regulate the market to protect the environment whilst pursuing a social programme based on a redistribution of wealth, equality and collective ownership. As the earlier discussion of decentralisation and the state revealed, many greens now attribute a key role to the state in delivering environmental protection policies.

Finally, it would be wrong to over-emphasise the significance of ecosocialism within the socialist tradition. Ecosocialism tends to draw on a very narrow body of socialist ideas, namely, the 'decentralist, non-bureaucratic, non-productivist socialism' (Dobson 2000: 187) of utopian socialists such as William Morris, G. D. H. Cole and Robert Owen. Their vision of a decentralised, self-sufficient community has much in common with ecologism, but it is not the dominant position within socialism, where the centralist, labourist heritage represents a sharp cultural barrier between the two movements.

The dialogue between these two ideologies has been particularly lively. Ecologism has certainly been sharpened by the socialist critique of capitalism. Socialism has also taken on board some of the lessons of ecologism; indeed, many socialists would agree that 'A socialism for the 21st century must put at its heart the ecological challenge and escape from the limits of productivist thinking' (Mellor 2006: 36). Yet critical differences remain on key issues, such as attitudes to human–nature relations, and in the institutional and cultural manifestations of each movement.

## ▶ Feminism

Ecofeminists are keen to correct the tendency for green politics to ignore feminist issues.[12] The deep ecology movement, and especially the US group

Earth First!, is often criticised for 'misogynistic proclivities' and for being 'saturated with male bravado and macho posturing' (Seager 1993: 226–7). Yet many women are active within the green movement and opinion polls frequently show that women are more concerned about environmental issues than are men. Just as there is no doubting the important contribution made by women to green politics, neither can the vibrancy of the burgeoning ecofeminist discourse be contested, with at least four broad approaches to ecofeminism identifiable: liberal, cultural, social and socialist (Merchant 2005). Yet the lack of agreement about the central message of ecofeminism may have diluted its impact on ecologism. The main source of conflict has been the dominance within ecofeminism of the 'difference' approach, which has been widely attacked within mainstream feminism.

'Difference' feminism, rather than seeking equality within the existing patriarchal society, emphasises the virtues of attributes such as nurture, kindness and care that are specifically feminine in that they are generally possessed by women (King 1983; Collard 1988). 'Difference' ecofeminists claim that these feminine values and forms of behaviour are precisely what will be needed in a green society, as opposed to the individualistic, instrumental rationality of patriarchal society, which, ecofeminists argue, is primarily responsible for the current abuse of nature. In short, ecofeminists identify a set of female traits, value them positively, and argue that the environment would be better protected if everyone (men and women) developed these traits. Ecofeminists also draw parallels between the domination of nature and the domination of women. They claim that, as women are closer to nature, they can better empathise with and understand its problems 'because we recognise the many faces of oppression' (Collard 1988: 97). Combining these arguments, ecofeminists claim that to solve ecological problems we must first remove patriarchy.

The 'difference' approach has been attacked on a number of fronts. Many feminists shudder at the way ecofeminists celebrate precisely the kind of stereotypical female traits that most feminists blame for the subjugation of women in contemporary society. Feminists might sympathise with the sentiment that the traditional undervaluing of female characteristics such as motherhood needs to be rectified, and that men should be encouraged to develop female traits – 'feminising' men. Nevertheless, there is a danger that this may turn out to be a reactionary path which exposes women to strong social pressures to conform to those subservient female forms of behaviour that patriarchal society allocates to them. Moreover, the task of trying to identify gender-specific traits may be fruitless. After all, men often display so-called feminine traits and women exhibit 'masculine' traits. Even if we could identify male and female traits, not all female traits (submissiveness?) may be desirable, and not all male traits (courage?) undesirable (Dobson 2000: 191–2). Moreover, if feminine traits immutably belong to women because of their biological make-up, how can men be expected to develop them?

Underlying these criticisms is the fundamental objection that this entire exercise smacks of 'essentialism': that female traits are biologically derived and, therefore, the female character does not vary across time, culture, race or class (Sargisson 2001). Evans objects that this essentialist celebration of the natural – the idea that women's biology is their destiny – 'could entrench more or less every aspect of the female condition many of us have fought to renounce. Having fought to emerge from nature, we must not go back' (Evans 1993: 187). Alert to the dangers of essentialism, several ecofeminists have qualified the nature–female link by arguing that gender roles are socially rather than biologically produced (King 1989; Plumwood 1993; Seager 1993). If femininity is a social construction, then it follows that men could learn female traits. Plumwood (1993) argues that we need a model of a 'degendered' human consisting of traits that are independently chosen rather than based on either male or female characteristics.

Alternatively, several ecofeminists, like ecosocialists, argue that female oppression and environmental degradation are both inextricably tied up with the power structures of capitalist society (Biehl 1991; Mellor 1992, 1997; Salleh 1997). These writers argue that it is women's gender – the nature of women's work and their roles in society – rather than their biology that brings women closer to nature. Both women and nature are materially exploited, by patriarchy and by capitalist institutions and mechanisms. It is through their social location that women frequently bear the brunt of ecological devastation, particularly in less developed nations where women's issues and poverty go hand in hand. Indeed, women have initiated many collective grassroots struggles to defend their environment, as illustrated by the protests of the Chipko women in India who famously used the non-violent strategy of 'tree-hugging' to protect their forests from multinational timber companies (Shiva 1989). Wider solutions to these problems would require the transformation of capitalist society, but ecofeminism, with its predominantly philosophical orientation, has only slowly engaged with these issues.

Ecofeminism highlights the need to incorporate feminist concerns into green theory and, 'by tapping into women's rage and despair at the destruction of our planet' (Seager 1993: 252), it may provide a catalyst for environmental activism. However, ecofeminism has made only a limited contribution to ecologism because it offers no coherent vision of a green society and no clear strategy for feminist environmental action.

## ▶ Anarchism

The profound influence of anarchism on the development of ecologism has already been established.[13] Anarchist writers such as Bahro (1986), Bookchin and Sale have made a major contribution to the ecological critique of contemporary society, the model of a sustainable society and green theories of agency. Anarchism is, in many respects, the political tradition apparently closest to an ecological perspective and, conversely, contemporary anarchism is itself shaped by ecological concerns (Eckersley 1992: 145). Core green principles such as decentralisation, participatory democracy and social justice are central features of the anarchist tradition, and many greens have inherited the anarchist distrust of the state. Anarchists have also helped shape the praxis of green politics by advocating grassroots democracy, extra-parliamentary activities and direct action.

Two main schools of ecoanarchism can be distinguished (Eckersley 1992; Pepper 1993): 'social ecology', which is primarily the product of Murray Bookchin's (1980, 1982, 1989) extensive writings, and ecocommunalism, which is a general category incorporating a range of more ecocentric positions, including the bioregionalism of Sale (1980, 1991). Ecocommunalism focuses on the relationship between society and nature and, in recommending greater integration of human communities with their immediate natural environment (for example, living within the carrying capacity of their bioregion), is closely linked with deep ecology and the ecocentric ideas discussed in Chapter 2. By contrast, social ecology attributes ecological degradation primarily to social causes. The discussion below focuses on Bookchin's explicit linkage of social hierarchy and environmental problems because it has made a notable theoretical contribution to the emancipatory message of ecologism.

The core message of social ecology is that the human domination of nature stems from 'the very real domination of human by human' (Bookchin 1989: 44). Echoing the thinking of the nineteenth-century anarchist Peter Kropotkin, Bookchin has a benign view of nature based on the belief that it is interdependent and egalitarian – 'ecology recognises no hierarchy on the level of the ecosystem. There are no "kings of beasts" and no "lowly ants"' (Bookchin 1980: 59). Bookchin argues that humans are naturally co-operative and will flourish best in a decentralised, non-hierarchical anarchic society, such as early pre-literate societies, which, he claims, were organic and at one with nature, seeking neither to dominate nor be dominated by it. Subsequently, as social hierarchies developed based on age, gender, religion, class and race, so humans acquired the apparatus and aptitude for domination of other humans and, by extension, non-human nature. Today, domination and hierarchy characterise society and shape a range of related dualisms: intellectual over physical work, work over pleasure and mental control over the sensuous body. Social ecology seeks the replacement of domination and hierarchy with equality and freedom. In short, if social hierarchy can be removed, then environmental degradation will also disappear.

Bookchin's thesis is vulnerable to the empirical criticism that there have been many societies characterised by social hierarchy, which have also lived in harmony with nature, such as feudalism. Conversely, a non-hierarchical egalitarian society, such as Marx's post-capitalist utopia, might still exploit nature (Eckersley 1992: 151). Nevertheless, Bookchin contributes an important social element to ecocentric thinking, which is intended to rectify the mystical flavour of deep ecology. Indeed, Bookchin has engaged in a series of vicious attacks on deep ecology, which he describes disparagingly as 'mystical eco-la-la', for its insensitivity to social issues. He has little patience with the deep green belief that change will come about simply through a transformation of individual world-views stimulated by better spiritual connections with nature. He also despises the misanthropic flavour of some deep green writing, detecting support for coercive forms of population control, immigration and aid policy, and he has engaged in vitriolic debate with the former leading Earth First! activist Dave Foreman (Bookchin and Foreman 1991). Notwithstanding their mutual hostility, social ecology and ecocommunalism share important principles, notably their belief that the state is intrinsically inimical to green ecological and social values (Barry 1999a: 98). Despite the growing acceptance of liberal democratic institutions amongst greens, the anarchist critique of the bureaucratic, centralised state and commitment to local political action continue to wield a strong influence over green theory and practice.

---

### Critical question 5
Can green ideas be satisfactorily accommodated within established political ideologies?

---

## ◗ Neither left nor right but in front?

Greens like to describe themselves as 'neither left nor right but in front' because they want to affirm their difference from other ideologies. What do they mean by this claim and is it accurate? Is ecologism a distinct ideology? If so, can it accommodate the many different green discourses discussed above, and where is ecologism located on the classic left–right ideological spectrum? Or is it necessary to use different criteria to categorise it?

Ecologism is characterised by two core ideas: the need to reconceptualise the human–nature relationship and the acceptance of the idea of limits to growth. At this point, consensus breaks down. Some writers hold that ecological imperatives require no specific political structures (Enzensberger 1974; Ryle 1988; Goodin 1992). Ryle, for example, believes that 'widely varying forms' of sustainable society are possible, including 'authoritarian capitalist' and 'barrack socialism', which would both be a far cry from the green model outlined above (Ryle 1988: 7). Others believe that ecological imperatives do imply certain political forms and exclude others. Martell (1994: 160), for example, argues that intervention and central co-ordination are needed, thus ruling out markets, capitalism and decentralisation. By contrast, Dobson believes that 'there is something about ecologism . . . that pushes it irrevocably towards the left of the political spectrum' (Dobson 2000: 73) – a position that acknowledges the powerful influence of the emancipatory ideologies (Eckersley 1992).

## 3.10 The technocentric–ecocentric dimension

*Technocentric orientation*

- an adherence to cornucopian assumptions that there are no limits to growth
- an unrestrained commitment to economic growth
- scientific and technological optimism that human ingenuity will find an answer to every ecological problem
- a strong emphasis on material values and resistance to widening public participation in decision-making
- an anthropocentric world-view

*Ecocentric orientation*

- a belief that there are both ecological and social limits to growth
- a development philosophy that seeks to minimise resource use and operate within the carrying capacity of ecosystems
- an appreciation of the complexities of ecosystems and the limits to human understanding and elitist expertise; i.e. we cannot solve every problem and we must adopt a cautious approach to the use of technology
- the belief that materialism for its own sake is wrong and an emphasis on non-material values such as education, fellowship, civic responsibility, democratic participation and community
- an ecocentric respect for nature and a belief that all lifeforms should be given the opportunity to pursue their own destinies

Modelled on O'Riordan (1981).

It is helpful to illustrate the relationship between ecologism and other ideologies diagrammatically. Conventional political discourse is dominated by distributive issues: who gets what, when and how? Thus ideologies are typically categorised along the familiar left–right dimension according to the position they take on key political dualisms such as 'state v. market' or 'equality v. hierarchy'. In contrast, ecologism, whilst not denying the importance of distributional issues, is driven by an ecological imperative, which is not picked up by the left–right dimension. By adapting O'Riordan's classic **technocentric**–ecocentric dimension (Box 3.10), it is possible to categorise different ideologies according to their perspective on environmental issues (see Figure 3.1).

**Technocentric:** A mode of thought which optimistically believes that society can solve all environmental problems, using technology and science, and achieve unlimited material growth.

The technocentric–ecocentric dimension cuts across the left–right dimension, thus giving some force to the green claim to represent a fundamentally different approach to politics. This sharp distinction holds good as long as we focus on those two ideas of non-anthropocentrism and limits to growth. However, as soon as the broader set of green principles is introduced into the equation, the distinction becomes more blurred. In Figure 3.2 the relationship between ecologism and other ideologies is illustrated by superimposing the technocentric–ecocentric dimension onto the conventional left–right dimension (based on attitudes to state intervention in the market).[14] If ecologism consists of the core ecological imperative supplemented by green principles of democratisation, decentralisation and social justice, then the

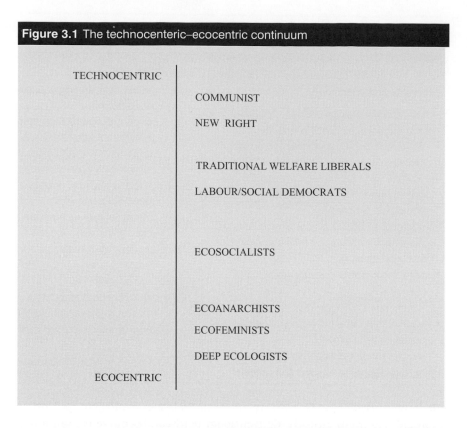

**Figure 3.1** The technocenteric–ecocentric continuum

TECHNOCENTRIC

COMMUNIST

NEW RIGHT

TRADITIONAL WELFARE LIBERALS

LABOUR/SOCIAL DEMOCRATS

ECOSOCIALISTS

ECOANARCHISTS

ECOFEMINISTS

DEEP ECOLOGISTS

ECOCENTRIC

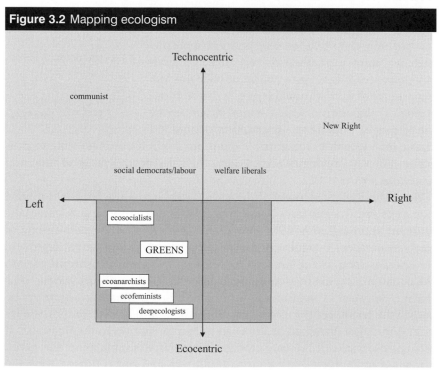

**Figure 3.2** Mapping ecologism

Technocentric

communist

New Right

social democrats/labour    welfare liberals

Left                                                                Right

ecosocialists

GREENS

ecoanarchists

ecofeminists

deepecologists

Ecocentric

shaded area in Figure 3.2 represents the broad area covered by ecologism. On this reading, ecologism clearly has most in common with those doctrines (socialism, anarchism, feminism) that (1) are critical of capitalism and have sought to transform it and (2) believe that human nature can and should be changed to make us less individualistic and less materialistic, although it has also drawn on reformist doctrines that seek to dilute the worst aspects of the market, such as welfare liberalism and social democracy. Thus ecologism stretches leftwards from just right of centre, but it does not reach the far left because greens want to control the market rather than remove it and their suspicion of the state means they reject any form of command economy. Ecologism goes no further to the right because sustainability is incompatible with an unfettered market economy. Moreover, greater participatory democracy and decentralisation would be impossible in either a command economy, by definition, or in a free market, where they would be curtailed by economic inequality and the capitalist dynamics of accumulation, competition and concentration. This approach leads to a conclusion that is slightly broader than that of Dobson: yes, ecologism does occupy broadly left-of-centre territory, but it draws in a wider range of perspectives than his anarchist–emancipatory framework. Although the model of a sustainable society outlined at the start of the chapter closely mirrored the ecoanarchist blueprint, the discussion of core green principles and the influence of other ideologies has highlighted weaknesses in this model and indicated the existence of several alternative perspectives *within* the green political arena. Indeed, it seems reasonable to expect that, just as there are many varieties of socialism, feminism and conservatism, the territory staked out by ecologism will have space for a range of green alternatives, including both the radical ecoanarchist and the 'pro-state' ecosocialist models.

This relatively relaxed approach to fixing the boundaries of ecologism is sensitive to the view that attempts to pin down a definitive 'correct' version of ecologism not only close down discussion (and put off potential adherents) but also understate the impact of green political theory on other political traditions. In this respect, there is much to commend Barry's (1999a) attempt to distinguish green political theory from the ideology of ecologism to enable a richer debate unencumbered by the need to adhere to a 'party line'.

Nevertheless, the central argument of this chapter is that the two core themes that underpin the ecological imperative (a reassessment of human–nature relations and the finitude of the Earth's resources), supplemented by a coherent set of principles drawn from other doctrines, is sufficient for us to talk legitimately about ecologism as an ideology in its own right. However, an important underlying theme is that many green theorists and activists have increasingly come to accept that liberal democracy is here to stay, so ecologism needs strategies for reforming it (Wissenburg 1998). It is this question that underpins the remainder of this book.

## ▶ *Further reading*

Dobson (2000) is the best introduction to ecologism, and is complemented by Barry (1999a), which includes good coverage of issues such as the green state, ecological citizenship and green political economy. Hay (2002) provides an exhaustive coverage of the many streams of thought influencing green political thought. Goodin (1992) is a clever and provocative book that demands attention. Dobson and Eckersley (2006) provides an excellent introduction both to the relationship between ecologism and other ideologies, and the way traditional political concepts have responded to the ecological challenge. For more detailed examination of the relationship between green theory and other ideologies, see Eckersley (1992), Pepper (1993), Hayward (1995) and de-Shalit (2000). Amongst the burgeoning literature relating green theory to traditional political concepts, see Smith (2003) on democracy, Eckersley (2004a) on the state and Dobson (1998, 1999) on justice. See the journals *Environmental Politics* and, for debates about the links between ecology and Marxism, socialism, anarchism and feminism, *Capitalism, Nature, Socialism*. Milbrath (1989) presents a fascinating vision of a sustainable society. Ernest Callenbach's novel *Ecotopia* offers one vision of a green 'utopia'.

NOTES

1 The *Limits to Growth* report was sponsored by the Club of Rome, a group of affluent industrialists, academics and civil servants.

2 The *Limits to Growth* report was so successful that it drew attention away from other important contemporary contributions, notably Georgescu-Roegen's (1971) work on the second law of thermodynamics. See Barry (1994).

3 Detailed discussions of future-generations arguments include Golding (1972), Barry (1991), Laslett and Fishkin (1992), de-Shalit (1995) and Dobson (1998, 1999).

4 Fuller discussions of the sustainable society can be found in Die Grünen (1983), Porritt (1984), Ekins (1986), Milbrath (1989), Goodin (1992), Tokar (1992), Pepper (1996), Barry (1999a) and Dobson (2000).

5 For a more detailed discussion of the green, or steady-state, economy, see Ekins (1986), Daly and Cobb (1990) and Barry (1999a).

6 Goodin's own theory of agency differs significantly from radical green perspectives in that he regards the liberal democratic central state as the best means of achieving green ends and he rejects (rather disparagingly) the green predilection for living simple individual lifestyles as misconceived and likely to detract from reaching green outcomes (Goodin 1992: 78–83, 120–3).

7 The discussion here focuses on political decentralisation rather than on the potential ecological benefits of a decentralised economy arising from small-scale production, appropriate technologies and reduced trade and travel.

8 McGinnis (1998) provides an introduction to bioregional writings.

9 For a critique of free-market environmentalism, see Eckersley (1993) and Barry (1999a: 150–5).

10 See also Wells (1978) and Scruton (2006).

11 For the relationship between Marxism and ecology, see also Grundmann (1991), Benton (1996), Barry (1998), Foster (2000) and Hughes (2000).

12 Good collections of ecofeminist writings include Caldecott and Leland (1983), Collard (1988), Plant (1989) and Warren (1994).

13 See Eckersley (1992), Pepper (1993) and Barry (1999a) for a wider discussion of ecoanarchism.

14 The contemporary blurring of left and right on their attitudes to the market undoubtedly reduces the usefulness of the state–market dimension, but it remains the dominant way of categorising ideologies. See also Paehlke (1989: 190) and Eckersley (1990).

# PART 2

# Parties and movements: getting from here to there

Part II examines the question of green agency; or how do we get from here to there? How do we achieve a sustainable society? One distinction to be made is that between collective action and individual lifestyle politics. The focus in Part II is on the main forms of collective action in environmental politics, namely green parties, the 'greening' of established parties and environmental groups, while the discussion of selected individual strategies, such as green consumerism, is left to Part III.[1]

A second distinction arises from the familiar *reformist* versus *radical* dilemma that underpins environmental politics. A broad strategic choice facing any political movement is whether to seek change through legislative institutions and the use of conventional forms of political activity or whether to adopt a more confrontational strategy that breaks the law and challenges the dominant rules and values of the political system. This tension lies at the heart of practical environmental politics: it underpins debates within green parties, colours their relationships with established parties and cuts across the wider environmental movement.

It is also important to place the rise of environmental politics within broader debates in political science about the trend towards a 'new politics' in advanced industrialised societies. To understand the 'new politics', we need first to understand what is meant by the 'old politics' that the 'new politics' is supposedly replacing. In the old politics, support for established parties is characterised by stable political cleavages and differences based on class, religion or regional divisions, of which the left–right pattern of partisan alignment is pre-eminent (Lipset and Rokkan 1967). The traditional values underlying political discourse relate to material issues of economics and security, such as economic growth, stable prices, public order, national security and the protection of traditional lifestyles. Political participation is low; for most people it extends no further than voting in national elections. Those citizens who are more active generally join movements such as trade unions or political parties, which pursue economic and political rights that will enhance the interests of their class.

Since the late 1960s, many observers have detected fundamental changes in the values and forms of political activity in industrialised nations. These changes, it is claimed, are transforming the issues that dominate the political agenda and creating new political cleavages which are contributing to a realignment of long-established party systems – the new politics (Inglehart 1990; Dalton 2006). There are three notable manifestations of this new politics. First, the emergence of **new social movements** (NSMs), such as the women's, peace, anti-nuclear and environmental movements,

> **New social movement:** A loose-knit organisation that seeks to influence public policy on an issue such as the environment, nuclear energy or peace, and which may use unconventional forms of political participation, including direct action, to achieve its aims.

which have been prepared to use unconventional forms of political participation, including civil disobedience and direct action, to achieve their aims. Secondly, the supporters of NSMs are drawn predominantly from what some theorists call a 'new middle class', of educated, professional service workers in industrialised societies. Lastly, a growing minority of citizens holds a set of postmaterial values emphasising equal rights, environmental quality and alternative lifestyles, which challenge the old materialist concerns of economic and physical security. If the new politics thesis is accurate, then it may help to explain contemporary environmental politics: from this perspective, green parties and environmental groups would be regarded as new social movements, most environmental activists would be from this new middle class, and environmental problems would be defined as postmaterial, quality-of-life issues. In short, a new politics account would interpret environmentalism as one element of a wider structural and cultural transformation of contemporary politics. One problem with such an approach is that it tends to denude environmental politics of its distinctive concern with ecological issues and dismisses the underlying 'objective' state of the environment as almost incidental in explaining its emergence.

These 'new politics' explanations are examined in detail in Chapter 4 to see whether they can account for the rise of green parties; they also inform the analysis of party politics and environmental groups in Chapters 5 and 6. It is argued that, whilst there is some mileage in the new politics thesis, it cannot alone provide an adequate explanation of contemporary environmental politics. Instead, Part II adopts a broad comparative approach to party politics and environmental groups, primarily in Europe and North America, with specific case studies of Germany, Britain, France and the USA, to argue that a range of institutional and political factors need to be included in any comprehensive analysis of environmental politics.

*Note*

1 There is also the radical option of attempting to opt out of capitalist society by setting
up alternative self-sufficient communities or green communes. Bahro (1986) makes
the case for communes and Pepper (1991) provides a study of commune experiments.
See Dobson (2000: ch. 4) for a wider discussion of strategies for change.

# Green parties: the rise of a new politics?

**4**

## Contents

## Key issues

▶ What is the 'new politics'?

▶ How can the emergence of green parties be explained?

▶ Who are the green voters?

▶ Why do people vote green?

▶ What factors explain variations in the electoral success of green parties?

Green parties have become a familiar feature of the political landscape, particularly in Europe. The first green parties were formed in Tasmania and New Zealand in 1972, and the Swiss elected the first green to a national assembly in 1979. By the late 1990s, green parties were sufficiently established to have joined national coalition governments in Belgium, Finland, France, Germany and Italy, to have deputies in several other national parliaments, and to be represented in sub-national chambers in many countries. In 2004, thirty-four Green MEPs from eleven countries were elected to the European Parliament. Several individual Green politicians have held high office, notably Joschka Fischer as German Foreign Minister and Michele Schreyer as the first Green European Commissioner between 1999 and 2004. The Greens have clearly arrived, and their message seems to have sufficient coherence and resonance to exert an electoral appeal that transcends national borders. How do we account for the rise of green parties? Do they simply reflect a specific public concern about the state of the environment, or are they part of a general shift towards a postmaterialist 'new politics'? To whom does the green message appeal? Why have green parties performed better in some countries than in others? Can green parties extend their appeal beyond a handful of rich industrialised nations? What is the impact of government participation on green electoral support? Are green parties here to stay or are they simply a 'flash party' that will soon disappear?

The chapter begins with a brief survey of green party electoral performance, identifying those countries where green parties have secured electoral success and those where they have not. The next section assesses three broad macro-level new politics explanations of green party development: new social movements, new class accounts and postmaterialism. These macro-level theories help explain the rise of green parties, but they cannot account for variations in green party success between countries. In the next section, the '**political opportunity structure**' (POS) framework, which combines these broad structural and cultural explanations with institutional factors such as the electoral system and party competition in individual countries, is applied to green party performance in Germany, France and the UK. Finally, although the POS framework does provide a more comprehensive and sensitive account, it can be criticised for underestimating the influence of ecological concerns in public support for green parties.

> **Political opportunity structure:** The dimensions of the political environment that either encourage people to use collective action or discourage them from doing so, and which shape the development of movements and parties.

## ▶ Green party electoral performance: an overview

Green parties have achieved their main electoral successes in Northern and Western Europe (see Table 4.1). In four countries – West Germany, Belgium, Switzerland and Luxembourg – green parties averaged at least 5 per cent of the vote during the 1980s and regularly won seats in national

## Table 4.1 Electoral performance of selected European green parties

| | First Green MP elected | Average % vote national elections | | | Number of MPs[a] |
|---|---|---|---|---|---|
| | | 1980s | 1990s | 2000–2006 | |
| Austria | 1986 | 4.0 | 6.0 | 10.3 | 21 |
| Belgium[b] | 1981 | 5.9 | 10.9 | 5.6 | 4 |
| Finland | 1983 | 2.8 | 6.9 | 8.0 | 14 |
| France | 1997 | 1.1 | 7.2 | 4.4 | 3 |
| Germany | 1983 | 5.1[c] | 6.3 | 8.4 | 51 |
| Ireland | 1989 | 1.0 | 2.1 | 3.7 | 6 |
| Italy | 1987 | 2.5 | 2.7 | 2.1 | 15 |
| Luxembourg | 1984 | 6.8 | 8.9 | 11.6 | 7 |
| Netherlands[d] | 1990 | – | 5.0 | 5.6 | 7 |
| Spain | 2004 | 0.9 | * | * | 1 |
| Sweden | 1988 | 2.9 | 4.3 | 4.9 | 19 |
| Switzerland | 1979 | 7.1 | 5.5 | 7.4 | 13 |
| UK | – | 0.3 | 0.5 | 0.9 | 0 |

*Notes:*
[a] At most recent election before January 2007.
[b] Combined results of Ecolo and Agalev/Groen!.
[c] This figure refers to West German elections.
[d] The figures refer to the Green Left, not the tiny De Groenen.
* There are several Spanish Green lists, so it is difficult to estimate their tiny vote.
*Source:* Keesings Archives.

parliaments. The German and Belgian greens have proved most successful. Germany boasts the largest and best-known green party, Die Grünen: it established itself as the third strongest German political party at the 1994 federal election and it joined with the Social Democrats to form a coalition government between 1998 and 2005.[1] The two Belgian green parties, the Flemish-speaking Groen! (formerly called Agalev) and French-speaking Ecolo, mirror the duplication of other Belgian parties on linguistic lines. After entering parliament in 1981 they steadily increased support, gaining a notable success in the 1999 election when a combined vote of 14.3 per cent and 20 MPs propelled them into governing coalitions at federal and sub-national levels. However, after four years in government both parties suffered a resounding defeat at the 2003 election, with Ecolo obtaining just four seats and Groen! failing to win a single seat. The Swiss Green Party is established as the largest alternative party outside the four-party government cartel.

In a second group of countries – Finland, France, Austria and the Netherlands – green parties did not average over 5 per cent of the vote in national elections until the 1990s. The Finnish Green League was the first green party to join a national government in 1995 and, after strengthening its position, it remained in the rainbow coalition government after the 1999 election. The Green League resigned from the coalition in 2002 after the Finnish parliament supported the government's decision to commission a new nuclear power station, but it achieved its best electoral performance in 2003 winning 8 per cent of the vote and fourteen seats. In France, Les Verts gained its first seven deputies in 1997 and joined the Lionel Jospin socialist-led coalition government, but the defeat of the government in 2002 saw Les Verts slip to three deputies. The Austrian Alternative Grüne Österreich (ALÖ), having absorbed most members of the moderate ecological party Vereinigte Grüne Österreich (VGÖ) in 1986, is now well established, gaining 11.1 per cent and twenty-one MPs in the 2006 election, making it the third largest party. In the Netherlands, a small 'dark' green party, De Groenen, has been completely eclipsed by the merger in 1990 of four small left-of-centre parties – communists, pacifists, radicals and an evangelical party – to form the Green Left. Although slow to take off, in 1998 it gained 7.3 per cent of the vote, slipping slightly by 2006 to 4.6 per cent and seven MPs. In addition to these 'successful' parties, the Swedish Miljopartiet entered parliament in 1988 and whilst it fell below the 4 per cent threshold in 1991, it has managed to remain just above the threshold since 1994, obtaining 5.2 per cent of the vote and nineteen seats in 2006.

Elsewhere, other European green parties have struggled to secure a firm electoral platform. The Italian Greens have consistently averaged around 2 per cent of the vote, yet they spent five years in the centre-left Olivo government between 1996 and 2001, and, after five years in opposition, they gained 2.1 per cent and fifteen MPs in 2006 as part of the centre-left alliance that formed the Prodi-led coalition government. The Irish Comhaontas Glas has grown steadily stronger, tripling its representation to six MPs in 2002. Green politics in Spain is highly factionalised: a national green party, Los Verdes, was not formed until 1992, although several other green lists are to be found in every national election. In 2004 Los Verdes agreed a coalition list with the Socialists and won its first seat. Another group of countries, including Britain, Norway and Denmark, have yet to elect a Green MP. It is debatable whether the Portuguese Os Verdes, which contests elections in coalition with the Communists, is a genuinely distinct party. Further afield, Greens have been elected to national assemblies in a disparate range of countries including the Czech Republic, Estonia, Latvia, Lithuania, Slovakia, Ukraine and Mexico. New Zealand boasts probably the most successful non-European green party, with six MPs elected in 2005. The absence of a single national green party in Australia has hampered progress, although a handful of Greens have been elected to the Senate and to state parliaments, notably in Tasmania. Green parties have had little success in North America, although the veteran consumer campaigner Ralph Nader attracted almost three million votes (2.7 per cent) on a green ticket in the 2000 US presidential election (see Box 5.5). In April 2006 there were over 232 greens holding minor elected office across twenty-eight American states (Green Party 2006).

This brief overview of green parties raises two main questions. How can the rise of green parties in recent years be explained? Why have they met with such variable electoral success? The following section assesses whether the 'new politics' thesis can account for the rise of green parties.

# ▶ Is there a new politics?

This section analyses the main components of the new politics thesis – the rise of new social movements, the emergence of a new middle class and the flourishing of postmaterial values – before assessing their contribution to the rise of green parties.

## ▶ *New social movements?*

'New social movements' (NSMs), notably the student, peace, anti-nuclear, feminist and environmental movements, were responsible for a major part of the collective social protest that swept Western Europe from the late 1960s. Scott (1990) distinguishes NSMs from old social movements, such as trade unions, according to their location, aims, organisational form and medium of action. First, while trade unions are located within the polity and typically seek to influence social democratic and labour parties, NSMs bypass the state by operating outside the established parties, trying to mobilise civil society rather than win power. Secondly, the aims of trade unions have been political integration, legislative reform and economic rights for workers, whereas NSMs focus on defending civil society against excessive political power (particularly of the state) and seek cultural changes to values and lifestyles. NSMs question the materialist assumptions, such as economic growth, that underpin the ideology of those movements representing capital and labour. Thirdly, trade unions adopt the bureaucratic and hierarchical forms of organisation prevalent in society, while NSMs are usually informal, decentralised and participatory organisations. Finally, trade unions generally work within the existing political institutions, whereas NSMs adopt innovative repertoires of action, including confrontation and direct action, often outside the law (see Box 4.1).

This characterisation of the NSM as participatory, issue-specific and geared to the mobilisation of public opinion, is an ideal type based on the NSM in its most radical and fundamentalist form. One obvious problem, therefore, is that it presents a snapshot of the NSM at one moment – its initial stage – when it 'has all the optimism of a new movement grounded in recent mobilisation, before the movement must reflect upon how it is to affect the social and political environment' (Scott 1990: 154). Once established, movements make compromises, usually by gradually adopting conventional organisational structures and strategies.

## 4.1 New social movements

There are two broad approaches to the study of social movements, commonly termed the European and American approaches (Klandermans and Tarrow 1988).

The *European* approach focuses on the structural transformations underpinning the rise of NSMs, i.e. *why* people take action in this way. Some theorists have made grand claims about their significance, suggesting that NSMs represent a radical new form of class politics (Touraine 1981), or that, in the modern information age, NSMs have a symbolic resonance reaching far beyond the scale of their activities (Melucci 1989).

The *American* approach, notably Resource Mobilisation Theory, sees politics as the mobilisation of resources. It examines *how* groups pursue goals by focusing on the role of organisation and of political entrepreneurs in turning grievances into political issues.

The *political opportunity structure* framework attempts to integrate these contrasting approaches by combining broad structural and cultural arguments with institutional factors.

These compromises have been so far-reaching that, 'by the end of the eighties, most of the new social movements in Western Europe appeared to be pragmatic reformist movements . . . closely connected to established politics in various dimensions' (Kriesi et al. 1995: xxi). It seemed that some of the more grandiose claims about the radical potential of NSMs (e.g. Touraine 1981; Melucci 1989) were misplaced. Nevertheless, the existence of a dynamic NSM milieu may provide an important *institutional* factor shaping the development of a green party.

▶ *Environmentalism as middle-class elitism?*

This explanation of the new politics focuses on fundamental changes in the economic and social *structures* of advanced capitalist societies in the post-war era. The contraction of traditional manufacturing industry and the growth of the service sector produced a major shift in occupational structures, with the decline in the traditional blue-collar working class mirrored by an expansion of the white-collar sector. Other factors, including improved material standards of living, the massive expansion of higher education and the information revolution, have also contributed to the blurring of traditional class divisions and loyalties in the 'postindustrial society' (Bell 1973). Some writers claim that a new middle class has emerged: highly educated, filling professional and welfare jobs and economically secure (Gouldner 1979; Kriesi 1993). It is argued that this new class is in some respects more alienated from the political system than the traditional working class and, crucially, more able and willing to criticise the established parties, the bureaucracy and the dominant materialist agenda.

The relevance of the 'new class' thesis to the study of environmental politics lies in the empirical claim that participants in new social movements generally, and environmentalists in particular, are predominantly drawn from the new middle class (Cotgrove 1982; Morrison and Dunlap 1986;

Rootes 1995a). Offe (1985) adds that two other groups are also active in NSMs: first, 'decommodified' groups who are peripheral to the labour market, such as students, housewives, pensioners and the unemployed; second, members of the 'old' middle class who are independent and self-employed, such as farmers, shop-owners and artisans. Significantly, all these groups fall outside the two traditional classes of capital and labour (i.e. the industrial working class).

New class explanations of NSMs assume that, as classes have interests, the domination of environmentalism by the new middle class must represent an attempt to further its own class interests. Indeed, some socialists have sought to dismiss environmentalism as an expression of middle-class elitism (Enzensberger 1974). However, class interest arguments are fraught with problems. In the first place, why should environmentalism serve exclusively middle-class interests? All classes suffer the consequences of pollution; indeed, it is usually the poorest and most disadvantaged groups who suffer the most direct and worst problems of environmental degradation and pollution in the workplace and in inner-city communities (Bullard 2000). Cotgrove (1982) suggests that the location of the new middle class in the non-productive sector marginalises it from the processes of decision-making at the economic and productive core of society. Hence new-middle-class frustration at its own powerlessness is manifested in protest activity and involvement in NSMs. It is not clear, however, why members of the new middle class feel alienated when, by definition, they are usually fully employed in professional and administrative jobs (Eckersley 1989). Alternatively, McAdams (1987) argues that they have an interest in the expansion of government, not least because it provides so many of the professional and welfare jobs they hold. Yet this argument cannot support the view that middle-class involvement in environmentalism is an expression of class interest because green arguments for slower economic growth threaten future expansion of the non-productive service sector, which employs so many of them. Thus, as Martell (1994) observes, new-middle-class concern for the environment may be 'class-based, but does not seem to be class-driven' (p. 130); there may be a disproportionate number of new-middle-class environmentalists, but there is no convincing argument why that concern should be in the material interests of that particular class.

Instead, it may be that the welfare professions encourage 'the development of emancipatory occupational cultures among radicals working in these fields' (Doherty 2002: 61); in other words, the nature of the job – notably its autonomy, its ambiguous role within capitalist society and its essentially political nature – nurtures the kinds of attitudes and values that make the new middle classes receptive to environmentalism. On the other hand, the causal relationship may operate in reverse, so that individuals with predisposed attitudes and values may be drawn to the welfare professions. If so, what is the origin of those attitudes? One possible explanation is provided by the postmaterialist thesis.

### ◗ *Environmentalism as postmaterialism?*

This explanation for the rise of green parties focuses on changes in the political culture and values of industrialised countries. Inglehart (1977, 1990) is the leading exponent of the postmaterialist thesis. He claims that there has been a 'silent revolution' involving 'the basic value priorities of Western publics . . . shifting from a Materialist emphasis toward a Postmaterialist one – from giving top priority to physical sustenance and safety toward heavier emphasis on belonging, self-expression and the quality of life' (Inglehart 1990: 66). This argument contains two core components: the scarcity hypothesis and the socialisation hypothesis. The *scarcity* hypothesis, modelled on Maslow's (1954) psychological theory of human motivation, claims that people place a higher priority on things that are in short supply. Inglehart argues that the post-war era of steady economic growth and unparalleled affluence produced a generation of young people who took their economic well-being for granted. When the lower-order needs of economic and physical security are satisfied, people direct attention to higher-order 'quality of life', or postmaterial, needs, such as the environment. According to Inglehart, the ascendancy of postmaterial values does not arise from individuals actually changing their values, but through the *socialisation* of a new generation that lives its formative, pre-adult, years in affluent times. Inglehart initially developed this theory to account for the student unrest that swept across the Western world in the late 1960s. Subsequently, it has been used to explain the dealignment of traditional partisan voting patterns, the involvement of this postmaterial generation in NSMs and the emergence of green parties: 'The rise of the West German Greens . . . reflects both the emergence of a Postmaterialist constituency whose outlook is not captured by the existing political parties and the emergence of a growing pool of voters who are politicized but do not feel tied to established parties' (Inglehart 1990: 369).

Although Inglehart's theory has gained many adherents, it has also been subjected to a barrage of criticisms, particularly aimed at the two hypotheses underpinning the model, and the methodology he devised to measure postmaterialism (see Box 4.2).[2] The scarcity hypothesis assumes that the satisfaction of material needs encourages individuals to shift attention to postmaterial values. Yet the hierarchy of needs adopts a static definition of those material needs – a roof over our heads, food on our plates, money in our pockets, the protection of law and order – when, in the modern consumer society, with greater affluence and an ever increasing range of available goods, our appetite for more and more material goods may be insatiable. Our definition of basic needs is steadily broadening: a washing machine was a luxury item in the 1960s, but many would now consider it a basic item – along with the dishwasher, computer and mobile phone. In short, greater affluence may simply encourage further materialism rather than nurture postmaterial values.

## 4.2 Measuring postmaterialism

Inglehart's methodology for measuring postmaterialism asks people to select their two most important goals from four options:

1. maintain order in the nation;
2. give people more say in the decisions of government;
3. fight rising prices;
4. protect freedom of speech.

Anyone choosing the second and fourth options is classified as a postmaterialist while someone choosing the first and third options is a materialist. All other combinations are placed in a 'mixed' category. Inglehart (1990) produced extensive comparative research across twenty-four countries to support his claim that Americans and Western Europeans have become substantially more postmaterialist since 1970 and he predicted that this trend will continue. A 1993 European survey found that postmaterialists are still in a minority and, almost everywhere, are outnumbered by materialists.

| % classified as | Germany | Britain | Italy | Spain |
|---|---|---|---|---|
| Postmaterialist | 23 | 11 | 12 | 12 |
| Mixed | 56 | 63 | 62 | 57 |
| Materialist | 21 | 26 | 25 | 31 |

*Source:* Bryson and Curtice (1998: 130).

*Methodological concerns*

1. Is it possible to make confident categorisations of individual value priorities on the basis of such a narrow battery of items?
2. The four-item battery contains no environmental item. Even Inglehart's expanded, but rarely used, twelve-item battery contains just one explicitly environmental item: 'trying to make our cities and countryside more beautiful'. How helpful is such a limited measure in evaluating why people vote green?

Inglehart bases the socialisation hypothesis on the critical pre-adult years, and largely dismisses the impact of any adult economic insecurity on values. His prediction that the proportion of postmaterialists will continue to rise rather downplays the impact of widespread economic insecurity during the 1970s and 1980s on subsequent cohorts. Even putting methodological objections aside and accepting that postmaterialism has increased, can this change be explained by the scarcity and socialisation hypotheses? Rather than NSMs being a product of postmaterialism, value change may actually be rooted in the NSM milieu. Instead of better living standards generating postmaterialism (and this brings us full circle), perhaps the growth of welfare-oriented jobs in education and public health has engendered value change (Martell 1994: 125; Doherty 2002: 61–3). On the specific question of the environment, the key variable linked to increased concern about the environment is experience of higher education, presumably because it helps people to process more information, enhances their job prospects and material security, and encourages a wider critical perspective (Offe 1985; Eckersley 1989; Rootes 1995a). A further problem with the postmaterialist thesis is that 'if environmentalism is simply a question of values, then environmental conflict is a conflict without interests' (Andersen 1990: 104–5). Yet the opponents of environmentalism are not individuals who simply hold different values, such as a preference for economic growth; rather, they are usually economic actors (employers, farmers, trade unions) who perceive their material interests (profits, livelihoods, jobs) as directly threatened by green measures. Notwithstanding these criticisms, there is sufficient empirical evidence of a spread of postmaterial values at least to treat it seriously as one partial explanation of the emergence of environmentalism.

The next section assesses how far these three broad 'new politics' arguments can account for the rise of green parties.

---

### Critical question 1
Is the environment a postmaterial or material issue?

---

## ▶ Green parties as new politics?

*New social movement* activity was certainly a catalyst for the development of green parties in some countries. The broad coalition of environmental and leftist groups that formed the anti-nuclear movements of the 1970s and 1980s was particularly conducive to green party formation in Germany, France, Luxembourg and Finland, and in Austria and Sweden green parties emerged from referendum campaigns against nuclear power (Rootes 1995b: 237). 'Eco-pax' coalitions between the environmental and the peace movements were also important, especially in Germany. The radical principles of NSM activists left a strong imprint on some green parties, notably the German Greens, which informed their reluctance to work with mainstream parties, the preference for participatory, decentralised organisational structures and a willingness to use extra-parliamentary action to achieve their aims. Nevertheless, although undoubtedly influenced by the counter-cultural NSM milieu, green parties cannot be regarded as NSMs. Just by contesting elections and operating within the political system, green parties set themselves clearly apart from the ideal-type NSM. Internal tensions over the extent to which green parties should engage with established political parties and institutions (see Chapter 5) are essentially about the *degree* of compromise, when the real compromise was the decision to form a party in the first place. Several green parties, notably in the UK, Ireland, Sweden and throughout Eastern Europe, are not rooted in the NSM milieu, which suggests that environmental concern may be qualitatively different from NSM concerns such as gender, race or peace (none of which has, with the odd exception, spawned its own political party).

Most European green parties do attract support overwhelmingly from new-middle-class voters. Academic studies and opinion polls show conclusively that, compared to supporters of other parties, green voters are younger, better educated, less likely to attend church and more likely to hold public sector and/or white-collar jobs (Müller-Rommel 1989, 1990; Richardson and

Rootes 1995). A detailed picture emerges from Germany which, because of the success of Die Grünen, has been subjected to intensive analysis. Here, until the mid-1990s, the majority of green voters were under thirty-six even though only one-third of the total German electorate was in that age group (Poguntke 1993; Scharf 1994: 79–89; Dalton and Bürklin 1996). Die Grünen has always drawn a disproportionately large share of support, around 50 per cent, from students and white-collar workers; conversely, it attracts relatively few older voters and blue-collar workers (Poguntke 1993; Dalton and Bürklin 1996; Gibowski 1999: 24–5). Greens are well educated: about half of green voters have gained an *Abitur* – which qualifies someone to enter university – compared to a national average of around a quarter (Poguntke 1993). The profiles of green electorates elsewhere, such as Austria (Lauber 2003: 140) and Finland, look remarkably similar. One study found that the Finnish Green League are 'the female-dominated party of the average to highly educated, and the relatively young, new middle classes' (Zilliacus 2001: 50).

Green party activists have an even more distinctive socio-economic profile. A 1990 survey of the UK Green Party reported that the typical member 'is 41 . . . has a university degree in an arts or social science subject (but not engineering, business or law), is an owner-occupier, and works as a "professional" in the public sector, most likely in education' (Rüdig et al. 1991: 30), a profile that had changed little by 2002 (Bennie 2004: ch. 8). Similar profiles were found in studies of Dutch (Voerman 1995), Belgian (Kitschelt 1989) and German (ibid.; Poguntke 1993) activists.

Greens, therefore, do seem to be drawn disproportionately from the so-called new middle class but, if Inglehart is right, they should also hold a wide range of postmaterial values. However, whilst levels of postmaterialism are high among party activists – 94 per cent of German Green Party delegates (Poguntke 1993: 93) and 74 per cent of Dutch Green Left delegates (Lucardie et al. 1995: 100) – the relationship is weaker in the wider electorate. German (Poguntke 1993: 58) and Dutch green voters do display a clear postmaterial orientation, but elsewhere green voters hold a broad spread of both material and postmaterial concerns, with the environment as the one theme in common (Jehlicka 1994). Typically, the evidence is suggestive rather than conclusive. In Sweden, for example, green voters are slightly more postmaterialist than those voting for other parties, but the statistical association is no more than 'modest' (Bennulf 1995: 135). More broadly, several surveys raise serious doubts about the existence of a direct link between postmaterial values and environmental concern (Nas 1995; Bryson and Curtice 1998).

These findings hint at a deeper problem with postmaterialist accounts of environmental politics: is it accurate to define all ecological hazards as postmaterialist concerns (Nas 1995: 288; Rootes 1997: 320–1)? Many environmental issues – about the safety of nuclear power and GM crops, or the links between air pollution and asthma – could all reasonably be defined as materialist problems because they affect personal security and health. As Beck (1992) has argued, people are increasingly motivated by the growing perception that we live in a 'risk society'. If so, perhaps the attachment to green politics is partly prompted by old-fashioned materialist values (albeit in a new guise), rather than, as Inglehart claims, the emergence of a new set of value priorities. Not least, this interpretation might explain why many 'materialists' vote for green parties.

On balance, 'new politics' arguments do help explain the rise of green parties; in particular, there is a remarkable cross-national uniformity in the socio-economic profile of green support. However, Inglehart's cultural explanation of green politics as reflecting the emergence of postmaterialist values remains unproven. Indeed, the socio-economic profile of green support suggests possible alternative explanations for the rise of green parties. The large number of greens with higher education lends support to Eckersley's (1989) claim that this variable may be critical. Also, while most greens do have reasonable economic security (or the prospect of future security), they tend to be located on the margins of society. This is not to say, as some have argued (Alber 1989; Bürklin 1987), that greens are profoundly alienated from society, for they clearly are not; teachers and social workers may not always represent the dominant values in society, but neither are they outsiders. However, many greens are shielded from the productive private sector of the economy where growth and its materialist spin-offs are central considerations. Whether this detachment is deliberately chosen by people already concerned by environmental issues, or reflects the experiences of working in specific occupations and sectors of the economy, is difficult to ascertain. However, it bodes well for the future prospects of the greens that they draw heavily for support on sectors of society – higher education, the service sector, health and welfare – that are expanding.

Conversely, there is growing evidence that the green vote in some countries is getting older, or 'greying'. Whereas 70.5 per cent of German Green voters were under thirty-five in 1980, by 1994 it was 51 per cent and in 2005 just 27.5 per cent (Hoffman 1999: 143; Federal Statistical Office 2006). In the 2002 federal election the Greens made most gains in older age groups and drew their biggest ever share of the 45–59 and 65 plus age groups (Saalfeld 2004: 186–7). This trend was repeated in the 2005 election with the share of Green voters in these two groups reaching 27.8 per cent and 16.0 per cent respectively (Federal Statistical Office 2006). Voters seem to have remained loyal to Die Grünen as they have got older, but the party is now less successful at recruiting first-time voters; so the centre of gravity of the party has shifted into the top end of the 35–45 age bracket. The same is true in Finland where the Green League, whilst still the prime representative of new politics, increasingly draws support from older voters, as well as a wider, more 'average', social base (Zilliacus 2001: 40–1). Perhaps there is a cohort of green voters working its way through the system who joined the student protests in the late 1960s and provided the NSM activists during the following two decades? If so, it could be bad for the long-term prospects of green parties. However, as yet there is insufficient evidence to confirm that greying is a universal trend. Indeed, there are several reasons why green parties might expect to remain popular with young voters. Voting green, particularly where the greens have not yet entered government, still represents a protest vote against the established parties and values, as shown by the success of the Belgian Greens in the 1999 national election and the popularity of Ralph Nader in the 2000 US presidential election. The increasing integration of environmental issues into the public domain, especially through the educational curriculum, should ensure that younger generations have a higher level of knowledge and understanding than older generations. Consequently, one speculative hypothesis is that, while older green supporters may be predominantly postmaterialist in outlook, the new generation of younger voters may be less postmaterialist, but influenced by a specific concern about the environment.

To summarise, new politics arguments identifying structural and cultural trends can provide only broad-brush, macro-level explanations for the rise of green parties. They do not account for differences between countries. This weakness can be illustrated by Inglehart's (1990: 93) own data. He reports that in the mid-1980s the three European countries with the highest proportion of postmaterialists were the Netherlands (25 per cent), West Germany (24 per cent) and Denmark (18 per cent). Yet green party development in these countries contrasts sharply: while Die Grünen has long been the leading light of the green movement, the Dutch Green Left only made a significant electoral breakthrough in the late 1990s while the Danish greens are so weak that they do not even contest national elections. Furthermore, there was an identical number of postmaterialists (15 per cent) in both Belgium and the UK, but while the Belgian green parties have achieved significant electoral successes, the Green Party in Britain has a dismal record in general elections. So, why have green parties developed earlier in some countries than in others, and why is their electoral performance so variable?

---

### Critical question 2
Is green politics a middle-class issue?

---

## ▶ The political opportunity structure and green party success

The political opportunity structure (POS) is a useful framework for analysing green party development because it looks beyond the broad macro variables that underpin the new politics thesis. The POS is concerned with the 'dimensions of the political environment which either encourage or discourage people from using collective action' (Tarrow 1994: 18).[3] Each writer tends to use a different combination of variables. The discussion here employs a model of the POS based on the work of Kitschelt (1986, 1988, 1990), who has used it to study green parties. His model incorporates the broad structural factors underpinning the new politics thesis, such as the development of modern welfare capitalism and contemporary economic prosperity, but draws particular attention to the institutional and political factors that might determine the openness of a political system to green parties. These include NSM activity, the form of electoral system, the nature of party competition and the existence of precipitating issues, such as the anti-nuclear protests, that may act as a catalyst for the emergence and development of a green party. The following short case studies of green party development in Germany, France and Britain focus on these critical features of the POS that help account for variations in green party performance.

### ▶ Germany[4]

Die Grünen has played a pioneering role in the development of the green movement. After entering parliament in 1983, it rapidly established itself in the German political system. After a blip in the 1990 post-unification election, when no Greens were returned in the former West Germany, the Greens edged past the liberal Free Democrats Party (FDP) to finish third in the 1994, 1998 and 2002 federal elections. Thus since the mid-1990s the party has become a serious political power-broker as a potential coalition partner for one of the two major parties, the Social Democrats (SPD) or the Christian Democrats (CDU). After the 1998 federal election the Greens joined the Social Democrats in a red–green government coalition until its defeat in 2005. Although attracting 8.1 per cent of the list vote in 2005 – only fractionally lower than in 2002 – the Greens slipped to fifth behind the FDP (9.8 per cent) and the new Left Party (8.7 per cent).

Die Grünen was rooted in social movement activity dating from the late 1960s and 1970s. Leading elements included a long-lasting student movement, citizen action groups (protesting about issues such as housing shortages, high rents and pollution), the anti-nuclear-power and women's movements. Many green activists were involved in the large peace movement, which campaigned against the siting of Pershing and Cruise missiles in Europe, and their 'eco-pax' agenda shaped the development of green ideology and practice. The acid rain issue was an important precipitating condition for the general increase in public concern about the environment in the early 1980s.

The electoral rules have generally proved very helpful to the Greens. German electoral law refunds campaign costs to any party gaining more than 0.5 per cent of the votes. Thus, from its early days the party was able to develop a national organisational structure without needing to attract rich sponsors. The additional member electoral system gives representation to every party receiving at least 5 per cent of the votes. This threshold was sufficiently low to be attainable, yet high enough to act as a force for unity for the disparate collection of green groups that mushroomed throughout West Germany in the late 1970s before forming Die Grünen in 1980. Progress was so rapid that the Greens gained twenty-seven MPs with 5.6 per cent of the vote in the 1983 federal election, matched by similar successes in subnational government. Subsequently, the party's progress was hampered by internal factionalism but, after the shock of losing all its deputies in the 1990 federal election, the discipline brought by the electoral rules enabled the moderate 'Realist' (see Box 5.2) wing of the party to win control of the party and push through a range of organisational reforms, a more moderate programme and a merger with the East German Bundnis 90. The federal structure of the German political system provided multiple access points for the Greens, enabling it to win seats in the *Länder* (states), which gave the party early publicity and credibility, and later acted as a laboratory for red–green coalitions with the SPD. European parliamentary elections have provided further electoral opportunities, with the Greens usually polling more strongly than in federal elections. The presence of a large and vocal group of Green MEPs in the European Parliament since 1984 gave the party another political platform (Bomberg 1998a).

The actions of the Green Party have also influenced its electoral success, notably its ideological development, internal party struggles and its performance in government. Ironically, for a party that is uneasy with the idea of leadership and suspicious of charismatic personalities, the Greens have produced two of the most popular and well-known German politicians of recent times, Petra Kelly and Joschka Fischer.

The Greens benefited from the political vacuum on the left of the German party system. The SPD – the leading left-wing party – shifted to the centre after a series of electoral defeats in the 1950s. As the dominant party in government between 1969 and 1982 it largely eschewed its socialist roots, to the despair of NSM activists. Consequently, in the absence of a communist party the Greens were able to fill the space to the left of the SPD by offering a new home for a sizeable constituency of disenfranchised leftists. However, since unification, the Greens have struggled in the old East Germany where the PDS (the former Communist Party) staked out the territory to the left of the SPD. Indeed, the Greens remain predominantly *West* German: in 2005 they gained 8.8 per cent there compared to 5.2 per cent in the old East Germany (Pulzer 2006: 569).

Finally, there are also some peculiarly German features to the success of the Greens. Markovits and Gorski (1993) stress the 'Holocaust effect', which covers a number of sensitive issues which have contributed to the significance of student politics and pacifism in post-war Germany. Although this last factor perhaps makes the German Greens untypical of green parties elsewhere, it is clear that institutional and political factors have played a critical role in the electoral performance of the party.

### ▶ *France*[5]

Although an ecological candidate contested the presidential election as far back as 1974 and Les Verts won eight seats in the 1989 European parliamentary elections, it was not until 1997 that the first Greens were elected to the French national assembly. During the 1970s, especially after the right-wing government launched a huge nuclear power programme in 1974, French environmentalism was dominated by the nuclear issue. When Mitterand, the newly elected Socialist president, broke his promise to place a moratorium on building new nuclear plants in 1981, environmental activists concluded that they needed a unified party to exercise greater influence in French politics. Consequently, Les Verts was formed in 1984 from the amalgamation of a disparate array of environmental and movement groups. After the success of Les Verts in the 1989 European election, a second green party, Génération Ecologie, was formed in 1990 by Brice Lalonde, a former environment minister in the Socialist government. Riding the crest of a green wave, both parties performed well in the 1992 regional elections, getting several hundred councillors elected. Subsequently, they put aside intense ideological and personal differences to form an Entente des Ecologistes to contest the 1993 legislative elections, but they failed to win any seats despite securing a respectable 7.8 per cent share of the vote. The Entente immediately collapsed. Factionalism prompted further fragmentation into a dozen small rival groups by 1995 (Faucher 1998). Yet, from this low point, Les Verts was able to establish itself as the dominant force in French green politics. In the 1997 legislative elections it agreed an electoral pact with Lionel Jospin's Socialists that returned seven Greens as part of a five-party 'plural left' alliance, enabling Les Verts to join the governing coalition with its national speaker, Dominique Voynet, initially holding the environment portfolio. In 2002, the best Green performance in a presidential election saw Noël Mamère attract 5.2 per cent of the vote, but this achievement could not compensate for the defeat of the Jospin 'plural left' government, with Les Verts winning just three seats with 4.4 per cent of the vote.

The political opportunity structure in France has constrained the development of green politics. Although the anti-nuclear movement contributed to the rise of ecological politics in the 1970s, it lost momentum in the 1980s because of conflict within the anti-nuclear movement and the obduracy of the Socialist government on this issue. Subsequently, no big ecological issue has provided a catalyst for the green parties.

France has a distinctive electoral system for legislative and presidential elections, based on two rounds of voting: if no candidate achieves 50 per cent of the vote in the first round, all candidates gaining at least 12.5 per cent can progress to the second round, which is a straight contest for the highest vote. This second-ballot system discriminates against minority parties as it is difficult to reach the 12.5 per cent threshold necessary to stay in a constituency contest, let alone win a seat. It was only an electoral pact, whereby Socialists and Greens stood down in favour of each other in around a hundred key seats to allow one candidate a clear run, that enabled Les Verts to overcome this obstacle to secure a handful of deputies in 1997 and 2002. Significantly, in European Parliament and regional elections, where proportional representation is used, ecological candidates have achieved more success.

French party politics has been dominated by a left–right cleavage, with a political discourse centred on class politics. For many years a four-party system consisting of two right-wing and two left-wing parties distributed the preferences of the electorate across the political spectrum. It was very difficult for new parties to enter the political arena and, unlike Germany, there was no vacant political space on the left for the greens to colonise. Nevertheless, greater instability characterised the political system during the 1980s: the rise of the far-right National Front suggested growing disillusionment with the established parties, particularly on the right. On the left, the greens benefited from the decline of the Communists and the shift rightwards by the Socialist government, giving them the opportunity to recruit disillusioned left-wing voters.

The electoral prospects of French green politics have been hampered by factionalism. For example, there have always been strong differences of opinion about whether Les Verts should eschew any dealings with other political parties or try building links with the left. These differences have been intensified by fierce personality clashes between leading activists, notably Voynet, Lalonde and Antoine Waechter, a deep green who eventually resigned from the party after it shifted leftwards. It was the ascendancy of Voynet, a keen advocate of closer links with the left, together with the departure of key fundamentalist factions that had strongly opposed them, that eventually led Les Verts to discard its opposition to coalitions. This move coincided with an opening up of the POS when the Jospin-inspired 'plural left' alliance was formed. However, after the defeat of the Jospin government in 2002 Les Verts was again embroiled in a crisis of various forms – organisational, leadership, financial and strategic direction. Thus the party continues to display an electorally damaging penchant for internal squabbling and weak leadership.

The electoral fortunes of Les Verts rest heavily on the continuation of its pact with the Socialists. In the March 2004 regional elections, for example, the unpopularity of the right-wing Raffarin administration produced a landslide for the left, which won twenty-five of twenty-six regional assemblies, with Les Verts doing well in the fifteen regions where it put forward a combined list with the Socialists. This dependency on the Socialists need not be a weakness. The long-term decline of the Communists means that Les Verts has the opportunity to establish itself as the uncontested second party of the left, and therefore vital in securing any future electoral victory for the centre-left, which would allow it to bargain from a position of some strength with the Socialists – providing it can overcome its self-destructive factionalist tendencies.

### ▶ *Britain*[6]

Although Britain boasted the first green party in Europe, the party has struggled to achieve any significant electoral success and performs feebly in national elections. The party, originally called People, was formed in 1973 by a small discussion group to campaign on environmental issues (McCulloch 1992).[7] It did not emerge from a NSM milieu and has remained quite separate from the broader environmental movement, although it has worked closely with the new wave of direct action protesters, such as the anti-roads and anti-GMO movements (see Chapter 6).

Small parties find it difficult to break into the British plurality electoral system in which most individual constituency contests are dominated by the major parties. Electors are unwilling to 'waste' their votes on a party with little chance of winning a seat. Only where a party can concentrate its vote geographically, as with the Welsh and Scottish nationalists, is there a chance of gaining representation, but the Greens have been unable to establish any regional base. Small parties are penalised by the need to pay a £500 deposit for each candidate in a parliamentary election, returnable only if they poll at least 5 per cent of the vote, and there is no state funding for political parties. The Green Party was left with a huge bill after the loss of all 253 deposits in the 1992 general election. Subsequently it became more selective about which seats it contested, standing in just 95 seats in 1997, although improvements in party fortunes enabled it to contest 202 (of 646) seats in 2005.

Party competition has left little space for the Greens to occupy. The Conservative and Labour parties have traditionally proved adept at providing a sufficiently broad church to incorporate a wide range of ideological positions. In particular, the relatively inclusive attitude of the Labour Party towards dissident social movements has encouraged leading NSMs, such as the Campaign for Nuclear Disarmament, to focus their efforts on persuading the Labour Party to change its policy, rather than by building links with what is widely seen as a narrow, single-issue, green party (Rüdig and Lowe 1986). The Green Party faces tough competition from the centrist Liberal Democrats and the Scottish and Welsh nationalist parties, who have all made some attempt to appeal to the environmentalist vote. The significance of party competition is illustrated by the 1989 European election, when the Greens won a remarkable 15 per cent of the vote (but no MEPs). The POS briefly opened up to allow the Greens to piggy-back on the contemporary growth in public interest in the environment and to benefit from a strong protest vote against the incumbent Conservative government and the weakness of the newly formed Liberal Democrats (Rootes 1995c). Subsequently, the Liberal Democrats became established and traditional material issues, such as the poll tax and the deepening recession, crowded out the environment, so that this window of opportunity closed again. Generally, however, the closed POS has meant that the focus of environmental politics in the UK has been on the established parties (see Chapter 5) and the large environmental lobby (see Chapter 6), rather than the Green Party. The pressure groups make a virtue of their non-partisan status, believing they will exercise most influence by lobbying politicians from all three major parties. They see little to gain from working with a weak Green Party; indeed, any partisanship might close the doors to government and risk alienating its membership. This vicious circle of exclusion has further weakened the Green Party.

Yet, in recent years, as a result of the Labour government's programme of constitutional reform the political opportunity structure has opened up a little to the advantage of the Green Party. The introduction of proportional representation in second-order elections enabled the Greens to secure election to the European Parliament and the new Scottish Parliament in 1999, and to the new Greater London Assembly in 2000. These successes were repeated during 2003/4, with the notable feat of gaining seven seats in the Scottish Parliament. These achievements seem to have had some positive impact on the party's performance in national elections. In 2005 the Greens won a record 283,486 votes, averaging 3.37 per cent in the seats contested and saving twenty-four deposits (Carter and Rootes 2006: 476), although the election of a Green MP still seems some way off.

## ▶ *Explaining green electoral performance*

The German, French and British examples illustrate how the institutional and political context influences the openness of a national political opportunity structure to green parties. In this section, drawing on the three case studies and green party experiences elsewhere, the critical institutional and political factors are identified.

The most striking institutional difference between the three countries appears to be the *electoral system*. The German experience suggests that green parties do better in electoral systems based on some form of proportional representation (PR). This hypothesis is supported by the relative success of green parties in Belgium, Finland, the Netherlands, Sweden and Switzerland, which all have PR systems, and their failure in the UK and North America, where non-proportional systems are used. The experience of the New Zealand Green Party before and after the introduction of PR illustrates the significance of the electoral system in shaping Green fortunes (see Box 4.3).

Yet in several countries with PR systems, including Norway, Denmark, Spain and Greece, green parties have had little or no success. The weakness of green parties in Southern Europe may reflect lower levels of economic

## 4.3 New Zealand Greens: proportional representation makes the difference

New Zealand was home to the world's first national green party, the Values Party, which contested the 1972 election. Values fought every seat in 1975, attracting an impressive 5.2 per cent of the national vote – enough to secure parliamentary representation in most countries, but not in New Zealand's plurality electoral system. After slipping to just 2.4 per cent in 1978, the party more or less disappeared from view, fighting a mere handful of seats in each election, until it relaunched as the Green Party in 1989. It gained 6.8 per cent of the vote in 1990, but again no seats, prompting the party to contest elections up to 1996 as part of the left-wing Alliance. Following a 1993 referendum New Zealand adopted a new 'mixed member proportional' system, resulting in the election of two Greens as Alliance MPs in 1996. Subsequently, the Green Party has again contested elections as a separate party. After gaining 5.2 per cent of the vote in 1999 and seven MPs, the Greens were propelled into the position of providing support for the minority Labour Government between 1999 and 2002, although it was not part of the coalition. The party quickly established itself as a serious political force (Bale 2003). However, it disagreed sharply with Labour over government support for the war in Iraq and its plan to lift the temporary moratorium on the release of genetically modified crops. After a stronger performance in 2002 when nine Green MPs were elected, the party slipped back to 5.3 per cent and six MPs in 2005. Since 2002 the Greens have adopted a halfway position between coalition and outright opposition, by either giving the Labour-led government support or by abstaining on key confidence and budget motions. Thus in 2005 the Greens signed an agreement with Labour giving them rights to consultation, access to ministers and involvement in developing specific policy and budget proposals (Bale and Wilson 2006: 401). It is therefore clear that the introduction of proportional representation has made a critical difference to the electoral performance and political influence of the New Zealand Greens.

development and, consequently, the presence of fewer postmaterialists, but Norway and Denmark are affluent, developed economies with many post-materialists. Moreover, the breakthrough of Les Verts in France shows that a plurality system is not an insuperable barrier, although this success was dependent on a pact with the Socialists. On balance, a facilitative electoral system is probably a necessary, but not a sufficient, condition for green party success.

Specific electoral rules may also shape green party development. The 5 per cent threshold in West Germany initially helped a fragmented environmental movement to unite into a single green party and, after the electoral defeat in 1990, contributed to the electorally driven internal transformation of the party. Similarly, after the Swedish Greens slipped below the 4 per cent threshold in 1991 to lose all its MPs, the party took a pragmatic turn, introducing organisational reforms and promoting itself as a conventional party (Bennulf 1995: 117). In Austria, the failure of the two small green parties to reach the 4 per cent threshold in 1983 led to their partial merger in 1986.

## Table 4.2  Green MEPs in the European elections, 2004

|  | MEPs | % vote |
|---|---|---|
| Austria (Die Grünen) | 2 | 12.9 |
| Belgium (Groen!) | 1 | 4.9 |
| Belgium (Ecolo) | 1 | 3.7 |
| Finland (Vihreä Liitto) | 1 | 10.4 |
| France (Les Verts) | 6 | 7.4 |
| Germany (Bündnis 90/Die Grünen) | 13 | 11.9 |
| Italy (Federazione dei Verdi) | 2 | 2.5 |
| Luxembourg (Dei Greng) | 1 | 15.2 |
| Netherlands (Groen Links) | 2 | 7.4 |
| Spain (Los Verdes & ICV) | 2 | * |
| Sweden (Miljopartiet de Grona) | 1 | 6.0 |
| United Kingdom (Green Party) | 2 | 6.2 |

*Note:* *The Spanish Green MEPs were elected from two separate coalition lists: Los Verdes united with the Socialist Party; the ecosocialist Catalonian ICV with the United Left, so it is impossible to isolate the green vote.
*Source:* Carter (2005)

Green parties have performed comparatively well in European Parliament and sub-national elections, where low turnouts and widespread protest voting can often reward smaller parties. The breakthrough election of thirty-one Green MEPs in 1989 was particularly significant, providing a major boost to the green profile across Europe. Their best performance to date was in the 1999 election when thirty-eight Green MEPs were elected, and they joined assorted regionalists to make the Green Group the fourth largest political grouping in the European Parliament (Carter 1999). In the 2004 election, the first following EU enlargement to twenty-five states, the Greens consolidated their position, with the return of thirty-four MEPs (see Table 4.2). The election of the first Spanish MEPs and gains in Germany were counter-balanced by the loss of both Irish members and five other countries returning fewer Green representatives (Carter 2005). The green message may be particularly apposite for elections to a supranational forum because environmental problems are widely regarded as requiring international solutions.

Conversely, sub-national elections, where the green message 'Think global, act local' may resonate with voters, have also provided an important base for several green parties. Certainly, in France and Germany, successes at supranational and sub-national levels have given both the party and its leading individuals a higher public profile and the opportunity to demonstrate that the Greens are a credible political force. Even in Britain, where the failure to gain access to Westminster severely limits the impact of the Greens on the national stage, their profile has been considerably boosted by their successes in the European and Scottish parliaments and the Greater London Authority.

Green parties have benefited from *federal* systems, as in Germany, Switzerland and Belgium, which offer more points of access, and hence more electoral opportunities, for a small party to gain visibility and representation. Yet federalism can be a double-edged sword. In Australia, whilst the Tasmanian Greens have attracted considerable attention, particularly when they held the balance of power after the 1989 state elections and agreed a governing 'Accord' with the Labour Party (Haward and Larmour 1993), the federal system discouraged inter-state co-operation between green parties and impeded the formation of a national Australian green party, thereby hampering electoral progress.

Electoral and institutional systems are relatively fixed institutional features of the POS that have clearly influenced the development of green parties, but they do not explain the lack of success of small green parties in Norway, Denmark or, until recently, the Netherlands. All three countries have structural and institutional conditions that might be expected to have facilitated the development of green parties: a relatively large number of postmaterialists, electoral systems based on PR, an active NSM sector and a high level of environmental consciousness.

*Political competition*, in particular Kitschelt's (1988) concept of the 'left-libertarian' party, may explain this puzzle. Kitschelt identifies a handful of 'left-libertarian' parties in Europe, which accept core elements of the socialist agenda – notably an egalitarian distribution of resources and a mistrust of the market – but, unlike the traditional left, reject authoritarian and bureaucratic statist solutions in favour of libertarian institutions that enhance autonomy and participatory democracy. Kitschelt identifies two groups of left-libertarian parties: first, a small group of left-socialist parties that emerged in the late 1950s/early 1960s in several countries; secondly, the green parties.[8] He argues that the emergence of left-libertarian parties is shaped by political opportunities, specifically the long-term incumbency of social democratic parties in government. When in opposition, social democratic parties appear more radical and offer hope to left-wing supporters, but once in power they shift rightwards, disappointing their radical base. Thus the first group of left-libertarian parties, including the Socialist People's Party in Denmark and in Norway, and the Pacifist Socialists in the Netherlands, flourished where social democratic parties had ruled in the 1950s. Later, when the environmental movement emerged, these existing left-libertarian parties provided a sympathetic platform for green concerns. Consequently, when small green parties appeared, such as De Groenen in the Netherlands, they found themselves crowded out because their 'natural' political space was already occupied and the loyalties of the green electorate committed elsewhere. In Sweden, the communist Left Party (VPK) became increasingly left-libertarian during the 1970s and now competes strongly with the Greens for the environmental vote. Kitschelt concludes that green parties have been less successful in countries where another left-libertarian party was already firmly established. By contrast, where social democratic parties dominated government throughout the 1970s, as in West Germany, Austria and Belgium, but there was no established left-libertarian party, green parties were able to colonise vacant political territory. The persuasiveness of the left-libertarian thesis is underlined by the keenness of many green parties to stress that they are not simply 'environmental' parties, but are also pledged to a wider left-libertarian political programme. One qualification to Kitschelt's thesis is that left-libertarian parties have generally done less well in countries, such as France, Italy, Greece, Portugal and Spain, where a strong Communist Party provided stiff competition for the left-wing electorate, at least during the 1970s and 1980s (Markovits and Gorski 1993: 17). Nevertheless, Kitschelt's left-libertarian thesis is important for underlining the significance of political competition in green party development.

The POS framework shows how the interplay between structural, institutional and political factors can explain variations in green party performance between countries. Yet the strength of the POS is also its weakness. Although providing a much fuller account of green party development, by throwing everything into the melting pot, the POS can end up looking like a catch-all typology: 'Used to explain so much, it may ultimately explain nothing at all' (Gamson and Meyer 1996: 275). The POS also conflates durable structural features of the political system, notably the electoral system, with contingent features, such as the state of party competition at a particular moment (Rootes 1995b). Whilst electoral systems rarely change (although the introduction of proportional representation in some British elections and the shift towards a plurality system in Italy show that they are not set in stone), the configuration of party competition can alter dramatically, as illustrated by the rightward shift of the German SPD and the thawing of traditional left–right party alignments in France since the 1980s. As long as these limitations are acknowledged, the POS provides a useful framework for testing how different institutional variables have influenced the development of green parties.

---

### Critical question 3

What is the principal factor determining the electoral success of green parties?

---

## ❯ Whatever happened to the environment?

One danger of using broad structural developments or institutional variables to explain the rise of green parties is that the underlying issue – the objective state of the environment – may be forgotten. Is it simply coincidence that the rise of green parties coincided with growing public knowledge and concern about the state of the environment? Perhaps there is no need for grand 'new politics' accounts to explain why people worry about the environment? Admittedly, there is no straightforward relationship between high levels of environmental consciousness and green party success. The environment has consistently ranked high as a salient political issue in Denmark and Norway, but neither has a significant national green party. Conversely, Belgian green parties have been very successful despite confronting the lowest level of environmental consciousness of any EU member state (Eurobarometer 1999). Nevertheless, there is also evidence that green parties have flourished as a direct response to specific environmental concerns. When the Swedish Greens achieved their electoral breakthrough in 1988, they attracted highest support in areas that had been most damaged by fall-out from the Chernobyl nuclear accident (Affigne 1990). The upsurge in green support in the 1989 European Parliament election came on the back of growing concern about environmental issues such as acid rain, climate change and ozone depletion. The success of the Belgian green parties in the 1999 elections was linked to a scandal involving the contamination of the poultry and dairy food chain with highly poisonous dioxins (Hooghe and Rihoux 2000). A strong concern about environmental issues sharply differentiates supporters of the Finnish Green League from supporters of other parties (Zilliacus 2001: 44). Thus in searching for sophisticated political science explanations for the rise of green parties we should not sacrifice the most straightforward interpretation: that in the 'risk society' (Beck 1992) support for the greens may be driven by a specific concern about the objective state of the environment, as much as it is a reflection of postmaterial values.

## ▶ New challenges

The fortunes of individual green parties may wax and wane, but the overall movement has established a reasonably secure and increasingly important role in several countries. Apart from the long-standing unfulfilled task of matching this achievement in the UK, USA, Australia, Canada and elsewhere, there are two important contemporary challenges facing the green movement.

One challenge in those five countries where green parties have entered government is to retain electoral support when they are no longer a party of protest. Green parties are likely to confront a particular tension: whilst judged by the wider public on their ability to act as responsible members of the government, many Green voters are expressing an anti-establishment protest and may be critical of their party's involvement in the dirty business of government. It may be impossible to satisfy both constituencies. It is too early to draw any firm conclusions about the electoral impact of government incumbency. On the one hand, the Finnish Green League slightly improved its electoral performance both in 1999, after four years in the coalition government, and again in 2003, despite (or because of?) having resigned from the coalition in the previous year over its opposition to the government's decision to build a new nuclear power station. The German Greens strengthened their position in 2002, and declined only marginally in 2005. By contrast, having entered government on the basis of a very strong performance in the 1999 election, both the Belgian green parties suffered humiliating electoral defeats four years later. The electoral fortunes of the French and Italian green parties, both of which agreed pre-election pacts with larger centre-left parties, were shaped by the electorate's assessment of the government as a whole at the end of its term in office, as was the return of the Italians to government in 2006 (even though their share of the vote has hardly changed in the last three elections). Perhaps all we can say so far is that entering government is not *necessarily* bad for green parties.

In seeking explanations for the variations in performance, two factors stand out (Rüdig 2006). First, the Greens themselves can make a difference, through the conduct of the party (both its leading politicians and the grassroots membership) and the popularity of Green policy initiatives. For example, government office brings a much higher profile for Green politicians, with both positive and negative results. Whilst the individual popularity of Germans Joschka Fischer and Renate Künast rose significantly after holding ministerial office, public perceptions of the competence of Belgian Green ministers, Martha Aelvoet and Isabelle Durant, plummeted. Secondly, institutional features, notably the links between the Greens and their coalition partners, can have an electoral impact. The German Greens benefited in 2002 especially from tactical voting by many SPD supporters who 'split their ticket' by voting for the Greens with their second 'list' vote, to help them reach the 5 per cent threshold that would ensure their presence in parliament and the continuation of the red–green coalition. However, the Belgian Greens, having resigned from the coalition government just two weeks before the 2003 election, probably lost support as potential voters switched to the Socialists to ensure the survival of the government (Rüdig 2006). Where a pre-election pact occurs it is vital that the Greens continue to perform well in second-order elections, such as the European and regional elections, to demonstrate their continued importance to the major coalition party.

The second challenge is for green parties to extend their electoral appeal beyond the small group of rich industrialised nations where they have achieved successes to date. In particular, a key objective must be to secure a foothold in the transitional states of Central and Eastern Europe, notably the recent EU accession member states. Ecological parties did achieve some short-lived successes in several countries, including Estonia, Lithuania,

Slovenia and Ukraine, as part of anti-Communist alliances in the early 1990s, only for them to disappear as an electoral force when these alliances broke up. In most countries, this brief Green success was a phenomenon peculiar to that particular historical juncture, when many dissidents joined ecological movements simply because they represented one of the few legal political organisations allowed under the former Communist regimes. One exception is Latvia where the green party combined with a farmers party to form the Green/Farmers Union party, gaining electoral success as part of the minority coalition government that came to power in 2004. The Czech Greens won six seats as part of a centre-right alliance in the June 2006 election. Otherwise it is barren ground for the Greens. Those fledgling green parties that do exist in the 'new' Europe badly need the resources, organisational know-how and experience of their counterparts in the 'old' Europe. However, no Green MEPs were elected from the ten accession states in the 2004 European Parliament elections, and the dismal performance of most Green candidates demonstrates the Herculean nature of the task ahead (Carter 2005: 109–10). There is little evidence of any groundswell of environmental concern in the transitional states, where the typical core green constituency – the new-middle-class, postmaterialist voters – remains relatively small. Nor will it be easy for green parties to carve out their own political space in the crowded party systems characteristic of these countries. Consequently, the prognosis for the Greens making a significant electoral breakthrough in the transitional states must be pessimistic.

# ▶ Conclusion

No single argument adequately explains the rise of green parties. There is some support for the claim that green parties are an expression of a new politics. Several green parties originally sprang from a vibrant new social movement milieu, with anti-nuclear protest acting as a critical mobilising condition. Green parties do draw support disproportionately from the 'new middle class', but this statistical relationship does not tell us very much, as the majority of this group supports other parties. Although Inglehart's cultural thesis that affluence and early socialisation have produced a population whose values are increasingly postmaterial has important theoretical and methodological weaknesses, there is considerable evidence that green parties do attract a relatively large share of postmaterial supporters. However, educational attainment, particularly possession of a higher degree in an arts or social science subject, may provide the strongest causal link with green support. Suggestions that the green constituency is gradually 'greying' could imply that there is a one-off generational cohort passing through the system, although the evidence is again inconclusive. The political opportunity structure helps to explain variation in green party performance by directing attention to institutional factors, such as the electoral system, and political competition. But perhaps all of these explanations understate the importance of the real cause of all the fuss: the state of the environment itself.

This discussion of electoral success raises broader questions about how green parties have adapted to the constraints of working within the parliamentary system and government, and how established parties have responded to the green challenge; we turn to these issues in the next chapter.

## ▶ *Further reading and websites*

Doherty (2002) contains several excellent chapters on the development of green parties. Burchell (2002) provides an interesting comparative analysis of green party development and change in four European countries. O'Neill (1997) covers a wide range of countries, but is very dated. Müller-Rommel (1998) is interesting on green party success. The journal *Environmental Politics* contains regular profile articles that update green party electoral performance in individual countries; see its 2002 special issue on green parties in government (also published as Müller-Rommel and Poguntke 2002). Dalton (2006) provides a good empirical survey of new politics issues, and della Porta and Diani (2006) is a general discussion of social movement theories.

The global green parties' page provides links to green parties worldwide (http://www.greens.org/) and the website of the European Federation of Green Parties (http://www.europeangreens.org/) provides links to most European national parties.

NOTES

1 The party is formally known as Bündnis 90/Die Grünen since merging in 1993 with the East German alliance of greens and civic action groups. The Greens were edged into fifth place by the FDP and the Left Party in the 2005 federal election.

2 See Abramson and Inglehart (1995) for a combative rebuttal.

3 The concept of the 'political opportunity structure' has been widely used in the social movement literature (Tarrow 1994; Kriesi et al. 1995; McAdam et al. 1996), although Rootes (1998) notes that several writers now prefer to use 'political opportunity' as the use of 'structure' undervalues the importance of 'agency'.

4 Detailed accounts of the development of the German Greens include Frankland and Schoonmaker (1992), Poguntke (1993), Markovits and Gorski (1993), Scharf (1994), and Mayer and Ely (1998).

5 See Faucher (1998) and Doherty (2002: ch. 4) for a fuller account of the development of the French green movement.

6 See McCulloch (1992) and Rootes (1995c) for fuller accounts of the early development of the Green Party.

7 The party name was changed to the 'Ecology Party' in 1975 and to the 'Green Party' in 1985. There is a separate Scottish Green Party.

8 Kitschelt categorises all green parties, apart from the Swiss, as left-libertarian. However, there are several small 'dark green' ecological parties, including the Dutch De Groenen and various French green factions, with a narrow ecological programme rather than a broader left-libertarian programme, which do not fit this label.

# Party politics and the environment

**5**

## Contents

## Key issues

▶ What is distinctive about green party organisation and strategy?
▶ What have green parties in government achieved?
▶ Has electoral success and entry to government changed green parties?
▶ Do party responses to the environment follow partisan lines?
▶ What factors influence the greening of established parties?

Chapter 4 charted the electoral appearance of green parties across Europe. Yet the simple fact of green representation does not guarantee any influence in the parliamentary arena, particularly as Green MPs frequently advocate radical policies and behave in unconventional ways. Where green parties gain electoral success, their political influence will partly be determined by the way they adapt to the pressures of conventional party politics. However, as green parties remain of marginal importance in most countries, much will depend, for the foreseeable future, on how the political elites respond to the broad environmental challenge. This chapter assesses the impact of environmental issues on party politics by looking at both these issues. The first part examines the experience of green parties in dealing with the transition from pressure politics to parliamentary opposition (focusing primarily on the German Greens) and, more recently, into government. The second half of the chapter uses case studies of Germany, Britain and the USA to assess how far established parties have absorbed environmental ideas and to identify the main factors shaping their responsiveness to the environmental agenda.

# ▶ Green parties in parliament

## ▶ The 'anti-party party' in theory

Green parties place great importance on *agency*: the means of achieving the sustainable society. Die Grünen is often regarded as the paradigmatic green party because its programme, organisation and electoral success have provided the dominant model for green parties elsewhere. The founders of Die Grünen set out to create a unique kind of party, which its leading activist, Petra Kelly, called the 'anti-party party' (APP). The APP has two core elements: a party organisation based on grassroots democratic principles, and a rejection of coalitions with established parties.

The principle of grassroots democracy, or *Basisdemokratie*, one of the four pillars of green politics discussed in Chapter 3 (see Box 3.5), underpins the organisational structure of Die Grünen (Frankland and Schoonmaker 1992: 100–5; Poguntke 1993: 137–9), in sharp contrast to most major political parties. Large, well-established parties are usually hierarchical, centralised, bureaucratic and professional; typically, they have a small, dominant parliamentary elite, a powerful professionalised national party machine, a rigid rule-bound organisational structure, and a weak, inactive party membership. These parties seem to confirm the 'iron law of oligarchy' identified by Robert Michels (1959) which stated that all political parties – even those with strong democratic principles – would always fall under the oligarchical control of a small ruling elite (see Box 5.1).

The organisational structure of Die Grünen was designed to avoid these oligarchical tendencies by preventing the emergence of a separate ruling class of professional politicians who might resist the radical demands of the grassroots membership (see Frankland and Schoonmaker 1992: ch. 5; Poguntke 1993: ch. 8). Party officers were elected and unsalaried. Enforced job rotation prevented anyone from being re-elected immediately to the same post. No one could hold a party post and a parliamentary seat simultaneously. There was no single party leader; instead, a principle of collective leadership produced three elected national speakers to share power and responsibility with

## 5.1 Michels's theory of oligarchy

> Who says organisation, says oligarchy.
>
> (Michels 1959 [1915]: 401)

The Swiss political scientist Robert Michels outlined an 'iron law of oligarchy' stating that all political parties will inevitably turn into oligarchies dominated by a small group of leaders. Three main factors contribute to these oligarchical tendencies:

1. Direct democracy is difficult to operate once an organisation grows beyond a certain size in terms of members and task differentiation, so hierarchy is more 'efficient'.

2. Individual rank-and-file party members lack the abilities, resources or motivation to participate effectively in complex organisations, so management is left to professionals.

3. Party leaders run the party in their own interests, notably a love of power and regular contacts with the ruling elite, not those of the rank-and-file members.

The German Greens were greatly influenced by the earlier 'oligarchisation' of the socialist SPD.

See Beetham (1977) and Kitschelt (1989) for a critique of the 'iron law of oligarchy'.

the federal party executive. Similar rules prevented a class of professional parliamentarians accumulating power over the wider party. A system of mid-term rotation required parliamentarians to step down halfway through their term of office in favour of a colleague lower on the party list. MPs had to live on an income equivalent to that of a skilled labourer, donating the remainder of their parliamentary salary to environmental causes. The 'imperative mandate' principle bound Green deputies to the resolutions or instructions of the party congress and the federal council. By restricting the trappings of office, the period of service, the accumulation of bureaucratic posts and the focus on individual leaders, the Greens hoped to prevent the personalisation of politics. The grassroots membership was also vested with a range of powers to enable it to keep a tight rein on the activities of party 'leaders'. Party meetings at every level, including the federal executive and the parliamentary party, were normally open to all members, as well as non-members. The party also pursued an aggressive policy of positive gender discrimination, with equal male/female representation on candidate lists and committees (Frankland and Schoonmaker 1992: 106–9).

The second element of the APP model, the rejection of coalitions, was intended to prevent the institutionalisation of the party into the established system of parliamentary politics. Activists wanted the party to act as the parliamentary arm of the new social movements and remain committed to a role of fundamental opposition. The idea of the 'movement-party' was captured in Petra Kelly's 'two-leg' soccer metaphor: the party in parliament was to be the free-moving leg and the extra-parliamentary movement was the more important supporting leg. Coalitions were rejected because they involved compromises that might lead the party to sacrifice its radical principles for short-term electoral or political gains. As Kelly observed, 'I am sometimes afraid that the greens will suddenly get

13 per cent in an election and turn into a power-hungry party. It would be better for us to stay at 6 or 7 per cent and remain uncompromising in our basic demands. Better to do that than have green ministers' (quoted in Markovits and Gorski 1993: 124).

Die Grünen therefore set out to be an alternative kind of party that would resist oligarchical tendencies and the corrupting temptations of the parliamentary arena. It was also hoped that this distinctive approach to politics might encourage a more participatory political culture throughout society.

### ▶ The 'anti-party party' in practice: no longer a protest party?

Can the APP concept 'work', and is it essential for green politics that it does? The organisational development of all political parties, including the Greens, is shaped by competition from other parties (Duverger 1954). Upon entering the parliamentary arena, a green party will immediately be subjected to strong pressure – the *logic of electoral competition* (Kitschelt 1990) – to replace the APP model with the hierarchical, bureaucratic and professional structures characteristic of established parties. However, vote maximisation is not the only factor shaping party organisation; in particular, the strength of ideological convictions of the party membership – the *logic of constituency representation* – might provide a counterbalance (Panebianco 1988). Die Grünen has faced the constant dilemma of choosing between radical strategies of fundamental opposition to conventional party politics and moderate strategies of compromise intended to achieve incremental policy change. Whilst the radical strategy may keep core green voters content, it is less likely to attract broader support; by contrast, whereas the moderate strategy may win more votes, the resulting dilution of the APP model could antagonise the grassroots membership.

This strategic tension has underpinned the internal conflict between the Fundamentalists (*fundis*) and the Realists (*realos*) that has plagued the party throughout its existence (see Box 5.2).[1] Broadly speaking, the two perspectives share the same long-term aim – to achieve an ecologically sustainable world – but disagree over the best means of getting there. Fundamentalists are firmly wedded to the APP and suspicious of the benefits of working within the parliamentary system. Realists believe that Greens can win significant incremental changes within the parliamentary system. Die Grünen was formed in 1980 when movement politics was in full swing and activists were hopeful that growing public awareness of the immediacy of the ecological crisis would provide the catalyst for radical change both inside and outside the parliamentary arena. However, during the 1980s, movement politics went into decline, leaving the Greens as the main voice of ecological concern. No longer was a transformation of the political system on the horizon; radical ambitions had to be tempered. The Greens had to come to terms with being a small party that regularly attracted no more than 10 per cent of the vote. From the mid-1980s, leading Realists, such as Joschka Fischer, argued

---

**5.2 The *fundi–realo* divide**

The *fundi–realo* divide reflects a strategic dispute over the role of green parties in achieving change.

**Fundamentalists**

- oppose the centralisation of the party organisation;
- reject coalitions with other parties;
- regard the state as the agent of the capitalist system;
- are therefore sceptical about the possibility of achieving radical change by parliamentary means;
- emphasise the grassroots extra-parliamentary base of the party.

**Realists**

- believe radical changes require a piecemeal parliamentary strategy;
- insist that some participatory principles must be sacrificed if the party is to become a credible force in electoral and parliamentary politics;
- are willing to build coalitions with other parties and to accept government office.

In short, the Fundamentalists have defended the 'anti-party party' model, whilst the Realists have sought to reform it.

---

that the 'anti-party' phase was over and that the Greens should become a normal party with a conventional organisational structure and prepared to form coalitions. The *fundi–realo* debate raged to and fro until, eventually, the shock of the 1990 electoral defeat shifted the balance of power decisively in favour of the Realists, whose position was cemented after the merger in 1993 with Bündnis 90, the moderate East German citizen alliance.

The Realists instigated a series of organisational reforms, including the abolition of the rotation principle and reform of the federal executive (see Box 5.3). Rotation was rejected as impractical in a parliamentary arena where effective politicians need time to develop a strong personal presence and master the complex procedures of the legislature. The principle of amateur politics also proved unworkable: how could the twenty-seven unpaid, part-time members of the federal executive hold the parliamentary group of almost 200 salaried, full-time staff to account (Poguntke 1993: 153)? Salaries were introduced for members of the federal executive. After entering government in the red–green coalition, organisational issues again came to the fore. Although a new Party Council was established to improve co-ordination between national and state MPs and the wider party, and two 'party chairs' replaced the former 'co-speakers', further Realist attempts to overhaul the party organisation foundered in the face of strong resistance from grassroots activists.

As for the second plank of the APP model, Die Grünen dropped its complete rejection of coalitions in 1985 when, after much internal wrangling, the first coalition with the SPD was formed in Hesse. The principle of fundamental opposition proved unworkable because, once in the parliamentary arena, politicians have to decide whether to support specific policies, and party groups are obliged to work alongside opponents, especially when a

## 5.3 How democratic is the 'anti-party party'?

Does the 'anti-party party' contain a paradox? Do rules that were designed to create a dynamic participatory democratic party have the unintended consequence of hampering internal democracy?

The grassroots democratic APP was built on the assumption that members will be highly motivated, committed and active participants. Rules that institutionalise democratic values in the party structure, such as rotation and the ban on joint office-holding, mean that there will be lots of jobs available throughout the party. Electoral success meant that Die Grünen needed more members to fill more party posts, but membership remained small at around 46,000. The principle of openness that allows non-members access to party meetings reduces the incentive to join the party. Many who do join, particularly the busy professional middle classes, leave quite quickly, put off by the demands of collective decision-making on their time: 'The more people taking part in meetings, and the more meetings strive for un-animity, the longer – and the more meetings – it takes to make any decision' (Goodin 1992: 140). The limited material incentives to take on party work – frequent enforced turnover of party positions, low pay for party officials, continuous supervision by the grassroots membership – may have the perverse anti-democratic effects of reducing the willingness of members to participate and of driving people out of the party. Ironically, the APP model may have the unintended consequence of denying power to one kind of elite by creating the conditions for the emergence of a new type of elite: the minority of people with the time, resources and endurance to play an active role in the party.

party holds the balance of power. The Hesse experiment was followed by red–green coalitions in several states (including a three-party coalition with the liberal FDP). By the mid-1990s, the Greens were actively seeking a coalition with the SPD at the federal level, which it achieved in 1998. By consistently working with the centre-left SPD rather than the right-wing CDU, the Greens were effectively dispensing with the old mantra 'neither left nor right but in front'.[2]

Despite these reforms, the Greens are still organisationally very different from other parties. The gender parity rules encouraging women to participate at all levels of the party provide a very visible difference; women generally make up at least 50 per cent of Green representatives in federal, state and local legislatures. So, too, does the refusal to have a single leader and, until recently, the incompatibility rule forbidding dual post-holding in party and parliament. Whilst the Greens have been quite willing to exploit the individual popularity of Joschka Fischer for electoral gain by, for example, running highly personalised campaigns, focused on him, in the 2002 and 2005 federal elections, the party activists repeatedly resisted attempts to give Fischer a formal leadership role in the party. However, in 2003 the Realists finally persuaded the party to lift the strict incompatibility rule. Other significant differences include the continued openness of party meetings and the left-libertarian values of the Green membership. The party retains a distinctive elite-challenging internal culture. Although the *logic of electoral competition* has seen the Realists triumph and the Greens enter government, the party remains structurally and temperamentally distinct from other parties, suggesting that the *logic of constituency representation* retains some influence. For example, the pre-election party congress in March 1998 saw the reaffirmation of several radical policies, including higher fuel taxes and drastic restrictions on personal air travel, that had little appeal to the wider electorate. In short, no single oligarchical elite of professional politicians dominates the party, although it is too early to declare Michels redundant.

The experiences of other green parties have much in common with Die Grünen. Most initially adopted elements of the APP organisational model, notably the principle of collective leadership and rotation (Burchell 2002; Doherty 2002; Rihoux 2006). The Swedish Greens, for example, elect two spokespersons (one man, one woman) who are regularly rotated; office-holders are discouraged from holding more than one post at a time and are expected to relinquish it after two parliamentary terms; and the central powers of the party are devolved to four functional party committees (Bennulf 1995: 132). However, green parties elsewhere have also found it difficult to square the radical principles of the APP with the demands of electoral politics. Sometimes a particularly sharp electoral setback, such as the disappointment of the French green *entente* at not winning any seats in the 1993 National Assembly election or the removal of all Swedish Greens from parliament after failing to reach the minimum electoral threshold in 1991 (see Chapter 4), has acted as a catalyst for internal party reform. Most green parties have become increasingly centralised and professional. One very visible example of change is the general shift away from collective leadership. Some green parties, whilst diluting the principle of collective leadership, have stopped short of electing a single leader, preferring to have two co-leaders or co-spokespersons, as in New Zealand, Sweden and Britain. The Finnish Green League and the Belgian Groen! elect, respectively, a party chair and a president, who acts as a single figurehead, but without the full range of powers of a typical party leader. A handful of green parties, including the Italian and Irish, have replaced collective structures with a single, elected leader. In Austria, the popular Alexander van der Bellen is both party spokesperson and chair of the parliamentary group, and is a *de facto* party leader. There has also been a general reduction in the power of party activists, particularly in those parties that have entered government where there are obvious practical obstacles to the involvement of party members in decision-making (Doherty 2002: 116–17; Poguntke 2002: 136–7; Rihoux 2006).

The prospect of power has also seen the lingering opposition to coalitions dissolve elsewhere, as Greens have entered national and sub-national government right across Europe and beyond. At national level, there has been considerable variety in the political make-up of these coalitions and pacts. Most have been dominated by the traditional party of the 'old left', notably the formal coalition with the Socialists in France, and the pacts that have seen green parties promise support in parliament that enabled the Swedish Social Democrats (1998–2006) and the New Zealand Labor Party (1999–2002) to govern. However, some green parties are also willing to do business with parties from the centre and even the right of the political spectrum. The Belgian coalition between 1999–2003 was a broad alliance of Green, Socialist and Liberal parties, whilst the Finnish Green League between 1995–2002 was in a five-party 'rainbow government' that included the ex-Communist Left Alliance, the Social Democrats and the Conservative National Coalition. After the 2002 Austrian election, the Green Party, despite its left-wing image, entered formal, though unsuccessful, discussions with the Conservative Party.

Overall, it seems that the *logic of electoral competition* has persuaded most green parties to shift towards a more professional, centralised party organisation and to display a willingness to work with established parties (Rihoux 2006). In those countries where green parties are now established, they are no longer a party of protest but a credible alternative party and, in some cases, a party of government.

### *Critical question 1*
Will electoral success inevitably undermine the 'anti-party party' model?

### ▌ *Greens in power*

As green parties have strengthened their presence in national and subnational assemblies they have been forced to confront the challenges of governance. By the late 1990s, Green politicians were at the heart of government making tough policy decisions: Joschka Fischer was the German foreign minister authorising German support for NATO bombing of Serbs; Dominique Voynet was the French environment minister charged with the task of solving traffic congestion in Paris; and Magda Aelvoet was the Green health minister with the responsibility for clearing up Belgium's food-contamination scandal. As Greens entered government, the nature of debate within green parties shifted from whether we *should* govern (Should we become a professional party? Should we enter parliament? Should we join a coalition?) to *how* we should govern (How do we cope with power? How do we exercise leadership? How do we handle the rank and file?). Many of the old strategic dilemmas remained, but they took different forms. The subsequent departure of most green parties from government has prompted further internal debate about future strategies (Was government a positive or negative experience? Should we remain close to our former coalition partners or seek to reassert our independence? Should we court new potential coalition partners? What further programmatic or organisational changes are needed to help us return to government? Or should we return to the role of protest party?). Although many of these debates are still raging, the Green experiences of government since 1995 in Belgium, Finland, France, Germany and Italy provide some important lessons.

For most voters, if not all green activists, the primary test of Green governance is its policy impact. In short, can the Greens make a difference? The ability of individual green parties to shape government policy has been limited by their status as junior partners in their coalitions, preventing them from securing their preferred ministerial portfolios and winning support for Green policy priorities. The nature of the coalition will also shape the influence of a green party. In Germany, a combination of ideological and political factors meant that the Greens were the only credible coalition partners for the SPD; in effect the red–green option was a 'minimum winning' two-party coalition, so the SPD was effectively dependent on the Greens to form a government, which strengthened their bargaining position. In Belgium the government did not need the votes of *both* green parties, but as Ecolo and Agalev had agreed only to enter a coalition together, or not at all, they could exercise some negotiating influence. By contrast, the Finnish Green League was part of a 'surplus coalition' where its involvement was not pivotal, so its departure would not bring down the government, as illustrated when it voluntarily left the government in 2002 (see below). In France and Italy the green parties were only in the government as a result of a multi-party centre-left pact within which the green parties were minor players. Consequently, the German and the Belgian green parties were the most successful at securing ministerial portfolios: Die Grünen received three cabinet posts, including the senior position of Foreign Minister for Joschka Fischer, while the Belgian green parties were also allocated three portfolios – transport, health and environment. By contrast, the Finnish, French and Italian green parties were initially rewarded only with the environment portfolio, although Finnish and Italian Greens later briefly controlled further ministries. The German Greens were also most effective at getting their policy priorities treated seriously: the closure of nuclear power stations and reform of German citizenship laws bore a strong Green imprint (see Box 5.4).

The policy impact of green parties has been shaped by the ministerial portfolios under their control, so, not surprisingly, they have had most impact on the environment. The iconic green issue of nuclear power has figured strongly, with mixed results. Although the red–green government encountered strong opposition in implementing its promise to initiate the shutting down of the German nuclear industry, a thirty-year closure programme was eventually agreed in 2001 (see Box 7.8). A more leisurely forty-year phase-out was approved in Belgium. However, in both cases agreement was only reached after offering significant concessions to the energy industry and these rather vague, long-term agreements could easily be altered or revoked by future governments. There were other setbacks. Green attempts to ban nuclear waste shipments through Germany and the export of Belgian nuclear material to Pakistan were rejected by coalition partners. The Finnish Green League was unable to prevent its coalition partners from supporting the construction of a new nuclear power station, and after the parliament supported the decision the Green League resigned from the coalition

---

**5.4 The political programme of the German red–green coalition**

After the 1998 federal election the SPD–Green coalition negotiations underlined the importance to the Greens of a broad left-libertarian agenda, rather than an exclusive concern with environmental issues. The final programme outlined three priorities (Lees 2000: 112):

1. reduction of unemployment by up to one million over four years;
2. rapid withdrawal from use of nuclear power and a parallel programme of eco-tax reform;
3. reform of citizenship laws to reflect the multicultural reality of German society.

By the 2002 federal election, this programme had achieved mixed results: underlying structural unemployment had continued to grow; a (long-term) nuclear closure programme had been agreed; and the citizenship laws had been radically liberalised. The 2002–5 government was dominated by traditional material issues: rising unemployment, growing public debt and Chancellor Schröder's efforts to implement a major economic and welfare reform programme, Agenda 2010. In short, environmental issues were of marginal importance.

---

government. In France, although the fast-breeder Superphenix nuclear power station was closed down, the Green environment minister, Dominique Voynet, failed to prevent production of Mox, halt reprocessing of nuclear waste or even impose a moratorium on the construction of new nuclear plants, and she provoked huge grassroots discontent by accepting a government decision in favour of underground storage of nuclear waste (Boy 2002: 68–9).

Another important theme was eco-taxation, where results were also mixed. An extensive range of eco-taxes was introduced in Germany: in particular, a tax on electricity and fuel was intended to lower energy consumption, whilst the revenues would be used to stabilise the social security system and stimulate job creation (see Chapter 12). Although unpopular with the public and the business community, these taxes have contributed to reductions in energy consumption and, to a lesser extent, in labour costs (Rüdig 2003: 259–61). The Finnish Green League played its part in achieving a shift in taxation away from labour and onto energy consumption (Paastela 2002: 30–1). However, in France, where Voynet emphasised eco-tax reform, her plans to reform taxation of water pollution, introduce an energy consumption tax and raise diesel fuel taxes were either abandoned or drastically diluted in the face of strong and effective opposition (Szarka 2003: 104–7). More generally, Green ministers have had little impact on the critical issue of transport policy: Voynet failed to stop plans to expand airport capacity, whilst German Greens were unable to prevent a series of new road-building programmes.

Green ministers have had most success where their ambitions have been more moderate. Voynet and her Italian counterpart, Ronchi, achieved significant increases in staff and resources for their environment ministries. Ronchi greatly improved the effective implementation of EU initiatives and existing government legislation that had been on the statute books but largely ignored (Biorcio 2002: 45–7). Green ministers have proven influential on several conservationist issues, particularly where backed by EU legislation. For example, the Finnish government implemented the Natura 2000 nature reserve network, despite strong lobbying from agricultural and forestry interests which wanted to reduce the size of the protected areas. The German Greens passed a new federal nature protection law in 2002. The presence of Greens in government may also have produced more progressive environmental policies in other policy areas. For example, the French Greens claimed they were responsible for various initiatives to reform food production and encourage more sustainable agriculture (Boy 2002: 74–5). Kunast, as German agriculture minister, made significant steps towards a more sustainable agricultural policy, particularly by encouraging organic farming, and strengthening food safety standards.

Green parties have certainly helped shape the left-libertarian policy agenda of their respective coalition governments. A range of liberal reforms giving greater protection to asylum-seekers, new rights to illegal immigrants and legal status to gay and lesbian relationships owed much to the presence of green parties. Perhaps, as Poguntke (2002: 140) suggests, it was the absence of core economic interests opposing these legislative initiatives, allied to their low financial cost, which enabled them to succeed here.

Perhaps the most important long-term outcome of their time in government was that Green ministers generally demonstrated to the electorate that they could be trusted to hold government office. Greens proved to be co-operative coalition partners and competent, responsible policymakers. They belied the expectation in some quarters that a protest party consisting of 'disorganised hippies' and 'left-wingers', and accountable to a radical, critical grassroots membership, would not cope with the pressures of office. To be sure, there were public spats, internal conflicts and a few humiliating moments, but these features are hardly unusual in coalition governments. Sometimes straddling the twin challenges of keeping the membership happy and winning wider public support proved impossible. Rank and file members were inevitably disappointed by some of the unpalatable compromises required of coalition government, as when Voynet climbed down over placing a moratorium on GM crops and Trittin complied with Chancellor Schröder's demand (in response to energetic lobbying by Volkswagen) that he veto a proposed EU directive on the recycling of cars. Unforeseen events also forced governments to make unpopular decisions. The Kosovo crisis led Joschka Fischer, as German foreign minister, to support military policies (NATO air strikes on Serbia) that flouted the long-standing green principle of pacifism. Later he overcame even stronger opposition within the party to support the US-led invasion of Afghanistan (Rüdig 2002: 93–6). Yet the German Greens survived these crises and were re-elected in 2002. Only the Belgian green parties left office with a somewhat tarnished reputation after two of their three ministers resigned in controversial circumstances: Magda Aelvoet (Agalev) resigned over her support for a government decision to grant a licence to export arms to Nepal, and Isabelle Durant (Ecolo) after her position on night flights from Brussels airport was publicly overruled by the Prime Minister (Hooghe and Rihoux 2003). By contrast, the Finnish Green League, after seven years in government, was widely regarded to have behaved honourably and responsibly in resigning from the government over the plan to build a new nuclear reactor.

Overall, the policy impact of the Greens has been quite modest, although they can boast a number of concrete achievements. Crucially, for their longer-term development, they have demonstrated that they are a serious political force and trustworthy coalition partners. The experience of government provided some important lessons too. When entering coalitions, Green ministers need coherent, deliverable policy goals so that they can demonstrate tangible achievements to their supporters. They also need good advisors; Green ministers often confronted unhelpful bureaucracies staffed by civil servants who were either ideologically unsympathetic or simply unused to the informal ways of working that the Greens brought to office. When the opportunity to enter government arises again, green parties should be much better prepared to cope with the challenges of office.

The ideological principles and policies of the Greens have been moderated and altered by the pragmatism required of power-sharing. The German Greens agreed a new 'Basic Programme' at their 2002 party conference, which stated explicitly that 'we are no longer the "anti-party party" but represent an alternative in the party system. The decisive difference for us was that, in order to stay successful, we wanted and needed to develop into a party of reform' (Bündnis 90/Die Grünen 2002: 16). This substantial document presents the Greens as a party of comprehensive societal reform: 'Ecological restructuring, social justice and democratic renewal remain key objectives, while reference to anti-capitalist, ecocentric or anti-modernist tenets has disappeared' (Blühdorn and Szarka 2004: 315). The Greens now seek to reform the political, economic and social institutions from within, rather than outside, the system. For example, Green enthusiasm for using eco-taxation and other incentives to encourage industry to adopt cleaner, less resource-intensive technologies, reflects an acceptance of the discourse of ecological modernisation (see Chapter 8) and a willingness to engage constructively with capitalist institutions and the market. Indeed, in Germany, where there has long been gridlock over the need to reform an increasingly unsustainable corporatist welfare state, the Greens were more willing to countenance neo-liberal reforms than their SPD coalition partner, which was constrained by its strong links to the trade unions. The new programme represents a strategic repositioning by the Greens that seeks to reconcile a range of elements within the party: the willingness to embrace certain neo-liberal economic measures marks a clear shift towards the political centre, but the commitment to a state-centred social justice system and a range of libertarian reforms demonstrates the persistence of left-libertarian principles. No longer outsiders, in those countries where they have held power, the Greens have demonstrated that they are a pragmatic party with a radical reform agenda, who can be trusted to hold office.

---

### Critical question 2

Do the achievements of green parties in government justify the compromises made on the road to power?

---

# ◗ The 'greening' of established parties

Historically, party systems in industrialised liberal democracies have proved adept at incorporating new political interests and denuding them of their radicalism. Political parties have appropriated new issues or cleavages by developing their own policies to address the problems identified by an emerging interest, such as race or gender. Yet the rise of environmentalism poses distinctive problems for established parties because the technocentric–ecocentric divide cuts across the left–right cleavage that underpins most party systems (see Box 3.10). Established parties, both left and right, share a technocentric commitment to maximising economic growth and are often linked closely to producer interests: generally, labour and social democratic parties are supported by trade unions, while conservative and liberal parties are closer to business groups. Despite their obvious differences, these producer interests are broadly united in supporting expansionary economic policies and opposing environmental interests. Political elites may also be nervous about adopting unpopular 'green' policies such as stringent eco-taxes or restrictions on consumerist lifestyles.

Nevertheless, most established parties have gradually adopted a more positive attitude towards environmental protection. This adjustment may involve little more than the use of greener rhetoric, but some parties have developed progressive environmental programmes. Such differences raise several questions. Why have some parties responded more positively than others? How significant is the presence of a successful green party in shaping the responsiveness of established parties? Do partisan divisions over the environment follow traditional left–right lines? Such questions are explored here by examining the **party politicisation** of the environment in two countries already examined in some detail and frequently compared in the green politics literature, Germany and Britain, as well as the USA, which is often ignored in this literature.[3]

> **Party politicisation**: A process whereby the environment ascends the political agenda to become electorally salient and the subject of party competition.

There is considerable variety among these three rich industrialised nations: Germany has a strong green party and a relatively open political opportunity structure (POS); Britain has a weak green party and a relatively closed POS; while the USA has no national green party but a pluralistic political system that is reasonably open to new challenges. Finally, 'party politicisation' is used here in a broad sense to refer to a process whereby the environment ascends the political agenda to become electorally salient and the subject of party competition, so that parties increasingly embrace environmental concerns, strengthen their policy programmes and attack their opponents for the inadequacy of their environmental record.

## ▶ Germany

Many observers agree that during the 1980s Germany 'moved from a position of reluctant environmentalism' (Weale 1992: 71) to become one of the '**pioneers**' of European environmental policy (Andersen and Liefferink 1997b). Under a succession of conservative CDU-led governments, German political and economic elites gradually accepted the core tenets of ecological modernisation (see Chapter 8) and legislated some of the most stringent pollution control standards and progressive environmental policies in Europe, while on the international stage Germany took the lead in pressing for tougher action on a wide range of issues.[4] Although the German reputation as an environmental pioneer has subsequently lost some of its lustre, all the established parties have accepted the central place of environmental issues on the political agenda.

**Pioneer states:** Those countries, mostly in Northern Europe, that have taken the lead in developing progressive environmental policies and setting high standards of environmental protection.

Die Grünen undoubtedly played a key role in this party politicisation of the environment (Markovits and Gorski 1993: 271–3; Jahn 1997: 176–8). It is even claimed that 'As a direct consequence of the Greens' engagement, the Federal Republic developed the strictest environmental protection laws anywhere in the world' (Joppke and Markovits 1994: 235). Widespread public concern about the environment in the early 1980s, stimulated by the acid rain and nuclear power issues, enabled the Greens to exploit the failure of the established parties to respond positively to environmental issues. The state of political competition was critical in an electoral system in which coalition government is the norm and small parties can exercise considerable influence. The established parties initially regarded the Greens as outsiders, but as the party grew stronger and the electoral strength of the FDP (the traditional liberal coalition partner of the CDU and SPD) waned, the established parties had to treat Die Grünen as a prospective coalition partner. Consequently, all the major parties started to emphasise environmental issues much more strongly and to strengthen the environmental commitments in their manifestos (Weale et al. 2000: 251).

Party competition rendered the SPD particularly vulnerable to the electoral challenge of Die Grünen whose entry into parliament in 1983 coincided with the defeat of the SPD, followed by years of internal crisis that produced a transformation in its attitude towards the environment. The SPD seemed to be the victim of a long-term dealignment of the electorate. It was losing support both to the Right, particularly amongst its traditional working-class base, and to the Left, with the Greens attracting the progressive post-materialist middle classes. The need to reconcile the aspirations and interests of these different constituencies posed a fundamental dilemma for the SPD: should it move rightwards to win back its core working-class supporters, or leftwards to counter the threat from the Greens (Scarrow 2004: 92–95). These tensions produced shifting SPD attitudes towards the green challenge, fluctuating from periods of co-operation and assimilation to bouts of non-co-operation and active opposition towards a party that many in the SPD regarded as irresponsible and unreliable.

By the mid-1990s, the SPD could no longer rule out the prospect of a red–green coalition because it offered the most realistic means of halting the long CDU tenure under Chancellor Kohl. Apart from this electoral imperative, several other factors encouraged the SPD to stop treating the Greens as maverick outsiders (Smith 1996: 66–7; Lees 2000). The bottom line was that the SPD felt less directly threatened by the Greens, whose national electoral support seemed to have stabilised at a level well below what once seemed possible (Scarrow 2004: 94). The success of SPD–Green coalitions in the *Länder*, where it became clear that the two parties could 'do business', encouraged a more co-operative approach. There was also considerable policy convergence between the two parties. SPD opposition to environmentalism weakened and the party adopted a stronger postmaterialist programme, including policies on nuclear power, gender equality and reform of citizenship laws (Markovits and Gorski 1993: 268–71; Lees 2000). Meanwhile, the ascendancy of the Realists heralded a considerable moderation of Green policies and institutional practices. By 1998, the party programmes of the SPD and the Greens shared so much common ground on key policies that a red–green coalition was clearly preferable to a SPD–CDU 'grand coalition' (Lees 2000). The success of the Greens was therefore critical in compelling established German parties, especially the SPD, to treat environmental issues more seriously.

It is important though not to overestimate the extent of party politicisation of the environment. Ironically, the Greens entered office just when their electoral fortunes seemed to have plateaued and the saliency of the environmental issue had diminished. Economic recession and the tumultuous impact of German unification pushed the environment down the political agenda during the 1990s, illustrated by the decreasing amount of space allocated to the environment by the established parties in their 1994 and 1998 federal election manifestos (Budge et al. 2001). They became more circumspect about advocating progressive environmental policies; for example, both the CDU and SPD moderated their support for a carbon tax because of the possible threat to jobs. The Greens were able to insist that key environmental issues, notably nuclear power, were addressed by the red–green government. At the 2002 federal election, Schröder and Fischer skilfully linked the dramatic floods that summer to climate change and presented the coalition government as the most effective for dealing with the problem.

| Table 5.1 German political parties: estimated positions and salience of environmental policy dimension | | |
| --- | --- | --- |
| | Position | Salience |
| CDU | 14.5 | 12.4 |
| FDP | 16.8 | 12.7 |
| Greens | 3.2 | 18.1 |
| PDS | 9.1 | 9.4 |
| SPD | 10.9 | 12.7 |

*Notes:*
*Position:* '1' represents 'supports the environment, even at the cost of economic growth' and '20' represents 'supports economic growth, even at the cost of damage to the environment'.
*Salience:* where '1' represents 'unimportant' and '20' represents 'very important'.
*Source:* Benoit and Laver (2006).

Subsequently, however, environmental issues were sidelined by the troublesome domestic economy and Schröder's controversial Agenda 2010 reforms.

An expert survey of German political scientists in 2002 (see Table 5.1), not surprisingly, shows that the environment is a very important issue for the Greens, far more so than for the other major parties, which gave it roughly equal emphasis, with the PDS trailing behind. Where the parties did differ was on their policy positions, with the left-of-centre SPD and PDS looking distinctly greener than the right-of-centre CDU and FDP. It is not yet clear what impact the defeat of the red–green coalition in the 2005 federal election will have on environmental politics. The Greens have the opportunity to exploit any neglect of environmental and left-libertarian issues by the CDU–SPD 'grand coalition' government, but the emergence of a new Left Alliance encompassing the PDS and various disaffected former SPD members, which did well in the 2005 election, represents real competition for the Greens in the political space to the left of the SPD. Clearly, the party politicisation of the environment in Germany remains fragile and heavily dependent on wider political developments.

The analysis of party politicisation in Germany has focused on the impact of the Greens on other parties, but as will be shown in the following sections on Britain and the USA, green parties have had little influence in those countries.

## ▶ Britain

The party politicisation of the environment in Britain has been slow, uneven and incomplete. Until the mid-1980s, there was little interest in the environment. Subsequently, the issue gradually moved up the policy agenda, with

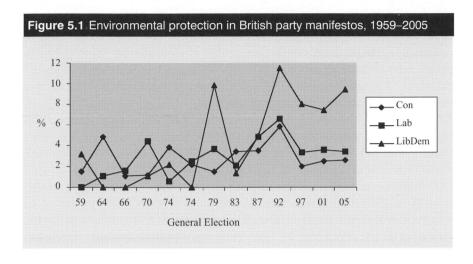

**Figure 5.1** Environmental protection in British party manifestos, 1959–2005

parties most responsive at the mid-term stage of the electoral cycle when public concern tends to be highest and leaders are more receptive to environmentalists within their parties (Flynn and Lowe 1992). For the next decade, a flurry of policy documents from the three established parties, each outlining a slightly tougher environmental programme than before, appeared roughly halfway between parliamentary elections. By the 1992 general election, the programmes of all three major parties included extensive environmental rhetoric. Yet Figure 5.1 shows that the space allocated to the environment peaked for every party in 1992. Although all the parties continued to develop their environmental programmes during the 1990s, the Conservative and Labour parties noticeably tempered their enthusiasm for the issue from the 1997 election onwards – it was only the twelfth most important issue in terms of content for both parties in their 2005 manifestos (Carter 2006: 755). By contrast, the Liberal Democrats have continued to give considerable emphasis to the environment, making it one of their top three issues in every manifesto since 1992. The reluctance of the Labour and Conservative parties to embrace the green challenge and the more positive response of the Liberal Democrats can be largely explained by electoral factors and party competition.

The principal reason for the limited party politicisation of the environment is that it is not a salient issue at general elections. Whilst opinion polls report that the British public is certainly worried about the environment and millions belong to environmental pressure groups (see Table 6.2), it tends to be regarded as a distant problem, and people often recoil at the personal costs involved in some proposed solutions, such as reducing car usage or higher energy taxes. When considered alongside other issues, the environment almost disappears from the radar. Between 1992 and 2000 monthly Gallup polls reported an average of no more than 1 per cent of people ranking the environment as the most important issue facing the country (King 2001: 270–3), and even when asked to identify several issues of importance, the environment is still mentioned by under 10 per cent of respondents (MORI 2005). With no sizeable environmental 'issue public' – people who include environmental considerations in their personal voting calculus – it is not surprising that environmental considerations have never been significant in a British general election.

Consequently, the Labour and Conservative parties have pursued a strategy of preference-accommodation. They have gradually adopted a greener rhetoric and developed a set of moderate policies to demonstrate that the environment would be safe in their hands, but they have resisted turning the environment into an arena of party competition.[5] One outcome of this strategy is that the environment in Britain is not generally perceived in party political terms or closely associated with either the 'Left' or the 'Right'. This situation is reinforced by the strong environmental lobby, which has scrupulously maintained a non-partisan approach, reasoning that an insider strategy will be most successful in the British political system if it can secure cross-party support. Despite the efforts of the Liberal Democrats to present themselves as environmental champions, none of the established parties is regarded as significantly greener than its rivals by the British electorate (Carter 2006: 760–1). To the extent that the public does associate one party with the environment, that party is the Greens. So if Labour or Conservative Party strategists try to compete on the environment, any electoral rewards arising from an increased political salience for the environment might simply accrue to the Green Party. The *logic of electoral competition* suggests, therefore, that as long as the Green Party remains insignificant, there is little incentive for either Labour or the Conservatives to raise the profile of the environment.

Party competition also explains the more positive response of the Liberal Democrats because they seem most vulnerable to the Greens, as illustrated by the 1989 European election when many of their supporters switched loyalties (Rootes 1995c). The Liberal Democrats also seem most at ease with the environment; indeed, Webb (2000: 106) identifies environmentalism as a defining feature of their ideology. However, their commitment to the environment is qualified. Where political capital can be gained the Liberal Democrats are quite willing to oppose progressive environmental initiatives: for example, they campaigned strongly *against* a proposed traffic congestion charge in Edinburgh in 2005 and they have opposed several wind farm proposals.

There are further ideological and political obstacles impeding the 'greening' of the major parties. Significantly, the Liberal Democrats have been historically free of the producerist interests – industrialists, farmers, trade unions – whose influence have made the Conservative and Labour parties ideologically less receptive to environmental ideas and encouraged them to remain committed to policies and spending plans that are dependent on continued economic growth (Carter 1992; Robinson 1992). Successive

Conservative governments between 1979 and 1992, enthused by Thatcherite deregulatory zeal, were certainly reluctant environmentalists. They were willing to act when necessary, but prepared to ignore, delay and dilute their responses whenever possible, although their record improved when John Gummer was Secretary of State for the Environment (1992–7). After entering opposition in 1997, the Conservative Party was consumed by self-destructive internal divisions and an obsession with the issue of 'Europe', and showed little interest in strengthening its environmental credentials until the election of David Cameron as party leader in 2005. He immediately identified the environment as an issue he could use to try to re-brand the Conservative Party and win back voters lost to the Labour and Liberal Democrat parties. It remains to be seen how long this Tory romance with the environment lasts, and whether Cameron is able to overcome business opposition to the kind of robust environmental protection proposals that will be necessary if he is to take on the Liberal Democrats on this issue.

Even when Britain was popularly dubbed the 'Dirty Man of Europe' in the 1990s for its poor pollution record, Labour showed a marked reluctance to attack Conservative governments on the issue, and none of the Labour leaders in opposition – Kinnock, Smith, Blair – showed any real interest in environmental issues. Although Labour briefly struck an upbeat attitude towards the environment in the immediate aftermath of its 1997 election victory, it failed to sustain this new-found enthusiasm. Like its Conservative predecessor, the Labour Government soon found itself ducking those environmental protection measures that might threaten competitiveness, jobs or its own popularity.

Why has 'New Labour' not embraced the environment? A critical moment occurred in its first term of office. The fuel blockade in September 2000 involved a sudden upsurge of popular opposition to high fuel taxation, which brought the country to a halt and saw Labour support in the polls plummet. It provided a powerful lesson to Labour about the political dangers of radical environmental initiatives. Thus although Blair has consistently highlighted climate change as a major threat and taken a lead in international climate change diplomacy, he has never made a concerted effort to turn it into an issue of domestic party politics, probably because of the potential unpopularity of many measures, such as fuel taxes. But New Labour's resistance to environmentalism may go deeper than mere electoral opportunism. According to Jacobs (1999: 9), New Labour is 'fundamentally suspicious of environmentalism', regarding it (not unreasonably) as a political movement with its own ideology and organisations. Certainly some of the radical ideas associated with green politics – anti-capitalism, anti-growth, anti-consumerism – are regarded by New Labour as 'anti-aspirational'. The bottom line is that Labour strategists believe that the lifestyle compromises implied by such ideas are irrelevant and unappealing to its target voters: 'Middle England drives cars, enjoys shopping, wants to own more material things and to go on more foreign holidays' (Jacobs 1999: 9). The contrast between these perspectives is illustrated by the opposing views over biotechnology and GM crops: Blair welcomed them with enthusiasm while environmentalists regarded them with deep suspicion.

So, although the Labour and Conservative parties have undoubtedly become considerably greener since the mid-1980s, their commitment has been half-hearted and often no more than rhetorical. The Liberal Democrats have sought to present themselves as the greenest of the major parties, by consistently making the environment a core campaigning issue. Yet the only party that the public clearly identifies as greener is the Green Party. Continued success in second-order elections in the new multilevel British polity, particularly if the Greens start to attract disillusioned left-wing voters, could pressure Labour to take the environment more seriously. Perhaps a more important influence on Labour will be the extent to which the Conservatives back up David Cameron's green rhetoric with progressive and far-reaching policy proposals.

## ▶ USA

The USA is like Britain in that it has no successful green party, it has a large environmental lobby (see Table 6.1), and the electoral saliency of environmental issues is low. Public concern about the environment increased steadily from the mid-1980s, with polls consistently reporting that Americans cared about a range of environmental problems, although there was a sharp decline after 2001, coinciding with the 11 September terrorist attacks, energy shortages and rising fuel prices (Bosso and Guber 2006: 82). Yet even at its peak, no more than about 5–6 per cent of the electorate – the environmental 'issue public' – included environmental considerations in deciding which way to vote, with under 2 per cent of respondents identifying the environment as the nation's 'most important problem' in September 2004 (Bosso and Guber 2006: 82). Notwithstanding the performance in 2000 of Ralph Nader, who stood on a Green Party ticket, the environment has generally been insignificant during presidential campaigns (Tatalovich and Wattier 1999: 173–5; Guber 2003: 119) (see Box 5.5).[6]

In comparison with the UK, environmental politics has taken a more partisan form in the USA, with the Democratic Party embracing environmentalism to a greater extent than the Republicans. Democratic Party platforms at presidential elections since 1976 have 'generally called for increased spending, additional government action, and overall stronger efforts to control pollution', whilst the Republicans have favoured 'little or no government intervention . . . and a relaxation of current pollution control restrictions so that economic growth is not impeded' (Kamieniecki 1995: 152). Admittedly, research shows that successful presidential candidates have a poor record in implementing their (limited) environmental pledges (Tatalovich and Wattier 1999). Nevertheless, studies of roll-call voting on environmental bills in Congress and state legislatures since the 1970s show that Democrat

Ralph Nader, the respected veteran consumer campaigner, contested the 2000 presidential election on a Green Party ticket. He ran an impressive high-profile campaign fought on a broad political programme headed by a fierce critique of excessive corporate power and demands for campaign finance reform and 'clean government', with the environment given lower priority. Nader's support for liberal policies such as affirmative action, tougher gun controls and an end to the death penalty, resulted in a programme similar in many respects to the left-libertarianism of European green parties.

Strong pre-election polling, giving Nader up to 10 per cent in some key states, prompted the Democratic candidate Al Gore to launch a negative 'A vote for Nader is a vote for Bush' campaign to persuade Nader sympathisers that, by failing to support Gore, they might put the Republican, George W. Bush, in the White House. In the event, Nader received a respectable 2,878,157 votes (2.73 per cent), a good result for a third-party candidate. Nader drew most support in the East and on the West Coast, including 10 per cent in Alaska and 418,000 votes (3.9 per cent) in California. Many Democrats blamed Nader for Gore's defeat because in Florida and New Hampshire, Nader's vote far exceeded Bush's majority over Gore. With polls reporting that in the absence of Nader his supporters would have voted 2:1 for Gore, victory in either state would have made Gore President.

Nader stood again in 2004, but as an independent, because the Green Party put up its own candidate. After four years of a distinctly anti-environment Bush presidency, most 'environmentalists' who had previously supported Nader decided that now the priority was to defeat Bush. Nader polled just over 400,000 votes, well under 1 per cent of the national vote. Rather than encouraging the Democrats to chase the environmental 'issue public' with a more radical left-libertarian programme, it seems that the long-term impact of Nader's success in 2000 in the context of an increasingly sharp partisan divide will be to remind potential defectors from the Democrat banner of the potentially dramatic consequences of supporting a third-party candidate.

representatives are more likely to support tougher environmental measures than their Republican counterparts (Kamieniecki 1995: 156), with recent figures (see Box 5.6) showing the gap between the two parties widening.[7]

Partisan differences became very pronounced during the Reagan presidency (1981–8) when the government enthusiastically pursued environmental deregulation through a combination of savage budgetary cutbacks and ideologically committed presidential appointees to key agency posts, including the Environmental Protection Agency (Long et al. 1999: 210–11). Hostilities were renewed after the 1994 congressional elections, when the Republican 'Contract with America' manifesto identified environmental regulations as a prime target for its conservative 'revolution', leading to further budget cuts and deregulation. Between these two periods, President Bush (1989–92), after declaring initially that he would be an 'environmental president', had briefly tried to strengthen the Republicans' green credentials (Sussman et al. 2002: 163). Yet, with the exception of the 1990 Clean Air Act, few new environmental initiatives were forthcoming. Moreover, Bush supported

## 5.6 Environmental partisanship in the USA

The League of Conservation Voters, a bipartisan pressure group, keeps an annual 'environmental scorecard' recording how Republicans and Democrats in Congress vote on key pieces of legislation affecting the environment. Records show clearly that Democrats are much more likely than Republicans to support environmental protection measures, and that the gap between the two parties is steadily widening.

| | Average % supporting environmental measures | | | | | |
|---|---|---|---|---|---|---|
| | House | | | Senate | | |
| | 1998 | 2001 | 2004 | 1998 | 2001 | 2004 |
| Democrats | 72 | 81 | 86 | 84 | 82 | 85 |
| Republicans | 24 | 16 | 10 | 12 | 9 | 8 |

This partisanship is further confirmed by an expert survey of American political scientists who placed the Democrats at 6.01 and the Republicans at 16.77 on a scale where '1' represents support for environmental protection over economic growth, and '20' represents priority to economic growth over environmental protection (Benoit and Laver 2006).

*Source*: http://www.lcv.org/index.htm

further deregulation, refused to sign the Earth Summit biodiversity convention and eventually resorted to condemning environmentalists as extremists who threatened American jobs. By contrast, Clinton, with the enthusiastic environmentalist Al Gore[8] as his running mate, contested the 1992 election on a pro-environment platform, and on a lower-profile, but still relatively strong, environmental stance in his 1996 re-election campaign, whilst Gore's personal commitment to the environment was a distinctive feature of his unsuccessful bid to become president in 2000. The election of George W. Bush saw another sharp swing against environmental interests, illustrated by his renouncement of US support for the Kyoto Protocol, his support for oil exploration in the Arctic National Wildlife Refuge and his efforts to rewrite environmental regulations to favour industry.

Why, given the limited saliency of environmental issues, have the Democrats proved greener than the Republicans? Institutional factors, notably the 'winner takes all' electoral system that characterises every level of the federal structure, make it extremely difficult for small, poorly funded parties to gain electoral success. However, the federal system and the weak political parties provide multiple opportunities for interest groups to lobby representatives in Congress and state legislatures, and to influence the relatively pluralistic policy process. As in the UK, rather than attempting to build a green party, environmentalists have focused on influencing the established parties. Unlike Britain, they have concentrated on one party, the Democrats, who are generally seen as less dependent on the support of business interests and more sympathetic to environmental causes. Indeed, environmental groups have become a leading part of the Democratic coalition; in some districts, particularly in the western states, the endorsement of key environmental groups and activists can play a critical role in securing the Democratic Party nomination. One reason for the less enthusiastic, even hostile, response of the Republicans may be their greater dependence on the financial backing of large corporations and polluting firms which have been most critical of the burden imposed by environmental regulations (Kamieniecki 1995: 164). It seems likely that the huge financial contributions by the major energy producers to the Republican presidential campaign in 2000 encouraged President George W. Bush to take a pro-industry stance on issues such as the Kyoto Protocol, and oil and gas drilling in the Arctic wilderness (*The Guardian*, 8 June 2005).

Although the relative greenness of the Democratic Party presents American voters with a clearer choice than their British counterparts, the significance of this partisan cue should not be exaggerated. Most American voters do not view the environment in as strongly partisan terms as the political elite: a clear majority of voters consistently detect no difference between the two parties (Kamieniecki 1995: 163; Guber 2003: ch. 6). The weakness of American parties dilutes the partisan cues communicated to the electorate. So, too, do the geographical and ideological differences encompassed by the loose coalitions that make up the Democratic and Republican Parties. Congressional roll-call voting patterns for environmental legislation show that Democrats and Republicans do not always vote along party lines, although instances of Republicans (especially in the eastern states) supporting environmental protection legislation and Democrats (especially from the Deep South) opposing them are becoming less common (see Box 5.6). The Democrats have found it easier to be greener in opposition than in power. Clinton, despite benefiting from Democratic majorities in both Houses between 1992 and 1994, did not give priority to environmental interests. Only after 1994, when confronted by a hostile Republican-majority Congress that effectively blocked his efforts in all these areas, was he more willing to speak out – almost as a voice of opposition – against its anti-environmental measures.

Where partisan differences do matter is in attracting the small environmental issue public to the Democrat banner. These core environmentalists have traditionally been loyal and committed Democrats; they are much more likely to identify with and vote for that party (Tatalovich and Wattier 1999: 176–7). In the 1992 presidential election, for example, this group voted for Clinton over Bush by a ratio of more than 5:1 (Vig 2006: 108). In short, they are a highly partisan sub-group compared to the electorate at large. Significantly, they seem to prefer the Democrats primarily as a reaction to the anti-environmentalism of the Republicans, rather than from a positive enthusiasm for, or confidence in, the Democrats. Before Nader's intervention in 2000, the implication was that as long as the Democrats remained *relatively* greener than the Republicans they would keep the loyalty of the environmental issue public, without having to adopt a radical programme that might alienate the wider Democrat constituency. However, Nader's success in appealing to this environmental issue public – even with the 'environmentalist' Gore as Democratic candidate – showed that their support for the Democrats cannot be taken for granted. The dilemma for Democrat strategists is that efforts to win over this group by offering a 'greener' agenda run the risk of alienating the far larger group of centrist independent swing voters that the party needs if it is to win elections (Guber 2003: 121–2).

In the USA, the environment is not an electorally salient issue and the major political parties have only partially embraced the environmental challenge. Yet environmental politics have become increasingly partisan and, with polling evidence showing that pro-environment attitudes among the wider public are now clearly associated with holding a liberal ideology and supporting the Democrats, whilst conservatives and Republicans are less likely to be pro-environment (Dunlap et al. 2001: 45; Dalton 2006: 143), that trend seems likely to continue. However, the bottom line is that on several key issues, notably climate change, the opposition to environmental measures – especially increased fuel taxes – is so strong that even the Democrats are wary about adopting a potentially unpopular green stance.

### *Critical question 3*

Does the party politicisation of the environment require the presence of a strong green party?

## ▶ Explaining party politicisation

This section draws a number of conclusions from the case studies about the nature and extent of the party politicisation of the environment. First, there has been a limited party politicisation of the environment in all three countries. The environment is now established on the political agenda and no party can afford to ignore it. A major factor driving this process everywhere has been the strength of public concern about environmental problems (Eurobarometer 1999; Dalton 2006: 113). Fluctuations in the level and intensity of public opinion help explain variation in the enthusiasm shown by parties for environmental issues (Guber 2003: ch. 3). Broadly speaking, people are most agitated about the environment during periods of economic prosperity and least interested when economic recession draws attention back to materialist issues. Thus the upsurge of interest in the mid/late 1980s, fuelled by growing knowledge about global problems and accentuated by precipitating events, such as the Chernobyl and *Exxon Valdez* accidents, undoubtedly contributed to the greening of German, British and American political parties during this period. Elsewhere, the intensity of public concern seems to be strongest in Scandinavia, where polls have suggested that at least a third of citizens believe environmental problems should get a higher priority than (and not just be equal with) economic growth (Aardal 1990; Eurobarometer 1995; Sairinen 1996). This finding may reflect higher numbers of postmaterialists amongst those populations, or a specific sensitivity to environmental issues. Either way, this deeper concern helps explain why all established parties in Scandinavia have generally developed greener platforms than elsewhere (Lester and Loftsson 1993).

Secondly, nevertheless, the environment has only rarely been an issue of genuine electoral salience. Typically, significantly fewer than 10 per cent of voters – around 5 per cent in the USA and Britain – regard it as one of the most important issues in national elections. Politicians are more likely to talk about the environment between elections – in party documents, or in the US president's 'State of the Union' speech (Tatalovich and Wattier 1999) – than in election campaigns, where it tends to disappear. This low saliency undoubtedly sets limits on the commitment of established parties to environmentalism (Guber 2003; Carter 2006).

Thirdly, the presence of a successful green party in Germany certainly acted as a catalyst for a broader politicisation of the environment, whereas the absence of one in Britain and the USA helps explain the lower intensity of environmental politics in these countries. Nevertheless, a flourishing green party does not guarantee a positive response from established parties. In Belgium, despite the presence of two electorally successful green parties, the main parties remained locked in a left–right materialist discourse and made few concessions to environmentalism (Kitschelt 1994: 190). The breakdown of these frozen party cleavages in the late 1990s, which allowed the Greens to join the government coalition, did not initiate a wider politicisation of environmental issues in Belgium. In Switzerland, Austria and Sweden, intense political competition in multiparty systems prompted established parties to develop comprehensive environment programmes before green parties gained electoral success, thereby preventing them from assuming a monopoly over environmental concern. The foundation of the Dutch Green Left in 1990 postdated the wider greening of established parties, which had stymied the progress of the small green party, De Groenen (Lucardie 1997: 187–8). Similarly, established parties in Norway and Denmark adopted progressive environmental platforms without any prompting from a green party, nipping in the bud the prospects of the nascent green parties (Lester and Loftsson 1993). It seems that the significance of green parties will be closely linked to the state of political competition in a particular country.

Fourthly, Rohrschneider (1993) argues that the policy responses of the major 'Old Left' parties, mediated by electoral laws, are particularly critical in shaping the way environmental orientations affect the partisanship of voters in each country. Where environmental cleavages mirror the traditional left–right dimension so that left-wing voters display stronger support for green issues than those on the right, environmentalism can pose a particularly strong threat to 'Old Left' parties. The vacillation of the German SPD between centrist and leftist strategies is just one example of an established leftist party threatened by the emergence of a green party. The Austrian and Danish Social Democrats have also attempted to counter the threat from green or left-libertarian parties by adopting stronger environmental programmes.

However, the environmental cleavage does not always mirror the left–right divide. In Britain, environmentalism largely transcends party lines (notwithstanding the efforts by the centrist Liberal Democrats to seize the green initiative) with the active environmental lobby remaining non-partisan. The absence of an effective green party makes the electorate less likely to link environmental issues with a wider left-libertarian programme. In a political system still dominated by two broad-church parties, both adept at absorbing factions and dissident opinion, the Labour Party has remained relatively unresponsive to environmentalism. US party politics is not structured along clear left–right lines, and there is no equivalent 'Old Left' party, although it is the more liberal and (relatively) left-wing Democratic Party that has taken a more environmentally progressive position. By contrast, in multiparty Norway and Sweden (Lester and Loftsson 1993) and Switzerland (Church 1995), social democrat, centrist and liberal parties have all competed equally vigorously for environmental votes; consequently, environmental issues are high on the agenda, but conflicts do not follow clear left–right lines.

Thus, to summarise, key institutional features of the political opportunity structure (POS) will shape the nature of environmental politics in each country. In Germany, the openness of the POS contributed to a sharp politicisation of the environment during the 1980s, whereas the relatively closed POS in Britain has enabled the major parties to get by with slightly greener rhetoric and actions. The POS in the USA has been sufficiently open for pressure to be placed on the Democrats to take a more partisan stance on the environment, but the low salience of the environment has placed firm limits on the overall response of the two major parties to environmentalism.

## Critical question 4
How important is it for established political parties to become 'greener'?

## ▶ Conclusion

Green parties like to claim that they are different from other parties and, indeed, they do remain distinct, both formally and culturally, from other parties. For example, most green parties have resisted appointing a single leader and can boast equal representation of women. However, the 'normalisation' of most green parties, as illustrated by Die Grünen, has seen them moderate the anti-party model in order to achieve electoral success and influence policy. The willingness of green parties to join governing coalitions suggests that they have to some degree been incorporated and deradicalised by the existing political system. The APP model has had little discernible effect on the way other parties conduct themselves, apart from adding to the general pressure to improve the representation of women. However, despite their inexperience and their position as junior coalition partners, green parties in government can point to some genuine policy achievements and have shown that they can be trustworthy and competent members of the government.

More broadly, the environment still lacks electoral saliency. Political discourse is still dominated by materialist issues, such as the state of the economy and taxation. Green electoral success has helped disrupt traditional party alignments in several countries. A strong green party presence can push the environment up the political agenda, forcing established parties to respond to this new agenda. Environmental politics is no longer – if it ever was – the exclusive preserve of green parties. Even where green parties are weak, as in Britain, other parties often claim to be the 'true' green party. Established parties have adopted greener rhetoric and promised new environmental initiatives, thereby appropriating and deradicalising parts of the environmental agenda. Consequently, it is vital that green parties, especially when they enter government, do not allow their broader role as agitators and protectors of a green conscience to be sacrificed on the altar of electoral success. The wider environmental movement outside parliament is struggling with a similar dilemma between radicalism and reformism, which we turn to in the next chapter.

## ▶ *Further reading and websites (see Chapter 4 for green party websites)*

General accounts of the organisational development of green parties can be found in Burchell (2002), Doherty (2002) and Rihoux (2006). The experience of the Greens in government is analysed in Müller-Rommel and Poguntke (2002) and a special issue of the *European Journal of Political Research* (2006). An interesting comparison of the French and German green parties can be found in Blühdorn and Szarka (2004). There is surprisingly little analysis of the greening of established parties: for Germany, see Lees (2000); for Britain, see Carter (2006); for the USA, see Tatalovich and Wattier (1999) and Bosso and Guber (2006).

### Germany
CDU (http://www.cdu.de/)
SPD (http://www.spd.de/)
FDP (http://www.fdp.de/)
Christian Social Union (CSU) (http://www.csu.de/)
Left Party (PDS) (http://sozialisten.de/sozialisten/aktuell/index.htm)

## UK

Labour Party (http://www.labour.org.uk/)
Conservative Party (http://www.conservative-party.org.uk/)
Liberal Democrat Party (http://www.libdems.org.uk/)
Scottish National Party (http://www.snp.org/)
Plaid Cymru (Welsh Nationalists) (http://www.plaidcymru.org/)

## USA

Democratic Party (http://www.democrats.org/index.html)
Republican Party (http://www.rnc.org/)

NOTES

1 There have also been several other factions, such as ecosocialists, within the German Greens. See Markovits and Gorski (1993), Doherty (2002) and Talshir (2002) for a fuller discussion of the *fundi–realo* debate.

2 See Blühdorn (2004) for an interesting discussion of the potential for a coalition between the Greens and the Christian Democrats.

3 No attempt is made here to judge which of these countries has the best environmental policies.

4 For an analysis of German environmental policy, see Rüdig (2003) and Wurzel (2004).

5 For an analysis of British environmental policy, see Carter and Lowe (1998), Jordan (2002) and Barry and Paterson (2005).

6 Davis and Wurth (2003), measuring different environmental variables from Guber (2003), argue that environmental factors were of significance in determining voting behaviour in the 1996 presidential election.

7 For an analysis of US environmental policy, see Sussman et al. (2002), Rosenbaum (2005a) and Vig and Kraft (2006a).

8 Al Gore had written a best-selling book, *Earth in the Balance*, which argued for environmental protection to be given high priority.

# Environmental groups

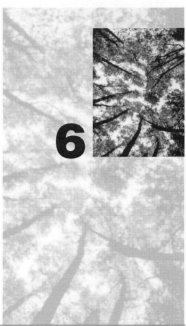

**6**

## Contents

## Key issues

▶ How powerful is the contemporary environmental movement?
▶ In what ways – size, organisation, strategy, tactics – do groups differ?
▶ How do groups exert influence?
▶ Why has there been a resurgence of grassroots activism?
▶ What impact have environmental groups had?

Environmental pressure groups (EPGs) are probably the most visible expression of contemporary environmental concern. The publicity-seeking stunts and daring deeds of the direct action protesters, whether tiny Greenpeace dinghies bobbing on the waves alongside ocean whalers or anti-road protesters perched at the top of trees, have attracted enormous public attention. Most pressure-group activity, however, involves rather more mundane conventional political activities such as lobbying and education. The rapid growth of the environmental movement since the mid-1980s has provided the resources for some groups to become highly professional organisations and to win regular access to policy elites. There is little doubt that environmental groups have been the most effective movement fighting for progressive environmental change, particularly in those countries such as the USA and UK where there is no successful green party and established parties have been largely unresponsive to environmental problems. Nevertheless, this process of institutionalisation involved compromises that blunted the radical edge of large groups such as Friends of the Earth and Greenpeace, and contributed to the resurgence of grassroots environmental groups during the 1990s, including the UK anti-roads protesters and the US environmental justice movement. Thus the environmental movement has confronted a dilemma familiar to many other political movements: should it maintain the reformist insider strategy of pressure politics, or should it pursue a radical outsider strategy of confrontational protest politics?

In this chapter, the development and achievements of the environmental movement are examined. The opening sections provide an audit of environmental groups and outline a typology that will be used to help make sense of this large and diverse movement. The following sections explore the dynamic tension between the *mainstream* environmental lobby and the less formally organised *grassroots* sector as a means of examining some central questions of green agency.[1] The main focus is on the strategic dilemmas facing any environmental group: should it adopt a professional or participatory organisational structure, and should it use conventional or disruptive forms of pressure? The next section examines the spread of transnational environmental action as one response to the challenge of globalisation and considers whether it represents the emergence of a new civil society. The final section offers a tentative evaluation of the impact of environmental groups. One theme running through the chapter is the extent to which the environmental movement represents a manifestation of the new politics.

## ▶ The environmental movement: an audit

The environmental movement, if judged simply by its sheer size and the scale of its activity, has clearly become a significant force in most industrialised countries. The USA boasts at least 150 national environmental organisations and 12,000 grassroots groups with a total estimated membership of 14 million (Sale 1993). There are around 200 national organisations and between 4 and 5 million members in the UK (Rawcliffe 1998; Rootes and Miller 2000) and about 900 organisations and 3.5 million members in Germany (Blühdorn 1995). The Dutch have the highest membership per capita: one survey found that a remarkable 45 per cent of Dutch adults claimed to be members of an environmental organisation, compared with 15 per cent of Americans, 13 per cent of Danish and under 3 per cent of German, British and French adults (Dalton 2005: 444).[2]

Two distinct waves of pressure-group mobilisation can be identified in most industrialised nations (Lowe and Goyder 1983; Dalton 1994; Brand

| Table 6.1 Membership of selected US environmental organisations ('000s) | | | | | |
|---|---|---|---|---|---|
| | 1971 | 1981 | 1992 | 1997 | 2004 |
| Sierra Club (1892) | 124 | 246 | 615 | 569 | 736 |
| National Audubon Society (1905) | 115 | 400 | 600 | 550 | 550 |
| National Parks & Conservation Assoc. (1919) | 49 | 27 | 230 | 375 | 375 |
| Izaak Walton League (1922) | 54 | 48 | 51 | 42 | 45 |
| Wilderness Society (1935) | 62 | 52 | 365 | 237 | 225 |
| National Wildlife Federation (1936) | 540 | 818 | 997 | 650 | 650 |
| Defenders of Wildlife (1947) | 13 | 50 | 77 | 215 | 463 |
| The Nature Conservancy (1951) | 22 | 80 | 545 | 865 | 972 |
| WWF-US (1961) | n.a. | n.a. | 970 | 1,200 | 1,200 |
| Environmental Defense Fund (1967) | 20 | 46 | 175 | 300 | 350 |
| Friends of the Earth (1969) | 7 | 25 | 30 | 20 | 35 |
| Natural Resources Defense Council (1970) | 5 | 40 | 170 | 260 | 450 |
| Greenpeace USA (1972) | n.a. | n.a. | 2,225 | 400 | 250 |

*Sources:* Bosso (2005: 54; Bosso and Guber 2006: 89).

1999).[3] The first wave, from the late nineteenth century to the 1950s, saw the emergence of the conservation movement with its focus on wildlife protection and the preservation of natural resources (see Box 2.5). Many major conservation groups today, including the Sierra Club and the National Audubon Society in the USA, the National Trust and the Royal Society for the Protection of Birds (RSPB) in the UK, and the Naturschutzbund Deutschland (NABU) in Germany, had their roots in this period. The founding in 1961 of the World Wildlife Fund, now World Wide Fund for Nature (WWF), a conservationist organisation but international in form and outlook, represented a bridge to a new type of international organisation. The second wave was a manifestation of 1960s modern environmentalism, which heralded an explosion in the number and size of groups. Reflecting the international nature of modern environmentalism, new groups such as Friends of the Earth (FoE) and Greenpeace rapidly became international organisations with national affiliates in many countries. They shared with new national groups, such as the Environmental Defense Fund and the Natural Resources Defense Council in the USA, a broader environmental, rather than conservationist, agenda incorporating industrial pollution, nuclear power and an expanding range of global problems. The growth of environmental concern at this time also greatly boosted the membership of traditional conservation groups and encouraged them to broaden their agendas to encompass a range of environmental and, in recent years, social justice issues.

Tables 6.1 and 6.2 show that membership has grown dramatically since the 1970s, becoming increasingly concentrated in a small number of large groups. Membership growth patterns show a cyclical form: periods of growth have been interspersed by periods of consolidation and standstill. After the

### Table 6.2 Membership of selected UK environmental organisations ('000s)

|  | 1971 | 1981 | 1991 | 1998 | 2004 |
|---|---|---|---|---|---|
| National Trust[a] | 278 | 1,046 | 2,152 | 2,557 | 3,400 |
| Royal Society for the Protection of Birds | 98 | 441 | 852 | 1,012 | 1,042 |
| Wildlife Trusts | 64 | 142 | 233 | 320 | 413 |
| WWF | 12 | 60 | 227 | 240 | 330 |
| Greenpeace |  | 30 | 312 | 194 | 221 |
| Friends of the Earth[a] | 1 | 18 | 111 | 114 | 100[b] |
| Campaign to Protect Rural England | 21 | 29 | 45 | 47 | 58 |

*Notes:*
[a] Data are for England, Wales and Northern Ireland only.
[b] Estimated.
*Source:* Office for National Statistics (2000); 2004 data from annual reports or correspondence with the groups.

initial spurt during the late 1960s/early 1970s, a second period of expansion reflected the escalation of public concern about global environmental problems during the mid/late 1980s. Subsequently, during the early 1990s, several environmental groups experienced a decline in membership; in particular, the membership of Greenpeace USA collapsed, resulting in the closure of regional offices and the reduction of salaried staff by a third (Bosso 2005: 92). Nevertheless, the major environmental groups now command substantial budgets owing to the massive increase in membership subscriptions and the development of professional fundraising activities (Jordan and Maloney 1997; Rawcliffe 1998; Bosso 2005). In particular, the US group The Nature Conservancy had an overall budget of $972.4 million in 2003, and is one of the biggest non-profit recipients of private support in the country (Bosso 2005: 101).

## A typology of environmental groups

The environmental movement is extraordinarily diverse, encompassing traditional conservation organisations (including RSPB and the Sierra Club), international NGOs (FoE and Greenpeace), radical direct action groups (Earth First! and Robin Wood) and a mass of local grassroots groups. Indeed, some observers argue that it is wrong to talk of a single environmental movement because the differences between groups are more significant than the similarities (Jordan and Maloney 1997; Bosso 1999). By contrast, Dalton (1994) refers to an all-inclusive 'green rainbow' in which differences between groups simply reflect tendencies along a continuum between a conservation orientation and an ecological orientation – ideal types that broadly correspond to the two historical waves of environmentalism. An inclusive approach to the environmental movement as encompassing all

**Table 6.3 A typology of non-partisan political organisations**

| | Forms of action | |
| --- | --- | --- |
| | Conventional pressure | Disruption |
| Professional resources | Public interest lobby | Professional protest organisation |
| Participatory resources | Participatory pressure group | Participatory protest organisation |

*Source:* Diani and Donati (1999: 16).

'broad networks of people and organisations engaged in collective action in the pursuit of environmental benefits' (Rootes 1999a: 2) is also used here. Nevertheless, one problem with inclusivity is that it can produce strange bedfellows, so the typology designed by Diani and Donati (1999) provides a helpful framework for making sense of this eclectic movement.

Diani and Donati (1999: 15–17) claim that all EPGs have to respond to two key functional requirements: **resource mobilisation** and political efficacy. *Resource mobilisation* involves securing the resources needed for collective action (see Box 4.1) (Tilly 1978; Zald and McCarthy 1987). There are two broad options: either to maximise support from the general public, through mass membership and fundraising, in order to fund a professional organisation; or to mobilise human resources by encouraging member activism. The basic choice is between a professional and a participatory organisation. *Political efficacy* refers to the choice of strategy and tactics. Again, there are two broad options: a conventional approach to political negotiation that complies with the political rules of the game or a strategy that disrupts routinised political behaviour by breaking those established rules.

> **Resource mobilisation:** An approach to collective action which focuses on the way groups mobilise their resources – members, finances, symbols – in turning grievances into political issues.

Two core dilemmas are therefore identified: between professional and participatory organisational models, and between disruptive and conventional forms of pressure (see Table 6.3). These choices produce four organisational types:

1. The *public interest lobby* is managed by professional staff, has low participation and uses traditional pressure tactics.
2. The *participatory protest organisation* emphasises participatory action, subcultural structures and disruptive protest.
3. The *professional protest organisation* combines professional activism and mobilisation of financial resources with use of confrontational tactics alongside conventional ones.
4. The *participatory pressure group* involves rank-and-file members and supporters but uses conventional pressure techniques.

The *institutionalisation* of the environment involves the growing acceptance of environmental values, concerns and organisations so that environmental collective action becomes a regular and normal feature of the established political system.

Van der Heijden (1997) identifies three aspects of institutionalisation:

1. *organisational growth* – in membership and income;
2. *internal institutionalisation* – professionalisation and centralisation of the organisation;
3. *external institutionalisation* – a shift from unconventional actions (e.g. direct action) to conventional actions (e.g. lobbying) as groups gain regular access to the policy process.

The following sections use this typology to analyse two key trends in the development of the environmental movement: the institutionalisation of the mainstream movement and the revitalisation of the grassroots sector.

### Critical question 1

Is it accurate or helpful to refer to a single environmental movement?

# ▶ The institutionalisation of the environmental movement

There is general agreement that the environmental movement in North America and Western Europe has become increasingly institutionalised (van der Heijden 1997, 1999; Brand 1999; Diani and Donati 1999; Dryzek et al. 2003; Rootes 2003; Bosso 2005) (see Box 6.1). Although there is considerable variation between countries, with institutionalisation most pronounced in Nordic countries, Germany and the Netherlands, and weakest in France and Southern Europe, overall it seems that the mainstream environmental movement has chosen reform over revolution. It has cast off any radical social movement roots in order to work within the political system; thus participatory principles and unconventional tactics have been replaced by professionalisation and conventional methods. This section analyses the nature and extent of this institutionalisation, using the criteria laid out in Box 6.1, by focusing in particular on the development of Friends of the Earth and Greenpeace.

First, the experience of 'environmental' groups should be distinguished from that of traditional conservation groups for whom institutionalisation is an unquestionable sign of success. Most conservation groups were 'born institutionalised' (Doyle and McEachern 2001: 101). They started out as elitist associations seeking moderate reforms within the existing socio-political order. The modern, mass-membership conservation groups remain hierarchical organisations, with limited democratic rights granted to members, and have used their enormous income to turn themselves into highly professional *public interest* groups. Where administration, legal advice and lobbying once depended on volunteers, today they employ professionals – managers, lawyers, fundraisers, lobbyists and scientists. Most conservation groups are wedded to conventional forms of pressure. Their political campaigning focuses on the dissemination of information, lobbying and using the legal system to protect the environment. Conservation groups have acquired growing influence within the policy process, engaging in regular dialogue with politicians and civil servants, and, by representing environmental interests in standard-setting and enforcement, they often play a formal role in policy implementation (Dryzek et al. 2003). Conservation groups are involved in a wide range of activities, from habitat protection to eco-labelling, often in partnership with state agencies, for which many groups receive significant public funding (Jamison 2001: ch. 5). Institutionalisation reaches its purest form where, as in Germany and the Netherlands, leading environmental groups are funded by the government 'with the declared objective to create a counter-lobby' (Brand 1999: 52). Conservation groups have become more institutionalised, therefore, in so far as they are now mass-membership organisations which have acquired greater legitimacy and better access to policymakers. Where some conservation groups have changed is in their willingness to broaden their agendas to include a range of transnational environmental issues because of the obvious threat to the natural habitats they seek to protect. For example, major Sierra Club campaigns include a 'global warming program', 'smart energy solutions' and 'safe and healthy communities' (Sierra Club 2006). The RSPB, recognising that the rich diversity of birds in the UK depends on the protection of the habitats of migratory birds in other continents from environmental hazards such as climate change, was an active participant in the 2002 World Summit on Sustainable Development (Rootes 2005: 31). However, apart from developing this wider environmental perspective, the massive growth of conservation groups has involved no fundamental transformation in their aims or strategies.[4] Organisations like the Sierra Club and the RSPB have always been *public interest* groups; now they are simply bigger and better at it.

The process of institutionalisation has proved more difficult for groups like Friends of the Earth (FoE) and Greenpeace, which started out as radical social movements. Both were products of the era of 'modern environmentalism'. FoE was formed in the USA in 1969 by David Brower, a former Sierra Club activist who was critical of that group's unwillingness to use confrontational methods. Greenpeace was founded in 1971 by Canadians protesting against a planned US nuclear test on a Pacific island.[5] Both groups quickly established a reputation for innovative campaigning, well-publicised protests and direct action. Greenpeace, in particular, attracted international attention through its dangerous, dramatic high-profile actions at sea against nuclear testing, whaling and the killing of seal pups. Today, both groups are huge international organisations: the FoE International federation has member groups in seventy countries (Friends of the Earth International 2006) and Greenpeace has a presence in forty countries (Greenpeace International 2006). Membership and income have also mushroomed.[6] Greenpeace International had 2.7 million 'supporters' (i.e. regular donors) and a net income of €158.5 million in 2004 (Greenpeace 2005). FoE International claims to have around 1.5 million 'members and supporters' (Friends of the Earth International 2006). FoE (England and Wales), for example, grew from eight local groups, 1,000 supporters, 6 staff and an annual budget of £10,000 in 1971 (Lowe and Goyder 1983: 133), to around 220 local groups, 100,000 supporters, 92 staff and an annual income of £5.5 million in 2004 (FoE 2004). Organisational growth of this order clearly satisfies the first category of institutionalisation (see Box 6.1), but can it be compatible with social movement aims and strategies?

The organisational structures of FoE and Greenpeace initially differed markedly. FoE, in its early days, resembled a social movement organisation – in each country it started life as a small campaigning group, usually with a central office to co-ordinate strategies, and autonomous local groups with independent control over budgets and campaigns. Today, the organisational structure of FoE varies between countries, ranging from the decentralised Australian group to the centralised US group with its focus on the Washington lobby (Doherty 2002: 130). However, where FoE attracted a mass membership it became increasingly centralised and professional. For example, as FoE (UK) expanded, the distance between the centre and local groups grew ever wider (Lowe and Goyder 1983). The centre initially resisted demands from local groups for a greater say in the organisation but, under growing pressure from members and campaign staff, it introduced a more democratic structure in 1983. Elected members do hold a majority on the board and local groups can influence strategy through the annual conference, but with the continued growth and further professionalisation of the organisation, it is a matter of some debate how democratic FoE is in practice (Jordan and Maloney 1997; Rawcliffe 1998). On balance, whilst the national level does effectively set the strategy (Doherty 2002: 129), it is also very keen to keep the grassroots membership content, hence its decision not to expand the national office and to locate any future increases in staff at the regional and local levels. Thus FoE (UK) has experienced a steady shift from an informal social movement towards a professional, centralised organisation, but elements of both 'types' remain in tension with each other, demonstrating that this transformation is not complete.

By contrast, Greenpeace has never claimed to be democratic. Its founders had a clear organisational blueprint of an elitist, hierarchical structure where control resided with full-time staff and professional activists. The intention was to free those activists from inefficient, time-consuming democratic controls to allow them to concentrate on direct action. Most Greenpeace 'members' are, in fact, 'supporters' whose subscription fee gives them no formal organisational rights, and the involvement of local groups and individual supporters is largely limited to fundraising. There are just a few hundred full members in each country. In Greenpeace Germany, for example, those members elect a management board which sets the agenda and appoints a directorate (one or two people) to head a management team that runs the national organisation (Blühdorn 1995: 191). This highly personalised and centralised executive structure has been described as 'authoritarian leadership' (Rucht 1995: 70).

The growing professionalisation of FoE and Greenpeace is reflected in the way that their national offices employ, in addition to campaigners and administrators, a significant number of marketing and fundraising specialists, and they depend decreasingly on volunteers (Jordan and Maloney 1997; Rawcliffe 1998: 82). Both groups invest significantly in mail-order recruitment. They purchase address lists of people with the demographic qualities – occupation, education, age, disposable income, political affiliations – likely to make them sympathetic to environmental causes, and willing to pay a subscription. One British study found that the typical FoE member is 'A well-educated middle-class female under 45 in a professional/managerial occupation from a relatively affluent household, who is a member of other campaigning organisations (most notably Greenpeace) and votes for a centre-left party' (Jordan and Maloney 1997: 121). Each new 'eco-crisis' is cleverly exploited with carefully chosen high-profile campaigns or stunts to draw media attention, combined with a massive mailshot to existing and potential supporters. An indication of the effectiveness of this strategy is that most British FoE members are recruited via a direct mail approach or advertisement, rather than through a social network of friends or colleagues (Jordan and Maloney 1997). Former Greenpeace activist Paul Watson has complained that Greenpeace has 'turned begging into a major corporate adventure' (*Time*, 10 June 1996).

Greenpeace and FoE both have a predominantly 'couch' membership that is quite willing to pay a subscription fee and let the leadership get on with running the organisation. Supporters seem to have only a limited emotional bond with the group; most do not wish to become activists and are unwilling to make major sacrifices to protect the environment. This passive support is probably no more than can be expected from a marketing strategy that asks for little more than a limited financial involvement from supporters in return for feeling good about helping the cause. Far from being new social movements, Jordan and Maloney (1997: 22) even describe Greenpeace and FoE as *protest businesses* modelled on private business practice because they emphasise investment in recruitment and marketing, make policy centrally, leave campaigning to professional staff and regard supporters as a source of income. This label may be more applicable to Greenpeace than to FoE as the latter still places considerable value on its links with its grassroots membership.

Further evidence of institutionalisation is found in the changes that both FoE and Greenpeace have made to their campaigning strategies. Whereas both groups were originally on the margins of the political system and made wide use of unconventional tactics, over time each has adopted a more conventional repertoire of actions. This shift from outsider to insider is most marked for FoE. In its early years, FoE frequently used direct action (usually within the law), such as the 1971 campaign to return non-returnable soft-drink bottles to Schweppes depots in Britain. Nevertheless, FoE has always employed a mixture of strategies; in particular, it pins great weight on the technical rationality of its case and likes to 'win the argument'. It gained considerable respect in Britain for its performance in the public inquiry into nuclear fuel reprocessing at Windscale in 1977, a success that encouraged it to move closer to the mainstream environmental lobby (Lowe and Goyder 1983). As it grew, FoE was able to devote more resources to monitoring government activities, publishing technical reports, using the judicial system and lobbying politicians and civil servants. Over time, the balance of its activities has gradually shifted from criticism and confrontation to practical, advice-based campaigning (McCormick 1991: 118). Today, FoE is regularly consulted by government and sometimes its representatives are found on official committees. Consequently, it eschews the grand confrontational gestures that helped build its reputation but which might now lose it the respectability needed for regular insider status. Where FoE once relished direct action, it is now hesitant to use it because it cannot afford to break the law for fear of having its financial assets sequestered by the courts.

Greenpeace remains more firmly wedded to the principle of direct action. It has always recognised the power of the media image, and quickly became associated with dramatic stunts that captured the attention of millions of viewers. A key event was the *Rainbow Warrior* incident in 1985. This Greenpeace ship, which was used to protest against French nuclear testing, was blown up by French government agents while it was docked in a New Zealand port, killing a crew member. The resulting publicity contributed to the rapid growth of Greenpeace as an international organisation. Yet this transformation brought new strategic dilemmas. Greenpeace had developed a symbiotic relationship with the media, based on its ingenious use of 'guerrilla theatre' to dramatise environmental destruction (Shaiko 1993: 97). These high-profile direct actions undoubtedly helped push issues such as whaling, sealing and the Antarctic into the limelight. The problem was that the tactics upon which Greenpeace built its reputation seemed to have a limited shelf-life; stunts needed to be ever more extreme to attract the interest of media that were becoming bored with repetition. As a big international NGO, Greenpeace now had the resources to develop new strategies (and, like FoE, it became increasingly reluctant to break the law),[7] so it adopted a more constructive 'solutions-led' approach (Rose 1993). This strategy built on the scientific expertise on which Greenpeace had always prided itself, by commissioning research, disseminating findings and appointing more scientists to key posts (Jamison et al. 1990: 117). It also reflected Greenpeace's belief that power has shifted significantly from governments to corporations. By

---

### 6.2 The changing nature of environmental pressure: solution-led campaigning

*The 'greenfreeze' refrigerator*

In 1992 Greenpeace Germany commissioned a prototype refrigerator with a hydrocarbon cooling agent instead of the ozone-depleting CFC-substitutes, HFCs and HCFCs. Large chemical companies were highly sceptical, declaring that the development of such technology was many years off. Yet Greenpeace persuaded a struggling East German company, Foron, to start commercial production of the refrigerator in 1993 (with government financial aid). Sales in Germany took off rapidly and within months major manufacturers such as Bosch began shifting to the new technology. By 1997, almost 100 per cent of German and approaching 80 per cent of production in Northern and Western Europe was 'greenfreeze'. In 2004 there were almost 150 million greenfreeze refrigerators in the world. The only significant market that it has failed to crack is North America.

See http://www.greenpeace.org/international/ campaigns/climate-change/solutions/solar_chill

---

using science to engage in a 'rational' debate with industry, Greenpeace was prepared to compromise its hostile attitude to its traditional 'enemy'. During the 1990s, the solutions-led strategy saw Greenpeace working closely with corporations in search of alternatives to environmentally damaging activities such as the use of chlorine-free paper for newspapers and fuel-efficient cars. As the successful 'greenfreeze' refrigerator campaign illustrates, a key aim was to use market pressures to change the behaviour of business (see Box 6.2). On occasion this 'constructive engagement' has even developed into 'partnership': Greenpeace UK has joined with an energy utility to invest in a wind power project, and it encourages consumers to purchase their electricity from this supplier. However, unlike many other established groups, such as WWF, Greenpeace has resisted going down the path of direct corporate sponsorship.

Greenpeace has not found the transition to greater respectability easy. Ironically, the shift to solutions-led campaigning upset both the old-guard activists and marketing staff. Hardline activists, several of whom left or were forced out of the organisation, accused the leadership of selling out by engaging in dialogue with corporations. Meanwhile, the marketing professionals were alarmed that the low profile of the solutions-led approach was not producing the racy headlines and evocative pictures necessary for fundraising. Since the mid-1990s, these internal pressures have encouraged Greenpeace to show a renewed enthusiasm for direct action, including the occupation of the Brent Spar oil-rig (see Box 6.3), an attempt to disrupt French nuclear testing in the Pacific Ocean (Bennie 1998), the destruction of GM crop experiments across Europe and temporarily stopping production of Land Rover sports utility vehicles (*Financial Times*, 17 May 2005). Direct action did not replace the policy of working with industry; rather, the two approaches are used in parallel. Gray et al. (1999) show how Greenpeace, in its various North Sea fishing industry campaigns, has used a broad range of unconventional and conventional strategies, ranging from confrontation to

### 6.3 Lessons of Brent Spar

Brent Spar was a redundant 14,500-tonne oil-platform which Shell, with the permission of the British government and acting on best scientific advice, had planned to dispose of deep in the North Atlantic. A high-publicity Greenpeace campaign against the 'dumping' during 1995, which included the occupation of Brent Spar, resulted in Shell abandoning the proposal.

Lessons:

1. *Direct action can be effective:* The brilliantly engineered media campaign stopped the dumping of Brent Spar and made the entire policy of deep-sea disposal of old oil-rigs politically unacceptable.
2. *The power of the moral message:* Greenpeace used a familiar, emotionally charged message – that dumping at sea was wrong and that the ocean should not be used as a dustbin – to take the moral high ground and project Shell and the government as the bad guys (Bennie 1998).
3. *The power of the market:* A key factor in Shell's climbdown was a European consumer boycott of its products, which was particularly effective in Germany where demand dropped by up to 30 per cent almost overnight.
4. *Lasting damage to Greenpeace's media image:* The subsequent admission that Greenpeace mistakenly overestimated the amount of pollutant material still in the platform lost it considerable respect in the media and undermined its reputation for scientific expertise. The media felt manipulated and have since become more critical of Greenpeace – a dangerous development for an organisation that is so dependent on media coverage.

dialogue, selecting whichever seems most appropriate to achieve a particular objective. Where Greenpeace once preferred to operate in isolation, now, like FoE, it frequently works with other EPGs, such as the Dolphin Coalition of forty groups which played a key role in securing legislation to protect the dolphin from tuna-fishing fleets in the eastern Pacific Ocean (Wright 2001).

It is clear that, measured by all three criteria, FoE and Greenpeace have undergone extensive (if not complete) institutionalisation. FoE started out as something close to a *participatory protest* organisation but, whilst it retains elements of democracy and participation, it is now much closer to the *public interest* model, with its professionalisation and emphasis on conventional strategies of publicity, lobbying, litigation and expert testimony. Greenpeace has also become more institutionalised, but its continuing commitment to direct action places it closer to the *professional protest* model. It is not an insider public interest group: its reluctance to engage in formal lobbying or to serve on government committees means it is often not trusted by government or the mainstream environmental lobby. Conversely, its dialogue with industry and its greater circumspection about law-breaking suggest to many environmental activists that even Greenpeace has lost its radical edge, although its renewed enthusiasm for direct action has restored some of its radical credentials. Nevertheless, many environmentalists have become increasingly disenchanted with the mainstream environmental movement, opting instead to get involved in grassroots activity.

### *Critical question 2*

Has the institutionalisation of Greenpeace and Friends of the Earth turned them into 'protest businesses'?

## ▶ The resurgence of grassroots environmentalism?

By the 1990s the growth of the environmental movement prompted widespread concern that its new-found success might also be its undoing, for a movement that could not mobilise its supporters against government or corporations would rapidly see a decline in influence. The institutionalisation of the movement had denuded its radical spirit, and environmental protests were apparently in decline.[8] Ironically, it was the grassroots environmental movement that came to the rescue. There has always been a grassroots sector alongside the major environmental organisations, but during the late 1980s and 1990s it was revitalised in several countries, notably in the UK and USA, very often as a direct response to the perceived failings of the institutionalised mainstream environmental movement. The term 'grassroots' conceals many differences, but three broad categories can be identified: first, radical social movements such as the Sea Shepherd Society, Robin Wood (Germany) and Earth First!; secondly, small local groups campaigning against a specific locally unwanted land use (LULU); and, thirdly, broad coalitions of groups, such as the US environmental justice movement and the UK anti-roads protesters, which may contain groups from both the other categories. This section assesses the significance of the grassroots sector by examining each of these three categories.

The first category of groups holds an explicitly ecological, counter-cultural orientation and makes up the most radical strand of the grassroots movement. Although many of these groups have developed a national, or even international, structure, they are grassroots in their commitment to participatory, decentralised structures and in their fierce rejection of all forms of institutionalisation. Many were set up by activists disillusioned with mainstream environmental groups. Robin Wood was formed by a breakaway group of Greenpeace Germany activists who wanted a more participatory organisation with an explicitly German agenda focusing on acid rain and forest decline (Blühdorn 1995: 197–200). Ex-Greenpeace activist Paul Watson founded the Sea Shepherd Society, which is notable for dramatic acts such as sinking two Icelandic whaling vessels in 1986 (Chatterjee and Finger 1994: 72). The most radical group is Earth First!, founded in the USA in 1980 by five activists critical of the bureaucratic structures and moderate stance of major conservation groups such as the Wilderness Society and the Sierra Club (Gottlieb 1993; Rucht 1995).

The founders of Earth First! were deep ecologists committed to confrontational direct action, including acts of civil disobedience and 'monkey-wrenching', or 'ecotage' (illegal actions such as tree-spiking and sabotaging bulldozers).[9] Our knowledge of Earth First! (USA) is rather murky because secrecy veils much of its (often illegal) activity. It is profoundly anti-institutional, with a highly decentralised structure of around a hundred groups, each with fifteen to twenty activists, plus supporting groups, and around fourteen operational centres co-ordinating national initiatives (Rucht 1995). Groups are autonomous, determining their own campaigns and raising their own finances. No one individual speaks for Earth First!. There are various organs of co-ordination and communication, including a magazine, an annual meeting and an activist conference. Earth First! has gained considerable attention and notoriety for its theatrical attention-seeking stunts, such as perching in trees destined to be chopped down for logging, and, most of all, for its acts of ecotage. Activists have gone far beyond the limits of civil disobedience by repeatedly destroying the technical equipment of companies engaged in logging, drilling, electricity supply and surveying. Whereas Greenpeace breaks the law infrequently, preferably where there is no moral ambivalence about the act and only when it has carefully calculated the impact on its public reputation, Earth First! is proud that it flouts the law and relishes any media backlash directed against it (Rucht 1995: 80). Indeed, it has attracted a highly critical response from the American media and from other environmental groups, even attracting violent counter-attacks, including a pipe bomb under a leading activist's car. By the early 1990s, Earth First! was badly split by ideological divisions between the older generation activists such as Dave Foreman, who emphasised a narrow 'deep ecology' zeal for wilderness and biodiversity issues, and a younger generation who disliked some of the misanthropic sentiments of the first group, preferring to develop a broader social agenda (Lee 1995; Doherty 2002: 158–60). Eventually, Foreman and his allies departed, allowing Earth First! to develop a wider environmental justice agenda. Earth First!, with its democratic, decentralised structure, its commitment to direct action and willingness to operate outside the formal political system, is a clear example of a *participatory protest* group. During the 1990s, Earth First! groups were formed in Britain, Ireland and the Netherlands. Ironically, inspired by the direct action movement in the UK (see below), a new shadowy militant group called the Earth Liberation Front emerged in the USA, claiming responsibility for numerous ecotage acts, notably a range of arson attacks on developers and logging companies (Doherty 2002: 160).

Most groups fall within the second category of grassroots group. They are based in a local community and are usually formed by residents as a 'not in my back yard' (NIMBY) response to a proposed LULU, such as a new road or incinerator, or from concern about the health risks of an existing hazard, such as a polluting factory or pesticide-spraying. These groups are usually participative and rely heavily on voluntary action, membership subscriptions and fundraising. Membership is likely to reflect the local base of the group: middle-class in an affluent area; working-class in poorer communities. A

## 6.4 The environmental justice movement

Environmental justice is broader than just preserving the environment. When we fight for environmental justice we fight for our homes and families and struggle to end economic, social and political domination by the strong and the greedy.

(Lois Gibbs, quoted in Schlosberg 1999b: 127)

The environmental justice movement emerged in the USA during the 1980s with the mushrooming of networks of grassroots groups, such as the Clearing House for Hazardous Waste (renamed, symbolically, in 1997 as the Centre for Health, Environment and Justice). It is a bottom-up movement that is rooted in the struggles of local communities against environmental hazards: people get involved through personal experience and local networks, not because they happen to be on a mailing list.

The key idea underpinning the environmental justice movement is the recognition that environmental hazards are closely linked to race and poverty. It is poor people who live in the worst environments, and in the USA the poorest people tend to be non-whites. Disproportionately large numbers of African-Americans and Hispanics live close to hazardous and toxic waste sites (Bullard 2000). In short, ecosystem destruction is often connected to racism. Hence the second principle of the environmental justice movement states that: 'Environmental justice demands that public policy be based on mutual respect and justice for all peoples, free from any form of discrimination or bias' (Environmental Justice Resource Center 2006).

For an analysis of the environmental justice movement, see Szasz (1994), Pulido (1996), Schlosberg (1999b), Roberts and Toffolon-Weiss (2001) and Visiglio and Whitelaw (2003).

notable feature of US grassroots groups is the prevalence of anti-toxic waste and environmental justice groups in many poor urban and rural communities, with a sharply different membership profile from the predominantly middle-class mainstream environmental movement. In particular, women of all classes are well represented in the anti-toxics movement (Gottlieb 1993) and they contain a much larger proportion of African-Americans and Latinos (Pulido 1996; Schlosberg 1999a; Visiglio and Whitelaw 2003). (See Box 6.4.)

NIMBY groups exist everywhere and employ a wide range of strategies. Some are *participatory pressure* groups employing conventional tactics, including lobbying, organising petitions, filing lawsuits or running candidates in local elections to publicise their case. Conventional methods often prove fruitless, prompting frustrated and increasingly politicised activists to adopt more confrontational, unconventional tactics, such as demonstrations, sit-ins and blockades. A famous 1978 incident involved the residents of Love Canal in New York holding two officials of the Environmental Protection Agency 'hostage' for several hours in order to publicise the danger of local toxic chemical pollution. Two days later, President Carter declared the area a disaster zone, which made the residents eligible for relocation assistance (Gibbs 1982). Although grassroots campaigns have achieved many individual successes, causing projects to be abandoned, delayed or amended, there have also been countless failed campaigns where the LULU gets built regardless. Typically, enthusiastic local campaigners are impotent against the combined power of profit-seeking corporations and governments anxious not to impede economic development (Gould et al. 1996). Where local campaigns are successful, it is usually because of external factors. One study of local campaigns in Britain shows how any limited success was largely 'dependent on action or inaction at other levels', such as national government, the European Commission, transnational corporations or the involvement of the mainstream environmental lobby (Rootes 1999b). Thus the conventional methods of the long-running (1979–96) local campaign against a proposed nuclear power station at Druridge Bay, Northumberland, finally succeeded when the British government introduced a moratorium on the building of all nuclear power stations (Baggott 1998).

Many local groups, recognising the limitations of operating in isolation, have built links with other like-minded grassroots groups. Consequently, the third category of grassroots group refers to the development of coalitions and networks among local environmental groups, which is particularly marked in the USA (Gould et al. 1996; Schlosberg 1999b). National coalitions that have co-ordinated campaigns against toxic hazards include the Centre for Health, Environment and Justice and the National Toxics Campaign, which claim to be in contact with up to 10,000 and 7,000 local groups respectively (Dowie 1995: 133). There are also many regional groups, such as the Silicon Valley Toxics Coalition in California and the Work on Waste (anti mass-burn incinerators/pro-recycling) in New York State. These coalitions have arisen from a common wish to share scientific and technical information, learn from each other's experiences and pool resources in jointly run campaigns. An additional catalyst has been a widespread disenchantment with the smooth professionalism of mainstream environmental groups. Grassroots activists frequently criticise the ineffectiveness of public interest group campaigning, the refusal of the established groups to endorse direct action, their willingness to get into bed with big corporations and their focus on the Washington lobby.

The environmental justice movement condemns the mainstream organisations for concentrating on 'universal' issues such as wildlife and natural resource protection, whilst ignoring those environmental hazards that hit poorer (often non-white) communities hardest (see Box 6.4). The environmental justice movement brings the issues of class, poverty, race and gender to the forefront of environmentalism. It holds that, because environmental hazards are inextricably linked to inequality, solutions will not be found in the middle-class issues of conservation and preservation, but in transforming entrenched economic and political structures. Environmental justice is thus a practical political expression of both the social justice principle of ecologism and the socialist critique of environmentalists as middle-class elitists (see Chapter 3). The environmental justice movement clearly offers a tough challenge to the 'whiteness' of the environmental movement. One of its achievements is its inclusiveness which, according to Schlosberg (1999a), has been nurtured by a form of discursive democracy based on respect for different identities and backgrounds, and with no attempt to impose any strong ideology on the movement.

The absence of an equivalent large working-class or non-white grassroots environmental justice movement in Europe may reflect different political opportunity structures, notably the more pluralistic nature of the American polity, and the greater possibility in Europe of expressing social justice issues in partisan terms through left-wing or green parties. Most networks of environmental groups in European countries still retain an explicitly environmental focus, whether campaigning on pollution, energy or nature conservation issues (Rootes 2003). In Germany, for example, protests through the 1990s were still dominated by the anti-nuclear issue. The one notable change in character was a shift away from protests against the construction of nuclear power stations – for no more were being built – towards protests against the transport and storage of nuclear waste (Rucht and Roose 2003; Fischer and Boehnke 2004). One recent example of an incipient environmental justice movement is the loose network of waste campaigns in the UK, particularly in opposition to proposed incinerators. Plans to site massive incinerators in socially deprived sites, such as Crymlyn Burrows, South Wales, have seen the language of environmental justice employed both by local campaigners and Friends of the Earth.

One of the most significant coalitions in Europe, the UK anti-roads protests, developed a mild social justice agenda, but it had a more overtly 'green' character than the American environmental justice movement. The anti-roads movement involved a series of linked struggles against the building of new roads as part of the Conservative government's massive construction programme, starting in 1992 with opposition to the M3 motorway extension at Twyford Down, and moving on to similar campaigns throughout the country. The loose coalition of some 250–300 anti-roads groups was co-ordinated by two volunteer umbrella groups, Road Alert and Alarm UK. An interesting feature of the anti-roads protests was that each individual campaign involved a coalition of two kinds of grassroots group (Doherty 1999: 276). There was always one group of local residents who had opposed the specific scheme for many years, primarily from NIMBY motivations, and had exhausted all legal avenues of opposition. They were then joined by a second group of activists from the green counter-culture, popularly known as 'eco-warriors' or eco-protesters. Thus the public was treated to graphic images of middle-aged, middle-class residents bringing food and drink to the eco-warriors in their treehouses and tunnels.

The radical eco-protester wing of the anti-roads movement, like the environmental justice movement, was born out of disillusionment with the perceived ineffectiveness of the mainstream, professional environmental groups, especially FoE and Greenpeace (Seel 1997: 121–2; Wall 1999). An important symbol of their impotence was the decision by FoE to withdraw from Twyford Down soon after construction began, when it was landed with a series of injunctions that threatened the sequestration of its assets. Into this political void stepped the eco-warriors, who were prepared to take those forms of direct action that frightened off the mainstream groups. The emergence of Earth First! (UK) in 1991 was critical: by 1997 there were around 60 active groups and its annual gathering was attended by about 400 activists (Doherty 1998: 68; Wall 1999). Not all eco-protesters identified with Earth First!, but common practices characterised the whole anti-roads movement. Organisationally, it was informal, decentralised and non-hierarchical. The activists were deeply alienated from the political parties, groups and institutions. Eco-protest appealed to a particular kind of person:

> Mostly young, in their twenties or late teens, in education or choosing to live on a low income . . . most are in effect full-time political activists. Becoming an eco-protester means making a commitment to a lifestyle based mainly in protest camps or communal houses, in which many possessions are shared, income is minimal, and codes of conduct that minimise impact on the environment are observed. [They] have little concern with formal ideology, even of a green kind, but share a belief that 'do-it-yourself political action' is the only viable means of improving democracy and overcoming the ecological crisis.
>
> (Doherty 1999: 276–7)

Although the road-building programme was their main focus, their concerns embraced broader questions about the centralised power of the British state, land ownership and the curtailments of civil liberties. The eco-protesters also campaigned against a second runway at Manchester Airport, open-cast mining and quarrying. As the anti-roads movement wound down around 1996, many individuals became involved in groups like Reclaim the Streets and The Land is Ours that developed a more positive agenda, linking existing patterns of car use and land ownership to environmental problems, and were more sharply influenced by social justice issues. From 1999, many joined the direct action protests against GM crop experiments or targeted multinationals such as McDonalds, Shell and BP, while others shifted attention to the Global Justice Movement (see below). Doherty's (1999) description of the eco-protesters as 'the first full expression of the new social movement type in British environmental politics' (p. 290) seems apt.[10]

### Critical question 3
Is a vibrant grassroots sector a sign of an effective environmental movement?

## ▶ A new civic politics?

The two preceding sections have shown that the environmental movement encompasses a rich mix of organisational forms, strategies and tactics

Environmental protests can involve a wide range of unconventional and indirect actions to influence policymakers:

1. The *logic of numbers:* to demonstrate the sheer size of support to the government and the wider public – around 20 million Americans celebrated the first Earth Day in 1970, a critical event in persuading policy elites that the public wanted legislation to protect the environment.
2. The *logic of damage:* to inflict material losses on business or government. Includes:
   (i) economic sanctions – the Greenpeace-orchestrated consumer boycott of Shell petrol stations during the Brent Spar campaign (Box 6.3);
   (ii) economic disruption – the anti-roads protests hoped the huge security costs of policing road-building sites would dissuade construction companies and the government from future developments;
   (iii) violence against property – Earth First! 'ecotage'; computer-hacking offers a new means of inflicting huge material damage on corporations and government.
3. The *logic of bearing witness:* to 'demonstrate a strong commitment to an objective deemed vital for humanity's future' (della Porta and Diani 2006: 176). It reinforces the moral message by showing that activists are willing to take personal risks because of the strength of their convictions:
   • in 1995 Greenpeace vessels sailed into the exclusion zone around Mururoa in the Pacific where the French were about to carry out nuclear tests.
   • ecological activists take up residence in treehouses or a maze of tunnels.

*Source*: della Porta and Diani (2006: 170–8).

(see Box 6.5). The typology (Table 6.3) reveals a dynamic movement in which the convergence amongst the major environmental groups in most countries towards the institutionalised 'public interest' model should, in many countries, be set against a thriving grassroots sector made up of both 'participatory pressure' groups of local citizens opposing specific LULUs and 'participatory protest' ecological social movements. Yet, contrary to the doubts of Bosso (1999), there does seem to be sufficient common ground to talk in terms of one broad environmental movement. Apart from the obvious points of similarity, such as a shared concern about environmental destruction, two particular manifestations of this unity are significant.

First, there seems to be a creative tension between the different wings of the movement. Certainly, the vitality of the grassroots sector is partly a result of the widespread negative perceptions of the mainstream movement amongst concerned citizens, with many grassroots groups springing directly from a deep-seated frustration at the perceived impotence of the environmental lobby, notably for their neglect of local campaigning. For their part, established groups, particularly those with radical roots, have tried to respond to the challenge from below. FoE (UK), for example, stung by criticisms that it has neglected its participatory principles, has used regional campaign co-ordinators to encourage its often moribund local groups to become more active – and has even trained some local groups in techniques of non-violent direct action. Greenpeace too has been sensitive to criticisms of its authoritarian, undemocratic structure. In 1995, for example, Greenpeace UK relaxed its prohibition on local support groups engaging in activities beyond fundraising and publicity in support of national and international campaigns; later, in 1999, it established a network of 'active supporters' to allow enthusiasts to become more involved in local actions (Rootes 2005: 38). Greenpeace USA has also worked closely with grassroots groups and made a concerted effort to recruit more staff from ethnic minorities (Dowie 1995: 147). One factor contributing to this change of heart was that, in common with other major groups, FoE and Greenpeace experienced a fall-off in support and a decline in income during the mid-1990s – a direct threat to the 'protest business' strategy. This stagnation may also be a function of the grassroots challenge. In the USA, the Sierra Club and National Audubon Society have faced internal criticism from members demanding that they should become more radical and less Washington-focused (Dowie 1995: 214–19). Thus there seems to be a symbiotic relationship between the mainstream and grassroots sectors that will probably regularly reproduce similar cycles of activity and stagnation across the 'green rainbow'.

Secondly, EPGs have shown an increasing willingness to form coalitions and networks to pursue their aims more effectively by pooling their resources. The established groups are regularly involved in international and national coalition activity, reflecting (and contributing to) the growing convergence between them. The big EPGs have years of experience working together in the lobby, on government committees and developing joint responses to consultative documents (Bosso 2005). The emergence of loose-knit coalitions with some grassroots groups, such as the anti-roads protesters and the environmental justice movement, suggests that there is sufficient common ground to work together on key issues. The successful conventional campaign against the proposal to build a Thames river-crossing through Oxleas Wood in London involved an alliance of FoE, WWF, Alarm UK and Earth First! (Doherty 1998: 284). Although the anti-roads campaigns initially saw considerable hostility between FoE and the eco-warriors, particularly at Twyford Down, they worked alongside each other in later campaigns (Seel and Plows 2000: 118). Elsewhere, German anti-nuclear protests typically involved a coalition of mainstream environmental groups, such as the Bund für Umwelt und Naturschutz Deutschland (BUND) and Greenpeace, and local groups (Rucht and Roose 2003: 102). Gould et al. (1996: 195–6) concluded from their study of local environmental mobilisation in the USA that groups are most effective when they build alliances with regional or national organisations. The massive international mobilisation of NGOs protesting against the World Trade Organisation (WTO) convention in Seattle in November 1999 involved a significant degree of co-ordination between mainstream and grassroots networks.

The Seattle events also identified the internationalisation of environmental politics as a key challenge for the contemporary environmental movement. In an interdependent global economic system the actions of non-democratic international capitalist institutions such as the WTO have a profound effect on the environment, and international environmental diplomacy between nation states has also expanded (see Chapters 9 and 10). With critical decisions increasingly being taken beyond the level of the nation state by international organisations, transnational corporations and national governments, how can environmental NGOs hope to compete against such powerful players?

Yet the international arena offers opportunities too. In recent years the environmental movement has shown its capacity to construct transnational alliances of NGOs, from both North and South, which have scored some notable successes, helping make possible international agreements preventing mineral exploitation of the Antarctic (Wapner 1996), banning ozone-depleting CFCs and protecting biodiversity (see Chapter 9). Major groups like Greenpeace and FoE have often shown their old dynamism at this international level, perhaps because global campaigns are more glamorous, attract wide publicity and offer different challenges to groups such as FoE that are increasingly shackled by domestic institutionalisation. Indeed, environmental NGOs are now so active at the international level that some writers see the emergence of a new *global civic society*, which is 'that slice of associational life that exists above the individual and below the state, but also across national boundaries' (Wapner 1996: 4; also Lipschutz 1996). They argue that, instead of identifying with the nation state, people are increasingly seeing themselves as part of a broader global community where they can be represented by environmental social movements: an international 'new politics'. While this inspiring vision may currently appear a little fanciful, it does nevertheless identify an important arena in contemporary environmental politics.

The most interesting example has been the global justice movement (GJM). This broad movement consists of a network of actors and organisations, engaged in collective action and sharing a common concern about a wide range of connected transnational issues, notably development, trade, debt, poverty and the environment. It involves activists from North and South, and makes important links between their respective concerns. The GJM incorporates both mainstream, moderate organisations, including aid and development charities, religious organisations and leading environmental groups such as WWF and FoE, as well as an eclectic array of direct action groups including environmental, anti-capitalist and anti-globalisation protesters. These different wings of the GJM have engaged (in their different ways) in conventional political activities, such as campaigns to reform the WTO and the Multilateral Agreement on Investment, high-profile public demonstrations including those at the Geneva WTO summit in 2002 and the Gleneagles G8 summit in 2005, and a range of conferences, such as the

European Social Forum. Not surprisingly, we have seen similar processes in the international arena as have occurred at the domestic level, with establishment NGOs expressing criticisms of the confrontational tactics of the direct action protesters as counter-productive, whilst the latter see the moderate tactics of the former as an ineffective 'sell-out'. Others, notably Friends of the Earth, which in the UK has made great efforts to adopt a transnational global justice agenda (Rootes 2005), prefer to see these differences as a creative tension, which will help propel issues onto the public agenda. However, whilst many environmental activists have thrown themselves wholeheartedly into the GJM, it is noticeable that, beyond the inclusion of some green rhetoric, the GJM has not given priority to environmental issues. Many of the biggest anti-globalisation events, such as the Prague demonstration against the IMF/World Bank in 2001, have had little direct environmental input. One reason may be the important role within the direct action anti-globalisation movement of left-wing activists, who have a wider political agenda and perhaps retain lingering suspicions of environmentalism. The growing significance within the GJM agenda of climate change, an explicitly environmental issue but one with profound social justice implications, may rectify this imbalance against the environment.

### Critical question 4
Is the global justice movement an effective defender of the environment?

## ▶ The impact of the environmental movement

The environmental movement has clearly become an important political actor in most advanced industrial liberal democracies, but it is very difficult to measure its overall impact, or to draw any firm conclusions about the relative effectiveness of conventional and unconventional strategies. It may be possible to assess the impact of an action in specific cases, such as the Greenpeace Brent Spar campaign, but how can the influence of the broader Greenpeace campaign for climate change prevention be measured? At best, we may only be able to make generalised, unquantifiable assessments. This section offers a tentative step in this direction by applying a framework that distinguishes five kinds of impact: individual identity, sensitising, procedural, structural and substantive (see Table 6.4).

One direct political aim of collective action is to raise the ecological consciousness of activists (who might then convert others to the cause). One yardstick is thus whether involvement in environmental groups affects individual political *identity*. This kind of politicisation is most likely in activist grassroots groups where individuals engage personally in a collective struggle. Involvement in those ecological social movements located in the counter-cultural milieu, such as Earth First!, is likely to provide a particularly powerful political experience, as illustrated by the anti-roads eco-protesters.

| **Table 6.4 Types of impact of environmental pressure groups** |
| --- |

**Internal**

*Impact on identity*
Politicisation of membership/supporters of group

**External**

*Sensitising impacts*
Changes in the political agenda and public attitudes

*Procedural impacts*
Access to decision-making bodies

*Structural impacts*
Changes in institutional or alliance structures, such as the creation of an environment agency or shift in attitude of parties

*Substantive impacts*
Material results: closure of a nuclear plant or new pollution legislation

*Source:* Based on Kriesi et al. (1995: 209–12) and van der Heijden (1999: 202–3).

Torgerson (1999) identifies the creation of a 'green political sphere', stretching beyond the radical fringe, characterised by an environmental discourse that allows people to live political lives, as a major achievement of the environmental movement. There is also evidence from the UK (Rootes 1999b: 298) and the USA (Szasz 1994) that even NIMBY activity can be a politically educative experience. Here, the key question, as Freudenberg and Steinsapir (1992) put it, is whether a NIMBY reaction can become a Not in Anyone's Back Yard (NIABY) belief. Does involvement in a struggle against a LULU encourage individuals to ask broader questions, such as 'If I don't want this incinerator in my neighbourhood, why should anyone else have to put up with it?' People might then start to ask wider questions about the nature of energy production and consumption. In short, they may begin to develop a wider ecological consciousness. The involvement of local groups in coalitions such as the National Toxics Campaign in the USA, by encouraging people to link their struggles with those of other communities, can play a vital role in this educative process. By contrast, 'couch' members of major environmental organisations may salve their environmental consciences through the limited act of paying a regular donation to a major group, whilst continuing their consumerist lifestyle. If an annual payment is the limit of an individual's activity, then involvement clearly has little additional politicising effect. Yet 'couch' membership should not be dismissed lightly. The very act of joining is a political statement. The access to magazines and campaigning literature may prove educative, encouraging people to reflect on their own and others' lifestyles. Membership may also be the first step towards a wider involvement, particularly if individuals become frustrated that their membership seems to be making little 'difference'.

The environmental movement has undoubtedly exerted a significant, and continuing, *sensitising* impact by helping place the environment on the political agenda and stimulating public support for environmental protection. Perhaps its main achievement has been to create a climate in which governments are expected to pay greater attention to environmental protection, even if it is not yet on a par with traditional material issues. Both insider and outsider strategies have played their part in this process of ecological sensibility. The established environmental lobby provides a constant educative and persuasive pressure on policy elites to consider the environment. Further from the heart of government, confrontational actions that capture media attention have repeatedly succeeded in pushing environmental issues into the public gaze. Together, the different parts of the environmental movement have all helped to shape the political discourse, from climate change to biodiversity, and from energy to waste.

One consequence has been a tranche of *structural* changes in the way governments treat environmental problems. In particular, environmental pressure was largely responsible for the creation of environment ministries in most governments (see Chapter 11).

The insider strategy has achieved some notable *procedural* successes. Everywhere the environmental lobby is listened to more closely and across much of Northern Europe, North America and Australasia it is now regularly consulted on many subjects. The international environmental lobby is represented in several UN and other international, including EU, consultation networks. A key question is whether procedural gains translate into influence. As Chapter 7 shows, environmental groups have achieved only limited access to the policy networks that shape core economic decisions – in finance, industry, trade, energy and agriculture – which are still dominated by corporate and producer interests. Where regular access is secured, as is widespread in corporatist Norway where the environmental movement is represented on a multitude of governmental policymaking committees (Dryzek et al. 2003: 22–5), there is a price to being an insider group, which involves compromise, obedience to the rules of the game and doing business with interests whose values and actions may be anathema to most environmentalists. In the USA, the incorporationary pressures of the Washington lobby, for example, were apparent in the negotiation of the North American Free Trade Agreement (NAFTA) in the early 1990s. Having opposed it when proposed by George Bush, most environmental groups eventually supported NAFTA in order to maintain their access to the Clinton White House and because they had been 'purchased' by large corporate donations, upon which they depend so heavily (Bosso 2005: 76, 115). Insider status can also prove fragile. In both the UK and the USA the environmental lobby found that the improved access to government that it achieved in the 1970s was dramatically reduced under the anti-environmentalist leadership of Thatcher and Reagan respectively (McCormick 1991; Dowie 1995) – and in the USA, after the doors began to reopen from the late 1980s onwards, they slammed shut again with the election of George W. Bush in 2000 (Bosso 2005: ch. 5). Even where green parties have entered government, as in Germany, environmental groups have found their access to ministers only marginally improved (Dryzek et al. 2003: 185–6; Rüdig 2003: 266).

The acid test of the environmental movement – its *substantive* impact – is particularly difficult to evaluate. Grassroots groups have certainly scored many individual local successes (although the prevention of a LULU in one location often results in it being built elsewhere). They have also endured many defeats: for example, most of the British roads that were the subject of an extensive anti-roads direct action campaign during the 1990s were eventually built. Grassroots campaigns have rarely proved decisive in the wider policy arena. The strongest claim for the British anti-roads protests is that these campaigns succeeded in pushing the road-building issue high up the political agenda and created the climate in which the Conservative government made dramatic cuts in the road-building programme, but it was not the decisive factor (Robinson 2000). In the USA, whilst some commentators are circumspect about the influence of grassroots groups (Gould et al. 1996), others argue that grassroots campaigns have helped change legislation on pollution control and right-to-know provisions, and encouraged business and government to take a more preventive approach to environmental contamination (Freudenberg and Steinsapir 1992: 33–5). The environmental justice movement seems to have persuaded the Clinton administration to issue Executive Order 12898 in 1994, which required agencies to take social and environmental justice concerns seriously (Roberts and Toffolon-Weiss 2001: 56). In Germany, confrontational strategies involving a combination of grassroots groups and more mainstream organisations, such as Greenpeace, have scored some notable victories, especially the anti-nuclear campaigns opposing the construction of nuclear reactors and transport of nuclear waste. Indeed, in an interesting comparative study of the environmental movements in Germany, Norway, the UK and the USA, Dryzek et al. (2003) identify Germany as the only country with 'significant pro-active policy in response to environmental activity in civil society' (p. 162).

The impact of the insider strategy pursued by the mainstream environmental movement has also been primarily defensive; a powerful, united green lobby can frequently repulse undesirable policy initiatives and block environmentally damaging development projects. It has had less success in building support for its own reforms or in bringing about major changes to the policy discourse, although its influence has varied between countries and over time. Obviously the policy impact of the environmental lobby in any individual country will depend on a wide range of contextual factors, including the openness of the political opportunity structure, public attitudes, the party politicisation of the environment, the strength of the producer lobby and the strategic choices made by the environmental groups themselves.

Dryzek et al. (2003) argue that an insider strategy will only be effective where a movement 'can attach its interest to one or more of the imperatives that constitute the state's core' (p. 192). However, the long-standing and familiar problem for the environmental movement is that its interests clash with the core state imperative of economic growth. Exceptionally, the American environmental movement was able to exercise considerable policy influence over the Nixon administration in the early 1970s, when the Environmental Protection Agency was formed and a tranche of environmental legislation enacted, because the core economic growth imperative was temporarily replaced by a legitimation imperative. Confronted by a range of controversial social and political issues (the Vietnam war, civil rights, student unrest etc.) and the emergence of a thriving counter-culture, Nixon saw the environment as one issue on which he could appease public discontent and diffuse the momentum behind the movement (ibid.: 34). Subsequently, the environmental movement in the USA and elsewhere had limited impact, with insider strategies turning out to represent a 'bad bargain, because the included group must either remain tame (avoiding core imperatives), frustrated (as it runs up against the core), or be deflected (to more minor issues at the periphery)' (ibid.: 163).

The rise of ecological modernisation, which regards economic and environmental concerns as potentially complementary, brought a change in the fortunes of the environmental movement in a handful of Northern European countries (see Chapter 8). Norwegian environmental groups, for example, were incorporated into government policymaking from the mid-1980s, resulting in undoubted policy advances (although it is hard to evaluate their impact on any particular policy). By contrast, in Germany, where ecological modernisation also arrived early, but the state was initially less willing to embrace environmental groups, the environmental movement pursued a dual insider–outsider strategy of seeking inclusion in the governmental policy process whilst retaining an active, often confrontational, involvement in civil society. The optimistic lesson is that the core imperatives of the state are not set in stone and that the alternative policy paradigm of ecological modernisation offers a firmer basis for an insider strategy. Consequently, the message for the environmental movement in its many and varied forms is to do all it can to shape the core imperatives of the state to make them congruent with the environmental imperative (Dryzek et al. 2003).

## ▶ Conclusion

Two main trends have characterised the contemporary environmental movement. The extensive convergence of major environmental organisations in most countries towards an institutionalised, professional public interest model has seen even once radical groups, such as FoE and Greenpeace, drawn increasingly into the establishment fold. Yet, in the UK and USA in particular, this trend contrasts sharply with the revitalisation of the grassroots sector, which has reaffirmed the importance of local activism and questioned the effectiveness of the moderate insider strategy of the big groups. Thus there is evidence of a new politics in the emergence of the environmental groups as a significant political force, in the innovative repertoires of protest and in the radical organisational forms and ideologies of ecological new social movements. However, the institutionalisation of the mainstream movement also suggests the continuing stability of established patterns of political behaviour. The overall impact of the environmental movement, although hard to measure, has been profound in setting agendas, shaping discourses and influencing policy. Yet the continued marginalisation of environmental considerations by policy elites fuels the rumblings of discontent and disappointment within the movement. Much now depends on the ability of the environmental movement to respond to the challenge of the transnational agenda associated with the increasing internationalisation of environmental politics. At this level, as at national and sub-national levels, environmental groups are just one actor in the policy process, and therefore cannot be judged in isolation. A complete assessment of the impact of the environmental movement, therefore, requires an understanding of their role within the policy process, which is the subject of Part III.

## ▶ *Further reading and websites*

Doherty (2002) is an excellent comparative analysis of the environmental movement from the perspective of social movement theory. The special issue of *Environmental Politics* (1999, vol. 8, no. 1) covers many debates about the environmental movement, and includes interesting comparative and country studies. Rootes (2003) provides a systematic comparative analysis of environmental protests in eight European countries, while Dryzek et al. (2003) is a thoughtful comparative analysis of the environmental movement in Germany, Norway, the UK and the USA. For specific countries, see Doyle (2000) on Australia; Rawcliffe (1998) and Rootes and Miller (2000) on the UK; and Duffy (2003) and Bosso (2005) on the USA. Visiglio and Whitelaw (2003) is a useful introduction to the issues raised by the environmental justice movement. Doyle (2004) offers an interesting comparison between environmental movements in the 'North' and the 'South'. For environmental movements and transnational politics, see the special issue of *Environmental Politics* (2006, vol. 15, no. 5).

### International websites
Earth First! (http://www.earthfirst.org/)
Friends of the Earth International (http://www.foei.org/)
Global Justice Movement (http://www.globaljusticemovement.net/)
Greenpeace International (http://www.greenpeace.org/)
World Wildlife Fund (http://www.panda.org/)

## UK websites

Campaign to Protect Rural England (http://www.cpre.org.uk/)
National Trust (http://www.nationaltrust.org.uk/)
Royal Society for Nature Conservation (http://www.rsnc.org/)
Royal Society for the Protection of Birds (http://www.rspb.org.uk/)

## USA websites

Defenders of Wildlife (http://www.defenders.org/)
Izaak Walton League of America (http://www.iwla.org/)
National Audubon Society (http://www.audubon.org/)
National Parks and Conservation Association (http://www.npca.org/)
National Wildlife Federation (http://www.nwf.org/)
Natural Resources Defense Council (http://www.nrdc.org/)
The Nature Conservancy (http://www.nature.org/)
Sierra Club (http://www.sierraclub.org/)
The Wilderness Society (http://www.wilderness.org/)

NOTES

1 'Grassroots' here refers to groups that are more bottom-up and decentralised, and have fewer members and financial resources, than large mainstream organisations.

2 Claims about the numbers of environmental organisations in individual countries and their membership levels must be treated with caution, as different studies have employed different methods of counting. See Dalton (2005) on membership density.

3 Although some writers, notably Lowe and Goyder (1983), distinguish different phases within these broad waves.

4 See Duffy (2003) for a detailed analysis of US environmental group activity, with a focus on new methods of issue definition and agenda-setting, particularly in the electoral process.

5 See Lamb (1996) for a history of Friends of the Earth and Pearce (1991) on the early Greenpeace.

6 Although an influential group, FoE now has a stagnant membership in the USA.

7 The significance of this threat was illustrated in August 1997 when BP obtained a legal injunction, backed by a freeze on Greenpeace assets, against a Greenpeace direct action campaign that was obstructing BP oil exploration in the North Atlantic.

8 Rootes (2003) provides an exhaustive analysis of environmental protests in eight European countries between 1988 and 1997, showing that, although there have been fluctuations over time and between countries, environmental protest did not consistently decline in this period, and in some countries it rose.

9 Monkey-wrenching was stimulated by the Edward Abbey novel *The Monkey Wrench Gang*. See also Foreman and Haywood (1985). Plows et al. (2004) analyses the role of ecotage in the UK direct action movement.

10 See Seel et al. (2000) and Doherty et al. (2003) for coverage of the direct action campaigns in the UK.

# PART 3

# Environmental policy: achieving a sustainable society

The discussion of environmental policy in Part III is in many respects a long way away from some of the abstract debates covered in Part I, or even the ambitious aspirations of some forms of environmental activism examined in Part II. It focuses on the practical challenges facing governments today. The interdependence of environmental issues poses a distinctive set of problems for policymakers. Few other policy areas can match it for sheer complexity. Nor are failures in most other policy areas likely to be as catastrophic or irredeemable as those affecting the environment, especially if the more pessimistic harbingers of environmental doom are correct.

The belief that economic growth must be given priority over environmental protection continues to govern the way many policymakers approach environmental issues. This traditional policy paradigm has proved inadequate for resolving the intractable problems posed by contemporary environmental issues. Consequently, since the late 1980s, the alternative policy paradigm of sustainable development has gradually come to dominate thinking about environmental policy. The central premise of sustainable development is that there need not be a trade-off between economic growth and environment; no longer need policymakers think in terms of the environment *versus* the economy. This message has made sustainable development politically appealing, with most governments, international institutions, political parties, business organisations and environmental NGOs now keen to proclaim their commitment to sustainable development. The broad aim of Part III is to examine the difficulties facing governments seeking to make the transition to sustainable development.

The two opening chapters analyse the competing policy paradigms that shape the way governments are responding to contemporary environmental problems. It is argued in Chapter 7 that the traditional policy paradigm, which emerged in the 1970s to deal with environmental problems, and which is still deeply entrenched among most policy elites, reflects the way power is distributed and exercised in all capitalist liberal democracies. Chapter 8 identifies the key features of the alternative policy paradigm of sustainable development and its close relation, ecological modernisation, and provides a broad analysis of the alternatives' respective strengths and weaknesses. The remaining chapters assess progress towards sustainable development and ecological modernisation by evaluating how far their key principles have been implemented. Two of these chapters focus on the international dimension of environmental policy. Chapter 9 examines the development of international co-operation to protect the global environment, with case studies of climate change and ozone depletion, then Chapter 10 analyses the relationship between globalisation, trade and the environment, focusing on three key institutions: the WTO, the NAFTA and the EU. The final two chapters shift down to the national level where most environmental policymaking, including the implementation of international agreements, takes place. Chapter 11 looks at a range of efforts to integrate environmental considerations into the policymaking process, while Chapter 12 focuses on implementation by assessing the relative merits of different policy instruments, with a particular focus on climate change strategies in the transport and energy sectors.

Throughout Part III many of the recurring themes arising from the relationship between politics and the environment reappear. Familiar issues in environmental politics, such as equity, social justice and democracy, lie at the very heart of environmental policy. Moreover, Part III shows that an understanding of environmental policy requires us to look beyond government to the central role played by industrial and producer interests, and by the wider public, as both citizens and consumers. Put differently, Part III highlights how difficult it is for governments to develop radical responses to environmental problems in a liberal democratic polity and a capitalist economic system.

# The environment as a policy problem

**7**

## Contents

## Key issues

▶ What are the core characteristics of environmental problems?
▶ What theories and models explain environmental policymaking?
▶ Where does power lie in environmental policymaking?
▶ What are the structural and institutional barriers to policy change?
▶ Why does policy change?

Policymakers have been slow to recognise or acknowledge that environmental problems might require special treatment. When new environmental imperatives emerged during the 1960s, forcing policymakers to confront the environment as a broad policy issue for the first time, all governments adopted a technocentric perspective, which regarded environmental problems as the unfortunate side-effects of economic growth (see Box 3.10). It was assumed that most environmental problems had solutions and that there was no need to question the underlying commitment to economic growth or to the political-institutional structures of the modern liberal democratic state. The standard approach to environmental problems – here called the 'traditional policy paradigm' – was reactive, tactical, piecemeal and end-of-pipe. This traditional paradigm has been found wanting, unable to stem long-standing problems of pollution and resource depletion or to deal with the new tranche of global problems that have emerged in recent years. Consequently, the traditional paradigm has increasingly been challenged by the alternative paradigm of sustainable development. Yet, despite the mounting environmental crisis and the rhetorical commitment of policy elites to sustainable development, many elements of the traditional model remain firmly entrenched, even in those countries that have pioneered progressive environmental policies (Andersen and Liefferink 1997a). Why has this traditional paradigm proved so resilient? What does its persistence tell us about the obstacles impeding the adoption of more progressive environmental policies?

The opening section of this chapter identifies the core characteristics that distinguish the environment as a policy problem and make it such a difficult problem for policymakers. The next part of the chapter examines the process of environmental policymaking by drawing on a range of theories of the policy process. It is argued that the resilience of the traditional paradigm is reinforced by the structural power of producer interests in capitalist society and the institutional segmentation of the policy process. However, policy change can and does occur, and in the second half of the chapter several models are used to assess the potential for policy change, ending with a case study of the nuclear power industry.

## ▶ Core characteristics of the environment as a policy problem

This section identifies seven core characteristics that distinguish the environment as a policy problem.[1]

### ▶ *Public goods*

Many environmental resources can be described as 'public goods'. By this we mean that 'each individual's consumption leads to no subtraction from any other individual's consumption of that good'.[2] Public goods are both 'non-rival' and 'non-excludable'. They are 'non-rival' because one individual's consumption does not limit the consumption of others: someone breathing clean air (normally) does not stop another individual also enjoying clean air. Public goods are 'non-excludable' in that, if one individual refrains from a polluting activity (e.g. driving a car), others cannot be excluded from the resulting benefits (cleaner air). By contrast, with private goods (a washing machine or a handbag), rivals can be excluded by the law of property (Weale 1992: 5).

The public nature of environmental problems has important consequences for policymakers because efforts to protect the environment may encounter significant collective-action problems. The benefits to be gained from using a public good are often concentrated among a handful of producers while the costs may be spread widely: for example, a power station releasing sulphur dioxide that will eventually fall as acid rain far away, or a factory dumping chemicals into a river that pollutes it for miles downstream. If a government wishes to prevent this pollution, the cost of dealing with the problem may fall largely on the polluter, which in these examples would be the electricity generator or the factory-owner. Consequently, a small number of spatially concentrated polluters who may have to pay for clean-up measures have an incentive to act collectively to protect their interests (perhaps by dissuading the government from taxing the pollution), whereas the individual citizens who suffer from the pollution are generally ill-informed, geographically dis-persed and insufficiently motivated to mobilise as a group in defence of their interests (Olson 1965).

Furthermore, if individuals cannot be excluded from the benefits that others provide, then each has the incentive to *free-ride* on the joint efforts of others to solve the problem (ibid.). So, if a government exhorts citizens to save water by refraining from 'unnecessary' activities such as washing cars or watering lawns, or it seeks to prevent air pollution by asking people to use their cars less, there will be a strong temptation for individuals to ignore these instructions in the expectation that others will be more dutiful. Free-riding will therefore result in a less than optimal provision of the collective benefit, which in these examples would be a constant water supply or clean air.

It is also useful to distinguish between *common-pool resources* (Ostrom 1990: 30) and *common-sink resources* (Weale 1992: 192–5). Common-pool resource systems are sufficiently large for it to be costly, though not impossible, to exclude potential beneficiaries from using them; they include fauna, forests and fish stocks. People benefit from these stocks by depleting the common pool, so the challenge for policymakers is to ensure that, say, the fishing fleets of different nations do not catch more fish than is prudent for the maintenance of the overall stocks. As common-pool resources can be indi-vidually appropriated – elephants can be shot, trees chopped down, fish caught – they are not pure public goods, although they share many attributes.[3] However, common-sink resources, such as fresh air, are pure

## 7.1 The Tragedy of the Commons

The idea of the 'Tragedy of the Commons' was popularised by Garrett Hardin. He invites us to picture a medieval village pasture that is open to all and to assume that each peasant will try to keep as many cattle as possible on this land. Eventually, the carrying capacity of the land will be reached. However, when confronted with a decision about whether or not to put an extra cow on the common land, the rational self-interested peasant will recognise that, whilst all the benefits of the extra cow accrue to her or him alone, the costs – the effects of overgrazing – will be shared with the other villagers. Thus each villager will keep adding more cows until the common land is destroyed:

> Therein is the tragedy. Each man is locked into a system that compels him to increase his herd without limit – in a world that is limited. Ruin is the destination toward which all men rush, each

pursuing his own best interest in a society that believes in the freedom of the commons. Freedom in a commons brings ruin to all.

> (Hardin 1968: 1244)

Hardin uses the common land of a medieval village as a metaphor for contemporary environmental problems to show how private benefit and public interest seem to point in opposite directions because individually rational actions may produce collectively irrational outcomes.

This metaphor can be used to analyse contemporary problems such as over-fishing and deforestation. Ostrom et al. (1999) argue persuasively that tragedies of the commons 'are real, but not inevitable' (p. 281). See Ostrom (1990) for a critical discussion of common-property issues.

public goods. The problem here is not about the consumption of air, but how individuals use this resource to dispose of waste materials such as sulphur dioxide or carbon dioxide. The collective challenge posed by common-sink resources is to control their level of pollution (Weale 1992: 192–3). Failure to protect either pools or sinks can lead to a 'tragedy of the commons' (Box 7.1) in which a resource is either completely exhausted or damaged beyond use.

## ▶ *Transboundary problems*

Problems of the global commons are frequently transboundary: for example, climate change, ozone depletion and marine pollution do not respect national borders. Global problems represent a major threat to the environment and can only be solved through concerted action by the international community. However, if one nation takes action to reduce ozone depletion or prevent global warming, it cannot exclude other nations from the benefits. Whereas an individual government can use the law of the land to require citizens or companies to change their behaviour, the doctrine of national sovereignty means that there is no equivalent international authority – no world government – that can force every country to conform. Consequently, as Chapter 9 shows, efforts by the international community to address transboundary problems have required unprecedented levels of co-operation between states and the building of new international institutions to persuade reluctant nations to support joint action.

# ◗ *Complexity and uncertainty*

Policymaking may be hampered by the complexity and uncertainty that characterise many environmental problems. It is often difficult to identify the complex and interdependent relationships between natural and human-made phenomena. The interconnectedness of ecosystems means that many problems are non-reducible: they cannot be resolved by addressing individual parts in isolation. Indeed, policies that deal with one discrete problem may have unintended and damaging consequences elsewhere. For example, in the 1950s local air pollution in Britain's industrial towns was reduced by building taller factory chimneys, only for it to be discovered many years later that this 'solution' had simply exported the pollution to fall as acid rain in Scandinavia. Similarly, cars can be fitted with catalytic converters to reduce the nitrogen oxide emissions that cause acid rain, but the resulting reduction in engine efficiency increases fuel consumption and, therefore, the carbon dioxide emissions that contribute to global warming.

Political constraints also contribute to the non-reducibility of problems. Thus solutions to the many environmental problems associated with modern farming practices (including soil erosion, river pollution, destruction of habitats) need to take account of broader public policies, such as national food production strategies, the rules governing international trade or, in EU member states, the price supports provided by the Common Agricultural Policy. Similarly, any government wishing to ban **genetically modified** crops may be stopped by World Trade Organisation rules that insist on free trade (see Chapter 10).

> **Genetically modified organisms:** New organisms created by human manipulation of genetic information and material.

Uncertainty surrounds many environmental problems. For example, is the climate changing? If it is, is this due to natural phenomena or to human activity? If the latter, what will be its impact and how quickly will its effects be noticed? Will planting new forests mitigate climate change by locking up carbon dioxide or exacerbate it by increasing methane emissions? Climate change may be an extreme case, but it is not exceptional. Are localised leukaemia clusters linked to emissions from nuclear power stations or caused by a virus? Are genetically modified organisms (GMOs) dangerous to human health or natural habitats? (See Box 7.2.)

Complexity and uncertainty underline the importance of science, scientists and professional expertise in environmental policymaking. Problems such as climate change and ozone depletion cannot even be identified without science. Some environmental degradation is reasonably visible, such as fumes from road traffic, or relatively easy to detect, such as falling fish stocks, but scientific knowledge is needed to make an accurate assessment of the nature of either problem. What is a safe level of lead in the atmosphere? What is a sustainable fish catch? Yet science frequently struggles to fulfil its role as objective arbiter among policy options. The scientific knowledge informing our understanding of environmental problems is often based on

---

### 7.2 Genetically modified food crops and scientific uncertainty

A GMO is 'any organism that has had its genetic material modified in a way that could not occur through natural processes' (Food Ethics Council 1999: 6).

GM food crops have many *potential* benefits, notably:

1. *Better for the environment* because their resistance to pesticides simplifies and reduces the spraying regime, i.e. there can be lower use of ecologically damaging pesticides (with a corresponding reduction in costs);
2. *Increased crop productivity* because their resistance to disease, pests and weeds, and to extreme weather conditions, increases crop yields;
3. *Improved human health* from 'functional foods' that can lower cholesterol or provide vital vitamins to supplement the diets of poor people.

Thus advocates of GM food crops suggest they may help combat world hunger and poverty.

However, if cross-pollination from GM plants results in the spread of pesticide-resistant genes in the wild population, then weeds and pests could spread uncontrollably and the species composition of wildlife communities could be altered, with devastating consequences for biodiversity.

We are not *certain* whether this cross-pollination will happen, or what the exact effects would be if it did. More broadly, there are other *political* solutions to problems of poverty and hunger, such as land redistribution and debt relief.

*Policy problem*: How strictly should we regulate the development and commercial release of GM crops as a precaution against the worst-case scenario? (See Box 7.6.)

---

a theory which is contestable and evidence that can be interpreted in several different ways, so scientific judgements will always be provisional and open to revision (Yearley 1991). The fluidity that characterises science can make it difficult for policymakers to make adequate responses to 'new' problems such as climate change, ozone depletion and GMOs. These issues may be subject to resistance or even denial by affected interests, such as industrialists or farmers, who may discourage or oppose fuller scientific inquiry into the environmental impact of such issues. There is also considerable disagreement within the scientific community concerning many long-established problems. For example, there are sharply contrasting views about whether bathing-water pollution should be prevented by building longer pipes to take sewage further out to sea, or by stopping all marine sewage disposal. Nor are scientists immune from twisting their findings to suit vested interests, such as their corporate funders, or even to increase their own chances of securing future research funding.

Uncertainty and complexity complicate policymaking. If policymakers understand the causes of a problem then it is obviously easier to design effective solutions, but frequently they have to act with incomplete information. Faced with uncertainty, should they adopt a precautionary approach to a problem, or continue depleting an environmental resource until scientific evidence proves that action must be taken? How policymakers respond will be shaped by their position on the ecocentric–technocentric divide (see Box 3.8), with ecocentrics opting for caution and technocentrics being more likely to assume optimistically that things will pan out satisfactorily. Moreover, in liberal democracies such dilemmas open decisions to political conflict by providing ammunition for both proponents and opponents of remedial action, which further complicates and politicises the decision-making process.

## ▶ *Irreversibility*

The problem of uncertainty is exacerbated by the irreversibility of many environmental problems. Once the Earth's carrying capacity is exceeded, then environmental assets may be damaged beyond repair. Scarce resources may be exhausted and species may become extinct. Some environmental assets are substitutable, although rarely is the process straightforward or costless. Technological advances may eventually enable solar energy and wind power completely to replace depleted fossil fuels as generators of energy, but probably only if there is also a massive overall reduction in energy consumption. Irreversibility places even greater pressure on policymakers to get it right, for unlike fiscal or welfare policy, where a poorly judged tax rate or benefit payment can be corrected in the following year's budget, it may not be possible to correct an earlier mistake.

## ▶ *Temporal and spatial variability*

Many environmental issues are complicated by the fact that their impact will be long-term, probably affecting future rather than present generations, whereas remedial policies need to be adopted before the full negative effects of a problem are felt. Indeed, there are serious pragmatic constraints on policymakers wishing to respond to the ethical concerns for future generations discussed in Part I. Although action to protect future generations may be needed now, politicians tend to have short-term concerns – tomorrow's papers, forthcoming opinion polls or the next election – and they know how difficult it is to persuade people to accept self-sacrifice today in order to protect those who are not yet born. In short, it is easier to make policy that responds to today's political pressures than addresses tomorrow's environmental problems.

Similarly, there are huge variations in the spatial impact of environmental problems. The depletion of Himalayan forests results in flooding downstream in Bangladesh. Rising sea-levels caused by global warming will cause most damage to low-lying lands such as Egypt and the Maldives. Sulphur dioxide emissions generated by British factories fall as acid rain in Scandinavia.

Spatial and temporal variability mean that the costs of environmental problems, and their solutions, are unevenly distributed. Inevitably, environmental policies will produce winners and losers. The challenge for governments is to balance competing interests, but this raises important issues of equity and social justice between current and future generations.

## ▶ *Administrative fragmentation*

The administrative structure of government is usually divided into distinct policy sectors with specific responsibilities such as education, defence or health care. A core group of economic ministries – typically finance, industry, employment, energy, agriculture and transport – make policy decisions affecting production, consumption, mobility and lifestyles that will frequently have negative consequences for the environment. Yet these individual ministries often engage in a blinkered pursuit of narrow sectoral objectives with little consideration for their environmental impact. A transport ministry might implement a massive road-building programme, or the agriculture ministry might encourage intensive farming methods, while responsibility for protecting the environment is typically given to a separate ministry. The instinct of bureaucrats is to break problems down into separate units, but the interdependence of economic and ecological systems does not respect these artificial administrative and institutional boundaries. Many environmental problems are cross-sectoral and require co-ordinated responses that transcend sectoral boundaries. An effective climate change strategy, for example, will need the involvement of the ministries responsible for transport, energy, industrial emissions, livestock and forestry, as well as for overall economic policy.

## ▶ *Regulatory intervention*

Environmental damage is frequently a by-product of otherwise legitimate activities; consequently, governments may have to intervene in the economy and society to regulate these damaging activities (Weale 1992: 6). Regulatory intervention can involve a mix of policy instruments, not just legal instruments: for example, setting factory emission standards or encouraging the recycling of waste paper. The regulatory character of much environmental policy contrasts with many other policy areas, notably welfare policy, where taxes and public spending are used to alter the distribution of resources. Although public spending is rarely the primary instrument of environmental policy, regulatory interventions will usually impose some kind of cost on key interests in society and may have significant distributive consequences. Consequently, regulatory proposals are likely to provoke howls of outrage from businesses and trade unions about the dangers of reduced competitiveness or jobs lost, or from consumers who have to pay higher prices for cleaner or safer goods. Thus the effectiveness of regulatory interventions may be limited by this historical tension between economic growth and environmental protection.

This section has identified seven core characteristics of environmental problems. The first five are intrinsic to the environment as a policy issue;

the remaining two characteristics reflect the institutional structures and policymaking processes of modern government.

---

### Critical question 1

Do the problems posed by the environment make it fundamentally different from other policy issues?

---

## ▶ The traditional policy paradigm

A policy paradigm provides policymakers with the terminology and a set of taken-for-granted assumptions about the way they communicate and think about a policy area. While none of the seven core characteristics identified in the previous section is unique to the environment, taken together they pose a range of problems that are particularly challenging to policymakers. Yet the traditional paradigm that emerged during the 1970s treated the environment like any other new policy area, rather than recognising the interdependency of the relationships between ecosystems and political, economic, social and cultural systems. The traditional paradigm has been characterised by Weale (1992: 10–23) in the following way (although he refers to it as 'old politics'). Government policies were reactive, piecemeal and tactical: few countries possessed a comprehensive national plan setting out an anticipatory, comprehensive and strategic approach to the environment. Instead, a specialist branch of government – an environment ministry – and various new agencies were formed to deal with environmental issues. Environmental policy was treated as a discrete policy area. Agencies had few powers over decisions taken in other policy sectors and there was little policy co-ordination and considerable scope for problem displacement. Pollution control, for example, typically involved the use of single-medium regulations to control industrial releases, whilst separate agencies dealt with discharges to air, water and land. End-of-pipe solutions were usually seen as adequate; policymakers preferred to deal with symptoms rather than causes. Administrative regulation was the policy instrument of choice. Many policies were prone to an 'implementation deficit' involving a shortfall between policy intent and outcome. For example, although major legislative programmes such as the US Clean Air Act 1970 and the UK Control of Pollution Act 1974 introduced stringent controls on pollutants and toxic substances, many deadlines and targets were missed and key provisions remained unimplemented many years later (Lundqvist 1980: 131–58; Ward 1998: 245–6). Above all, a balance had always to be struck between environmental protection and economic growth, with the latter frequently taking priority. The traditional paradigm was not reproduced identically in all countries, but something akin to it could be identified everywhere.

This traditional paradigm was fundamentally flawed in design and practice. Most indicators and trends showed that the 'objective' state of the environment in advanced industrialised nations worsened through the 1970s with a general deterioration in key pollution indicators, including sulphur dioxide, nitrogen oxide, particulates, carbon monoxide and carbon dioxide (OECD 1991). Although some trends were reversed in the 1980s, notably a decline in sulphur dioxide emissions, others, notably carbon dioxide, worsened (European Environment Agency, http://www.eea.eu.int/), whilst the appearance of new problems such as acid rain and climate change posed novel challenges to policymakers. The weaknesses in the traditional paradigm have become increasingly apparent to policy elites, yet, despite the emergence of the alternative paradigm of sustainable development, the traditional paradigm has proved very resistant to change.

# ▶ Political obstacles to change

The traditional paradigm is bolstered by two core characteristics of the policy process: first, the privileged position of business and producer groups; secondly, sectoral divisions within the institutional structure of government both reflect and reinforce a special-interest approach to public policy in which each ministry tends to act as a sponsor for the key producer or professional groups within its policy sphere. This section uses theories of state–group relations and policy network analysis to show how the power of producers and the fragmented nature of government have reinforced the traditional paradigm.

## ▶ *The power of producers*

In political science, it is common to explain policy outcomes in terms of the power exercised by competing interests. This section uses some central theories of state–group relations (pluralist, neo-pluralist, neo-Marxist)[4] and the theory of three-dimensional power (Lukes 1974) to explain the continuing strength of the traditional paradigm in shaping environmental policy outcomes.

The *pluralist* model regards public policy as the outcome of competition among different groups. For every environmental issue there will be a wide range of institutions, organisations and interest groups seeking to influence the formation and implementation of public policy. Each interest group will use the resources at its disposal – expertise, finance, membership, public opinion – to influence policy outcomes. It is assumed that power is diffuse: no single group or set of interests dominates the decision process, many groups can gain access to government and, if sufficiently determined, most groups can achieve at least some of their objectives. The government will obviously have its own preferences on many subjects, but it will consult widely and respond to powerful outside demands (Dahl 1961).

Of course, not every group has equal influence. In particular, a primary aim of any government is to manage the economy, so in core economic sectors it regularly consults and seeks the co-operation of business groups (Truman 1951). Environmental policy often has a direct impact on businesses, so they will mobilise against proposed (or existing) regulations or eco-taxes, or to win approval for a new development such as a motorway or a dam. As insider groups, businesses will usually remain within the law: lobbying politicians and civil servants, financing publicity campaigns or funding sympathetic pressure groups. Sometimes producers may threaten to flout legislation or even take direct action to make their case; French farmers have an unrivalled record in achieving their aims by blocking roads and ports.

Pluralist accounts therefore concede that producers have both the motivation and the means to play an active role in the policy process, but they do not regard business as a privileged participant. Businesses may exercise disproportionate influence compared to environmental groups because they have more resources at their disposal. The pluralist would anticipate that when environmental groups are able to mobilise sufficient resources to counter the strength of business, they too should win better access to government and a matching influence over policy outcomes (unless, like Greenpeace, they deliberately resist entry for fear of being 'captured'). Yet, in practice, in many key areas affecting the environment, those 'insider' pressure groups operating closest to government typically consist of a handful of powerful producer interests.[5] Governments regard the views of key producer groups as legitimate and important, so they benefit from good access to ministers and civil servants to discuss matters affecting their interests and they are regularly consulted by government officials. Conversely, environmental and consumer groups are often 'outsider' groups excluded from the corridors of power; they are less routinely consulted and they may struggle to get their voice heard by government. Consequently, more often than not, policy outcomes show the interests of producer groups trumping those of environmentalists.

One weakness of pluralism is its use of an incomplete, one-dimensional model of power which underestimates the influence of business interests (Lukes 1974) (see Box 7.3). Pluralists focus on *observable* influence, examining each individual decision to assess whether the preferences of business groups hold sway. However, Bachrach and Baratz (1962) argue that observable power measures only one aspect of power. They identify a second dimension of power – 'non-decision-making' – which refers to the ability of powerful groups to keep issues off the agenda. Producer groups can manage conflict before it even starts by using political routines to produce or reinforce dominant values and interests, suppress dissenting demands or co-opt challenging groups, a process that Schattschneider (1960) called the 'mobilisation of bias'. In practice, observable 'pluralist' decision-making is frequently confined to safe issues that do not threaten the fundamental interests of the dominant (producer) groups, while the grievances of those interests excluded from the policy process, such as environmental

---

**7.3 The three dimensions of power**

*First dimension*

A has power over B to the extent that A can get B to do something that B would not otherwise do. A defeats B by mobilising superior bargaining resources in open conflict over clearly defined issues.

*Second dimension*

A constructs a barrier against the participation of B in decision-making – A engages in 'non-decisions' and uses the 'mobilisation of bias' to suppress or thwart challenges to A's values or interests by B.

*Third dimension*

A influences or shapes the consciousness of B to accept inequalities (through myths, information control, ideology) and to induce a sense of powerlessness and acceptance in B. Very difficult to detect.

Based on Lukes (1974). See discussion of Crenson (1971) for examples of each dimension.

---

groups, are marginalised. Indeed, opposition groups may not even raise their dissenting views in the formal policy process because of a fatalistic assumption that they will be rejected by the dominant producer interests.

A classic environmental illustration of non-decision-making is provided in Crenson's (1971) study of air pollution in two neighbouring American steel towns: East Chicago and Gary. Whereas East Chicago introduced legislation controlling air pollution in 1949, Gary delayed acting until 1963, even though the pollution problem was identical in the two towns. A key difference between the towns was that, whilst many steel companies were located in East Chicago, just one big corporation, US Steel, dominated Gary. US Steel did not lobby overtly against regulation, but it was able to exercise enormous indirect influence because local political leaders feared that the company might leave the town if anti-pollution laws were introduced. Environmental groups saw little point in even seeking to raise the issue of air pollution because they anticipated the negative reaction of US Steel were they to do so. Yet no observable decision opposing anti-pollution legislation was ever taken; it was a 'non-decision'. By contrast, the fragmentation of the steel industry in East Chicago made the negative employment impact of legislation less risky and allowed proponents of legislation to get pollution control on the agenda much earlier.

This broader two-dimensional model of power underpins the *neo-pluralist* theory of state–group relations which, like pluralism, sees businesses as exercising power through their ability to mobilise resources in the political arena but, in contrast to pluralism, claims that they also possess structural power. Lindblom (1977) provides a forceful elaboration of the view that business holds a privileged interest within the political system owing to its structural importance in the capitalist economy. Any government in a liberal democracy will routinely take account of producer interests in its decision-making because the overall performance of the economy is likely to influence its popularity, and hence its chances of re-election. Governments therefore assume responsibility for creating the conditions under which business can make profits. In anticipating the needs of business, a government will take decisions that reflect commercial interests without businesses having to take any observable action, not even to organise as a lobby. Lindblom does not see business as uniformly privileged across all policy areas: he distinguishes 'grand majority' issues affecting significant economic interests over which the public can exercise only limited influence, from secondary issues that do not impinge directly on powerful business interests and where the policy process is more competitive, or pluralistic (for example, land-use planning). The contribution of neo-pluralism is to point to the privileged position of business in many core economic policy sectors affecting the environment, without claiming that business will always determine policy outcomes, or keep all 'undesirable' issues off the agenda.

Nevertheless, from a more radical perspective, the two-dimensional model still does not capture all aspects of the concept of power. Structuralist explanations, notably *neo-Marxism*, emphasise the significance of the underlying economic structure in determining the distribution of political power in favour of a ruling elite, or class. A key contribution made by structuralists is to identify an ideological dimension to power in which the role of the state is to support and promote the process of capitalist accumulation. Offe (1974) argues that within capitalist societies there are various mechanisms, or exclusion rules, which identify those issues that merit attention and filter out issues that threaten the values and rules of capitalist societies. Broad principles, such as the right to private property, provide the legitimacy to screen out undesirable challenges to the status quo, including some of those posed by environmentalism. Within individual policy sectors, non-decision-making mechanisms keep certain issues off the agenda and ideological mechanisms will define issues and problems in ways that produce a systematic bias in favour of capitalist interests. This ideological role of the state reflects what Lukes (1974) calls 'third-dimension' power whereby the 'very wants' of individuals are shaped to accept the preferences of the ruling elite, or class (even when they run counter to their own 'objective' interests), so that conflicts remain latent. Thus, returning to the Crenson study, the selective perception within the local community in Gary that jobs and economic development were the only real concerns – even though air pollution might be damaging public health – may indicate that political institutions had managed to mould citizen preferences to reflect the interests of capital.[6]

Structuralist and neo-pluralist theories of the state help explain how business interests have retained a privileged position within the policy process despite the increasingly large, vocal and professional environmental lobby. Business can exercise the second and third dimensions of power to reinforce the traditional paradigm and to resist more strategic and holistic approaches to environmental policy. Of course, this structural power is not deterministic. Sometimes environmental interests will prevail and governments do overrule producer objections, as illustrated by the raft of environmental regulations introduced over the past thirty years. Nor should it be assumed that producers will always oppose measures to protect the environment. Sometimes producers are persuaded by the environmental 'argument' to change their behaviour; sometimes – as the discussion of ecological modernisation in Chapter 8 demonstrates – there is a commercial advantage to be gained. Certainly the current shift towards organic farming in many countries is driven by both considerations, whilst wind turbine manufacturers and many energy generators are strong advocates for an expansion of wind power. However, on balance, it seems that business power has been used to reinforce the traditional paradigm.

### Critical question 2
Is industry the main villain in environmental policy?

## ▶ *Administrative fragmentation*

Another factor giving some interest groups disproportionate access to the policy process is the institutional structure of the state. The fragmentation of government into sectoral divisions produces a special-interest approach to public policy in which each ministry tends to act as a sponsor for the key groups of producers or professionals within its policy sphere. Agriculture ministers typically see themselves as speaking on behalf of farmers, rather than acting to protect consumer interests or the environment. Similarly, energy ministers see their role as protecting the commercial interests of the major energy producers in the coal, oil, gas and nuclear industries, so they may downplay the environmental damage associated with the energy sector. Each policy sector is characterised by administrative arrangements that reflect the underlying power relations between the concerned interest groups. Thus in most countries, pluralistic patterns of environmental policymaking seem to be the exception rather than the rule. Even in the USA, a relatively pluralistic political system, the widely used 'iron triangle' metaphor acknowledges the enormous influence of producer groups in key policy areas where decision-making is dominated by three powerful actors: congressional committee, administrative agency and producer group (Cater 1965). The congressional sub-committee provides money and monitors regulations, the bureau hands over the money or enforces the regulation, and the producer group is the benefiting special interest. Each actor needs the others, so this cosy relationship would break down without the participation of the others; conversely, it is in their mutual interest to limit the access of other actors to the policy process. Thus it is an 'iron' triangle because it is largely impenetrable to outsiders.[7] In this section a similar institutional model of the policy process – *policy network analysis* – is used to support the argument that the sectoral fragmentation of government further entrenches the structural power of producer groups over many areas of environmental decision-making.

Policy network analysis examines the relationship between actors involved in the public policy process (Rhodes 1988; Marsh and Rhodes 1992; Smith 1993) and there is evidence that policy networks exist in most countries, including the USA (Heclo 1978), Canada (Pross 1992), several European countries (Kickert et al. 1997; Marsh 1998) and within the EU policy process (Peterson and Bomberg 1999). Policy networks are clusters of public and private actors connected to each other by resource dependencies, such as information, expertise, money and legitimacy, and separated from other clusters by breaks in the structure of resource dependencies. Marsh and Rhodes (1992) distinguish two ideal types of policy network at opposite ends of a continuum: policy communities and issue networks.

The *policy community* has a closed and stable membership, usually involving a government ministry or agency and a handful of privileged producer groups, who regularly interact and share a consensus of values and predispositions, almost a shared ideology, about that policy sector that sets the community apart from outsider groups. The cement that joins the members of the policy community together is their mutual resource dependency: each has resources that can be exchanged or bargained with so that a balance of power prevails, allowing every member to benefit from a positive-sum game. Through their ability to control the agenda, the members produce continuity and stability in policy outcomes that transcend changes in the political complexion of government and are largely immune from the gaze and control of either the legislature or the public. According to Smith (1993: 66–74), policy communities provide the state with four advantages: a consultative policymaking environment; a consensual, depoliticised policy arena; predictable, stable surroundings; and a reinforcement of policy segmentation by the building of barriers against encroachment by other ministries.

In contrast, the open *issue network* has many competing groups with fluctuating membership and less regular interaction. The government tends to consult rather than bargain with members of this more pluralistic network. As a result, policy outcomes are far less stable and predictable. It is important to note that the policy community and issue network are at opposite ends of a continuum, and various hybrid networks exist between these two poles.[8]

The significance of policy network analysis in explaining the strength of the traditional paradigm lies in the prevalence of policy communities in those policy sectors where environmental issues impinge on major economic interests and the government is dependent on producer groups for implementation. Here the power and interests of producers and the fragmented administrative structure become mutually reinforcing; neither producers nor the state want anything to disrupt this cosy situation. So, how common are policy communities and, where they exist, how do they influence environmental policy outcomes?

The empirical evidence supporting the widespread existence of closed policy communities is strongest in Britain, where it reflects central features of the political system such as the strong executive and the culture of secrecy (Marsh and Rhodes 1992; Smith 1993). For example, during the post-war period transport policy has generally emerged from a policy community consisting of officials from the Department of Transport and representatives from the motor industry, road construction industry, oil industry and various road haulage and motoring organisations (Dudley and Richardson 1996; Rawcliffe 1998: 121–3). Consequently, British transport policy has been heavily biased towards road-building and encouraging car use, with little interest in alternative, less environmentally damaging forms of transport such as railways or cycling. Similarly, for many years a policy community dominated by the Atomic Energy Authority and its scientific experts underpinned the strong commitment of successive governments to the development of the nuclear power industry as a clean, cheap source of electricity (Greenaway et al. 1992: 233–4; Saward 1992). Tight policy communities have also been identified in other areas affecting the environment, including the energy and water industries (Ward and Samways 1992; Maloney and Richardson 1994). Several studies suggest that policy communities are also to be found in environmental policymaking elsewhere in Europe, including the water (Bressers et al. 1994) and energy (Kasa 2000) sectors.

The *agriculture sector* provides a classic illustration of how policy communities have hampered the development of sustainable environmental policies in a range of European countries, including Denmark (Daugbjerg 1998), Finland (Jokinen 1997), the Netherlands (Glasbergen 1992) and Britain (Cox et al. 1986; Smith 1990). In each case the policy community normally consists of officials from the agriculture ministry and leading farmers' groups. The British policy community, for example, primarily involves the Department for Environment, Food and Rural Affairs (until 2001, Ministry of Agriculture, Fisheries and Food) and the National Farmers' Union (NFU). It first emerged in the late 1930s and was formalised in the Agriculture Act 1947 when farmers were given a statutory right to be consulted over policy. The members were bound together by the shared belief that farmers should maximise the output and efficiency of their land. The state deliberately created the policy community to ensure a secure war-time food supply and, to do so, it was prepared to guarantee prices to farmers (Smith 1990). It suited both the farming ministry and the NFU to plan a mutually beneficial expansionist agricultural policy and to maintain this arrangement after the war. The policy community was, therefore, a result of a structural feature – a political context that demanded a secure food supply – that subsequently institutionalised the power of the NFU.

In most of the EU-15 states, but particularly in Britain, Denmark and the Netherlands, the objective of agricultural policy has been to stimulate the competitive position of the agrarian sector by adopting increasingly intensive farming methods. Livestock production, wherever possible, has maximised the use of factory farming methods. The specialisation of arable production has seen the appropriation of every possible piece of land and the lavish use of chemical fertilisers and pesticides. The benefits are obvious: a stable farming sector, readily available and affordable farm produce for the consumer and a food surplus that has contributed to exports; but the environmental damage has also been immense. The British countryside, for example, has been transformed since the mid twentieth century by the massive destruction of hedgerows, ancient woodlands, wetlands and lowland heaths, which has harmed many species of animals, birds and insects. Intensive farming gradually erodes soil quality and consumes vast amounts of water, and run-off from slurry pollutes rivers and underlying water tables. Yet the efforts of environmental and consumer groups to get new issues onto the agricultural agenda were, for many years, effectively rebuffed by policy communities across Europe (Cox et al. 1986; Smith 1990; Glasbergen 1992). Until recently, any group questioning the underlying expansionist ideology of agricultural policy was marginalised. Typically, when a new environmental issue emerges, the agricultural policy community will initially seek to deny the existence of the problem or to play down the danger. As concern grows, delaying tactics are employed, such as a call for further research or the setting up of a commission of inquiry (Glasbergen 1992). When action can no longer be avoided, problems are dealt with in ways that suit the interests of the policy community. Some issues, such as the Dutch problem of surplus manure, are depoliticised by defining them as 'technical' problems – i.e. uncontroversial – which can be solved by expert insiders. Alternatively, the EU set-aside scheme, which encourages conservation by farmers through financial compensation, also created a new justification for high public support for the agrarian sector. British farmers' groups have tried to deflect criticism from environmentalists of their destructive methods by using the concept of set-aside to recast their role to become 'stewards of the countryside'. Thus agricultural policy communities, by institutionalising the power of farmers, have managed to keep new issues off the policy agenda or, where this is impossible, impeded or diluted policies intended to reduce the environmental damage from agri-industry – although agricultural policy communities have become increasingly unstable in recent years (see below, pp. 199–200).

The example of the agricultural sector shows how the state, by facilitating the formation of a closed policy community, has helped institutionalise the structural power of producer groups within individual policy sectors. Producer groups derive structural power from the policy network because 'rules, procedures and beliefs support the interests of the powerful without the powerful having to decide on every occasion what should be allowed on that agenda' (Smith 1990: 39). Hence the values underpinning sectoral policy communities frequently produce policy outcomes that are explicitly expansionist and likely to damage the environment. If a policy community is forced to address an environmental issue, the major actors will seek solutions that require no questioning of the principles shared by the policy community, such as the commitment to agricultural price support. When environmental issues grew in importance after the 1970s, policy networks were already well established in sectors such as agriculture, energy and industry (Daugbjerg 1998), so that environmental groups confronted entrenched institutional frameworks that were resistant to the penetration of new ideas and issues, and sought to prevent access to environmental groups (Rawcliffe 1998). Policy communities also reinforce a sectoral approach to environmental policymaking. Individual ministries, such as agriculture or energy, are wary of co-ordinated strategies to address cross-sectoral problems such as climate change, fearing disruption of established sectoral patterns of policymaking. In short, the institutional structure of the state has reinforced the traditional environmental policy paradigm.

However, policy communities are neither ubiquitous nor static. Even in Britain some policy areas, usually those concerned with 'secondary issues' (Lindblom 1977) such as nature conservation and countryside recreation, where there is no major threat to the interests of economic or professional groups, are characterised by more pluralistic issue networks. Elsewhere, particularly in North America, pluralistic relations are more common. Moreover, where policy communities do exist, these institutional arrangements are not set in stone and environmental policy change can occur. The next section examines the dynamics of policy change.

---

### Critical question 3

Does the capitalist state present insuperable barriers to a co-ordinated environmental policy?

---

## ▶ Achieving policy change

Despite the powerful structural and institutional factors reinforcing the traditional environmental policy paradigm, policy change is not impossible. In recent years, all governments have introduced new measures to improve environmental protection, although evidence of *radical* change is scarce (see Box 7.4). This section draws selectively from the wide literature on policymaking by highlighting the agenda-setting, advocacy coalition and network approaches as useful frameworks for exploring the potential for policy change and, in particular, to indicate how the traditional paradigm might be superseded by an alternative framework.

### ▶ *Agenda-setting*

The agenda-setting stage of the policy process is a critical point at which policy change can be initiated. Amongst several models that seek to explain

## 7.4 Defining policy change

Hall (1993) outlines a three-level taxonomy of policy change:

*First-order* change affects the levels or settings of basic policy instruments, such as adjustments to an emissions standard or a tax rate.

*Second-order* change also sees no change in the overall policy goals, but involves alterations in the instruments used to achieve them, perhaps the replacement of an emissions standard by an eco-tax.

First- and second-order changes can be seen as 'normal policymaking', in which policy is adjusted without challenging the existing policy paradigm.

*Third-order* change is marked by a radical shift in the overall goals of policy that reflects a fundamental paradigm shift (such as the transition from Keynesianism to monetarism in economic policy). Such radical changes are rare and usually follow a wide-ranging process of societal debate and reflection on past experience, or 'social learning'.

Although incremental changes in environmental policy are possible within the traditional paradigm, an accumulation of first- and second-order changes will not automatically lead to third-order changes, because genuinely radical change requires the replacement of the traditional paradigm with an alternative.

## 7.5 Downs's issue attention cycle

Stage 1 *Pre-problem*: Knowledge exists about a problem, experts and interest groups may be worried, but public interest is negligible.

Stage 2 *Alarmed discovery and euphoric enthusiasm*: A dramatic event or discovery makes the public aware of and alarmed by the problem. People demand action and the government promises solutions.

Stage 3 *Counting the cost of progress*: Both politicians and the public become aware of what 'solving' the problem

will cost in terms of financial cost and personal sacrifices.

Stage 4 *Gradual decline of intense public interest*: People have second thoughts. Attention is distracted by new issues.

Stage 5 *Post-problem*: Public interest wanes but the institutions, policies and programmes set up to solve the problem remain in place.

Source: Downs (1972).

how issues can get onto and ascend agendas, a crude but influential model, specifically designed to account for the rise and fall of environmentalism in America in the early 1970s, was the **issue attention cycle** (Downs 1972) (see Box 7.5).

**Issue attention cycle:** The idea that there is a cycle in which issues attract public attention and move up and down the political agenda.

The notion that environmental issues go through cycles of attention is attractive because it resembles the way that public and media interest latches onto one issue before lurching off in pursuit of another. Moreover, evidence from the USA suggests that peak periods of relevant organisational activity (new institutions, programmes and policies) often coincide with peak periods in the attention cycle, implying that governments do respond to public concern (Peters and Hogwood 1985). More cynically, it could be suggested that policymakers are simply making sure they are seen to be 'doing something', even if their action has minimal impact on the problem (Parsons 1995: 119). Indeed, Downs presents an essentially pessimistic view of the importance of agenda-setting as a process which generates a temporary public fascination with the topic of concern, but has little long-lasting importance. This pessimism is particularly appropriate where policy communities exist because, even if an issue attracts widespread public attention, a policy community may be strong enough to resist pressure for substantial change, confident that public attention will not sustain an issue long enough to define a new agenda (Smith 1993: 90).

Other theorists have argued more optimistically that these brief moments of public interest are occasions when structural changes can be forced through, which may permanently alter the rules of access and participation. Kingdon (1995) outlines a sophisticated model of agenda-setting based on a dynamic picture of the policy process. Agenda change occurs when problems, policy solutions and political receptivity combine in a 'window of opportunity': a compelling problem is recognised, a technically viable solution exists and the political circumstances are right for change. Similarly, Baumgartner and Jones's (1993) model of 'punctuated equilibrium' characterises the policy process as having long periods of stability in which only incremental changes occur, interspersed with short periods of instability when major policy change occurs. Disruption to the equilibrium may allow access by new groups seeking to challenge the dominant policy paradigm. Sometimes that challenge is sufficiently powerful and persuasive to overthrow the dominant policy consensus and to replace it with new perspectives, institutions and policies. A key role during these moments of instability is played by the media, which can direct public attention to new issues or developments, or offer a new perspective on familiar issues. Suddenly issues that are normally confined to policy sub-systems are thrown open to wider scrutiny. New participants from other sub-systems may become interested in the debates so that previously low-profile policy arrangements are permanently disrupted (see Box 7.6).

Baumgartner and Jones (1993: 93–102) use developments in the American pesticides industry as one illustration of their argument. Pesticides attracted enormous public attention immediately after the Second World War because of the claims that new synthetic organics such as DDT could achieve amazing results, including the eradication of malaria and increased food production to the point of ending world hunger. The popular wave of enthusiasm for pesticides saw the emergence of an iron triangle of the Department of Agriculture, farm and chemical interests, and congressional agriculture and appropriations committees, which controlled the regulation of these chemicals and set up an institutional structure that promoted the industry for decades to come, long after public interest had waned. However, during the

## 7.6 GM crops and agenda-setting

During the 1980s and 1990s the rapid commercialisation of GM crops, led by large multinational corporations such as Monsanto, resulted in their widespread use throughout the USA. The EU had been gradually developing a system for the regulation of the release of GM crops, so it seemed that it was just a matter of time before European farmers followed suit. Early in 1999 the British prime minister, Tony Blair, enthusiastically declared: 'There is no scientific evidence on which to justify a ban on GM foods and crops . . . we should resist the tyranny of pressure groups.' Just one year later a chastened prime minister conceded that there was 'legitimate public concern' about their 'potential for harm' to health and the environment (*Guardian*, 28 March 2000).

During 1998–9 a 'window of opportunity' opened, allowing the GM issue to be catapulted dramatically on to the political agenda and prompting a huge increase in public concern throughout the EU:

1. *A compelling problem was identified*
   A series of well-publicised scientific findings alerted the public to a problem:
   (i) Professor Arpad Pusztai claimed that the immune systems of rats had been damaged by eating GM potatoes;
   (ii) American scientists reported that GM crops harmed the Monarch butterfly;
   (iii) a series of reports – from English Nature, the British Medical Association and Christian Aid – highlighted the environmental and food safety risks posed by GM crops.

2. *The right political circumstances*
   (i) a decision by Monsanto to mix GM and non-GM grain;
   (ii) the imminent approval by the EU of a range of GM crops;
   (iii) high public sensitivity and distrust of science and politicians regarding food safety issues following the BSE crisis;

   (iv) an obvious 'bad guy' – the multinational corporation Monsanto;
   (v) high-profile pressure group campaigning, especially by Greenpeace, and repeated direct action by eco-protesters that destroyed many of the British government's GM crop trials.

3. *Viable short-term solutions existed*
   (i) Although eighteen GM products had been approved up to April 1998, the EU Council of Environment Ministers announced its refusal to approve further releases of GM crops until a tougher regulatory regime, governing labelling and tracing of products through the food chain, was approved.
   (ii) At a national level, the British government agreed a voluntary three-year moratorium on the commercial planting of GM crops with the biotechnology industry, pending further crop trials testing their safety.

The agenda-setting framework shows how significant policy change can occur. However, the period of alarmed discovery about GM crops has passed. Pressure from the WTO (and especially the USA) and several member-state governments (particularly those with a large biotechnology industry) brought the moratorium, step-by-step, to an end. A new EU directive on the deliberate release of GMOs came into force in October 2002, but a blocking minority of states – Denmark, Greece, France, Italy and Luxembourg – continued to refuse approval to new products until May 2004 when Bt11 maize was authorised for use in food, although as of January 2006 no products had been approved for cultivation.

See Rosendal (2005) and Lieberman and Gray (2006).

1960s, growing awareness of the dangers of some of these pesticides, stimulated by a series of food scares and by Rachel Carson's (1962) best-seller *Silent Spring*, produced a new, negative wave of interest, that eventually peaked with the banning of DDT in 1969 and several new pieces of legislation regulating pesticide use. Thus positive issue attention in the late 1940s provided a window of opportunity to create a producer-dominated iron triangle promoting the pesticide industry, whilst negative issue attention during the 1960s provided a second window of opportunity that contributed to the collapse of this cosy network and ushered in policy change.

This example of punctuated equilibrium suggests that the Downs model overlooked the longer-term institutional legacies of agenda-setting, which can produce change through an unfolding historical process. As the 'euphoria' surrounding an issue fades away and public attention turns elsewhere, the organisations created during that period of heightened interest remain (Baumgartner and Jones 1993). Another example arose from the huge public interest provoked by the *Exxon Valdez* oil-tanker disaster in Alaska Sound in 1989, which disrupted a previously complacent policy network responsible for marine safety in the Sound and led to the creation of new institutions. After the public interest died away, the institutional legacy remained, notably a regulatory framework introduced to oversee the implementation of improved safeguards in Alaska Sound and a new regional citizens' advisory council that has acted as an effective 'sentinel' by promoting further policy change to improve safety (Busenberg 1999).

## ▶ *The advocacy coalition framework*

Sabatier (1988) argues that it is unrealistic to distinguish agenda-setting so sharply from the wider policy process as a major source of policy change. His advocacy coalition framework (ACF) is a comprehensive model of the policy process emphasising the role of ideas, information and analysis as factors contributing to policy change at all 'stages' of the policy process (ibid.; Sabatier and Jenkins-Smith 1993, 1999). A central claim of the ACF is that an understanding of policy change requires a focus on elite opinion and the factors that encourage shifts in elite belief systems over time.

The ACF, like network theory, focuses on the policy sub-system which is composed of all the actors – politicians, bureaucrats, interest groups, academics, journalists, professionals – who are actively concerned with a particular policy issue such as air pollution control, and who regularly seek to influence public policy on that issue. Within each sub-system these actors may form several 'advocacy coalitions' drawing together people who share the same normative and causal beliefs about how policy objectives should be achieved. The belief systems of each coalition are organised into a three-level hierarchy: (1) *deep core beliefs* are the broad philosophical values that apply to all policy sub-systems (e.g. left–right); (2) *policy core beliefs* are the fundamental values and strategies across that specific policy sub-system

## 7.7 Discourse coalitions

Several writers on the environment have applied discourse analysis to the study of policy change (Hajer 1995, 2003; Fischer 2003; Dryzek 2005). A discourse is 'a shared way of apprehending the world. Embedded in language, it enables those who subscribe to it to interpret bits of information and put them together into coherent stories or accounts. Discourses construct meanings and relationships, helping to define common sense and legitimate knowledge' (Dryzek 2005: 9). 'Discourse coalitions' are held together not so much by shared beliefs as by 'storylines' that interpret events and courses of action; its members share a particular way of thinking about and discussing environmental issues.

Whereas the 'advocacy coalition' involves individuals co-ordinating their political activities, the members of a discourse coalition might never meet, but their independent actions will reinforce a particular storyline. Thus, as Chapter 8 demonstrates, people all round the world can share, sustain and reproduce the sustainable development storyline without ever meeting or co-ordinating their political activities. If discourse analysts are correct in ascribing a central role to language in the policymaking process, then discourse coalitions, such as the sustainable development discourse coalition, can be important vehicles for achieving policy change.

See Fischer (2003: ch. 5).

(e.g. the seriousness of the problem and the best policy instruments to deal with it); (3) *secondary aspects* are the narrower beliefs about specific aspects of the problem and policy implementation. Typically, a policy sub-system will be dominated by one powerful coalition, with several competing minority coalitions each seeking to impose its approach on the policy process. Sabatier, like Hall (see Box 7.4), argues that change will normally be incremental because it is secondary beliefs that are most prone to change, usually as a result of 'policy-oriented learning' by coalitions as they acquire new information and reflect on the best methods of achieving their policy objectives. Changes to policy core beliefs are less frequent and will normally only occur when non-cognitive factors are disrupted by exogenous shocks from outside the sub-system, such as macro-economic developments or a change in government. At these infrequent moments, the opportunity exists for a minority coalition to impose its belief system on the policy process. (See Box 7.7 for an alternative form of coalition.)

The ACF provides considerable insight into the way policy changes. By emphasising the importance of belief systems, it complements the policy network focus on interests and power. The ACF is particularly relevant to issues where there is some technical complexity and open political conflict: it has been widely applied to environmental and energy policy issues in North America, such as air and water pollution, where there is plenty of scope for policy-oriented learning through the analysis of quantitative data and its application to natural systems (Sabatier and Jenkins-Smith 1999).

The ACF (and the agenda-setting model) is underpinned by pluralistic assumptions, no doubt reflecting its American origins. Consequently, it may be less applicable in countries where conflict is less open, as in the étatist French system, or where closed policy communities prevail, as in Britain (but see Sabatier 1998). Nevertheless, where policy processes are pluralistic, which is often the case with environmental issues, the ACF can be a useful tool for explaining policy outcomes. Within EU institutions, for instance, much policymaking affecting the environment is made within open issue networks that offer interest groups better access to policy elites than is normally available at the national level (Bomberg 1998b). Coalitions made up of lobbyists and politicians have frequently emerged around divisive issues such as the biotechnology, waste packaging and auto-emissions directives, with each coalition seeking to control the policy networks in order to shape policy outcomes.

According to all these ideas-based approaches – agenda-setting, the ACF and even the discourse framework (see Box 7.7) – change in environmental policy is easier to achieve where policymaking is relatively pluralistic than where it is dominated by closed policy networks (although there is no guarantee that the policy outcomes will be better for the environment as industry coalitions will often prevail over environmental coalitions because they can mobilise more resources in an exercise of one-dimensional power). Even then, however, *radical* change is rare because without major exogenous changes there are few windows of opportunity to provide access to different interests and advocacy coalitions that can push new issues and ideas onto the policy agenda.

## ▶ *Policy communities and exogenous change*

The strength of policy network analysis lies in its capacity to explain continuity and stability, but it has been widely criticised for offering a static model that is poor at explaining policy change (Dowding 1995; Dudley and Richardson 1996). After all, if a policy community is stable, why should it ever introduce changes that are not directly in the interests of its members? Yet no sub-system is immune from external developments. Just as Sabatier recognised that radical change requires the belief systems of policy elites to be shaken up by exogenous non-cognitive factors, similarly network analysts have identified a number of structural factors that may destabilise a strongly institutionalised policy community and so make policy change more likely (Smith 1993: 93–7). In short, exogenous factors can play a catalytic role in changing power relations. Five external factors seem particularly significant in shaping environmental policy.

1. A *sudden crisis* may throw a policy community into disarray. The discovery of a link between bovine spongiform encephalopathy (BSE) and the human disease new-variant Creutzfeld–Jakob disease in 1996 provoked a food scare so enormous that the EU introduced a complete ban on the export of British beef, profoundly weakening the powerful agricultural policy community. During 2000–1, the discovery of BSE elsewhere in Europe

and an outbreak of foot-and-mouth disease provoked a public debate about the nature of intensive agriculture that destabilised agricultural policy communities across Europe. The 1989 *Exxon Valdez* oil spill in Alaska Sound produced immediate local improvements in the safeguards against marine oil pollution (Busenberg 1999).

2. A policy community may also be disturbed when a government is confronted by a *new problem,* such as climate change or food safety, for which the dominant interests in the policy community have no immediate solution. In such circumstances governments seeking answers to policy puzzles may turn to alternative interests outside the established network. The need to reduce carbon emissions from road traffic has prompted policymakers to look beyond powerful road lobbies in their search for alternative transport policies. The development of new technologies such as GMOs may similarly disrupt established methods of consultation in the agricultural sector, forcing governments to listen to a wider range of interests, including consumers and environmentalists.

3. Changes in *external relations* can disrupt the structural conditions underpinning a policy community. International agreements such as the ban on chlorofluorocarbons (CFCs) or commitments to reduce greenhouse gas emissions impose new external obligations that may require a national government to override the resistance of powerful producer interests. The extensive privatisation of public assets since the 1980s has also undermined some established policy communities, particularly in Britain where, for example, greater competition transformed the energy market (resulting in a major shift from coal to gas as the source of electricity generation) and therefore disrupted the established energy policy community (see Box 12.5). EU environmental directives in those areas where policy has been most stringent, such as drinking- and bathing-water quality, have destabilised some policy networks (Maloney and Richardson 1994). In the British water industry, the combination of regulatory restructuring arising from privatisation and tough European directives prised open a previously cohesive policy community (consisting of engineers and water scientists) to provide a window of opportunity for environmental groups to politicise water quality issues. This flux eventually forced the government to make several significant policy changes, including a shift away from the established policy of low-cost, long-pipe sewage disposal at sea that was blamed by many for the low quality of bathing water in many tourist resorts (Jordan 1998).

4. The emergence of *new social movements and pressure groups* has contributed to the growing importance of environmental issues on the political agenda. It has become harder for politicians, civil servants and even producer groups to ignore these issues and many environmental groups are now routinely consulted by most governments across a wide range of issues (see Chapter 6).

5. Political actors, notably ministers, have the capacity to use their *despotic power* to break up a policy community and to allow access to new groups.

Mainstream political leaders may come to accept that certain powerful environmental groups can no longer be excluded from the policy process, so they force a change upon a sub-system. A change of government can have the same outcome: the Green involvement in the German coalition government in 1998 led directly to the decision to phase out nuclear power.

Indeed, nuclear power provides an interesting example of policy change because, as the following case study shows, a combination of exogenous factors has profoundly disrupted established patterns of policymaking to produce a radical reversal of the previous pro-nuclear consensus – although this transformation may not be permanent.

## Critical question 4

Under what conditions is radical reform of environmental policy possible?

## ▶ The rise and fall (and rise again?) of nuclear power

The potential threats to human safety and the environment posed by the use of nuclear power highlight many of the core characteristics of environmental policy identified in this chapter. As the catastrophic explosion at the Chernobyl nuclear reactor in 1986 demonstrated, there can be few other issues that pose such a *potentially* irreversible, transnational and long-term threat to the environment as nuclear power – even if the actual risk of damage is statistically extremely low. Despite these concerns, from the late 1950s to the 1980s, as strong pro-nuclear policy communities developed, most industrialised nations invested heavily in the expansion of nuclear energy. Yet, remarkably, since the 1980s, an extraordinary coincidence of exogenous factors has profoundly weakened these entrenched policy communities, resulting in a dramatic reversal of the enthusiastic pro-nuclear consensus amongst policy elites. By the mid-1990s, most North American and Western European nations had abandoned all plans to build new nuclear reactors and the industry appeared to be in terminal crisis. A decade on, there is growing evidence of renewed government interest in nuclear power in an ironic new guise: as a carbon-free energy solution to mitigate climate change.

Historically, decisions about nuclear power generally emerged from tight-knit, closed policy communities or corporatist institutional arrangements. In Britain, for example, the policy process was dominated by the Atomic Energy Authority (UKAEA) – a government-funded, largely unaccountable, cross-breed between a ministry and a nationalised industry – and its scientific experts – with the Department of Energy only a secondary actor in the policy community (Greenaway et al. 1992: ch. 6; Saward 1992). The government gave the policy community its full support and ensured that it was subject to minimal democratic control via Parliament.

In the 1950s and 1960s, two key factors explained government support for nuclear power. First, for nuclear powers such as Britain, France and the USA, the military objective to develop nuclear weapons generated a demand for plutonium (for weapons), which could only be extracted from reprocessed spent uranium (from nuclear power-stations). This military–industrial link was critical in the decision to push ahead with what was, even to its most enthusiastic supporters in the 1950s, still an uncommercial technology. Secondly, the belief that nuclear power offered a modern, technological solution to future energy requirements was widespread. All governments, including many with no pretensions to develop nuclear weapons, were persuaded that nuclear power had the potential to provide an abundant supply of cheap energy to underpin future economic growth. Other factors contributed to this growing love affair with nuclear energy. Concern about pollution from coal-fired plants was a major stimulus to the US nuclear programme in the 1960s. The Middle East oil crisis of 1973–4 prompted several European countries, notably West Germany and France, to launch huge construction programmes in order to reduce their dependence on oil supplies from volatile overseas markets. By 2006 there were some 440 nuclear reactors in operation across the world in 31 countries generating 16 per cent of global electricity (World Nuclear Association 2006). The USA has the biggest nuclear sector, with 103 reactors generating 788.6 billion kilowatt hours of electricity (or 20 per cent of its total electricity), whilst in France, with the second largest nuclear capacity, 78 per cent of electricity is generated by the nuclear sector.

Yet, since the mid-1990s, the nuclear industry has been in deep crisis. In 2001, there were no reactors under construction anywhere in Western Europe or North America, with a moratorium on the construction of new reactors in five out of eight European nations with nuclear power. Britain had no plans for further expansion and the US nuclear industry had come to a complete standstill. Sweden launched its policy of abandoning nuclear power – the source of half its electricity – by closing the Barsebäck-1 reactor in November 1999. Germany and Belgium also initiated gradual phase-outs of nuclear power. In short, it amounted to a truly dramatic policy reversal. Significantly, all five exogenous factors identified in the previous section contributed to the destabilisation of pro-nuclear policy communities.

First, the nuclear industry was hit by a series of major crises. The partial meltdown of a reactor at the Three Mile Island plant in 1979 prompted a major global debate about nuclear safety and destroyed the industry in America: no new nuclear power stations were ordered there after 1978. The 1986 accident at Chernobyl had a similar impact on the nuclear consensus in Europe: Italy held three referenda on nuclear power in 1987, the German SPD declared its commitment to a phase-out of nuclear power and opposition in Scandinavia strengthened. Only in France did the powerful pro-nuclear elite consensus produce a complacent response to Chernobyl (Liberatore 1995).

Secondly, a range of operational problems has undermined the political case for nuclear energy; in particular, it has failed to deliver on its promise to be reliable and safe. Many nuclear plants have been beset by malfunctions that have put them out of action for long periods of time. Public fears have been repeatedly rekindled by the frequency of accidental releases of low-level radioactive materials and heated debates about the potential dangers (e.g. links with cancers) of living in close proximity to nuclear plants. In the aftermath of the Cold War, there was widespread concern in the West about the safety of the large stock of Russian-designed reactors in Eastern Europe, prompting the German government to close all the plants in the former East Germany immediately after unification. Austria – a non-nuclear state that closed its sole nuclear power-station after a 1978 plebiscite – tried unsuccessfully to make the closure of the unreliable Czech Temelin power-station, close to the Austrian border, a condition for the accession of the Czech Republic to the EU in 2004 (Axelrod 2004).

Perhaps most important is the still largely unresolved problem of how the growing stockpile of spent fuel and waste – some of which will be active for 1,000 years – should be safely stored. In the USA, where most waste is stored on site, there have been long-running and unresolved disputes over plans to build a national nuclear waste repository at Yucca Mountain, Nevada, and interim sites elsewhere (Rogers and Kingsley 2004). In Britain, despite the identification of several hundred possible sites for the storage of nuclear waste (*Guardian*, 11 June 2005), all efforts to provide a long-term repository for the 100,000 tonnes of existing nuclear waste have failed. Indeed, only a handful of such facilities have been completed anywhere.

Thirdly, external changes have opened up pro-nuclear political communities and led to serious challenges to the economic case for nuclear energy. The policy communities managed to conceal the true costs of nuclear power behind the veil of state ownership and regulatory structures for many years, but privatisation and liberalisation of European electricity markets have made this more difficult. Most existing nuclear power-stations were built either directly by state-owned companies or by private developers in receipt of huge state subsidies; today those options are often unavailable. For example, proposals by the Conservative government to privatise the British nuclear power industry in the late 1980s unintentionally helped break up the nuclear policy community because the exposure to financial scrutiny required for market flotation revealed the true (i.e. enormous and previously unquantified) costs of the industry (Greenaway et al. 1992). Although uranium fuel is cheap and plentiful, the capital cost of building a nuclear plant – which may take ten years to complete – is enormous compared to, say, a gas-fired power station. In the USA, the failure of the completed $5.5 billion Shoreham nuclear plant on Long Island, New York, to open, after the local authorities rejected evacuation plans, means that any company considering building a nuclear reactor runs the risk of its credit rating taking a hit and its bonds dropping to junk status (*Financial Times*, 10 August 2004). Moreover, the massive costs of decommissioning reactors were never properly included in the cost–benefit analysis of nuclear energy. In short, cheap nuclear energy proved to be a myth.

Fourthly, the anti-nuclear movements in the 1970s and 1980s were among the most popular, persistent and successful new social movements, especially in Germany (Flam 1994); indeed, nuclear power is often defined as a classic postmaterial issue (see Chapter 4). They have played an important part in turning the public against nuclear power and persuading many mainstream parties to alter or moderate their former pro-nuclear stances. At the local level, combined opposition from environmental groups and local citizen action groups has made it almost impossible for most Western governments to secure support for a new nuclear plant. This mobilising potential of the anti-nuclear movement remains an important factor in the nuclear debate (Fischer and Boehnke 2004).

Lastly, as green parties have entered government, their anti-nuclear roots have prompted them to lead a direct assault on the nuclear industry. The German red–green coalition government in 1998 agreed a complete phase-out of nuclear energy in 2001 (see Box 7.8). The appointment of a Green environment minister in France, Dominique Voynet, also produced the first crack – albeit quickly sealed – in the powerful bipartisan French pro-nuclear consensus when she closed the Creys-Malville Super Phenix nuclear generator in 1998. The involvement of the green parties in the 1999–2003 Belgian coalition government resulted in legislation prohibiting the construction of new nuclear reactors and limiting the lives of existing ones to forty years. The Finnish Green League resigned from the government in 2002 over its opposition to the construction of a new nuclear reactor.

To summarise, exogenous factors have disrupted established patterns of policymaking, leading many Western countries to call a halt to their nuclear expansion programmes. Certainly the decline of the nuclear lobby provides clear evidence that even the strongest of policy communities can be destabilised and broken down, although it took a remarkable combination of events to produce this transnational decline. For Baumgartner and Jones (1993: ch. 4), the rise and fall of the US nuclear industry is a classic example of punctuated equilibrium: popular enthusiasm about the promise of nuclear technology, followed by years of policy stability and industry growth under the control of a powerful policy community (or, as they call it, a 'policy monopoly'), to be replaced by growing questioning of the nuclear industry which peaked with the Three Mile Island accident in 1979 and the subsequent disintegration of the policy community.

However, the death certificate of the nuclear industry should not be signed prematurely, for there seems to be considerable life in it yet. Even whilst it was in crisis in North America and Europe, several industrialising nations, notably South Korea, China and India, were investing heavily in nuclear

## 7.8 German nuclear shutdown?

The phasing out of nuclear power has always been an article of faith for the German Greens, so they made it a condition of the October 1998 SPD–Green coalition agreement that the government would launch a decommissioning programme for Germany's nineteen nuclear power-stations. Jürgen Trittin, the Green environment minister, wanted a rapid decommissioning programme with all reactors being closed within twenty years, and an end to the export of nuclear waste by January 2000. His proposals met strong resistance from the energy industry:

1. German nuclear energy companies had firm contracts, guaranteed by the government, to export nuclear waste to Britain and France for reprocessing. To renege on these contracts would be diplomatically damaging and make the government liable to pay massive financial compensation.
2. The nuclear energy companies responded with a strong campaign calling for a longer lifespan for their reactors. By focusing their efforts on the SPD, they were able to exploit the weakness of the red–green coalition during 1999–2000 as it stumbled from one crisis to another and suffered a series of setbacks in *Länder* elections.
3. Nuclear power contributed around 36 per cent of German energy capacity. If reactors were to be closed, the lost generating capacity, at least in the short term, would be replaced by fossil fuel sources, which would raise carbon emissions.

The arguments dragged on for over eighteen months, causing serious tensions between the SPD and the Greens, until a decommissioning package was eventually agreed with the energy producers, and formally approved in 2001. This package provided that:

- each nuclear plant would be set an operating life on the basis of an average overall lifespan of thirty-two years from the start of commercial production (but productive capacity could be switched between plants so the early closure of one plant might allow another to stay open longer than thirty-two years).
- recycling of waste would be halted 'as soon as possible'.

This diluted package bears witness to the capacity of a united and powerful industry sector to influence policy. Indeed, the German nuclear industry should not be written off yet, for much could change by 2021 (when most reactors are due to be phased out), which could yet see this agreement torn up. Indeed, Angela Merkel campaigned in the 2005 federal election on a promise to allow German nuclear power-stations to operate beyond 2021. However, the SPD insisted that the new Merkel-led CDU-SPD government leave the agreement intact. But the issue will not disappear whilst Germany is under pressure to reduce carbon emissions to prevent climate change and to ensure energy security in the face of new international threats to its oil and gas supplies.

power. In 2005, thirty reactors were under construction around the world, mostly in Asia, including nine in India, while South Korea expects to have built a further eight reactors by 2015 (World Nuclear Association 2006). Elsewhere, governments have found it much easier to stop building new plants than to close existing ones. Nuclear reactors have high capital costs but, once built, they are relatively cheap to operate. Closure will harm the nuclear industry and make many people unemployed. The combination of international and domestic obstacles encountered by the German government in trying to agree a decommissioning programme illustrates the continuing strength of the pro-nuclear advocacy coalition (see Box 7.8). The longer the nuclear industry in each country can delay the implementation of a serious closure programme, the more chance it has that new exogenous factors may swing the argument back in its favour. Ironically, the threat of global warming has provided a boost for the industry because many countries will be unable to meet their carbon emissions reduction commitments if they close their nuclear plants. Given the small size of the renewable energy sector in most countries, one short-term cost of closing nuclear reactors is almost certain to be an increased dependence on electricity generated by fossil fuels. Consequently, most countries have delayed further closures of reactors by upgrading existing nuclear stock, improving capacity and lengthening their expected lifespan.

There is also growing evidence of renewed support for nuclear power among Western policy elites. The EU Energy Commissioner, Loyola de Palacio, stated that nuclear power could help ensure the stability of energy prices and supply: 'Five years ago no one was talking about it, but now [the debate about nuclear energy] is on the table . . . there are not many alternatives' (*Financial Times*, 10 August 2004). In short, EU carbon emission reduction targets may only be met by building new nuclear reactors to replace declining stock. Western European governments provided financial support for the construction of two new nuclear power-stations in the Ukraine to replace the Chernobyl plant. The Finnish parliament approved the construction of a fifth reactor in 2002. The French government has chosen a site in Normandy where the prototype of a new generation of European pressurised water reactors will be built, ready to replace the ageing French stock from about 2015. A review of UK energy policy published in 2006 concluded that new nuclear power-stations would be a significant source of low carbon electricity generation (DTI 2006: 17), effectively backing the Prime Minister, Tony Blair, who had already declared his support for the construction of more nuclear reactors. Following a series of power cuts in California, President Bush championed the new Energy Policy Act 2005, which specifically promotes the construction of new nuclear plants. The federal government will provide significant financial aid to encourage developers to take advantage of a new, more relaxed permit regime designed to make it easier for companies to win construction and operating licences. So the future of the nuclear industry remains in the balance: whilst there is growing pro-nuclear sentiment among policy elites in many countries, most Western European governments, let alone the wider public, have still to be convinced by the safety, economic and political arguments for renewed nuclear expansion.

What does the nuclear case study tell us about the potential for radical policy change? The reversal of the commitment to nuclear expansion undoubtedly represents a radical policy change; in Hall's taxonomy, it resembles third-order change. Nevertheless, the pro-nuclear paradigm has not yet been replaced by a new, alternative paradigm, such as a commitment to a sustainable energy policy. Significantly, although frequently defined as a postmaterial issue, the radical change in nuclear policy has been driven primarily by two *materialist* arguments: the risk it poses to human safety and the collapse of the economic case for nuclear power. Moreover, there has been no process of social learning in which policy elites have questioned the sustainability of the core assumptions underpinning energy policy. Drawing on Sabatier, the changes have affected the *policy core* beliefs within one subsystem, resulting in expectations about the contribution of nuclear energy to overall energy production to be scaled down – although in recent years the need to cut carbon emissions has prompted renewed interest in the nuclear option. Crucially, the *deep core* beliefs about the wider role of energy production and consumption in the economy remain largely intact. In a consumerist society in which energy conservation remains a low priority and where profit-seeking energy utilities encourage increased energy consumption, it is not surprising that few countries have made any serious attempt to develop an alternative energy strategy, and the door remains ajar for the return of nuclear power (see Chapter 12).

## *Critical question 5*
Will climate change save the nuclear industry?

## ▶ Conclusion

This chapter has identified a major problem: why has the traditional paradigm proved so resilient, despite its patent inadequacy in dealing with the complex challenges thrown up by contemporary environmental problems? Familiar concepts in political science – interests, ideas, institutions and power – and the relationship between them have been used to explain this resilience.

It has been argued that the traditional paradigm is underpinned by the structural power of producer interests, the segmentation of the policy process and the belief systems of policy elites. Policymakers are informed by a technocentric commitment to economic expansion, which encourages them to define the interests of the state as largely synonymous with those of producers and, therefore, to 'recognise some social interests as more legitimate than others and privilege some lines of policy over others' (Hall 1993: 292). More often than not, the interests of producer groups trump those of environmental groups, and economic growth takes priority over environmental protection. The expansionist paradigm and the institutional structure of government are mutually reinforcing: organisational structures, administrative procedures and policy networks are designed to implement the dominant ideas and, in turn, sustain and support them (Jordan 1998: 34). Even where policy processes are more pluralistic, producer groups are often able to dominate policymaking by mobilising sufficient resources to exercise effective first-dimensional power. The need to overcome powerful structural and institutional obstacles makes the replacement of the traditional paradigm no easy task, and probably dependent on the capacity for significant exogenous changes to disrupt the power of established interests. Even then, as the nuclear case study reveals, a radical policy reversal in one sector may not be matched by the adoption of a more strategic approach to energy policy. The nuclear industry may be wounded, but fossil fuel suppliers remain in the ascendant everywhere. It would seem therefore that policymakers will be best equipped to overcome the various structural and institutional obstacles to change when 'armed with a coherent policy paradigm' (Hall 1993: 290) such as sustainable development. In identifying the importance of belief systems, both Sabatier and Hall show that paradigm change is also dependent on a process of social learning by government and business policy elites (and wider society). The success of the alternative paradigms of sustainable development and ecological modernisation will depend on their capacity to win the hearts and minds of policy elites and to persuade them that their interests are compatible with a sustainable society.

## ◗ *Further reading*

Weale's (1992) study of pollution policies includes an insightful critique of the traditional environmental paradigm. Crenson (1971) is a classic treatment of power and environmental policymaking. Parsons (1995) and Hill (2005) are good general introductions to the policymaking literature, while Dovers (2005) provides a useful analysis of environmental policymaking. The innovative contributions by Kingdon (1995), Baumgartner and Jones (1993), Sabatier and Jenkins-Smith (1993, 1999) and Fischer (2003) all contain interesting case studies relevant to the environment.

NOTES

1 This list echoes similar categorisations found in Weale (1992) and Jordan and O'Riordan (1999).
2 Samuelson, quoted in Mueller (1989: 10).
3 See Ostrom (1990: 32–3) for a discussion of the distinction between common-pool resources and public goods.
4 See Hay et al. (2006) for a review of state theory.
5 See Grant (1995) for a discussion of insider and outsider groups.
6 Other 'environmental' applications of the three-dimensional model include two British case studies of pollution from a brickworks (Blowers 1984) and of agricultural pollution (Hill et al. 1989). The three-dimensional model of power is not without its critics (see Polsby 1980). See Hill (2005: ch. 2) and Parsons (1995: 134–45) for a general discussion of the model.

7 Heclo (1978) argued that the 'iron triangle' metaphor was overplayed, and that it is now less applicable anyway. However, Peters (1998a: 29) warns against the complete rejection of the iron triangle and notes the persistence of elite dominance in many sectors.

8 See Dowding (1995) for a critical discussion of the policy network approach, and the rejoinder by Marsh and Smith (2000).

# Sustainable development and ecological modernisation

**8**

## Contents

## Key issues

▶ What is sustainable development?
▶ Why is it such a complex and contestable concept?
▶ What are its core principles?
▶ What is ecological modernisation?
▶ What are its strengths and weaknesses?

The tension between economic growth and environmental protection lies at the heart of environmental politics. The concept of sustainable development is a direct attempt to resolve this dichotomy by sending the message that it is possible to have economic development whilst also protecting the environment. Not surprisingly, policymakers the world over, told that they can have their cake and eat it, have seized on the idea. Almost every country is now committed, at least on paper, to the principles of sustainable development. Yet sustainable development is an ambiguous concept, with a meaning that is contested and complex. This elusiveness is both a strength and a weakness: it allows a multitude of political and economic interests to unite under one banner, while attracting the criticism that it is an empty slogan with little substance. Policymakers have also found it difficult to turn this loose set of ideas into practical policies. Indeed, in those industrialised countries that boast the most progressive environmental policies, the narrower concept of ecological modernisation has acquired increasing resonance.

Sustainable development and its half-sister, ecological modernisation, offer an alternative policy paradigm to the traditional model of environmental policy. The first part of this chapter examines the various meanings attributed to sustainable development and identifies five core principles underpinning most definitions of the concept. The second half outlines the key features of ecological modernisation before analysing its strengths and limitations.

# ▶ Sustainable development

## ▶ *Spreading the word*

Sustainable development has rapidly become the dominant idea, or discourse (Dryzek 2005), shaping international policy towards the environment. The concept was first endorsed in the World Conservation Strategy (IUCN/UNEP/WWF 1980) produced by three international NGOs. This document was primarily concerned with ecological sustainability, or the conservation of living resources, and directed little attention to wider political, economic or social issues. Sustainable development was given a broader social meaning in *Our Common Future*, published by the World Commission on Environment and Development (WCED 1987) and commonly known as the Brundtland Report (see Box 8.1). The Brundtland Report popularised sustainable development so successfully that it has since been taken up by almost every international institution, agency and NGO. The principles of sustainable development underpinned the Rio Earth Summit agenda where approval was given to the Agenda 21 document outlining a 'global partnership for sustainable development' (see Box 8.2). This massive document addresses a wide range of environmental and developmental issues and is intended to provide a strategy for implementing sustainable development throughout the world. The UN Commission on Sustainable Development (see http://www.un.org/esa/sustdev/csd/review.htm) was established to monitor and promote the implementation of Agenda 21 in each country and it now provides policy guidance for the Johannesburg Plan

## 8.1 The Brundtland Commission

The United Nations General Assembly established the World Commission on Environment and Development in 1983 in response to growing concerns about both environmental degradation and the economic crisis. The Commission, chaired by Gro Harlem Brundtland, the Norwegian prime minister, consulted widely for four years, soliciting reports from expert bodies and holding public meetings in several countries. In 1987 it produced its final report, *Our Common Future*, popularly known as the Brundtland Report (WCED 1987), which popularised the concept of sustainable development worldwide.

To understand the Commission's approach to sustainable development, it is important to be aware of the political context in which it operated. Since the 1972 Stockholm Conference there had been growing awareness of the severity of environmental problems, accentuated by new worries about the global problems of climate change, ozone depletion and biodiversity loss. However, the environmental agenda had been largely hijacked by the affluent North. Meanwhile, poorer countries in the South were experiencing major economic problems with the collapse in commodity prices, the debt crisis and economic stagnation all contributing to worsening poverty (and environmental degradation). Against this background the continuing East–West tensions associated with the Cold War raised serious security concerns.

This political context explains why the Commission deliberately designed sustainable development as a *bridging* concept that could unite apparently diverse and conflicting interests and policy concerns (Meadowcroft 2000). Specifically, it sought to bring together the environmental agenda of the North with the developmental agenda of the South; hence the title of the final report, *Our Common Future*.

## 8.2 Agenda 21

Agenda 21 (UNCED 1992) provides the blueprint for implementing sustainable development agreed at the 1992 Earth Summit (and approved by over 170 nations). This substantial document covers an enormous number of environment and development issues, with forty chapters ranging from 'Changing Consumption Patterns' and 'Combating Deforestation' to 'Children and Youth in Sustainable Development' and 'Strengthening the Role of Farmers'. Indeed, a key feature of Agenda 21 is that it does not confine itself to the traditional agenda of environmental degradation and conservation, but devotes considerable attention to the political, economic and financial aspects of sustainable development. Thus twenty-five of the forty chapters focus on non-ecological issues.

Agenda 21 website: http://www.un.org/esa/ sustdev/documents/agenda21/english/ agenda21toc.htm.

of Implementation (see Box 8.3), although it has few powers to force compliance. Most industrialised countries have published national sustainable development strategies (Jänicke and Jörgens 1998; Lafferty and Meadowcroft 2000a) and many local authorities have launched Local Agenda 21 strategies (Lafferty 2001).

---

**8.3 World Summit on Sustainable Development 2002 (WSSD)**

The WSSD was held in Johannesburg in 2002. Its objectives were to review progress in the ten years since the Rio Earth Summit, and to give a kick-start to the global sustainable development process. It was the largest ever international conference, and alongside it 40,000 people attended the parallel Global People's Forum of NGOs, yet the most powerful world leader, President Bush, refused to go. Although the WSSD briefly put the environment back on the international agenda, it disappointed most observers. The key outcome was the 'Plan of Implementation' for Agenda 21, which identifies the processes necessary to deliver sustainable development. Yet there are few specific targets, apart from new commitments to improve sanitation and access to drinking water; in particular, the absence of commitments on renewable energy was a major failing. One focus of the WSSD was the promulgation of new forms of partnership between government, businesses and NGOs, giving a much bigger role to the corporate sector. Indeed, some critics felt that the summit was effectively hijacked by corporate interests – leading to a 'privatisation of sustainable development' (von Frantzius 2004: 469). Overall, despite some limited achievements, the WSSD was a wasted opportunity. Undermined by the USA, and let down by the lack of leadership from the EU, it was too big, too unwieldy and too complex to be successful.

See Seyfang (2003), Wapner (2003), von Frantzius (2004) and Baker (2006: 64–9).

---

The reach of sustainable development has extended far beyond government into the world of business and civil society. The World Bank has sought to throw off its poor reputation with environmentalists by developing an environmental strategy document, *Making Sustainable Commitments*, publishing annual environmental reports, holding regular seminars and sponsoring research on a wide range of environmental issues (see http://www.worldbank.org/). The World Bank is host to the Global Environment Facility, which is the institution responsible for channelling financial assistance for sustainable development from Northern to Southern nations (see Box 9.3). The World Business Council for Sustainable Development, established in its current form in 1995, is a coalition of around 180 international companies from 35 countries and 20 industrial sectors, linked to a global network of 50 national and regional business councils of over 1,000 business leaders. Its mission is 'to provide business leadership as a catalyst for change toward sustainable development and support the business licence to operate, innovate and grow in a world increasingly shaped by sustainable development issues' (WBCSD 2006). Many trade associations have also declared their support for sustainable development; for example, the insurance industry (which potentially has much to lose if climate change leads to rising sea-levels, floods and storms) has issued a Statement of Environmental Commitment signed by over ninety leading insurance companies from twenty-seven countries (see http://www.unepfi.org/). These international efforts have been widely replicated at the national level, where state-sponsored round-tables have brought together representatives from all sections of society – politicians, business, trade unions, churches and environmental and consumer groups – to discuss how sustainable development can be implemented. Despite this widespread enthusiasm, the precise meaning of sustainable development remains elusive.

## ▶ A complex and contested concept

The sheer proliferation of definitions of sustainable development is evidence of its contestability; for example, Pearce et al. (1989: 173–85) provide a 'gallery' of over forty definitions. The most widely used definition, taken from the Brundtland Report, is that 'sustainable development is development that meets the needs of the present without compromising the ability of future generations to meet their own needs' (WCED 1987: 43). This definition sets out the two fundamental principles of intragenerational and intergenerational equity, and contains the two 'key concepts' of needs and limits (ibid.: 43). The concept of *needs* demands that 'overriding priority' should be given to the essential needs of the world's poor, both North and South. Poverty and the unequal distribution of resources are identified as major causes of environmental degradation: 'Sustainable development requires meeting the basic needs of all and extending to all the opportunity to satisfy their aspirations for a better life' (ibid.: 44). Crucially, the Brundtland Report stresses that these goals can only be achieved if consumption patterns in the richer countries are readjusted. Secondly, the concept of *limits* recognises that the current state of technology and social organisation imposes limits on the ability of the environment to meet present and future needs, so we must moderate our demands on the natural environment. Yet Brundtland rejects the crude anti-growth arguments of the 1970s, asserting that 'Growth has no set limits in terms of population or resource use beyond which lies ecological disaster' (ibid.: 45). Indeed, Brundtland demands a revival of growth in developing countries to help alleviate poverty and provide basic needs, although it seeks a more 'eco-friendly' type of growth that is 'less material- and energy-intensive and more equitable in its impact' (ibid.: 52).

A central distinguishing feature of sustainable development as a policy paradigm is that it shifts the terms of debate from traditional environmentalism, with its primary focus on environmental protection, to the notion of sustainability, which requires a much more complex process of trading off social, economic and environmental priorities. Box 8.4 shows that the Brundtland definition is as much concerned with economic and social development as it is with environmental protection. *Development* is a process of transformation which, by combining economic growth with broader social and cultural changes, enables individuals to realise their full potential. The dimension of *sustainability* brings the recognition that

## 8.4 Core elements of sustainable development

Sustainable development is a normative concept used to prescribe and evaluate changes in living conditions. Such changes are to be guided by four Brundtland aspirations:

1. To satisfy basic human needs and reasonable standards of welfare for all living beings. (*Development*)
2. To achieve more equitable standards of living both within and among global populations. (*Development*)

3. To be pursued with great caution as to their actual or potential disruption of biodiversity and the regenerative capacity of nature, both locally and globally. (*Sustainability*)
4. To be achieved without undermining the possibility for future generations to attain similar standards of living and similar or improved standards of equity. (*Sustainability*)

From Lafferty (1996: 189).

development must also adhere to the physical constraints imposed by ecosystems, so that environmental considerations have to be embedded in all sectors and policy areas. Brundtland's unapologetic anthropocentrism, displayed in its concern for human welfare and the exploitation of nature, in preference to an ecocentric interest in protecting nature for its own sake, has opened up environmental politics to a wider audience.[1] The promise of sustainable development is that it seems to offer a way out of the economy versus environment impasse; no longer need there be a trade-off between growth and environmental protection. Far from it: growth is seen as a 'good thing' because it enables less developed countries to develop and so improve the standard of living of their impoverished citizens, while the material quality of life in the affluent North can be maintained. All these benefits . . . and environmental protection too!

Sustainable development, like beauty, is in the eye of the beholder; it promises something for everyone. As Lele has put it, with just a hint of irony, 'Sustainable development is a "metafix" that will unite everybody from the profit-minded industrialist and risk-minimising subsistence farmer to the equity-seeking social worker, the pollution-concerned or wildlife-loving First Worlder, the growth-maximising policy maker, the goal-oriented bureaucrat, and, therefore, the vote-counting politician' (Lele 1991: 613). This universal appeal is enhanced by the apparent ideological neutrality of sustainable development. It offers no clear vision of an ideal end state, whether green utopia or otherwise, and no set of political or economic arrangements is specifically promoted. Instead, sustainable development involves a *process of change* in which core components of society – resource use, investment, technologies, institutions, consumption patterns – come to operate in greater harmony with ecosystems.

These chameleon characteristics attract a wide array of supporters, but they also make sustainable development a highly contestable concept. Some aims appear radical: the elimination of poverty, the pursuit of global equity, reductions in military expenditure, wider use of appropriate technologies, democratisation of institutions and a shift away from consumerist lifestyles. Other themes, such as the acceptance of the capitalist economic system and the need for continued economic growth, seem to accept the status quo. The core concepts also beg many hoary but unresolved political questions. For example, what are basic needs? Should they reflect the needs of citizens in the USA or Bangladesh? How far will the living standards of rich industrialised nations have to be readjusted to achieve sustainable consumption patterns? Different answers to these questions produce conflicting interpretations of sustainable development. These ambiguities have not been helped by the absence of a detailed framework in the Brundtland Report to help individual countries turn these broad principles into practical policy measures. Consequently, policymakers have been able to pick and choose from the pot-pourri of often contradictory ideas in the Agenda 21 document while the endless stream of reports and books seeking to give flesh to sustainable development has fuelled disagreement as much as it has brought consensus.

The proliferation of meanings is not just an exercise in academic or practical clarification but a highly political process of 'different interests with different substantive concerns trying to stake their claims in the sustainable development territory' (Dryzek 2005: 146). As it has become more important, key interests have tried to define sustainable development to suit their own purposes. Thus an African government might emphasise the need for global redistribution of wealth from North to South in order to eliminate poverty, while a transnational corporation might insist that sustainability is impossible without vibrant economic growth to conquer poverty, stabilise population levels, provide for human welfare and, of course, maintain profit levels.

With so much ambiguity surrounding the meaning of sustainable development, there have been several attempts to construct typologies distinguishing different 'versions' of sustainable development (Pearce et al. 1993; O'Riordan 1996; Baker 2006, *inter alia*). Most typologies identify 'weak' and 'strong' forms of sustainable development, with some normatively outlining a transition from weaker to stronger versions. Baker (2006) has designed a 'ladder' of sustainable development (see Table 8.1), which is a useful heuristic device to identify different forms or discourses of sustainable development. The ladder 'identifies the political scenarios and policy implications associated with each rung', and links them to different philosophical beliefs about nature (ibid.: 28). The bottom rung is the technocentric *pollution control* approach, which believes that human ingenuity will solve any environmental problem. It assumes the existence of an environmental 'Kuznets curve' in which the high pollution associated with early industrialisation will decline as economic development continues into a post-industrial stage. *Weak sustainable development* aims to integrate capitalist growth and environmental concerns. Its objective is to keep the overall stock of human capital and natural capital (i.e. natural resources and ecological processes) constant over

**Table 8.1 The ladder of sustainable development: the global focus**

| Model of sustainable development | Normative principles | Type of development | Nature | Spatial focus |
|---|---|---|---|---|
| *Ideal model* | Principles take precedence over pragmatic considerations (participation, equity, gender equality, justice; common but differentiated responsibilities) | Right livelihood; meeting needs not wants; biophysical limits guide development | Nature has intrinsic value; no substitution allowed; strict limits on resource use, aided by population reductions | Bioregionalism; extensive local self-sufficiency |
| *Strong sustainable development* | Principles enter into international law and into governance arrangements | Changes in patterns and levels of consumption; shift from growth to non-material aspects of development; necessary development in Third World | Maintenance of critical natural capital and biodiversity | Heightened local economic self-sufficiency, promoted in the context of global markets; green and fair trade |
| *Weak sustainable development* | Declaratory commitment to principles stronger than practice | Decoupling; reuse, recycling and repair of consumer goods; product life-cycle management | Substitution of natural capital with human capital; harvesting of biodiversity resources | Initial moves to local economic self-sufficiency; minor initiatives to alleviate the power of global markets |
| *Pollution control* | Pragmatic, not principled, approach | Exponential, market-led growth | Resource exploitation; marketisation and further closure of the commons; nature has use value | Globalisation; shift of production to less regulated locations |

*Source*: Baker (2006: 30–1).

| Governance | Technology | Policy integration | Policy tools | Civil society–state relationship | Philosophy |
|---|---|---|---|---|---|
| Decentralisation of political, legal, social and economic institutions | Labour-intensive appropriate, green technology; new approach to valuing work | Environmental policy integration; principled priority to environment | Internalisation of sustainable development norms through ongoing socialisation, reducing need for tools | Bottom-up community structures and control; equitable participation | Ecocentric |
| Partnership and shared responsibility across multilevels of governance (international, national, regional and local); use of good governance principles | Ecological modernisation of production; mixed labour and capital-intensive technology | Integration of environmental considerations at sector level; green planning and design | Sustainable development indicators; wide range of policy tools; green accounting | Democratic participation; open dialogue to envisage alternative futures | |
| Some institutional reform and innovation; move to global regulation | End-of-pipe technical solutions; mixed labour- and capital-intensive technology | Addressing pollution at source; some policy co-ordination across sectors | Environmental indicators; market-led policy tools and voluntary agreements | Top-down initiatives; limited state–civil society dialogue; elite participation | |
| Command-and-control state-led regulation of pollution | Capital-intensive technology; progressive automation | End-of-pipe approach to pollution management | Conventional accounting | Dialogue between the state and economic interests | Anthropocentric |

time, although it accepts substitution between the various kinds of capital so that the natural resources might dwindle providing they are compensated for by the extension of human capital. Following the work of environmental economists, such as Pearce et al. (1989), it holds that the best way to protect the environment is to put a value or price on it (see Chapter 12). The third rung is *strong sustainable development*, which regards environmental protection as a pre-condition for economic development. It asserts that there are some forms of 'critical' natural capital that are essential for life – ozone, tropical rainforests, coral reefs – which cannot be replaced by technology and should be preserved absolutely. The top rung represents the *ideal form* of sustainable development which equates with radical forms of green politics such as bioregionalism and deep ecology, and is characterised by a steady-state economy, local social, political and economic self-reliance and a redistribution of property rights through burden-sharing. Of course, there are great variations *within* each category and there is often an overlap between them. Currently, most countries have managed only to make a tentative step onto the *weak sustainable development* rung.

To what extent is sustainable development compatible with ecologism? Many deep greens are understandably suspicious of a strategy that seems incompatible with the radical changes they demand. Thus Richardson (1997: 43) condemns sustainable development for being a 'political fudge' that 'seeks to bridge the unbridgeable divide between the anthropocentric and biocentric approaches to politics'. Others regard sustainable development as compromised by its acceptance of capitalism, arguing that sustainable development is a contradiction in terms because much economic growth cannot be ecologically sustainable; instead, capitalism must be replaced by a more decentralised, self-sustaining social and economic system. The top rung of the ladder incorporates these radical positions, some of which eschew using the term 'sustainable development'. However, most contemporary green activists are firmly committed to the principles of sustainable development: the original four pillars of the German Greens (see Box 3.5), for example, emphasise the centrality of development issues such as social justice, equality and democracy. Many greens hold views that fall into both the top and the second rung of the ladder. So whilst a strict definition of ecologism would include only the ideal model, as the boundary between the top two rungs is rather blurred there is scope for ecologism to encompass elements of strong sustainable development.

Does it matter that so many versions of sustainable development exist and that there is so much disagreement about its meaning? One view holds that without a clear meaning almost anything could be said to be sustainable, leaving it as little more than an empty political slogan. A universally acceptable definition is needed, with a list of measurable criteria against which it would be possible to judge progress towards sustainability. Better to have clarity and risk losing a few unwanted adherents, than retain a vacuous 'anything goes' approach. Policymakers would also benefit from a clear technical definition to help them implement sustainable development. Yet this perspective may undervalue one of the great strengths of sustainable development, which is that the fluidity of the concept should be celebrated rather than condemned. Rather like other political concepts such as democracy or justice, sustainable development is widely seen as a 'good thing' and has a generally accepted common-sense meaning within broad boundaries, but within those parameters there is deeper contestation around its constituent ideas (Dryzek 2005: 147; Baker 2006: 27). On this view the contestability of sustainable development has several virtues. Its 'all things to all people' quality has helped the message to resonate around the world and attract followers to the flag. Hajer (1995) suggests that the 'coalition for sustainable development can only be kept together by virtue of its rather vague story-lines at the same time as it asks for radical social change' (p. 14), whereas insistence on a precise formulation of the term is more likely to deter potential supporters. Thus the 'motherhood' idea of sustainable development can win broader acceptance for radical ideas such as equity and democratisation.

These debates can be a dynamic and positive feature of the incremental process of change. At the international level the sustainable development discourse has provoked fierce political struggles – particularly between North and South – which have pushed many environmental and development issues up the diplomatic agenda. International institutions such as the Commission on Sustainable Development have tried to drive the debate down to national and sub-national levels. The proliferation of sustainable development round-tables and Local Agenda 21 strategies has helped diffuse the idea throughout society and generated many practical initiatives. Even when governments pay only lip-service to international commitments, they may indirectly initiate change simply by creating new institutions and promulgating different ideas which can disrupt established patterns of policymaking and alter the belief systems of policy elites. By signing up to Agenda 21, for example, governments were obliged to produce national sustainable development strategies (see Chapter 11), which provided a window of opportunity for concerned actors to bring environmental issues to the attention of other ministries.

So the ambiguity and contestability that make sustainable development such a complex concept may also be a political strength. Its optimistic message offers something for everyone and allows all actors to speak the same language (even if it means different things to different people). But can this elusive concept be turned into practical policy proposals? Although the wide-ranging Agenda 21 document contains many practical suggestions, and despite the laudable efforts of many institutions and individuals, there is still no compact toolkit setting out the policies and instruments needed for sustainable development. The next section identifies five fundamental principles which, nevertheless, seem to underpin all versions of sustainable development.

---

*Critical question 1*
Is sustainable development too vague to be helpful to policymakers?

---

▶ *Core principles of sustainable development*

## Equity

> Our inability to promote the common interest in sustainable development is often a product of the relative neglect of economic and social justice within and amongst nations.
>
> (WCED 1987: 49)

Equity is a central feature of environmental policy. Governments always consider the distributional implications of any measure to prevent or alleviate environmental degradation. Will a tax on domestic energy consumption fall disproportionately on the poor, or a petrol tax unfairly harm people dependent on cars such as rural dwellers? Will tough emission standards requiring companies to invest heavily in cleaner technology reduce their competitiveness and lead to job losses? In short, most environmental measures generate winners and losers.

When environmentalism emerged onto the international stage in the 1970s, its main focus was on intergenerational equity, with its emphasis on the *Limits to Growth* discourse and the need to protect fragile ecosystems for future generations. The ascendancy of sustainable development has deflected some of the criticisms of 1970s environmentalism that it was an elitist doctrine which placed the concerns of nature and the environment above the immediate basic needs of the world's poorest people. The Brundtland Report emphasised two key features of the poverty–environment nexus. First, environmental damage from global consumption falls most severely on the poorest countries and the poorest people, who are least able to protect themselves. Secondly, the growing number of poverty-stricken and landless people in the South generates a struggle to survive that places huge pressure on the natural resource base. The resulting resource depletion – desertification, deforestation, overfishing, water scarcity, loss of biodiversity – continues the downward spiral of impoverishment by forcing more people onto marginal, ecologically fragile, lands. By underlining the interdependence between environmental and developmental issues, the Brundtland Report drew attention to the environmental impact of key North–South issues such as trade relations, aid, debt and industrialisation. It concluded that sustainable development is impossible while poverty and massive social injustices persist; hence the importance attributed to intragenerational equity alongside the more straightforwardly environmental principle of intergenerational equity.

However, putting intragenerational equity into practice can generate enormous political conflict, particularly along North–South lines. The principle of 'common but differentiated responsibilities', which was written into the

Rio Declaration, recognises that every country has to act to protect the environment in the interests of guarding the common fate of humanity, but it also acknowledges that not every country has made the same contribution to the current eco-crisis, and that countries have different capacities to address these problems. Thus a major issue in international environmental diplomacy is the extent to which the rich North is willing to accept the political and financial responsibility for addressing global problems such as climate change and ozone depletion, which were primarily caused by the industrialisation of the developed world, but where the policy focus is now increasingly on preventing developing countries from exacerbating these problems (see Chapter 9).

The concept of *sustainable consumption* is an equally contentious equity issue. The Brundtland Report was rather quiet on the need to change consumption patterns in the North, no doubt because its authors recognised that the issue was political dynamite. Subsequently, following its inclusion in Agenda 21, growing interest in sustainable consumption has helped direct attention onto the disparities between mass consumption in affluent countries and the billion or more of the poorest people in the South whose basic consumption needs are not being met (UNDP 1998). Sustainable consumption is the use of goods and services that respond to basic needs and bring a better quality of life, while minimising the use of natural resources, toxic materials and emissions of waste and pollutants over the life-cycle, so as not to jeopardise the needs of future generations. According to the 1998 Human Development Report (UNDP 1998), consumption must be: (1) *shared* – ensuring basic needs for all; (2) *strengthening* – building human capabilities; (3) *socially responsible* – so the consumption of some does not compromise the well-being of others; (4) *sustainable* – without mortgaging the choices of future generations.[2]

Numerous initiatives have been launched with the twin aims of reducing the direct impact of Northern consumption on scarce resources and improving the social and economic lot of the communities who supply those resources. The UN Department of Social and Economic Affairs, for example, sponsors over 300 sustainable development partnerships.[3] The 'fair-trade' movement, which has grown rapidly in recent years, is dedicated to helping poor and disadvantaged producers in developing countries by establishing direct links with consumers in the North and eliminating intermediaries in the trading chain. A Fairtrade label has been established guaranteeing that products meet certain minimum standards regarding the price paid, workers' rights, health and safety, and environmental quality.[4] Fair trade is concerned primarily with equity: the alleviation of poverty through enabling small producers to compete by ensuring that they receive a fair and stable price for their products. Indeed, one of the most common definitions of fair trade asserts that it contributes to sustainable development, 'by offering better conditions to, and securing the rights of, marginalised producers and workers – especially in the South' (European Fair Trade Association 2006). Whilst the explicitly environmental element may only involve, say, a maximum level of a permitted pesticide, in practice many fair-trade products, such as coffee, chocolate and bananas, are organically produced. Small farmers are less likely to use pesticides on a large scale (as it is not cost-effective) than are big producers, so simply by enabling the former to compete, fair trade is indirectly benefiting the environment. Café Direct is a British scheme in which a group of 'alternative' trading organisations, including Oxfam, Traidcraft and Twin, buy directly from farming organisations in less developed countries such as Nicaragua, with a fixed minimum price, prepayment of orders and a commitment to a long-term trading partnership. Many of the producer co-operatives then invest their profits directly in community development projects, such as new schools. The success of several organic coffee blends has enabled Café Direct to encourage and help several producers to shift to organically certified farming.[5]

Of course, equity is not an exclusively North–South concern. According to the UNDP human poverty index,[6] from 7 per cent (Sweden) to almost 30 per cent (Italy) of the population in industrial countries is poor (UNDP 2005: 230). Homelessness, unemployment and social exclusion are common in rich nations too. Poor, socially deprived households are the least likely to pursue sustainable consumption. The pressures of competitive spending and conspicuous consumption in affluent societies exacerbate disparities between rich and poor, encouraging poorer households to go deeper into debt in their unsuccessful attempt to meet rising consumption standards, thereby crowding out spending on food, education and health. Achieving sustainable consumption will therefore involve both an overall readjustment in the levels and patterns of consumption in rich countries and the provision of basic needs to the socially excluded poor.

Thus the sustainable development paradigm, by emphasising the complex links between social, economic, political and environmental factors, introduces a new layer of dilemmas to the issue of equity and environment (as illustrated by the controversial debate over trade in ivory outlined in Box 8.5). In so doing, it underlines how 1970s environmentalism misdiagnosed the problem, with its narrow and inaccurate focus on economic growth, over-population and nature protection.

## Democracy and participation

> Sustainable development requires: a political system that secures effective citizen participation in decision making . . .
>
> (WCED 1987: 65)

Sustainable development emphasises the importance of democracy and participation in solving environmental problems. The traditional paradigm saw no direct link between democracy and environmental problems, whereas sustainable development holds that the achievement of intragenerational

During the 1980s the African elephant was officially defined as an endangered species: one estimate reported the elephant population crashing from 1.3 million in 1979 to 609,000 in 1989, especially in East Africa. The primary cause was the thriving international trade in ivory, concentrated in Japan, which encouraged widespread poaching. The plight of the elephant became a *cause célèbre* for environmental organisations such as WWF and Western governments, including Britain, France and the USA. In 1989 the Convention on International Trade in Endangered Species (CITES) banned the ivory trade by placing elephants on its Appendix I list of sacrosanct creatures. The ban had an immediate impact on Western demand for ivory, slashing its price and reducing poaching, and the elephant population began to recover during the 1990s.

Several southern African states lobbied hard for a partial relaxation of the ban because:

1. Rather than being under threat, the elephant population in their countries is too large. Zimbabwe claimed that its elephant population had grown from 30,000 to 70,000 in recent years, which is about 25,000 more than its scrubland can support, causing the government to cull elephants and build up a huge stockpile of ivory.

2. Is it right that Western governments, by banning the ivory trade, should deny poor African countries the opportunity to make money from one of their few natural resources? Nor is the ban costless; elephant herds often trample precious crops and damage property.

In 1997 CITES allowed a partial relaxation of the ban on ivory trade so that Zimbabwe, Botswana and Namibia agreed a one-off sale of stockpiled ivory to Japan. Almost 50 tonnes (5,446 tusks) was sold to Japan for some US$5 million in 1999. In 2002, CITES agreed a further sale of existing ivory stocks by Botswana (20 tonnes), Namibia (10 tonnes) and South Africa (30 tonnes). However, this sale had still not taken place in January 2007 because of the failure to establish robust baseline data on the elephant population and on poaching levels.

*The case for a ban (preservation)*

1. Any trade in ivory legitimates it and makes it difficult to regulate: it is hard to tell whether ivory has been legally or illegally traded. Poaching in Kenya increased when the one-off sale took place in the late 1990s.

2. Many Westerners adopt the preservationist position that it is simply wrong to kill any elephant.

3. Elephants may be worth more to local people alive as a tourist attraction.

4. As it is difficult to measure elephant populations accurately, we cannot be sure that they are flourishing.

Conclusion: The relaxation of the ban will stimulate a massive increase in poaching and an illegal ivory trade, sending the elephant population back into decline.

*The case for trade (sustainable utilisation)*

1. The existence of large stockpiles of ivory from elephants that died naturally or were culled is a waste of a valuable resource.

2. A strictly regulated, limited trade in stockpiled ivory will bring much-needed revenue to impoverished indigenous communities. In Zimbabwe, the Campfire community-based programme permits local communities to sell lucrative hunting licences so that rich Western tourists shoot elephants as trophies, with the revenues being ploughed back into conservation (although critics claim that most revenue goes to the safari companies and very little trickles down to local people).

3. Sustainable utilisation provides an incentive for local communities to protect their elephant population in return for a share of the revenues.

Conclusion: The partial lifting of the ban represents a shift from preservation to sustainable development because (in theory) the environment is protected whilst social injustices are reduced.

See Barbier et al. (1990). CITES website: http://www.cites.org/.

equity will require measures to help poor and disadvantaged groups, and that these groups should have the opportunity to define their own basic needs. Although this democratic message was particularly aimed at developing countries, the encouragement of community participation through consultative processes, citizen initiatives and strengthening the institutions of local democracy is equally applicable in developed countries. It is vital that all local interests, whether poor inner-city or isolated rural communities, can participate in policy and planning decisions, such as urban development and transport planning, that have a direct effect on their lifestyles.

Democracy can also play an important legitimation role, particularly in richer countries, where it is necessary to win public support for environmental initiatives that may have a detrimental effect on lifestyles, such as new eco-taxes or the regulation of car use. If information is widely available and people can participate in decision-making, they may come to see the need for action and be more willing to accept sacrifices in their material quality of life.

## The precautionary principle

In order to protect the environment, the precautionary approach shall be widely applied by States according to their capabilities. Where there are threats of serious or irreversible damage, lack of full scientific certainty shall not be used as a reason for postponing cost-effective measures to prevent environmental degradation.                    (Agenda 21, Principle 15 (UNCED 1992))

The sustainable development paradigm deals with the complexity and uncertainty that surrounds so much environmental policymaking, particularly where technical and scientific issues are involved, by insisting on the widespread application of the precautionary principle. This principle states that the lack of scientific certainty shall not be used as a reason for postponing measures to prevent environmental degradation.

The precautionary principle is consistent with the notion of ecological sustainability in that it is about relieving pressure on the environment and giving it more 'space'. It is also a practical expression of intergenerational equity because to protect the world for our descendants we need to be sure that our actions will not cause irreparable harm to the environment. The debate around genetically modified organisms provides a good illustration of this issue (see Durant and Boodphetcharat 2004). The great promise of GM crops is that by increasing agricultural productivity they can make a real contribution to preventing food shortages in the poorest countries of Africa, Asia and Latin America. Yet GMOs are also characterised by chronic uncertainties about the possible threat they pose to ecosystems (see Box 7.2). Should companies be given free rein to develop these products, as has largely been the case in North America, or should governments invoke the precautionary principle to justify a step-by-step approach employing strict safeguards on trials and imposing moratoriums on production, as has occurred in Europe (Rosendal 2005; Lieberman and Gray 2006)? The Cartagena Protocol on Biosafety, agreed in 2000, explicitly invokes the precautionary principle by giving countries the right to refuse to accept the import of GM agricultural products. The principle of intragenerational equity also drives the precautionary principle when industrial countries accept the burden of helping poorer countries prevent damage, such as climate change, that might arise from their future economic development.

It is important to note two qualifications within the above UNCED definition. First, the qualification 'according to their capabilities' implies that less developed countries might not have to apply the approach so rigorously – this idea has informed the use of the precautionary principle in the ozone and climate change treaties (see Chapter 9). Secondly, it is not clear what kind of cost–benefit analysis should determine whether measures are 'cost-effective'. Are these internal or external costs? How should future costs be discounted and, given the uncertainties involved, at what stage of decision-making should they be applied? Not surprisingly, there is plenty of disagreement about precisely what the precautionary principle involves.[7] A strong interpretation would effectively reverse the burden of proof so that the responsibility is vested with the polluter (the factory that wants to release toxic chemicals into the atmosphere or the water company wishing to dump sewage in a river) to prove that an activity is safe before it is allowed. Similarly, if damage has already occurred, the relevant industry would have to prove it was not responsible: guilty until proven innocent! The advantage of this tough approach should be that industries would be less inclined to risk releasing a pollutant if the onus rested with them to prove that they had not done so. A weaker version may simply encourage policymakers to act cautiously in accordance with the old adage that 'it is better to be safe than sorry', although it is less clear what this might mean in practice.[8] It is significant that O'Riordan's suggested rules for applying the precautionary principle (see Box 8.6), no doubt influenced by difficulties encountered by the British government in dealing with both BSE and GMOs, are underpinned by strong democratic principles of openness and participation.

## Policy integration

> The objective of sustainable development and the integrated nature of the global environment/development challenges pose problems for institutions . . . that were established on the basis of narrow preoccupations and compartmentalised concerns.
>
> (WCED 1987: 9)

The problems for the environment posed by the segmentation of the policy process into distinct sectors such as industry, agriculture, transport and energy were discussed in Chapter 7. Individual ministries pursue

### 8.6 Six rules for a precautionary world

Tim O'Riordan has identified the following guidelines to help policymakers put the precautionary principle into practice:

1. Where unambiguous scientific proof of cause and effect is not available, it is necessary to act with a duty of care.
2. Where the benefits of early action are judged to be greater than the likely costs of delay, it is appropriate to take a lead and to inform society why such action is being taken.
3. Where there is the possibility of irreversible damage to natural life-support functions, precautionary action should be taken irrespective of the forgone benefits.

4. Always listen to calls for a change of course, incorporate representatives of such calls into deliberative forums, and maintain transparency throughout.
5. Never shy away from publicity and never try to suppress information, however unpalatable. In the age of the internet, someone is bound to find out if information is being distorted or hidden.
6. Where there is public unease, act decisively to respond to that unease by introducing extensive discussions and deliberative techniques.

From Economic and Social Research Council (1999: 17).

narrow sectoral objectives with little consideration for their overall environmental impact. This fragmentation of responsibility is a major obstacle to sustainable development because environmental considerations need to be integrated into the formulation and implementation of policies in every sector. Individual ministries must broaden their horizons and discard their narrow compartmentalised concerns. Integration involves the creation of new structures, the reform of existing institutions and the transformation of established policymaking processes. In short, it requires an administrative revolution. However, as the previous chapter showed, there are many structural and political barriers impeding integration.

## Planning

Sustainable development must be planned. Only free-market environmentalists believe that the unfettered market can, of its own volition, produce sustainable development. There are too many complex interdependencies between political, social and economic factors to leave it to chance; equally, those same complexities set limits as to what can be achieved by planning. What is at issue is not 'whether' but 'how much' planning should take place – and which policy instruments should be used.

Agenda 21 makes clear that every level of government – supranational, national, regional and local – has to plan sustainable development strategies. This exhortation is not a recipe for a state-planned economy. An active planning role does not mean that the government has to shoulder the responsibility for implementing sustainable development alone. On the contrary, the sustainable development discourse is enthusiastic about partnerships with a wide range of non-state actors.

Moreover, government intervention in the market and society can take many forms. Policymakers can select from a range of instruments to tackle environmental problems – regulations, market mechanisms, voluntary mechanisms and government expenditure – which may all involve some form of intervention in the market (see Chapter 12). The sustainable development discourse is agnostic about these instruments, displaying no *a priori* preference for one type of measure: they all have a role to play, with the precise balance between them varying according to the particular problem and the political, administrative and judicial traditions of each country. However, whatever the mix of policy instruments, they need to be part of a strategic plan that is designed, co-ordinated and supervised by the government.

## ◗ *Sustainable development: reform or revolution?*

Few proponents of sustainable development would dissent from any of the five principles identified above (although some might suggest additional principles), but the nature and degree of support for each will vary. Different actors will attribute varying meanings to each principle; for example, as Chapter 9 shows, several fundamentally different interpretations of the equity principle have been applied to climate change negotiations. The relative importance attributed to each principle will also differ. The five principles are central to the discourse initiated by Brundtland, which is driven by a firm commitment to the development ethos, but this message has not been taken up with equal enthusiasm by all supporters of sustainable development. A Northern government, for example, may be more concerned about addressing domestic environmental problems than alleviating global poverty and social injustices, so it might emphasise planning, integration and the precautionary principle rather than equity.

The enormity of the barriers confronting the successful implementation of sustainable development should not be underestimated. In particular, the structural and institutional factors underpinning the traditional paradigm identified in Chapter 7 pose problems for all five principles. Thus the clarion call for greater democracy focuses on the first dimension of power by seeking more participation where decisions are observable, yet the wider use of democratic mechanisms alone may have little impact if business is still able to exercise structural second-dimension power. Attempts to apply the precautionary principle more extensively are likely to encounter strong commercial and developmental pressures to allow new products such as GM crops, or to proceed with a project such as a new dam. The quest for greater integration and strategic planning will be obstructed where the institutional segmentation of government reinforces the influence of producer interests. Not least, the demand for greater equity goes to the very heart of the capitalist system, which underpins the structural power of business interests.

Indeed, critics of Brundtland argue that in trying to find the middle ground between North and South a solution was found that posed no serious threat to the dominant neo-liberal ideology of the day because there was no call for slower economic growth or any transformation of the capitalist system. The Brundtland emphasis on continued wealth creation (albeit environmentally sustainable growth) to overcome poverty arguably understates the links between excessive consumption and environmental degradation (despite the subsequent interest in 'sustainable consumption'). For critics such as Sachs (1999), who regard economic globalisation as profoundly bad for the environment, the willingness of Brundtland to embrace globalisation suggests that sustainable development will do little to protect the ecological limits of the planet (see Chapter 10). Moreover, there is increasing evidence that on the global stage the discourse of sustainable development is increasingly influenced by (moderate) market liberal ideas. Certainly, corporate interests played a major role at the Johannesburg WSSD (see Box 8.3) encouraging richer countries, particularly the USA and Australia, to emphasise the role of economic globalisation and free trade in delivering development goals, in contrast to their efforts to focus on the environmental agenda at previous international summits on the environment and development (Wapner 2003). In short, sustainable development does little to challenge the hegemony of global capitalism.

Yet the potential radicalism of the sustainable development discourse should not be underestimated. Sustainable development may accept the underlying capitalist system, but if the five principles were implemented as part of a strategy of strong sustainable development then the outcome would be a very different form of capitalism from that which exists today. Even an incremental process of weak sustainable development might eventually gather sufficient momentum to generate extensive change. The strength of sustainable development is that the compromises it makes with the current political and economic system may produce a more feasible programme of change than that outlined by deep ecologists. Sustainable development is driven by practical politics. It is an antidote to the romantic visions of a green utopia popular among ecocentrics, and it is preferable to 1970s-style survivalist predictions that the catalyst for change will be a planetary eco-crisis. The proponents of sustainable development recognise that a wide and diverse range of interests needs to be won over for lasting change to take place. By looking to reconcile the environment versus development dichotomy, sustainable development confronts the practical issues of agency that ecocentric ideologies tend to avoid or ignore. Sustainable development may be incrementalist, accommodationist and reformist, but (in the right hands) it could still be radical.

### Critical question 2
How radical is sustainable development?

# ▶ Ecological modernisation: the practical solution?

It is clear that the implementation of sustainable development is likely to confront many deep-seated obstacles. In a capitalist world it will certainly be difficult to make real progress without appealing to the economic interests of the business sector. The progress of environmental protection in individual countries may also be constrained by the centrality of North–South issues and the development agenda in the sustainable development discourse. An alternative approach to greening capitalism can be found in the concept of ecological modernisation, a variation of sustainable development that has emerged in a handful of the most industrialised countries which, significantly, boast the best records of environmental protection. Ecological modernisation has its roots in the work of the German social scientist Joseph Huber, who observed that from the late 1970s some policymakers in a few countries such as Germany and the Netherlands had begun to adopt a more strategic and preventive approach to environmental problems.[9]

## ▶ *The concept*

Ecological modernisation concedes that environmental problems are a structural outcome of capitalist society, but it rejects the radical green demand for a fundamental restructuring of the market economy and the liberal democratic state. The political message of ecological modernisation is that capitalism can be made more 'environmentally friendly' by the reform of existing economic, social and political institutions,[10] so that the 'opposing' goals of economic growth and environmental protection can be reconciled by further, albeit 'greener', industrialisation. Ecological modernisation focuses attention on transforming the nature of industrialisation, particularly the production process. Two key ideas underpinning ecological modernisation are *dematerialisation*, which means that for each unit of output (e.g. a car, a mobile phone or a chocolate bar) there will be progressively fewer environmental resources used in its production, and which at an aggregated societal level can lead to a *decoupling* of economic growth and resource use, so that continued improvements in income and living standards become decreasingly dependent on the input of natural resources and result in less environmental degradation.[11]

The focus on greening capitalist industrialisation distinguishes ecological modernisation with its forceful and positive utilitarian claim that *pollution prevention pays* (Hajer 1995: 26) from the sustainable development discourse; in short, business can profit by protecting the environment. Consequently, ecological criteria must be built into the production process. On the supply side, costs can be reduced by improving productive efficiency in ways that have environmental benefits. Savings can be made by straightforward technological fixes to reduce waste, and hence pollution, but also through a

227

more fundamental rethinking of manufacturing processes so that large-scale production systems such as 'smoke-stack' industries, that can never be made ecologically sound, are gradually phased out. On the demand side, there are growing markets in green technologies such as pollution abatement equipment and alternative forms of energy. The rise of 'green consumerism' has stimulated demand for goods that minimise environmental damage both in the way they are made (by using recycled materials or minimising packaging) and in their impact when used (by containing less harmful chemicals, as in phosphate-free washing powders).

Several kinds of social and institutional transformations flow from these core ideas (Jansen et al. 1998; Mol and Spaargaren 2000). First, science and technology, although contributing to many environmental problems, are also regarded as central to their resolution. Ecological modernisation rejects standard technocentric end-of-pipe solutions in favour of a holistic 'pollution in the round' approach that recognises the complex and interdependent nature of environmental problems, which often renders them capable of solution only at source (Weale 1992). Through concepts such as integrated product policies, environmental considerations should be built into the design, production, use and final disposal of all products and technologies. Secondly, the market will play a central role in the transmission of ecological ideas and practices, with producers, financial institutions and consumers all playing their parts. A key requirement is that the external costs of environmental damage must be made calculable by their internalisation into the price of a product or service (Hajer 1995: 26). This message is directed especially at businesses and governments. Businesses can take account of environmental factors through techniques such as environmental management systems, but they may need some encouragement to drop their focus on short-term profits. The government can provide such an incentive by applying the polluter pays principle, notably through the use of market-based instruments such as eco-taxes and tradeable permits, which penalise environmentally damaging activities (see Chapter 12). Thirdly, the role of government therefore changes under ecological modernisation from the traditional centralised, regulatory nation state towards a more flexible, decentralised state that employs a range of instruments to 'steer' production and consumption in more efficient, environmentally benign directions. The emphasis will be on partnership and co-operation between government, industry, scientists and those moderate environmental groups that are willing to be co-opted into the system.

### ◗ *Ecological modernisation as a positive-sum game?*

Ecological modernisation clearly has much to offer. A country that seizes the commercial opportunities it offers – lower costs, niche markets, new advanced products – will prosper in terms of jobs, wealth and a better environment: truly a positive-sum game (Hajer 1995: 26). Ecological modernisation also discards much of the political baggage of sustainable development, notably the 'development' agenda of North–South issues, inequalities, social justice and democracy, which can prove controversial and costly to implement.[12] Moreover, while sustainable development struggles to provide a clear, precise blueprint for policymakers, ecological modernisation seems to offer a practical set of principles and techniques for dealing with the problems facing advanced industrialised countries. Its model of a flexible and enabling state reflects contemporary developments in the idea of 'governance' as involving 'steering' rather than 'rowing', whereby governmental organisations set strategic objectives but leave day-to-day implementation to other actors (Rhodes 1997).

Perhaps the most distinctive feature of ecological modernisation is that it directly addresses the business sector, whose support, as shown in Chapter 7, is vital for any transition towards a more sustainable society. Although industry's contribution to environmental degradation is highlighted in the sustainable development literature, the Brundtland Report offers little to win over businesses beyond some mild words of exhortation, such as '[industry] should accept a broad sense of social responsibility and ensure an awareness of environmental considerations at all levels' (WCED 1987: 222). By contrast, by appealing to business in a language it understands and respects – profit! – ecological modernisation may encourage the industrial sector to treat environmental protection more seriously.

Ecological modernisation theory also reflects developments in several industrialised countries where policymaking elites have adopted a more holistic, strategic approach to environmental issues. With its roots in countries such as Germany, the Netherlands, Sweden, Norway, Finland and Denmark, which are consistently picked out as having the best records of environmental performance in the world, ecological modernisation offers a good lesson in 'best practice' environmental policymaking. The Dutch National Environmental Policy Plan (see Chapter 11) is presented as an ideal model of the way environmental criteria can be integrated into every aspect of government, whilst Lundqvist (2004) reports similar developments in Sweden. Another success story is the expansion of the environmental technology sector in the German economy (Weale 1992). All these countries have adopted elements of ecological modernisation – environmental policy integration, the precautionary principle, the polluter pays principle, integrated pollution control – in several policy sectors, although nowhere has it been universally implemented. The fifth EU Environmental Action Plan (1993–2000) was also explicitly couched in the language of ecological modernisation.

## ▶ *Limitations of ecological modernisation*

Ecological modernisation is not, however, immune from criticism. In the first place, although it is a narrower, less ambitious and therefore more cogent concept than sustainable development, ecological modernisation does not escape definitional problems. Whilst there is a reasonable consensus about the core characteristics of ecological modernisation, there are sufficient differences between writers to distinguish between 'weak' and 'strong' versions along a continuum (Christoff 1996b). In its weaker 'techno-corporatist' form, ecological modernisation focuses on the development of technical solutions to environmental problems through the partnership of economic, political and scientific elites in corporatist policymaking structures (Hajer 1995). It is a narrow understanding of the concept, 'a discourse for engineers and accountants' (Dryzek 2005: 172), that largely excludes consideration of development and democratic issues. The stronger 'reflexive' version of ecological modernisation adopts a much broader approach to the integration of environmental concerns across institutions and wider society, envisaging extensive democratisation and recognising the international dimensions of environmental issues (Hajer 1995). Seen in this light it is not clear how far the stronger version differs significantly from sustainable development; indeed, Hajer (1995) identifies the Brundtland Report as 'one of the paradigm statements of ecological modernisation' (p. 26). This strong version of ecological modernisation is perhaps best regarded as a particular variant of sustainable development that focuses on the role of business and the problems of industrialised countries. Paradoxically, the weaker version of ecological modernisation is more distinct from sustainable development, although, as 'little more than a rhetorical rescue operation for a capitalist economy confounded by ecological crises' (Dryzek 2005: 174), that vision may have less appeal. Mol and Spaargaren (2000) suggest that this simplistic dichotomy reflects a dated interpretation of the literature that does not take account of the mushrooming of theoretical and empirical studies since the mid-1990s. In particular, they argue that the narrow conceptualisation of ecological modernisation as involving little more than the introduction of 'add-on' technologies misrepresents the way the discourse has moved on to consider fundamental structural changes to socio-technical systems.

Secondly, although ecological modernisation is attractive to Northern policy elites precisely because its narrower focus omits the political baggage (i.e. the development agenda) that comes with sustainable development, perhaps the omission of social justice issues is its Achilles' heel. For example, techniques such as 'life-cycle assessment' are increasingly used to analyse the environmental impact of a product 'from cradle to grave' to include all the inputs of raw materials and energy and all the outputs of air, water and solid waste emissions generated by the production, use and disposal of a product. Life-cycle assessment offers enormous potential benefits but it largely ignores the issues of equity and social justice raised by the broader sustainable development discourse. Ecological modernisation is predicated on the utilitarian argument that by making pollution prevention pay, all actors – government, business, consumers, environmental groups – can play a positive-sum game in which everyone benefits and everyone participates.

One problem is that many people will be unable to participate because their basic needs are not being met. Social justice issues are prominent in the sustainable development literature precisely because, as noted above, most environmental issues involve distributional questions that can rarely be resolved without winners and losers. As Hajer (1995: 35) observes, it may be rather naive to believe that ecological modernisation can avoid addressing basic social contradictions (see Reitan 1998).

Indeed, with a few exceptions, ecological modernisation is strangely silent on North–South issues. It is not hard to envisage a scenario in which large transnational companies operate along 'ecomodernist' lines in the North, with efficient clean technologies and products, while locating their more polluting activities in developing countries where environmental regulations are weaker (Christoff 1996b; Goldfrank et al. 1999). Perhaps ecological modernisation requires a large periphery of poor countries to act as a waste tip for the polluting activities of a rich core of nations?

Thirdly, furthermore, concerns about its relevance to the developing world have contributed to the specific criticism that ecological modernisation is 'Eurocentric' (Blowers 1997), which if true would rather limit its global appeal as a feasible national-level environmental reform programme. Not surprisingly, as Mol (2003: 66) notes, several critics question whether in an increasingly globalised world of economic interdependence, global political interactions and the standardisation of science, technology, production and consumption, there is sufficient scope for developing countries to develop their own 'ecologically sound development path'. Some observers have also suggested that ecological modernisation has limited applicability outside the core pioneer states of Northern Europe, particularly in the USA and Canada (Cohen 1998). Although several recent studies have demonstrated that elements of ecological modernisation are operating at the local level in the USA (González 2002; Scheinberg 2003), this questioning of the geographical reach of ecological modernisation has inspired a debate about the kind of state in which it can flourish (see next section).

Finally, in its attentiveness to production and the message that pollution prevention pays, ecological modernisation generally understates the importance of consumption, especially the overall *level* of consumption (Carolan 2004). The implicit assumption seems to be that greening the production process allows consumption to be infinite. Despite its name, ecological modernisation is only superficially *ecological* because it largely ignores the integrity of ecosystems and the cumulative impact of industrialisation on them (Christoff 1996b: 486). Its technocentric view of nature recognises no limits to growth and assumes that all problems are open to solutions. Yet even if businesses do adopt every available ecologically sound technique, the environmental benefits are likely to be offset by economic growth. If, for example, ecological modernisation leads to the replacement of 8 million fuel-inefficient cars with 10 million more fuel-efficient cars, then, contrary to the decoupling thesis, the overall impact on the environment may be little different. Many environmental problems can only be solved if individual citizens accept their share of the responsibility by changing both the nature and the level of consumption.

One phenomenon that is consistent with the ecological modernisation discourse is the rise of 'green consumerism', whereby 'knowledgeable' consumers apply environmental criteria when making purchasing choices with the aim of influencing the economic activities of businesses (Spaargaren and van Vliet 2000: 70). Thus the 'green' consumer is the driving force of market transformation (Seyfang 2005: 294), encouraging manufacturers and retailers to advertise the environmental friendliness of their products with the intention of winning the custom of a more discerning and usually affluent shopper. The Body Shop, for example, grew exponentially in the 1990s by selling its franchises worldwide on the back of the cosmetics market for 'beauty without cruelty'. Ethical investment, a broad term for any investment activities that aim to influence companies to adopt policies that benefit society and the environment, has also become big business. In 2003, total ethical assets in the USA reached $151 billion, the value of European ethical funds was €12.2 billion, and £4.2 billion was invested in UK ethical unit trusts (Carter and Huby 2005: 258).

It is easy to decry green consumerism. The ecological modernisation of domestic consumption requires knowledgeable consumers, but consumers are frequently subjected to false or misleading claims about products: washing powders that never contained phosphates are suddenly marketed as 'phosphate-free' whilst refrigerators are described as 'ozone-friendly' when, although CFC-free, they contain ozone-depleting HFCs. Stricter advertising codes of practice and tough eco-labelling standards could remedy some of these flaws. A bigger problem is that green consumerism remains a minority activity; too few people engage in it on too few occasions. An important equity issue is that many people cannot afford the higher prices that characterise most 'green' products. Yet many middle-income consumers are also only intermittent green consumers, either because they are selective about which high prices they will pay, or because there are numerous lifestyle sacrifices, such as giving up the second car (let alone dispensing altogether with a car) or dishwasher, that they are not prepared to make.

More fundamentally, green consumerism appears to be a contradiction in terms, for how can we *consume* our way out of the environmental crisis? By encouraging us to alter the type, rather than the level, of consumption, 'shopping to save the planet' does nothing to halt the inexorable overall growth of consumption. Indeed, there is a danger that individuals will think they have done their bit by buying a few green products, while maintaining their high-consumption lifestyle. Consumers need to undergo a much deeper process of social learning. However, Press and Mazmanian's (1999) observation that in the USA 'There is simply no visible governmental or corporate leadership devoted to reducing extreme consumption and the perceived need for high-volume, high-polluting, high-obsolescence products'

(p. 277) is universally true. Despite efforts to redress the balance (Spaargaren and van Vliet 2000; Spaargaren 2003), ecological modernisation theory has given insufficient attention to the consumption side of the sustainability equation.

## Critical question 3

Is ecological modernisation only suitable for a handful of affluent industrialised nations?

## ▶ Ecological modernisation in practice

This section offers some broad empirical observations about the role of two key actors in the ecological modernisation discourse: the state and industry.

### The state

Despite the enthusiasm for it in some circles, there are still only a few policy developments that clearly fit within the ecological modernisation framework, most of which are concentrated in a handful of 'pioneer' nations (Andersen and Liefferink 1997a). Some political systems appear more open to ecological modernisation than others; in particular, it has taken root most firmly in countries with policy styles containing significant corporatist traits, notably a culture of planning, intervention and nurturing a close working relationship between the state and industry (Dryzek 2005: 166–7). Where there is a corporatist tradition of seeking co-operative relations with powerful non-state interests, there may also be a willingness to deal with emerging environmental and consumer groups. Thus the Norwegian government 'has expanded Norway's traditional consensus-corporatist style of policy-making into the environment field' (Jansen and Mydske 1998: 188; see also Dryzek et al. 2003) by gradually including environmental groups in most phases of the routine policy process. Sweden, where the corporatist culture has also traditionally sought consensus, has intermittently included environmental groups in planning and decision-making (Lundqvist 2004). It is ironic that corporatist arrangements that were originally intended to maximise economic growth by giving privileged access to business and trade union groups have produced a consultative policy style that is relatively open to environmental interests that challenge some of those expansionist assumptions. Indeed, cross-national comparative studies suggest that **corporatism** produces better environmental outcomes than pluralism (Crepaz 1995; Scruggs 2003).[13]

> **Corporatism:** A system in which major organised interests (traditionally, capital and labour) work closely together within the formal structures of government to formulate and implement public policies.

In a comparative study of pollution control policy, Weale (1992) showed how German policymakers were more receptive to elements of ecological modernisation during the 1980s than their counterparts in Britain. German policy elites recognised the link between economic intervention-ism and the growth potential of the emerging pollution control industry. Consequently, by investing heavily in the green technology sector and apply-ing the concept of 'best available technology' (BAT), which makes the award of an operating licence conditional on a company installing the most mod-ern, cleanest equipment, the German state provided a massive stimulus to the green technology sector. By contrast, British policy elites failed to make this connection. The absence of close links with peak economic associations, combined with its particular ideological objection to interventionism, ren-dered the Thatcher government unable and unwilling to consider a proactive developmental role for the state. The consensual, interventionist policy style required by ecological modernisation may make it less suitable for English-speaking countries in general, such as the USA, Britain, Australia and New Zealand, where environmental groups generally remain outsiders in the policy process and market liberal ideologies have exercised most influence (Dryzek 2005: 177–8).

Yet the pioneer states are not paragons of ecological virtue; the empiri-cal basis of ecological modernisation is actually very limited. The ecological modernisation paradigm has not yet colonised the belief systems of all pol-icy elites. One authoritative study of the Dutch response to the acid rain problem found that a discourse of ecological modernisation co-existed with traditional, sectoral policy responses (Hajer 1995). Consequently, 'anticipa-tory story-lines were combined with end-of-pipe solutions', so that rather than reducing sulphur and nitrate emissions by attacking the source of the problem – discouraging road traffic, cutting cattle stocks or conserving energy – the Dutch fell back on the remedial solutions associated with the traditional paradigm, such as requiring catalysts in cars, building slurry-processing plants and fitting FGD equipment to power stations (Hajer 1995: 267). Similarly, German pollution policies focus on symptoms rather than causes, so they too mainly employ end-of-pipe solutions rather than attempt-ing to change behaviour by, for example, reducing speed limits on the autobahn (Weale 1992: 84–5). A study of Norwegian climate change policy found little evidence that the state was promoting ecological restructuring; indeed, several key state institutions such as the Ministry of Industry and Energy actively impeded attempts to reconcile economic and environmental objectives by levying a carbon tax (Reitan 1998: 22). Efforts to institutionalise environmental values across a range of Norwegian public policy issues have usually broken down whenever 'significant economic interests have been at stake' (Jansen and Mydske 1998: 203). In the pioneer states, as elsewhere, governments still provide many perverse subsidies that encourage pollution and environmental damage. Lastly, although they are the favoured policy instrument of the ecological modernisation discourse, market-based instru-ments, such as eco-taxes, are still used sparingly (see Chapter 12).

## Industry

If state structures show tardiness in adapting to ecological modernisation, evidence of genuine conversion in the business world is also scarce. Whilst many business leaders proclaim the virtues of greening industry, the rhetoric is not always matched by behavioural changes. For every company that has made a serious attempt to build ecological criteria into its operations – and there are an increasing number of innovators – there are dozens more that have done little or nothing. Many companies are selective in their adoption of ecological modernisation. Most major energy suppliers, for example, have developed a renewable energy business – electricity supply companies have built wind farms, oil companies have invested in biomass and hydrogen (BP has even rebranded itself 'Beyond Petroleum') – whilst their core businesses continue to use or supply massive amounts of fossil fuels. Other corporations have appropriated successful niche 'ecologically-sound' businesses – Cadbury Schweppes purchased Green & Black's, the organic chocolate company, and Unilever bought Ben & Jerry's ethical ice cream company – whilst their core businesses have remained unchanged.

The slow progress of ecological modernisation within European industry can be illustrated by the limited impact of initiatives to promote environmental improvement at the enterprise level. The voluntary EU Eco-Management and Audit Scheme (EMAS) involves firms publishing an externally verified environmental statement of their operations. EMAS is a very weak eco-audit scheme. Firms can select the sites they wish to enter and set their own objectives and targets (which do not even have to match the industry-best environmental practice), so the external audit does little more than check that the documentation is in order (Neale 1997). Even so, take-up is low. EMAS was introduced in 1995, yet ten years later just 3,225 companies were registered throughout the EU and Norway, of which 1,499 were in Germany, where external verification requirements are lower than elsewhere (ENDs 1998). Many European firms have chosen to register with the international standard ISO 14001 which, as it involves no independently verified statement, is even less demanding than EMAS. Recognising these weaknesses, the EU adopted a new EMAS regulation in 2001, extending the scheme to all areas of economic activity including local authorities, encouraging greater employee participation and transparency, and incorporating ISO 14001 as part of a tougher environmental statement. Of course, many firms carry out environmental audits without bothering to register with official programmes, but the general indifference to schemes that would publicly advertise their green credentials indicates the limited penetration of ecological modernisation in the industrial sector (see Box 8.7).

One reason for the general reluctance to embrace ecological modernisation may be ignorance. Many industrialists, particularly in small and medium-sized firms, may lack the opportunity or resources to gain access to the ecological modernisation discourse. Even when the 'pollution

## 8.7 Eco-labelling: business fails to embrace ecological modernisation?

Eco-labelling is a voluntary system that seeks to harness market forces by helping consumers identify products that are less harmful to the environment. Manufacturers pay for the right to display a logo demonstrating the 'greenness' of their products. If this logo proves attractive to consumers, then other manufacturers have a market incentive to make their products greener – a clear example of the 'pollution prevention pays' principle. The widespread use of eco-labelling would be an indicator that industry was absorbing the message of ecological modernisation.

Some eco-labelling schemes have proved relatively successful, but most have not. The German Blue Angel label had been awarded to over 3,600 products produced by 580 companies in March 2006, encouraging innovation and diffusion in some product categories, including returnable bottles, recycled paper and heating appliances (Müller 2005). The EU scheme launched in 1992 has had a more limited impact: by February 2006 just 289 companies had been awarded a licence to use the 'Flower' symbol. Italy topped the list with eighty-two companies, but only five UK companies had a licence. The most popular products with the Flower were textiles, paints and varnishes, and tourist accommodation.

*Problems*

1. Eco-labelling depends on the willingness of industry to compete for the logo, but trade associations dislike schemes that pit their members against each other or might impose new costs on them. Consequently, many industry trade associations have lobbied against the introduction of eco-labelling schemes or persuaded their members to boycott them once in place (Harrison 1999).

2. Opponents of eco-labelling, including many less developed countries, argue that the criteria used to award eco-labels are biased in favour of domestically produced goods, i.e. they are a barrier to free trade (and flout World Trade Organisation (WTO) rules).

Blue Angel website: http://www.blauer-engel.de/
EU eco-label website:
http://europa.eu.int/comm/environment/ecolabel/
index_en.htm.

prevention pays' message has been absorbed, individual firms may still make the economic calculation that the costs of greening outweigh the benefits. Certainly, the transaction costs of green innovations may be significant: investments in new cleaner technologies are likely to be 'lumpy', requiring a major short-term expenditure in anticipation of long-term benefits. Firms may be reluctant or unable to make such a commitment, especially if it threatens short-term competitive advantage.

Consequently, several writers have argued that progress in greening industry is most likely to occur at the sectoral level (Porter 1990; Press and Mazmanian 1999). Here the transaction costs of change can be reduced by sharing the financial burden and integrating technical expertise so that industry-wide networks of companies can gain sectoral advantages in the global market. If an entire sector acts in unison then the problems of collective action are reduced; individual firms are more likely to innovate if they believe their direct competitors will too. In the USA, one sector where such voluntary initiatives have achieved notable advances in recent years is the pulp and paper industry, where major changes include reducing emission levels and energy intensity, phasing out the use of chlorine and other toxic chemicals, and increasing the volume of recycled waste (Press and Mazmanian 1999: 275–6). The lesson is that governments might be wise to adopt a strategy of ecological modernisation that targets particular (highly polluting) sectors by working with the relevant trade associations and encouraging voluntary industry self-regulation.

Overall, the greening of industry remains an aspiration. Many companies are increasingly aware of the environmental impact of their activities, but business elites have not yet absorbed the ideology of ecological modernisation and there is only limited evidence of ecological criteria being built into production processes. Even in 'pioneer' countries, industry has been selective about which ideas are adopted, with huge variations among sectors. The business community has shown little interest in state-sponsored schemes to encourage ecological modernisation and close state–industry collaboration remains the exception rather than the rule. Indeed, as the following chapters show, many industries are actively hostile to ecological modernisation initiatives, opposing the use of innovative policy instruments such as eco-taxes that are specifically designed to implement the 'pollution prevention pays' principle.

---

### Critical question 4
Why has ecological modernisation struggled to win the hearts and minds of business leaders?

---

## ▶ Conclusion

The significant contribution of sustainable development has been to question the long-standing assumption that there is an inevitable trade-off between environmental and economic objectives. By setting environmental considerations in a broader social, economic and political context, it has also produced a development agenda that can marry the often conflicting aims of rich and poor countries. Despite the many different meanings attributed to sustainable development, it has become the dominant paradigm driving the discourse about contemporary environmental policy. While all governments claim to be committed to its principles, some Northern policy elites have been drawn to the narrower concept of ecological modernisation. As a 'half-sister' to sustainable development, they share many aims, principles and policies, but ecological modernisation is lauded as a more practical and effective means of transforming the traditional paradigm because it directly addresses the issue of producer power. By offering a utilitarian incentive to industry to build environmental considerations into the profit calculus, ecological modernisation anticipates that business elites will recognise the instrumental advantages of better environmental protection. It also provides an incentive for the state to transform itself by identifying a key role for it in facilitating industrial change. The 'discourse of reassurance' (Dryzek 2005: 172) offered by ecological modernisation is particularly attractive to policymakers and residents of prosperous industrialised countries, who are confronted with fewer hard choices than are posed by stronger versions of sustainable development. Yet, as one comparative study of ecological modernisation concludes, 'even environmental front-runners display major shortcomings . . . [with regard to] . . . general resource consumption, biodiversity, and inter and intragenerational equity', and they retain a continuing preference for 'standard solutions based mainly on technical progress' (Weidner 2002a: 1364). In short, the jury is still out on whether or not ecological modernisation offers a practical programme for achieving sustainability.

One lesson to take from this chapter is that the widespread agreement that sustainable development is a good thing belies deep conflict over its meaning and, therefore, its implementation. The following chapters explore how far there has been a shift from the traditional paradigm towards sustainable development or ecological modernisation. One measure of change will be evidence that the core principles identified here are shaping policy practice. In the next chapter, particular attention will be given to the significance of equity, democracy and the precautionary principle in international environmental politics.

## ▶ *Further reading*

There is a huge literature on sustainable development. A good place to start is the Brundtland Report itself (WCED 1987). For an academic analysis, see Lafferty (1996), Meadowcroft (2000), Redclift (2005) and Baker (2006). For a critical perspective, see Luke (2005). Dryzek (2005: chs. 7 & 8) presents a perceptive comparison of the discourses of sustainable development and ecological modernisation. Good surveys of the ecological modernisation literature can be found in Christoff (1996b) and Mol and Sonnenfeld (2000). Mol (2003) examines the relationship between ecological modernisation and globalisation. Weale (1992) and Hajer (1995) provide excellent empirical studies of ecological modernisation in a comparative context. The journals *Environmental Politics* and *Sustainable Development* carry numerous articles on these issues.

NOTES

1 The Brundtland Report contains a few isolated non-anthropocentric observations (Achterberg 1993: 86), but the overall tone is anthropocentric.

2 A wider discussion of sustainable consumption can be found in UNDP (1998), Cohen and Murphy (2001), Jackson and Michaelis (2003) and Seyfang (2005).

3 See http://www.un.org/esa/sustdev/partnerships/partnerships.htm.

4 The Fairtrade Labelling Organisation International (FLO) is responsible for certification and standard-setting of the Fairtrade label. Global retail sales under this label in 2004 exceeded US$1 billion (FLO Annual Report 2004–5, http://www.fairtrade.net/).

5 See http://www.cafedirect.co.uk/about/gold_support.php (accessed 21 February 2006). By contrast, the Rainforest Alliance, a US conservation charity, runs a rival certification scheme that emphasises ecological criteria, rather than equity issues; in coffee production it focuses on the use of sustainable agricultural practices, rather than providing a guaranteed price.

6 The UNDP Human Poverty Index, HPI-2, is a multidimensional composite measure designed specifically for industrial countries, and is based on human longevity, knowledge, standard of living and social exclusion (UNDP 2005).

7 See Wildavsky (1995, Conclusion) for a robust critique of the precautionary principle.

8 Myers and Raffensperger (2005) analyse the practical application of the precautionary principle in US environmental policy. Christoforou (2004) shows that the precautionary principle has acquired constitutional status in many EU states, but not in the USA. O'Riordan et al. (2001) provide a range of perspectives and examples.

9 Key early ecological modernisation studies include Jänicke (1991), Weale (1992) and Hajer (1995).

10 Mol (1996) distinguishes two broad approaches within the ecological modernisation discourse: one, those writers who regard (and promulgate) ecological modernisation as a political programme for contemporary environmental politics; two, environmental sociologists who have constructed a social theory labelled ecological modernisation. The discussion here focuses on the former; for the latter, see Spaargaren and Mol (1992).

11 Some proponents of ecological modernisation are persuaded by the notion of an environmental Kuznets curve, which suggests that there is a direct relationship between per capita income and environmental quality: as income rises, environmental degradation will initially increase up to a point, after which it declines. In short, economic growth is ultimately good for the environment. For a critical discussion, see Arrow et al. (1995) and Stern et al. (1996).

12 There are exceptions, notable Hajer (1995), who stresses the importance of democracy.

13 See Hukkinen (1995) for an alternative view.

# Global environmental politics

**9**

## Contents

## Key issues

▶ What are environmental regimes?

▶ How can the growth of international environmental co-operation be explained?

▶ What are the obstacles to international environmental co-operation?

▶ Are environmental treaties effective?

▶ Has international environmental co-operation contributed to sustainable development?

Environmental problems at a global and international scale pose major challenges to the achievement of sustainable development. The distinguishing feature of an *international* environmental problem is that it does not respect national boundaries. Several transboundary issues, such as the conservation of endangered wildlife, natural habitats and marine life, have been around for many years. Some problems that were once predominantly regional or

**Table 9.1 Some major multilateral environmental treaties**

| | |
|---|---|
| 1946 | International Convention for the Regulation of Whaling |
| 1973 | Convention on International Trade in Endangered Species of Wild Fauna and Flora (CITES); Convention on the Prevention of Pollution from Ships (MARPOL) |
| 1979 | Geneva Convention on Long-Range Transboundary Air Pollution (LRTAP) |
| 1982 | UN Convention on the Law of the Sea |
| 1985 | Vienna Convention for the Protection of the Ozone Layer |
| 1989 | Basle Convention on the Control of Transboundary Movements of Hazardous Wastes and Their Disposal |
| 1992 | UN Framework Convention on Climate Change |
| | UN Convention on Biological Diversity |
| 1994 | UN Convention to Combat Desertification |
| 2000 | Cartegena Protocol on Biosafety |

local in cause and effect, such as deforestation, desertification and water scarcity, now have international dimensions. A 'new' range of issues, including climate change, ozone depletion and biodiversity loss, are truly *global* in that they affect everyone. All states contribute to problems of the global commons and all suffer the consequences, although the extent to which each country is culpable for causing a particular problem and vulnerable to its effects varies enormously.

Global environmental problems require international solutions; they cannot be solved by nation states acting alone. Only if individual nation states co-operate with each other can environmental problems be resolved. As governments have grown increasingly aware of their mutual vulnerability, environmental issues have become firmly established on the international policy agenda. The UN conferences at Stockholm in 1972 and Rio de Janeiro in 1992 were important milestones in this transition. Multilateral environmental agreements (MEAs) did exist before 1972, covering issues such as wildlife conservation and maritime pollution, but the Stockholm Conference marked the start of a wide-ranging debate about the environment in international politics. Twenty years later the Rio Earth Summit pushed the environment centre-stage; it was then the largest ever gathering of world leaders and was attended by a host of non-governmental organisations (NGOs) and interest groups. Two conventions on climate change and biodiversity were agreed and Agenda 21 was launched, committing the international community to the principles of sustainable development. Today the rising tide of international co-operation has produced around 200 MEAs and spawned a plethora of institutional structures to monitor, enforce and strengthen them (see Table 9.1).

Yet the mere existence of these agreements, which are undoubtedly a real achievement of environmental diplomacy, is something of a puzzle because they represent a degree of international co-operation that seems to fly in the face of traditional realist assumptions about the way states behave in a system of international relations where, historically, conflict and mistrust have been the norm. This chapter starts with a short conceptual discussion of this paradox, drawing principally on neo-realist and institutionalist theories of international relations. The next section outlines the emergence of two of the most important recent MEAs, dealing with ozone depletion and climate change, and the following section provides a wide-ranging discussion of the factors determining whether or not nation states choose to co-operate to protect the global commons. Although a MEA may represent a diplomatic triumph, it does not guarantee that the problem addressed will be resolved, and the next section assesses some of the difficulties confronting the implementation of MEAs, emphasising how the capacity of states to enforce environmental agreements is inextricably linked to wider issues of international political economy. The chapter concludes with an assessment of the relationship between international environmental politics and sustainable development.

## ◗ The paradox of international co-operation

International environmental co-operation may be desirable, but severe collective action problems make it difficult to achieve. As Hurrell and Kingsbury (1992) ask: 'Can a fragmented and often highly conflictual political system made up of over 170 sovereign states and numerous other actors achieve the high (and historically unprecedented) levels of cooperation and policy coordination needed to manage environmental problems on a global scale?' (p. 4). Unlike a domestic political system where a national government can regulate behaviour and levy taxes, there is no central sovereign authority in the international arena to co-ordinate policy responses to problems of the global commons or to ensure that sovereign states comply with agreements. According to the neo-realist perspectives that long dominated academic international relations, individual sovereign states operate in an anarchic system in which their behaviour is almost exclusively shaped by considerations of power politics (Morgenthau 1978). The primary aim of each nation state is to survive by accumulating more power relative to other countries. As no nation can fully trust the intentions of others, individual countries are unlikely to co-operate to protect the global commons. If individual states cannot solve global environmental problems by acting alone, there is little point in one state changing its behaviour without the assurance that others will too. On the contrary, game theory can be used to show that it is rational for states *not* to co-operate (i.e. to free-ride) if some other states are co-operating because the benefits of co-operation, such as pollution prevention, will be secured anyway (Weale 1992: 191).[1]

## 9.1 Environmental security: a contested concept

One approach to environmental security simply adds the 'environment' to the list of potential threats to the external security of individual sovereign states: in short, will environmental degradation lead to violent conflict or war? From this perspective, the key threats to the environment arise from resource conflict as states seek control over increasingly scarce resources such as water, arable land, forests and fisheries. Water shortages, particularly in the politically volatile Middle East, where several countries compete for the limited waters supplied by a few major rivers, are often mentioned as a potential cause of conflict (Bulloch and Darwish 1993). Another is the growing pressure on arable land, especially due to rapidly rising populations, and resulting food shortages (Homer-Dixon 1999). As these problems worsen, exacerbated by climate change, environmental refugees threaten to become a major source of destabilisation. Up to 25 million environmental refugees flee annually from drought, famine, deforestation and degraded land; they are a particular source of conflict when seeking safety by crossing national borders.

An alternative critical approach condemns the traditional security discourse for using the language of the 'military model' of states, conflict and territorial security to analyse environmental problems. After all, military solutions to such environmental threats seem self-defeating because war wreaks massive environmental destruction, as illustrated by the use of the Agent Orange defoliant in Vietnam and the burning Kuwaiti oilfields during the 1991 Gulf War. Instead, the threat to the environment demands a demilitarisation of security away from defining threats nationalistically as coming from other states, towards a recognition that most environmental problems are transboundary and require international co-operative solutions that address their root causes, rather than the symptoms (Dalby 2002; Deudney 2006).

See Elliott (2004: ch. 9), Deudney (2006) and Swatuk (2006) for overviews of the environmental security debate.

Realists, therefore, treat the environment primarily as a security issue in so far as problems of the global commons could be a source of conflict between states (see Box 9.1). But the rising tide of international environmental co-operation poses a problem for the realist view that in international politics 'Anarchy and conflict are the rule, order and co-operation the exception' (Hurrell and Kingsbury 1992: 5). One explanation is that it may be rational for actors to co-operate when they are assured that others will co-operate too.[2] If individual states have common interests, such as to prevent pollution, then the mutual recognition that each state will have to interact repeatedly with others over the long term might build the trust necessary to provide the assurance that co-operation will be forthcoming and that other states will not free-ride (see Paterson 1996: 101–8). Realists may be also inaccurate in characterising all international relations as concerned with power politics; for example, the claim that states seek to maximise *relative* gains can be replaced with the reasonable assumption that they pursue *absolute* gains. If each state is seeking to improve its absolute position rather than always seeking to 'win' each play of the game (i.e. to accept an absolute gain even if it is lower than the gains accruing to another country), then co-operation is more likely because everyone can end up a winner. Such assumptions underpin institutionalist perspectives, which regard environmental co-operation as perfectly rational whenever self-interested states judge that the benefits of co-operation will outweigh the costs (Keohane 1989).[3]

The apparent paradox of international co-operation may, therefore, not be so 'irrational' as realists suggest. Of course, realist reservations should not be dismissed lightly. Collective action problems, not least the incentive to free-ride on the efforts of others to co-operate, ensure that each MEA will represent a hard-won diplomatic triumph. Nevertheless, the existence of so many concrete examples of co-operation suggests that the obstacles are not insuperable. Instead, following the lead of institutionalist writers, and also drawing on constructivist approaches (e.g. Haas 1999), it is more productive to focus on the factors that influence the emergence of international treaties addressing problems of the global commons.

## ⟩ Environmental regimes: the ozone and climate change treaties

**Regimes** are 'sets of implicit or explicit principles, norms, rules, and decision-making procedures around which actors' expectations converge in a given area of international relations' (Krasner 1983: 2) (see Box 9.2). Part of the significance of a

> **Regime**: The principles, norms, rules and decision-making procedures which form the basis of co-operation on a particular issue in international relations.

regime is that, by agreeing to it, a government voluntarily accepts external interference in the way it exploits resources within its own sovereign territory. The growth of MEAs since the early 1970s is evidence of growing international co-operation to deal with problems of the global commons. This section describes the processes leading to the signing of the ozone depletion and climate change treaties. These treaties are interesting not only because they address two of the most serious contemporary global atmospheric problems but also because they offer a contrast between one apparently successful regime (ozone) and one that has had little success (climate change).

---

### 9.2 Regime terminology

A *convention*, or treaty, is the main form of multilateral legal instrument, containing binding obligations, rules and regulations.

A *framework convention* is negotiated in anticipation of later texts and may contain only a broad set of principles and aims relating to the issue. Subsequently, maybe over several years, it is strengthened by the negotiation of protocols and amendments.

A *protocol* spells out specific, binding obligations, such as specific emission reduction targets.

From Porter et al. (2000: 13–14).

| Table 9.2 Ozone protection – key developments | |
| --- | --- |
| 1974 | Scientists hypothesise that CFCs might cause ozone depletion. |
| 1977 | UNEP Co-ordinating Committee on the Ozone Layer established to assess ozone depletion. |
| 1982 | Twenty-four states begin discussions towards an ozone convention. |
| 1985 | Vienna Convention signed by twenty states and European Community: to co-ordinate reporting and monitoring (came into force 1988). British scientists discover 'hole' in ozone layer over Antarctic. |
| 1987 | Montreal Protocol signed by twenty-four states and the European Community: to regulate consumption and production of CFCs and halons (came into force 1989). |
| 1988 | Ozone Trends Panel report confirms the link between CFCs and the ozone hole. |
| 1989 | EC and USA agree to phase out all production of CFCs by 2000. |
| 1990 | London Amendments to Montreal Protocol: all CFC/halon production to be phased out by 2000 (came into force 1992); more substances banned. |
| 1992 | Interim Multilateral Fund established; USA, then EC, announce CFC production to halt by 1996; Copenhagen Amendments – HCFC controls agreed leading to ban by 2030. |
| 1997 | Montreal Amendment finalises schedule for phasing out of methyl bromide. |
| 1999 | Beijing Amendment agreed immediate phase-out of bromochloromethane. |

See UNEP (http://ozone.unep.org/index.asp) and International Institute for Sustainable Development (http://www.iisd.ca/) for developments in ozone diplomacy.

▶ *Ozone protection*[4]

The stratospheric ozone layer plays a critical part in protecting life on Earth by absorbing harmful ultraviolet radiation. In 1974 two American-based scientists suggested that the concentration of ozone in the atmosphere could be extensively damaged by anthropogenic chemicals, notably chlorofluorocarbons (CFCs), used as propellants in aerosols, refrigerants, solvents, foam products, and halons, which are used in fire extinguishers. These synthetic chemicals leak into the atmosphere, then rise into the stratosphere where they release chlorine and bromine, which destroy ozone. A thinner ozone layer would increase skin cancers and cataracts, harm human and animal immune systems (which will weaken resistance to infectious diseases) and damage ecosystems. The sheer volume of these chemicals in the stratosphere is indicative of their significance in modern industrialised economies, being safe (i.e. non-inflammable and non-toxic), stable and versatile. Consequently, any attempt to limit their use was sure to encounter strong resistance from economic interests, notably the major chemical corporations that manufactured them, such as Dupont (USA) and ICI (UK).

The first steps towards international action were tentative, as scientific fact-finding, consensus-building and policy developments proceeded hand in hand (see Table 9.2). Initially, it was essential to establish the scientific basis of the ozone problem, so in 1975 the UN Environment Programme (UNEP) funded a study by the World Meteorological Society to examine the link between CFCs and ozone depletion. Two years later a UN conference of experts from thirty-two countries drew up a World Plan of Action on the Ozone Layer to co-ordinate future research, but not until the discovery in 1985 of a 'hole' in the ozone layer above the Antarctic – regular springtime decreases of ozone in excess of 40 per cent between 1977 and 1984 – did a scientific consensus about the existence of ozone depletion begin to emerge. This consensus was completed in 1988 when the Ozone Trends Panel, representing over a hundred leading atmospheric scientists from ten countries, concluded that the ozone layer in the Northern Hemisphere had been reduced by up to 3 per cent between 1969 and 1986: 'ozone layer depletion was no longer a theory; at last it had been substantiated by hard evidence' (Benedick 1991: 110). Crucially, the panel also confirmed that CFCs and other synthetic chemicals were the primary cause of ozone depletion.

Meanwhile, international negotiations had gradually picked up pace. In 1977, the USA, Canada, Norway, Sweden and Finland (collectively known as the Toronto Group) together urged UNEP to consider remedial action; when this was not forthcoming they took unilateral action to ban non-essential aerosol uses of CFCs. The European Community (EC), which accounted for 45 per cent of world CFC production, strongly resisted such action. In the absence of firm scientific evidence, EC member states were subjected to strong industrial lobbying to protect export markets and avoid the costs of developing substitutes. When multilateral negotiation of a framework convention commenced in 1982, the representatives from twenty-four nations were broadly divided between the Toronto Group, which pushed for a complete ban on non-essential uses of CFCs, and the European Community, which would only consider a cap on production. Unable to resolve this fundamental conflict, the resulting 1985 Vienna Convention for the Protection of the Ozone Layer represented little more than an agreement to co-operate on monitoring, research and information exchange, for it imposed no targets or controls to reduce CFC production, although the USA was able to win an important commitment to start negotiations for a binding protocol (Benedick 1991: 45–6). Nevertheless, the Vienna Convention was significant because it was signed without firm scientific evidence that ozone depletion was happening – the first instance of international environmental law based (implicitly) on the precautionary principle.

During the nine months of negotiations leading up to the signing of the Montreal Protocol in September 1987, the European Community and Japan shifted from resistance to any cut in production to acceptance of a compromise proposal to reduce CFC production by 50 per cent of 1986 levels by 1999 and to freeze halon production at 1986 levels by 1992. Several factors contributed to this dramatic change of heart. Opponents were subjected to energetic US diplomatic manoeuvring. The negotiations were handled skilfully by Mustafa Tolba, UNEP's executive director. European states were increasingly split as West Germany, under strong domestic political pressure to make concessions, disagreed with the other major CFC producers, France, Italy and the UK. Most important, though, was the firming up of scientific evidence following the discovery of the ozone hole, which had a profound impact on national representatives and even influenced industrial interests (Brenton 1994: 140–1). Again, as the Ozone Trends Panel report proving the link between CFCs and ozone depletion only appeared several months *after* the Montreal Protocol was signed, it was significant that politicians had signed an agreement in advance of scientific evidence supporting their action (Seaver 1997: 33–4).

Soon after the Ozone Trends Panel report Dupont declared that it would accelerate research into substitutes and stop manufacturing all CFCs and halons by the end of the century – a declaration swiftly followed by other major international chemical producers (Benedick 1991: 111–15). This scientific evidence led to further strengthening of the regime at follow-up meetings of the signatories, both by ratcheting forward reduction and phase-out dates so that production of CFCs, halons and three other chemicals had halted in developed countries by 1996, and by extending the Protocol to further chemicals, such as hydrochlorofluorocarbon (HCFC) and bromochloromethane.

One major problem unresolved at Montreal was the need to persuade developing countries to participate in the regime. Industrialised nations, representing 25 per cent of the world's population, were responsible for almost 90 per cent of global CFC consumption, with a per capita consumption more than twenty times higher than in less industrialised nations (Benedick 1991: 148–9), so it was obviously incumbent on the former to take the initiative in reducing emissions. However, the long-term success of the regime was in jeopardy without the involvement of developing countries, notably China and India, where the consumption of ozone-depleting substances in refrigeration and air-conditioning systems would grow with further industrialisation. Developing countries complained that they should not be expected to incur the costs for resolving a problem that they did not cause, and insisted that either they be allowed to continue using CFCs or that they receive financial and technological help to develop substitutes. The Montreal Protocol contained no such facility, so only a handful of developing states signed it; the three largest countries – Brazil, China and India – refused to do so (Porter et al. 2000: 90). Industrialised countries were reluctant to make open-ended commitments to pay for a fund, with the USA particularly concerned about the possible precedent for future environmental regimes, notably climate change. It was increasingly apparent that the success of the Protocol depended on providing sufficient incentives to persuade developing countries to sign up. Consequently, the London meeting in 1990 established a multilateral fund for financial and technology transfer to help developing countries. The fund was $160 million, rising to $240 million if China and India signed (which they eventually did), to be administered by UNEP, UNDP and the World Bank. The allocation was subsequently increased and the multilateral fund had dispersed $1.86 billion by the end of 2005 (UNEP 2005: 8).

By November 2005 the Montreal Protocol and London Amendments had 189 and 179 ratifications respectively (ibid: 3).

## ▶ *Climate change*[5]

The major climate change issue concerns the 'greenhouse effect', a natural phenomenon whereby various atmospheric gases keep the Earth's temperature high enough to sustain life as we know it. These gases, which include carbon dioxide ($CO_2$), methane, nitrous oxide and halocarbons, allow radiation from the Sun to pass through but then absorb radiation reflected back from the Earth's surface, trapping heat in the atmosphere. Without the natural greenhouse effect it is estimated that the average global temperature would be about 33 degrees centigrade lower. However, it seems that human activities, notably carbon emissions from burning fossil fuels and deforestation, and methane emissions from agricultural activities such as livestock and paddy fields, have strengthened the greenhouse effect by increasing the concentration of these gases in the atmosphere. It is the fear that a human-made process of global warming is taking place with a range of potentially devastating implications for the planet that makes climate change the most important contemporary global environmental issue.

Scientific research has focused on three key questions. Is there evidence of global warming? If so, is it caused by human activities or is it a natural cyclical fluctuation in temperature? What is the likely impact of global warming? There have been huge advances in the science of climate change in recent years, co-ordinated by the work of the Intergovernmental Panel on Climate Change (IPCC), but the direct relationship between rising temperatures, emission levels, higher concentrations of gases and, crucially, their combined impact remains uncertain. Nevertheless, there is now a broad consensus on the answers to the three questions. Climatological evidence shows that the Earth is getting warmer; global mean surface temperature rose by about 0.6 degrees centigrade over the last century, and is projected to increase by between 1.4 and 5.8 degrees (relative to 1990) by 2100 (IPCC 2001; see also Dessler and Parson 2006: ch. 3). Concentrations of the key gases in the atmosphere have increased substantially during the twentieth century. Most scientists now agree that these gases have contributed to temperature increases and that human activities have produced these higher concentrations. If temperatures continue to rise at a similar rate, the impact of global warming could be devastating.[6] A rise in global average sea-level of between 9 and 88 centimetres by 2100 (IPCC 2001) will flood many low-lying lands, while the disruption of global weather systems will alter patterns of land use, reduce agricultural yields, increase water stress and create millions of environmental refugees. Although it remains in the world of informed speculation precisely which countries and regions will suffer most, how soon and by how much, it is certain that less developed countries will suffer the worst

## Table 9.3 Climate change – key developments

| 1970s | Growing scientific concern about impact of human activities on climate expressed at series of international conferences. |
|-------|--------------------------------------------------------------------------------------------------------------------------|
| 1979 | First World Climate Conference – agreed that human activities had increased levels of $CO_2$ and that more $CO_2$ may contribute to global warming, which could have damaging consequences. |
| 1985 | Villach Conference – scientific consensus that increased $CO_2$ was linked to global warming. |
| 1988 | Toronto Conference – recommended 20 per cent cut in carbon emissions by 2005. IPCC established. |
| 1990 | Preliminary IPCC report and Second World Climate Conference confirmed scientific consensus and called for policy response. |
| 1992 | Framework Convention on Climate Change signed by over 150 nations at Rio Summit. |
| 1995 | Berlin Mandate (COP-1) – agreed timetable to negotiate stronger commitments. IPCC Second Report: scientific consensus strengthened. |
| 1997 | Kyoto Protocol (COP-3) – agreed legally binding targets and timetables for developed countries. |
| 2000 | Collapse of COP-6 talks at The Hague, primarily due to intransigence of a small group of industrialised nations led by USA. Key disagreement over how to treat carbon sinks for the purpose of measuring carbon emissions. |
| 2001 | IPCC Third Assessment report presented 'new and stronger evidence that most of the observed warming of the last 50 years is attributable to human activities'. Binding agreement at Bonn on implementing Kyoto targets – excluding USA. Confirmed in Marrakesh Accords (COP-7). |
| 2004 | Russia finally ratifies Kyoto Protocol. |
| 2005 | Kyoto Protocol came into force. COP-11 at Montreal agreed to fund Clean Development Mechanism, launched Joint Implementation and established a compliance regime. Initiated post-Kyoto dialogue. |

See IPCC (http://www.ipcc.ch/), IISD (http://www.iisd.ca/process/climate_atm.htm) and the UN (http://unfccc.int/2860.php) for developments in climate change negotiations.

effects, partly because most are located in tropical and sub-tropical zones, but also because their weak infrastructures limit their capability to adapt to these changes.

The scientific consensus emerged slowly during the 1980s and 1990s (see Table 9.3). The World Climate Programme conference at Villach, Austria, in 1985 produced the confident scientific conclusion that increased carbon dioxide concentrations would lead to a significant rise in mean surface temperatures (Paterson 1996: 29). Over the next five years this scientific consensus rapidly strengthened as the quality of the data and the climate models improved. The scientific community also started to reach out to the wider political world. The 1988 Toronto Conference, attended by leading scientists and policymakers from many countries, recommended a 20 per cent reduction in $CO_2$ emissions by 2005 (Paterson 1996: 34). Toronto prompted a host of follow-up intergovernmental conferences and encouraged some countries, including all European Community and European Free Trade Association members, to make unilateral commitments to stabilise carbon emissions. A key role was played by the IPCC, formed by UNEP and the World Meteorological Organisation in 1988; its first report confirmed the scientific consensus that human activities were contributing to climate change, and called for immediate policy action to reduce carbon emissions (Houghton et al. 1990). The combination of growing scientific consensus, intergovernmental conferences and unilateral commitments generated a political momentum that resulted in the international convention on climate change agreed at the 1992 Rio Earth Summit.

The Framework Convention was initially signed by 155 countries and the EU, and entered into force in March 1994. It identified a set of principles – precaution, equity, co-operation and sustainability – and a wide range of measures to enable the international community to stabilise greenhouse gas concentrations at levels that should mitigate climate change. However, no firm targets or deadlines were agreed; developed countries were simply given the 'voluntary goal' of returning greenhouse gas emissions to 1990 levels (Elliott 2004: 85). The principle of 'common but differentiated responsibilities' was written into the convention, so developed countries were expected to take the lead in combating climate change and to transfer financial and technological resources to developing countries to help them address the problem, but no one was committed to anything specific, apart from establishing a fund under the auspices of the newly formed Global Environment Facility (see Box 9.3).

Nevertheless, an elaborate institutional framework was established to continue negotiations aimed at strengthening what everyone acknowledged was just the first step towards an effective climate change regime. The first Conference of the Parties to the Framework Convention (COP-1) in Berlin in 1995 was unable to agree any new commitments, although the 'Berlin mandate' recognised the need to work towards a protocol that set targets and strengthened commitments to reduce greenhouse emissions. Eventually, the Kyoto Protocol, hammered out over ten days of intense negotiations in December 1997 (COP-3), agreed legally binding targets for developed countries (so-called Annex 1 countries) intended to achieve an overall reduction in GHG emissions of 5.2 per cent of 1990 levels in the period 2008 to 2012 (see Box 9.4).

Each stage of the regime strengthening process, in Rio, Berlin and Kyoto, was greeted with both acclamation and criticism. Praise for the environmental diplomacy that brokered each agreement in the face of apparently irresolvable political conflicts was matched by criticism about the weakness of the commitments and sanctions in the treaty. These contrasting responses reflected the compromises that had to be made if agreement was to be reached between sharply opposing negotiating positions. However, subsequent efforts to firm up the details agreed at Kyoto floundered at The

## 9.3 The Global Environment Facility (GEF)

The GEF was established in 1991 as a joint programme between the UNDP, the UNEP and the World Bank. The GEF provides funding to help less developed countries implement measures to protect the global environment.

The GEF has six priority areas:

- biological diversity
- climate change
- international waters
- ozone layer
- land degradation
- persistent organic pollutants (POPs)

Projects financed by GEF include alternative energy programmes, conservation measures and grassroots/community NGOs.

There was some distrust of the GEF because it was located in the World Bank, which is treated with enormous suspicion by developing nations as it is dominated by industrialised countries, acts as standard-bearer of neo-liberal ideologies and has been historically insensitive to environmental concerns. The GEF has been criticised for the lack of transparency in decision-making, the absence of participation by NGOs and local communities and its pursuit of a Northern agenda (e.g. a small GEF-funded biodiversity project in the Congo provided a green veneer for a much larger World Bank loan for road-building and industrial logging).

However, the South has won some important concessions in the way GEF operates, including some reform of GEF decision-making structures, and it is now regarded as one of the most transparent international organisations (Elliott 2004: 101–2). The GEF has dispensed around $4.5 billion in grants and generated $14.5 billion in co-financing schemes that have funded some 1,300 projects in 140 countries. It was pledged a budget for 2002–6 of $3 billion. Although this budget is small in global terms, the GEF does represent an important step in addressing the issue of intragenerational equity.

See GEF (http://www.gefweb.org/) and UNEP (http://www.unep.org/gef/).

Hague (COP-6) in 2000, and the following year the newly elected President Bush renounced the Kyoto Protocol. As the USA was responsible for around 25 per cent of global greenhouse gas emissions this decision prompted a major crisis because the Kyoto Protocol could not come into force until it had been ratified by (a) fifty-five countries, which (b) represented at least 55 per cent of the GHG emissions of the Annex 1 countries. Frenzied diplomatic activity amongst the other developed countries resulted in the Bonn agreement in July 2001, where Japan and Russia were persuaded to sign a binding agreement, but it was not until November 2004 that Russia, after winning several concessions through hard bargaining, finally ratified the agreement. Yet, as the Kyoto Protocol came into force, attention had already switched to what happens next, with the dialogue about a post-Kyoto agreement after 2012 being launched at the Montreal COP-11 in 2005.

Two fundamental tensions have dogged the climate regime bargaining process, neither of which has yet been satisfactorily resolved. First, there are divisions among developed countries regarding their willingness to make firm commitments. Resistance has coalesced around the resistance

## 9.4 The Kyoto Protocol

The 1997 Kyoto Protocol strengthens the UN Framework Convention on Climate Change agreed at Rio in 1992 by committing developed countries (Annex 1) to reducing their collective emissions of six key greenhouse gases (GHGs) by at least 5 per cent below 1990 levels throughout the 2008–12 period (which, in effect, means 10 per cent below 2000 levels and 30 per cent below what would be expected in 2010 without emissions-control measures).

*Individual targets*
GHG emissions to *decrease* by:

| | |
|---|---|
| 8 per cent | The EU, Switzerland, most central/east European states |
| 7 per cent | USA |
| 6 per cent | Canada, Hungary, Japan, Poland |
| 0 per cent | Russia, New Zealand, Ukraine |

GHG emissions to *increase* by:

| | |
|---|---|
| 1 per cent | Norway |
| 8 per cent | Australia |
| 10 per cent | Iceland |

The EU 'bubble' of 8 per cent contains wide variations between member states: some richer states have to make large reductions, e.g. Denmark (21 per cent), Germany (21 per cent), UK (12.5 per cent); others merely need to stabilise emissions, e.g. France and Finland; while less developed members can increase emissions, e.g. Portugal (27 per cent), Greece (25 per cent), Spain (15 per cent) and Ireland (13 per cent).

The Protocol also agreed three new flexibility mechanisms to reduce the costs of reducing emissions:

- An international emissions trading regime allowing industrialised countries to buy and sell emission credits amongst themselves.
- A Joint Implementation procedure enabling industrialised countries to implement projects that reduce emissions or remove carbon in another Annex 1 country in exchange for emission reduction credits.
- A 'clean development mechanism' permitting developed countries to finance emissions-reduction projects in developing countries and receive credit for doing so.

Although the USA subsequently rejected the Protocol, 178 countries managed to reach a binding agreement for its implementation and the Kyoto Protocol eventually came into force on 16 February 2005.

See http://www.unfccc.de/

of the USA (plus Australia and Canada and Japan) to agree greenhouse gas reduction targets. Clearly, as the world's largest producer of greenhouse gas emissions, the inclusion of the USA in any regime is vital to its success. Yet, while the EU and other industrialised nations pressed for quantified targets throughout the negotiations, the US government was initially reluctant to sign the Framework Convention at Rio and blocked agreement on targets or timetables at Berlin. Before eventually agreeing to a 7 per cent reduction target at Kyoto, the USA won significant concessions, including the introduction of a tradeable permit system (see Chapter 12) that would allow rich polluting nations (i.e. the USA) effectively to buy the right to maintain high emission levels from countries emitting less than their target. The main sticking point at the unsuccessful Hague Conference in 2000 was the insistence of the US government that it be allowed to offset its emissions against its carbon sinks (i.e. its vast forests). Disagreements between developed countries can be attributed primarily to differences in energy resources and the structure of the energy industry (Paterson 1996). Countries that rely on fossil fuels for export income, such as Middle Eastern oil-producing states, and those with large energy resources, including the USA, have been most resistant to cuts.

The USA has an abundance of fossil fuel energy: it is the world's second largest oil and natural gas producer, and the largest coal producer. America has developed a 'gas-guzzler' culture of cheap, available energy, which generates strong resistance to improving energy efficiency. The economic and political costs of implementing emission cuts are therefore seen as higher in the USA than elsewhere and because climate change is not perceived to be as serious a problem in America as it is across the Atlantic, the US government believes the costs of adapting to climate change are affordable. Furthermore, American politicians have been subjected to strong pressure from a powerful domestic industrial lobby, particularly motor and energy interests (which bankrolled Bush's presidential campaigns), to obstruct the regime-building process (Newell and Paterson 1998). Consequently, the Bush administration has played the role of veto state with some aplomb, doing its best to reframe the climate change debate on its terms (Schreurs 2004: 219–22). For example, in the face of growing scientific consensus about climate change, the US government has exploited remaining uncertainties, such as the heavy dependence on scientific modelling, although it subsequently shifted ground by conceding that whilst human activities had contributed to climate change it was too late to do anything about it, and that Kyoto was certainly doomed to fail (ibid.: 221–2). Support for emissions cuts was also inconsistent with Bush's domestic agenda of hijacking the California energy shortages to justify the exploitation of oil reserves in Alaska on the grounds that there was a huge demand for more energy (Lisowski 2002). By contrast, most European governments regard climate change as a much greater threat. EU countries are heavily dependent on imported energy and there is no gas-guzzling culture as in the USA, while governments have a stronger balance-of-payments incentive to cut carbon emissions because of the knock-on effect of reducing imports of fossil fuels. There is a stronger tradition in Europe of government intervention in economic decision-making, so governments are expected to take a lead in dealing with climate change and there is general approval of the proactive role played by the EU in climate change diplomacy.

However, there is evidence of growing opposition in the USA to the President's intransigent position. Several states have developed their own climate change strategies: California has passed laws requiring vehicles to cut carbon emissions and all major industrial producers to cut emissions by 25 per cent by 2020 in order to reduce greenhouse gas emissions to 1990 levels by 2020

(*Financial Times*, 18 October 2006). Some north-eastern states are attempting to regulate regional greenhouse gas emissions, by limiting emissions from power stations (Schreurs 2004: 225). There are signs that the flooding of New Orleans in 2005, which many have (rightly or wrongly) linked to climate change, has led to a shift in domestic public opinion.[7] Indeed, this may be evident in President Bush's changing rhetoric on climate change, as illustrated by his trumpeting of the Asia-Pacific Partnership on Clean Development and Climate, a 2005 initiative with Australia, China, India, Japan and South Korea, which is intended to find voluntary ways of reducing emissions by accelerating 'the development and deployment of clean energy technologies' (http://www.asiapacificpartnership.org/default.htm). Not surprisingly, critics, such as Greenpeace, see it as a way of trying to circumvent the Kyoto Protocol.

A second fundamental tension dogging negotiations has been the North–South divide. Although the principle of 'common but differentiated responsibilities' was enshrined in the Convention, there has been bitter disagreement over what this means in practice (see below). For example, by imposing targets only on Annex 1 countries, the US government has been able to criticise the Kyoto Protocol for effectively absolving developing nations from taking action to reduce carbon emissions. Conversely, the major developing countries, such as China and India, have ensured that the issues of development, sovereignty and equity have had a prominent place on the agenda. Many disputes boil down to conflict over the transfer of financial and technological resources from North to South. There has been little disagreement with the principle that developed countries should transfer resources to help developing countries invest in energy-efficient technology, but putting it into practice has thrown up many knotty problems. Developed countries have been unwilling to put their hands in their pockets, and big private corporations are reluctant to relinquish control of technologies without economic or financial compensation (e.g. access to markets); hence the paucity of firm obligations in the Framework Convention and the Kyoto Protocol. It is important to note that the simple North–South dichotomy does not capture the complexity of climate change politics; just as there are divisions between developed nations over what should be done, there are also opposing interests among developing countries. For example, the Alliance of Small Island States (whose members are particularly vulnerable to rising sea-levels caused by climate change) has lobbied for firm targets and commitments, whereas oil-producing states have opposed them.

Underlying both these key tensions is the familiar trade-off between economic and environmental interests. Short-term concerns about economic growth and development have outweighed the longer-term need to mitigate climate change. With little visible immediate evidence of global warming that might whip up public concern, it is all too easy for governments to bow to producer and consumer resistance to costly remedial measures such as carbon taxes. Certainly, international efforts to mitigate climate change have been far less successful than action on ozone depletion.

---

### Critical question 1

Why has it been easier to obtain international co-operation to prevent ozone depletion than climate change?

---

## ▶ Accounting for regimes

This section identifies the key factors determining the success of environmental regime bargaining, drawing in particular on the ozone and climate change treaties.

Regime formation is aided by the willingness of a powerful nation, or group of nations, to take a leadership role by cajoling or bullying weaker states into supporting a treaty. A *lead state* will be committed to achieving effective international action on an issue; it will accelerate the bargaining process and seek the support of other states for a regime (Porter et al. 2000: 36). The USA, the most powerful country in the world, is the obvious candidate to play a hegemonic role in a way similar to its imposition of the Bretton Woods system of trade liberalisation and stable currencies on the international community in the aftermath of the Second World War (Gilpin 1987). However, although the USA played a leading role in ozone diplomacy, its record in the Antarctic, acid rain, biodiversity and climate change treaty negotiations shows that it has more often obstructed international co-operation. Consequently, it has fallen to other economically powerful states to take a lead role. Australia and France were instrumental in pushing for the 1991 Madrid Protocol banning mineral extraction in the Antarctic (Elliott 1994). On acid rain, Sweden and Norway were lead states in bringing about the Geneva Convention on Long Range Transboundary Air Pollution (LRTAP) in 1979, while Germany later took the lead in reaching agreement on the Helsinki Protocol (Levy 1993). During the Vienna Convention ozone negotiations, Finland and Sweden submitted the initial draft agreement before the USA adopted a lead role in proposing the 95 per cent reduction in CFCs. Groups of states can also make a significant contribution, as illustrated by the Toronto Group in ozone diplomacy and the EU in pushing for firm emission reduction commitments at the Kyoto Summit. Indeed, the EU, representing a rich and powerful bloc of industrialised nations, is an increasingly important player in environmental diplomacy (see Chapter 10).

Conversely, a *veto state* will impede negotiations or stall implementation of an agreement. Veto states are most significant where the involvement of a particular country, or group of countries, is essential for the negotiation of an effective regime. Thus, knowing that any climate change agreement would be ineffective without its involvement, the US government was able to wring important concessions at Kyoto, as did the Russian government prior to its ratification of the Protocol. The LRTAP regime was initially weakened without support from Britain, the major source of acid precipitation in Northern Europe. A ban on the ivory trade is meaningless without the support of Japan as the largest market for ivory. Key veto states are usually OECD countries, but the largest developing states, notably China and India, have played an astute veto role in extracting important concessions, as in the ozone negotiations. Lead states need to persuade veto states of the error of their ways, a task that will usually involve offering them some form of compromise or incentive to drop their opposition, such as the payments to China and India that persuaded them to sign the London Amendments on ozone depletion, or accepting the American proposal at Kyoto to set up a tradeable permit scheme.

The resistance of veto states is usually motivated by a desire to protect vital economic interests. European states initially resisted attempts to freeze CFC production because their chemical industries had not yet developed substitutes. Japan, Iceland and Norway have championed their coastal communities by resisting bans on commercial whaling (Stoett 1997). British opposition to an acid rain agreement reflected a wish to protect its energy industries from the enormous costs of compliance (Boehmer-Christiansen and Skea 1991). In each case, governments have been subjected to strong lobbying from powerful domestic economic interests opposing the regime. One of the most effective lobby groups was the Global Climate Coalition, which was instrumental in President Bush's refusal to sign the Climate Convention at Rio in 1992 and later in persuading the Clinton presidency to take a tough negotiating stance at Berlin and Kyoto. It should be noted that economic interests do not always oppose international environmental co-operation. The insurance industry, for example, is relatively sympathetic towards action on climate change because damage to property from rising sea-levels and the disruption of weather patterns is likely to generate massive insurance claims (Brieger et al. 2001; Jagers et al. 2005). Moreover, where it is clear that a changing political climate makes environmental regulations inevitable, then government and industry may unite to win the deal that best suits their national self-interest. The US government was encouraged to pursue its lead role in ozone diplomacy after 1988 by the American chemical conglomerate Dupont, which hoped to snatch a competitive advantage over rival European chemical manufacturers in the development of CFC alternatives (Benedick 1991: 30–4). Nevertheless, on balance, economic interests tend to push governments towards a veto rather than a lead role.

Conversely, domestic political pressure from environmental groups, the media or public opinion may persuade a government to become a lead state. When the West German government swung from veto to lead state on acid rain in the early 1980s, it was influenced by the rising importance of environmental issues and the emergence of the Green Party as an electoral force. The decision of the Australian Labor Party to reject an Antarctic minerals treaty and push for a moratorium on minerals extraction was a result of its pro-green stance at the 1987 election aimed at winning the support of environmentally concerned voters (Elliott 1994).

Another consideration is the availability of salient solutions (Young 1994: 110–11). Some problems have identifiable and feasible solutions, such as the bans on whale-hunting, the ivory trade and the exploitation of Antarctic mineral resources. Technological progress can make political co-operation more likely: the availability of substitutes helped achieve co-operation on phasing out CFC production, and agreement to reduce acid precipitation was eased by the development of catalytic converters and flue-gas desulphurisation equipment to cut emissions from cars and coal-fired power stations. By contrast, one of the continuing obstacles to progress on climate change has been the absence of viable and affordable alternatives to fossil fuels in energy production and road transport.

Regime formation may be hastened by exogenous shocks such as ecological disasters. Within six months of the accident at the Chernobyl nuclear power-station in 1986 an international agreement on dealing with nuclear accidents was signed. The discovery of the hole in the ozone layer gave a massive boost to the negotiations that led to the Montreal Protocol. In contrast, the absence of any similar disaster or dramatic discovery has probably hampered the progress of climate change diplomacy. Scientists may play a vital role in regime formation because the uncertainty surrounding each new environmental issue increases the dependency of governments on expert advice throughout the policy process. Scientists are critical in identifying problems, evaluating their significance, developing solutions and monitoring the effectiveness of remedial action. Consensus within the scientific community about a particular problem is likely to be a catalyst for international co-operation, as occurred in ozone diplomacy after the discovery of the hole in the ozone layer and the subsequent hardening of scientific knowledge. Conversely, where scientific uncertainty remains, co-operation may prove elusive. During the 1970s and 1980s, the British government cited the inconclusiveness of scientific findings to justify its refusal to reduce acid emissions (Boehmer-Christiansen and Skea 1991; Weale 1992). However, science is not always of paramount importance in regime formation; it played only a limited role in reaching agreements on whaling, the ivory trade, hazardous waste, tropical deforestation and Antarctic minerals (Porter et al. 2000: 142).

Furthermore, scientists are not just passive reporters of 'neutral' scientific knowledge and advice; they may also adopt a highly pro-active role in the policy process (Andresen et al. 2000). The influence of scientists has been analysed through the idea of 'epistemic communities', which Peter Haas (1990) defines as 'knowledge-based groups of experts and specialists who share common beliefs about cause-and-effect relationships in the world and some political values concerning the ends to which policies should be addressed' (p. xviii). Having identified an environmental problem, groups of scientists (usually from several countries) are sufficiently moved to intervene in the political process to encourage international action. Their capacity to influence the political process rests on their ability to persuade others that their knowledge is valid and sufficiently important to require a policy response. Haas (1990) showed how epistemic communities helped spur the international co-operation that produced the Mediterranean Action Plan (1975) dealing with sea pollution. Asked initially to investigate the problem of oil pollution from tanker traffic in the Mediterranean, scientists were able to broaden the focus of policy concern to encompass a wider range of pollution sources, including agricultural run-off, river flows and atmospheric deposition (Haas 1990; Weale 1992). By showing that land-based sources were the most important cause of pollution, epistemic communities helped persuade doubting nations, such as Algeria, of the benefits of co-operation. The Ozone Trends Panel and the IPCC have played a similar role promoting international action against ozone depletion and global warming.

The political activities of scientific organisations also offer a broader lesson about the importance of non-state actors in environmental diplomacy, particularly in informing, educating and shaping cognitions. International institutions can provide astute political leadership, as illustrated by the skill of Mustafa Tolba, UNEP's executive director, in facilitating and guiding the negotiations that led to the ozone protection regime. These 'institutions for the earth' (Haas et al. 1993) can encourage co-operation by setting agendas, winning over doubters and co-ordinating policy responses.

International environmental NGOs, such as Greenpeace, WWF and FoE, have acquired a growing role in international environmental politics, although it is difficult to evaluate their influence (see Chapter 6). There is certainly scope for NGOs to play a part at all stages of environmental diplomacy. By whipping up public concern about a wide range of global issues, communicating the findings of scientists and co-ordinating campaigns against governments and companies, they have contributed to domestic pressure on governments to act (Litfin 1998a; Haas 1999; Young 1999; Newell 2000). They have also gained increasing access to international conferences, with thousands of NGO representatives at both the Rio Earth Summit and the Johannesburg WSSD, although Arts (1998) questions their influence at Rio. However, Betsill (2006: 190–1) argues that the Climate Action Network – a transnational advocacy network – played a significant role at Kyoto both by pressing the EU to stand firm on its relatively tough reduction target and by persuading Al Gore to attend the negotiations and to instruct the US delegation to be more flexible. Greenpeace and other NGOs were a powerful voice in the rejection of an Antarctic minerals treaty in favour of a further moratorium on mineral extraction (Elliott 1994) and in persuading sufficient non-whaling nations to join the International Whaling Commission (IWC) to enable a moratorium on whaling to be passed in 1985 (Stoett 1997; Skodvin and Andresen 2003). Benedick (1991) credits NGOs with a significant role in bringing about the Montreal Protocol by proposing key policy alternatives to negotiators. On balance, NGOs have exerted a growing, but rarely decisive, influence in environmental diplomacy.

Another factor in regime formation may be the nature of the problem itself, perhaps by influencing the strength of the opposition to co-operation or shaping the choice of solutions. Weale (1992: 194) identifies three reasons why it should be easier to agree regimes for the protection of common-pool resources such as fisheries stocks and endangered species than for common-sink resources such as clean air (see also Young 1994: ch. 1). First, as the benefits of common-pool resources can be individually appropriated it should be easier to monitor compliance with an agreement (e.g. to check whether a fishing vessel has exceeded its catch), whereas the non-appropriability of common-sink problems creates collective-action problems. However, there are exceptions; for example, the limited number of CFC manufacturers has meant that it has proven relatively easy to monitor compliance with the ozone regime. Secondly, where benefits are not appropriable for common-sink problems, proxy measures are often devised with the aim of negotiating reductions from that baseline figure (as with the 1990 figures for carbon emissions used in the Kyoto Protocol), but the inevitable arbitrariness of such baseline figures places some countries at a comparative disadvantage to others. For example, the marginal costs of reducing emissions in economies that were in recession in the base year (i.e. relatively low emission levels) will be higher than where the economy was booming. However, the fierce disputes between EU member states over the fishing quotas underpinning the Common Fisheries Policy (Gray 1997) suggests that the agreement of burden-sharing arrangements that are regarded as equitable by all parties is a problem confronting both common-pool and common-sink problems. Lastly, the exhaustion of common-pool resources hurts those that benefit from them most, whereas the over-exploitation of common-sink resources may not fall on those who cause the problem. Thus fishing communities who will suffer from over-fishing have an incentive to co-operate in order to protect their own livelihoods, unlike those UK companies whose emissions are responsible for acid rain in Scandinavia.

Overall, a number of factors might influence regime formation; none stands out as decisive. Efforts to secure international co-operation to solve an environmental problem will be shaped by a complex mix of scientific, economic, political and social factors. To return to the ozone and climate change examples, it is clear that climate change is one of the most complex and perplexing issues confronting policymakers today. Compared to ozone diplomacy, international co-operation over climate change has been harder to achieve because the various obstacles – powerful veto states, strongly opposed economic interests, scientific uncertainty, a multitude of distributional and equity issues, non-appropriability and the unwillingness of citizens to make lifestyle sacrifices – have proved much harder to overcome. A key difference is the cost and availability of solutions. In ozone diplomacy, CFCs were not critical to the economy and substitutes (now) exist for most uses. Solutions to ozone depletion are largely technological and can be dealt with by co-operation between the state and a small number of key manufacturers with little observable impact on citizens. In contrast, energy production and consumption is of central economic importance. Affordable and practicable solutions, such as **renewable** sources of energy (wind, solar, waves) or cleaner technologies (electric cars), may not be readily available or acceptable. Effective measures to com-

> **Renewable energy:** Energy sources, such as wind, geothermal and hydroelectric, that never run out.

bat climate change will inevitably involve fundamental socio-economic changes affecting economic growth, energy production, transport and individual lifestyles. There are few votes to be won and many to be lost on these issues. Not surprisingly, no country has yet committed itself to such radical solutions (see Chapter 12).

---

### Critical question 2

Is the role of environmental NGOs in securing international environmental co-operation undervalued?

---

# ▶ Regime implementation

How successful are environmental regimes in solving the problems they address? Hurrell (1995) has observed that 'the weakest link in the chain of international environmental cooperation may well not lie in the difficulties of negotiating formal agreements but, rather, in ensuring that those arrangements are effectively implemented' (p. 141). Despite extensive coverage of the formation and strengthening of environmental regimes, until recently implementation issues were relatively neglected, but this gap in the literature has been plugged by a wave of implementation studies since the mid-1990s (Victor et al. 1998; Young 1999; Kütting 2000; Miles et al. 2002). None the less, with many regimes still evolving, it is difficult to draw overall conclusions about their effectiveness.

It is important, first, to be clear about the meaning of 'effectiveness' (Young 1994: ch. 6; Kütting 2000; Wettestad 2005). One approach regards a regime as successful if the institutional arrangements it creates can change the behaviour of states, for example by overcoming the objections of veto states or persuading countries to sign up to new or tougher targets. This definition is only really a proxy measure of effectiveness, for it works on the assumption that commitments made on paper will be implemented – but that is an heroic assumption.

Even if some or all commitments are implemented, a comprehensive assessment of effectiveness must also determine whether a regime contributes to the improvement of the environmental problem it addresses. At best, has the problem been resolved? One obvious proxy measure is whether the objectives of an agreement have been achieved. More realistically, has the regime achieved a 'relative improvement' in the problem (Wettestad 2005: 300–1)? Put differently, what would be the situation if the regime did not exist? For if regimes matter we need to be sure that any measurable improvements, such as reduced levels of pollution, are a result of regime activity rather than other factors. This methodological problem is illustrated by the 1979 LRTAP Convention and subsequent protocols on $SO_2$ and $N_2O$ emissions and depositions. There is no doubt that overall emissions in Europe of both gases have fallen steadily and significantly (EEA 2005a: 256–9). However, it is less clear whether reduced emissions are a direct result of the measures introduced by the various agreements, such as flue-gas desulphurisation equipment to coal-fired power-plants, or are the (often unintentional) consequences of developments such as economic restructuring in Eastern Europe, which closed many old polluting factories and power-stations, and the privatisation of the UK energy utilities, which prompted a rapid switch to gas-fired power-stations (ibid.; see also Wettestad 2005: 313–15).

The Antarctic Treaty banning the mining of minerals on that continent is one clear example of a regime where the successful achievement of the objective can be directly attributed to the regime. The Montreal Protocol on ozone depletion is widely regarded as a success. Total global consumption of CFCs fell from 1.1 million tonnes in 1986 to 70,000 tonnes in 2004, and over that period consumption in developed countries fell dramatically from 1 million tonnes to just 2,000 tonnes and by around 60 per cent in developing countries. It has been estimated that, without the Montreal Protocol, the depletion of the ozone layer would have been about ten times worse than current levels by 2050 (UNEP 2005: 4–6). Other regimes generally regarded as successful include the Oslo Convention for the Prevention of Marine Pollution by Dumping from Ships and Aircraft and the Convention on the Conservation and Management of Highly Migratory Fish Stocks [notably tuna fisheries] in the Western and Central Pacific (Miles et al. 2002). Yet the success of a regime is often much less clear-cut than in these examples. For many years after its formation in 1946 the International Whaling Commission (IWC) was hopelessly ineffective in protecting whales; indeed, more whales were caught than before regulation was introduced. It was only after anti-whaling nations seized control of the IWC and forced the implementation of a moratorium from 1986, leading to a dramatic reduction in the number of whales killed, that the regime institutions began to achieve their objectives. Although the IWC itself has no sanctions, the reluctance of whaling nations, notably Japan and Norway, to incur the wrath of the anti-whaling nations and of international NGOs such as Greenpeace, has ensured their broad, if uneven, compliance with the ban (Stoett 1997), although the hostility between the two camps has made the regime increasingly unstable in recent years (Miles et al. 2002: 400).

All regimes face serious implementation difficulties. Even the Montreal Protocol on ozone depletion will have to overcome major obstacles to achieve long-term success. Several countries, notably Russia and China, have admitted that they will be unable to comply with the CFC phase-out timetable. The efforts of industrialising countries have been hampered by the failure of some richer countries to honour their payments to the multilateral fund. Another serious problem is the flourishing illegal trade in CFCs. It is estimated that since CFC production ceased in developed countries, up to 20,000 tonnes of CFCs are illegally traded annually in industrialised countries (UNEP 2005: 10). The major source of smuggling seems to be Russia, which is still manufacturing CFCs, from where virgin products are either smuggled as unlicensed imports or, more commonly, falsely substituted for recycled CFCs, which can still legally be traded.

Sometimes the problem lies with a weak regime agreement. A framework convention may be a triumph of diplomacy, but its substance is initially often rather thin, as illustrated by the ineffective voluntary carbon emission targets agreed at Rio which few developed states met. For example, only three EU member states (Britain, Germany, Luxembourg) reduced carbon emissions between 1990 and 1998 (EEA 2000). States generally prefer non-binding targets and schedules, but without meaningful sanctions and effective monitoring systems it is difficult to hold countries to their commitments. Much may depend on the effectiveness of the institutional structures that oversee implementation. Sustained political commitment is also critical. The good intentions of a government during regime negotiations, perhaps spurred on by a supportive enthusiastic public and environmental lobby, may have diminished by the time it comes to act on its promises. Where the solutions are very expensive, such as fitting scrubbers to power-stations, or politically unpopular, such as an eco-tax, governments may give priority to short-term domestic considerations. Consequently, environmental pressure groups can help implementation by constantly pressing governments to fulfil their commitments and monitoring. The International Institute for Environment and Development, WWF and Greenpeace played a critical role in the implementation of the conservation features of the International Tropical Trade Agreement (Princen and Finger 1994: 5). Greenpeace's pro-active 'greenfreeze' refrigerator campaign (see Box 6.2) forced chemical manufacturers to produce CFC/HFC-free refrigerators much sooner than they had planned.

Sometimes, a government may be simply unable to implement an agreement. Environmental regimes are agreed between nation states, but governments often have only limited control over the behaviour of actors (notably corporations and individual citizens) and the activities they have promised to change. Even rich developed countries with strong political structures and a culture of compliance with the law have problems in implementing global agreements; for example, ten out of the fifteen EU Annex 1 states are predicted to miss their 'binding' 2012 Kyoto emissions reduction targets (UNFCCC 2005).

But many governments lack the state capacity to meet their regime obligations. First, some countries lack the political and social infrastructure that enables a government to enforce its policy decisions. Not surprisingly, Russia, where the government is undermined by its chronic inability to collect tax revenues and where corruption is endemic, has no effective recovery and recycling system for CFCs and cannot prevent them from being smuggled abroad. In developing countries that are wracked by political conflicts and civil unrest, or where deep-set poverty and inequalities are widespread, government pronouncements about global warming, ozone depletion or loss of biodiversity will receive low priority. Secondly, many governments have insufficient resources to implement the costly changes needed to meet environmental commitments. Developing economies are often dependent on the export of one or two commodities or cash crops, rendering them highly vulnerable to market fluctuations and changes in the terms of trade. Many economies have not recovered from the debt crisis of the 1980s and 1990s and have been subjected to stringent structural adjustment programmes imposed by the International Monetary Fund (IMF) and the World Bank, which have further reduced the state's capacity to implement environmental policies. Without financial and technical aid, it is unlikely that investment in energy efficiency measures or the recovery of CFCs will materialise. Thirdly, some Northern transnational corporations (TNCs) are so powerful that they are almost autonomous from national governments and can ride roughshod over the law. Many developing countries have weaker environmental regulations and laxer enforcement than in the North, and their governments, desperate to attract investment and jobs, may turn a blind eye to the environmentally damaging industrial activities of TNCs.

These examples of state incapacity underline the important role of domestic factors in the implementation of environmental regimes and, in turn, how the analysis of implementation cannot be separated from the broader international political economy that contributes to that state incapacity. One conclusion is that some implementation problems lie beyond the reach of institutional solutions. Institutional structures may bring opposing parties to the negotiating table, facilitate co-operation and enhance the capacity of individual governments to implement regime commitments by administering financial and technical transfers. Yet environmental regimes can do little to transform the system of capitalist development that underpins the increasingly globalised world economy in which some powers have shifted from the nation state to transnational actors, financial institutions and international economic institutions such as the WTO, IMF and World Bank. The resulting 'quasi-sovereignty' is at its sharpest in the poorest developing countries where the key features of global economic interdependence, such as the international trading system, aid programmes and the structures of debt relief, exacerbate the interlinked problems of poverty, inequality and environmental degradation (Jackson 1990). National governments struggle to resolve these problems because they lack the autonomy to choose their own economic path or the capacity to deliver the radical policies that might benefit the environment. Thus many forms of environmental degradation are inextricably tied up with the working of the global capitalist economy (Stevis and Assetto 2001). The next chapter examines the relationship between the international political economy and global environmental politics, focusing on the relationship between international trade and the environment.

### Critical question 3

What is the best way to evaluate the effectiveness of environmental treaties?

## ◗ Global environmental politics and sustainable development

Global environmental politics has implications for all five core principles of sustainable development identified in Chapter 8, but three in particular have been highlighted in this chapter: the *precautionary principle*, *equity* and *democracy*.

First, recent environmental diplomacy has undoubtedly strengthened the importance of the *precautionary principle*. Both the ozone and climate change conventions and the Cartagena Biosafety Protocol have either implicitly or explicitly applied the precautionary principle to a problem still characterised by scientific uncertainty. Whereas earlier regimes addressed problems that were already apparent and requiring urgent action (such as declining whale populations or polluted seas), by promising to ban CFCs, reduce greenhouse gas emissions or limit the trade of genetically modified products, states have agreed to act before there is conclusive proof of a problem.

Secondly, *equity* considerations have dominated environmental diplomacy, particularly the climate change and ozone depletion negotiations. By accepting the principle of 'common but differentiated responsibilities' developed states have conceded their historic responsibility for causing the problems and that they continue to be the major contributors to it. By setting up mechanisms such as the Global Environment Facility (see Box 9.3) and the Multilateral Ozone Fund they have acknowledged that poorer countries need help to implement environmental agreements. Conversely, less developed countries have (more or less) conceded that Northern concern about the environment is not an 'eco-colonial' device to deny them the fruits of economic growth. They accept that these global environmental problems will harm everyone – North and South, rich and poor – and require preventive action. Indeed, environmental diplomacy may offer new bargaining opportunities for the South. Although the interests of developed countries have generally prevailed in regime bargaining, it is the mutual vulnerability of all states to global problems that has persuaded developed states to concede limited financial and technology transfers.

However, turning the principle of equity into something concrete has generated considerable conflict. The success of regime bargaining will depend on all participants accepting that the proposed arrangements are both effective and fair. Yet the concept of equity is highly contestable. Climate change politics have generated several competing interpretations of what constitutes a 'fair' allocation of carbon emission reductions between different countries (Grubb et al. 1992; Rose 1992; Rowlands 1997). Grubb et al. (1992: 312–14), for example, identify seven possible equity rationales applicable to greenhouse gas burden-sharing, ranging from the idea that all humans should be entitled to an equal share in the atmospheric commons, through the 'polluter pays' principle that countries should pay for the pollution that they have generated, to a 'status quo' position that accepts a state's current rate of emissions almost as a 'squatter's right'. The different perspectives are informed by a wide variety of philosophical concepts of justice, including egalitarian rights, utilitarianism, Rawlsian and basic-needs approaches (Grubb 1995). These concepts, in turn, raise other tricky issues, such as whether a 'right to pollute' exists and how responsibility should be allocated, which have implications for the way history is treated. For example, does historical usage create a kind of common-law right to continue producing at a particular level, or should countries pay for their historic responsibility in using up a disproportionate share of a global resource (Rowlands 1997: 5–6)? Whilst the concept of 'common but differentiated responsibilities' has been widely adopted in recent regimes in 'an attempt to meet Northern concerns that all countries have obligations and Southern concerns that those obligations are not the same' (Elliott 2004: 174), it has done little to resolve equity conflicts, because it allows the South to argue for reductions based on historic responsibility (i.e. placing the burden on the North), while the North can argue that future emission levels must be built into the equation (i.e. the South must make commitments too). Thus the fact that the richest 20 per cent of the world's population is currently responsible for about 60 per cent of greenhouse gases (and that figure exceeds 80 per cent if past contributions are included) was critical in persuading the developed world to agree the Kyoto Protocol, but with China set to overtake the USA as the largest emitter of greenhouse gases by around 2020, any post-Kyoto agreement must surely impose targets on many of the fast-growing industrialising nations.

Each approach to equity will affect countries very differently (Rowlands 1997). Within Europe, those states with the biggest populations – Germany, France, Italy, the UK – are responsible for the largest *volume* of greenhouse gas emissions. By contrast, per capita emissions vary by at least a factor of three, between, for example, one of the lowest, France, which has a large nuclear industry, and the highest, Luxembourg, with its important metallurgical industry (EEA 2006b). Not surprisingly, countries tend to lobby for the equity principle that best matches their national self-interest. At Kyoto, the EU tried to resolve such conflicts through a Community-wide 'bubble' strategy that set an overall reduction target for Community emissions but incorporated different targets for individual states so that increased emissions in poorer states such as Greece and Portugal would be offset by larger cuts in richer states such as Germany and Britain (see Box 9.4). The bubble approach attracted criticism from non-Annex 1 states who wanted all industrialised countries to make the same percentage cut in emissions, and from some, such as the USA, who believed this collective strategy conferred unfair advantages on the EU. The bubble strategy certainly allowed the EU to take a lead role in pushing for tougher targets, but meant it was allocated a larger share of the emissions reduction burden. Thus equity is a source of conflict between developed countries as well as between North and South.

Lastly, international environmental co-operation raises some interesting issues of *democracy* because national sovereignty, and the role of the state in delivering sustainable development, is threatened in several ways (Litfin 1998b). Obviously, the transboundary nature of an international environmental problem puts it beyond the competence of an individual state to defend itself unilaterally from damage. Consequently, the creation of a complex structure of international treaties, institutions and laws has required nation states to concede some authority and control to these higher bodies – what Hurrell (1995) calls 'the erosion of sovereignty from above' (p. 136). This growing network of international institutions has taken power even further away from the local communities and indigenous peoples who many environmentalists argue should be at the centre of sustainable development initiatives. Conversely, sovereignty is also threatened from below by the inability of many developing states to implement environmental commitments. Yet, while state sovereignty may be ebbing away in a globalising world, the willingness of governments to defend this principle at all costs has been a major bone of contention in environmental diplomacy. Few countries have been prepared to sacrifice even small areas of sovereignty, hence MEAs rarely include meaningful sanctions that have any force over the sovereign territory of nation states. Developing countries have been particularly suspicious of Northern attempts to control their economic development, a sentiment that underpinned Malaysian opposition at the Rio Earth Summit to a convention to protect forests that would have imposed external constraints on the way it exploited its own resources (although it subsequently came out in support of a convention as a means to secure technology transfer, financial assistance and debt relief) (Humphreys 1998).

It could be argued that whatever sovereignty a state surrenders by participating in a regime is partly compensated by the benefits it gains from collective action, and by the resulting influence it is able to exercise over the activities of other states. The importance of the EU as an actor in environmental diplomacy is certainly linked to the strength it derives from the willingness of each member state to transfer a range of environmental competencies to it. Institutionalists claim that regimes enhance the capacity of weaker states by transferring finance and technologies to them (as illustrated by the Global Environment Facility and the Multilateral Ozone Fund), or by providing the support and resources to resist TNC power, so that their sovereignty is effectively enhanced (Haas et al. 1993; Conca 1994). If developed countries press for tougher, more effective regimes, as occurred in ozone diplomacy, they effectively strengthen the bargaining position of less developed nations, particularly bigger players such as China, India, Brazil, which enables them to extract better concessions.

---

### Critical question 4

For poor nations in the South, is 'sovereignty lost, influence gained'?

---

## ▶ Conclusion

The growth of environmental diplomacy, with its accompanying baggage of international treaties, institutional arrangements and policy initiatives, is evidence of the substantial progress made by the international community in addressing problems of the global commons. International co-operation can be a perfectly rational strategy for states to pursue, although collective-action problems mean that the agreement of each new regime represents a considerable diplomatic achievement.

However, caution is necessary. Much of the momentum engendered by the Rio process has dissipated. The attempt at the Johannesburg WSSD in 2002 to kick-start the global sustainable development process was widely regarded as a failure and progress on climate change since Kyoto has been slow and acrimonious. The enthusiasm for environmental issues expressed by many Northern governments in the late 1980s/early 1990s has waned. Although recent treaties have applied the precautionary principle and made genuine efforts to grapple with equity issues, many aspects of environmental diplomacy are still permeated by the traditional paradigm. Most international problems are treated in isolation and end-of-pipe technical solutions remain the norm. Not surprisingly, institutional responses have had only limited success. Many MEAs, notably the climate change treaty, still represent an inadequate response to the problem; considerable regime strengthening is required. Serious implementation gaps impair the effectiveness of most regimes. These difficulties demonstrate how the narrow institutionalist focus on regime formation and strengthening needs to be supplemented by the recognition that many sources of environmental degradation may be beyond the reach of environmental diplomacy, because they reside in broader structural factors such as globalisation and the system of international trade, to which we turn in the next chapter.

## ▶ *Further reading and websites*

Porter et al. (2000), Elliott (2004) and Clapp and Dauvergne (2005) provide good introductions to global environmental politics. Betsill et al. (2006) is an excellent review of the major theoretical approaches to the study of international environmental politics. On specific approaches and issues, see Deudney (2006) and Swatuk (2006) on environmental security; Young (1994) and Vogler and Imber (1996) for a conceptual discussion of regime formation; Andresen et al. (2000) on the role of science in regime formation; and Young (1999), Kütting (2000) and Miles et al. (2002) for an evaluation of regime effectiveness. Haas (1999) provides a critique of institutionalist approaches. Stevis and Assetto (2001) analyse international political economy and the environment. Levy and Newell (2005) is a collection of readings on the role of business actors in global environmental politics.

See the journals *Global Environmental Politics*, *Environmental Politics*, *Global Environmental Change* and *International Affairs* for developments in international environmental politics. For details and updates on recent developments in environmental diplomacy, see the *Earth Negotiations Bulletin* published by the International Institute for Sustainable Development (http://www.iisd.ca/). Useful websites for other key conventions include: http://www.unfccc.de/ (climate change); http://ozone.unep.org/index.asp (ozone); http://www.biodiv.org/ (biodiversity); http://www.unccd.int/ (combating desertification); http://www.basel.int/ (hazardous wastes); and http://www.cites.org/ (CITES).

NOTES
1 See Axelrod (1984) for an analysis of game-theoretic approaches to international relations.
2 Put in game-theoretic language, repetitive, or iterated, playing of games like the 'prisoner's dilemma' can come to resemble an 'assurance game' where 'cooperation is an individually rational strategy provided that the actor contemplating cooperation can be assured that others will cooperate' (Weale 1992: 191; see also Axelrod 1984).
3 The term 'institutionalist' is used here to refer to a wide range of approaches, notably neo-liberal institutionalism, but also those from alternative epistemological perspectives, which emphasise the role of international institutions in managing conflict and solving collective-action problems – the focus that has dominated the study of international environmental politics (e.g. Young 1994, 1999; Rowlands 1995). For a critique of this perspective, see Paterson (1996: ch. 6), Haas (1999), Kütting (2000) and Broadhead (2002).
4 Detailed accounts of ozone diplomacy include Benedick (1991), Litfin (1994) and Rowlands (1995). Seaver (1997) analyses ozone diplomacy using a range of international relations theories.

5 Detailed accounts of the politics of climate change include Paterson (1996), Victor (2004) and Dessler and Parson (2006).

6 Dessler and Parson (2006) provide an excellent accessible analysis of the science, including predicted outcomes, of climate change.

7 See Schreurs (2004) for a comparison of the US and EU role in climate change negotiations, and Lisowski (2002) specifically on US opposition to the Kyoto Protocol.

# Globalisation, trade and the environment

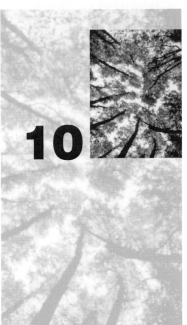

**10**

## Contents

## Key issues

▶ What is the relationship between globalisation and the environment?

▶ Is free trade good for the environment?

▶ Does the WTO protect the environment?

▶ Is NAFTA a 'green' treaty?

▶ Why has the EU developed such an extensive and progressive body of environmental legislation?

The previous chapter examined the high politics of international environmental diplomacy – the negotiation of environmental treaties between nations – but it also introduced the international political economy perspective to help understand problems in implementing those treaties. This chapter focuses more squarely on the relationship between the global capitalist economy, specifically international trade, and the environment. The discussion is based on the assumption that globalisation has had a profound impact on the global economy over the last thirty years, although its nature and extent are widely debated. Whilst many of the processes of globalisation are hardly new – the expansion, extension and integration of international economies has been happening for several hundred years – as Lipschutz (2004) observes, 'What is new is the scale and volume of capitalist expansion and the commodification of things never before exchanged in markets, such as genes, air pollution, and whale watching' (p. 122). Thus economic globalisation has seen a massive growth in global trade, investment and finance, but the implications for the environment are hotly contested; some see globalisation as a positive development, whilst others regard it in profoundly negative terms. A similar debate surrounds the specific issue of free trade, which is a key driver of globalisation. The opening sections of this chapter therefore introduce debates about the relationship between globalisation and the environment, and between international trade and the environment. The chapter then examines the major institutions governing global trade today. First, it analyses the way the environment is treated by the World Trade Organisation (WTO), which is the global institution responsible for applying international trade rules. It then assesses the impact on the environment of the two most important regional trading agreements: the North American Free Trade Agreement (NAFTA) and the European Union (EU).

## ▶ Globalisation and the environment

Globalisation is a hotly contested idea. With major disagreements over what the term even refers to, it is hardly surprising to find sharply contrasting views of its significance. Some observers regard it as involving a fundamental transformation of the world over the last thirty years or so, while others deny that any major change has occurred.[1] There is also considerable disagreement over the extent of the empirical changes involved in globalisation. Rather than engage in a definitional debate, 'globalisation' will be used here quite narrowly to refer to those processes that are integrating the global economy: an intensification of capitalist production indicated by the increasing mobility and velocity of capital, the deregulation of economic activity, an increasingly global division of labour, the absence of social protection, a changing role for the state and the rapid growth in communication links.[2] Furthermore, there seems to be a general acceptance within the study of environmental politics that globalisation is happening, with the battle-lines having been drawn up over whether or not globalisation is good or bad for the environment. Consequently, the discussion here accepts this assumption and focuses on its implications for the environment.

The case that globalisation is beneficial for the environment is made most enthusiastically by market liberals, such as Bhagwati (2004). The thrust of their argument is that globalisation is an 'engine of wealth creation': the globalisation and liberalisation of trade, investment and finance is increasing the global wealth (measured by per capita GDP) that will fund environmental improvements (Clapp and Dauvergne 2005: 26–7). Market liberals are persuaded by the Kuznets curve thesis (see Chapter 8) that as societies become richer the process of industrialisation initially results in greater pollution, but a point is eventually reached when there is a decoupling of economic activity and pollution. In the style of Lomborg (see Chapter 3) they emphasise the historical trends that show how the standard of living for the majority of the world's population is far higher than in the 1970s, despite the rapidly rising population, and that the record of the developed world demonstrates that the best form of population control is to bring education and prosperity to the masses. Globalisation, by delivering the 'development' side of the sustainable development equation, will solve the social problems that contribute to ecological degradation; indeed, environmentalist opponents of globalisation are condemned for being 'eco-imperialists' for trying to deny poor countries the right to develop (Bhagwati 2004). Market liberals make the cornucopian claim that the planet is still replete with unused natural resources and unfilled waste sinks, and the technocentric argument that history shows that human ingenuity has consistently overcome environmental problems.

By contrast, the dominant view in environmental politics, among both academic commentators (e.g. Sachs 1999: ch. 8) and the ranks of anti-globalisation political activists (see Chapter 6), is that globalisation is unremittingly bad for the environment. By underpinning rapid economic growth, globalisation is responsible for the over-consumption of natural resources and the filling of waste sinks. It involves the movement of capital, technology, goods and even labour to areas with high returns on investment, without regard to the impact on the communities and people moved or those left behind (Lipschutz 2004: 121). Globalisation stretches the chains of production and consumption over great distances and across many locations, which increases the temporal and spatial separation between the sources of an environmental problem and their impact in specific places. For example, the division of labour associated with economic globalisation results in the increased transport of raw materials, commodities, semi-processed materials, parts, finished goods and waste, greater energy consumption and more pollution (including higher carbon emissions) – plus the risk of major environmental accidents (Mol 2003: 71–2). As well as changing production patterns in environmentally damaging ways, globalisation reinforces the sharp inequalities between the North and South. For example, the ready availability throughout the year in the supermarkets of the developed world of almost every vegetable or fruit is the result of a shift from subsistence farming to intensive cash cropping in developing countries. In addition to the significant environmental externalities of flying these products to Northern markets, cash cropping brings questionable benefits to developing countries. Lipschutz notes that 'Farming for export relies on chemicals for uniformity, machinery for volume, and high quality land for productivity' (p. 126). It is a capital-intensive business concentrating wealth on a limited number of agri-industrial corporations and rich farmers, but generating few jobs. As agri-business acquires the best quality land, poor farmers are forced to cultivate low-quality, marginal land, contributing to soil erosion and habitat destruction.

In practice, the dynamic and multifaceted complexity of globalisation suggests that it will have both positive and negative effects on the environment, which is reflected in the existence, between these two polarised positions, of many other perspectives, which neither wholly glorify nor vilify globalisation. Liberal institutionalists, for example, whilst generally regarding globalisation in a positive light, recognise that it will have some detrimental impact on the environment. None the less, they believe that most major environmental problems can be resolved through the institutions of global governance, notably international environmental regimes, but also the greening of global economic institutions such as the World Bank and the WTO, and the influence of regional supranational organisations such as the EU and NAFTA. Mol (2003) offers a sober assessment of the negative environmental consequences of globalisation, but uses the ecological modernisation framework to argue that globalisation is also contributing to a greening of many global production and consumption processes, primarily by the export of green practices from richer to poorer countries. Even amongst its fiercest opponents, it is recognised that globalisation opens up new opportunities and sites of protest that have encouraged the emergence of a vibrant global civil society, including international environmental groups and the anti-globalisation movement, as a counter-balance to the hegemony of neo-liberalism.

### Critical question 1

On balance, is globalisation good or bad for the environment?

## ▶ International trade and the environment

At the heart of the debate about the relationship between globalisation and the environment is the impact of international trade on the environment and the extent to which international trade organisations should integrate environmental considerations into their activities. The liberalisation of international trade and the growing importance of global institutions such as the WTO and regional trade organisations such as NAFTA and the EU are key empirical elements of globalisation. The sheer growth of international trade – from 25 per cent of global GDP in 1960 to 58 per cent in 2001 – indicates the potential significance of its impact on the environment. One of the principal reasons for this expansion has been the steady removal of government barriers to trade. The tariffs that industrialised countries impose on manufactured goods have fallen from about 50 per cent in 1948 to an average of 3.7 per cent today (Brack 2005: 2).

The relationship between trade and the environment is as fiercely contested as the globalisation debate; indeed, many of the arguments overlap.[3] Thus one core argument behind the claim that trade is positive for the environment is the neo-liberal thesis that free trade contributes to economic growth, which generates the wealth necessary to fund environmental improvements. Of course, market liberals make a brave and perhaps overly optimistic assumption that firms will spend their extra wealth on greener technologies such as pollution abatement equipment, rather than just taking it as profit, although it is likely that as incomes rise citizens will demand higher environmental standards. Proponents of free trade argue that it has other environmental benefits; in particular, that it allocates resources more efficiently than any other system, which results in lower usage and therefore fewer wasted resources (Clapp and Dauvergne 2005: 123–7). It does so, first, by the specialisation of production based on the economic theory of comparative advantage, whereby countries specialise in those products that they are better at producing, which is more efficient than pursuing national self-sufficiency in a wide range of goods. Secondly, free trade removes trade restrictions that distort markets, such as tariffs, quotas and export subsidies, because such protectionism reduces the incentive to develop greener technologies and encourages over-consumption by underpricing goods on the domestic market. Another argument for free trade, which also informs the ecological modernisation perspective (Mol 2003), is the claim that countries will adopt the higher environmental standards of richer countries to enable their businesses to compete in those lucrative markets. Vogel (1995) provides several examples showing how the lure of green markets in the USA and EU has encouraged developing countries to raise their standards, particularly in the automobile industry (see Chapter 12).

Many environmentalists, however, have deep reservations about the proclaimed advantages of global free trade. A basic problem lies with the contribution of trade to economic growth. Even if the market liberals are correct that free trade makes production more 'efficient', any resulting benefits in terms of lower resource use will rapidly be overshadowed by the overall growth in the economic activity encouraged by free trade. For example, steady improvements in the fuel efficiency of aircraft have been outstripped by the dramatic growth in air passenger traffic (IPCC 1999). Indeed, more trade means more pollution simply from transporting more finished and partially completed goods around the globe. Moreover, if efficiency gains result in falling prices for a particular good, then greater demand for those goods will lead to increased consumption (Clapp and Dauvergne 2005: 127–8). Free trade also fails to take account of the external environmental costs of economic activity: the price a consumer pays for a good does not include the full value of the natural resource (e.g. its irreplaceability) or of the transportation costs (e.g. costs to society of addressing pollution problems and higher $CO_2$ emissions), so increased trade leads to more environmental destruction (see Chapter 12).

Free trade may also exacerbate economic inequities and environmental damage. Ecological economists, such as Daly and Cobb (1990: ch. 11), argue that the theory of free trade and comparative advantage is based on the long-outdated assumption that goods are mobile but capital and labour are relatively immobile – that they cannot cross borders. Today, one of the features of globalisation is that capital is highly mobile, and labour is much more mobile too, as illustrated by the millions of migrant workers in the developed world. Consequently, the specialisation of production is likely to concentrate pollution in particular locations, typically in developing countries and regions, whilst the richer countries enjoy the benefits of the goods whilst suffering only limited environmental damage. In the developing world, production for export is generally heavily dependent on the unsustainable use of natural resources (such as forestry, fishing, coffee and palm oil plantations) or on mass production exploiting cheap labour and low health and safety standards (Elliott 2004: 192; Clapp and Dauvergne 2005: 128–9). Indeed, the 'pollution haven' thesis suggests that free trade may encourage a developing country to exploit a possible comparative advantage by using low environmental regulations as a kind of non-tariff subsidy to encourage polluting industries to locate there (see Box 10.1). Critics of free trade therefore suggest that rather than encourage a 'race to the top' or what Vogel (1995) calls 'trading up', it is more likely to provoke a 'race to the bottom' to 'lowest-common-denominator' environmental standards (Esty 1994; Porter 1999; Elliott 2004: 193).

## Critical question 2

Are the core assumptions of the 'trading-up' argument sound?

Between these two opposed positions there are many other perspectives in the free trade debate. Significantly, many observers, including those sympathetic to free trade, recognise that the international system is out of balance, because those institutions responsible for governing trade (primarily the WTO) are much more powerful than those protecting the environment, so the interests of big corporations receive higher priority than environmental protection or the concerns of local communities (Brack 2005: 3). The issue, therefore, is about how best to 'manage' trade to ensure it minimises environmental damage (Clapp and Dauvergne 2005: 132). Thus the fiercely contested debate about the relationship between trade and the environment has a practical outlet in the contemporary conflicts surrounding the evolution of world trading agreements and institutions, notably the WTO.

## 10.1 Does free trade result in 'industrial flight' to 'pollution havens'?

One of the main drivers of globalisation is foreign direct investment by the rapidly growing number of transnational corporations (TNCs). A major criticism of TNCs is that they locate their most polluting operations in countries with weak or poorly enforced environmental regulations. 'Industrial flight' takes place when environmental standards are raised in one country, prompting industry to move to another country with lower standards. A 'pollution haven' is a country that sets its environmental standards inefficiently low (in economic terms) to attract foreign direct investment and where there is clear evidence that an industry does relocate there to avoid pollution abatement costs. There are clearly many developing countries that have low environmental standards and suffer from high levels of pollution, but those features do not in themselves make them pollution havens.

Several econometric studies of US manufacturing firms, mostly from a pro-free trade perspective, have argued that industrial flight is unlikely, primarily because other costs, such as labour or technology, are much higher than environmental costs. Whilst not denying that polluting industries have grown in developing countries, proponents of free trade blame changes in domestic production and consumption, rather than relocation by TNCs. Local firms lack resources to invest in modern cleaner technologies, the products from dirty production methods tend to be for domestic markets and they often find it easier to avoid compliance with environmental regulations because they are smaller and more dispersed. By contrast, TNCs operate to higher environmental standards and use greener, more efficient technologies. So, different environmental standards are inevitable, but they do not result in industrial flight.

Critics argue that the most polluting, high-impact industries, such as mining, oil drilling and logging, have a high concentration of TNCs. Many TNCs operate double standards, stricter in industrialised countries, laxer in developing countries. There are numerous case studies of highly polluting TNCs in developing countries, including the *maquiladora* manufacturing plants in Mexico, where around 2,000 American companies, mostly in polluting chemical, electronics and furniture industries, have moved in, partly in response to higher regulations in the USA, and partly attracted by laxer enforcement of standards across the border. It is argued that economic globalisation means that even the smallest of cost differences can be enough to persuade TNCs to relocate, whilst governments in poorer countries are put off raising environmental standards for fear of driving firms away.

One reason why this debate rumbles on is that it is very difficult to *prove* either interpretation is correct.

Based on Clapp and Dauvergne (2005: 161–9). See Clapp (2001) and Neumayer (2001).

## ◗ The WTO and the environment

Defenders of the WTO argue that it can and does protect the environment; its opponents claim that the WTO and the international trade rules it governs are biased against environmental interests. This section analyses this question by examining the impact of the WTO disputes procedures and assesses the relationship between the rules governing international trade and the multilateral treaties that underpin environmental regimes.

The removal of trade barriers in the post-war era was co-ordinated and promoted under the General Agreement on Tariffs and Trade (GATT). Formally agreed in 1947, GATT underwent eight rounds of negotiation, culminating in the Uruguay round completed in 1994, which established the WTO as a permanent body to oversee the implementation of GATT and related agreements, and a quasi-judicial system of dispute resolution that requires consensus among WTO members to overturn any of its decisions (Brack 2005: 2). The WTO has 149 members and accounts for 97 per cent of world trade (WTO 2006).

GATT was established long before any major global environmental concerns arose, so its rules – still the main mechanism for governing trade – contain few references to the environment, although the preamble to the Agreement Establishing the WTO does include sustainable development and environmental protection among its objectives. The one GATT rule that does appear to address environmental issues is the general exceptions clause, Article XX, which allows trade restrictions where they are 'necessary to protect human, animal or plant life or health' (Article XX(b)) or relate 'to the conservation of exhaustible natural resources' (Article XX(g)). However, such exceptions are subject to a range of qualifications, notably that they must be *necessary* (i.e. there is no alternative), that *domestic restrictions* must also be imposed and that any trade measures must not be *arbitrary* or *unjustifiable*. There is also disagreement about whether measures intended to protect natural resources outside a country's border are allowed and whether measures can discriminate on the grounds of their *process and production methods*, which in many cases – because they produce transboundary pollution or deplete natural resources such as fish or timber – are environmentally unsustainable (Brack 2005: 8; Clapp and Dauvergne 2005: 136–7).

The restrictiveness of these rules, apparently reflected in some early decisions of the disputes procedure, has led many environmentalists to condemn the GATT/WTO for failing to protect the environment. They cite, in particular, the two decisions on the tuna–dolphin dispute. The first case was brought by Mexico against the USA on the grounds that a US import ban on Mexican tuna caught in 'dolphin-unfriendly' nets was discriminatory. In 1991, the dispute panel said that Article XX did not apply because the USA was trying to apply national laws beyond its own jurisdiction and that anyway the US ban was in breach of GATT rules by discriminating against a product on the basis of the way it was produced rather than because of its own characteristics. In 1994, a second decision found in favour of the EU because the US secondary ban on third-party sellers of tuna was unilateral and arbitrary. Another similar case was the 1996 WTO ruling against a US law on gasoline cleanliness, which was found to discriminate against imports from Brazil and Venezuela. Yet, as DeSombre and Barkin (2002) observe, the problem in most cases where the WTO has ruled against a regulation is that 'the regulations were not particularly good; they were either clear attempts at industrial protection dressed up in environmentalist clothes, or they were poorly thought through and inappropriate tools for the environmental management intended' (p. 18).

Significantly, subsequent WTO decisions, notably the final outcome of the shrimp–turtle dispute, appear to have 'changed things fundamentally' (Neumayer 2004: 2). This case involved a US embargo on imports of shrimp caught by methods that killed endangered species of sea turtles, i.e. because of the process and production method. The disputes panel initially found against the USA in 1998, on the grounds that the rules were applied in a discriminatory way and were too rigid. However, in 2001 the appellate body found in favour of the USA, ruling that regulations aimed at the process and production method *are* admissible under WTO rules, providing they are applied justly and in a non-arbitrary manner. The panel was sympathetic to the US reform of the original law so that shrimp imports were allowed on a shipment-by-shipment basis, providing it could be shown that the shrimp had been caught in ways that did no harm to turtles, even if the shipments came from countries, such as Malaysia, that could not provide assurances that all shrimp was caught in this way. This finding has potentially significant implications for the development of regulations directed at transboundary environmental problems, a development that not every environmentalist opponent of free trade has acknowledged (DeSombre and Barkin 2002).

Another central area of dispute in the trade–environment debate concerns the relationship between WTO rules and international environmental regimes. Of approximately two hundred MEAs about twenty of the most significant contain trade-restrictive measures that address transboundary ecological problems (Eckersley 2004b: 27). The ozone treaty, for example, imposes stringent restrictions on trade in ozone-depleting substances and products (such as refrigerators and aerosols) that contain them. Such restrictions appear to flout various WTO rules, particularly where different restrictions are applied to parties and to non-parties to the agreement. To date, this tension is theoretical insofar as no cases have arisen that challenge an MEA for contravening WTO rules, which may be evidence of WTO members showing sensible restraint (Neumayer 2004: 4). But it may only be a matter of time before a challenge emerges, particularly as several countries, notably the USA, have refused to ratify various key MEAs, including the Kyoto and Cartagena Protocols. Yet the relative status of the two sets of rules remains ambiguous. Moreover, commentators such as Eckersley (2004b) argue that the awareness of a possible WTO challenge to an MEA has resulted in a conservative implementation of existing MEA trade restrictions and is having a 'chilling' effect on ongoing multilateral negotiations. It is acknowledged on all sides that this tension between the WTO rules and MEAs needs to be resolved. When the WTO was created, a Committee on Trade and the Environment was established to review the relationship between trade rules and the environment, but over ten years on, it has still not produced any conclusive decisions (Eckersley 2004b; Brack 2005: 7; see also Williams 2001).

The WTO is certainly an easy target for environmentalists, both activist and academic. As a symbol of globalisation, free trade and corporate interests, and with very limited environmental NGO participation in its decision-making processes (Mason 2004), it has proved a mobilising force for environmental activists, most notably when the WTO talks in Seattle were disrupted in 1999. Many academics have condemned the WTO for its negative impact on the environment (Conca 2000; Williams 2001; Eckersley 2004b; Thomas 2004, *inter alia*). Yet, as several commentators have suggested (DeSombre and Barkin 2002; Neumayer 2004), the past record of the WTO is in some respects unfairly criticised. Perhaps the absence of stringent environmental measures should be blamed on the callowness of national governments rather than on WTO rules (Neumayer 2004: 5)? Young (2005), noting how few formal challenges are made to WTO rules, argues that by exaggerating the power of the WTO, environmental and consumer activists do harm to the very regulations that they favour, by dissuading governments from making a challenge.

However, the WTO itself has done little to promote environmental protection. Significantly, it is reluctant to incorporate the precautionary principle (Neumayer 2004: 5–6; Brack 2005: 7–8). Currently, only one WTO agreement, on the Application of Sanitary and Phytosanitary Measures, contains reference to the precautionary principle. Even this agreement only allows trade restrictions based on the precautionary principle to be provisional, which effectively ignores the possibility of persistent, or at least long-term, scientific uncertainty on issues such as the environmental or health impact of GM products. Indeed, the onus is on the member state(s) to 'prove', with the help of risk assessment (see Chapter 11), the existence of a danger, which, given the nature of uncertainty, seems very difficult to do (Neumayer 2004: 6). Consequently, the disputes procedure has found against the EU's import ban on beef treated with hormones (although the EU continued the ban and accepted the retaliatory trade sanctions allowed by the WTO) and in 2006 it backed the US complaint against the EU's 'moratorium' on the import of GM foods (see Box 7.6). This decision exacerbated political tensions with the EU, where public resistance to GM foods remains strong, and with the developing world, because it will help US GM companies gain access to their markets, thereby strengthening the widespread view that the WTO supports the interests of the developed world, especially the USA.

The prospects for any fundamental reform of WTO rules regarding the environment seem slim. At the time of writing, the ongoing Doha round of trade negotiations had stalled over the reform of agricultural subsidies, which inflict major harm on the environment. Although the MEA/WTO tension is on the Doha agenda, it has a low priority. Moreover, the bottom-line is that the member states will not agree on reform. The developing world is deeply suspicious of the environmental agenda, regarding it as an excuse for Northern protectionism; the developed world is split on key issues, notably the unwillingness of the USA to endorse MEAs that incorporate the precautionary principle. Thus there is a sharp divide between the minority of states who want clear and explicit rules to exempt MEAs from a WTO challenge, and a majority who want no further environmental compromise of trade rules (Mason 2004; Eckersley 2004b: 33). Consequently, with little prospect of the stalemate being resolved, it seems that, on balance, the environmental cause remains poorly served by the WTO, although its negative impact is perhaps not quite as devastating as many environmentalists suggest.

### Critical question 3
Would trade be greener without the WTO?

## ▶ North American Free Trade Agreement

If the WTO has struggled to reconcile tensions between trade and the environment, to what extent have they been resolved by regional trading agreements such as NAFTA and the EU (see next section)? NAFTA was negotiated between Canada, Mexico and the USA in the early 1990s, and is often described as a 'green' trading agreement because it addresses the environment explicitly both in the preamble and in several chapters of the text (Sanchez 2002). The bargaining process took place at a time of high concern about environmental issues and generated heated debates, with several environmental NGOs, including the Sierra Club and Greenpeace, and some trade unions complaining that it favoured corporate interests. The Clinton administration was therefore prepared to offer concessions to the green lobby. Thus the agreement states explicitly that the trade provisions in certain MEAs – including CITES, the Basle Convention on Hazardous Wastes and the Montreal Protocol – take precedence over NAFTA. It also includes an innovative side agreement, the North American Agreement on Environmental Cooperation (NAAEC), specifically on the environment (although it is not formally part of NAFTA) and established the Commission on Environmental Cooperation (CEC) to oversee NAAEC. The CEC has some limited powers, including reporting on various environmental issues (such as the life-cycle of products), acting as a disputes panel on the enforcement of environmental laws related to trade and the right to impose fines (on Canada alone) or trade sanctions for failure to implement environmental laws. Unlike the WTO, environmental NGOs have the right to participate, by making submissions and advising the CEC. NAFTA seeks to prohibit a member state from lowering environmental regulations to become a 'pollution haven'.

Although NAFTA included these environmental provisions, in practice few of the mechanisms have worked as environmentalists had hoped (Sanchez 2002: 1388). The environmental provisions in NAFTA, the NAAEC side agreement and the CEC have not generated a broader discussion of trade and environmental interactions. After their successes in the initial bargaining process, the opportunities provided for environmental NGO participation have not been realised; indeed, American and Mexican environmental NGOs have reduced their involvement in the implementation of NAFTA (Sanchez 2002: 1381). By contrast, businesses have been strengthened by NAFTA and have ensured that the three federal governments and NAFTA institutions have interpreted NAFTA/NAAEC quite narrowly in trade terms, so that the environment has been treated primarily as an *obstacle* to free trade (ibid.: 1388).

On the wider question of NAFTA's environmental impact, the jury is still out. Most studies seem to report a mix of findings, some positive, some negative (Deere and Esty 2002; Markell and Knox 2003). The key Mexican–US environmental issue is transboundary pollution. Many Mexican standards have been raised, Mexican companies have signed compliance action plans and when NAFTA was launched the enforcement of regulations became much stricter, but subsequently enforcement has slackened, and Mexican government funding to help firms with compliance has declined (Vogel 2006: 367). Overall, there seems little evidence of any significant improvement in Mexican environmental degradation. Environmental standards in the USA have changed little as a result of NAFTA, and Canada's post-NAFTA record is even less impressive (Clapp and Dauvergne 2005: 151–2). There is consensus that the CEC has had little impact, although it has helped produce agreement between the three federal governments to phase out a range of dangerous chemicals and pesticides (Vogel 2006: 366).

On balance, despite its early green image, NAFTA has disappointed the environmental lobby. Its environmental innovations have struggled to make any significant impact on the trade–environment nexus. It is not surprising that environmental NGOs regard President Bush's proposed free trade agreement with Central and Latin America with considerable trepidation (Deere and Esty 2002; Vogel 2006: 368).

## ▌ The European Union

In many respects it is unproductive to compare the EU with NAFTA, for the EU is a unique supranational institution with unprecedented powers to remove sovereignty from member states in pursuit of the twin aims of economic and political integration. Yet the driving objective behind it has always been trade liberalisation within a common market, which has forced the EU to confront familiar trade and environment tensions, but with a very different outcome from NAFTA.

The Treaty of Rome that established the Common Market in 1957 was committed to the promotion of 'continuous expansion' and made no mention of environmental protection, let alone sustainable development (see Box 10.2). As environmental issues rose up the global agenda in the early 1970s, European leaders increasingly recognised the need to introduce

## 10.2 The European Union: from traditional paradigm to sustainable development?

*Treaty of Rome* (came into effect 1957)
Article 2 stated that the Community should promote 'a harmonious development of economic activities, a continuous and balanced expansion'. No mention of environmental protection.

*Single European Act* (1987)
For the first time provided a formal, legal underpinning for EU environment policy. Article 130r(2) established a new principle of integration: 'environmental protection requirements shall be a component of the Community's other policies'.

*Maastricht Treaty* (1993)
Introduced the word 'sustainable' (not sustainable development) to the formal aims of the EU. Hence Article 2 was amended so that 'continuous expansion' was replaced by 'sustainable and non-inflationary growth respecting the environment' while Article B of

the Common Provisions stated that a Community objective was 'to promote economic and social progress which is balanced and sustainable'.

*Treaty of Amsterdam* (1999)
Introduced the term 'sustainable development' so that Article 2 seeks 'to promote throughout the Community a harmonious, balanced and sustainable development of economic activities' and a new Article 6 strengthens the integration principle: 'Environmental protection requirements must be integrated into the definition and implementation of the Community policies and activities referred to in Article 3 [i.e. the full range of EU policies] in particular with a view to promoting sustainable development.'

*Treaty of Nice* (2003)
No significant extension of environmental aims or powers.

environmental protection measures, but with no reference to the environment in the Treaty the European Community had no power to enact legislation in that area. Instead, environmental policy was dressed up as a market regulation intended to ensure that common standards existed across member states – a 'level playing-field' – to prevent some countries from gaining a competitive advantage by having lower environmental standards (and therefore lower industrial costs) than others. Using this approach to integration, a growing range of environmental protection legislation was passed. Moreover, a series of Environmental Action Plans (see Chapter 11) encouraged a more strategic approach to environmental policy. The informal status of the environment was ended by its inclusion for the first time in the 1987 Single European Act, and subsequent treaties have established sustainable development as an overall aim of the EU (see Box 10.2), although to ease proposals through the labyrinthine and slow policymaking process, officials still tend to emphasise the 'single market' justification to win cross-departmental support (Lenschow 2005: 308). From the mid-1980s, a tranche of environmental legislation was passed, affecting water, air, waste, chemicals and nature. Today, the environmental *acquis* – the laws, rules and procedures governing environmental policy – encompasses some 500 legislative items and represents a substantial corpus of progressive and far-reaching environmental legislation. Many of these policies far exceeded 'any conceivable standards that would be strictly necessary by a concern to ensure a single functioning market' (Weale 2005: 128). By making the environmental *acquis* an entry requirement to be met by all accession states, the expansion of the EU to twenty-five member states – with more to follow – has directly raised legislative and regulatory standards across much of Europe.

The EU has also expanded its role as an international actor (Vogler 1999; Sbragia 2005). Since its early foot-dragging resistance to the Vienna Convention on ozone depletion, the Union has sought to establish itself as a normative power pushing a sustainable development agenda on the international stage (Lightfoot and Burchill 2004). Thus the EU has taken a proactive role – as a lead 'state' – in negotiating the Kyoto and Cartegena protocols on climate change and biosafety (see Chapter 9). At the Johannesburg World Summit on Sustainable Development it managed to keep sustainable development on the agenda by playing a mediating role between less developed countries and a group of developed countries including the USA, Japan and Australia who were pressing an economic globalisation agenda (Lightfoot and Burchill 2004: 339). Environmental NGOs now look to the EU to adopt a leadership role in international diplomacy, pushing the sustainable development agenda.

The EU is able to assume this role because of its economic weight in the global economy. To perform it effectively, it is vital to secure member state agreement before negotiations; for example, by agreeing the emissions 'bubble' prior to Kyoto (see Box 9.4), the EU was able to exercise great influence in those negotiations. If there are splits between member states, as in ozone diplomacy in the mid-1980s, then it is harder for the EU to exercise influence. One constraint is its lack of a coherent legal identity on the world stage. Other countries have sometimes resisted the EU acting as a signatory to international agreements – for example, it has not been allowed to accede to CITES (Lenschow 2005: 323). The compromise carved out in both the ozone and climate change conventions is a form of 'mixed agreement', whereby both the Union and the member states sign, but this still involves some complicated wrangling over who holds legal competence to deal with a particular problem. Is it the EU or the member states, and, within the EU, is it the Commission or the Council of Ministers? Significantly, the need to resolve these issues and to co-ordinate responses is itself an additional pressure on the EU to 'put its own house in order' by pursuing a more effective sustainable development strategy within the Community (Lightfoot and Burchill 2004: 343).

Why has the EU adopted such a relatively positive approach to the environment? It is important to note that unlike other trading agreements, the EU is a much more ambitious project involving the active pursuit of both economic and political integration in Europe. During the 1980s, European public opinion became increasingly concerned about the environment, which was widely seen as a natural 'European' issue requiring international co-operation to resolve transboundary problems such as acid rain. The success of green parties, both domestically and in elections to the European Parliament (see Chapter 4), and the growing influence of environmental groups in Brussels, brought growing pressure on member state governments to respond. So, apart from delivering the level playing-field necessary for the single economic market, EU elites identified the development of a progressive environmental policy as a source of legitimacy for the EU and a strategy to encourage political integration. A crucial enabling factor has been the willingness of all the key actors in the EU policy process, at various times, to play a proactive role in EU environmental policy.

Probably the key actor is the European Commission, which is responsible for initiating most environmental legislation, primarily through the Directorate-General for Environment. Historically, the Commission was often prepared to take a proactive role promoting tougher environmental rules than many member states wanted to accept, 'thus seeking to conflate "Europeanness" and "greenness"' (Lenschow 2005: 313), although in practice it could do so only with the support of key member states who have been prepared to grasp the environmental baton. The EU has traditionally tended to divide roughly on North–South lines, with the group of richer 'pioneer' countries – Denmark, Germany and the Netherlands, and, after becoming EU members in 1995, Austria, Finland and Sweden – seeking to persuade the poorer 'laggards' from Southern Europe – Greece, Italy, Portugal, Spain – to adopt tougher environmental measures (Andersen and Liefferink 1997a). Often, pioneer states, encouraged by an environmentally concerned electorate, have introduced stringent regulations at home so they are keen to reduce any competitive disadvantage by requiring all member states to adopt them. A further reward for the proactive member state is that implementation costs are lower if its own national model is adopted as the Community standard. One example of such 'regulatory competition' (Heretier 1996; Börzel 2002) in the mid-1980s saw the German government lobby hard to ensure that the EU car emissions directive reduced emissions by requiring new cars to be fitted with catalytic converters (which German car manufacturers had invested in) rather than the lean-burn engine technology (championed by the UK) (Weale et al. 2000: 397–407). By contrast, in Southern Europe the environment generally has lower political salience, with public concern focused primarily on economic development. To ease the compliance burden on the Southern states, the EU set up a Cohesion Fund in 1993, with about half its budget spent on environmental projects. Of course, this simplistic North–South characterisation is not always accurate; in particular, on issues where environmental protection might impose domestic costs, pioneers can become laggards (Weale et al. 2000: ch. 14; Börzel 2003).

As the European Parliament has acquired more formal powers and greater influence, it has developed a reputation as an 'environmental champion', particularly through its Environment Committee, and is widely acknowledged to have played a constructive role in pushing the EU's environmental agenda, often working closely with the Commission (Burns 2005). The European Court of Justice has also contributed positively to the development of environmental policy. Before the Single European Act its decisions developed legal norms that established the legitimacy of environmental measures; subsequently, it has emancipated the environment from the single market agenda, most notably in the Danish bottle case, which ruled that the principle of the free movement of goods can be overridden if it helps to achieve common environmental objectives (Koppen 2005; Lenschow 2005: 317). Environmental NGOs have been able to exercise some influence in Brussels, with a small, institutionalised lobby of core groups, such as the European Environmental Bureau, FoE and WWF, who all – except Greenpeace – receive some EU funding (Lenschow 2005: 318). The lobby concentrates its resources on the policy formulation stage of the legislative process, lobbying the parliament and member states and offering expert advice to policymakers, although it also does its best to highlight the implementation failures in EU policy (see Chapter 12) (McCormick 2001: 116–22). However, in recent years the business lobby has become much better organised and effective in resisting costly regulations (ibid.: 111–13; Pesendorfer 2006).

Of course, there is a litany of problems facing EU environmental policy that qualify its impact on the environment. The momentum driving the legislative onslaught has diminished noticeably since the mid-1990s (although some important legislation has been passed, including directives addressing the problem of electronic waste and establishing a framework of environmental liability based on the polluter pays principle). There is also some evidence that it is increasingly hard to agree new stringent environmental regulations. For example, the REACH programme on chemicals policy originally included some far-reaching proposals based on the precautionary principle that were intended to strengthen environmental regulations governing a wide range of chemicals. However, the Commission's commitment to the neo-liberal elements of the Council's Lisbon agenda, namely the drive for greater competitiveness and a more dynamic market, encouraged it to accept business lobbying that many of the proposals would harm economic competitiveness, with the result that many proposals were significantly watered down (Pesendorfer 2006). The enlargement of the EU from fifteen to twenty-five states in 2004 almost certainly made it harder to achieve agreement over any policy (Tsebelis and Yataganas 2002); the addition of several relatively poor Central and Eastern European industrialising states may also have strengthened the laggard camp, although it is too early to be certain (Vandeveer and Carmin 2004: 325–6). There are major implementation problems involving both the transposition of EU environmental legislation into national law and the actual delivery of policies (see Chapter 11). The EU is also responsible for many environmentally degrading policies. Most notably, the Common Agricultural Policy – by far the largest EU budget item – has subsidised the development of intensive farming practices that have been hugely damaging to the environment (see Chapter 7). But the most profound criticism of the EU is that its *raison d'être* – economic integration based on creating a free internal market – has stimulated and accelerated the free movement of goods, capital and people, which inflicts damage on the environment that far outweighs the benefits arising from its progressive environmental policies. This debate about the overall impact of the EU on the environment mirrors the wider free trade debate. Significantly, whereas in the past many green parties and environmentalists opposed European integration, in recent years their position has mostly shifted to one of accepting integration but working for the 'greening' of that process (Bomberg and Carter 2006).

The EU is a fascinating supranational institution that over the last thirty years or so has tried to address the complex relationship between globalisation, trade and the environment by developing a body of often ambitious and far-reaching environmental policy. Although a process of 'Europeanisation' can be clearly detected, there is little evidence that the domestic environmental policies and processes of member states have converged to produce a common European model of policy (Jordan and Liefferink 2004a); indeed, the precise impact of 'Europeanisation', as opposed to other factors, such as domestic pressure from pressure groups and public opinion, is remarkably varied (see Box 10.3). The EU policy process involves hard bargaining and plentiful compromises, so the preferences of greener pioneer nations on each particular policy initiative are rarely completely satisfied.

## 10.3 The Europeanisation of environmental policy?

The process of 'Europeanisation' refers to the impact of the EU on the domestic politics, policies and administrative structures of member states. There are several different definitions of the concept, but the most common and simplest confines itself to the top-down influence deriving from European decisions on member states.

A rigorous comparative analysis of ten countries (nine EU-15 states and Norway) using this definition found that the EU has 'affected the content of national policy much more deeply than national policy structures and policy style' (Jordan and Liefferink 2004a: 230). Significantly, every dimension of national policy has been Europeanised to some extent, even in the pioneer states, but more so where the EU promoted a preventative, source-based policy paradigm that was fundamentally at odds with

common practice (as in Ireland and the UK) or the use of explicit emission standards where few existed before (Finland, France, the UK). In short, the EU has produced a 'trading up' of environmental protection regulations across the Community rather than a 'race to the bottom'.

Yet the degree of Europeanisation should not be exaggerated. It has not changed policy structures significantly, as most large changes in the machinery of government, such as the creation of environment ministries (see Chapter 11), were introduced for domestic reasons. Nor has it altered policy styles much, and it has had only limited impact on the selection of policy instruments, such as regulations or eco-taxes, at national level (see Chapter 12). In short, there is little evidence of convergence on a single European model of environmental policy.

Drawn from Jordan and Liefferink (2004a)

However, the overall impact of legislation has been to raise environmental standards across the Community – and beyond, as firms wanting access to the European market must adopt the same standards.[4]

---

**Critical question 4**
Why is the EU so much 'greener' than NAFTA?

---

# ▶ Conclusion

Many of the debates about the international political economy are too often presented as stark dichotomies: market liberals laud globalisation and free trade as the only effective way to reduce pollution; environmentalists are unstinting in their eagerness to condemn them as devastating for the environment. This chapter has demonstrated the need for more balanced and nuanced debates. Certainly the environmental impact of globalisation and trade is neither all good nor all bad. On a positive note, globalisation and free trade provide the mechanisms to spread the ecological modernisation discourse worldwide, far beyond the narrow confines of the pioneer nations (Mol 2003). Even the much maligned – in environmentalist circles – WTO has perhaps been unfairly treated in terms of some of its judgements, whilst the quest for a European common market has seen the emergence of the EU as a progressive environmental force, both within the twenty-five member states and as an international actor. There are also undoubted negative entries on the balance sheet. To date, the environmental benefits of trade seem to have been outweighed by the sheer scale of growth in production, consumption and waste associated with the expansion of the global economy. One strength of the Brundtland Report was its assumption that globalisation was already happening, and that ecological sustainability required solutions to the economic, political and social problems thrown up by global capitalism, the inequitable international trading system and the power of TNCs. Recent trends, such as the dominance of corporate interests at the Johannesburg World Summit on Sustainable Development, the likely failure to implement an environmental agenda in the Doha trade round, and the resistance of global economic institutions to applying more than a thin coat of 'greenwash' to their activities, indicate that the sustainable development discourse is still struggling to shape the global economy.

## ▶ *Further reading and websites*

Clapp and Dauvergne (2005) and Lipschutz (2004) provide very good, contrasting introductions to global environmental politics and globalisation. Sachs (1999) provides a critical assessment of the relationship between globalisation and the environment, whilst Mol (2003) offers a more sympathetic analysis from an ecological modernisation perspective. Neumayer (2001) analyses the trade and environment relationship, and Eckersley (2004b) and Young (2005) examine the WTO. Deere and Esty (2002) present a range of readings on NAFTA. For EU environmental policy, see Lenschow (2005) for a short introduction, and Weale et al. (2000), McCormick (2001), Jordan and Liefferink (2004b) and Jordan (2005) for fuller accounts. Vig and Faure (2004) examine USA–EU links.

See the journals *Global Environmental Politics*, *Environmental Politics*, *Global Environmental Change* and *International Affairs* for developments in international environmental politics. The key institutional websites are: http://www.wto.org/ (WTO); http://www.nafta-sec-alena.org/DefaultSite/index_e.aspx?ArticleID=1 (NAFTA); http://www.europa.eu.int/pol/env/index_en.htm (EU Directorate-General for Environment); http://www.eea.eu.int/ (European Environmental Agency).

## NOTES

1 Good places to start on the massive globalisation debate are Held et al. (2005) and Scholte (2005). See Mol (2003) specifically on globalisation and the environment.
2 Broader definitions of globalisation, which are particularly common in sociology, distinguish between economic, political and cultural forms.
3 For a fuller discussion of the trade and environment relationship, see Esty (1994), Neumayer (2001) and Clapp and Dauvergne (2005: ch. 5)
4 Moreover, when the three 'green' states – Austria, Finland and Sweden – joined the EU in 1995 they negotiated a special right to maintain their existing higher environmental standards.

# Greening government

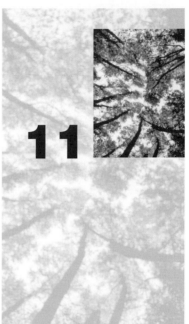

**11**

## Contents

## Key issues

- How should the principles of sustainable development change the way governments work?
- How might administrative methods improve the integration of environmental considerations throughout government?
- What is green planning?
- How democratic is environmental policymaking?
- Can institutional reforms overcome the political and economic obstacles to greener government?

> Governments' general response to the speed and scale of global changes has been a reluctance to recognise sufficiently the need to change themselves . . . Those responsible for managing natural resources and protecting the environment are institutionally separated from those responsible for managing the economy. The real world of interlocking economic and ecological systems will not change; the policies and institutions concerned must.
>
> [The Brundtland Report] (WCED 1987: 9)

In the final two chapters the focus moves down to the nation state where most environmental policy is made and implemented: Chapter 11 is concerned with the way governments build environmental considerations into the policymaking process and Chapter 12 examines the policy instruments that governments use to implement policy. An underlying theme is the emergence of 'environmental governance', in which governments increasingly work collaboratively with other actors, including business, NGOs and individual citizens, to achieve sustainable development.

Sustainable development, even in its weaker forms, has major implications for the way government works. Environmental governance means that institutions, administrative procedures and decision-making processes all need to be overhauled. Policy elites have to rethink the way they perceive the world so that environmental considerations are integrated across government and penetrate routine policymaking processes within every sector. In short, to achieve the environmental policy integration necessary for sustainable development, government must first transform itself.

**Environmental impact assessment:** A systematic non-technical evaluation, based on extensive consultation with affected interests, of the anticipated environmental impact of a proposed development such as a dam or road.

**Risk assessment:** An evaluation of the potential harm to human health and the environment from exposure to a particular hazard such as nitrates in drinking water.

This chapter assesses the shift towards greener government by examining progress towards the implementation of three core principles of sustainable development: integration, planning and democracy. The opening section distinguishes two broad mechanisms for achieving greater *integration*: first, through organisational reforms such as the creation of new environment ministries and agencies; secondly, through the use of administrative techniques, notably **environmental impact assessment**, **risk assessment** and cost–benefit analysis. The next section evaluates efforts to improve policy co-ordination through better strategic *planning* of sustainable development at European Union, national and local levels of government. To complement the discussion of democracy in terms of the independence of the sovereign state in Chapter 9, the final section analyses the role of *democracy* in environmental decision-making within the nation state by assessing the contribution of public inquiries and other democratic or participatory mechanisms to advancing sustainable development.

**11.1 Forms of integration**

Two notions of integration can be distinguished:

The *inter*sectoral approach pursues a co-ordinated and coherent strategy of environmental protection across different sectors and media. For example, a climate change strategy aimed at reducing carbon emissions must encompass different sectors (notably transport, energy and economic policy) and media (land, water, air).

The *intra*sectoral approach focuses on the integrated management of a single natural resource. For example, a sustainable water management strategy has to reconcile conflicting demands on water for drinking, irrigation, fishing, leisure uses and waste disposal.

The two forms of integration often overlap, sometimes complementing, sometimes conflicting, but each is an essential ingredient of sustainable development.

# ▶ Integration

The concept of 'environmental policy integration' (EPI) has moved increasingly centre-stage in recent years (Lenschow 2002; Lafferty and Hovden 2003; EEA 2005b). Although there is some debate about the exact meaning of the term, two broad notions of integration can be distinguished (see Box 11.1). A similar, if slightly narrower, institution-based definition distinguishes between horizontal EPI – the extent to which a central authority has developed a comprehensive cross-sectoral EPI strategy – and vertical EPI – the extent to which a government sector has adopted and implemented environmental objectives as a key feature of its portfolio (Lafferty and Hovden 2003: 12, 14). Reforms of the machinery of government, such as the creation of new organisations and committees, are primarily, but not exclusively, intended to improve inter-sectoral, or horizontal, integration, while the use of administrative techniques such as environmental impact assessment can enhance intrasectoral, or vertical, integration by encouraging policymakers in each sector to consider the environmental consequences of their actions routinely and more comprehensively.

## ▶ *Integration through organisational reform*

In many countries, initial attempts to improve horizontal integration saw the creation of a new ministry of the environment (ME). The first MEs were formed in the early 1970s in Denmark, the Netherlands, Norway, Austria and Britain, although Germany, Finland, Italy and Sweden delayed until the mid-1980s, while Iceland and Spain waited until 1990 and 1996 respectively.[1] Most OECD countries now have an ME, although not the USA. Typically, the decision to create an ME was symbolic of the traditional paradigm: a visible token of a government's concern with environmental protection, whilst neatly categorising it as a separate policy area. However, in practice, separation has usually meant marginalisation.

MEs have only partially resolved horizontal co-ordination problems. Although they bring together a range of functions that had previously been carried out by other departments and agencies, many overtly environmental competencies initially remained outside the ambit of MEs. Over time there has been greater consolidation of functions, but some fragmentation persists everywhere; for example, water management is the responsibility of other ministries in the Netherlands, Croatia and the Czech Republic (EEA 2005b: 19). The emergence of global issues such as climate change, which require greater co-ordination of strategies encompassing energy and transport policies, has increased pressure to amalgamate some economic and environmental functions. The British government, therefore, created a new 'super-department' of Environment, Transport and the Regions in 1997, but this unwieldy and internally divided ministry was broken up again in 2001 when environment was combined with the agriculture and food safety portfolios in a new Department of Environment, Food and Rural Affairs (DEFRA). One progressive initiative is in Sweden where a Ministry of Sustainable Development has been created combining energy, construction and housing with the traditional environmental responsibilities (such as nature conservation and biodiversity), and with a specific remit to co-ordinate sustainable development and climate policy across government. However, attempts to extend the jurisdiction and power of an ME frequently stumble into turf wars with established 'economic' ministries, such as transport or energy, anxious not to relinquish their functions (Jansen et al. 1998: 302).

Two broad models of environment ministry can be identified. One has an exclusively environmental remit, which produces a clear but narrow policy focus. A danger here is that the ME might be politically isolated. A small, unimportant department, often with a correspondingly weak minister, may be a lone, ineffective voice for the environment within government. The French Ministry of the Environment, for example, has a clear mission, but it possesses few independent policymaking powers and can only get things done by working with other departments. Although it bangs the drum of environmental protection loudly, the Ministry has been marginalised, frequently behaving more like 'an internal government pressure group than the central focus of a major sectoral policy domain' (Buller 1998: 77; see also Szarka 2003: 96–7). Similarly, even the more powerful German Ministry for the Environment has little or no influence over many core 'environmental issues' that fall within the competency of other ministries, such as transport and agricultural policy, and like most MEs it has a small budget (Weidner 2002b: 155). A second, generalist, ME model involves the merger of several environmental and non-environmental functions within one department. Common partners for the environment are the portfolios for housing (Finland, the Netherlands, Sweden), local government (Ireland and, until 2001, the UK), agriculture/rural affairs (Austria, UK), heritage (Australia,

Ireland) and food safety (Iceland, the UK). Even more broadly, Belgium has a Ministry for Social Affairs, Public Health and the Environment. Whilst a bigger ministry might give a minister more influence within the government, sometimes environmental issues may struggle to reach the top of the ME agenda.

The power of an ME is influenced by various factors. The political context is critical, notably the level of public concern about the environment and the salience of the issue, which will largely determine the degree of leadership interest. Critical internal factors include the size of the budget and a healthy staff complement, particularly if, as in Norway, the ME has its own field organisation of inspectors, scientists and other professionals (Jansen et al. 1998: 303). For the ME to act as an effective advocate for the environment, its staff may need to be drawn from a wide variety of backgrounds, so that hard-nosed technocrats, such as engineers, agronomists and economists, are balanced by biologists and environmental managers who by instinct and training are more likely to be 'environmentalists'.

The concentration of environmental responsibilities in a single ministry has undoubtedly given greater prominence to environmental matters within government and improved policy co-ordination. The restructuring of functional responsibilities arising from the formation of an ME may disrupt established policy networks or advocacy coalitions, perhaps bringing policy areas traditionally dominated by producer groups within the remit of an ME more willing to listen to the environmental lobby. Where MEs are relatively strong, notably in Denmark, Finland, Norway, Sweden and the Netherlands (Andersen and Liefferink 1997b: 32), they have sufficient autonomy to provide the focus for more powerful coalitions of environmental and consumer interests. Territorial wars may result from attempts by an ME, particularly as it becomes more established, to contest responsibility for a particular policy area. Thus land use and food safety issues have traditionally been the responsibility of agriculture ministries, but MEs have increasingly demanded control over these activities because they have a major impact on the environment. Yet neither the small, focused model nor the large, wide-ranging model has overcome the entrenched sectoral divisions of government. Conflict between MEs and the economic ministries remains endemic. Politically weak and often faced by an alliance of opposing ministers, the ME is frequently outgunned in interministry disputes, unless the minister is a particularly astute coalition-builder. This is a major problem because in most countries the ME has responsibility for implementing sustainable development across government.

The ME is usually the sponsor for a range of regulatory agencies responsible for the implementation of environmental legislation and policy. The administrative history of environmental regulation typically follows a similar pattern to that of the development of MEs, with an increasing concentration of responsibilities that were previously fragmented across many different departments and levels of government. The pioneering

## 11.2 The US Environmental Protection Agency

The EPA has responsibility for implementing all or part of thirteen major pieces of federal environmental legislation dealing with clean air, solid waste disposal, safe drinking water, pesticides, toxic substances and radiation. It is the federal government's largest and costliest regulatory agency, with around 18,000 employees and a budget of just over $8 billion in 2005. The EPA can boast some important achievements, notably in the areas of air quality, pesticide control and toxic waste, but it has had a troubled history and experienced a major onslaught from the Reagan administration and the Republican-controlled Congress after 1994. Major criticisms of the EPA include:

- many missed programme deadlines
- failure to achieve numerous key regulatory objectives
- spiralling costs of administration and litigation
- the lack of flexibility to set its own policy priorities
- the financial burden of regulation

Yet many of these problems arise from inadequacies in the environmental legislation that the EPA has to implement: the heavy dependency on 'command and control' regulation, unrealistic programme objectives, little cross-media pollution control and, crucially, the lack of guidance on how the EPA should allocate priorities between different pieces of legislation and the seventy congressional committees it has to serve. One independent report concluded that 'The EPA lacks focus, in part, because Congress has passed more than a dozen environmental statutes that drive the agency in a dozen directions, discouraging rational priority-setting or a coherent approach to environmental management' (quoted in Rosenbaum 2006: 173).

The pressures for change led in 1995 to the launch of a major programme to 'reinvent' the entire system of regulatory control through greater use of community-based environmental protection, collaborative decision-making, public–private partnerships, enhanced flexibility in rule-making and enforcement, and major cuts in red tape and paperwork. Yet it has had limited success. The agency remains strapped by its cumbersome organisational structure and culture, which saw its major 'media offices' refusing to surrender the powers and resources required of the various reinvention initiatives. Congress continues to lambast the EPA at every opportunity, instead of taking on the politically dangerous task of initiating a fundamental restructuring of the EPA's regulatory mission.

*Sources*: Rosenbaum (2006) and EPA website (http://www.epa.gov/).

model of a powerful cross-sectoral agency was the US Environmental Protection Agency (EPA), a federal agency formed in 1970 with legislative and judicial backing to enforce environmental laws and regulations across states and sectors (see Box 11.2). The Swedish EPA, formed in 1967, has similarly wide-ranging responsibilities and has also become an influential actor in Swedish environmental policy (Lundqvist 1998). Other countries have opted for a weaker model: in Britain the wide range of agencies dealing with air-borne, water-borne, solid and radioactive waste was gradually rationalised until a unified, but relatively weak, Environment Agency was set up in 1996 (Carter and Lowe 1995; Bell and Gray 2002).

As the principles of sustainable development have gained wider currency, many governments have launched various 'managerial' initiatives to improve policy co-ordination, including new 'in-house' cabinet committees, interdepartmental working groups and departmental 'green' ministers, as well as the formation of specialist advisory groups operating alongside the formal administrative structure. Some of the more promising reforms are to be found in those countries, such as Norway, Sweden, Canada and the UK, which have taken a 'whole of government' approach that aims to integrate the responsibility for sustainable development across the public sector (Lafferty and Meadowcroft 2000b: 350). Norway established a State Secretary Committee for Environmental Matters in 1989 to co-ordinate its sustainable development strategy. A major feature of its approach has been the development of sectoral environmental action plans by each ministry. The Swedish government used a Delegation for Ecologically Sustainable Development, consisting of cabinet ministers of environment, agriculture, taxation, schools and labour, to initiate a range of EPI strategies. Subsequently, a Co-ordination Unit for Sustainable Development, within the Ministry of Sustainable Development, was formed to co-ordinate work within the government, act as a think-tank and develop the national sustainable development strategy. In Canada, the office of Commissioner of Environment and Sustainable Development, an independent officer of Parliament, was created in 1995, with a remit that includes making an independent, public assessment of each departmental sustainable development strategy, which has to be updated every three years (Toner 2002: 88–92). The British government set up a Sustainable Development Unit within the environment ministry to promote its strategy across government, and a new parliamentary Environmental Audit Committee to evaluate government policy. In each country, the aim is to co-ordinate and institutionalise environmental considerations into the routine decision-making of every department.

However, it seems that these reforms have mostly had only a limited impact. Despite the raft of Norwegian integration initiatives, in 2005 the environment ministry still reported that 'sectoral responsibilities for environmental policy need to be further clarified and strengthened. In particular, better co-ordination is needed to deal with diffuse environmental problems and problems that need to be solved by means of close co-operation between several sectors and the other parties involved' (Ministry of the Environment 2005). Ironically, in Canada, although the office of Commissioner has been a success, its positive reputation is partly based on its scathing criticisms of the 'lack of coordination and integration' (Toner 2002: 111) across the federal government in environmental policy, as illustrated by the Commissioner's 2005 annual report, which observed that 'Canadians and parliament have no clear idea of the government's plan for sustainable development, how it will carry out that plan, and what progress it has made' (Commissioner of Environment and Sustainable Development 2005). Similarly, in the UK, the new Environmental Audit Committee has established its reputation with a series of hard-hitting, well-researched reports. Its assessment of the government's sustainable development strategy found that the Sustainable Development Unit needed more powers to enable it to shift from being merely a 'communication centre' to working for cross-departmental co-operation (Environmental Audit Committee 2003–04: paras. 6.1, 6.4). Overall, the Committee found 'little evidence of any government department embedding and mainstreaming sustainability in *all* their processes and actions, although some are doing better than others' (ibid.: para. 3.3) and 'there is a fundamental problem, from the global to the local community level, of too many plans and processes with too little coordination and linkage amongst them' (ibid.: para. 3.6). The Swedish reforms seem to have been most successful; whilst acknowledging the persistence of conflicts between sectoral and environmental strategies, Lundqvist (2004: 143–7) concludes that definite progress has been achieved.

The Agenda 21 process has also spawned numerous specialist advisory groups and round-tables that sit alongside the formal administrative structure. Unfortunately, in some countries, initiatives that emerged in the early 1990s, during the peak of public environment concern and backed by particular administrations, have (as Downs's issue attention cycle predicts – see Box 7.5) faded in importance or have even been disbanded. President Clinton created a President's Council on Sustainable Development in 1993, comprising twenty-five leaders from business, government and NGOs, with the aim of finding ways of reconciling economic and environmental objectives. However, after meeting over six years and issuing several reports, it disbanded in the face of indifference and hostility from the Republican-dominated Congress (Bryner 2000; Vig and Kraft 2006b: 375). The Ecologically Sustainable Development process in Australia set up nine working groups consisting of representatives from government, universities, industry, trade unions, environmental and consumer groups, which were each given the responsibility for producing strategic recommendations in a core policy area such as agriculture, manufacturing and transport. Although many of the recommendations in their 1991 reports were taken on board, these groups were allowed to disappear, and no effort was made to institutionalise their 'productive and promising discourse' into government (Walker 2002: 264; Howes 2005: 115–26).

Elsewhere, the reform process has put down deeper roots. Early British government initiatives setting up advisory groups and round-tables drawing on representatives from civil society, were subsumed into a new Sustainable Development Commission in 2000, an 'independent watchdog' that reports direct to the Prime Minister and whose first head was the environmental activist, Jonathan Porritt. The Finnish government set up a National Commission on Sustainable Development in 1993 whose members included the prime minister, senior ministers and representatives from local government, churches, trade unions and the media. While none of these groups has exercised great influence, they mostly persevere, drip-feeding ideas and reports into the policy process which gradually trickle down to sub-national government. Some, notably the Swedish National Committee for Agenda 21, have engaged in extensive consultation and education throughout civil society.

Although there is evidence that in some of the more enthusiastic countries, such as Sweden and Norway, these reforms have exerted a creeping impact on the way government thinks about environmental issues, overall they have brought only limited improvements in intersectoral integration of environmental policy, as departments still display only minimal engagement with the sustainable development agenda (Lafferty and Meadowcroft 2000b). Perhaps this is not surprising, as the wider history of administrative reform indicates that the perennial quest for better horizontal co-ordination in government has repeatedly encountered insurmountable barriers (Peters 1998b). Indeed, Rhodes (1997) argues that the increasing complexity of policymaking and the 'hollowing out' of the modern state now make co-ordination of all policies – not just environmental ones – even more difficult. Nevertheless, the prospects for better environmental integration have not been helped by government initiatives that frequently appear timid in design and half-hearted in execution. In particular, it seems that the rhetoric of sustainability has not yet penetrated the hearts and minds of policymakers in economic sectors where the traditional paradigm still generally holds sway.

### Critical question 1

Should the environment ministry be responsible for co-ordinating sustainable strategies across government?

## ▶ *Integration through administrative techniques*

Another means by which governments might improve integration is through the use of administrative techniques that bring environmental issues into the decision-making process in a 'rational' way, so that decisions are based on full scientific and technical knowledge, and expertise rather than short-term political motivations. The three techniques discussed in this section – environmental impact assessment (EIA), risk assessment and cost–benefit analysis (CBA) – offer the promise of bringing environmental considerations routinely into decision-making in individual policy sectors. All are used quite widely, if sporadically and inconsistently, in policy sectors where actions frequently have significant environmental implications.

*Environmental impact assessment* (EIA) is the only one of the three techniques that was designed specifically to identify potential environmental problems in order to pre-empt them. It provides a systematic process for the evaluation of the anticipated environmental impact, incorporating social, political and cultural factors, of a proposed development such as a dam, power-station or out-of-town shopping complex.[2] An environmental impact statement (EIS) is a non-technical report based on extensive consultation with a wide range of affected government agencies, professional experts, interest groups and the public. The aim of EIA is to encourage the developer, whether government department or private company, to incorporate environmental considerations into its decision-making processes. The USA led the way in the use of EIA when its National Environmental Policy Act 1969 required that an EIS accompany all major legislative proposals or federal actions that might affect the human environment. After an initial burst of some 2,000 EIA reports in 1971, the annual figure has settled down to around 500 since the mid-1980s (NEPAnet 2006). In the European Union, an EIA is required for a wide range of public and private projects. Approximately 14,000–15,000 EIAs are carried out each year within the EU, although the number in each state ranges widely from around 10 in Austria to 7000+ in France (European Commission 2002: 51).

*Risk assessment* evaluates the potential harm to human health and the environment from exposure to a particular hazard such as nitrates in drinking water, lead in the air or toxic waste on a derelict industrial site. Risk is often expressed as a dose–response assessment, which measures quantitatively the relationship between the amount of exposure to a substance and the degree of toxic effect from it, or as an overall risk characterisation, which assesses the health risk from exposure to a hazard; for example, the additional risk of developing cancer from exposure to a particular chemical over an average lifetime might be estimated at one in a million people. Risk assessment is now used extensively to evaluate environmental risk, especially in the USA where it is 'the dominant language for discussing environmental policy in the EPA' (Andrews 2006: 215).

*Cost–benefit analysis* (CBA) is a long-established economic technique that can be applied to almost any decision. The costs and benefits of an intervention, such as a plan to build a new road or regulate the use of a harmful pesticide, are weighed up to determine 'objectively' whether the proposal will increase or decrease total social welfare. To ensure that like is compared with like, CBA places a monetary value, or shadow price, on every potential cost and benefit. Historically, CBA tended to ignore or undervalue environmental costs, allowing many environmentally damaging projects to proceed. Yet many environmental economists argue that, as most decisions are made on financial grounds, an extended CBA that properly values environmental harms can be an excellent way of protecting the environment. By valuing the environment in the same 'currency' as other costs and benefits, policymakers are forced to look beyond the narrow economic benefits of a proposal to give proper consideration to its environmental impact (Pearce et al. 1989).[3] CBA is used worldwide across all areas of public policy, although it is applied to environmental regulation much more extensively in the USA than in Europe. Pearce (1998: 4–5) offers two explanations for its relative popularity in the USA. First, CBA has been regarded, especially by Republicans, as an instrument to improve the efficiency of government. Secondly, the widespread use of liability legislation and a greater proclivity to use the courts than in Europe have seen the extensive employment of CBA to determine court settlements.

To summarise, the environmental case for all three techniques is twofold: they offer a rational means of building environmental considerations, particularly those characterised by scientific uncertainty, into formal decision-making processes and, therefore, they should also encourage policymakers to anticipate and address the environmental implications of their actions more routinely. Yet the techniques generate widespread criticism, particularly from environmentalists; indeed, many experts suggest that these techniques may *harm* environmental interests rather than advance them. The debate about their strengths and weaknesses focuses on five key themes.

First, each technique claims to be a rational tool of analysis, yet none is an exact science. Risk assessment, for example, is usually empirically based on either animal studies or epidemiology, but often neither is reliable or accurate enough to support conclusive risk assessments (Wildavsky 1995; Armour 1997). The scientific claims of risk assessment are based on a supposedly rigorous methodology that, in practice, usually relies on 'a multitude of assumptions and subjective judgements as much as it depends upon empirical observation or testing' (Rosenbaum 1997: 42). Consequently, many risk estimates are very tentative, making them vulnerable to challenge from further scientific research, which can have embarrassing and expensive consequences for policymakers. Thus, in 1974, when studies revealed that dioxins contained in waste oil sprayed on roads in Times Beach, Missouri, might be highly carcinogenic and have contributed to ill-health in children and horses, government officials ordered all residents to evacuate the city at a cost of $139 million. A few years later the senior official responsible testified that subsequent studies suggested that the evacuation, although based on the best available scientific evidence, had been unnecessary (Rosenbaum 1997: 43). When the science underpinning risk assessment is rapidly advancing into new territory, as is currently the case with GMOs, definitive risk assessment is almost impossible. The bottom line for risk assessment, as the respected Royal Commission on Environmental Pollution (1998) in Britain put it, is that 'No satisfactory way has been devised of measuring risk to the natural environment, even in principle, let alone defining what scale of risk should be regarded as tolerable' (para. 9.49).

Similarly, a serious methodological problem with CBA is the difficulty of putting a price on environmental harms, such as the loss of scarce habitats or damage from acid rain. Techniques do exist that attempt to overcome this problem, such as contingent valuation, which asks people how much they would pay to protect a threatened habitat (Pearce et al. 1989: 69–71). There are also several techniques for calculating the value of human life. However, they cannot disguise the imprecision and subjectivity that lie at the heart of CBA (ironically, many policymakers like the way CBA produces a single, definitive figure for each proposal that allows them to announce a decision apparently based on incontrovertible objective criteria). Conversely, whilst an EIA can also be undermined by unreliable or incomplete data, it is the qualitative methodology and the openness of its conclusions that may reduce its authority. The terms of reference for an individual EIA may also produce biased outcomes, particularly where, as in Australia, it is the responsibility of the private developer, rather than an independent body, to carry out the EIA. Overall, although promulgated as objective tools of rational analysis, each of the three techniques contains fundamental conceptual and technical weaknesses that render it vulnerable to charges of bias, unreliability and imprecision.

Secondly, these methodological weaknesses contribute to the uneasy interface between science and politics that characterises many environmental problems. Even risk assessment practitioners are unable to reach a consensus about what constitutes an 'acceptable' level of risk; instead, they hand the problem over to the policymaker, who may be guided by public opinion when deciding how to manage a particular risk. Yet public perceptions of risk are socially constructed and depend on a wide range of factors, including the position of an individual in society, and whether the possible consequences of an action are delayed or immediate (Adams 1995; Liberatore 1995). Thus 'NIMBYism' is often fuelled by a gross exaggeration of the real risk to health from a proposed development such as an incinerator or landfill site, but fierce public opposition may persuade the politician to override a scientific risk assessment that judges the proposal to be safe. By contrast, people are more tolerant of risks they bear voluntarily, such as smoking, or where, as with car ownership, halting an activity might have high personal costs.

From an ecocentric standpoint, CBA is morally unacceptable because it places a monetary value on wildlife or wilderness. It might be countered that the practice of valuing human life is common in healthcare provision, where the allocation of scarce resources involves similar difficult trade-offs between priorities, so why not extend it to nature? A more persuasive objection to CBA is that, while monetary valuation may be meaningful for some small-scale incidences of localised air or noise pollution, many important environmental goods are simply not commensurable in this way (Jacobs 1991). How can a value be placed on an endangered species, irreplaceable rainforest or an undamaged ozone layer? A CBA may provide useful information for policymakers but, like risk assessment, its claims to objectivity often leave them no better equipped to arbitrate between different interests. Ultimately, this apparent weakness may be no bad thing, for political decisions cannot – and should not – be reduced to a mathematical exercise: 'such choices must be a matter of judgement, not computation' (ibid.: 219). In this respect, whereas CBA reduces the flexibility for political judgement by providing a cut-and-dried calculation about whether the benefits of a proposal exceed the costs (Pearce 1998), an advantage of EIA is that underpinning its longer checklist of potential impacts and lack of a definitive conclusion is the recognition that broader social, cultural and political considerations must be taken into account.

Thirdly, once in the political arena, all three techniques are open to contestation and manipulation. The uncertainties inherent in risk assessment make it a weapon to be used in the conflicts between regulators and regulated, or the developers and the public (Armour 1997). Some of the methodologies commonly used in risk assessment, such as 'worst case scenarios' and the inclusion of an 'extra margin of safety', are often accused of overestimating risk (Armour 1997; Rosenbaum 1997; Andrews 2006). While neoliberal critics believe that this conservative bias may unnecessarily alarm the public and encourage the government to regulate more than is necessary, environmentalists applaud the 'better to be safe than sorry' approach to human and environmental safety, which chimes well with the precautionary principle. In practice, a risk assessment is open to wide and contrasting interpretations. Why a particular insecticide is legal in one country, but not in another – despite similar risk assessments – can be largely explained by the different advocacy coalitions, drawn from industrial, farming, consumer and environmental interests, lined up for and against a ban in each country.

These administrative techniques are also open to manipulation. Policymakers may use them to justify decisions they have already taken. Or, faced by public opposition to a controversial project such as a new incinerator, civil servants might employ an EIA not because it makes the decision more rational but because 'it enhances the *appearance* of rationality and thus serves to undermine environmental opposition to development projects' (Amy 1990: 63). Not surprisingly, opinion is therefore divided about the impact of EIAs on specific agency decisions. In the USA, few projects are stopped directly as a result of an EIA; rather EIAs 'are more likely to compel incremental, though sometimes environmentally valuable, modifications in major federal programs' (Rosenbaum 2005b: 201). Similarly, in the EU very few projects are discarded as a result of an EIA. In Sweden, major infrastructure developments during the 1990s, notably the ring-road round Stockholm and the Öresund bridge linking Sweden and Denmark, were approved after an EIA had produced no conclusive evidence regarding their environmental acceptability. In short, they proceeded because powerful economic interests supported them (Lundqvist 1998: 246–7). None the less, as one Danish study reveals, EIAs often result in limited modifications to the design, and in a minority of cases major changes are required (Christensen et al. 2003).

CBA is also vulnerable to political manipulation, notably to 'institutional capture' by government and public agencies. In particular, it is relatively easy to use the discount rate, which calculates future costs and benefits, to justify decisions made on other (political) grounds. By choosing a low discount rate, public agencies have been able to justify many projects, notably dam and irrigation works in the USA, in the face of strong environmental objections (Amy 1990; Hanley and Spash 1993: 161). Indeed, owing to its

focus on monetary cost, CBA has found support amongst right-wing opponents of 'excessive' environmental regulation who believe that the wider use
of CBA would reduce the regulatory burden on industry and help inculcate
bureaucrats with a greater sensitivity to costs. Both the Reagan administration in the early 1980s and the Republican Congress in 1995 extended the
range of issues for which federal agencies were required to use CBA before
introducing any significant new regulation (Rosenbaum 1997: 36–7). In the
UK, the Conservative government ensured that legislation setting up a new
Environment Agency required it to carry out CBA before making any significant intervention, a requirement that environmentalists claimed would
undermine its capacity to protect the environment (Carter and Lowe 1995:
55). With such friends, it is not surprising that many environmentalists are
suspicious of CBA.

Fourthly, there is a strong anti-democratic element inherent in all three
techniques because their administrative rationalism legitimates 'government by the experts' and denies citizens the opportunity to voice their views
(Dryzek 2005: ch. 4). By allocating a primary role to professional experts
such as economists, scientists or lawyers, these techniques privilege certain
elite stakeholders, particularly when the detailed analysis is not made public. CBA limits conflict about a decision to those parties with something at
stake for which they are willing to pay, and who know about or are immediately affected by the conflict. Indeed, CBA can be a way of preventing a
conflict from breaking into the public realm, where it might come to the
attention of democratic institutions such as legislatures, political parties,
courts and the press (Sagoff 1988: 96–7). Proponents of CBA defend it as
democratic on the economic argument that its values are those of the public expressed through their private choices in the market-place (Amy 1990:
68), but Sagoff (1988) argues persuasively that our choices as consumers may
be quite different from our choices as citizens. As consumers we may prefer the convenience of plastic disposable bottles, but as citizens we might
vote to ban them as ecologically damaging. From the point of view of sustainable development, it might be better if policymakers put their trust
in the citizen's long-term concern to protect the environment rather than
the consumer's short-term individual preference. By contrast, EIA has more
democratic potential because it involves a formal, public process of consultation with a wide range of stakeholders including public agencies, private
organisations and groups representing environmental, consumer and citizen interests. EIA provides an opportunity for environmental and citizen
groups to engage in the decision process by giving them access to information, the right to comment on draft reports and to apply for judicial review
of the EIA preparation. In Australia, governments have used EIA as a means
of gauging public opinion on a project but also as a means of deferring
difficult decisions (Papadakis 1993: 112).

Finally, these techniques, if insensitively applied, ignore distributional
and equity considerations. Risk assessment often glosses over any unequal

distribution of risk among different groups, yet this begs some important political questions, such as whether a risk that is concentrated on certain groups is more or less acceptable than one that is evenly distributed. There are also wider environmental justice issues concerning the extent to which socially and economically disadvantaged groups are exposed to higher levels of risk. Certainly, in the USA, heavily polluting factories, incinerators and waste disposal units appear disproportionately located in neighbourhoods populated by minority ethnic groups (Bullard 2000). Similarly, few CBAs identify variations in the incidence of costs and benefits on different groups (Pearce 1998). EIA, in theory, is more likely to pick up these distributional issues, provided the terms of reference are drawn sufficiently widely to cover the full range of distributional impacts.

To assess whether these administrative techniques improve integration, we can return to the twofold case that they bring a more rational approach to environmental decision-making and, in so doing, encourage policymakers to consider environmental factors more routinely. Clearly, in most countries, techniques such as EIA are not yet a routine part of government decision-making; few bureaucrats automatically consider environmental factors in the way that they automatically check the financial cost of new proposals. Indeed, the three techniques are still treated with ambivalence or hostility by many environmentalists: they promise a more systematic and rigorous treatment of environmental factors, but they are frequently used (or misused) to the detriment of the environment. Yet they are only administrative *tools* providing information to improve the policymaking process. Once certain methodological improvements are made these techniques are not necessarily inherently biased against the environment. Instead, it is the way that powerful actors, particularly government agencies representing economic interests, use and manipulate these tools to serve their own political ends that can unfairly prejudice environmental interests. Despite their flaws, these techniques, particularly EIA, can help introduce environmental considerations into the bureaucratic mindset and contribute to social learning by policy elites (Bartlett 2005: 54–6). Some positive environmental outcomes will probably rub off on agency policies simply as a result of their engagement in the preparation of EIAs, as several American studies confirm. There may be a creative tension between EIA specialists and other bureaucrats that contributes to greater environmental awareness among all staff. Policymakers and developers may learn to anticipate certain environmental objections and pre-empt a critical EIA by amending proposals accordingly (Rosenbaum 1995: 212–15). At the very least, the techniques force policymakers to think about the environment – even if they are only looking for ways to defeat environmentalist objections to a project.

One wider problem is that all three techniques still tend to be used within the traditional paradigm in that they are applied to specific decisions rather than the underlying policy. Thus, although several of the individual road schemes that provoked anti-road protests in Britain during the 1990s were the subject of an EIA, the environmental impact of the Conservative government's underlying massive road-building programme was never assessed. There is evidence of a gradual shift from this 'tactical' EIA focus on individual projects towards strategic environmental assessment. A new EU directive on Strategic Environmental Assessment came into force in 2004, extending environmental assessment to plans, programmes and overall policies, which the European Commission believes is a vital step towards the full integration of sustainable development across core economic sectors.[4] One of the most innovative examples of this strategic shift is the New Zealand Resource Management Act 1991, which made it mandatory for all regional policies, regional and district plans, and resource consent applications to be accompanied by an EIA, and for the authorities to monitor the impact of their activities on the environment (Bartlett 1997). This kind of strategic framework is most likely to emerge where a national government is taking sustainable development planning seriously.

### Critical question 2
Are risk assessment, EIA and CBA friends or foes of the environment?

## ▶ Planning

Sustainable development needs to be planned at several levels of government. Traditionally, central government has usually taken responsibility for controversial or dangerous issues such as nuclear power, hazardous waste or air pollution, leaving sub-national government to deal with other environmental matters, including land use planning, where flexibility and local knowledge may produce better policy. In federal systems, such as in Germany, Australia and the USA, the states have retained extensive environmental competencies. In recent years, twin-pronged pressures have shifted the locus of policymaking towards central government. From the supranational level, national governments have encountered increasing pressure to introduce new legislation and policy in order to fulfil international treaty commitments such as carbon emission reductions or, in the EU, to implement environmental directives. Conversely, from within the nation state, the worsening condition of the environment and its growing political salience have encouraged most national governments to rein in responsibilities that traditionally resided at the sub-national level (although the decentralised Danish system is an exception). Nevertheless, the achievement of sustainable development will still require a multilevel approach, preferably based on the principle of subsidiarity, so that responsibilities lie at the lowest appropriate level of government. Thus, to return to the centralisation–decentralisation dilemma discussed in Chapter 3, subsidiarity contains a primary principle of administrative effectiveness underpinned by a secondary principle of decentralisation. With this multilevel approach in mind, this section examines efforts to improve planning at three levels of government: supranational, national and local.

## ▶ EU Environmental Action Plans

The environmental programmes of the EU are a unique attempt to co-ordinate and integrate environmental policy across national boundaries.[5] The first Environmental Action Plan (EAP) was launched in 1973 when the European Community began approving environmental regulations aimed at ensuring that common standards existed across member states (see Chapter 10). Although the first EAP established several important and progressive principles, notably the need for preventive action, in practice the first three EAPs pursued a regulatory, end-of-pipe approach that lay firmly within the traditional paradigm. After an integration clause was included in the 1987 Single European Act (see Box 10.2), the fourth EAP (1987–92) identified an ambitious nineteen priority areas and took tentative steps towards integrating environmental considerations into other EU policies.

The fifth EAP (1992–2000), significantly titled *Towards Sustainability* (European Commission 1992) and suffused with the language of ecological modernisation, outlined a bold strategy to improve integration focused on five key sectors – tourism, industry, energy, transport and agriculture – using a wide range of policy initiatives and instruments, including sustainable tourism, industrial eco-audits and eco-labels, energy conservation schemes, carbon taxes and set-aside schemes protecting environmentally sensitive areas (Liberatore 1997; Wilkinson 1997). Although several of these initiatives were implemented, an official evaluation of the fifth EAP acknowledged that 'practical progress towards sustainable development has been rather limited' (European Communities 2000: 9). It proved especially difficult to persuade other Directorates-General (ministries) inside the Commission to place environmental issues above their own sectoral priorities, so there was little progress towards intersectoral integration, apart from in the industry sector. It seems that the EU mirrors many national governments in struggling to achieve the kind of deep-seated social learning by policy elites that might usher in greater integration of environmental considerations. Furthermore, the evaluation report bemoaned the absence of 'clear recognition of commitment from member states and stakeholders' (ibid.: 9); for example, their failure to agree a fundamental reform of the Common Agricultural Policy far outweighed any marginal benefits from set-aside schemes. An effort to kick-start the integration process at the Cardiff Summit of EU leaders in June 1998 by generating stronger political commitment and identifying key strategies and tools needed to bring it to fruition had some positive effect, albeit uneven across sectors (Baker 2006: 149), although 'the commitment of the EU's political leadership to environmental integration remains volatile, especially during difficult economic times' (Lenschow 2005: 321).

The aim of the sixth EAP, *Environment 2010: Our Future, Our Choice* (2001–10), is to correct some of the failings of its predecessor. It has four priorities – climate change; protecting nature and biodiversity; environment and health; resource and waste management – and five thematic strategies, including environmental policy integration and more effective implementation of existing policies. Significantly, the EU launched a separate sustainable development strategy document, *A Sustainable Europe for a Better World*, prepared for the Johannesburg World Summit on Sustainable Development, which set out a three-pronged approach based on pursuing economic growth, social inclusion and environmental protection hand-in-hand. A brief interim review in 2005 observed that despite some progress having been made, much remained to be done; in particular, it called for 'clearer objectives, targets and related deadlines' to give focus and allow accurate monitoring of progress (European Commission 2005: 51) – a demand constantly repeated for national and local level plans. Subsequently, a renewed strategy document was published in June 2006 with four objectives: environmental protection; social equity and cohesion; economic prosperity; and meeting the EU's international responsibilities (Council of the EU 2006: 3–4).

Currently, there is little to suggest that the sixth EAP will succeed where its predecessor failed, or that the ploy of producing a separate sustainable development strategy will reap markedly better rewards. The ambitions are worthy, limited improvements – both in the nature of policymaking and in policy content – can and will be identified, but well over a decade of EU plans based explicitly on sustainable development principles have failed to break down the deeply entrenched sectoral divisions. One problem is the lack of member state commitment, but that is hardly surprising given its absence from the domestic planning process too.

## ▶ National green plans

Since the late 1980s, most OECD countries, including nineteen of the EU25 states (EEA 2005b: 15), have published national sustainable development strategies, or 'green plans', setting out long-term goals, policies and targets, which are also intended to improve both horizontal and vertical integration (Jänicke and Jörgens 1998; Lafferty and Meadowcroft 2000a). The most comprehensive initiatives have come from countries such as Norway, Sweden and the Netherlands where the assumption that there must be a trade-off between environmental and economic goals had been challenged long before the Agenda 21 process pushed the idea of green plans onto the international stage (see Andersen and Liefferink 1997a). Australia was also briefly ahead of the pack with its 'ecologically sustainable development' process in 1990 to produce its National Strategy document. However, many documents were produced simply to satisfy the Agenda 21 requirement that all governments produce a national plan and made few commitments regarding implementation. In the USA and Canada, Agenda 21 has virtually no domestic political salience (Lafferty and Meadowcroft 2000a), whilst the German document was not translated into German or even published there (Beuermann and Burdick 1997: 90). These plans are a step towards a more strategic and comprehensive approach to environmental policy, but one comparative study of sixteen green plans concluded that they are little more than 'pilot strategies . . . a first step towards intersectoral communication' (Jänicke and Jörgens 1998: 47). The goals are generally inadequate, there are few new policy initiatives, the commitments are vague and only a handful of (mostly qualitative) targets are identified. The timidity of these plans usually reflects the compromises that governments have to make with powerful economic sectors and producer interests. Another comparative study, whilst acknowledging the limitations and instability of many of these plans, does identify two positive trends. First, there is a tendency for goals, especially in Sweden, Britain and Canada, to become more carefully defined over time, with measurable targets to judge success. Indeed, several countries, such as Sweden and Britain (DEFRA 2005a), have subsequently produced new or significantly updated strategy documents. Secondly, there is a strengthening of collaborative and participatory dimensions within the strategic planning process in several countries, notably the Netherlands, as governments recognise the need to consult more widely to find and legitimate solutions to complex environmental challenges (Lafferty and Meadowcroft 2000b: 356–72).

The pioneering model of a green plan is the Dutch National Environmental Policy Plan (NEPP), a wide-ranging and ambitious strategy that, from its launch in 1989, was widely praised as a genuine 'success' (Weale 1992; Jänicke and Jörgens 1998). The aim of NEPP was to improve both intersectoral co-ordination of policy and intrasectoral integration of environmental considerations into the day-to-day policy processes in core ministries such as transport, energy and agriculture. NEPP explicitly rejected the reorganisation of the *structure* of government in favour of an approach based on inventing *processes* of policy planning that establish co-ordination and integration (Weale 1992: 148). At its core was a set of 50 strategic objectives, with over 200 specific quantitative targets to be achieved by various dates up to 2010. The objective of reducing acidification, for example, was accompanied by costed targets setting out percentage reductions in the level of emissions of critical chemicals such as $SO_2$ and $N_2O$, which in turn were broken down into individual targets for different activities such as traffic, energy supply, industry and households (Weale 1992: 125–6). This process of target-setting was repeated for other environmental problems including climate change, eutrophication and waste disposal. Having been agreed by the four key ministries of environment, economics (industry), transport and agriculture, NEPP provided the environment ministry with the tools to co-ordinate a national environmental strategy – NEPP acquired a legal basis in 1993 – and significant political clout to enforce it. The co-operative process of agreeing and implementing the plan also helped to integrate environmental considerations more effectively across a full range of public policies, and provided a framework for 'social learning' so that policymakers in all sectors 'think environment' routinely (Weale 1992). The 'target group policy' of structured consultation and negotiation of targets in the form of voluntary agreements (covenants) between government representatives and key industrial interest groups aided implementation by encouraging target groups to accept more responsibility for environmental protection by developing a sense of ownership of the targets, whilst allowing them the flexibility to achieve them in their own way.

One study showed that around half the targets set for 1995 were met and that even where targets were not attained nearly every trend showed an improvement on the pre-NEPP period (Jänicke and Jörgens 1998: 45–6). Hanf and van de Gronden (1998) reported that cuts in key pollutants such as $SO_2$, $N_2O$ and phosphate had 'achieved a marked reduction of pressures on and threats to the environment' (p. 178).

No single factor explains the relative success of NEPP, but it benefited from a fortunate congruence of two phenomena: one, the consensual style of Dutch politics which places a high premium on avoiding conflict and seeking negotiated solutions; two, the redefinition of environmental problems, encouraged by the discourse of ecological modernisation, as requiring the participation of economic actors who were once seen as the cause of environmental problems, but are now regarded as an essential part of their solution (ibid.: 153). This situation persisted through the 1990s, partly because successive Dutch governments provided sustained political support for NEPP (backed by sympathetic public opinion), but also because fundamental clashes between economic and environmental interests were largely avoided. One concern is that industry may have reached the limits of its willingness to act voluntarily out of self-interest, particularly with regard to the fundamental changes required to meet climate change targets. With declining public enthusiasm for environmental issues, the government has increasingly struggled to follow through on the challenge of implementing the ambitious NEPP goals (van Muijen 2000: 172). Indeed, the fourth NEPP, published in 2001, may be the last. In a speech announcing that NEPP would be replaced by the 'Future Environment Agenda', the environment minister identified a number of problems hampering progress towards sustainable development, including a lack of public support and problems with the Dutch economy. The minister also said (in an implicit criticism of NEPP) that while many of the easier environmental problems had been addressed successfully, the Dutch environmental record was 'only average', with little progress in dealing with the intractable 'wicked problems' such as climate change (Dekker 2005). Nevertheless, the NEPP remains a powerful model for the design of green plans elsewhere.

## 11.3 Local Agenda 21 in Sweden: a qualified success?

By 1996 all 288 Swedish municipalities had reported to UNGASS that they had launched a LA21 process and 70 per cent had adopted an action plan. Key features:

* Most had given responsibility for co-ordination of LA21 to the overall council rather than the environment department, i.e. LA21 was not regarded as just about the environment.
* In 2001 65 per cent had a full or part-time Agenda 21 co-ordinator, which decreased to 52 per cent in 2004.
* Initially, there was central government funding for LA21 activities, but over time central funding has been reallocated to a massive local investment programme for ecological sustainability that has partly taken over the role of LA21, although activities now have a more technical focus.

* Public awareness of LA21 is widespread, but public participation is rather low and decreasing over time.
* Activities range from waste and water management and 'green purchasing' to renewable energy, biodiversity and auditing systems. More recently, public health and consumer issues have been included.
* A core group of 40–60 'pioneer' authorities has implemented quite radical changes to infrastructure, resource use and individual lifestyles; elsewhere the impact is limited, and there is widespread evidence of waning interest.

Based on Rowe and Fudge (2003) and Dahlgren and Eckerberg (2005).

## ▶ *Local Agenda 21*

There is enormous potential for planning and integration at the local level, where there are many examples of individual municipalities implementing innovative sustainability programmes. An important catalyst was the Local Agenda 21 (LA21) process, which gained a firm footing in several countries. Chapter 28 of Agenda 21 (see Box 8.2) focuses on the local authority role in implementing sustainable development because it is the level of government closest to the people. LA21 does not provide a single blueprint to follow, but it makes two important recommendations: first, that the local authority will take a leading role in planning and facilitating change; secondly, that sustainable development requires ongoing consultation and partnership with a wide range of actors in the local community. All local governments were asked to engage in a process of consultation and consensus-building with their citizens, local organisations and businesses to produce an LA21 action plan for sustainable development. A 2002 survey found that over 6,400 municipalities had got involved in LA21 in 113 countries, of which over 80 per cent were in Europe (Baker 2006: 112; ICLEI 2006).

Although there are huge variations in the take-up of LA21 both between and within countries, overall progress seems rather limited (Lafferty 2001). Nevertheless, there are some exceptions, particularly in Britain and Sweden (see Box 11.3). The reasons for the relative success of LA21 in these two countries seem, in some respects, to be quite different. In Britain, where the Thatcher era had seen a significant reduction in the autonomy, functions and power of local government, LA21 was regarded as an opportunity to carve out a new role for local authorities, building on their traditional responsibilities for implementing environmental regulations. Local governments were especially attracted by the potential of LA21 to restore their legitimacy by improving public participation and contributing to local economic development (Mason 1999: ch. 6). In short, LA21 took off despite a lack of support from central government. By contrast, the baseline for many Swedish local authorities was that they already possessed sufficient autonomy and powers to develop innovative and far-reaching programmes for sustainable development, including the use of various eco-taxes (Eckerberg and Brundin 1999). Moreover, the Swedish national government provided much more support for LA21 in terms of publicity and support networks and by allocating financial resources specifically for LA21 projects. One critical factor common to both countries is the presence of individual politicians and bureaucrats, or 'firebrands' (ibid.), dedicated to bringing sustainability onto the local political agenda. In recent years interest in LA21 seems to have ebbed in both Sweden (Rowe and Fudge 2003) and the UK, where central government has encouraged a shift in emphasis onto the development of sustainable communities and regeneration (Bulkeley and Betsill 2005: 44). By contrast, there is evidence that after a slow start, LA21 has started to take off in Germany (Kern et al. 2007) and Italy (Sancassiani 2005).

Overall, the plethora of green plans emerging at all levels of government reflects the widespread recognition of the need for a more integrated, strategic approach to sustainable development. Most green plans have proved unimpressive in design and execution; in particular, despite tentative efforts to plan better integration, governments everywhere have found it difficult to generate sectoral environmental responsibility in core polluting sectors such as transport, energy and agriculture. Nevertheless, lesson-drawing from those green national plans, such as the NEPP, that have had some success, has identified some key characteristics of 'successful' plans (see also Jänicke and Jörgens 1998: 48–9). In particular, as in the NEPP sectoral target system it is important to have effective monitoring and measurement systems in place; otherwise it is difficult to include meaningful targets in plans or to evaluate progress in achieving sustainable development. To this end, many international organisations and national governments have tried to develop robust and comprehensive sustainability indicators (Bell and Morse 1999; OECD 2003). The British government, for example, has published a (revised) set of twenty 'headline indicators' backed up by a further forty-eight core indicators to provide a select, but manageable toolkit to record progress in achieving the targets set out in the national sustainable development strategy (DEFRA 2005b) (see Box 11.4). Ultimately, the most important lesson is that effective planning requires strong, sustained political leadership that can be institutionalised across policy sectors through legislation, institutional reform, target-setting and monitoring of progress. One way of

| 11.4 Headline indicators of sustainable development in the UK | |
|---|---|
| 1. Greenhouse gas emissions | 12. Workless households |
| 2. Resource use | 13. Childhood poverty |
| 3. Waste | 14. Pensioner poverty |
| 4. Bird population | 15. Education |
| 5. Fish stocks | 16. Health inequality |
| 6. Ecological impacts of air pollution | 17. Mobility |
| 7. River quality | 18. Social justice |
| 8. Economic output | 19. Environmental equality |
| 9. Active community | 20. Well-being |
| 10. Crime | |
| 11. Employment | *Source:* DEFRA (2005b: 12). |

stimulating and sustaining this political momentum might be to extend the use of participatory mechanisms in the policy process at every level of government.

### Critical question 3
Can the Dutch NEPP model be transferred elsewhere?

## ▶ Democracy and participation

The central argument for extending democracy and participation in decision-making, echoing the green case for democracy discussed in Chapter 3, is that ordinary citizens must play a key role in the achievement of sustainable development. As the Brundtland Report put it: 'The law alone cannot enforce the common interest. It principally needs community knowledge and support, which entails greater public participation in the decisions that affect the environment' (WCED 1987: 63). A complementary argument holds that greater democracy will improve the quality of decision-making about complex environmental matters because by listening to a full range of voices, including environmental, consumer and citizen viewpoints, the government is more likely to anticipate problems and build environmental considerations into policy. This section briefly assesses the role of democracy in environmental decision-making.

Most liberal democracies have long recognised that where major environmental decisions mobilise deeply held competing interests, then democratic mechanisms may be the best form of conflict resolution. The public inquiry is often used when controversial projects provoke conflict. In Britain, for example, there have been several large public inquiries into proposed nuclear installations (notably the THORP reprocessing plant at Windscale (now Sellafield) and a pressurised water reactor at Sizewell B, Suffolk), airport developments (including a third London airport and new terminals at Heathrow and Manchester airports) and numerous major road schemes. Public inquiries into major wilderness developments have been commonplace in Australia, such as proposed uranium mining in the Kakadu National Park, and in Canada, notably the Berger inquiry into an oil and gas pipeline from the Arctic and an inquiry into proposed logging in Clayaquot Sound (Torgerson 2003).

A public inquiry is chaired by an individual who will receive numerous depositions and listen to many witnesses representing a wide range of interests before producing an assessment based on that evidence. The inquiry report is then considered by the relevant government authority when deciding on the proposal. In theory, this participatory process allows all information to be gathered and every interest to have its say, before a 'rational' planning decision is made. However, although public inquiries may appear to provide an open, pluralistic forum where all views can be expressed, much depends on the terms of reference given to the inquiry, the independence of the presiding 'judge' and the resources available to the various interests giving evidence.[6] These variables are often biased in favour of the developers; most obviously, a well-researched case will require a huge financial outlay for research, expert witnesses and legal fees. Large corporations can usually mobilise far greater resources – the UK Central Electricity Generating Board spent £20 million on the Sizewell B inquiry (O'Riordan et al. 1988) – than are available to environmental groups. The formal proceedings, dominated by legalistic jargon and techniques of cross-examination, intimidate community groups and individuals and so impede genuine public participation (Rydin 1998: 258–9). One comparative study of public inquiry processes concluded that everywhere the public holds an ambiguous attitude towards them: while people strongly demand participation, there is a widespread perception that inquiries are no more than a 'mock consultation' intended to give legitimacy to decisions that have effectively already been made (Mason 1999: 78).

Nevertheless, even when a government uses a public inquiry to legitimise a decision it wants to make, or when developers lavish vast resources in presenting their side of the argument, the openness of the forum can still provide a window of opportunity to be exploited by environmentalists (Kingdon 1995; Torgerson 2003). At the very least, opponents can gain publicity, and even win modifications to the project. Sometimes proposals are abandoned, as was a plan to sand-mine on Fraser Island on the Australian barrier reef. The British campaigner, John Tyme, by astute political tactics and clever use of the mass media, was able to cause such disruption to a series of inquiries into individual road schemes during the 1970s that the government was forced to reappraise its entire road-building programme (Tyme 1978; Dudley and Richardson 1996: 74–5). Other democratic mechanisms can also act as 'focusing events' (Kingdon 1995) around which environmental groups can mobilise and which they can use to push new issues onto public agendas. Referenda, for example, which are frequently used for specific decisions in Switzerland and California, and for local planning decisions in many countries, allow groups to campaign and may raise public awareness about environmental issues. Indeed, one outcome of the 1980 Swedish referendum on its nuclear power programme was that activists involved in the 'No' campaign went on to form the Green Party.

One drawback of big public inquiries and referenda, as with EIA, is that they are unique events that are designed to resolve a particular conflict; they do not turn participation in decision-making into a regular routine. Even where, as in Britain, the public inquiry is widely used within the land use planning process, each decision is unique and discrete. Alternative dispute resolution, increasingly employed in the USA, takes a step further by drawing a range of affected interests into a mediation process. Again, this practice usually addresses a specific environmental issue, but by absorbing political conflict into the administrative process it allows the possibility for mutual learning and compromise solutions that result in neither complete victory nor defeat for either 'side' of a dispute (Lee 1993; O'Leary et al. 2004; Dryzek 2005: 103).

The sustainable development discourse envisages this kind of learning through deliberation and dialogue becoming an ongoing, routine part of the administrative process, 'by promoting citizens' initiatives, empowering people's organisations and strengthening local democracy' (WCED 1987: 63). Thus many of the round-table and advisory initiatives associated with Agenda 21 were designed to encourage such dialogue by providing a forum in which representatives from a wide range of interest groups discuss environmental problems and make recommendations for action (see above, pp. 298–9).

More radically, there is growing interest in a range of innovative techniques, including citizen juries, consensus conferences and deliberative opinion polls, which enhance citizen deliberations within the policy process based on principles of green democracy (Ward 1999; Smith 2003: 86–93; Ward et al. 2003; Meadowcroft 2004; Niemeyer 2004). These particular techniques share several features: citizens are brought together over three to four days; participants are given extensive information; they hear the opinions of experts and concerned interests; and independent facilitators ensure the fairness of the proceedings. They differ on the number of participants, ranging from several hundred for a deliberative poll to just twelve to twenty-five for the other techniques. Whilst all three techniques use forms of random sampling to select participants, the small size of citizen juries means that the sample is stratified, and applicants for a consensus conference are selected on socio-economic criteria. Finally, whilst citizen juries and consensus conferences make a collective decision, the individual decisions of citizens are recorded in a deliberative poll (Smith 2003: 86–7). Although still quite rare, there is growing evidence of the transformative power of these various citizen forums, with participants becoming much better informed and often changing their judgements and preferences. For example, deliberative polls run by Texas public utilities asked citizens to choose between four resource planning options: renewable energy; fossil fuel plants; investment in energy conservation; or importing energy from elsewhere. Before deliberation, citizens wanted renewable energy; afterwards, while still keen on it, they swung strongly behind energy conservation as the most cost-effective solution (ibid.: 88; Fishkin 1997: 200–3). Both citizen juries (used in several countries, especially Germany where they are called planning cells) and consensus conferences (common in Denmark) produce recommendations that take environmental concerns far more seriously than existing policy, whilst demonstrating that citizens are capable of deliberating about complex issues. All three techniques are open to criticism; for example, over whether they should be representative, or whether they are open to manipulation, or whether they suppress conflict (Smith 2003: 90–3; Meadowcroft 2004). Nor should they replace existing democratic mechanisms. But they do offer a very promising complement to representative structures by obtaining citizen opinions about tricky environmental issues and providing useful recommendations that can be fed into the policy process (Smith 2003: 93).

However, it is important to recall that democratic mechanisms do not guarantee environmentally benevolent outcomes (see Chapter 3). They may open up policymaking but pluralistic processes are frequently hijacked by powerful actors, especially as producer interests can exercise first-dimensional power by mobilising greater resources in their cause. Alternatively, radical voices may be co-opted into the policy process and tamed. Even if the 'democratic will' (whatever that may be) does prevail over power politics, it may not represent a victory for sustainable development. As the example of UK wind energy illustrates, local planning decisions may produce conflict between the democratically expressed preferences of a local community and the sustainable development strategy of the elected national government (see Box 11.5). More broadly, as the next chapter shows, elected governments frequently desist from implementing radical environmental initiatives such as regulating car use or imposing eco-taxes for fear of upsetting the will of the majority at the next election.

Such dilemmas are in the nature of democracy, and they underpin a difference in emphasis between sustainable development and ecological modernisation. Sustainable development acknowledges the imperfections in democracy but believes in its potential to educate citizens to behave more considerately towards the environment and to improve environmental policymaking. By contrast, ecological modernisation places greater trust in the capacity of technological innovation and the market-place, rather than the wilfulness of democratic mechanisms, to bring about a sustainable society.

### 11.5 Opposition to wind power: democracy or NIMBYism?

Renewable sources contributed just 3.6 per cent of UK electricity generation in 2004. The British government's climate change strategy has set a target of increasing this share to 10 per cent by 2010 and 15 per cent by 2015. Wind power is expected to contribute a significant share of that amount. It is a safe, clean technology, producing no carbon emissions, which uses an unlimited natural resource, and Britain has the largest potential for wind power in Europe. Who could be against it? Indeed, opinion polls consistently show that the public supports wind energy.

Yet, despite significant government subsidies, the wind energy sector remains tiny. In 2005, the amount of installed wind power was 1,353MW, compared to 18,428MW in Germany, 10,027MW in Spain and 3,122MW in Denmark.

This shortfall can be explained partly by local planning decisions, often involving a planning inquiry: between 1994 and 1998, of eighteen wind developments that went before planning inquiries, just two small schemes won approval (RCEP 2000: 216). The number of consents has increased subsequently, with 35 projects for 733MW power approved in 2005, but 25 proposals were refused (BWEA 2006). Many proposals encounter fierce local resistance from residents and interest groups, such as the CPRE, the RSPB and the Ramblers Association. The main objections to wind farms focus on perceptions of their:

*visual impact* – they scar the countryside and may damage tourism
*noise* – from the blades
*ecological damage* – to birds and to habitats
*expense* – cost more than energy from fossil fuels
*variable efficiency* – the wind does not blow all the time

The main reason for most planning refusals is their *visual impact*. Unfortunately, the windiest areas of Britain that are most suitable for the turbines are also areas of outstanding beauty – and countryside protection is a major environmental concern in Britain.

The slow development of the UK wind power sector illustrates the complex relationship between democracy and sustainable development. The climate change strategy of the democratically elected national government is being undermined by the democratic opposition of local communities. Is this an example of self-interested 'NIMBYism', or does it underline the importance of strong grassroots democracy in protecting local environmental and economic interests?

The British Wind Energy Association offers counter-arguments to these objections: http://www.bwea.com/energy/myths.html. See also Toke (2002), Szarka (2004) and Bell et al. (2005).

---

### Critical question 4
Will increased democracy and participation improve the quality of environmental governance?

---

## ◗ Conclusion

Since the early 1990s, spurred on by the Agenda 21 programme, governments have begun to change the way they approach environmental issues. Most have adopted a more strategic approach that at least genuflects in the direction of (very weak) sustainable development. The plethora of institutional and administrative reforms intended to improve integration and planning, and to encourage a wider democratic dialogue around the concept of sustainable development, have undoubtedly led some policymakers to consider environmental issues more routinely. In short, there is evidence of a gradual shift away from the traditional paradigm. However, progress towards environmental governance is slow: most reforms are still in their infancy and have exerted only a limited impact on the way government actually operates. In particular, the weakness of environmental ministries, agencies and green plans has hampered efforts to improve the co-ordination of cross-sectoral environmental initiatives across government. It seems that, as Chapter 7 showed, there are many deep-seated obstacles to the successful implementation of sustainable development. Not least, with the political salience of environmental issues remaining low, few governments have been willing to provide strong, sustained leadership. Without such political leadership, sustainable development may promise to end the economy/environment trade-off but, in practice, policy continues to emerge from a sectoral administrative structure where economic growth is the priority, producer interests prevail and environmental considerations too often remain an afterthought.

## ▶ *Further reading and websites*

The Brundtland Report (WCED 1987) is a good place to start reading about environmental governance, after which move on to Dryzek (1987, 2005), Jansen et al. (1998), Durant et al. (2004) and Paehlke and Torgerson (2005), which cover many of the issues and mechanisms discussed in this chapter. Lafferty and Meadowcroft (2000a) provide a comparative assessment of progress in nine OECD countries towards implementing Agenda 21. On environmental policy integration, see Lenschow (2002) and Lafferty and Hovden (2003). Smith (2003) provides an excellent theoretical and empirical analysis of the relationship between democracy and the environment.

Information about all aspects of EU environmental policy can be found on the Environment Directorate website (http://www.europa.eu.int/pol/env/index_en.htm). The European Environmental Agency website (http://www.eea.eu.int/) provides excellent links to national environmental ministries, agencies and institutions in most European nations and detailed information about the state of the environment in Europe. For the USA, consult the EPA (http://www.epa.gov), and, for Canada, Environment Canada (http://www.ec.gc.ca/envhome.html).

NOTES

1 Detailed accounts of the institutional arrangements for environmental policy in various developed countries can be found in Hanf and Jansen (1998), Lafferty and

Meadowcroft (2000a) and Desai (2002). For the USA, see Rosenbaum (2005a) and Vig and Kraft (2006a).

2 See Wood (1995) for an account of environmental impact assessment methodology.

3 See Hanley and Spash (1993) for a balanced assessment of the use of CBA in environmental decision-making.

4 See Wood (2005) for a comparative analysis of the use of strategic environmental assessment.

5 Weale et al. (2000: 56–62) provide a brief account of the first five EAPs.

6 The openness of the inquiry process differs between countries: for example, it is open to a much wider range of interests in France than in Germany (Mason 1999: 77).

# Policy instruments and implementation

## Contents

## Key issues

▶ What are the main environmental policy instruments?
▶ What are the strengths and weaknesses of regulatory and market-based instruments?
▶ How do national regulatory styles differ?
▶ Why are there so few market-based instruments?
▶ How can policy instruments be used to prevent climate change?

Chapter 11 assessed progress towards sustainable development by examining various ways in which governments have tried to build environmental considerations into the policymaking process. Another aspect of judging progress towards sustainable development is to examine the policy outputs that emerge from that process. A key element in the policymaking and implementation process concerns the choice of policy instrument, or levers, by which a government tries to achieve its policy objectives. Policy instruments should be enforceable, effective and educative: they should change the behaviour of target groups, achieve the stated policy objectives and help spread environmental values throughout society.

It is conventional to distinguish four broad types of policy instrument available for a government to use in pursuing its environmental objectives: regulation, voluntary action, government expenditure and market-based instruments (MBIs).[1] A distinguishing characteristic of the traditional environmental policy paradigm was its reliance on regulatory, or 'command and control', instruments. During the 1970s and 1980s, new environmental legislation created an extensive regulatory framework in most countries, but as many environmental problems continued to worsen despite this growing regulatory 'burden', the use of regulation was increasingly criticised, particularly by economists, industrialists and right-wing politicians. Consequently, there has been growing support for MBIs as a more efficient and effective alternative to regulations. Ecological modernisation in particular is underpinned by an explicit assumption that it is the market that will deliver sustainability, so a growing interest in MBIs may be one indicator of a general shift away from the traditional paradigm towards ecological modernisation.

A central argument of this chapter is that the choice of policy instrument is only partly a technical matter of selecting the instrument that offers the most efficient or effective means of delivering policy objectives. It is also a highly *political* process in which decisions are shaped by competing interests. Policy instruments are intended to alter the behaviour of producers and/or consumers, so it is hardly surprising that affected interests will mobilise resources to influence those choices. Indeed, political considerations have informed the way the 'command and control versus MBI' debate is often stylised as a choice between two sharply contrasting approaches when, in practice, the differences are not so clear-cut.

The first part of this chapter analyses the strengths and weaknesses of different policy instruments, concentrating on the central debate between regulation and MBIs. It also identifies some important contextual features which influence their implementation, such as variation in national regulatory styles. The second part provides a broad overview of climate change strategies in the energy and transport sectors – probably the most pressing and perplexing policy arena for contemporary policymakers – to illustrate some of the issues raised earlier in the chapter.

# ❭ Regulation and regulatory styles

## ❭ *The case for regulation*

Regulation is the most widely used instrument of environmental policy. Broadly defined, regulation involves any attempt by the government to influence the behaviour of businesses or citizens, but it is used here to refer to what many observers, rather pejoratively, call 'command and control' or 'coercive' regulation. It involves the government specifying the standards of pollution control that a process or product has to meet, and then using state officials, backed up by the legal system, to enforce its rules. Regulatory standards usually take one of three forms. *Ambient* standards place limits on the total concentration of pollutants permitted in a particular area, such as a street, river or bathing waters. *Emission* standards limit what an individual source can emit: the gases released from factories, exhaust emissions from vehicles and discharges of agricultural silage into rivers are all typically regulated in this way. *Design* standards require the use of a specific type of pollution-control technology or production process, such as a catalytic converter in a car, or the use of particular materials or products, such as unleaded petrol. In addition, stringent controls limit the dumping of hazardous waste. Many chemicals such as DDT, once widely used as a pesticide, are completely banned or else their use is tightly controlled. Some regulations are aimed directly at the behaviour of individual citizens. Clean Air Acts have created urban smokeless zones where the burning of coal is banned; traffic-congested cities such as Florence and Athens limit the number of cars entering the city centre; while many local municipalities require citizens to separate their household waste for recycling. Regulation is also the main instrument used by international regimes to deal with both common-sink problems (e.g. banning ozone-depleting substances) and common-pool problems (banning whaling).

Regulation is the policy instrument most associated with the traditional environmental paradigm. When the political salience of pollution rose during the 1970s, governments concentrated their initial legislative responses on the large industrial polluters responsible for the bulk of harmful emissions. As there were relatively few firms compared to consumers, they appeared easy to police; industry had the resources to invest in abatement and factory smoke-stacks and waste-pipes were highly visible symbols of pollution (Braadbaart 1998). The huge extant legislative programmes designed to achieve pollution abatement still make regulation the most widely used environmental policy instrument. In the USA, for example, eight new regulatory programmes, or major amendments to existing ones, were introduced between 1980 and 1994. The EU has introduced over 600 regulations directly affecting the environment (Haigh 1998). Environmental policy today is still primarily concerned with the content and implementation of regulations.

Regulation has an obvious appeal to policymakers. It appears to offer precision, predictability and effectiveness: an exact standard is set, the regulator and regulated both know what is expected of them and enforcement is ensured by a regulatory agency backed up by the force of law. Regulations can be administratively efficient, especially when a substance or an activity is completely banned, as they do not require complete information about a problem. Assuming there is a high level of compliance, they can also be inexpensive as there is no need to investigate each individual case. As the application of uniform standards and rules means that, in theory, all polluters are treated identically, regulations are widely perceived by producers and consumers as equitable. The political, judicial and administrative back-up they receive from the state should make regulations reasonably immune from manipulation and enhance their public legitimacy. There are countless examples of successful regulations, ranging from the world's first comprehensive air pollution control legislation, the Clean Air Act 1956, which dramatically improved air quality in British cities, to the Montreal Protocol banning CFC production in developed countries.

Yet the use of regulations has come under increasing attack from many quarters. There was a widespread neo-liberal backlash against the 'regulatory burden', which informed the deregulatory efforts of the Reagan and Thatcher governments during the 1980s, and later inspired the Congressional Republican Party's 'Contract with America' in the mid-1990s, which attempted to make a bonfire of 'unnecessary' regulations. Most advocates of wholesale deregulation have little sympathy for 'environmentalism'. They are most vocal in the USA where their populist rhetoric has chimed with industry complaints about an excessive regulatory burden (Kraft and Vig 2006: 18–19). Vitriolic criticism has been heaped upon the many inadequacies of the EPA, the impact on competitiveness of 'unnecessary' regulations and the cost to the taxpayer (see Box 11.2). One rhetorical success of the neo-liberal backlash was to gain wide acceptance of the term 'command and control' in preference to 'regulation'. In practice, as shown below, regulations are rarely applied in a coercive way, so 'command and control' is a misnomer. Nevertheless, it represents a clever political achievement; after all, how many people will opt for coercion over the 'free' market (Dryzek 2005: 135–6)?

Not all criticism of regulation is so partisan. Despite the ever-expanding volume, reach and stringency of environmental regulations in most developed countries, it became increasingly clear that the overall environmental record remained poor. Research showed that pollution control policies introduced during the 1970s in the USA, UK, Germany and elsewhere had failed to deliver the standards, targets and procedures set out in the legislation (Weale 1992: 17). There were isolated examples of improved environmental performance, and some countries certainly performed better than others, but generally it seemed that the huge resources invested in regulatory programmes had disappointing outcomes. One high-profile example was the US

Superfund programme for decontaminating toxic waste sites. Here costs have multiplied – averaging around $1.6 billion per year in the early 1990s – owing to the 'extensive litigation involved in determining responsibility for clean-ups, wasteful spending on elaborate remediation plans, and long delays in implementation' (Vig and Kraft 1999: 376). Congress refused to reauthorise the taxes needed for the Superfund in 1995 and although the costs were eventually borne by the taxpayer, the funds allocated (about $1.25 billion in 2005) are 'woefully inadequate for the task' (Vig and Kraft 2006b: 380). Indeed, despite the enormous cost of the programme, clean-up had been completed on only 1,244 sites by April 2006, a small proportion of contaminated sites (http://www.epa.gov/superfund/). Thus Superfund has, arguably, failed to achieve its most basic objective.

Broadly speaking, the criticisms of regulation fall into two categories: that it is inefficient, and that it is ineffective. The alleged *inefficiency* of regulation will be discussed in the section on MBIs below (pp. 332–4). The claim that it is *ineffective* is essentially concerned with the implementation deficit – defined here as a failure to achieve policy objectives – that characterises so much environmental regulation. Ineffective regulation can be explained both by the incapacity of the state to monitor and enforce regulations and by variations in national regulatory styles.

### Critical question 1

How persuasive is the political case against 'command and control' regulations?

## ▶ *Implementation deficit and state failure*

Regulatory regimes are often weak. The government, or a state agency such as the EPA, is usually responsible for the monitoring, compliance and enforcement elements of environmental regulation. These activities can be very costly and time-consuming, so problems may arise when inadequate funding prevents regulatory agencies from carrying them out properly. In the USA, personnel and budgetary shortages have severely affected the ability of many agencies to implement environmental policy (Kraft and Vig 2006: 19–20). As one new environmental programme followed another, Congress frequently underestimated the workload generated by new regulations that produced unrealistic deadlines, excessive administrative rules and virtually unattainable programme objectives (Rosenbaum 2006: 171–3). However, the full explanation for the underfunding was more pernicious: the Reagan administration deliberately sought to reduce the power of the EPA and other natural resource agencies by slashing their operating budgets (Kraft and Vig 2006: 19–20). Problems can be particularly acute where responsibility for implementation is passed down from one level of government to another. US states complain loudly about the financial and administrative burden caused by the implementation of federal environmental regulations, such as the need to issue thousands of industrial permits as required by the Clean Water Act 1990.

EU environmental policy has also encountered a range of implementation problems. Crucially, the responsibility for implementing EU environmental regulation lies with the member states and there is no 'European' environmental inspectorate with powers of enforcement. Not surprisingly, there are sharp differences between member state governments in their approach to the environment (Weale et al. 2000; Jordan and Liefferink 2004b). One oft-cited cleavage is that between the 'pioneer' ecologically modernising countries of the North and the less developed 'laggard' Southern European nations. For example, the Southern member states – Greece, Italy, Spain and Portugal – have generally been slower at transposing EU environmental directives into national legislation and, more importantly, have been rather lax about enforcing them (Weale et al. 2000: 299–303). This record partly reflects basic infrastructural problems, such as an administrative incapacity to deal with the costly burden of EU directives (in all policy sectors). Whereas Northern European states have generally managed to adapt existing structures to respond to specific directives, in the absence of any tradition of environmental control Southern European states have had to build new institutions and structures. Some observers also refer, rather controversially, to a 'Mediterranean syndrome', meaning a civic culture that sanctions non-co-operative and non-compliant behaviour and impedes the enforcement of regulative policies (La Spina and Sciortino 1993). Whilst there is evidence of a gap between North and South on environmental policy, it is a rather crude dichotomy, and several observers argue that the perception of a 'Southern problem' in EU environmental policy is neither accurate nor helpful. Weale et al. (2000: 330) point out that Spain's 'more effective' record is closer to that of the UK, than to those of Italy and Greece, whilst Börzel (2003), in a comparison of Spanish and German environmental policy, reveals that on some issues Germany has been the laggard. The North–South gap has also been reduced by various EU distributive programmes, notably the Cohesion Fund which directed around €18 billion to environmental projects in Spain, Portugal, Greece and Ireland, and the structural funds for disadvantaged regions (Lenschow 2005: 322). It is too early to tell whether the ten new EU member states will, as some commentators predict, join the ranks of 'laggards' (Vandeveer and Carmin 2004: 325–6).

## ▶ *Implementation deficit and national regulatory styles*

Most regulatory mechanisms face a fundamental administrative dilemma. One advantage of regulation is that standards and rules should be applied uniformly across an industry; in practice, there are strong pressures undermining this principle. Pollution control is a highly complex process with an informational asymmetry favouring the polluter, which may oblige regulatory agencies to build close relationships with those whom they regulate simply to gain an understanding of each situation. Once a relationship is established, officials will often bargain with the polluter over targets, timetables and investment in new technologies. The regulator will make judgements and exercise discretion about whether to enforce rules fully, or whether to negotiate compliance, taking into account individual local circumstances such as culpability, negligence and the likelihood of future compliance (Weale 1992: 17–18; Fiorino 2004: 395–401; Rosenbaum 2005a: 174–7). The dilemma is that the benefits of flexibility have to be weighed against the costs of diluting standards so that slippage may occur between policy and implementation. The exact way in which this dilemma is played out may depend on the regulatory style prevailing in each country (Richardson 1982).

One characteristic of a national regulatory style is the extent to which regulation relies on judicial or on administrative procedures. The approach to environmental control pursued in many European countries is primarily formal and legalistic. In France the aim is to establish clear legal frameworks and procedures, backed up by state agencies and the judiciary (Buller 1998: 70). Germany and Austria both have a preference for detailed command-and-control regulations imposing uniform emissions standards and setting clear rules (Lauber 2004: 52; Wurzel 2004: 102–3). In principle, a judicial approach should minimise the opportunity for regulatory officials to exercise discretion when implementing policy in individual cases. By contrast, where environmental control is pervaded by administrative procedures, as in Britain, the style is more informal, accommodative and technocratic (Lowe and Flynn 1989). Legislation tends to be broad and discretionary with an avoidance of legislatively prescribed standards and quality objectives:

> It has long been traditional to rely upon, where practicable, the characteristics of the local natural environment as a sensible disposal and dispersal route for potential pollutants. This underlying approach in theory requires that agencies should be given complete independence and discretion to determine, in the light of local circumstances, the degree of seriousness of a potential pollutant and the appropriate control measures. (Macrory 1986: 8)

A second feature of any regulatory style is the way environmental policy is enforced: some systems are confrontational, others more co-operative. In a comparison of British and American environmental practice, Vogel (1986) noted that, despite key similarities in political and cultural traditions, common environmental conflicts and even shared organisational responses, there were sharp differences between environmental controls in the United Kingdom and the United States: 'Americans rely heavily on formal rules, often enforced in the face of strong opposition from the institutions affected by them, while the British continue to rely on flexible standards and voluntary compliance – including, in many cases, self-regulation'

(p. 77). The British, because they are 'reluctant to adopt rules and regulations with which they cannot guarantee compliance' (ibid.), draft regulations that allow officials to negotiate specific arrangements with firms that will be accepted by their superiors and the courts. Consequently, government officials seek to 'persuade' industrial and farming interests of the need to modify their behaviour and, when laws are broken, officials usually choose not to prosecute. By contrast, in the USA there is a greater willingness to resort to the courts to prosecute polluters and enforce compliance. Yet the existence of a strongly legalistic administrative culture does not necessarily imply that laws will be enforced rigidly with frequent recourse to judicial action. In Austria, for example, producer interests are often accommodated so that criminal courts play a negligible role, allowing most polluters either to go unpunished or to pay insignificant fines, although one outcome of Europeanisation is a shift away from this consensual style (Lauber 2004).

The concept of regulatory style inevitably involves some generalisation and should be applied advisedly. Vogel's characterisation of the USA as formalistic and confrontational was based primarily on a study of just two policy areas, air pollution and land use, although subsequent studies confirm his broad findings (Fiorino 2004: 396–401). If the idea of a regulatory style has some resonance, one obvious question arises: which regulatory style produces the best environmental outcomes?

The main criticism of the British style is that its extreme flexibility allows the polluter to escape a tight regulatory embrace. The preference for administrative discretion over judicial interpretation, the bureaucratic obsession for secrecy and the way secret site-level negotiations between polluter and inspector remain at the heart of industrial pollution control, create the perfect conditions for 'regulatory capture' (Skea and Smith 1998: 268). The widely used concepts of 'best practicable means' (BPM) of controlling pollution and 'best available technique not entailing excessive costs' (BATNEEC) have ensured that regulatory authorities are sensitive to the economic and practical constraints that businesses face. Put differently, British regulators have accepted too readily the standards and practices of the regulated (Richardson et al. 1983).

So, does a more formalistic regulatory style provide better protection for the environment? Vogel (1986: 23), whilst not claiming that British environmental controls were particularly effective, argued that the emphasis on voluntary compliance had proved no less effective than the more adversarial and legalistic approach adopted by American policymakers. Although American standards were higher, the level of compliance was much lower, resulting in a serious implementation deficit. Industries complained that they could not afford to implement strict emission standards. The EPA, constrained by limited resources, frequently took only the most obvious and gross violators to court. This more conflictual style generated bad feeling between the enforcement agencies and industry, which, in turn, encouraged further flouting of the law. Although Vogel's work is now very dated, the continuing troubles besetting the EPA, the widespread criticism of the inflexibile US regulatory style and the repeated attempts to reform it, suggest that these observations remain pertinent (Fiorino 2004: 399). Observing that the more co-operative relations between regulator and regulated in Britain ensured that the lower standards were at least implemented effectively, Vogel concluded that different national regulatory styles have little impact on policy outcomes. An alternative lesson might be that some kind of halfway house is desirable between these two flawed regulatory systems. Thus membership of the EU, with its high volume of environmental regulation, may have produced some limited convergence of national regulatory styles among member states (Jordan and Liefferink 2004a). Britain, for example, has adopted stricter standards, uniform targets, explicit monitoring and review mechanisms and reduced discretion for local officials across a wide range of environmental matters (Jordan 2002).

Although contextual factors, such as differing regulatory styles, may influence the effectiveness of regulations, the wide-ranging criticism of command-and-control methods has encouraged policymakers to cast around for alternative policy instruments to achieve environmental policy goals. The following sections first provide brief accounts of voluntary action and government expenditure, and then a more detailed examination of market-based instruments.

---

### Critical question 2

To what extent does the effectiveness of 'command-and-control' instruments depend on the national regulatory style?

---

# ▶ Voluntary action

Voluntary action involves individuals or organisations doing things to protect the environment that are neither required by law nor encouraged by financial incentive. Voluntary action is the main way in which individuals, by changing their lifestyles and acting as ecological citizens, can contribute to the achievement of a more sustainable society. Individuals can engage in a wide range of voluntary activities, including green consumerism, ethical investment (see Chapter 8), recycling and voluntary conservation work. The government can encourage voluntary action through a range of communicative strategies such as information campaigns setting out the environmental benefits of recycling drink containers or newspapers, extending citizen rights to environmental information and making it easier for individuals and organisations to take polluters to court.

Businesses may also choose to consider the environmental impact of their activities, although the incentive is often to increase profits. Many firms, encouraged by governments, have adopted Eco-Management and Audit

It is difficult to evaluate the effectiveness of a voluntary agreement: proponents want to measure improvements against some base year; critics want to evaluate performance against what could have been achieved by regulatory instruments or MBIs. Both approaches are flawed, as the former cannot distinguish changes from developments that might have happened anyway and the latter is based on a hypothetical situation. None the less, based on historical trends, both examples below seem to have been successes (albeit open to criticism).

*USA – 33/50 Program for Toxic Emissions*
This was an EPA initiative representing a voluntary 'add-on' to the Toxic Release Inventory. It set national goals for seventeen prioritised toxic chemicals of a 33 per cent reduction of releases by 1992 and a 50 per cent cut by 1995 compared with 1988 levels. Of 5,000 companies invited, some 1,300

corporations agreed to join the agreement, succeeding in making 50 per cent cuts in their emissions by 1994, although overall cuts among all firms on the Toxic Release Inventory had reached only 42 per cent by 1995 and 45 per cent by 1998 (Sterner 2003: 303).

*German climate change agreement*
In 1995 the German government, having set an ambitious $CO_2$ emission reduction target of 25 per cent by 2005, made a voluntary agreement with fifteen (later nineteen) industry associations representing 80 per cent of industry energy emissions. In exchange for industry promises to make emission cuts of up to 20 per cent by 2005, the government agreed to withhold additional regulatory measures. Initially criticised for being unambitious, subsequent agreements set increasingly tougher emissions reduction targets, which were achieved well before 2005 (Hatch 2005a).

Schemes (EMAS), environmental management standards such as ISO 14001 and eco-labelling (see Chapter 8). The most significant instrument is the environmental 'voluntary agreement', which is a commitment undertaken by firms or trade associations, usually in consultation or negotiation with a public authority, although normally there will be no sanctions if commitments are not fulfilled. Environmental agreements have become increasingly common since the late 1980s: a comparative study of eight OECD countries reported that they had 'grown significantly' everywhere (Jordan et al. 2003a: 211), with several thousand in Japan, and the Netherlands and Germany having the largest share in the EU. While the Dutch NEPP has produced agreements, or 'covenants', in almost all policy areas (see Chapter 11), most countries have just a handful of agreements concentrated in a few core polluting areas, notably the energy, chemical, agriculture, tourism and transport sectors. Some environmental agreements represent a co-ordinated industry response to a legislative development; for example, all EU member states have concluded agreements that implement the European Commission directive on packaging waste.

Environmental agreements have several potential advantages (see Box 12.1). They offer a flexible and cost-effective means of achieving policy objectives because they give producers the freedom to decide how best to meet goals and encourage speedy implementation and compliance, whilst requiring little or no 'policing' by the state. Voluntary agreements may generate constructive co-operation between the state and industry along the lines of ecological modernisation, leading to changes in the environmental values and behaviour of both state officials and producers. Nevertheless, voluntary agreements have their weaknesses too; indeed, the OECD (2003b) has concluded that their environmental effectiveness is questionable and their economic efficiency is low. They are often unambitious, involving commitments at the level of the lowest common denominator acceptable to the least enthusiastic signatories to the agreement. An industry will often only establish a voluntary agreement as a means of forestalling the threat of a tougher regulation or eco-tax. Thus Swedish firms agreed voluntarily to ban the use of chlorine in paper-bleaching, presumably to gain good publicity and create a future bargaining tool, only when the EPA was drafting laws to proscribe it (Sterner 2003: 121). Generally, voluntary agreements made in anticipation of legislation are likely to set easier targets and more relaxed deadlines than the government would impose by other means. Voluntary agreements are also not backed up by mechanisms for enforcing compliance. The absence of sanctions may make implementation very difficult, with free-riding a real possibility.

The effectiveness of voluntary agreements is also influenced by regulatory styles. There have been very few voluntary agreements in the UK: most have been unambitious and very weak – 'many are more like codes of best practice than what continental Europeans would classify as negotiated agreements' (Jordan et al. 2003: 192) – yet they have still largely failed to meet their commitments. It seems that the British voluntarist tradition co-exists with an entrenched bias in favour of corporate interests, nurtured by the continued domination of closed policy communities in key sectors. However, whilst voluntarism inevitably involves some compromise, it does not have to be as sympathetic to corporate interests as it is in Britain. The discussion of the NEPP in Chapter 11 showed how it too has nurtured self-regulation within Dutch industry, but as a means to implement ambitious pollution reduction targets negotiated with particular sectors (see Mol et al. 2000; Weale et al. 2000: 174–5, 220–1). The Dutch regulatory style is emblematic of ecological modernisation as it involves close but transparent co-operation between the state and industry, resulting in a framework characterised by a combination of high standards and tough target-setting, but with the flexibility to respond to individual needs and local circumstances. Yet even in the Netherlands sustainable development will not be achieved through industry voluntary agreements alone. Although industry might sometimes regard the voluntary agreement as an alternative to other policy instruments, most observers believe it is just a useful supplement to other measures (Sterner 2003: 121–2; Fiorino 2004: 413).

## ▶ Government expenditure

Government expenditure can help achieve environmental goals where the costs of taking remedial action are too great for individual producers or citizens to bear (Jacobs 1991: ch. 13). The classic form of government expenditure is a subsidy, which might encourage producers to buy cleaner technologies, farmers to shift to less intensive forms of agriculture, or citizens to insulate their homes. Some forms of voluntary action may also benefit from government investment in basic infrastructure, such as the provision of recycling facilities or public transport, that must exist before people will recycle bottles and newspapers, or reduce car usage. Governments can subsidise nascent green industries such as wave or wind energy. Subsidies are, however, an inefficient means of changing behaviour, notably because they cannot discriminate between people who were going to do something (e.g. fit loft insulation) anyway, and those who were only persuaded to do so by the subsidy. Even so, there is scope for governments to adopt a far more ambitious approach to public expenditure in pursuit of sustainable development. For example, in many Northern European countries a publicly funded home energy conservation programme could create employment, reduce carbon emissions, slash domestic energy bills and even prove popular with the electorate – truly a win–win strategy. However, despite the benefits of reduced welfare payments and higher tax revenues from the new jobs, the huge cost of such massive public works programmes obviously limits the potential of government expenditure as a policy instrument.

## ▶ Market-based instruments

### ▶ *The case for market-based instruments*

In addition to its alleged ineffectiveness, regulation is criticised for its *inefficiency* as a means of achieving policy objectives (Turner et al. 1994: 144). Where a regulation imposes a technology or emissions standard on individual factories it may be costly for the government regulator to obtain information from the polluter in order to agree, monitor and enforce these rules. Some polluters will find it easier than others to reduce pollution. Rather than impose a single standard that all polluters have to meet, it might be more efficient to concentrate effort on those who can reduce their pollution most cheaply. Regulations offer no incentive for polluters to reduce their pollution beyond what is required by law. MBIs can provide that incentive.

The aim of MBIs is to prevent market failure by applying the polluter pays principle (PPP). Market failure occurs when environmental resources are over-exploited because of open access to goods whose market price does not incorporate the external costs of using those environmental resources. The PPP holds that the price of a good or service should fully reflect the total cost

## 12.2 Market-based instruments

A market-based instrument internalises into the price of a good or product the external costs to the environment of producing and using it.

Eco-taxes

| | |
|---|---|
| *User charges* | Fees payable for treatment, collection and disposal costs of wastes or other environmental administration |
| *Emission charges* | Charges on the discharge of pollutants into air, water or soil (i.e. directly linked to quantity and quality of pollutant), e.g. taxes on sulphur emissions, or water effluent charges. |
| *Product charges* | Charges on harmful products, e.g. fertilisers, pesticides, low sulphur petrol, plastic bags, batteries. |
| *Tradeable permits* | Environmental quotas that are tradeable, e.g. $SO_2$ and $CO_2$ emissions, fishing quotas. |
| *Deposit-refunds* | Charge on a polluting product that is refunded if the product is returned after use, e.g. beverage containers. |

*Sources*: Turner et al. (1994); OECD (1997); EEA (2006a).

of production, including the use of public goods such as air, water or land for emissions. An MBI internalises these external costs into the price of a good (Turner et al. 1994: 145) by means of an explicit government intervention in the market.[2] The MBIs with most potential are eco-taxes and tradeable permits (see Box 12.2). The refundable deposit, such as the returnable deposit imposed on drink containers in Denmark and several US states (Rabe 2006: 40), can also be an effective means of rewarding environmental concern and punishing neglect.[3]

*Eco-taxes* are levied on pollution or on the goods whose production generates pollution. Direct effluent charges are most appropriate where pollution is concentrated, such as chemical emissions from a power-station or factory discharges in a river. Where pollution is widely dispersed, as with farm waste containing fertiliser nitrates or $CO_2$ from vehicle exhausts, it may be easier to tax the source, namely the fertiliser containing nitrate or the fuel containing carbon (Jacobs 1991: 141). The rationale for eco-taxes is that the government decides the ambient standard of pollution it wants to achieve and sets a tax at a level that will achieve that outcome. Unlike a regulatory standard, a tax allows the individual polluter the flexibility to decide how (and how far) it will reduce pollution. Those firms that can cut pollution relatively cheaply will pursue abatement further than those for whom it is relatively expensive (who will pay more tax). Thus eco-taxes are more efficient than regulation because the same level of pollution abatement should be achieved for a lower overall cost to industry. Moreover, whereas regulation offers no incentive for firms to reduce pollution below the ambient standard, eco-taxes provide a constant incentive for industry to reduce pollution further to cut the tax bill (Pearce et al. 1989; Pearce and Turner 1990).

Whereas an eco-tax is a price-based mechanism, a *tradeable permit* is a rights-based mechanism that combines regulation with a financial incentive. The government calculates the overall level of allowable emissions for an area and sets a target that either corresponds to that total, or is lower. The overall target level is divided into individual emission permits, each giving the owner the right to release a specific volume of emissions. These permits are then sold or auctioned to polluters.[4] The government sanctions a market in the permits, which gives firms an incentive to reduce pollution and sell any surplus permits for a profit, while firms that do nothing to reduce pollution will at least pay something towards the cost of environmental damage. Permits offer firms the flexibility to reduce pollution in the most cost-effective way, whilst also giving the government the opportunity to cut the overall level of emissions by withdrawing permits, buying them back or cutting their entitlement.

Beyond their greater efficiency, proponents claim that MBIs have further advantages. They raise revenues which can be reinvested in environmentally beneficial ways: for example, money from water pollution taxes in France, Germany and the Netherlands is reinvested in water quality improvement (Andersen 1994). Taxes have a potential educative and communicative role by providing a signal to producers and consumers that they should change their behaviour. Many experts also claim that eco-taxation offers a potential 'double dividend', by delivering both environmental protection and additional jobs (see Box 12.3). Among several administrative benefits, it is claimed that compliance will be cheaper and more effective because the tax is gathered by the existing revenue collection framework instead of being policed by infrequent on-site inspection.

Yet environmental MBIs remain the exception rather than the rule. Until recently, tradeable permits hardly existed outside the textbook. The USA has led the way with several small-scale experiments arising from various Clean Air Acts. One big scheme, underpinning a major drive to prevent acid rain, saw the introduction in 1995 of a permit system to control $SO_2$ emissions. Each source (usually a coal-burning power-station) was issued with permits equal to a percentage of its historic emissions level, with permits reduced to the overall emissions target level from 2000. The Dutch have set up an $NO_x$ trading scheme, Denmark and the UK have introduced national carbon trading systems and in January 2005 the EU established a trading scheme for greenhouse gas emissions – the first EU-wide MBI. Individual transferable quotas have been used for several years to control fishing in Iceland, Australia and New Zealand, and in several EU states such as Portugal and Denmark.

Eco-taxes have been around longer: water charges were introduced in France in 1969 and the Netherlands in 1972 (Braadbaart 1998). Yet they are still used sparingly. There are very few in the USA beyond the local

## 12.3 Eco-taxes and the double dividend

All governments are currently interested in fiscal reform. One key idea involves shifting the burden of taxation from environmental 'goods', such as enterprise, employment and savings, on to environmental 'bads', such as pollution and inefficient use of energy and resources. Proponents argue that a double dividend is possible: eco-taxes protect the environment and, by removing inefficient subsidies and tax distortions, they also stimulate employment. Although the existence of the double dividend is hotly debated among economists (O'Riordan 1997), an OECD (2001) overview found that using eco-tax revenues to reduce labour taxes and social security contributions, particularly of unskilled labour, can generate jobs.

Recent examples of taxes, or tax packages, that apply these principles include the following:

| | |
|---|---|
| Finland | Cuts to income and labour taxes in 1997 were partly compensated by a landfill tax and increased energy taxes. |
| Germany | The first in a series of energy tax increases by the SDP/Green coalition government in 1999 raised taxes on gas, heating oil, diesel and petrol, and imposed a new electricity tax (subsequent annual increases were smaller and levied only on transport fuels and electricity). The aim was to cut $CO_2$ emissions and to use the extra revenue to stimulate employment by reducing social security contributions. |
| UK | The revenue from the UK climate change levy on industry, introduced in 2001, is recycled to business through a cut in their National Insurance contributions and government support for energy efficiency measures. |

municipality. The total tax revenues of EU member states raised from environmental taxes (on energy, transport and pollution) was only 6.5 per cent in 2002, having slipped from 6.7 per cent in 1997 (EEA 2006a: 31). Moreover, many of those taxes were imposed primarily for revenue-raising reasons rather than to shape environmental behaviour. However, the number of eco-taxes in the EU-25 has grown steadily since the mid-1990s, with a much wider range of taxes applied to carbon emissions, sulphur in fuels, waste disposal, raw materials and some new product taxes, such as plastic bags, batteries and tyres (ibid.: 26–7). Denmark stands out as the country with the widest spectrum of eco-taxes in Europe, contributing almost 10 per cent of its total tax revenue (ibid.: 16).

Here then is a paradox. There seems to be a convincing economic case that MBIs are more efficient and, possibly, more effective at achieving environmental outcomes than conventional regulatory methods. Influential international organisations such as the OECD (2001, 2004), the EU in its fifth and sixth EAPs, and national green tax commissions, as in Norway and the Netherlands, have strongly recommended wider use of MBIs – indeed, along with the voluntary agreement, they are the preferred policy instruments of ecological modernisation. Yet, eco-taxes and tradeable permits still play only a limited role in environmental policy. How can this paradox be explained? The following discussions of the practical and political obstacles to MBIs suggest that the case in favour of them is less persuasive than it first appears.

## ▶ Weaknesses in the economic case for market-based instruments

One problem with the MBI versus regulation debate is that it often involves a highly stylised and sharply distinguished comparison of perfect 'laboratory' MBIs with flawed real-life regulations. In practice, MBIs encounter implementation difficulties that are either ignored or glossed over in the economics textbooks.

One common claim is that MBIs will not encounter the informational asymmetries that force regulators to use resources to discover how polluters behave. Yet economic theory places great importance on setting a tax at the correct level, so that it both builds in the external environmental costs of the polluting activity in question and that it is set sufficiently high to offer a real incentive for firms to reduce pollution and hence to maximise the potential efficiency of the tax. To ensure such accuracy the regulator will need detailed technical information, which may only be obtainable from the polluter or technically very difficult to assess. Indeed, the UK landfill tax is a rare instance of an eco-tax where the tax rate is based on the marginal cost of the activity – managing landfills (EEA 2006a: 24–5). Further, the need to monitor performance and update assumptions about pollution levels, demand elasticities and the relative value of goods, might – in theory – oblige the regulator to make frequent adjustments to the tax level; in practice, this would be costly and disruptive to both industry and government planning, as illustrated by the (now withdrawn) Dutch MINAS manure tax (OECD 2005a). Crucially, if a proposed tax is perceived as too onerous, then the government may encounter strong resistance from businesses, trade unions or consumers. Not surprisingly, eco-taxes are therefore often set below the optimal level, which limits the efficiency gains, as with French water pollution charges (Andersen 1994). A sub-optimal rate also limits their effectiveness because, as in the case of fertiliser taxes in several countries, the price was set too low to have any significant effect on sales (Eckerberg 1997: 31); indeed, they have been withdrawn in Austria, Finland and Norway (EEA 2006a: 7). In practice, the environmental benefits of earmarked taxes may not come from persuading polluting firms or consumers to change behaviour but from investing the revenues raised in environmentally beneficial ways, such as subsidising firms to adopt cleaner technologies (Andersen 1994).

Similarly, the case for MBIs seems to have been 'developed in an imaginary world where market solutions are self-enforcing and therefore require little or no policing' (Braadbaart 1998: 143). The flaws of real-world regulations are compared to apparently perfect textbook MBIs, but MBIs encounter implementation problems too. It is unlikely that all polluters will be honest citizens. After all, if polluters are prepared to ignore regulatory standards when they think they can avoid detection, then surely they may also cheat or lie in order to avoid taxes? The introduction of a landfill tax on waste in Britain in 1996, for example, led to a huge increase in illegal fly-tipping of waste materials to avoid paying duties. An assessment of the Dutch MINAS manure tax found that the 'high cost for administration is in part caused by exploitation of loopholes, fraud, juridical procedures' (OECD 2005a: 5). Thus eco-taxes still need to be policed. Although the responsibility for this task may fall to the established revenue collection system of a finance ministry rather than a regulatory agency, any savings made are likely to be small. Similarly, a tradeable permit system also needs to be monitored by a regulatory agency to ensure that firms do not exceed their permitted emissions levels.

These technical and practical reservations are given further credence by the lack of definitive assessments of the performance of MBIs, although as new schemes flourish, more studies are appearing. The USA provides the most reliable evidence about tradeable permit schemes because European schemes remain in their infancy. US emissions trading has clearly generated considerable cost savings for firms. One evaluation of the US sulphur emissions trading system suggests that significant cuts in both emissions and costs have been achieved: during Phase 1 (1995–9) it is estimated that savings over direct regulations averaged $358 million per annum, rising to a predicted $2.3 billion per annum in Phase 2 (2000–7) (Ellerman et al. 2003: 11–18; see also Cole and Grossman 2005). The limited impact of the programme on acid rain has led to some circumspection about its environmental benefits, although the problem seems to lie with the timid emissions baseline set by the regulator rather than the operation of the trading scheme itself (Bryner 2005: 178–82). In Europe, there is a lively new market trading in carbon permits, but wild price fluctuations – rising from around €7 per tonne of carbon in January 2005 to just over €30 in April 2006, before collapsing almost overnight to €11 (*Financial Times*, 3 May 2006) – suggest that the system is still finding its feet amid criticisms that some businesses have made huge profits from the free allocation of permits and several member states have issued far too many permits.

There is more evidence available regarding eco-taxes, with several successful examples (see Box 12.4). Dutch water pollution charges have reduced organic emissions into waterways at low cost and encouraged firms to introduce cleaner technologies, although similar schemes in France and Germany have had mixed results (Andersen 1994). Swedish sulphur dioxide and nitrogen oxide taxes have produced significant emission reductions (EEA 1996: 31). The Swiss heavy goods vehicle fee has greatly increased the efficiency of heavy goods road transport (OECD 2005b). Several waste taxes have proved successful, including the Irish tax on plastic bags, the Dutch nutrient surplus charge and Danish taxes on waste disposal and batteries (EEA 2006a: 7). However, the verdict is not always clear-cut. During the 1990s, many EU states introduced tax differentiation between leaded and unleaded petrol to

---

**12.4 Some successful eco-taxes**

*Swedish sulphur tax*
The introduction of this tax in 1991 resulted in a reduction in the sulphur content of fuel oils by almost 40 per cent beyond the legal standard and the tax stimulated emission abatement measures in combustion plants (OECD 1997).

*Water pollution charges in the Netherlands*
Earmarked water effluent charges have been highly cost-effective because they (a) provided an incentive to polluters to control discharges and (b) generated revenues that were used to subsidise firms investing in pollution control technologies (Andersen 1994).

*Irish plastic bags tax*
A tax of 15 cents per bag was imposed in 2002 on every plastic bag given away by shops. Official estimates claim that plastic bag consumption has fallen by around 90 per cent, from 1,200 million per annum to 115 million in 2004, generating €13.5 million in revenue that is invested in waste management and environmental projects (DEHLG 2005: 14).

---

encourage consumers to shift to unleaded petrol but, as the tax coincided with new regulations requiring petrol stations to supply unleaded fuel and new EU emission standards for motor vehicles requiring catalytic converters, it is difficult to disentangle the precise effect of this tax. On balance, it is likely that the tax differentials hastened a trend that would, eventually, have happened anyway (leaded petrol was eventually banned throughout the EU in 2000). Several countries have since imposed a sulphur tax to encourage motorists to shift to low sulphur fuels, with some success. Overall, the efficiency advantages of MBIs over regulation, although real, are probably less significant than many textbooks claim, whilst their effectiveness will depend on the nature of the problem.

## ▶ *The politics of market-based instruments*

Several political obstacles also limit the wider use of MBIs. Policymakers are apprehensive about MBIs. Bureaucracies tend to be conservative institutions, which prefer tried and trusted mechanisms such as regulations. They want concrete examples of success before they are prepared to experiment with new techniques and the inconclusive evidence about MBIs does little to dispel their apprehension. Nevertheless, these reservations are diminishing as the demonstration effect of wider application and successful lesson-drawing slowly overcomes bureaucratic reservations. MBIs also fall foul of the administrative fragmentation identified in Chapter 7, as illustrated by the issue of hypothecation. An environment ministry might wish to raise revenue from a hypothecated, or earmarked, eco-tax to reinvest directly in environmental 'goods', perhaps by subsidising the development of renewable energy technologies. However, finance ministries usually dislike earmarked taxes because hypothecation undermines the fundamental principle that tax-based programmes of public expenditure never relate directly to tax payments by citizens, as such a system would be unworkable (see

O'Riordan 1997). Yet, attitudes are changing, with either the explicit or *de facto* hypothecation of eco-taxes revenues in several countries, including the Irish plastic bags tax, the UK landfill tax and the Swedish $NO_x$ charge.

Some environmentalists, especially deep greens, offer the ethical objection that, by putting a price on the environment, MBIs effectively allow firms or individuals to buy the right to carry on polluting. Yet, in this respect, MBIs are little different from regulations, which, by imposing an emissions standard, are effectively granting a right to pollute up to a certain level – free of charge! At least MBIs invoke the polluter pays principle by requiring the polluter to pay some of the costs of environmental damage.

A more persuasive ethical objection concerns their potential inequity, or regressive impact. By raising the price of some environmentally sensitive goods such as water or energy, eco-taxes discriminate against lower income groups because a larger share of their disposable income goes on these basic needs than is spent by higher income groups. For example, a Danish water consumption tax introduced in 1994 was estimated to cost an extra 0.38 per cent of the salaries of the lowest income group, but only 0.14 per cent of those of the highest income group (OECD 1997: 39). An assessment of the distributional impact of all Danish eco-taxes found that energy and water taxes were regressive, pollution taxes about neutral and transport taxes progressive (although they hit rural dwellers harder than urban dwellers) (EEA 2006a: 16). An illustration of the political sensitivity surrounding the regressive nature of eco-taxes was a rebellion by British Conservative backbench MPs in the mid-1990s after their own government raised value added tax on domestic fuel from 8 per cent to 17.5 per cent. Consequently, when eco-taxes are levied on items of basic need, there are strong ethical and pragmatic grounds for taking action to offset their regressive impact. One option is to return the revenue raised by the eco-tax directly to low-income groups, perhaps through cuts in income tax or increased welfare payments. The Dutch small energy users' tax sets a tax-free threshold of energy use, which ensures that average energy users are no worse off under the tax, but that higher and lower energy users in each income bracket are respectively worse and better off. This transparent 'fairness' won public acceptance for the tax, although it helped that it was not set at a very high level (EEA 1996: 37).

Active political support for MBIs is also weak, not least among two constituencies – right-wing politicians and businesses – who might appear to have most affinity to the market rhetoric of the economists who enthusiastically advocate MBIs. Support for MBIs from the neo-liberal right is rather half-hearted and even disingenuous; their support for MBIs is driven primarily by a dislike of regulations rather than enthusiasm for improving environmental protection. The pro-market rhetoric of the UK Conservative government in the 1990s was, in practice, a recipe for inaction: its deregulatory zeal led to many 'unnecessary' regulations being removed, but the only eco-taxes it introduced were a discriminatory tax on leaded petrol and a landfill tax.

Nor do MBIs inspire enthusiasm within the business community. Again, this might appear strange as, in theory, industry should benefit from the greater cost efficiency of MBIs. Yet proposals for new eco-taxes are typically met by fierce producer resistance (Andersen et al. 1998; Kasa 2000; Daugbjerg and Pedersen 2004). The most common business objection is that eco-taxes increase business costs and reduce international competitiveness. Indeed, many businesses prefer regulation to market incentives, notably where a regulatory agency has been so effectively 'captured' by the industry that it will act in its interests, perhaps by helping to exclude new entrants into a market. Leading companies might regard the replacement of existing regulations by an eco-tax as a potential threat to their market position by removing a barrier against the entry of new firms. Moreover, whereas a regulation requires a company to make only those environmental improvements necessary to meet the required standard, a tax is levied on all its discharges, not just those exceeding the standard, making it more onerous (albeit supposedly more efficient) for many firms (Jacobs 1996: 121).

In practice, the typical response of business is to resist *any* form of imposition on their activities, whether tax or regulation. If change is seen as inevitable, an industry, provided it is sufficiently organised, may offer a voluntary agreement as a means of preventing or delaying a new regulation or MBI, in the hope that the government will regard it as quicker and less costly. If the path of self-regulation is closed, then industry will lobby for the instrument – whether regulation or MBI – that better suits its self-interest, and it seems that tradeable permits are preferred to taxation, because when permits are allocated by grandfathering to established firms, they may provide a windfall profit for some participants and may act as a barrier to entry if new firms have to purchase pollution permits to enter the market.

However, not all the blame should be placed on the business community. The bottom-line everywhere is that taxes are deeply unpopular with the public. Certainly the unfavourable political environment is a key factor explaining the remarkably low number of eco-taxes in the USA (Fiorino 2004: 406). In particular, with transport a prime target for taxation amidst contemporary concern about climate change (see below), governments were made aware of public sensitivity on this issue by the fuel protests throughout Europe in 2000 demonstrating popular hostility to the high taxation of petrol that had forced the pump price up (see Chapter 6). Not surprisingly, democratically elected governments are nervous about upsetting their electorates with new eco-taxes. As Prime Minister Tony Blair observed in February 2005, in response to calls for an aviation tax, 'How many politicians facing . . . a potential election at some point in . . . the not so distant future would vote to end cheap air travel' (*The Observer Magazine*, 18 June 2006, p. 7).

To summarise, the relative scarcity of MBIs is less puzzling than at first appears. The theoretical case for MBIs, that they are more efficient and effective at delivering environmental policy objectives than regulations, has several technical and practical weaknesses, and there are significant political obstacles impeding the wider application of MBIs. The next section explores some of the points raised here by examining the use of different policy instruments to prevent climate change in the energy and transport sectors – a policy goal that must be central to any sustainable development strategy.

---

### Critical question 3
Should MBIs be the main environmental policy instrument?

---

# ▶ Policy instruments and climate change

The energy supply and transport sectors are the major contributors of greenhouse gas emissions; for example, they accounted for 59 per cent (from fossil fuel combustion in electricity and heat production, refineries, manufacturing industries, households and services) and 21 per cent ($CO_2$ from fossil fuel combustion and $N_2O$ from catalytic converters) of total EU-15 GHG emissions respectively in 2004 (EEA 2006b: 38). For most governments to reach even the relatively unambitious GHG emission reduction commitments promised at Kyoto (see Box 9.3) will require fundamental policy changes in these sectors, including extensive strategic planning, effective cross-sectoral co-ordination, the use of a mixed package of policy instruments and a willingness to impose stringent measures on both businesses and consumers.

## ▶ *Energy policy*

Historically, national energy policies have been designed to guarantee supplies of cheap energy to industry and the home, whilst ensuring sufficient fuel diversity to avoid the kind of dependence on imported fuels that led to economic disruption during the oil crises of the 1970s. Sustainable energy strategies must address both the supply and demand sides of the energy equation: electricity generation must shift away from a dependency on fossil fuels, notably coal and oil, towards renewable energy sources such as hydroelectric power (HEP), wind, solar, wave and biomass, which emit low or zero carbon; energy consumption must be reduced in both industrial and domestic sectors through improved energy efficiency and conservation measures. To date, little significant progress has been made towards sustainability in either the generation or consumption of electricity.

On the supply side, few countries boast a large renewable energy sector. Renewable energy provided just 14.7 per cent of EU-15 electricity in 2004 (compared to 13.4 per cent in 1990), mostly from HEP (EEA 2006b: 41–2).

Although HEP is very important in some countries, notably Austria, Norway and Sweden, its growth potential is limited not only by geography, but by the strong political opposition to the damage to habitats and communities arising from the construction of giant dams. So the development of alternative renewable sources is essential. Yet several serious obstacles make this a challenging policy goal, including powerful energy producers, competitive liberalised energy markets, discriminatory fossil fuel subsidies and technological problems. Where energy supply is provided by a large domestic industry, such as coal and oil in the USA, governments are reluctant to take action that might harm it. As Jansen et al. (1998) observe, even in Norway, where environmental consciousness is high, 'environmental quality counts, but national economic interests decide' (p. 198). If oil or gas is imported, powerful energy generators will resist any attempt to reduce their market share. Where significant changes in the energy mix have occurred, they usually owe little to sustainable energy policies, as illustrated by the UK (see Box 12.5).

Nor do renewables face a level playing field. In many countries, subsidies have historically favoured fossil fuel and nuclear production: one estimate put direct government subsidies for fossil fuel energy sources and technologies worldwide at around $200 billion annually, of which $100 billion is provided by the US government (Hempel 2006: 305). Alongside the small scale of operations and lack of investment, it is not surprising therefore that electricity from renewable energy is usually more expensive than from fossil fuels. The balance did start to shift during the 1990s as many governments began to introduce subsidies and other forms of protection to stimulate the nascent renewable sector. The declining output of the nuclear sector – notwithstanding its recent revival (see Chapter 7) – has also encouraged greater urgency in the search for alternatives. When the German government agreed its nuclear power-station closure programme (see Box 7.8), it instigated a radical programme, complete with ambitious targets and backed by annual subsidies of €2 billion, to expand its renewable energy industry.

Wind is the largest renewable energy source after HEP. The total global capacity for generating electricity through wind power was about 59.4 GW in 2005 (GWEC 2006). Although still contributing only a tiny share of the total global electricity-generating capacity and representing just a fraction of the *potential* wind energy capacity, the sector is growing rapidly, increasing by 25 per cent in 2005 alone. Technological improvements, notably the development of more efficient turbines, have seen the price of electricity from onshore wind farms drop significantly. Generation in the EU-15 grew by a factor of seventy-five between 1990 and 2004, helped by generous price tariffs in Germany and Spain (EEA 2006b: 42). Elsewhere, tax breaks were a catalyst for steady growth in the USA, although wind power still contributed less than 1 per cent of total electricity generation in 2006 (AWEA 2006). The fastest growth is in India, which is now the fourth-largest generator in

## 12.5 Tensions in UK energy policy

Britain should exceed its Kyoto target of a 12.5 per cent reduction of 1990 levels in six greenhouse gases by 2010, despite lacking a long-term sustainable energy strategy. This success in cutting greenhouse emissions is almost entirely due to one fortuitous factor: a dramatic change in the energy mix from coal to gas. In 1990 coal generated 67 per cent of UK electricity but by 2004 it had fallen to 28 per cent; in the same period gas rose from less than 1 per cent to 40 per cent. This 'dash for gas' was made possible by the privatisation of the energy industry during the 1980s and the liberalisation of the electricity market. Freed of historic state-imposed commitments to purchase expensive coal, the privately owned energy suppliers rapidly invested in gas-fired power stations.

*Yet British energy policy is currently unsustainable*

- Gas is a non-renewable fuel source and will eventually be exhausted; as domestic gas supplies decline, Britain will become a net importer of gas sometime after 2010, primarily from Russia.

- The nuclear sector contributed 19 per cent of electricity in 2004, but without the construction of new reactors it will rapidly decline.
- The renewable sector is tiny, with a current market share of just 3.6 per cent in 2004; it will struggle to meet the government target of 10 per cent by 2010.
- Domestic energy consumption continues to rise, helped by the Labour government's decision to cut VAT on domestic fuel to 5 per cent in 1997.

*Main government initiatives*

- A Climate Change Levy on industry introduced in 2001, but with limited impact after the initial 'entry effect'.
- The Renewables Obligation introduced in 2002 requires all energy suppliers to deliver a specified and growing proportion of electricity from renewable sources, with a target of 10 per cent by 2010, 15 per cent by 2015 and rising to 20 per cent thereafter.
- DTI (2006): the government commits to nuclear energy as a low carbon solution and promises a raft of measures to improve energy efficiency.

*Sources*: DTI (2005, 2006).

the world (GWEC 2006). Other renewable sources such as solar power and biomass are also expanding rapidly, but their overall contribution remains small (EEA 2006b: 42–3). Wave power, which has great potential as a large and predictable source of energy, is still a relatively untested technology. The EU-15 target for 2010 of a 22 per cent share of gross electricity generation from renewable energy sources will not be met; indeed, few if any individual member states will meet their national targets (EEA 2006b: 42). It is unlikely that renewable energy will become a significant source of electricity generation without the imposition of a carbon tax on fossil fuels that is set sufficiently high to make the fledgling renewables sector more competitive and (as in Denmark) tax revenues are reinvested in the renewables sector for research and design, subsidies and preferential agreements (Andersen et al. 1998).

On the demand side, progress in containing, let alone reducing, energy consumption is extremely slow. There are numerous ways of improving domestic and industrial energy efficiency. Some governments have set high mandatory energy efficiency standards for buildings, subsidised home conservation and low-energy light bulbs, and agreed energy efficiency classification systems for consumer goods such as washing machines. There are many examples of industry voluntarily introducing energy-saving measures, notably the detailed energy efficiency targets agreed by Dutch industry covering over 90 per cent of its total energy use. The British government used the threat of a new climate change levy to negotiate agreements with several industrial sectors to reduce carbon emissions. In many countries, increasing numbers of consumers have voluntarily chosen to insulate their homes or purchase efficient domestic goods to conserve energy. Nevertheless, existing regulations, subsidies and voluntary actions, although helpful, will not achieve the necessary reductions in energy consumption. Perhaps only more stringent carbon and energy taxes can provide the necessary incentive to change industrial and consumer behaviour.

Carbon and energy tax proposals have encountered fierce opposition from domestic business communities, primarily on the grounds that their international competitiveness would be severely affected. Eight EU member states had carbon taxes in 2004, with mixed results (EEA 2006a: 27). Sweden imposed a stiff carbon tax on industry in 1991, but the government reduced it a year later, declaring that the resulting competitive advantage to Swedish industry would create over 10,000 jobs (EEA 1996: 40). Subsequent green tax reforms have involved high carbon taxes balanced by reduced employment taxes (Government of Sweden 2006). In Finland, the carbon tax introduced in 1990 had such a detrimental impact on industry that it was replaced by a consumption tax in 1996 (Sairinen 2003: 83–4). President Clinton, in the face of pressure from the fossil fuel lobby and energy-intensive industries, failed in 1993 to get congressional support for his proposed 'Btu tax', a broad-based tax on the heat content of fuels (Hempel 2006: 306–7). After strong and co-ordinated industry lobbying, the UK climate change levy was a watered-down version of the original proposal, although there is evidence that it initially had some positive impact on the behaviour of firms (HM Treasury 2006). Business resistance helped persuade the Kohl government to drop plans for a carbon tax in Germany for competitive reasons (Schreurs 2002: 160), although the SPD–Green coalition subsequently introduced an ambitious range of energy taxes in 1999 (Kohlhaas and Meyer 2005).

Overall, national carbon and energy taxes have had a marginal impact on behaviour because, to make them politically acceptable, they have been levied at too low a level. Clearly, carbon taxes pose a classic free-rider problem: unless states co-ordinate their actions to impose a uniform tax collectively, then industry in those countries where a tax is levied will be competitively disadvantaged. However, attempts by the Danish, Dutch and

German governments to agree a EU carbon tax in the mid-1990s encountered equally fierce industry lobbying of the European institutions and foundered on the opposition of several countries, notably the UK and France (Zito 2000: ch. 4). Without an EU tax no member state is likely to impose carbon taxes at sufficiently stringent levels to produce fundamental improvements in energy efficiency, reductions in energy consumption, or a shift to renewable sources of energy. Having failed to agree a carbon tax, it is tempting to regard the creation of the EU emissions trading scheme in 2005, in which thousands of permits were simply given away free of charge, as a 'business-friendly' fall-back measure.

## ▶ Transport policy

Transport policies in most countries have traditionally adopted a 'predict and provide' approach to the expansion of road and air transport: *predict* the anticipated growth in each sector and *provide* the roads and airports necessary to support it. Some governments, notably in the USA and Canada and the Thatcher government in the UK, adopted a pro-roads stance with particular ideological fervour, directly linking road construction to economic growth and freedom of the individual. By 2000, global passenger car production reached 40.9 million vehicles, contributing to a global total of around 532 million vehicles, with the annual distance travelled by each driver rising steadily (Whitelegg and Haq 2003a: 4–5). Climate change prevention requires a fundamentally different approach to transport policy. A sustainable transport policy has to address both supply and demand: on the supply side, air and road transport need to produce fewer polluting emissions; on the demand side, traffic volume must be reduced so that fewer journeys are made by car and plane.[5] All governments now recognise the need to change, but few have made a genuine paradigm shift, for they are reluctant to do anything that might damage the economy or prove unpopular with the public (see Box 12.6).

Policymakers have pinned their hopes on the supply-side objective of developing 'greener' motor vehicles (Hempel 1995; Whitelegg 1997). In recent years, the impact of individual cars on the environment has been lessened through engine modifications, anti-pollution devices, alternative fuels and new types of vehicle. Several major vehicle manufacturers have launched new models that use biomass products, such as ethanol and methanol, or liquefied petroleum gas or run on electricity. They are also working with oil companies, such as BP, to develop alternatives, such as hydrogen fuel-cell technology. To date, none of these alternatives has been a major commercial success, although there are small but growing markets for biofuels and liquefied petroleum gas, and for hybrid vehicles, which combine a fuel-efficient petrol engine with batteries and an electric drive train.

Sometimes technological advances have been helped by voluntary agreements, which may stimulate the development of innovative solutions. For example, car manufacturers agreed to limit the average carbon emissions of new cars sold in the EU to 140 g/km – by 2008 for European car-makers and 2009 for Japanese and Korean car-makers (EEA 2006c: 28). However, with current trends going in the wrong direction (notably the availability of heavier, more powerful vehicles, the specific boom in sales of SUVs and the growing demand for extra equipment such as air conditioning) it seems unlikely that even this modest target will be achieved (EEA 2006c: 28; *Financial Times*, 26 April 2006). The Commission admits that its medium-term target of 120 g/km is not yet within reach.

Regulation has proved a stronger catalyst for the commercial development of new technologies. Vogel (1995) identifies the significance of the 'California effect': this state has long boasted the strictest American automotive pollution control standards, obliging motor manufacturers to make technological improvements if they want access to California's large and wealthy car market. The US Clean Air Act 1970 permitted California to set stricter vehicle emissions standards than other states, which directly contributed to the development of the catalytic converter. EU emission legislation since the late 1980s has also imposed tough vehicle emission standards, which have hastened technological improvements. The 1998 Auto/Oil programme, for example, set new vehicle emission and fuel quality standards in an attempt to force manufacturers to develop catalysts for diesels and new low sulphur fuels which are necessary for future emission reductions. More radically, a 1990 Californian mandate (later adopted by several other states) required 10 per cent of the state's new vehicles sold in 2003 to be 'zero emission', such as electric cars. Although subsequently much amended, for example to allow manufacturers to earn credits for low (rather than zero) emission vehicles, the mandate has contributed to the development of cleaner technologies (Shaheen et al. 2004).

Although regulatory competition has, on balance, made motor vehicles cleaner and more fuel-efficient, there are many limitations to the 'techno-fix' solution. The overall environmental impact is usually complex. For example, while the widespread use of catalytic converters has reduced nitrogen oxide emissions, their lower fuel efficiency has increased carbon emissions. The bottom-line is that technological solutions all avoid the core problem of traffic volume; indeed, techno-fixes may even encourage the false belief that driving a 'greener' car will not seriously damage the environment. Yet the increase in emissions resulting from the inexorable growth in traffic volume (more vehicles, greater frequency of use and increased average journey length) has consistently cancelled out the benefits from techno-fixes, and has been exacerbated by the current fashion for SUVs (see Vanderheiden 2006).

Policymakers have begun to address the consumption side of the equation. Perhaps the best example of strategic planning is the Netherlands, which has long boasted a well-integrated national intermodal transport network. But governments almost everywhere and at every level are increasingly using transport planning systems both as a stick to discourage car use and as a carrot to encourage alternative forms of travel such as public transport, cycling and walking. Many cities have experimented with a range of sticks, such as car-sharing requirements and restrictions on car access and parking capacity, and carrots, notably schemes to give priority to trams and buses. Cycling and walking are encouraged by the use of speed restrictions, traffic-calming schemes and segregated cycle lanes to make streets safer. Walking is made more attractive by pedestrianised zones, better pavements and safe crossing points. Yet traffic management can exert only a marginal impact without stronger incentives to discourage car use.

Policymakers have therefore become increasingly interested in using MBIs to alter travelling habits. There is a strong economic case for using MBIs to correct market failure because existing taxes on motoring, such as sales, vehicle and fuel taxes, cover only a small proportion of its external costs. Indeed, there are still subsidies promoting petrol-driven vehicles, particularly in the USA (Litman 2003), and tax breaks for road transport generally, such as company cars. Road transport tax regimes have traditionally focused on raising general tax revenue. Where the aim is to alter behaviour, such as setting lower taxes for low sulphur fuels, or linking road taxes to engine size, there has been no impact on traffic volume. A few countries, including Britain, the Netherlands, Norway and Sweden, have increased fuel taxes for explicitly environmental reasons, but with little impact on consumption. For example, a 10 per cent Norwegian $CO_2$ tax introduced in 1991 is estimated to have reduced motor vehicle emissions by just 2–3 per cent per annum (OECD 1997: 26). The inelasticity of demand for petrol will require a substantial increase, perhaps over 40 per cent, to have any significant impact on consumption, but politicians are understandably resistant to taking such a radical step. None the less, with taxes (excluding VAT) making up 40–60 per cent of the sales price of motor fuels in Europe – far higher than in the USA – it is no coincidence that the European car fleet is far more energy-efficient and that per capita carbon emissions are much lower than in the USA (EEA 2006c). One positive trend is that more countries are basing vehicle taxes on $CO_2$ emissions.

There is growing interest in road pricing schemes using microwave technology or satellite positioning equipment which, by charging motorists for every journey, could reduce non-essential trips and hence the overall volume of journeys. Several cities, including London, Melbourne, Singapore and Toronto, have introduced successful schemes. The weekday congestion charge in London, introduced in 2003, was intended to reduce congestion in the city centre, with revenues used to improve public transport (mainly buses and the Underground). The charge has produced an average 30 per cent reduction in congestion, an 18 per cent reduction in traffic and significant growth in bus use (Transport for London 2005: 2–3). By creating a substantial financial disincentive and making the driver aware of the cost of each journey, road-pricing systems may represent the most potent incentive to reduce traffic volume. As part of a wider package of vehicle, fuel and road taxes, they can generate revenue to invest in vital public transport improvements, as in London. Massive capital investment programmes are needed to expand rail networks, improve rolling stock and increase the frequency and reliability of trains. Modern high-speed rail links, such as the French TGV, have shown that trains can compete successfully for long-distance travellers and freight traffic. Without the carrot of fast, efficient, convenient and affordable public transport, it is unlikely that people will be persuaded to leave their cars at home.

To summarise, the main conclusion of this brief analysis of climate change policies is that progress in implementing sustainable energy and transport policies remains slow. Although energy and transport sectors are generally in a state of flux, there are few signs of the kind of paradigm shift necessary for even weak sustainable development. Governments still rely heavily on the technical solutions that characterise the traditional paradigm, such as more fuel-efficient engines or exhaust-pipe emissions control, when it seems clear that the reduction of emissions from the transport sector is likely to require a broad mix of policy instruments. The absence of comprehensive stringent carbon taxes, in particular, indicates that policymakers have not yet accepted that sustainability requires solutions which have a significant impact on the lifestyles of citizens. Yet, there are encouraging signs of innovation, ranging from road-pricing schemes to tradeable permits, which suggest that some policymakers in some instances, are starting to take the climate change challenge seriously.

**Critical question 4**
Does popular opposition to 'excessive' fuel duties demonstrate the
limitations of eco-taxes?

## ▶ Conclusion

Rarely does the choice of policy instrument involve a simple exercise of
selecting the technically best (i.e. the most efficient or effective) option.
There are clearly some environmental problems that can only be resolved
satisfactorily by regulation. Where the objective is the *complete* prevention of a damaging activity – for example, the removal of a dangerous
substance, such as lead from petrol – then legal prohibition, provided
it is effectively implemented, is the only way to guarantee a successful
outcome; an MBI allows the possibility that a polluter may be prepared
to pay any price to continue its dangerous behaviour. Regulations are also
faster-acting; a legal prohibition can take effect immediately, whereas an
incentive, such as an emissions tax aimed at persuading firms to invest in
cleaner technology, may take longer to influence behaviour. However, most
problems can be addressed by a wide range of different policy instruments,
and the process of choosing between them will be suffused with political
considerations.

The wider political context has contributed to the growing interest in
MBIs. The ascendancy of neo-liberal ideas has shifted the terms of debate
against the use of regulatory measures by focusing on their negative
attributes of inefficiency and inflexibility. The growing influence of the
ecological modernisation discourse has also strengthened the support for
alternatives. Policymakers seem more prepared to draw on a wider armoury
of measures and, significantly, the alternatives to regulation seem to be
used most widely in 'new' policy areas such as climate change, where the
demand for radical solutions is most acute. The pace of change is, however, slow. Currently, ecological modernisation is most apparent as a discourse rather than as an activity. Regulations are, and will continue to be,
widely used everywhere, not least because they satisfy administrative convenience, retain public legitimacy and suit industry. The knee-jerk resistance
in the business community to any new eco-tax hardly suggests that it is
persuaded by ecological modernisation. If it is to change, then the initiative will have to come from those governments that are willing to intervene
actively in the market to steer business and consumer behaviour, which
again suggests that ecological modernisation is more likely to flourish in
some countries than in others (see Chapter 8). The wider use of eco-taxes
in Scandinavia reflects public acceptance of a high taxation burden, which
is justified in terms of the established institutional logic of the welfare

state: that taxes are necessary to improve the common good (Jansen et al. 1998: 312). By contrast, where neo-liberal ideas are predominant, as in Australia, Britain and the USA, there is a stronger anti-tax culture and greater resistance to state intervention, which may be less conducive to ecological modernisation.

It is important not to become fixated on the highly stylised regulation versus MBI dichotomy. In practice, policymakers select a mix of instruments to achieve a policy objective. MBIs, in particular, are usually introduced as part of a package of measures alongside regulations that are kept to ensure that minimum standards are maintained. Although the literature often implies that they are polar opposites, there is considerable common ground between regulations and MBIs because both require active state intervention in the economy; indeed, tradeable permits explicitly involve a combination of regulation and market forces. Perhaps the focus on different types of instrument obfuscates the real issue: whether the package of instruments selected is sufficiently *stringent* to achieve the desired outcomes.

Here, a useful distinction can be made between low- and high-cost environmental policies (Daugbjerg 1998). *Low-cost policies* favour the interests of producers: advice and information are preferred to measures that may impose costs, but where regulations are used, they are couched in broad terms to allow flexible implementation to suit local conditions. Eco-taxes are used rarely but, if imposed, they are set at low levels and producers are often reimbursed through subsidies. Tradeable permit schemes issue too many permits at too low a price. *High-cost policies*, by contrast, emphasise more extensive use of eco-taxes, less generous tradeable permit schemes and universal regulations setting standards and targets. Put differently, the presence of stringent MBIs at the centre of a broad package of policy instruments may be a good indicator of a serious approach to sustainable development.

As high-cost policies would normally affect key producer, consumer and environmental interests, the distribution of power within the policy process will play a critical role in determining the stringency of policy instruments. Daugbjerg (1998) compares agri-environmental policy in Denmark and Sweden and argues that in sectors characterised by policy communities, low-cost policies will be introduced, whereas high-cost policies will be associated with issue networks. Danish nitrate policymaking shows that a tight policy community sharing a consensus on policy principles produced a low-cost nitrate policy. By contrast, the open Swedish policy network, with its weaker links between state and farmers and a significant role for environmental interests, has resulted in a high-cost policy consisting of tougher nitrate reduction targets, a higher fertiliser tax, relatively inflexible universal regulations and lower subsidies than in Denmark.

The climate change case study bears the clear imprint of powerful producer interests. Corporate interests were instrumental in dissuading EU member states from introducing a Community-wide carbon tax. Within each country business interests have fiercely, and usually effectively, resisted the imposition of domestic energy and fuel taxation. In Norway, a powerful policy community of employers' organisations, trade unions and the energy and industry ministries successfully blocked repeated proposals to extend the existing $CO_2$ tax to a wider range of exempted emission-intensive industries, such as metallurgical production (Kasa 2000). Everywhere, resistance to road taxation is typically organised around pro-roads advocacy coalitions consisting of oil companies, vehicle manufacturers, construction companies, trade unions and groups representing car drivers and the road haulage industry. Business resistance is aided by the administrative fragmentation of the state, which has enabled the energy and roads lobbies to find plenty of allies at the heart of government. The importance of both energy and road transport in the modern economy has ensured that industry and finance ministries have also proved receptive to their interests. Transport ministries have only slowly begun to temper their enthusiasm for the motor vehicle and road construction, and most remain avowedly 'pro-roads'.

Policymakers seem even more reluctant to impose MBIs on consumers. Politicians fear that stringent eco-taxes on items of basic need, such as domestic energy consumption, or key lifestyle goods, such as cars, would provoke huge public hostility. Car ownership has become a central part of the culture of the modern consumer society, symbolising individual freedom and personal achievement. Changing consumer behaviour will be no easy task. Moreover, all energy and road taxes are potentially regressive. Fuel taxes, for example, exert a disproportionate impact on low-income groups, who may need extra heating or be dependent on motor vehicles by virtue of ill-health, infirmity, disability or the absence of alternatives. Politicians have become more nervous about introducing unpopular taxes since the wave of fuel protests that swept across Western Europe during 2000, forcing concessions from panicky governments. The reluctance of successive American presidents to agree to carbon emissions reductions is influenced partly by the powerful energy producers and car manufacturers, but also by the strong gas-guzzling American culture founded on the availability of cheap gasoline.

Arguably, it is precisely this strong resistance that makes the case for eco-taxes so persuasive: by sending the clear financial signal that people should conserve energy or change their travelling patterns, they seem to offer most hope of changing consumer behaviour. The enthusiasm for MBIs amongst environmental groups, who were once wary of them, underlines this point. Green parties are also converts, with eco-tax packages forming key planks of coalition agreements in Belgium and Germany. While the use of market mechanisms was once condemned as a reformist blind alley, today many greens have embraced these market measures with enthusiasm, underlining their readiness to accept the capitalist economic system, just as their entry into national parliaments and then into government declared their willingness to work within liberal democracy.

## ▶ *Further reading and websites*

Vogel (1986), although very dated, still merits reading for an interesting comparison of the US and UK regulatory styles. Dryzek (2005: ch. 6) provides an interesting discussion of the ideas behind market approaches, although it is advisable to dip into the economic textbooks to get a real grasp of the technical arguments for and against different policy instruments: Jacobs (1991), Turner et al. (1994) and Sterner (2003) provide accessible and reasonably non-technical introductions to the subject. Jordan et al. (2003b), Hatch (2005b) and EEA (2006a) are comparative analyses of practical developments in the use of policy instruments. Mol et al. (2000) analyse the development and effectiveness of voluntary agreements in the EU. Hempel (2006) assesses American climate change policy. See Toke (2002) and Szarka (2004) for comparative studies of wind energy. Whitelegg and Haq (2003b) provide a useful international comparison of transport issues and the EEA (2006b) analyses key transport trends and issues in the EU.

See the websites at the end of Chapter 11 for data on national climate change, energy and transport policies, and see the excellent European Environment Agency website (http://www.eea.eu.int/).

NOTES

1 Some writers use the term 'economic instrument' in preference to MBI.
2 It is this active state intervention that distinguishes the work of environmental economists, such as Pearce et al. (1989), from free market environmentalism (see Chapter 3), which holds that the environment will only be protected by the normal operation of free markets.
3 The EEA (2006a) also regards liability and compensation schemes as MBIs, but this is not universally accepted.
4 The allocation of permits is itself a highly political issue. Permits are usually allocated according to past emissions levels, but this 'grandfathering' method may be inequitable because it effectively grants pollution 'rights' to companies on the basis of their previous record of pollution.
5 For reasons of space the discussion concentrates on road transport.

# Conclusion

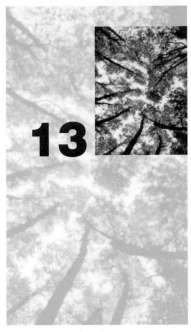

**13**

Chapter 12 ended with the observation that the environmental movement has become so reconciled to the continuation of capitalism that it is now positively enthusiastic about the role of the market as a tool to protect the environment. This sentiment seems a long way from the anti-industrialism and the anarchistic blueprint of a sustainable world discussed in Part I. Indeed, it reflects the shift in the centre of gravity of environmental politics in recent years from a radical rejection of the existing economic and political system towards a reformist acceptance of capitalism and liberal democracy. This concluding chapter draws together some of the themes discussed in the book by analysing the state of environmental politics some forty years after the emergence of 'modern environmentalism'. More specifically, it examines the significance of ecologism, assesses progress towards sustainable development and speculates about the future path of environmental politics.

A central argument of the book is that ecologism should be regarded as an ideology in its own right. It offers a persuasive critique of (capitalist) industrial society and the liberal democratic polity, holding them largely responsible for the current ecological crisis; it outlines a vision of an alternative sustainable society; and it suggests strategies of change that might achieve that utopian vision. The most distinctive theoretical contribution of ecologism, as discussed in Part I, resides in its two core ideas: the need to reassess human–nature relations and the belief in ecological limits to growth. These core ideas have been supplemented by a set of principles drawn from other doctrines but reworked to fit green purposes: notably social justice, participatory democracy and decentralisation. These principles are regarded as essential components of a sustainable society and they also inform green theories of agency for getting to that sustainable world.

Ecologism and the environmental movement pose important challenges to established political traditions at the levels of ideas, action and policy. First, Part I showed how the distinctive, if contentious, theoretical contribution of ecologism has forced political philosophers to engage with the notion that we might have duties towards nature and to future generations of unborn humans. Greens also make new demands of familiar concepts such as participatory democracy and social justice. Participatory democratic decision-making, for example, is expected not only to improve the quality of the democratic polity, but also to raise ecological consciousness and generate greener policy outcomes. Individualist theories of justice need to be reworked to address the distribution of collective environmental goods. Moreover, by invoking familiar political concepts, greens can draw important lessons from mainstream political philosophy; after all, they are not the first to think about participatory democracy or social justice. So, green theorists must be aware of the conceptual baggage these principles carry with them. For example, what are the implications of basing an environmental ethical theory on utilitarianism? Would it be better to ground a green theory of justice on equality or on rights? The flourishing environmental movement has forced other ideologies, especially those on the left, to address environmental issues, such as the possibility that there may be ecological limits to growth. Conversely, green politics has drawn on other political traditions, notably socialism, for a critique of capitalism, and from anarchism for its suspicion of the state. The creative tension that exists where ecologism engages with other ideologies is illustrated by the emergence of hybrid doctrines, such as ecosocialism, ecoanarchism and ecofeminism.

Ecologism is theoretically less distinctive in dealing with political action; indeed, it offers a rather incoherent strategy for change. Radical ecologism has thrown up a hotch-potch of approaches, which reflect its anarchistic and libertarian roots. Some writers recommend opting out of the existing system by setting up communes or adopting alternative lifestyles; others demand direct action that confronts the existing system. Within the environmental movement there is a strong, albeit diminishing, fundamentalist purity about grassroots democracy, which reflects the 'new social movement' origins of many environmental groups and green parties. Yet many environmental activists have found these strategies impractical (most people simply do not want to opt out of the system or to break the law) and ineffective as a means of engaging in practical political activity. Consequently, as environmental politics has become increasingly mainstream, so environmental activism has become increasingly reconciled to reformist strategies that work within the legislative process and the boundaries of civil society. How should this development be assessed? Is it sensible pragmatism to bring environmental politics in from the margins or is it a sign of its failure to achieve real change?

Proponents of the reformist strategy point to the undoubted impact of environmental politics on contemporary political behaviour. Chapters 4 and

5 showed how the electoral success of green parties has contributed to a thawing of frozen party cleavages and voter alignments in several European countries and forced most parties to treat the environment more seriously, at least by developing a greener rhetoric and strengthening policy programmes. The presence of green parties in red–green and rainbow coalition governments at all levels of government has had a visible, albeit limited, impact on policy outcomes. Yet the potential of green electoral politics is circumscribed by the low salience of the environment: traditional materialist issues continue to dominate electoral politics and less than 10 per cent of the electorate regard the environment as a major issue. A majority green government remains a distant prospect. However, environmental groups are important actors in the policy process. Chapter 6 showed how the enormous resources and public support that the largest groups can now mobilise have contributed to the institutionalisation of the mainstream movement. While environmental groups remain less influential than business interests in most critical policy areas, they have undoubtedly changed policy agendas and influenced many specific decisions.

By contrast, critics of reformism counter that the limited 'success' of environmental politics actually illustrates the failure of this approach in that it symbolises the incorporation or co-option of green politics by dominant interests. From this perspective, the radicalism of green parties will inevitably be compromised by their need to ensure continued electoral success – the *logic of electoral competition* – and to win the support of partners in a coalition government. Similarly, the institutionalisation of the environmental movement, which has seen international NGOs invited to join UN bodies such as the Commission for Sustainable Development and major domestic groups regularly consulted and funded by national governments, and even Greenpeace now sitting down to talk business with Shell and Monsanto, has arguably denuded environmentalism of its radical principles and prevents it from achieving substantive change. It has been this suspicion of reformism – of getting into bed with the enemy – that has contributed to the grassroots backlash of eco-protesters employing confrontational methods of protest, such as the actions of the British anti-road movement and the anti-globalisation demonstrations at the meetings of the WTO. Ultimately, the relative merits of each approach will be judged by the impact of environmental politics on policy outcomes.

Yet ecologism is perhaps at its weakest in dealing with practical issues because its utopian vision of a sustainable society offers few concrete suggestions to help policymakers deal with immediate problems. Not surprisingly, it is sustainable development that has become the dominant policy discourse for governments, international organisations, businesses and for the environmental movement itself. In part, this reflects a disenchantment and frustration among many environmental activists with the narrow ecological concerns of green politics; or at least with the widespread public perception that it is a single-issue movement. By declaring that environmental protection need not be bought at the expense of economic growth, sustainable development is immediately more appealing to a wider public. More important, though, is its broad development agenda which, by linking poverty, inequality and North–South issues to environmental degradation, offers a more comprehensive analysis of the contemporary ecological crisis than, say, deep ecology. Seen in this light, the emergence of sustainable development has much in common with the left-libertarian programme represented by the four pillars of green politics discussed in Chapter 3. Some radical greens believe sustainable development falls outside the boundaries of ecologism: it is human-centred, denies (or at least doubts) the existence of limits to growth and seeks to reform rather than overthrow capitalism. However, the implementation of strong versions of sustainable development would certainly result in a form of capitalism so radically different as to be virtually unrecognisable, which points to the adoption of an inclusive definition of ecologism that encompasses strong versions of sustainable development that seek to reform, rather than overthrow, capitalism and liberal democracy. Either way, the centre of gravity in environmental politics has undoubtedly shifted from a *radical* rejection of industrialism and a *narrow* concern with ecological issues, to a *reformist* acceptance of capitalism and liberal democracy based on a *broader* (and, in many respects, more radical) social justice agenda.

To date, although sustainable development has been almost universally adopted as the policy paradigm driving strategies to protect the environment, no country has yet got anywhere close to achieving even the very weakest forms of sustainability. Despite the deteriorating state of the environment, there is still a wide gap between the rhetoric and reality of sustainable development. Policymakers are willing to make symbolic gestures but reluctant to approve concrete policy measures. Progress towards sustainable development is slow, piecemeal and insubstantial. Certainly there have been many initiatives and some real achievements in the name of sustainable development, but these improvements have only scratched the surface of the problem. Chapter 9 identified many examples of international environmental co-operation. New international institutions and projects, including the UNEP, CSD and Agenda 21, have been given considerable responsibility for ensuring that international agreements are enforced and that the sustainable development message trickles down to all levels of government and throughout civil society. International environmental regimes have generated some genuine success stories: in particular, ozone diplomacy has directly resulted in a massive reduction in the manufacture of ozone-depleting chemicals. However, since the massive Rio jamboree in 1992, the environment has slipped down the agenda of international politics. Other issues, notably armed conflicts in the Middle East, Europe and Africa, have helped push it aside, but governments have also begun to count the domestic costs of implementing some international treaty commitments, which helps explain the difficulty in securing agreement on carbon emission reductions. With many countries unlikely to achieve even the minimum targets agreed in the Kyoto Protocol and the United States resolute in its rejection of it, the international community is still struggling to get to grips with the most serious environmental problem currently confronting the world.

Similarly, most governments, as outlined in Chapter 11, have taken tentative steps towards environmental governance by introducing a myriad of institutional and administrative reforms with the intention of improving integration, planning and participation in the policy process. Environmental groups have gained better access to policymaking processes, which has allowed them to win isolated victories preventing specific proposals or introducing particular amendments to legislation, but they have rarely been able to seize the policy initiative from industrial interests. Even in those pioneer countries where ecological modernisation has taken root, politicians still tend to 'talk' sustainable development without routinely thinking through the environmental considerations of their actions. Reforms of the machinery of government have done little to resolve the administrative fragmentation that institutionalises the power of sectoral producer interests such as energy companies, the roads lobby or farmers, let alone alter the structural factors that privilege these industrial interests. Consequently, administrative techniques that could build environmental considerations into decision-making processes, such as EIA and risk assessment, rarely disrupt the dominance of industrial interests.

Not surprisingly, therefore, government policies in most areas remain insufficiently stringent, as illustrated in Chapter 12 by the inadequacy of climate change policies in the energy and transport sectors. The share of electricity generated from renewable sources remains tiny and no government has managed (or even tried) to transform the transport sector away from private cars and freight towards a fully integrated public transport infrastructure. Governments are increasingly prepared to employ a wider toolkit of policy instruments, notably market-based instruments and voluntary agreements, thus reducing the traditional dependence on regulatory measures, which have been widely criticised for being inefficient and ineffective. Yet the continuing absence of a tranche of stringent market-based instruments reflects the sensitivity of governments to powerful business lobbying and their fear of an electoral backlash against unpopular taxes.

On balance, the benefits from the many environmental protection measures that are in place, such as reductions in certain pollutants and the adoption of cleaner technologies, are outweighed by the accelerating growth of ecologically unsustainable consumption and resource depletion arising from the apparently inexorable advance of global capitalism and the still rapidly growing world population. The debates about globalisation and free trade discussed in Chapter 10 are particularly pertinent given the rapid expansion of major industrialising nations such as China and India. Many argue that the extraordinary transformation of China into a nascent hegemonic power is being achieved at a dreadful cost to the environment (Liu and Diamond 2005), although amidst the litany of woes there are some positive signs of change (Carter and Mol 2006).

Does this provide evidence to support the rejectionist stance of radical greens who question the possibility of achieving a sustainable society without transforming the capitalist system? Or is there any evidence suggesting that the reformist approach can be successful? The answers to these questions seem largely to lie in the relationship between three key actors: the state, business, and the individual citizen, and this discussion will close with a few speculative comments about each of these.

Governments at all levels have a key role to play in ensuring that the sustainable development process gains a momentum of its own. There will be further structural reforms as environmental ministries and agencies gradually acquire more powers and wider responsibilities. Green planning will become more extensive, with wider use of sustainability indicators linked to tougher sectoral targets and the development of green national accounting measures to complement traditional methods (Ogle 2000). Efforts to extend participation will increase, especially at the local level. Crucially, the growing international pressure to develop more effective responses to climate change is sure to see more experimentation with MBIs, notably the establishment of an international emissions trading market. Over time these initiatives may build up to exert a substantive effect, although the challenge of integrating environmental considerations across government – crucially, persuading major economic departments routinely to 'think green' – seems almost insurmountable. Moreover, politics, as this book shows, is not all about the state. Governments may be held back from taking more stringent measures by the lack of support from two key actors whose active support and participation are essential for the successful implementation of sustainable development: business and citizens.

Business remains a major obstacle to sustainable development. As Chapter 7 showed, business retains its privileged position in the policy process, reinforced by the administrative fragmentation of the state, producer-dominated policy networks and pro-industry advocacy coalitions. Not surprisingly, the traditional environmental policy paradigm still prevails in most policy areas. If capitalism is to be reformed, industry must be a willing partner. Hence the potential attraction of ecological modernisation is that the 'pollution prevention pays' principle demonstrates that business has an economic incentive to care for the environment. Certainly, by working in partnership with industry, the state can play a critical role in facilitating social learning by business elites and providing a framework of regulations and financial incentives to nurture ecological modernisation in specific policy areas. The evidence discussed in Part III suggests an ambivalent view of ecological modernisation. To date, it has colonised only a small minority of business boardrooms in certain sectors in a handful of mostly Northern European nations, which begs important questions about its applicability elsewhere, particularly in less developed countries. An important problem with ecological modernisation identified in Chapter 8 is that the literature seems focused on the production side of the equation, identifying the possibility of efficiency savings to be gained from adopting less polluting production technologies and practices. By contrast, the consumption side has been relatively ignored. Yet the market can only act as an instrument for change if consumers play their part. Currently, gestures towards green consumerism, such as increased levels of recycling or a switch to organic food products, are swamped by the dominance of consumer capitalism, which seems to feed off an apparently insatiable desire to consume more and more. While there is some scope for businesses to help shape consumer preferences by, for example, providing information about the energy efficiency of products, there is no incentive for businesses to persuade people to consume *less*. On the contrary, the logic of capitalism – the drive for capital accumulation and profit-maximisation – implies that business must encourage greater consumption.

One lesson of this book is that the transition to a sustainable society involves more than institutional restructuring by governments and social learning by policy elites. Neither businesses nor governments are likely to change their behaviour until they can be assured that consumers and citizens will support them. The market will continue to provide the goods that consumers demand (although business can of course stimulate and shape those consumer preferences) and, as long as the environment lacks electoral salience, few governments will risk unpopularity by introducing high eco-taxes on, say, domestic fuel or petrol. In short, in a capitalist liberal democracy the individual consumer, or citizen, may be a major obstacle to sustainable development.

It seems that sustainable development also requires a transformation in the beliefs, attitudes and behaviour of individuals along the lines of the 'ecological citizenship' models increasingly discussed by green theorists (Christoff 1996a; Barry 1999a; Dobson 2003; Dobson and Bell 2006). Although sustainable development does not require the dramatic sacrifices towards frugal living anticipated by deep ecologists, it will nevertheless still involve some significant changes in individual lifestyles if there is to be a shift from a *consumer* society towards a *conserver* society. Such changes will only take root if people accept the underlying ethos and voluntarily make the necessary alterations. The use of MBIs can play a role here. However, ecological citizenship will clearly involve a degree of ecological responsibility towards non-citizens, notably animals and ecosystems, and civic loyalty must stretch beyond the boundaries of the nation state to encompass global considerations, such as poverty in the less developed world. Ecological citizenship in practice will range from ethical investment to participation in

LETS schemes, and from green consumerism to voluntary involvement in community and environmental programmes. If ecological citizenship were to take root, even its weakest forms would act as a potential market stimulus to ecological modernisation.

How might ecological citizenship be nurtured? There are certainly plenty of opportunities for governments to facilitate ecological citizenship through policies that might even prove popular. Not least, policies aimed at the alleviation and removal of poverty and inequality would be critical. Institutional reforms, notably the democratisation and decentralisation of state structures, could encourage greater deliberation and participation by citizens.

Crucially, the state can also invest in education. At a general level, people are mystified or bewildered by the complexity of most global environmental issues. Public understanding of global warming, for example, remains at an alarmingly low level. Things are slowly changing. Today the environment is a familiar feature on the school curriculum from the moment children start formal education. Younger generations are undoubtedly much better informed about environmental issues than their predecessors. The growing significance of the Internet as a source of knowledge, education and communication may enhance this trend (it also offers unknown potential to expand the repertoire of protest, as illustrated by the activist networking behind the global justice movement). Furthermore, there is evidence that higher levels of education enhance public understanding of environmental issues (Rootes 1999b). Here again there is reason for optimism. The proportion of people with higher education is growing in most countries, so public awareness and understanding of environmental issues is likely to grow.

Of great importance, though, is evidence that environmental activism is positively linked to higher education, so a more educated citizenry may also be more willing and more capable of acting on its concerns by changing lifestyles and participating in the political process. One way to persuade people to change their lifestyles would be to educate people to consider the impact of their ecological footprint and to encourage them to reduce its impact. Another form of political education is through the experience of struggle. Most people encounter an environmental conflict at the local level, perhaps resisting a new road or incinerator, but a local struggle frequently involves direct confrontation with a multinational corporation and/or a national government. Local groups may then look to national and international NGOs for support, which might act as a catalyst for individuals to make links between their local struggle and wider issues, a process of learning and reflection that has the potential to stimulate a wider ecological consciousness. It is the prospect of this reflexivity occurring on a large scale that has led some writers to enthuse about the emergence of a global civil society of international NGOs such as Greenpeace, FoE and WWF linking civil society across national boundaries and providing a new source of identity for individual citizens beyond their own nationality

(Lipschutz 1996; Wapner 1996). At present, this kind of ecological citizenship remains, for the most part, at the level of aspiration; whether or not it develops will depend on many factors, notably the interdependence of the state, business and the citizen within the wider structure of global capitalism. Hopefully, if this book helps cast light on these complex relationships, then it might make a small contribution to the development of that ecological citizenship.

# References

Aardal, Bernt (1990) 'Green Politics: A Norwegian Experience', *Scandinavian Political Studies*, 13(2): 147–64.

Abbey, Edward (1975) *The Monkey Wrench Gang*, New York: Avon.

Abramson, Paul and Inglehart, Ronald (1995) *Value Change in Global Perspective*, Ann Arbor: University of Michigan Press.

Achterberg, Wouter (1993) 'Can Liberal Democracy Survive the Environmental Crisis?', in Andrew Dobson and Paul Lucardie (eds.), *The Politics of Nature*, London: Routledge, pp. 81–101.

Adams, John (1995) *Risk*, London: UCL Press.

Affigne, Anthony (1990) 'Environmental Crisis, Green Party Power: Chernobyl and the Swedish Greens', in Wolfgang Rüdig (ed.), *Green Politics One*, Edinburgh University Press, pp. 115–52.

Alber, Jens (1989) 'Modernization, Cleavage Structures and the Rise of Green Parties and Lists in Europe', in Müller-Rommel (ed.), pp. 195–210.

Amy, Douglas (1990) 'Decision Techniques for Environmental Policy: A Critique', in Robert Paehlke and Douglas Torgerson (eds.), *Managing Leviathan: Environmental Politics and the Administrative State*, London: Belhaven Press, pp. 59–79.

Andersen, Jorgen Goul (1990) '"Environmentalism", "New Politics" and Industrialism: Some Theoretical Perspectives', *Scandinavian Political Studies*, 13(2): 101–18.

Andersen, Mikael Skou (1994) *Governance by Green Taxes*, Manchester University Press.

Andersen, Mikael Skou, Christiansen, Peter Munk and Winter, Soren (1998) 'Denmark: Consensus Seeking and Decentralisation', in Hanf and Jansen (eds.), pp. 40–59.

Andersen, Mikael Skou and Liefferink, Duncan (eds.) (1997a) *European Environmental Policy: The Pioneers*, Manchester University Press.

(1997b) 'Introduction: The Impact of the Pioneers on EU Environmental Policy', in Andersen and Liefferink (eds.), pp. 1–39.

Anderson, Terry and Leal, Donald (1991) *Free Market Environmentalism*, Boulder: Westview Press.

Andresen, Steinar, Skodvin, Tora, Underdal, Arild and Wettestad, Jørgen (2000) *Science and Politics in International Environmental Regimes*, Manchester University Press.

Andrews, Richard (2006) 'Risk-Based Decision-Making: Policy, Science and Politics', in Vig and Kraft (eds.), pp. 215–38.

Armour, Audrey (1997) 'Rethinking the Role of Risk Assessment in Environmental Policymaking', in Lynton Caldwell and Robert Bartlett (eds.), *Environmental Policy: Transnational Issues and National Trends*, Westport, CT: Quorum Books, pp. 37–59.

Arrow, Kenneth (and ten others) (1995) 'Economic Growth, Carrying Capacity and the Environment', *Science*, 268: 520–1.

Arts, Bas (1998) *The Political Influence of Global NGOs: Case Studies on the Climate and Biodiversity Conventions*, Utrecht: International Books.

Attfield, Robin (1983) *The Ethics of Environmental Concern*, Oxford: Blackwell.

(1993) 'Sylvan, Fox and Deep Ecology: A View from the Continental Shelf', *Environmental Values*, 2: 21–32.

AWEA [American Wind Energy Association] http://www.awea.org/pubs/factsheets.html (accessed 1 May 2006).

Axelrod, Regina (2004) 'Nuclear Power and EU Enlargement: The Case of Temelín', *Environmental Politics*, 13(1): 153–72.

Axelrod, Robert (1984) *The Evolution of Cooperation*, New York: Basic Books.

Bachrach, Peter and Baratz, Morton (1962) 'The Two Faces of Power', *American Political Science Review*, 56: 947–52.

Baggott, Rob (1998) 'Nuclear Power at Druridge Bay', *Parliamentary Affairs*, 51: 384–96.

Bahro, Rudolf (1986) *Building the Green Movement*, London: GMP.

Baker, Susan (2006) *Sustainable Development*, London: Routledge.

Baker, Susan, Koussis, Maria, Richardson, Dick and Young, Stephen (1997) *The Politics of Sustainable Development: Theory, Policy and Practice within the European Union*, London: Routledge.

Bale, Tim (2003) '"As You Sow, So Shall You Reap": The New Zealand Greens and the General Election of 2002', *Environmental Politics*, 12(2): 140–4.

Bale, Tim and Wilson, John (2006) 'The Greens', in Raymond Miller (ed.), *New Zealand Government and Politics*, 4th edn, South Melbourne: Oxford University Press, pp. 392–404.

Barber, Benjamin (1984) *Strong Democracy*, Berkeley: University of California Press.

Barbier, Edward, Burgess, Joanne, Swanson, Timothy and Pearce, David (1990) *Elephants, Economics and Ivory*, London: Earthscan.

Barry, Brian (1991) *Liberty and Justice: Essays in Political Theory*, Oxford: Clarendon Press.

Barry, John (1994) 'Beyond the Shallow and the Deep: Green Politics, Philosophy and Praxis', *Environmental Politics*, 3(3): 369–94.

(1996) 'Sustainability, Political Judgement and Citizenship: Connecting Green Politics and Democracy', in Doherty and de Geus (eds.), pp. 115–31.

(1998) 'Marxism and Ecology', in Andrew Gamble, David Marsh and Tony Tant (eds.), *Marxism and Social Science*, Basingstoke: Macmillan, pp. 259–79.

(1999a) *Rethinking Green Politics*, London: Sage.

(1999b) *Environment and Social Theory*, London: Routledge.

Barry, John and Eckersley, Robyn (eds.) (2005) *The State and the Global Ecological Crisis*, Cambridge, MA: MIT Press.

Barry, John and Paterson, Matthew (2005) 'Globalisation, Ecological Modernisation and New Labour', *Political Studies*, 52(4): 767–84.

Bartlett, Robert (1997) 'Integrated Impact Assessment: The New Zealand Experiment', in Lynton Caldwell and Robert Bartlett (eds.), *Environmental Policy: Transnational Issues and National Trends*, Westport, CT: Quorum Books, pp. 157–71.

(2005) 'Ecological Reason in Administration: Environmental Impact Assessment and Green Politics', in Hatch (ed.), pp. 47–58.

Baumgartner, Frank and Jones, Bryan (1993) *Agendas and Instability in American Politics*, University of Chicago Press.

Beck, Ulrich (1992) *Risk Society*, London: Sage.

Beckerman, Wilfred (1995) *Small Is Stupid*, London: Duckworth.

(2002) *A Poverty of Reason: Sustainable Development and Economic Growth*, Oakland, CA: The Independent Institute.

Beetham, David (1977) 'From Socialism to Fascism: The Relation between Theory and Practice in the Work of Robert Michels', *Political Studies*, 25: 3–24, 161–81.

Bell, Daniel (1973) *The Coming Crisis of Post-Industrial Society*, New York: Basic Books.

Bell, Derek (2002) 'How Can Political Liberals be Environmentalists?', *Political Studies*, 50: 703–24.

Bell, Derek and Gray, Tim (2002) 'The Ambiguous Role of the Environment Agency in England and Wales', *Environmental Politics*, 11(3): 76–98.

Bell, Derek, Gray, Tim and Haggett, Claire (2005) 'The "Social Gap" in Wind Farm Siting Decisions: Explanations and Policy Responses', *Environmental Politics*, 14(4): 460–77.

Bell, Simon and Morse, Stephen (1999) *Sustainability Indicators*, London: Earthscan.

Benedick, Richard (1991) *Ozone Diplomacy*, Cambridge, MA: Harvard University Press.

Bennie, Lynn (1998) 'Brent Spar, Atlantic Oil and Greenpeace', *Parliamentary Affairs*, 51: 397–410.

(2004) *Understanding Political Participation: Green Party Membership in Scotland*, Aldershot: Ashgate.

Bennulf, Martin (1995) 'Sweden: The Rise and Fall of Miljöpartiet de Gröna', in Richardson and Rootes (eds.), pp. 128–45.

Benoit, Kenneth and Laver, Michael (2006) *Party Policy in Modern Democracies*, London: Routledge.

Benson, John (1978) 'Duty and the Beast', *Philosophy*, 53: 529–49.

Benton, Ted (1993) *Natural Relations*, London: Verso.

(ed.) (1996) *The Greening of Marx*, New York: Guilford.

Betsill, Michelle (2006) 'Transnational Actors in International Environmental Politics', in Betsill et al. (eds.), pp. 172–202.

Betsill, Michelle, Hochstetler, Kathryn and Stevis, Dimitris (eds.) (2006) *International Environmental Politics*, Basingstoke: Palgrave.

Beuermann, Christine and Burdick, Bernhard (1997) 'The Sustainability Transition in Germany: Some Early Stage Experiences', *Environmental Politics*, 6(1): 83–107.

Bhagwati, Jagdish (2004) *In Defence of Globalisation*, Oxford University Press.

Biehl, Janet (1991) *Rethinking Ecofeminist Politics*, Boston: South End Press.

Biorcio, Roberto (2002) 'Italy', in Müller-Rommel and Poguntke (eds.), pp. 39–62.

Blowers, Andrew (1984) *Something in the Air: Corporate Power and the Environment*, London: Harper and Row.

(1997) 'Environmental Policy: Ecological Modernisation or the Risk Society?', *Urban Studies*, 34(5–6): 845–71.

Blühdorn, Ingolfur (1995) 'Campaigning for Nature: Environmental Pressure Groups in Germany and Generational Change in the Ecology Movement', in Ingolfur Blühdorn, Frank Kruse and Thomas Scharf (eds.), *The Green Agenda: Environmental Politics in Germany*, Keele University Press, pp. 167–220.

(2004) '"New Green" Pragmatism in Germany – Green Politics beyond the Social Democratic Embrace?', *Government and Opposition*, 39(4): 564–86.

Blühdorn, Ingolfur and Szarka, Joseph (2004) 'Managing Strategic Positioning Choices: A Reappraisal of the Development Paths of the French and German Green Parties', *Journal of Contemporary European Studies*, 12(3): 303–19.

Boehmer-Christiansen, Sonja and Skea, Jim (1991) *Acid Politics*, London: Belhaven.

Bomberg, Elizabeth (1998a) *Green Parties and Politics in the European Union*, London: Routledge.

(1998b) 'Issue Networks and the Environment: Explaining European Union Environmental Policy', in Marsh (ed.), pp. 167–84.

Bomberg, Elizabeth and Carter, Neil (2006) 'The Greens in Brussels: Shaping or Shaped?', *European Journal of Political Research*, 45: S99–S125.

Bookchin, Murray (1980) *Towards an Ecological Society*, Montreal: Black Rose.

(1982) *The Ecology of Freedom*, Palo Alto, CA: Cheshire.

(1989) *Remaking Society*, Montreal: Black Rose.

Bookchin, Murray and Foreman, Dave (1991) *Defending the Earth*, Boston: South End Press.

Börzel, Tanja (2002) 'Pace-setting, Foot-dragging and Fence-sitting: Member State Responses to Europeanization', *Journal of Common Market Studies*, 40(2): 193–214.

(2003) *Environmental Leaders and Laggards in Europe*, Aldershot: Ashgate.

Bosso, Christopher (1997) 'Seizing Back the Day: The Challenge to Environmental Activism in the 1990s', in Norman Vig and Michael Kraft (eds.), *Environmental Policy in the 1990s*, 3rd edn, Washington, DC: CQ Press, pp. 53–74.

(1999) 'Environmental Groups and the New Political Landscape', in Norman Vig and Michael Kraft (eds.) *Environmental Policy*, 4th edn, Washington, DC: CQ Press, pp. 55–76.

(2005) *Environment, Inc.: From Grassroots to Beltway*, Lawrence: University of Kansas Press.

Bosso, Christopher and Guber, Deborah (2006) 'Maintaining Presence: Environmental Advocacy and the Permanent Campaign', in Vig and Kraft (eds.), pp. 78–99.

Botzler, Richard and Armstrong, Susan (eds.) (1998) *Environmental Ethics*, 2nd edn, London: McGraw-Hill.

Boy, Daniel (2002) 'France', in Müller-Rommel and Poguntke (eds.), pp. 63–77.

Braadbaart, Okke (1998) 'American Bias in Environmental Economics: Industrial Pollution Abatement and "Incentives Versus Regulations"', *Environmental Politics*, 7(2): 134–52.

Brack, Duncan (2005) *The World Trade Organisation and Sustainable Development: A Guide to the Debate*, Briefing Paper EEDP BP 05/03, London: Royal Institute of International Affairs.

Bramwell, Anna (1985) *Blood and Soil: Walther Darré and Hitler's 'Green Party'*, Bourne End, Bucks.: Kensal Press.

(1989) *Ecology in the Twentieth Century*, New Haven: Yale University Press.

Brand, Karl-Werner (1999) 'Dialectics of Institutionalisation: The Transformation of the Environmental Movement in Germany', *Environmental Politics*, 8(1): 35–58.

Brennan, Andrew (1986) 'Ecological Theory and Value in Nature', *Philosophical Inquiry*, 8: 66–96 [reprinted in Elliot (ed.) (1995)].

(1988) *Thinking about Nature*, London: Routledge.

(1992) 'Moral Pluralism and the Environment', *Environmental Values*, 1: 15–33.

Brenton, Tony (1994) *The Greening of Machiavelli*, London: Earthscan.

Bressers, Hans, O'Toole, Laurence and Richardson, Jeremy (eds.) (1994) *Networks for Water Policy: A Comparative Perspective*, Newbury Park: Frank Cass.

Brieger, Tracey, Fleck, Trevor and MacDonald, Douglas (2001) 'Political Action by the Canadian Insurance Industry on Climate Change', *Environmental Politics*, 10(3): 111–26.

Broadhead, Lee-Anne (2002) *International Environmental Politics*, Boulder: Lynne Rienner.

Brown, Lester (1978) *The Twenty-Ninth Day*, New York: Norton.

Bryner, Gary (2000) 'The United States: "Sorry – Not Our Problem"', in Lafferty and Meadowcroft (eds.), pp. 273–302.

(2005) 'The Costs and Benefits of Emissions Trading', in Hatch (ed.), pp. 169–93.

Bryson, Caroline and Curtice, John (1998) 'The End of Materialism?', in Roger Jowell et al. (eds.), *British – and European – Social Attitudes: The 15th Report*, Aldershot: Ashgate, pp. 125–48.

Budge, Ian, Klingemann, Hans-Dieter, Volkens, Andrea, Bara, Judith and Tanenbaum, Eric (2001) *Mapping Policy Preferences*, CD dataset, Oxford University Press.

Bulkeley, Harriet and Betsill, Michelle (2005) 'Rethinking Sustainable Cities: Multilevel Governance and the "Urban" Politics of Climate Change', *Environmental Politics*, 14(1): 42–63.

Bullard, Robert (2000) *Dumping in Dixie: Race, Class and Environmental Quality*, 3rd edn, Boulder: Westview Press.

Buller, Henry (1998) 'Reflections across the Channel: Britain, France and the Europeanisation of National Environmental Policy', in Philip Lowe and Stephen Ward (eds.), *British Environmental Policy and Europe*, London: Routledge, pp. 67–83.

Bulloch, John and Darwish, Adel (1993) *Water Wars: Coming Conflicts in the Middle East*, London: Victor Gollancz.

Bündnis 90/Die Grünen (2002) *The Future is Green*, http://www.gruene.de/index.htm.

Burchell, Jon (2002) *The Evolution of Green Politics*, London: Earthscan.

Bürklin, Wilhelm (1987) 'Governing Left Parties Frustrating the Radical Non-Established Left: The Rise and Inevitable Decline of the Greens', *European Sociological Review*, 3(2): 109–26.

Burns, Charlotte (2005) 'The European Parliament: the European Union's Environmental Champion?', in Jordan (ed.), pp. 87–105.

Busenberg, George (1999) 'The Evolution of Vigilance: Disasters, Sentinels and Policy Change', *Environmental Politics*, 8(1): 90–109.

BWEA [British Wind Energy Association] (2006) *Statistics – 2005*, http://www.bwea.com/statistics/2005.asp (accessed 16 October).

Caldecott, Leonie and Leland, Stephanie (eds.) (1983) *Reclaim the Earth: Women Speak Out for Life on Earth*, London: Women's Press.

Callenbach, Ernest (1978) *Ecotopia*, London: Pluto.

Callicott, J. Baird (1985) 'Intrinsic Value, Quantum Theory, and Environmental Ethics', *Environmental Ethics*, 7: 257–75.

(1986) 'On the Intrinsic Value of Nonhuman Species', in Bryan Norton (ed.), *The Preservation of Species: The Value of Biological Diversity*, Princeton University Press, pp. 138–72.

Carolan, Michael (2004) 'Ecological Modernization Theory: What about Consumption?' *Society and Natural Resources*, 17: 247–60.

Carson, Rachel (1962) *Silent Spring*, Boston: Houghton Mifflin.

Carter, Neil (1992) 'The Greening of Labour', in Martin Smith and Joanna Spear (eds.), *The Changing Labour Party*, London: Routledge, pp. 118–32.

(1996) 'Worker Co-operatives and Green Political Thought', in Doherty and de Geus (eds.), pp. 56–75.

(1999) 'The Greens in the 1999 European Parliamentary Elections', *Environmental Politics*, 8(4): 160–7.

(2005) 'Mixed Fortunes: the Greens in the 2004 European Parliament Election', *Environmental Politics*, 14(1): 103–11.

(2006) 'The Party Politicisation of the Environment in Britain', *Party Politics*, 12(6): 747–67.

Carter, Neil and Huby, Meg (2005) 'Ecological Citizenship and Ethical Investment', *Environmental Politics*, 14(2): 255–72.

Carter, Neil and Lowe, Philip (1995) 'The Establishment of a Cross-Sector Environment Agency', in Tim Gray (ed.), *UK Environmental Policy in the 1990s*, Basingstoke: Macmillan, pp. 38–56.

(1998) 'Britain: Coming to Terms with Sustainable Development?', in Hanf and Jansen (eds.), pp. 17–39.

Carter, Neil and Mol, Arthur (eds.) (2006) *Environmental Governance in China*, London: Routledge.

Carter, Neil and Rootes, Christopher (2006) 'The Environment and the Greens in the 2005 Elections in Britain', *Environmental Politics*, 15(3): 473–8.

Cater, Douglass (1965) *Power in Washington*, London: Collins.

Cavalieri, Paola and Singer, Peter (eds.) (1993) *The Great Ape Project: Equality Beyond Humanity*, London: Fourth Edition.

Chambers, Nicky, Simmons, Craig and Wackernagel, Mathis (2000) *Sharing Nature's Interest*, London: Earthscan.

Chatterjee, Pratap and Finger, Matthias (1994) *The Earth Brokers*, London: Routledge.

Christensen, Per, Kørnøv, Lone and Nielsen, Eskild Holm (2003) *The Outcome of EIA in Denmark*, University of Aalborg.

Christoff, Peter (1996a) 'Ecological Citizens and Ecologically Guided Democracy', in Doherty and de Geus (eds.), pp. 151–69.

(1996b) 'Ecological Modernisation, Ecological Modernities', *Environmental Politics*, 5(3): 476–500.

Christoforou, Theofanis (2004) 'The Precautionary Principle, Risk Assessment and the Comparative Role of Science in the European Community and the US Legal Systems', in Vig and Faure (eds.), pp. 17–51.

Church, Clive (1995) 'Switzerland: Greens in a Confederal Polity', in Richardson and Rootes (eds.), pp. 146–67.

Clapp, Jennifer (2001) *Toxic Exports: The Transfer of Hazardous Wastes from Rich to Poor Countries*, Ithaca: Cornell University Press.

Clapp, Jennifer and Dauvergne, Peter (2005) *Paths to a Green World: The Political Economy of the Global Environment*, Cambridge, MA: MIT Press.

Clark, Stephen (1977) *The Moral Status of Animals*, Oxford: Clarendon Press.

Cohen, Maurie (1998) 'Science and the Environment: Assessing Cultural Capacity for Ecological Modernization', *Public Understanding of Science*, 7: 149–67.

Cohen, Maurie and Murphy, Joseph (eds.) (2001) *Exploring Sustainable Consumption*, Oxford: Pergamon.

Cole, Daniel and Grossman, Peter (2005) 'Institutional and Technological Constraints on Environmental Instrument Choice: A Case Study of the US Clean Air Act', in Hatch (ed.), pp. 225–44.

Cole, H., Freeman, Christopher, Jahoda, Marie and Pavitt, K. (1973) *Thinking about the Future: A Critique of the Limits to Growth*, Brighton: Sussex University Press.

Collard, Andree (1988) *Rape of the Wild*, London: Women's Press.

Commissioner of Environment and Sustainable Development (2005) *Report 2005*, http://www.oag-bvg.gc.ca/domino/reports.nsf/html/c2005menu_e.html.

Commoner, Barry (1971) *The Closing Circle: Nature, Man and Technology*, New York: Alfred Knopf.

Conca, Ken (1994) 'Re-thinking the Ecology–Sovereignty Debate', *Millennium*, 23(3): 701–11.

(2000) 'The WTO and the Undermining of Global Environmental Governance', *Review of International Political Economy*, 7(3): 484–94.

Connelly, James and Smith, Graham (2003) *Politics and the Environment*, 2nd edn, London: Routledge.

Cotgrove, Stephen (1982) *Catastrophe or Cornucopia?* Chichester: Wiley.

Council of the European Union (2006) *Review of the EU Sustainable Development Strategy: Renewed Strategy*, 10117/06, 9 June, Brussels.

Cox, Graham, Lowe, Philip and Winter, Michael (1986) 'Agriculture and Conservation in Britain: A Policy Community under Siege', in Graham Cox, Philip Lowe and Michael Winter (eds.), *Agriculture: People and Policies*, London: Allen and Unwin, pp. 181–215.

Crenson, Matthew (1971) *The Unpolitics of Air Pollution*, Baltimore: Johns Hopkins University Press.

Crepaz, Markus (1995) 'Explaining National Variations of Air Pollution Levels: Political Institutions and their Impact on Environmental Policy-Making', *Environmental Politics*, 4(3): 391–414.

Dahl, Robert (1961) *Who Governs?*, New Haven: Yale University Press.

Dahlgren, Katrin and Eckerberg, Katarina (2005) *Status för Lokal Agenda 21 – en enkätundersökning 2004* [Status of LA21: A Survey, 2004], Umeå: Hållbarhetsrådet, http://www.hallbarhetsradet.se/upload/publikationer/LA21.pdf.

Dalby, Simon (2002) *Environmental Security*, University of Minneapolis Press.

Dalton, Russell (1994) *The Green Rainbow: Environmental Groups in Western Europe*, New Haven: Yale University Press.

(2005) 'The Greening of the Globe? Cross-national Levels of Environmental Group Membership', *Environmental Politics*, 14(4): 441–59.

(2006) *Citizen Politics: Public Opinion and Political Parties in Advanced Industrial Democracies*, 4th edn, Washington, DC: CJ Press.

Dalton, Russell and Bürklin, Wilhelm (1996) 'The Two Electorates', in Russell Dalton (ed.), *Germans Divided*, Oxford: Berg, pp. 183–207.

Daly, Herman (1992) *Steady State Economics*, 2nd edn, London: Earthscan.

Daly, Herman and Cobb, John (1990) *For the Common Good*, London: Green Print.

Daugbjerg, Carsten (1998) 'Linking Policy Networks and Environmental Policies: Nitrate Policy-Making in Denmark and Sweden 1979–95', *Public Administration*, 76: 275–94.

Daugbjerg, Carsten and Pedersen, Anders Branth (2004) 'New Policy Ideas and Old Policy Networks: Implementing Green Taxation in Scandinavia', *Journal of Public Policy*, 24(2): 219–49.

Davis, Frank and Wurth, Albert (2003) 'Voting Preferences and the Environment in the American Electorate: The Discussion Extended', *Society and Natural Resources*, 16: 729–40.

de-Shalit, Avner (1995) *Why Posterity Matters: Environmental Policies and Future Generations*, London: Routledge.

(2000) *The Environment Between Theory and Practice*, Oxford University Press.

Deere, Carolyn and Esty, Daniel (eds.) (2002) *Greening the Americas: NAFTA's Lessons for Hemispheric Trade*, Cambridge, MA: MIT Press.

DEFRA [Department for Environment, Food and Rural Affairs] (2005a) *Securing the Future – UK Government Sustainable Development Strategy*, Cm 6467, London.

(2005b) *One Future – Different Paths: The UK's Shared Framework for Sustainability*, London.

DEHLG [Department of the Environment, Heritage and Local Government] (2005) *Annual Report 2004*, Dublin.

Dekker, Sybilla (2005) 'Better off with Brussels?', speech (4 July), http://international.vrom.nl/pagina.html?id=9555.

della Porta, Donatella and Diani, Mario (2006) *Social Movements*, 2nd edn, Oxford: Blackwell.

Des Jardins, Joseph (2002) *Environmental Ethics*, 3rd edn, Belmont, CA: Wadsworth.

Desai, Uday (ed.) (2002) *Environmental Politics and Policy in Industrialized Countries*, Cambridge, MA: MIT Press.

DeSombre, Elizabeth and Barkin, J. Samuel (2002) 'Turtles and Trade: the WTO's Acceptance of Environmental Trade Restrictions', *Global Environmental Politics*, 2(1): 12–18.

Dessler, Andrew and Parson, Edward (2006) *The Science and Politics of Global Climate Change*, Cambridge University Press.

Deudney, Daniel (2006) 'Security', in Dobson and Eckersley (eds.), pp. 232–51.

Devall, Bill (1990) *Simple in Means, Rich in Ends: Practising Deep Ecology*, London: Green Print.

Devall, Bill and Sessions, George (1985) *Living as if Nature Mattered*, Layton, UT: Peregrine and Smith.

Diani, Mario and Donati, Paolo (1999) 'Organisational Change in Western European Environmental Groups: A Framework for Analysis', *Environmental Politics*, 8(1): 13–34.

Dickens, Peter (1992) *Society and Nature*, Hemel Hempstead: Harvester Wheatsheaf.

Die Grünen (1983) *Programme of the German Green Party* (trans. Hans Fernbach), London: Heretic Books.

Dobson, Andrew (1998) *Justice and the Environment*, Oxford University Press.

(ed.) (1999) *Fairness and Futurity: Essays on Environmental Sustainability and Social Justice*, Oxford University Press.

(2000) *Green Political Thought*, 3rd edn, London: Routledge.

(2003) *Citizenship and the Environment*, Oxford University Press.

(2006) 'Ecological Citizenship: A Defence', *Environmental Politics*, 15(3): 447–51.

Dobson, Andrew and Bell, Derek (eds.) (2006) *Environmental Citizenship*, Cambridge, MA: MIT Press.

Dobson, Andrew and Eckersley, Robyn (eds.) (2006) *Political Theory and the Ecological Challenge*, Cambridge University Press.

Dobson, Andrew and Sáiz, Ángel Valancia (eds.) (2005) *Citizenship, Environment, Economy*, London: Routledge.

Doherty, Brian (1996) 'Green Parties, Nonviolence and Political Obligation', in Doherty and de Geus (eds.), pp. 36–55.

(1998) 'Opposition to Road-Building', *Parliamentary Affairs*, 51: 370–83.

(1999) 'Paving the Way: The Rise of Direct Action against Road-Building and the Changing Character of British Environmentalism', *Political Studies*, 47(2): 275–91.

(2002) *Ideas and Actions in the Green Movement*, London: Routledge.

Doherty, Brian and de Geus, Marius (eds.) (1996) *Democracy and Green Political Thought*, London: Routledge.

Doherty, Brian, Plows, Alexandra and Wall, Derek (2003) '"The Preferred Way of Doing Things": The British Direct Action Movement', *Parliamentary Affairs*, 56: 669–86.

Dovers, Stephen (2005) *Environment and Sustainability Policy*, Annandale, NSW: Federation Press.

Dowding, Keith (1995) 'Model or Metaphor? A Critical Review of the Policy Network Approach', *Political Studies*, 43: 136–58.

Dowie, Mark (1995) *Losing Ground: American Environmentalism at the Close of the Twentieth Century*, Cambridge, MA: MIT Press.

Downs, Anthony (1972) 'Up and Down with Ecology – the "Issue Attention Cycle"', *The Public Interest*, no. 28.

Doyle, Timothy (2000) *Green Power: the Environmental Movement in Australia*, Sydney: University of New South Wales Press.

(2004) *Environmental Movements in Minority and Majority Worlds*, New Brunswick, NJ: Rutgers University Press.

Doyle, Timothy and McEachern, Doug (2001) *Environment and Politics*, 2nd edn, London: Routledge.

Drengson, Alan (1989) *Beyond Environmental Crisis*, New York: Peter Lang.

Dryzek, John (1987) *Rational Ecology*, Oxford: Blackwell.

(1990) *Discursive Democracy*, Cambridge University Press.

(2005) *The Politics of the Earth*, 2nd edn, Oxford University Press.

Dryzek, John, Downes, David, Hunold, Christian, Schlosberg, David and Hernes, Hans-Khristian (2003) *Green States and Social Movements*, Oxford University Press.

Dryzek, John and Schlosberg, David (eds.) (2005) *Debating the Earth: The Environmental Politics Reader*, 2nd edn, Oxford University Press.

DTI [Department of Trade and Industry] (2005) *UK Energy in Brief – July 2005*, http://www.dti.gov.uk/energy/inform/energy_in_brief/index.shtml (accessed 1 May 2006).

(2006) *The Energy Challenge*, Cm. 6887, London: The Stationery Office.

Dudley, Geoffrey and Richardson, Jeremy (1996) 'Why Does Policy Change over Time? Adversarial Policy Communities, Alternative Policy Arenas and British Trunk Roads Policy 1945–95', *Journal of European Public Policy*, 3(1): 63–83.

Duffy, Robert (2003) *The Green Agenda in American Politics*, Lawrence: University of Kansas Press.

Dunlap, Riley, Xiao, Chenyang and McCright, Aaron (2001) 'Politics and Environment in America: Partisan and Ideological Cleavages in Public Support for Environmentalism', *Environmental Politics*, 10(4): 23–48.

Durant, Robert and Boodphetcharat, Thanit (2004) 'The Precautionary Principle', in Durant et al. (eds.), pp. 105–43.

Durant, Robert, Fiorino, Daniel and O'Leary, Rosemary (eds.) (2004) *Environmental Governance Reconsidered*, Cambridge, MA: MIT Press.

Duverger, Maurice (1954) *Political Parties*, London: Methuen.

Dworkin, Ronald (1993) *Life's Dominion*, New York: Alfred Knopf.

Eckerberg, Katarina (1997) 'Comparing the Local Use of Environmental Policy Instruments in Nordic and Baltic Countries – The Issue of Diffuse Water Pollution', *Environmental Politics*, 6(2): 24–47.

Eckerberg, Katarina and Brundin, Pia (1999) *A Survey of Swedish Municipalities' Work with Agenda 21*, Swedish Ministry of Environment/Swedish Association of Local Authorities, Stockholm: Kommentus Förlag.

Eckersley, Robyn (1989) 'Green Politics and the New Class: Selfishness or Virtue?', *Political Studies*, 37: 205–23.

(1990) 'The Green Political Ball Park: An Overview of Positions and Players', unpublished paper.

(1992) *Environmentalism and Political Theory*, London: UCL Press.

(1993) 'Free Market Environmentalism: Friend or Foe', *Environmental Politics*, 2(1): 1–19.

(1996) 'Greening Liberal Democracy: The Rights Discourse Revisited', in Doherty and de Geus (eds.), pp. 212–36.

(2004a) *The Green State*, Cambridge, MA: MIT Press.

(2004b) 'The Big Chill: The WTO and Multilateral Environmental Agreements', *Global Environmental Politics*, 4(2): 24–50.

Economic and Social Research Council (Global Environmental Change Programme) (1999) *The Politics of GM Food: Risk, Science and Public Trust*, Special Briefing No. 5, Falmer: University of Sussex.

EEA [European Environment Agency] (1996) *Environmental Taxes: Implementation and Environmental Effectiveness*, Copenhagen: EEA.

(2000) *European Community and Member States Greenhouse Emission Trends 1990–1998*, Copenhagen: EEA.

(2005a) *European Environment: State and Outlook 2005*, Copenhagen: EEA.

(2005b) *Environmental Policy Integration in Europe: State of Play and an Evaluation Framework*, Copenhagen: EEA.

(2006a) *Using the Market for Cost-Effective Environmental Policy*, Copenhagen: EEA

(2006b) *Greenhouse Gas Emission Trends and Projections 2006*, Copenhagen: EEA.

(2006c) *Transport and the Environment: Facing a Dilemma*, Copenhagen: EEA.

Ehrlich, Paul (1968) *The Population Bomb*, New York: Ballantine.

Ekins, Paul (1986) *The Living Economy*, London: RKP.

Ellerman, Denny, Joskow, Paul and Harrison, David (2003) *Emissions Trading in the US: Experience, Lessons and Considerations for Greenhouse Gases*, Pew Center on Global Climate Change, http://www.pewclimate.org/global-warming-in-depth/all_reports/emissions_trading/index.cfm.

Elliot, Robert (ed.) (1995) *Environmental Ethics*, Oxford University Press.

Elliott, Lorraine (1994) *International Environmental Politics: Protecting the Antarctic*, Basingstoke: Macmillan.

(2004) *The Global Politics of the Environment*, 2nd edn, Basingstoke: Macmillan.

ENDs [Environmental Data Services] (1998) *ENDs Report*, No. 281.

Environmental Justice Resource Center (2006) *Principles of Environmental Justice*, http://www.ejrc.cau.edu/princej.html (accessed 20 October).

Environmental Audit Committee (2003–4) 'The Sustainable Development Strategy: Illusion or Reality?', 13th Report, Volume 2, House of Commons, HC624-1.

Enzensberger, Hans-Magnus (1974) 'A Critique of Political Ecology', *New Left Review*, 84: 3–31.

Esty, Daniel (1994) *Greening the GATT: Trade, Environment and the Future*, Washington, DC: Institute for International Economics.

Eurobarometer (1995) *Europeans and the Environment*, Brussels: European Commission.

(1999) *What Do Europeans Think about the Environment?*, Brussels: European Commission.

European Commission (1992) *Towards Sustainability*, COM(92)23 final, Luxembourg.

(2002) *How Successful are the Member States in Implementing the EIA Directive?*, Brussels, http://www.europe.eu.int/comm/environment/eia/report_en.pdf.

(2005) *Review of the Sustainable Development Action Strategy: A Platform for Action*, COM(2005)658 final, Brussels, http://ec.europa.eu/sustainable/sds2005/index_en.htm.

European Communities (2000) *The Global Assessment. Europe's Environment: What Directions for the Future?*, Luxembourg, http://europa.eu.int/comm/environment/newprg/99543_en.pdf.

European Fair Trade Association (2006), http://www.eftafairtrade.org/ (accessed 21 February).

Evans, Judith (1993) 'Ecofeminism and the Politics of the Gendered Self', in Andrew Dobson and Paul Lucardie (eds.), *The Politics of Nature*, London: Routledge, pp. 177–89.

Faucher, Florence (1998) 'Is There Hope for the French Ecology Movement?', *Environmental Politics*, 7(3): 42–65.

Federal Statistical Office (2006) http://www.destatis.de/presse/englisch/wahl2005/p6001211.htm (accessed 26 June).

Fiorino, Daniel (2004) 'Flexibility', in Durant et al. (eds.), pp. 393–425.

Fischer, Corinna and Boehnke, Klaus (2004) '"Obstruction Galore": A Case Study of Non-violent Resistance against Nuclear Waste Disposal in Germany', *Environmental Politics*, 13(2): 393–413.

Fischer, Frank (2003) *Reframing Public Policy: Discourse Politics and Deliberative Practices*, Oxford University Press.

Fishkin, James (1997) *The Voice of the People*, New Haven: Yale University Press.

Flam, Helena (1994) *States and Anti-Nuclear Movements*, Edinburgh University Press.

Flynn, Andrew and Lowe, Philip (1992) 'The Greening of the Tories', in Wolfgang Rüdig (ed.), *Green Politics Two*, Edinburgh University Press, pp. 9–36.

Food Ethics Council (1999) *Novel Foods: Beyond Nuffield*, Southwell: Food Ethics Council.

Foreman, Dave and Haywood, Bill (1985) *Ecodefense: A Field Guide to Monkeywrenching*, Tucson: Ned Ludd.

Foster, John Bellamy (2000) *Marx's Ecology: Materialism and Nature*, New York: Monthly Review Press.

Fox, Warwick (1990) *Toward a Transpersonal Ecology*, Boston: Shambhala.

Frankel, Boris (1987) *The Post Industrial Utopians*, Cambridge: Polity Press.

Frankland, E. Gene and Schoonmaker, Donald (1992) *Between Protest and Power: The Green Party in Germany*, Oxford: Westview Press.

Freudenberg, Nicholas and Steinsapir, Carol (1992) 'Not in Our Backyards: The Grassroots Environmental Movement', in Dunlap and Mertig (eds.), *American Environmentalism: The US Environmental Movement 1970–1990*, New York: Taylor and Francis, pp. 27–37.

Friends of the Earth (2004) *Annual Report 2004*, London.
  (2005) http://www.foe.co.uk/ (accessed 5 June).

Friends of the Earth International (2006) http://www.foei.org/ (accessed 5 June).

Gamson, William and Meyer, David (1996) 'Framing Political Opportunity', in McAdam et al. (eds.), pp. 275–90.

Garner, Robert (2005) *Animal Ethics*, Cambridge: Polity Press.

Gauthier, David (1986) *Morals by Agreement*, Oxford University Press.

Georgescu-Roegen, Nicholas (1971) *The Entropy Law and the Economic Process*, Cambridge, MA: Harvard University Press.

Gibbs, Lois (1982) *Love Canal: My Story*, Albany: SUNY Press.

Gibowski, Wolfgang (1999) 'Social Change and the Electorate: An Analysis of the 1998 *Bundestagswahl*', *German Politics*, 8(2): 10–32.

Gilpin, Robert (1987) *The Political Economy of International Relations*, Princeton University Press.

Glasbergen, Pieter (1992) 'Agri-Environmental Policy: Trapped in an Iron Law? A Comparative Analysis of Agricultural Pollution Control in the Netherlands, the United Kingdom and France', *Sociologia Ruralis*, 32(1): 30–48.

Goldfrank, Walter, Goodman, David and Szasz, Andrew (eds.) (1999) *Ecology and the World-System*, London: Greenwood Press.

Golding, Martin (1972) 'Obligations to Future Generations', *The Monist*, 56: 85–99.

Goldsmith, Edward, Allen, Robert, Allaby, Michael, Davoll, John and Lawrence, Sam (1972) *A Blueprint for Survival*, Harmondsworth: Penguin.

González, George (2002) 'Local Growth Coalitions and Air Pollution Controls: The Ecological Modernisation of the US in Historical Perspective', *Environmental Politics*, 11(3): 121–44.

Goodall, Jane (1986) *The Chimpanzees of Gombe*, Cambridge, MA: Harvard University Press.

Goodin, Robert (1992) *Green Political Theory*, Cambridge: Polity Press.

Gore, Albert (1992) *Earth in the Balance*, New York: Houghton Mifflin.

Gorz, Andre (1980) *Ecology as Politics*, Boston: South End Press.

Gottlieb, Robert (1993) *Forcing the Spring: The Transformation of the American Environmental Movement*, Washington, DC: Island Press.

Gould, Carol (1988) *Rethinking Democracy*, Cambridge University Press.

Gould, Kenneth, Schnaiberg, Allan and Weinberg, Adam (1996) *Local Environmental Struggles*, Cambridge University Press.

Gouldner, Alvin (1979) *The Future of Intellectuals and the Rise of the New Class*, Basingstoke: Macmillan.

Government of Sweden (2006), 'Climate Policy', http://www.sweden.gov.se/sb/d/5745/a/21787 (accessed 5 May).

Grant, Wyn (1995) *Pressure Groups, Politics and Democracy in Britain*, 2nd edn, Hemel Hempstead: Harvester Wheatsheaf.

Gray, John (1993) *Beyond the New Right*, London: Routledge.

Gray, Tim (1997) 'The Common Fisheries Policy in the European Union', *Environmental Politics*, 6(4): 150–8.

Gray, Tim, Gray, Mark and Hague, Rod (1999) 'Sandeels, Sailors, Sandals and Suits: The Strategy of the Environmental Movement in Relation to the Fishing Industry', *Environmental Politics*, 8(3): 119–39.

Greenaway, John, Smith, Steve and Street, John (1992) *Deciding Factors in British Politics*, London: Routledge.

Green Party (2006) http://www.greens.org/elections/ (accessed 5 June).

Greenpeace (2005) *Annual Report 2005*, http://www.greenpeace.org/international/press/reports/annual-report-2005.

Greenpeace International (2006) *About Greenpeace*, http://www.greenpeace.org/international/about/ (accessed 20 October).

Grove, Richard (1995) *Green Imperialism*, Cambridge University Press.

Grubb, Michael (1995) 'Seeking Fair Weather: Ethics and the International Debate on Climate Change', *International Affairs*, 71(3): 463–96.

Grubb, Michael, Sebenius, James, Magalhaes, Antonio and Subak, Susan (1992) 'Sharing the Burden', in Irving Mintzer (ed.), *Confronting Climate Change*, Cambridge University Press, pp. 305–22.

Gruen, Lori (1993) 'Animals', in Peter Singer (ed.), *A Companion to Ethics*, Oxford: Blackwell, pp. 343–53.

Gruen, Lori and Jamieson, Dale (1994) *Reflecting on Nature: Readings in Environmental Philosophy*, Oxford University Press.

Grundmann, Reiner (1991) *Marxism and Ecology*, Oxford: Clarendon Press.

Guber, Deborah (2003) *The Grassroots of a Green Revolution*, Cambridge, MA: MIT Press.

GWEC [Global Wind Energy Council] (2006) *Global Wind 2005 Report*, http://www.gwec.net (accessed 1 May).

Haas, Peter (1990) *Saving the Mediterranean*, New York: Columbia University Press.

(1999) 'Social Constructivism and the Evolution of Multilateral Environmental Governance', in Aseem Prakash and Jeffrey Hart (eds.), *Globalization and Governance*, London: Routledge, pp. 103–33.

Haas, Peter, Keohane, Robert and Levy, Marc (eds.) (1993) *Institutions for the Earth: Sources of Effective International Environmental Protection*, Cambridge, MA: MIT Press.

Haigh, Nigel (1998) *Manual of Environmental Policy*, London: Elsevier/Institute for European Environmental Policy.

Hailwood, Simon (2004) *How to be a Green Liberal*, Chesham: Acumen.

Hajer, Maarten (1995) *The Politics of Environmental Discourse: Ecological Modernisation and the Policy Process*, Oxford University Press.

(2003) 'A Frame in the Fields: Policy-Making and the Reinvention of Politics', in Maarten Hajer and Hendrik Wagenaar (eds.), *Deliberative Policy Analysis: Understanding Government in the Network Society*, Cambridge University Press, pp. 88–110.

Hall, Peter (1993) 'Policy Paradigms, Social Learning and the State', *Comparative Politics*, 25: 275–96.

Hanf, Kenneth and Jansen, Alf-Inge (eds.) (1998) *Governance and Environment in Western Europe*, Harlow: Addison-Wesley Longman.

Hanf, Kenneth and van de Gronden, Egbert (1998) 'The Netherlands: Joint Regulation and Sustainable Development', in Hanf and Jansen (eds.), pp. 152–80.

Hanley, Nick and Spash, Clive (1993) *Cost–Benefit Analysis and the Environment*, Cheltenham: Edward Elgar.

Hardin, Garrett (1968) 'The Tragedy of the Commons', *Science*, 162: 1243–8.

(1977) 'Living on a Lifeboat', in Garrett Hardin and John Baden (eds.), *Managing the Commons*, San Francisco: W. H. Freeman, pp. 261–79.

Harrison, Kathryn (1999) 'Racing to the Top or the Bottom? Industry Resistance to Eco-labelling of Paper Products in Three Jurisdictions', *Environmental Politics*, 8(4): 110–37.

Harrison, Paul (1993) *The Third Revolution*, London: Penguin.

Hatch, Michael (2005a) 'Voluntary Agreements: Cornerstone or Fig Leaf in German Climate Change Policy?', in Hatch (ed.), pp. 97–124.

(ed.) (2005b) *Environmental Policymaking: Assessing the Use of Alternative Policy Instruments*, Albany: SUNY Press.

Haward, Marcus and Larmour, Peter (eds.) (1993) *The Tasmanian Parliamentary Accord and Public Policy 1989–92*, Canberra: Federalism Research Centre.

Hay, Colin, Lister, Michael and Marsh, David (eds.) (2006) *The State: Theories and Issues*, Basingstoke: Palgrave.

Hay, Peter (2002) *A Companion to Environmental Thought*, Edinburgh University Press.

Hayward, Tim (1995) *Ecological Thought*, Cambridge: Polity Press.

(2006a) 'Ecological Citizenship: Justice Rights and the Virtue of Resourcefulness', *Environmental Politics*, 15(3): 435–46.

(2006b) 'Ecological Citizenship: A Rejoinder', *Environmental Politics*, 15(3): 452–3.

Heclo, Hugh (1978) 'Issue Networks and the Executive Establishment', in Anthony King (ed.), *The New American Political System*, Washington, DC: American Enterprise Institute, pp. 87–124.

Heilbroner, Robert (1974) *An Inquiry into the Human Prospect*, New York: Norton.

Held, David, et al. (2005) *Debating Globalization*, Cambridge: Polity Press.

Hempel, Lamont (1995) 'Environmental Technology and the Green Car: Towards a Sustainable Transportation Policy', in Frank Fischer and Michael Black (eds.), *Greening Environmental Policy*, London: Paul Chapman, pp. 66–86.

(2006) 'Climate Policy on the Installment Plan', in Vig and Kraft (eds.), pp. 288–310.

Heretier, Adrienne (1996) 'The Accommodation of Diversity in European Policy-Making and its Outcomes: Regulatory Policy as Patchwork', *Journal of European Public Policy*, 3(2): 149–76.

Hill, Michael (2005) *The Public Policy Process*, 4th edn, Harlow: Pearson Longman.

Hill, Michael, Aaronovitch, Sabrina and Baldock, David (1989) 'Non-Decision Making in Pollution Control in Britain: Nitrate Pollution, the EEC Drinking Water Directive and Agriculture', *Policy and Politics*, 17(3): 227–40.

HM Government (2006) *Climate Change: the UK Programme 2006*, cm 6764, London: HMSO (http://www.defra.gov.uk/environment/climatechange/uk/ukccp/index.htm).

HM Treasury (2006) *The Climate Change Levy Package*, London: Stationery Office.

Hoffman, Jürgen (1999) 'From a Party of Young Voters to an Ageing Generation Party: Alliance'90/The Greens after the 1998 Federal Election', *Environmental Politics*, 8(3): 140–6.

Homer-Dixon, Thomas (1999) *The Environment, Scarcity and Violence*, Princeton University Press.

Hooghe, Mark and Rihoux, Benoît (2000) 'The Green Breakthrough in the Belgian General Election of June 1999', *Environmental Politics*, 9(3): 129–36.

(2003) 'The Harder the Fall: the Greens in the Belgian General Elections of May 2003', *Environmental Politics*, 12(4): 120–6.

Houghton, John, Jenkins, Geoffrey and Ephraims, J. (eds.) (1990) *Climate Change: The IPCC Scientific Assessment*, Cambridge University Press.

Howes, Michael (2005) *Politics and the Environment: Risk and the Role of Government and Industry*, London: Earthscan.

Hughes, Jonathan (2000) *Ecology and Historical Materialism*, Cambridge University Press.

Hukkinen, Janne (1995) 'Corporatism as an Impediment to Ecological Sustenance: The Case of Finnish Waste Management', *Ecological Economics*, 15: 59–75.

Humphreys, David (1998) 'The Report of the International Panel on Forests', *Environmental Politics*, 7(1): 214–21.

Hurrell, Andrew (1995) 'International Political Theory and the Global Environment', in Ken Booth and Steve Smith (eds.), *International Relations Theory Today*, Cambridge: Polity Press, pp. 129–53.

Hurrell, Andrew and Kingsbury, Benedict (1992) 'The International Politics of the Environment: An Introduction', in Andrew Hurrell and Benedict Kingsbury (eds.), *The International Politics of the Environment*, Oxford University Press, pp. 1–47.

ICLEI [Local Governments for Sustainability] (2006) www.iclei.org/index.php? id=798 (accessed 16 April).

Inglehart, Ronald (1977) *The Silent Revolution*, Princeton University Press.
(1990) *Culture Shift*, Princeton University Press.

IPCC [Intergovernmental Panel on Climate Change] (1999) *Aviation and the Global Atmosphere*, http://www.ipcc.ch/pub/av(E).pdf
(2001) *Climate Change 2001: Impacts, Adaptation, Vulnerability*, Geneva: UNEP/World Meteorological Organisation.

IUCN/UNEP/WWF [International Union for the Conservation of Nature and Natural Resources/UNEP/WWF] (1980) *World Conservation Strategy: Living Resource Conservation for Sustainable Development*, Gland, Switzerland.

Jackson, Robert (1990) *Quasi-States: Sovereignty, International Relations and the Third World*, Cambridge University Press.

Jackson, Tim and Michaelis, Laurie (2003) *Policies for Sustainable Consumption*, Oxford: Sustainable Development Commission.

Jacobs, Michael (1991) *The Green Economy*, London: Pluto.
(1996) 'Financial Incentives: The British Experience', in Robyn Eckersley (ed.), *Markets, the State and the Environment*, Basingstoke: Macmillan, pp. 113–28.
(1997) 'Introduction: The New Politics of the Environment', in Michael Jacobs (ed.), *Greening the Millennium?*, Oxford: Blackwell, pp. 1–17.
(1999) *Environmental Modernisation: The New Labour Agenda*. London: Fabian Society.

Jagers, Sverker, Paterson, Matthew and Stripple, Johannes (2005) 'Privatising Governance, Practicing Triage: Securitization of Insurance Risks, and the Politics of Global Warming', in Levy and Newell (eds.), pp. 249–74.

Jahn, Detlef (1997) 'Green Politics and Parties in Germany', in Michael Jacobs (ed.), *Greening the Millennium?*, Oxford: Blackwell, pp. 174–82.

Jamison, Andrew (2001) *The Making of Green Knowledge*, Cambridge University Press.
(2004) 'Learning from Lomborg: Or Where Do Anti-Environmentalists Come From?', *Science as Culture*, 13(2): 173–95.

Jamison, Andrew, Eyerman, Ron, Cramer, Jacqueline and Laessoe, Jeppé (1990) *The Making of the New Environmental Consciousness*, Edinburgh University Press.

Jänicke, Martin (1991) *The Political System's Capacity For Environmental Policy*, Berlin: Free University.

Jänicke, Martin and Jörgens, Helge (1998) 'National Environmental Policy Planning in OECD Countries: Preliminary Lessons from Cross-National Comparisons', *Environmental Politics*, 7(2): 27–54.

Jansen, Alf-Inge and Mydske, Per Kristen (1998) 'Norway: Balancing Environmental Quality and Interest in Oil', in Hanf and Jansen (eds.), pp. 181–207.

Jansen, Alf-Inge, Osland, Oddgeir and Hanf, Kenneth (1998) 'Environmental Challenges and Institutional Changes: An Interpretation of the Development of Environmental Policy in Western Europe', in Hanf and Jansen (eds.), pp. 277–325.

Jehlicka, Petr (1994) 'Environmentalism in Europe: An East–West Comparison', in Chris Rootes and Howard Davis (eds.), *A New Europe? Social Change and Political Transformation*, London: UCL Press, pp. 112–31.

Jokinen, Pekka (1997) 'Agricultural Policy Community and the Challenge of Greening: The Case of Finnish Agri-Environmental Policy', *Environmental Politics* 6(2): 48–71.

Joppke, C. and Markovits, Andrei (1994) 'Green Politics in the New Germany', *Dissent*, Spring: 235–40.

Jordan, Andrew (1998) 'Private Affluence and Public Squalor? The Europeanisation of British Coastal Bathing Water Policy', *Policy and Politics*, 26(1): 33–54.

(2002) *The Europeanisation of British Environmental Policy: A Departmental Perspective*, Basingstoke: Palgrave.

(ed.) (2005) *Environmental Policy in the European Union: Actors, Institutions and Processes*, 2nd edn, London: Earthscan.

Jordan, Andrew and Liefferink, Duncan (eds.) (2004a) 'Europeanisation and Convergence: Comparative Conclusions', in Jordan and Liefferink (eds.), pp. 224–45.

(2004b) *Environmental Policy in Europe*, London: Routledge.

Jordan, Andrew and O'Riordan, Tim (1999) 'Environmental Problems and Management', in Paul Cloke, Philip Crang and Mark Goodwin (eds.), *Introducing Human Geographies*, London: Arnold, pp. 133–40.

Jordan, Andrew, Wurzel, Rüdiger and Zito, Anthony (2003a) '"New" Environmental Policy Instruments: An Evolution or a Revolution in Environmental Policy?', *Environmental Politics*, 12(1): 201–24.

(2003b) *'New' Instruments of Environmental Governance: National Experiences and Prospects?*, London: Frank Cass (also published as a special issue of *Environmental Politics*, 12(1)).

Jordan, Andrew, Wurzel, Rüdiger, Zito, Anthony and Brückner, Lars (2003) 'Policy Innovation or "Muddling Through"? "New" Environmental Policy Instruments in the UK', *Environmental Politics*, 12(1): 179–98.

Jordan, Grant and Maloney, William (1997) *The Protest Business?*, Manchester University Press.

Kamieniecki, Sheldon (1995) 'Political Parties and Environmental Policy', in James Lester (ed.), pp. 146–67.

Kasa, Sjur (2000) 'Policy Networks as Barriers to Green Tax Reform: The Case of $CO_2$ Taxes in Norway', *Environmental Politics*, 9(4): 104–22.

Keohane, Robert (1989) *International Institutions and State Power: Essays in International Relations Theory*, Boulder: Westview Press.

Kern, Kristine, Koll, Claudia and Schophaus, Malte (2007) 'The Diffusion of Local Agenda 21 in Germany', *Environmental Politics*, 16.

Kickert, Walter, Klijn, Erik-Hans and Koppenjan, Jap (1997) *Managing Complex Networks*, London: Sage.

King, Anthony (ed.) (2001) *British Political Opinion*. London: Politico's.

King, Ynestra (1983) 'The Ecofeminist Perspective', in Leonie Caldecott and Stephanie Leland (eds.), *Reclaim the Earth*, London: Women's Press, pp. 9–14.

(1989) 'The Ecology of Feminism and the Feminism of Ecology', in Plant (ed.), pp. 18–28.

Kingdon, John (1995) *Agendas, Alternatives and Public Policies*, 2nd edn, New York: HarperCollins.

Kitschelt, Herbert (1986) 'Political Opportunity Structures and Political Protest: Anti-Nuclear Movements in Four Democracies', *British Journal of Political Science*, 16: 58–95.

(1988) 'Left-Libertarian Parties: Explaining Innovation in Competitive Party Systems', *World Politics* 40(2): 194–234.

(1989) *The Logics of Party Formation: Ecological Politics in Belgium and West Germany*, Ithaca: Cornell University Press.

(1990) 'New Social Movements and the Decline of Party Organization', in Russell Dalton and Manfred Kuechler (eds.), *Challenging the Political Order: New Social and Political Movements in Western Democracies*, Cambridge: Polity Press, pp. 179–208.

(1994) *The Transformation of European Social Democracy*, Cambridge University Press.

Klandermans, Bert and Tarrow, Sidney (1988) 'Mobilization into Social Movements: Synthesizing European and American Approaches', *International Social Movement Research*, 1: 1–38.

Kohlhaas, Michael and Meyer, Bettina (2005) 'Ecological Tax Reform in Germany', in Hatch (ed.), pp. 125–49.

Koppen, Ida (2005), 'The Role of the European Court of Justice', in Jordan (ed.), pp. 67–86.

Kraft, Michael and Vig, Norman (2006) 'Environmental Policy from the 1970s to the Twenty-First Century', in Vig and Kraft (eds.), pp. 1–33.

Krasner, Stephen (1983) *International Regimes*, Ithaca: Cornell University Press.

Kriesi, Hanspeter (1993) *Political Mobilisation and Social Change: The Dutch Case in Comparative Perspective*, Aldershot: Avebury.

Kriesi, Hanspeter, Koopmans, Ruud, Dyvendak, Jan and Giugni, Marco (1995) *New Social Movements in Western Europe*, London: UCL Press.

Kütting, Gabriela (2000) *Environment, Society and International Relations*, London: Routledge.

La Spina, Antonio and Sciortino, Giuseppe (1993) 'Common Agenda, Southern Rules: European Integration and Environmental Change in the Mediterranean States', in Duncan Liefferink, Philip Lowe and Arthur Mol (eds.), *European Integration and Environmental Policy*, London: Belhaven, pp. 217–36.

Lafferty, William (1996) 'The Politics of Sustainable Development: Global Norms for National Implementation', *Environmental Politics*, 5(2): 185–208.

(ed.) (2001) *Sustainable Communities in Europe*, London: Earthscan.

Lafferty, William and Hovden, Eivind (2003) 'Environmental Policy Integration: Towards an Analytical Framework', *Environmental Politics*, 12(3): 1–22.

Lafferty, William and Meadowcroft, James (eds.) (2000a) *Implementing Sustainable Development*, Oxford University Press.

(2000b) 'Patterns of Governmental Engagement', in Lafferty and Meadowcroft (eds.), pp. 337–421.

Lamb, Robert (1996) *Promising the Earth*, London: Routledge.

Laslett, Peter and Fishkin, James (eds.) (1992) *Justice Between Age Groups and Generations*, New Haven: Yale University Press.

Lauber, Volkmar (1997) 'Austria: A Latecomer Which Became a Pioneer', in Andersen and Liefferink (eds.), pp. 81–118.

(2003) 'The Austrian Greens after the 2002 Elections', *Environmental Politics*, 12(3): 139–44.

(2004) 'Austria', in Jordan and Liefferink (eds.), pp. 47–63.

Lee, Kai (1993) *Compass and Gyroscope: Integrating Science and Politics for the Environment*, Washington, DC: Island Press.

Lee, Martha (1995) *Earth First!: Environmental Apocalypse*, New York: Syracuse University Press.

Lees, Charles (2000) *The Red–Green Coalition in Germany*, Manchester University Press.

Lele, Sharachchandra (1991) 'Sustainable Development: A Critical Review', *World Development*, 19(6): 607–21.

Lenschow, Andrea (ed.) (2002) *Environmental Policy Integration*, London: Earthscan.

(2005) 'Environmental Policy', in Helen Wallace, William Wallace and Mark Pollack (eds.) *Policy-Making in the European Union*, Oxford University Press, pp. 305–27.

Leopold, Aldo (1949) *A Sand County Almanac*, Oxford University Press.

Lester, James (ed.) (1995) *Environmental Politics and Policy: Theories and Evidence*, 2nd edn, Durhem, NC: Duke University Press.

Lester, James and Loftsson, Elfar (1993) 'The Ecological Movement and Green Parties in Scandinavia: Problems and Prospects', in Sheldon Kamieniecki (ed.), *Environmental Politics in the International Arena*, Albany: SUNY Press, pp. 113–28.

Levy, David and Newell, Peter (eds.) (2005) *The Business of Global Environmental Governance*, Cambridge, MA: MIT Press.

Levy, Marc (1993) 'European Acid Rain: The Power of Tote-Board Diplomacy', in Haas et al. (eds.), pp. 75–132.

Liberatore, Angela (1995) 'The Social Construction of Environmental Problems', in Pieter Glasbergen and Andrew Blowers (eds.), *Perspectives on Environmental Problems*, London: Arnold, pp. 59–83.

(1997) 'The Integration of Sustainable Development Objectives into EU Policy-Making: Barriers and Prospects', in Baker et al. (eds.), pp. 107–26.

Lieberman, Sarah and Gray, Tim (2006), 'The So-called "Moratorium" on the Licensing of New Genetically Modified Products by the European Union 1998–2004: A Study in Ambiguity', *Environmental Politics*, 145(4): 592–609.

Light, Andrew and Rolston, Holmes (eds.) (2003) *Environmental Ethics: An Anthology*, Oxford: Blackwell.

Lightfoot, Simon and Burchill, Jon (2004) 'Green Hope or Greenwash? The Actions of the European Union at the World Summit on Sustainable Development', *Global Environmental Change*, 14: 337–44.

Lindblom, Charles (1977) *Politics and Markets*, New York: Basic Books.

Lipschutz, Ronnie (with Judith Mayer) (1996) *Global Civil Society and Global Environmental Governance: The Politics of Nature from Place to Planet*, Albany: SUNY Press.

Lipschutz, Ronnie (2004) *Global Environmental Politics*, Washington: CQ Press.

Lipset, Seymour Martin and Rokkan, Stein (1967) 'Cleavage Structures, Party Systems and Voter Alignments: An Introduction', in Seymour Martin Lipset and Stein Rokkan (eds.), *Party Systems and Voter Alignments: Cross-National Perspectives*, New York: Free Press, pp. 1–67.

Lisowski, Michael (2002) 'Playing the Two-Level Game: US President Bush's Decision to Repudiate the Kyoto Protocol', *Environmental Politics*, 11(4): 101–19.

Litfin, Karen (1994) *Ozone Discourses: Science and Politics in Global Environmental Cooperation*, New York: Columbia University Press.

(1998a) 'The Greening of Sovereignty: An Introduction', in Litfin (ed.), pp. 1–27.

(ed.) (1998b) *The Greening of Sovereignty in World Politics*, Cambridge, MA: MIT Press.

Litman, Todd (2003) 'Regional Transport Issues in North America', in Whitelegg and Haq (eds.), pp. 203–12.

Liu, Jianguo and Diamond, Jared (2005) 'China's Environment in a Globalizing World', *Nature*, 435 (30 June): 1179–86.

Lomborg, Bjørn (2001) *The Skeptical Environmentalist*, Cambridge University Press.

Long, Carolyn, Cabral, Michael and Vandivort, Brooks (1999) 'The Chief Environmental Diplomat: An Evolving Arena of Foreign Policy', in Soden (ed.), pp. 189–226.

Lowe, Philip and Flynn, Andrew (1989) 'Environmental Politics and Policy in the 1980s', in John Mohan (ed.), *The Political Geography of Contemporary Britain*, Basingstoke: Macmillan, pp. 255–79.

Lowe, Philip and Goyder, Jane (1983) *Environmental Groups in Politics*, London: Allen and Unwin.

Lucardie, Paul (1993) 'Why Would Egocentrists Become Ecocentrists? On Individualism and Holism in Green Political Theory', in Andrew Dobson and Paul Lucardie (eds.), *The Politics of Nature*, London: Routledge, pp. 21–35.

(1997) 'Greening and Ungreening the Netherlands', in Michael Jacobs (ed.), *Greening the Millennium?*, Oxford: Blackwell, pp. 183–91.

Lucardie, Paul, van der Knoop, Jelle, van Schuur, Wijbrandt and Voerman, Gerrit (1995) 'Greening the Reds or Reddening the Greens? The Case of the Green Left in the Netherlands', in Wolfgang Rüdig (ed.), *Green Politics Three*, Edinburgh University Press, pp. 90–111.

Luke, Tim (1988) 'The Dreams of Deep Ecology', *Telos*, 76: 65–92.

(2005) 'Neither Sustainable nor Development: Reconsidering Sustainability in Development', *Sustainable Development*, 13: 228–38.

Lukes, Steven (1974) *Power: A Radical View*, Basingstoke: Macmillan.

Lundqvist, Lennart (1980) *The Hare and the Tortoise: Clean Air Policies in the United States and Sweden*, Ann Arbor: University of Michigan Press.

(1998) 'Sweden: From Environmental Restoration to Ecological Modernisation', in Hanf and Jansen (eds.), pp. 230–52.

(2004) *Sweden and Ecological Governance*, Manchester University Press.

McAdam, Doug, McCarthy, John and Zald, Mayer (1996) *Comparative Perspectives on Social Movements*, Cambridge University Press.

McAdams, John (1987) 'Testing the Theory of the New Class', *Sociological Quarterly*, 28(1): 23–49.

McCormick, John (1989) *Reclaiming Paradise*, Bloomington: Indiana University Press.

(1991) *British Politics and the Environment*, London: Earthscan.

(2001) *Environmental Policy in the European Union*, Basingstoke: Palgrave.

McCulloch, Alistair (1992) 'The Green Party in England and Wales: Structure and Development', *Environmental Politics* 1(3): 418–36.

McGinnis, Michael (ed.) (1998) *Bioregionalism*, London: Routledge.

McLaughlin, Andrew (1993) *Regarding Nature*, New York: SUNY Press.

McMichael, A. J. (1995) *Planetary Overload*, Cambridge University Press.

Macrory, Richard (1986) *Environmental Policy in Britain: Reaffirmation or Reform?*, Berlin: International Institute for Environment and Society.

Maloney, William and Richardson, Jeremy (1994) 'Water Policy-Making in England and Wales: Policy Communities under Pressure?', *Environmental Politics*, 3(4): 110–38.

Markell, David and Knox, John (eds.) (2003) *Greening NAFTA: The North American Commission for Environmental Cooperation*, Stanford University Press.

Markovits, Andrei and Gorski, Philip (1993) *The German Left: Red, Green and Beyond*, Cambridge: Polity Press.

Marsh, David (ed.) (1998) *Comparing Policy Networks*, Buckingham: Open University Press.

Marsh, David and Rhodes, R. A. W. (eds.) (1992) *Policy Networks in British Government*, Oxford University Press.

Marsh, David and Smith, Martin (2000) 'Understanding Policy Networks: Towards a Dialectical Approach', *Political Studies*, 48: 4–21.

Martell, Luke (1994) *Ecology and Society*, Cambridge: Polity Press.

Martinez-Alier, Joan (2003) *Environmentalism of the Poor: A Study of Ecological Conflicts and Valuation*, Cheltenham: Edward Elgar.

Maslow, Abraham (1954) *Motivation and Personality*, New York: Harper Row.

Mason, Michael (1999) *Environmental Democracy*, London: Earthscan.

(2004) 'Representing Transnational Environmental Interests: New Opportunities for Non-Governmental Organisation Access within the WTO?', *Environmental Politics*, 13(3): 566–89.

Mathews, Freya (1991) *The Ecological Self*, London: Routledge.

Mayer, Margit and Ely, John (1998) *The German Greens: Paradox between Movement and Party*, Philadelphia: Temple University Press.

Meadowcroft, James (2000) 'Sustainable Development: A New(ish) Idea for a New Century?', *Political Studies*, 48: 370–87.

(2004) 'Deliberative Democracy', in Durant et al. (eds.), pp. 183–217.

Meadows, Donella, Meadows, Dennis and Randers, Jorgen (1992) *Beyond the Limits: Global Collapse or a Sustainable Future?*, London: Earthscan.

Meadows, Donella, Meadows, Dennis, Randers, Jorgen and Behrens, William (1972) *The Limits to Growth*, London: Earth Island.

Meadows, Donella, Randers, Jorgen and Meadows, Dennis (2004) *The Limits to Growth: The Thirty Year Update*, London: Earthscan.

Mellor, Mary (1992) *Breaking the Boundaries*, London: Virago.

(1997) *Feminism and Ecology*, Cambridge: Polity Press.

(2006) 'Socialism', in Dobson and Eckersley (eds.), pp. 35–50.

Melucci, Alberto (1989) *Nomads of the Present: Social Movements and Individual Needs in Contemporary Society*, London: Hutchinson Radius.

Merchant, Carolyn (2005) *Radical Ecology*, 2nd edn, London: Routledge.

Michels, Robert (1959 [1915]), *Political Parties*, New York: Dover.

Midgley, Mary (1983) *Animals and Why They Matter*, Harmondsworth: Penguin.

Milbrath, Lester (1989) *Envisioning a Sustainable Society*, Albany: SUNY Press.

Miles, Edward, Underhal, Arild, Andresen, Steinar, Wettestad, Jørgen, Skjærseth, Jon Birger and Carlin, Elaine (2002) *Environmental Regime Effectiveness*, Cambridge, MA: MIT Press.

Miller, David (1999) 'Social Justice and Environmental Goods', in Dobson (ed.), pp. 151–72.

Ministry of the Environment (2005) *The Government's Environment Policy and the State of the Environment in Norway*, White Paper, Report 21 (2004–5), http://odin.dep.no/md/english/doc/white_paper/bn.html.

Mol, Arthur (1996) 'Ecological Modernisation and Institutional Reflexivity: Environmental Reform in the Late Modern Age', *Environmental Politics*, 5(2): 302–23.

(2003) *Globalization and Environmental Reform*, Cambridge, MA: MIT Press.

Mol, Arthur, Lauber, Volkmar and Liefferink, Duncan (2000) *The Voluntary Approach to Environmental Policy*, Oxford University Press.

Mol, Arthur and Sonnenfeld, David (eds.) (2000) 'Ecological Modernisation around the World: Perspectives and Critical Debates', *Environmental Politics*, Special Issue, 9(1).

Mol, Arthur and Spaargaren, Gert (2000) 'Ecological Modernisation Theory in Debate: A Review', *Environmental Politics*, 9(1): 17–49.

Moran, Alan, Chisholm, Andrew and Porter, Michael (eds.) (1991) *Markets, Resources and the Environment*, North Sydney: Allen and Unwin.

Morgenthau, Hans (1978) *Politics Among Nations*, 5th edn, New York: Alfred Knopf.

MORI (2005) http://www.mori.com/polls/ (accessed 22 May).

Morrison, Denton and Dunlap, Riley (1986) 'Environmentalism and Elitism: A Conceptual and Empirical Analysis', *Environmental Management*, 10(5): 581–9.

Mueller, Dennis (1989) *Public Choice II*, Cambridge University Press.

Müller, Edda (2005) 'Environmental Labeling, Innovation, and the Toolbox of Environmental Policy: Lessons Learned from the German Blue Angel Program', in Hatch (ed.), pp. 17–44.

Müller-Rommel, Ferdinand (ed.) (1989) *New Politics in Western Europe*, Boulder: Westview Press.

(1990) 'New Political Movements and "New Politics Parties" in Western Europe', in Russell Dalton and Manfred Kuechler (eds.), *Challenging the Political Order: New Social and Political Movements in Western Democracies*, Cambridge: Polity Press, pp. 209–31.

(1998) 'Explaining the Electoral Success of Green Parties: A Cross-National Analysis', *Environmental Politics*, 7(4): 145–54.

Müller-Rommel, Ferdinand and Poguntke, Thomas (eds.) (2002) *Green Parties in National Governments*, London: Frank Cass.

Myers, Nancy and Raffensperger, Carolyn (2005) *Precautionary Tools for Reshaping Environmental Policy*, Cambridge, MA: MIT Press.

Naess, Arne (1973) 'The Shallow and the Deep, Long-Range Ecology Movement', *Inquiry*, 16: 95–100.

(1989) *Ecology, Community and Lifestyle*, Cambridge University Press.

Nas, Masja (1995) 'Green, Greener, Greenest', in Jan van Deth and Elinor Scarbrough (eds.), *The Impact of Values*, Oxford University Press, pp. 275–300.

Nash, Roderick (1989) *The Rights of Nature: A History of Environmental Ethics*, Madison: University of Wisconsin Press.

Neale, Alan (1997) 'Organising Environmental Self-Regulation: Liberal Governmentality and the Pursuit of Ecological Modernisation in Europe', *Environmental Politics*, 6(4): 1–24.

NEPAnet (2006) http://ceq.ch.doe.gov/nepa/EIS_Statistics_1970_to_2004.pdf (accessed 14 April).

Neumayer, Eric (2001) *Greening Trade and Investment: Environmental Protection Without Protectionism*, London: Earthscan.

(2004) 'The WTO and the Environment: Its Past Record is Better than Critics Believe, but the Future Outlook is Bleak', *Global Environmental Politics*, 4(3): 1–8.

Newell, Peter (2000) *Climate for Change: Non-State Actors and the Global Politics of the Greenhouse*, Cambridge University Press.

Newell, Peter and Paterson, Matthew (1998) 'A Climate for Business: Global Warming, the State and Capital', *Review of International Political Economy*, 5(4): 679–704.

Niemeyer, Simon (2004) 'Deliberation in the Wilderness: Displacing Symbolic Politics', *Environmental Politics*, 13(2): 347–72.

Norton, Bryan (1991) *Towards Unity amongst Environmentalists*, Oxford University Press.

Nozick, Robert (1974) *Anarchy, State and Utopia*, Oxford: Blackwell.

Nussbaum, Martha (1986) *The Fragility of Goodness: Luck and Ethics in Greek Tragedy and Philosophy*, Cambridge University Press.

OECD (1991) *Environmental Indicators: A Preliminary Set*, Paris.

(1997) *Environmental Taxes and Green Tax Reform*, Paris.

(2001) *Environmentally Related Taxes in OECD Countries: Issues and Strategies*, Paris.

(2003a) *Environmental Indicators: Development, Management and Use*, Paris, http://www.oecd.org/dataoecd/7/47/24993546.pdf.

(2003b) *Voluntary Approaches for Environmental Policy*, Paris.

(2004) *Tradeable Permits: Policy Evaluation, Design and Reform*, Paris.

(2005a) *Manure Policy and MINAS: Regulating Nitrogen and Phosphorus Surpluses in Agriculture in the Netherlands*, Paris, http://www.oecd.org/env/taxes.

(2005b) *The Window of Opportunity: How the Obstacles to the Introduction of the Swiss Heavy Vehicle Fee Have Been Overcome*, Paris, http://www.oecd.org/env/taxes.

Oelschlaeger, Max (1991) *The Idea of Wilderness*, New Haven: Yale University Press.

Offe, Claus (1974) 'Structural Problems of the Capitalist State', in Klaus von Beyme (ed.), *German Political Studies*, vol. I, London: Sage, pp. 31–57.

(1985) 'New Social Movements: Challenging the Boundaries of Institutional Politics', *Social Research*, 52(4): 817–68.

Office for National Statistics (2000) *Social Trends 30: 2000 Edition*, London: The Stationery Office.

Ogle, Greg (2000) 'Accounting for Economic Welfare: Politics, Problems and Potentials', *Environmental Politics*, 9(3): 109–28.

O'Leary, Rosemary, Nabatchi, Tina and Bingham, Lisa (2004) *Environmental Conflict Resolution*, in Durant et al. (eds.), pp. 323–54.

Olson, Mancur (1965) *The Logic of Collective Action*, Cambridge, MA: Harvard University Press.

O'Neill, John (1993) *Ecology, Policy and Politics*, London: Routledge.

O'Neill, John, Turner, Kerry and Bateman, Ian (eds.) (2001) *Environmental Ethics and Philosophy*, Cheltenham: Edward Elgar.

O'Neill, Michael (1997) *Green Politics and Political Change in Contemporary Europe*, Aldershot: Ashgate.

Ophuls, William (1977) *Ecology and the Politics of Scarcity*, San Francisco: Freeman and Co.

O'Riordan, Timothy (1981) *Environmentalism*, 2nd edn, London: Pion.

(1996) 'Democracy and the Sustainability Transition', in William Lafferty and James Meadowcroft (eds.), *Democracy and the Environment: Problems and Prospects*, Cheltenham: Edward Elgar, pp. 140–56.

(ed.) (1997) *Ecotaxation*, London: Earthscan.

O'Riordan, Timothy, Cameron, James and Jordan, Andrew (2001) (eds.), *Reinterpreting the Precautionary Principle*, London: Cameron May.

O'Riordan, Timothy, Kemp, Ray and Purdue, Michael (1988) *Sizewell B: An Anatomy of the Inquiry*, Basingstoke: Macmillan.

Ostrom, Elinor (1990) *Governing the Commons*, Cambridge University Press.

Ostrom, Elinor, Burger, Joanna, Field, Christopher, Norgaard, Richard and Policansky, David (1999) 'Revisiting the Commons: Local Lessons, Global Challenges', *Science*, 284: 278–82.

Paastela, Jukka (2002) 'Finland', in Müller-Rommel and Poguntke (eds.), pp. 17–38.

Paehlke, Robert (1989) *Environmentalism and the Future of Progressive Politics*, New Haven: Yale University Press.

Paehlke, Robert and Torgerson, Douglas (eds.) (2005) *Managing Leviathan: Environmental Politics and the Administrative State*, 2nd edn, Peterborough, Ont.: Broadview Press.

Panebianco, Angelo (1988) *Political Parties*, Cambridge University Press.

Papadakis, Elim (1993) *Politics and the Environment*, St Leonards, NSW: Allen and Unwin.

Parfitt, Derek (1984) *Reasons and Persons*, Oxford University Press.

Parsons, Wayne (1995) *Public Policy*, Cheltenham: Edward Elgar.

Pateman, Carol (1970) *Participation and Democratic Theory*, Cambridge University Press.

Paterson, Matthew (1996) *Global Warming and Global Politics*, London: Routledge.

Paterson, Matthew, Doran, Peter and Barry, John (2006) 'Green Theory', in Hay et al. (eds.), pp. 135–54.

Pearce, David (1998) 'Cost–Benefit Analysis and Environmental Policy', *Oxford Review of Economic Policy*, 14(4): 84–100.

Pearce, David, Markandya, Anil and Barbier, Edward (1989) *Blueprint for a Green Economy*, London: Earthscan.

Pearce, David and Turner, R. Kerry (1990) *Economics of Natural Resources and the Environment*, Hemel Hempstead: Harvester Wheatsheaf.

Pearce, David (and twelve others) (1993) *Blueprint 3: Measuring Sustainable Development*, London: Earthscan.

Pearce, Fred (1991) *Green Warriors*, London: Bodley Head.

Pepper, David (1991) *Communes and the Green Vision*, London: Green Print.
   (1993) *Ecosocialism*, London: Routledge.
   (1996) *Modern Environmentalism*, London: Routledge.

Pesendorfer, Dieter (2006) 'EU Environmental Policy under Pressure: Chemicals Policy Change between Antagonistic Goals?', *Environmental Politics*, 15(1): 95–114.

Peters, B. Guy (1998a) 'Policy Networks: Myth, Metaphor and Reality', in Marsh (ed.), pp. 21–32.
   (1998b) 'Managing Horizontal Government: The Politics of Co-ordination', *Public Administration*, 76: 295–311.

Peters, B. Guy and Hogwood, Brian (1985) 'In Search of an Issue-Attention Cycle', *Journal of Politics*, 47: 238–53.

Peterson, John and Bomberg, Elizabeth (1999) *Decision-Making in the European Union*, Basingstoke: Macmillan.

Pickering, Kevin and Owen, Lewis (1997) *An Introduction to Global Environmental Issues*, 2nd edn, London: Routledge.

Pilbeam, Bruce (2003) 'Natural Allies? Mapping the Relationship between Conservatism and Environmentalism', *Political Studies*, 51(3): 490–508.

Plant, Judith (ed.) (1989) *Healing the Wounds: The Promise of Ecofeminism*, London: Green Print.

Plows, Alexandra, Wall, Derek and Doherty, Brian (2004) 'Covert Strategies: Ecotage in the UK', *Social Movement Studies*, 3(2): 199–219.

Plumwood, Val (1993) *Feminism and the Mastery of Nature*, London: Routledge.
   (1996) 'Has Democracy Failed Ecology? An Ecofeminist Perspective', *Environmental Politics*, 4(4): 134–68.

Poguntke, Thomas (1993) *Alternative Politics: The German Green Party*, Edinburgh University Press.

(2002) 'Green Parties in National Governments: From Protest to Acquiescence', in Müller-Rommel and Poguntke (eds.), pp. 133–45.

Polsby, Nelson (1980) *Community Power and Political Theory: A Further Look at Problems of Evidence and Inference*, 2nd edn, New Haven: Yale University Press.

Ponting, Clive (1992) *A Green History of the World*, London: Penguin.

Porritt, Jonathon (1984) *Seeing Green*, Oxford: Blackwell.

Porter, Gareth (1999) 'Trade Competition and Pollution Standards: "Race to the Bottom" or "Stuck at the Bottom"', *Journal of Environment and Development*, 8(2): 133–51.

Porter, Gareth, Brown, Janet Welsh and Chasek, Pamela (2000) *Global Environmental Politics*, 3rd edn, Boulder: Westview Press.

Porter, Michael (1990) *The Competitive Advantage of Nations*, New York: Free Press.

Pratt, Vernon, with Jane Howarth and Emily Brady (2000) *Environment and Philosophy*, London: Routledge.

Press, Daniel and Mazmanian, Daniel (1999) 'Understanding the Transition to a Sustainable Economy', in Norman Vig and Michael Kraft (eds.), *Environmental Policy*, 4th edition, Washington, DC: CQ Press, pp. 257–80.

Princen, Thomas and Finger, Matthias (1994) 'Introduction', in Thomas Princen and Matthias Finger (eds.), *Environmental NGOs in World Politics*, London: Routledge.

Pross, Paul (1992) *Group Politics and Public Policy*, 2nd edn, Oxford University Press.

Pulido, Laura (1996) *Environmentalism and Social Justice*, Tucson: University of Arizona Press.

Pulzer, Peter (2006) 'The German Federal Election of 2005', *West European Politics*, 29(3): 560–72.

Rabe, Barry (2006) 'Power to the States: The Promise and Pitfalls of Decentralisation', in Vig and Kraft (eds.), pp. 34–56.

Rawcliffe, Peter (1998) *Environmental Pressure Groups in Transition*, Manchester University Press.

Rawls, John (1973) *A Theory of Justice*, Oxford University Press.

Raz, Joseph (1986) *The Morality of Freedom*, Oxford: Clarendon Press.

RCEP [Royal Commission on Environmental Pollution] (1998) *Setting Environmental Standards*, 21st Report, Cm. 4053, London: The Stationery Office.

(2000) *Energy – the Changing Climate*, 22nd Report, Cm. 4794, London: The Stationery Office, http://www.rcep.org.uk/energy.htm.

Redclift, Michael (2005) 'Sustainable Development (1987–2005): An Oxymoron Comes of Age', *Sustainable Development*, 13: 212–27.

Regan, Tom (1983) *The Case for Animal Rights*, London: RKP.

Reitan, Marit (1998) 'Ecological Modernisation and "Realpolitik": Ideas, Interests and Institutions', *Environmental Politics*, 7(2): 1–26.

Rhodes, R. A. W. (1988) *Beyond Westminster and Whitehall: The Sub-Central Government of Britain*, London: Unwin Hyman.

(1997) *Understanding Governance*, Buckingham: Open University Press.

Richardson, Dick (1997) 'The Politics of Sustainable Development', in Baker et al. (eds.), pp. 43–60.

Richardson, Dick and Rootes, Chris (eds.) (1995) *The Green Challenge*, London: Routledge.

Richardson, Genevra, Ogus, Anthony and Burrows, Paul (1983) *Policing Pollution*, Oxford University Press.

Richardson, Jeremy (ed.) (1982) *Policy Styles in Western Europe*, London: Allen and Unwin.

Ridley, Matt (1995) *Down to Earth: A Contrarian View of Environmental Problems*, London: Institute of Economic Affairs.

Rihoux, Benoît (2006) 'Governmental Participation and the Organizational Adaptation of Green Parties', *European Journal of Political Research*, 45: S69–S98.

Ringquist, Evan (1995) 'Evaluating Environmental Policy Outcomes', in Lester (ed.), pp. 303–27.

Roberts, J. Timmons and Toffolon-Weiss, Melissa (2001) *Chronicles from the Environmental Justice Frontline*, Cambridge University Press.

Robertson, James (1985) *Future Work*, Aldershot: Gower.

Robinson, Mike (1992) *The Greening of British Party Politics*, Manchester University Press.

Robinson, Nick (2000) 'The Politics of the Car: The Limits of Actor-Centred Models of Agenda-Setting', in Seel et al. (eds.), pp. 199–217.

Rodman, John (1980) 'Paradigm Change in Political Science', *American Behavioral Scientist*, 24(1): 49–78.

Rogers, Kenneth and Kingsley, Marvin (2004) 'The Politics of Interim Radioactive Waste Storage: The United States', *Environmental Politics*, 13(3): 590–611.

Rohrschneider, Robert (1993) 'New Party versus Old Left Realignments: Environmental Attitudes, Party Policies and Partisan Affiliations in Four Western European Countries', *Journal of Politics*, 55(3): 682–701.

Rolston, Holmes (1988) *Environmental Ethics: Duties to and Values in the Natural World*, Philadelphia: Temple University Press.

    (1991) 'Environmental Ethics: Values in and Duties to the Natural World', in F. Herbert and Stephen Kellert (eds.), *The Broken Circle*, New Haven: Yale University Press, pp. 73–96.

Rootes, Christopher (1995a) 'A New Class? The Higher Educated and the New Politics', in Louis Mahen (ed.), *Social Movements and Social Classes: The Future of Collective Action*, London: Sage, pp. 220–35.

    (1995b) 'Environmental Consciousness, Institutional Structures and Political Competition in the Formation and Development of Green Parties', in Richardson and Rootes (eds.), pp. 232–52.

    (1995c) 'Britain: Greens in a Cold Climate', in Richardson and Rootes (eds.), pp. 66–90.

    (1997) 'Environmental Movements and Green Parties in Western and Eastern Europe', in Michael Redclift and Graham Woodgate (eds.), *The International Handbook of Environmental Sociology*, Cheltenham: Edward Elgar, pp. 319–48.

(1998) 'Political Opportunity Structures: Promise, Problems and Prospects', *La Lettre de la Maison Française*, no. 10, pp. 75–97.

(1999a) 'Environmental Movements: From the Local to the Global', *Environmental Politics*, 8(1): 1–12.

(1999b) 'Acting Globally, Thinking Locally? Prospects for a Global Environmental Movement', *Environmental Politics*, 8(1): 290–310.

(ed.) (2003) *Environmental Protest in Western Europe*, Oxford University Press.

(2005) 'A Limited Transnationalization? The British Environmental Movement', in Donatella della Porta and Sidney Tarrow (eds.), *Transnational Protest and Global Activity*, Lanham, MD: Rowman and Littlefield, pp. 21–43.

Rootes, Christopher and Miller, Alexander (2001) 'The British Environmental Movement: Organisational Field and Network of Organisations', paper at ECPR Joint Sessions, Copenhagen, 14–19 April.

Rose, Adam (1992) 'Equity Considerations of Tradeable Carbon Emission Entitlements', in UNCTAD, *Combating Global Warming*, Geneva: UNCTAD, pp. 55–83.

Rose, Chris (1993) 'Beyond the Struggle for Proof: Factors Changing the Environmental Movement', *Environmental Values*, 2(4): 285–98.

Rosenbaum, Walter (1995) 'Bureaucracy and Environmental Policy', in Lester (ed.), pp. 206–41.

(1997) 'Regulation at Risk: The Controversial Politics and Science of Comparative Risk Assessment', in Sheldon Kamieniecki, George Gonzalez and Robert Vos (eds.), *Flashpoints in Environmental Policy-Making*, Albany: SUNY Press, pp. 31–61.

(2005a) *Environmental Politics and Policy*, 6th edn, Washington: CQ Press.

(2005b) 'Environmental Impact Statements: Gift Box or Black Box', in Hatch (ed.), pp. 195–223.

(2006) 'Improving Environmental Regulation at the EPA: The Challenge in Balancing Politics, Policy and Science', in Vig and Kraft (eds.), pp. 169–92.

Rosendal, Kristin (2005) 'Governing GMOs in the EU: A Deviant Case of Environmental Policy-Making?' *Global Environmental Politics*, 5(1): 82–104.

Rowe, Janet and Fudge, Colin (2003) 'Linking National Sustainable Development Strategy and Local Implementation: A Case Study of Sweden', *Local Environment*, 8(2): 125–40.

Rowell, Andrew (1996) *Green Backlash: Global Subversion of the Environmental Movement*, London: Routledge.

Rowlands, Ian (1995) *The Politics of Global Atmospheric Change*, Manchester University Press.

(1997) 'International Fairness and Justice in Addressing Global Climate Change', *Environmental Politics*, 6(3): 1–30.

Rucht, Dieter (1995) 'Ecological Protest as Calculated Law-Breaking: Greenpeace and Earth First! in Comparative Perspective', in Wolfgang Rüdig (ed.), *Green Politics Three*, Edinburgh University Press, pp. 66–89.

Rucht, Dieter and Roose, Jochen (2003) 'Germany', in Christopher Rootes (ed.), *Environmental Protest in Western Europe*, Oxford University Press, pp. 80–108.

Rüdig, Wolfgang (2003) 'The Environment and Nuclear Power', in Stephen Padgett, William Paterson and Gordon Smith (eds.), *Developments in German Politics 3*, Basingstoke: Palgrave, pp. 248–68.

(2006) 'Is Government Good for Greens? Comparing the Electoral Effects of Government Participation in Western and East-Central Europe', *European Journal of Political Research*, 45: S127–S154.

Rüdig, Wolfgang, Bennie, Lynn and Franklin, Mark (1991) *Green Party Members: A Profile*, Glasgow: Delta.

Rüdig, Wolfgang and Lowe, Philip (1986) 'The Withered "Greening" of British Politics: A Study of the Ecology Party', *Political Studies*, 34: 262–84.

Rydin, Yvonne (1998) *Urban and Environmental Planning*, Basingstoke: Macmillan.

Ryle, Martin (1988) *Ecology and Socialism*, London: Radius.

Saalfeld, Thomas (2004) 'Party Identification and the Social Bases of Voting Behaviour in the 2002 Bundestag Election', *German Politics*, 13(2): 170–200.

Sabatier, Paul (1988) 'An Advocacy Coalition Framework of Policy Change and the Role of Policy-Oriented Learning Therein', *Policy Sciences*, 21: 129–68.

(1998) 'The Advocacy Coalition Framework: Revisions and Relevance for Europe', *Journal of European Public Policy*, 5: 98–130.

Sabatier, Paul and Jenkins-Smith, Hank (eds.) (1993) *Policy Change and Learning: An Advocacy Coalition Approach*, Boulder: Westview Press.

(1999) 'The Advocacy Coalition Framework: An Assessment', in Paul Sabatier (ed.), *Theories of the Policy Process*, Boulder: Westview Press, pp. 117–66.

Sachs, Wolfgang (1999) *Planet Dialectics*, London: Zed Books.

Sagoff, Mark (1988) *The Economy of the Earth*, Cambridge University Press.

Sairinen, Rauno (1996) *The Finns and Environmental Policy*, Helsinki: Central Statistics Office, Research Report 217.

(2003) 'The Politics of Regulatory Reform: "New" Environmental Policy Instruments in Finland', *Environmental Politics*, 12(1): 73–92.

Sale, Kirkpatrick (1980) *Human Scale*, London: Secker and Warburg.

(1991) *Dwellers in the Land: The Bioregional Vision*, 2nd edn, Philadelphia: New Society Publishers.

(1993) *The Green Revolution: The American Environmental Movement 1962–92*, New York: Hill and Wang.

Salleh, Ariel (1997) *Ecofeminism as Politics*, London: Zed Books.

Sancassiani, Walter (2005) 'Local Agenda 21 in Italy', *Local Environment*, 10(2): 189–200.

Sanchez, Roberto (2002) 'Governance, Trade and the Environment in the Context of NAFTA', *American Behavioral Scientist*, 45(9): 1369–93.

Sargisson, Lucy (2001) 'What's Wrong with Ecofeminism?', *Environmental Politics*, 10(1): 52–64.

Sarkar, Saral (1999) *Ecosocialism or Ecocapitalism?*, London: Zed Books.

Saward, Michael (1992) 'The Civil Nuclear Network in Britain', in Marsh and Rhodes (eds.), pp. 75–99.

(1996) 'Must Democrats Be Environmentalists?', in Doherty and de Geus (eds.), pp. 79–96.

Sbragia, Alberta (2005) 'Institution-Building from Below and Above: The European Community in Global Environmental Politics', in Jordan (ed.), pp. 201–24.

Scarrow, Susan (2004) 'Embracing Dealignment, Combating Realignment: German Parties Respond', in Peter Mair, Wolfgang Müller and Fritz Plasser (eds.), *Political Parties and Electoral Change*, London: Sage, pp. 86–110.

Scharf, Thomas (1994) *The German Greens*, Oxford: Berg.

Schattschneider, E. E. (1960) *The Semi-Sovereign People*, New York: Holt, Rinehart and Winston.

Scheinberg, A. (2003) 'A Change by Any Other Name: Re-examining the Urban Recycling Experience in North America and its Implications for Ecological Modernisation Theory', *Environmental Politics*, 12(4): 49–75.

Schlosberg, David (1999a) *Environmental Justice and the New Pluralism*, Oxford University Press.

(1999b) 'Networks and Mobile Arrangements: Organisational Innovation in the US Environmental Justice Movement', *Environmental Politics*, 8(1): 122–48.

Scholte, Jan Aart (2005) *Globalization: A Critical Introduction*, 2nd edn, Basingstoke: Palgrave.

Schreurs, Miranda (2002) *Environmental Politics in Japan, Germany and the United States*, Cambridge University Press.

(2004) 'The Climate Change Divide', in Vig and Faure (eds.), pp. 207–30.

Schumacher, E. F. (1975) *Small Is Beautiful*, London: Sphere.

Scott, Alan (1990) *Ideology and the New Social Movements*, London: Unwin Hyman.

Scruggs, Lyle (2003) *Sustaining Abundance*, Cambridge University Press.

Scruton, Roger (2006) 'Conservatism', in Dobson and Eckersley (eds.), pp. 7–19.

Seager, Joni (1993) *Earth Follies*, London: Earthscan.

Seaver, Brenda (1997) 'Stratospheric Ozone Protection: IR Theory and the Montreal Protocol on Substances that Deplete the Ozone Layer', *Environmental Politics*, 6(3): 31–67.

Seel, Benjamin (1997) 'Strategies of Resistance at the Pollok Free State Road Protest Camp', *Environmental Politics*, 6(4): 108–39.

Seel, Benjamin, Paterson, Matthew and Doherty, Brian (eds.) (2000) *Direct Action in British Environmentalism*, London: Routledge.

Seel, Benjamin and Plows, Alex (2000) 'Coming Live and Direct: Strategies of Earth First!', in Seel et al. pp. 112–32.

Sen, Amartya (1994) 'Population: Delusion and Reality', *New York Review of Books*, 22 September.

Sessions, George (ed.) (1995) *Deep Ecology for the 21st Century*, London: Shambala.

Seyfang, Gill (2003) 'Environmental Mega-Conferences – from Stockholm to Johannesburg and Beyond', *Global Environmental Change*, 13: 223–8.

(2005) 'Shopping for Sustainability: Can Sustainable Consumption Promote Ecological Citizenship?', *Environmental Politics*, 14(2): 290–306.

Shaheen, Susan, Wright, John and Sperling, Daniel (2004) *California's Zero Emissions Vehicle Mandate*, Institute of Transportation Studies, University of California, Davis.

Shaiko, Ronald (1993) 'Greenpeace USA: Something Old, New, Borrowed', *The Annals*, July, pp. 88–100.

Shiva, Vandana (1989) *Staying Alive: Women, Ecology and Development*, London: Earthscan.

Sierra Club (2006) http://www.sierraclub.org/vision/ (accessed 23 June).

Simon, Julian (1981) *The Ultimate Resource*, Princeton University Press.

Singer, Peter (1976) *Animal Liberation*, London: Jonathan Cape.

—— (1979) *Practical Ethics*, Cambridge University Press.

Skea, Jim and Smith, Adrian (1998) 'Integrating Pollution Control', in Philip Lowe and Stephen Ward (eds.), *British Environmental Policy and Europe*, London: Routledge, pp. 265–81.

Skodvin, Tora and Andresen, Steinar (2003) 'Nonstate Influence in the International Whaling Commission, 1970–1990', *Global Environmental Politics*, 3(4): 61–86.

Smith, Gordon (1996) 'The Party System at the Crossroads', in Gordon Smith, William Paterson and Stephen Padgett (eds.), *Developments in German Politics 2*, Basingstoke: Macmillan, pp. 55–75.

Smith, Graham (2003) *Deliberative Democracy and the Environment*, London: Routledge.

Smith, Mark (1999) *Thinking through the Environment*, London: Routledge.

Smith, Martin (1990) *The Politics of Agricultural Support in Britain*, Aldershot: Dartmouth.

—— (1993) *Pressure, Power and Policy: State Autonomy and Policy Networks in Britain and the United States*, Hemel Hempstead: Harvester Wheatsheaf.

Soden, Dennis (ed.) (1999) *The Environmental Presidency*, New York: SUNY Press.

Spaargaren, Gert (2003) 'Sustainable Consumption: A Theoretical and Environmental Policy Perspective', *Society and Natural Resources*, 16: 687–701.

Spaargaren, Gert and Mol, Arthur (1992) 'Sociology, Environment and Modernity: Ecological Modernisation as a Theory of Social Change', *Society and Natural Resources*, 5(4): 323–44.

Spaargaren, Gert and van Vliet, Bas (2000) 'Lifestyles, Consumption and the Environment: The Ecological Modernisation of Domestic Consumption', *Environmental Politics*, 9(1): 50–76.

Stephens, Piers (2001) Green Liberalisms: Nature, Agency and the Good', *Environmental Politics*, 10(3): 1–22.

Stern, David, Common, Michael and Barbier, Edward (1996) 'Economic Growth and Environmental Degradation: The Environmental Kuznets Curve and Sustainability', *World Development*, 24: 1151–60.

Sterner, Thomas (2003) *Policy Instruments for Environmental and Natural Resource Management*, Washington: Resources for the Future.

Stevis, Dimitris and Assetto, Valerie (eds.) (2001) *The International Political Economy of the Environment*, Boulder: Lynne Rienner.

Stoett, Peter (1997) *The International Politics of Whaling*, Vancouver: UBC Press.

Sussman, Glen, Davies, Byron and West, Jonathan (2002) *American Politics and the Environment*, New York: Addison Wesley Longman.

Swatuk, Larry (2006) 'Environmental Security', in Betsill et al. (eds.), pp. 203–36.

Sylvan, Richard and Bennett, David (1994) *The Greening of Ethics*, Cambridge: White Horse Press.

Szarka, Joseph (2003) 'The Politics of Bounded Innovation: "New" Environmental Policy Instruments in France', *Environmental Politics*, 12(1): 93–114.

(2004) 'Wind Power, Discourse Coalitions and Climate Change: Breaking the Stalemate?', *European Environment*, 17(6): 317–30.

Szasz, Andrew (1994) *Ecopopulism: Toxic Waste and the Movement for Environmental Justice*, Minneapolis: University of Minnesota Press.

Talshir, Gayil (2002) *The Political Ideology of Green Parties*, Basingstoke: Palgrave.

Tarrow, Sydney (1994) *Power in Movement: Social Movements, Collective Action and Mass Politics*, Cambridge University Press.

Tatalovich, Raymond and Wattier, Mark (1999) 'Opinion Leadership: Elections, Campaigns, Agenda Setting and Environmentalism', in Soden (ed.), pp. 147–87.

Taylor, Bob Pepperman (1991) 'Environmental Ethics and Political Theory', *Polity*, 23: 567–83.

(1992) *Our Limits Transgressed: Environmental Political Thought in America*, Lawrence: University Press of Kansas.

Thomas, Urs (2004) 'Trade and the Environment: Stuck in a Political Impasse at the WTO after the Doha and Cancun Ministerial Conferences', *Global Environmental Politics*, 4(3): 9–21.

Tilly, Charles (1978) *From Mobilization to Revolution*, Reading: Addison-Wesley.

Tokar, Brian (1992) *The Green Alternative*, San Pedro: R. & E. Miles.

Toke, Dave (2002) 'Wind Power in the UK and Denmark: Can Rational Choice Help Explain Different Outcomes?', *Environmental Politics*, 11(4): 83–100.

Toner, Glen (2002) 'Contesting the Green: Canadian Environmental Policy at the Turn of the Century', in Desai (ed.), pp. 71–120.

Torgerson, Doug (1999) *The Promise of Green Politics*, Durham, NC: Duke University Press.

(2003) 'Democracy through Policy Discourse', in Maarten Hajer and Hendrik Wagenaar (eds.), *Deliberative Policy Analysis*, Cambridge University Press, pp. 113–38.

Touraine, Alain (1981) *The Voice and the Eye: An Analysis of Social Movements*, Cambridge University Press.

Trainer, F. E. (1985) *Abandon Affluence!*, London: Zed Books.

Transport for London (2005) *Central London Congestion Charging: Impacts Monitoring*, 3rd Annual Report, London.

Truman, David (1951) *The Governmental Process*, New York: Alfred Knopf.

Tsebelis, George and Yataganas, Xenophon (2002) 'Veto-Players and Decision-Making in the EU after Nice', *Journal of Common Market Studies*, 40(2): 283–308.

Turner, R. Kerry, Pearce, David and Bateman, Ian (1994) *Environmental Economics: An Elementary Introduction*, Hemel Hempstead: Harvester Wheatsheaf.

Tyme, John (1978) *Motorways versus Democracy*, Basingstoke: Macmillan.

UNCED [United Nations Conference on Environment and Development] (1992) *Agenda 21: A Programme for Action for Sustainable Development*, New York: United Nations.

UNDP [United Nations Development Programme] (1998) *Human Development Report 1998*, Oxford University Press.

(2005) *Human Development Report 2005*, http://hdr.undp.org/reports/global/2005/.

UNEP [United Nations Environment Programme] (2005) http://ozone.unep.org/Public_Information/press_backgrounder.pdf (accessed 10 May 2006).

UNFCCC (United Nations Framework Convention on Climate Change) (2005) *Key GHG Data*, http://unfccc.int/essential_background/background_publications_htmlpdf/items/3604txt.php (accessed 10 May 2006).

Van der Heijden, Hein-Anton (1997) 'Political Opportunity Structure and the Institutionalisation of the Environmental Movement', *Environmental Politics*, 6(4): 25–50.

(1999) 'Environmental Movements, Ecological Modernisation and Political Opportunity Structures', *Environmental Politics*, 8(1): 199–221.

Van Muijen, Marie-Louise (2000) 'The Netherlands: Ambitious on Goals – Ambivalent on Action', in Lafferty and Meadowcroft (eds.), pp. 142–73.

Vanderheiden, Steve (2006) 'Assessing the Case Against the SUV', *Environmental Politics*, 15(1): 23–40.

Vandeveer, Stacy and Carmin, Joann (2004) 'Assessing Conventional Wisdom: Environmental Challenges and Opportunities Beyond Eastern Accession', *Environmental Politics*, 13(1): 315–31.

Venetoulis Jason and Talberth, John (2006) *Ecological Footprint of Nations, 2005 Update*, Oakland, CA: Redefining Progress, http://www.ecologicalfootprint.org/.

Victor, David (2004) *The Collapse of the Kyoto Protocol and the Struggle to Slow Global Warming*, Princeton University Press.

Victor, David, Raustiala, Kal and Skolnikoff, Eugene (eds.) (1998) *The Implementation and Effectiveness of International Environmental Commitments: Theory and Practice*, Cambridge, MA: MIT Press.

Vig, Norman (2006) 'Presidential Leadership and the Environment', in Vig and Kraft (eds.), pp. 100–23.

Vig, Norman and Faure, Michael (eds.) (2004) *Green Giants: Environmental Policies of the United States and the European Union*, Cambridge, MA: MIT Press.

Vig, Norman and Kraft, Michael (eds.) (1999) 'Toward Sustainable Development?', in Norman Vig and Michael Kraft (eds.), *Environmental Policy*, 4th edn, Washington, DC: CQ Press, pp. 370–88.

(eds.) (2006a) *Environmental Policy: New Directions for the Twenty First Century*, 6th edn, Washington, DC: CQ Press.

(2006b) 'Toward Sustainable Development?', in Vig and Kraft (eds.), pp. 374–94.

Vincent, Andrew (1993) 'The Character of Ecology', *Environmental Politics*, 2(2): 248–76.

Visiglio, Gerald and Whitelaw, Diana (eds.) (2003) *Our Backyard: a Quest for Environmental Justice*, Lanham, MD: Rowman and Littlefield.

Voerman, Gerrit (1995) 'The Netherlands: Losing Colours, Turning Green', in Richardson and Rootes (eds.), pp. 109–27.

Vogel, David (1986) *National Styles of Regulation*, Ithaca: Cornell University Press.

(1995) *Trading Up: Consumer and Environmental Regulation in a Consumer Economy*, Cambridge, MA: Harvard University Press.

(2006) 'International Trade and Environmental Regulation', in Vig and Kraft (eds.), pp. 354–73.

Vogler, John (1999) 'The European Union as an Actor in International Environmental Politics', *Environmental Politics*, 8(3): 24–48.

Vogler, John and Imber, Mark (1996) *The Environment and International Relations*, London: Routledge.

Von Frantzius, Ina (2004) 'World Summit on Sustainable Development Johannesburg 2002: A Critical Analysis and Assessment of the Outcomes', *Environmental Politics*, 13(2): 467–73.

Wackernagel, Mathis and Rees, William (1996) *Our Ecological Footprint: Reducing Human Impact on the Earth*, Gabriola Island, BC: New Society.

Walker, K. J. (2002) 'Environmental Policy in Australia', in Desai (ed.), pp. 249–93.

Wall, Derek (1994a) 'Introduction', in Wall (ed.), pp. 1–15.

(ed.) (1994b) *Green History*, London: Routledge.

(1999) *Earth First! and the Anti-Roads Movement*, London: Routledge.

Wapner, Paul (1996) *Environmental Activism and World Civic Politics*, Albany: SUNY Press.

(2003) World Summit on Sustainable Development: Toward a Post-Jo'burg Environmentalism', *Global Environmental Politics*, 3(1): 1–10.

Ward, Hugh (1999) 'Citizens' Juries and Valuing the Environment: A Proposal', *Environmental Politics*, 8(2): 75–96.

Ward, Hugh, Norval, Aletta, Landman, Todd and Pretty, Jules (2003) 'Open Citizens' Juries and the Politics of Sustainability', *Political Studies*, 51(2): 282–99.

Ward, Hugh and Samways, David (1992) 'Environmental Policy', in David Marsh and R. A. W. Rhodes (eds.), *Implementing Thatcherite Policies*, Buckingham: Open University Press, pp. 117–36.

Ward, Neil (1998) 'Water Quality', in Philip Lowe and Stephen Ward (eds.), *British Environmental Policy and Europe*, London: Routledge, pp. 244–64.

Warren, Karen (ed.) (1994) *Ecological Feminism*, London: Routledge.

WCED [World Commission on the Environment and Development] (1987) *Our Common Future*, Oxford University Press [The Brundtland Report].

Weale, Albert (1992) *The New Politics of Pollution*, Manchester University Press.

(2005) 'Environmental Rules and Rule-Making in the European Union', in Jordan (ed.), pp. 87–105.

Weale, Albert, Pridham, Geoffrey, Cini, Michelle, Konstadakopulos, Dimitrios, Porter, Martin and Flynn, Brendan (2000) *Environmental Governance in Europe*, Oxford University Press.

Webb, Paul (2000) *The Modern British Party System*, London: Sage.

Weidner, Helmut (2002a) 'Capacity Building for Ecological Modernization: Lessons from Cross-National Research', *American Behavioral Scientist*, 45: 1340–68.

(2002b) 'Environmental Policy and Politics in Germany', in Desai (ed.), pp. 149–201.

Wells, David (1978) 'Radicalism, Conservatism and the Environment', *Politics*, 13(2): 299–306.

Weston, Joe (1986) *Red and Green* London: Pluto.

Wettestad, Jørgen (2005) 'The Effectiveness of Environmental Policies', in Betsill et al. (eds.), pp. 299–328.

White, Lynn (1962) *Medieval Technology and Social Change*, Oxford: Clarendon Press.

Whitelegg, John (1997) *Critical Mass: Transport, Environment and Society in the Twenty-First Century*, London: Pluto Press.

Whitelegg, John and Haq, Gary (2003a) 'The Global Transport Problem: Same Issues but a Different Place', in Whitelegg and Haq (eds.), pp. 3–25.

(eds.) (2003b) *World Transport: Policy and Practice*, London: Earthscan.

Wildavsky, Aaron (1995) *But Is It True?* Cambridge, MA: Harvard University Press.

Wilkinson, David (1997) 'Towards Sustainability in the EU? Steps within the European Commission towards Integrating the Environment into Other EU Policy Sectors', *Environmental Politics*, 6(1): 153–73.

Williams, Bernard (1973) 'A Critique of Utilitarianism', in J. J. C. Smart and Bernard Williams, *Utilitarianism: For and Against*, Cambridge University Press, pp. 75–150.

Williams, Marc (2001) 'In Search of Global Standards: The Political Economy of Trade and the Environment', in Stevis and Assetto (eds.), pp. 39–61.

Williamson, Peter (1989) *Corporatism in Perspective: An Introductory Guide to Corporatist Theory*, London: Sage.

Wissenburg, Marcel (1998) *Green Liberalism*, London: UCL Press.

(2006) 'Liberalism', in Dobson and Eckersley (eds.), pp. 20–34.

Wood, Christopher (1995) *Environmental Impact Assessment: A Comparative Review*, Harlow: Longman.

(ed.) (2005) *Strategic Environmental Assessment and Land Use Planning: An International Evaluation*, London: Earthscan.

World Business Council for Sustainable Development (2006) http://www.wbcsd.org (accessed 16 June).

World Nuclear Association (2006) http://www.world-nuclear.org/ (accessed 16 June).

Worldwatch Institute (2006) *State of the World 2006: The Challenge of Global Sustainability*, London: Earthscan.

Wright, Brian (2001) 'Environmental NGOs and the Dolphin–Tuna Case', *Environmental Politics*, 9(4): 82–103.

WTO [World Trade Organisation] (2006) http://www.wto.org/ (accessed 5 April).

Wurzel, Rüdiger (2004) 'Germany: from Environmental Leadership to Partial Mismatch', in Jordan and Liefferink (eds.), pp. 99–117.

Yearley, Steven (1991) *The Green Case*, London: HarperCollins.

Young, Alasdair (2005) 'Picking the Wrong Fight: Why Attacks on the WTO Pose the Real Threat to National Environmental and Public Health Protection', *Global Environmental Politics*, 5(4): 47–72.

Young, Oran (1994) *International Governance*, Ithaca: Cornell University Press.
(ed.) (1999) *The Effectiveness of International Environmental Regimes*, Cambridge, MA: MIT Press.

Zald, Mayer and McCarthy, John (1987) *Social Movements in an Organizational Society*, New Brunswick, NJ: Transaction.

Zilliacus, Kim (2001) '"New Politics" in Finland: The Greens and the Left Wing in the 1990s', *West European Politics*, 24(1): 27–54.

Zito, Anthony (2000) *Creating Environmental Policy in the European Union*, Basingstoke: Macmillan.

# Index